A Constructive Christi ⎯ ⎯⎯⎯GY
for the Pluralistic World

HOPE AND COMMUNITY

Veli-Matti Kärkkäinen

WILLIAM B. EERDMANS PUBLISHING COMPANY

GRAND RAPIDS, MICHIGAN

Wm. B. Eerdmans Publishing Co.
2140 Oak Industrial Drive NE, Grand Rapids, Michigan 49505
www.eerdmans.com

2019-04

ISBN 978-0-8028-6857-2

Library of Congress Cataloging-in-Publication Data

Names: Kärkkäinen, Veli-Matti, author.
Title: Hope and community / Veli-Matti Kärkkäinen.
Description: Grand Rapids : Eerdmans Publishing Co., 2017. | Series: A constructive Christian
   theology for the pluralistic world ; Volume 5 | Includes bibliographical references and index.
Identifiers: LCCN 2017008129 | ISBN 9780802868572 (pbk. : alk. paper)
Subjects: LCSH: Hope—Religious aspects—Christianity. | Eschatology. | Communities—
   Religious aspects—Christianity. | Christianity and other religions.
Classification: LCC BV4638 .K37 2017 | DDC 234/.25—dc23
   LC record available at https://lccn.loc.gov/2017008129

Contents

Abbreviations

AG	*Ad Gentes: Decree on the Mission Activity of the Church* (Vatican II). http://www.vatican.va/archive/hist_councils /ii_vatican_council/documents/vat-ii_decree_19651207 _ad-gentes_en.html
Aquinas, *ST*	*The Summa Theologica of St. Thomas Aquinas.* 2nd and rev. ed. 1920. Literally translated by Fathers of the English Dominican Province. Online edition. Copyright © 2008 by Kevin Knight. http://www.newadvent.org/summa/
Barth, *CD*	Karl Barth. *Church Dogmatics.* Edited by G. W. Bromiley and T. F. Torrance. Translated by G. W. Bromiley. Edinburgh: T. & T. Clark, 1956–1975. Online edition by Alexander Street Press, 1975
BC	*The Book of Concord. The Confessions of the Evangelical Lutheran Church.* Translated by Theodore G. Tappert. Philadelphia: Fortress, 1959
BCSC	*The Blackwell Companion to Science and Christianity.* Edited by J. B. Stump and Alan G. Padgett. Malden, Mass., and Oxford: Blackwell, 2012
BEM	*Baptism, Eucharist and Ministry.* Faith and Order, 1982
	BEM-B = Baptism section
	BEM-E = Eucharist section
	BEM-M = Ministry section
CA	Confessio Augustana (= Augsburg Confession)
CCCIT	*The Cambridge Companion to Classical Islamic Theology.*

x

	Edited by Tim Winter. Cambridge: Cambridge University Press, 2008. Online edition
CC-LCE	*The Church as Communion: Lutheran Contributions to Ecclesiology.* Edited by Heinrich Holze. Geneva: Lutheran World Federation, 1997
CTCV	*The Church: Towards a Common Vision.* Faith and Order Paper no. 214. 2013
CWMRW	*Christian Witness in a Multi-Religious World: Recommendations for Conduct.* World Council of Churches, Pontifical Council for Interreligious Dialogue, World Evangelical Alliance, 2011
DAR	*Death and Afterlife: Perspectives of World Religions.* Edited by Hiroshi Obayashi. London: Praeger, 1992
DIRW	*Death and Immortality in the Religions of the World.* Edited by Paul Badham and Linda Badham. New York: Paragon House, 1987
EPCW	*Evangelization, Proselytism, and Common Witness: The Report from the Fourth Phase of the International Dialogue between the Roman Catholic Church and Some Classical Pentecostal Churches and Leaders, 1990–1997.* http://www.prounione.urbe.it/dia-int/pe-rc/doc/i_pe-rc_pent04.html
ER	*Encyclopedia of Religion.* Edited by Lindsay Jones. 15 vols. 2nd ed. Detroit: Macmillan Reference USA/Gale, Cengage Learning, 2005
EWEG	*The End of the World and the Ends of God: Science and Theology on Eschatology.* Edited by John Polkinghorne and Michael Welker. Harrisburg, Pa.: Trinity, 2000
FFU	*The Far-Future Universe: Eschatology from a Cosmic Perspective.* Edited by George F. R. Ellis. Philadelphia and London: Templeton Foundation Press, 2002
GDT	*Global Dictionary of Theology.* Edited by Veli-Matti Kärkkäinen and William Dyrness. Assistant editors, Simon Chan and Juan Martinez. Downers Grove: InterVarsity, 2008
Haight, CCH	Roger Haight, SJ. *Christian Community in History.* Vol. 1, *Historical Ecclesiology.* Vol. 2, *Comparative Ecclesiology.* Vol. 3, *Ecclesial Existence.* New York and London: Continuum, 2004, 2005, 2008

JBC	*Jesus beyond Christianity: The Classic Texts.* Edited by Gregory A. Barker and Stephen E. Gregg. Oxford: Oxford University Press, 2010
JWF	*Jesus in the World's Faiths: Leading Thinkers from Five Religions Reflect on His Meaning.* Edited by Gregory A. Barker. Maryknoll, N.Y.: Orbis, 2008
Kasper, *HTF*	Cardinal Walter Kasper. *Harvesting the Fruits: Basic Aspects of Christian Faith in Ecumenical Dialogue.* London and New York: Continuum, 2009
LDWR	*Life after Death in World Religions.* Edited by Harold Coward. Maryknoll, N.Y.: Orbis, 1997
LG	*Lumen Gentium: The Dogmatic Constitution on the Church.* Solemnly Promulgated by His Holiness Pope Paul VI on November 21, 1964 (Vatican II). http://www.vatican .va/archive/hist_councils/ii_vatican_council/documents /vat-ii_const_19641121_lumen-gentium_en.html
LW	*Luther's Works.* American ed. (Libronix Digital Library). Edited by Jaroslav Pelikan and Helmut T. Lehman. 55 vols. Minneapolis: Fortress, 2002
NMC	*The Nature and Mission of the Church: A Stage on the Way to a Common Statement.* Faith and Order Paper no. 198. 2005
NPNF[1]	*A Select Library of the Nicene and Post-Nicene Fathers of the Christian Church.* Edited by Philip Schaff. 1st ser. 14 vols. Edinburgh, 1886. Public domain; available at www .ccel.org
NPNF[2]	*A Select Library of the Nicene and Post-Nicene Fathers of the Christian Church.* Edited by Philip Schaff and Henry Wace. 2nd ser. 14 vols. Edinburgh, 1890. Public domain; available at www.ccel.org
OBTMR	*One Baptism: Towards Mutual Recognition; A Study Text.* Faith and Order Paper no. 210. 2011
OHE	*Oxford Handbook of Eschatology.* Edited by Jerry L. Walls. New York: Oxford University Press, 2009. Online edition
OHGR	*The Oxford Handbook of Global Religions.* Edited by Mark Juergensmeyer. New York: Oxford University Press, 2006
OHM	*The Oxford Handbook of Millennialism.* Edited by Catherine Wessinger. New York: Oxford University Press, 2011. Online edition

OHRD	*The Oxford Handbook of Religious Diversity*. Edited by Chad Meister. Oxford: Oxford University Press, 2010
Pannenberg, ST	Wolfhart Pannenberg. *Systematic Theology*. Translated by Geoffrey W. Bromiley. 3 vols. Grand Rapids: Eerdmans, 1991, 1994, 1998
PC	*Physics and Cosmology: Scientific Perspectives on the Problem of Natural Evil*. Edited by Nancey Murphy, Robert John Russell, William R. Stoeger, SJ. Vol. 1. Vatican City and Berkeley, Calif.: Vatican Observatory and Center for Theological and the Natural Sciences, 2007
PE	*The Problem of Evil*. Edited by M. M. Adams and R. M. Adams. Oxford: Oxford University Press, 1990
Pelikan, CT	Jaroslav Pelikan. *The Christian Tradition: A History of the Development of Doctrine*. Vol. 1, *The Emergence of the Catholic Tradition (100–600)*. Vol. 2, *The Spirit of Eastern Christendom (600–1700)*. Vol. 3, *The Growth of Medieval Theology (600–1300)*. Vol. 4, *Reformation of Church and Dogma (1300–1700)*. Chicago: University of Chicago Press, 1971, 1974, 1978, 1984
PIR	*Personal Identity and Resurrection: How Do We Survive Our Death?* Edited by Georg Gasser. Surrey, UK: Ashgate, 2010
QCLN	*Quantum Cosmology and the Laws of Nature: Scientific Perspectives on Divine Action*. Edited by Robert John Russell, Nancey Murphy, and C. J. Isham. Vatican City: Vatican Observatory Publications, 1993
RCCC	*Routledge Companion to the Christian Church*. Edited by Gerard Mannion and Lewis S. Mudge. New York: Routledge, 2012
RTSA	*Resurrection: Theological and Scientific Assessments*. Edited by T. Peters, R. J. Russell, and M. Welker. Grand Rapids: Eerdmans, 2002
SBE	*Sacred Books of the East*. Translated by Max Müller. 50 vols. Oxford: Oxford University Press, 1879–1910. Also available at www.sacred-texts.com
Schleiermacher, CF	Friedrich Schleiermacher. *The Christian Faith*. Edited by H. R. Mackintosh and J. S. Stewart. London and New York: T. & T. Clark, 1999
SPDA	*Scientific Perspectives on Divine Action: Twenty Years of*

	Challenge and Progress. Edited by Robert John Russell, Nancey Murphy, and William R. Stoeger, SJ. Vatican City and Berkeley, Calif.: Vatican Observatory and Center for Theological and the Natural Sciences, 2008
TCW	"Towards Common Witness: A Call to Adopt Responsible Relationships in Mission and to Renounce Proselytism." WCC and the Vatican, 1997
Tillich, *ST*	Paul Tillich. *Systematic Theology.* 3 vols. Chicago: University of Chicago Press, 1951, 1957, 1963
TTL	*Together towards Life: Mission and Evangelism in Changing Landscapes.* Commission on World Mission and Evangelism/WCC, 2012
UR	*Unitatis Redintegratio: Decree on Ecumenism* (Vatican II)
WA	Weimarer Ausgabe (the Weimar edition of Luther's works)
WCC	World Council of Churches

Bible references, unless otherwise indicated, are from the Revised Standard Version of the Bible, copyright 1952 (2nd ed. 1971) by the Division of Christian Education of the National Council of the Churches of Christ in the United States of America. Used by permission. All rights reserved.

Unless otherwise indicated, all citations from patristic writers come from the standard series listed above.

Josephus's writings are from the Sacred Texts Web site: http://www .sacred-texts.com/jud/josephus/index.htm.

Unless otherwise indicated, contemporary Roman Catholic documents, documents of Vatican II, papal encyclicals, and similar works are quoted from the official Vatican Web site: www.vatican.va. This includes also dialogue documents with Lutherans, Reformed, Anglicans, Methodists, and Pentecostals.

Contemporary World Council of Churches documents are quoted from their official Web site, http://www.oikoumene.org/, unless otherwise indicated.

The sources used for postbiblical Jewish literature are as follows:

Midrashic commentary literature is from *Midrash Rabbah*. Translated and edited by H. Freedman and Maurice Simon. 10 vols. 3rd imprint. London: Soncino Press, 1961 (1939). Available at https://archive.org/details /RabbaGenesis.

Talmud references are from *The Babylonian Talmud*. Translated and edited by I. Epstein. 35 vols. London: Soncino Press, 1952. Available at http:// www.come-and-hear.com/tcontents.html.

Mishnah texts are from eMishnah.com (2008) at http://www.emishnah .com/Yoma.html.

All others, unless otherwise noted, are from http://www.earlyjewishwrit ings.com/ (e.g., Philo of Alexandria).

The Qur'anic references, unless otherwise indicated, are from *The Holy Qur'ān: A New English Translation of Its Meanings* © 2008 Royal Aal al-Bayt Institute for Islamic Thought, Amman, Jordan. This version of the Qur'an is also available online at http://altafsir.com.

Hadith texts are from the Hadith Collection Web site: http://www.hadith collection.com/ (2009–).

Buddhist texts, unless otherwise indicated, are from "Tipitaka: The Pali Canon." Edited by John T. Bullitt. *Access to Insight*, May 10, 2011. Available at http://www.accesstoinsight.org/tipitaka/index.html.

Bhagavad-Gita texts are from the translation by Ramanand Prasad. EAWC Anthology, 1988.

All other Hindu texts, unless otherwise indicated, are from the Sacred Texts Web site: http://www.sacred-texts.com/hin/index.htm.

Preface

This book is one of the five volumes in the series titled CONSTRUCTIVE CHRIS-
TIAN THEOLOGY FOR THE PLURALISTIC WORLD. The goal of the series is to
present a novel, dynamic constructive Christian theology for the pluralistic
world shaped by cultural, ethnic, sociopolitical, economic, and religious diversity, as well as the unprecedented influence of the sciences. While robustly
Christian in its convictions, building on the deep and wide tradition of biblical, historical, philosophical, and contemporary systematic traditions, this
project seeks to engage our present cultural and religious diversity in a way
Christian theology has not done in the past. Although part of a larger series,
each volume can still stand on its own feet, so to speak, and can be read as an
individual work.

The current book is the fifth and last one in the series, following *Christ
and Reconciliation* (2013), *Trinity and Revelation* (2014), *Creation and Humanity* (2015), and *Spirit and Salvation* (2016). Along with traditional topics,
constructive theological argumentation in this series also engages a number
of topics, perspectives, and issues that systematic theologies are missing, such
as race, environment, ethnicity, inclusivity, violence, and colonialism. A consistent engagement with religious and interfaith studies is a distinctive feature
of this series. The current volume, similarly to the third one, majors also in a
deep and wide dialogue with natural sciences, including cosmology, physics,
quantum theory, and neurosciences.

The introductory chapter gives a brief orientation to overall methodology; this is more extensively discussed in the lengthy introduction to volume
1 and, thereafter, more briefly in each succeeding volume. Furthermore, at the

beginning of each major topic, the honing and clarification of methodological issues continue, in this case with regard to eschatology and ecclesiology. The project is funded by the conviction that the material presentation of theological themes itself helps shape and clarify the method — and of course, vice versa. I fully agree with the American Reformed theologian David Kelsey's observation that in the real sense of the word, the clarification of methodology is "largely retrospective," if not for other reasons, then because "[t]he intellectual and imaginative challenges peculiar to different theological topics are so diverse that any set of methodological rules purporting to cover them all would have to be so general as to be useless."[1] Although I hesitate to go as far as Moltmann, who confessed that the methodological "road emerged only as I walked it,"[2] neither am I following Pannenberg, who devoted decades to a most detailed clarification of all kinds of methodological issues before venturing into a tightly presented *summa*.

Having now finished the whole five-volume series of constructive theology, totaling close to three thousand pages, I am more convinced than ever of the admission I made earlier (quoting the noted American Lutheran science-theology expert Philip Hefner): that I have "mixed different types of thinking . . . without justifying the mixture or clarifying how the recipe would work," and that "age has simply intensified what were once distracting youthful tendencies."[3] I fear that in my case this "mixing" is even worse because not only do I lack the breadth and width of the knowledge of the masters, but my project is, if possible, even more hybrid and ambitious in its goal. On the other hand, humbly — and boldly — stated, I believe that something like what is attempted in this project will be the "normal" mode of systematic/constructive Christian theology in the near future, that is, interconfessional, interdisciplinary, and interreligious. Or to put it more modestly, something like this project might well be *a* major direction for constructive theology to come. In any case, theology should break out from its self-made limitations and become truly interdisciplinary and also interfaith sensitive. Broadly speaking, it seems to me that whereas the European systematic theological work (often named "dogmatics") is still content with endless clarification of questions of the past, the American fascination with everything new and novel too often fails to appreciate tradition. Theologians in the Global South, almost exclusively trained in and under the Euro-American academia, oscillate between the two. The way forward is

1. Kelsey, *Eccentric Existence*, 1:12.
2. Moltmann, *Experiences in Theology*, p. xv.
3. Hefner, *The Human Factor*, p. xiii.

to hold tightly to the best of tradition in order to critique and transcend it. That is what happened with Saint Athanasius, Saint Augustine, Saint Thomas Aquinas, Calvin and Luther, Schleiermacher and Barth, as well as, say, Elizabeth Johnson and Gustavo Gutiérrez. For them what is now called systematic theology was not merely the preservation of the past; they were standing on the legacy of tradition and seeking new ways of renewing it.

The writing of this volume, similarly to the others in this series,[4] has taken place in the midst of a full, indeed, consistently overloaded, teaching career at Fuller Theological Seminary and my annual intensive docent-teaching trips at the University of Helsinki. It has given me an opportunity over the years to test these materials both with master's and doctoral students coming from all Christian churches and all continents; I have also taught many parts of the project as a guest professor in Australia, Africa, and Europe. Fuller's generous sabbatical program made it possible for me to finish the project according to its (overly) ambitious timetable, one volume per year. More than a decade of high-level editorial assistance from Fuller Theological Seminary's School of Theology faculty publications editor, Susan Carlson Wood, has meant more to my publishing career than I am able to express in words. Finally, I could not survive without the competent and dedicated research assistants, doctoral students funded by the Center for Advanced Theological Studies, who collaborated in all aspects of the research process. For this volume, Dan Brockway, Christopher O'Brian, Jongsoeck Shin, and Joseph Muthalali worked for innumerable hours helping find resources. Jongsoeck also went to the extreme work of checking all references against the original sources, not a small task for a project that encompasses several disciplines, many religions, and numerous languages, ancient and contemporary. The index was compiled by Viktor Toth.

My most heartfelt thanks go to my wife and life companion of thirty-six years, Anne-Päivi, with whom I have lived on three continents, traveled all over the globe, learned new languages, and enjoyed life beyond measure. Every morning we begin with a cup of coffee and devotional in bed; the rest of the day, whether teaching or writing, is but the continuation of the blessing and happiness of life shared in *koinonia*.

4. Except for vol. 3, for which I received a partial stipend for one semester from the Lilly Foundation, matched by my own institution, and a partial fellowship from the Center for Christian Theology at Biola University, during my regular sabbatical.

Introduction: In Search of a New Methodological Vision for Constructive Theology

As orientation to the current volume, this introduction briefly outlines the methodological vision of the project, presented and defended in earlier volumes.[1] The vision for doing constructive theology in a religiously pluralistic and culturally diverse "post-world" — postmodern, postfoundationalist, poststructuralist, postcolonial, postmetaphysical, postpropositional, postliberal, postconservative, postsecular, post-Christian — can be sketched like this:

> Systematic/constructive theology is an integrative discipline that continuously searches for a coherent, balanced understanding of Christian truth and faith in light of Christian tradition (biblical and historical) and in the context of the historical and contemporary thought, cultures, and living faiths. It aims at a coherent, inclusive, dialogical, and hospitable vision.

The nomenclature "systematic" is most unfortunate since the ultimate goal of constructive theology is not a "system"! Rather, constructive theology seeks a coherent and balanced understanding. Regarding the theory of truth, it follows coherence theory. One current way of speaking of coherence compares it to a web or a net(work) that underwrites postfoundationalist rather than foundationalist epistemology. That metaphor is fitting, as it speaks of an

---

1. This section repeats the materials from vol. 3, *Creation and Humanity*, which similarly engages robustly not only other faith traditions but also the natural sciences. Since the discussion in vol. 1, *Christ and Reconciliation*, contains detailed bibliographic references, they are not repeated here, except for direct citations.

attempt to relate every statement to other relevant statements and ultimately to the "whole." Coherence has not only to do with inner-textual coherence but also with the "fit" of theological statements with "reality."[2]

With classical tradition (and say, Pannenberg, among contemporary theologians), in a qualified sense, we can still speak of systematic theology as the "science of God,"[3] as it presupposes the existence of truth apart from human beings and human beings' social construction thereof.[4] That said — without subscribing to any particular form of late modern/postmodern episte-mology — we hasten to add that we humans never have a direct, uncontested access to the infinitely incomprehensible God.[5] Rather, human grasp of truth is only provisional.[6] Rather than on firm "foundations," theological argumen-tation builds on a *post*foundationalist epistemology because of "*the contested nature of theological truth claims.*"[7] A postfoundationalist approach or episte-mology seeks "to engage in interdisciplinary dialogue within our postmodern culture while *both* maintaining a commitment to intersubjective, transcommu-nal theological argumentation for the truth of Christian faith, *and* recognizing the provisionality of our historically embedded understandings and culturally conditioned explanations of the Christian tradition and religious experience."[8]

Constructive theology's nature as an "integrative" discipline is its most distinctive feature. To practice well constructive theology, one has to utilize the results, insights, and materials of all other theological disciplines, that is, biblical studies, church history and historical theology, philosophical theology, as well as ministerial studies. Closely related fields of religious studies, ethics, and missiology also belong to the texture of systematic work. That alone is a tall order. But since theology operates in a particular context and religiously pluralistic world, the insights from cultural studies as well as the study of liv-ing faiths (in this project, Judaism, Islam, Buddhism, and Hinduism) are also invoked. Finally — alas! — even more resources are needed for the discussion of certain theological topics such as creation, anthropology, and eschatology — namely, the natural sciences, whether cosmology, physics, quantum theory,

---

2. Murphy, *Beyond Liberalism and Fundamentalism*, pp. 98–108.

3. Aquinas, *ST* 1a.1.7.

4. Pannenberg, *ST* 1:50.

5. Pannenberg, *ST* 1:4-6; for a full discussion, see his *Theology and the Philosophy of Science*, pp. 297–326 particularly.

6. See further Pannenberg, "What Is Truth?" pp. 1–27; Vainio, *Beyond Fideism*, p. 132.

7. Clayton, *Adventures in the Spirit*, p. 28, emphasis in original (commenting on Pan-nenberg's theology).

8. Shults, *The Post Foundationalist Task of Theology*, p. 18, emphasis in original.

or brain study. The use of all these materials and insights, however, is guided by the principle according to which the systematician must listen carefully to related disciplines but also go beyond their input, domains, and questions. From the beginning to the end, this project is a *theological* enterprise.

A methodological approach that "celebrates diversity, pluralism, and contextuality, while at the same time pursuing shared resources of human rationality and interdisciplinary conversation,"[9] is particularly appropriate in an investigation undertaken in the matrix of theology, religious studies, and the sciences. This kind of interdisciplinary discourse, "a complex, multileveled transversal process,"[10] breaks through the limitations of any specific discipline with standard borders. It seeks mutual learning, interaction, and engagement in its quest for a coherent vision. The term "transversal" indicates "a sense of extending over, lying across, and intersecting with one another."[11]

That principle, however, does not float freely in the air, as it were; it is not a smorgasbord where one can pick and choose as one wishes, to use another metaphor. Rather, it acknowledges the theory-laden nature of each inquiry but also the rootedness of such an inquiry in a particular tradition. For the theologian, the guiding tradition is the biblical-historical and contemporary theological wisdom, the deposit of faith. That tradition, however, is neither a straitjacket that limits creative pursuit of knowledge nor a basis for mere repetition and defense. Rather, remaining "tied to specific communities of faith without being trapped by these communities,"[12] the investigation honors contextuality and builds on a shared identity of the wider community of faith. Appreciation and critique of tradition are part of the task.[13] Following Alasdair MacIntyre, it can be said that "the idea that there can be a kind of reason that is supra-cultural and that would enable us to view all the culturally conditioned traditions of rationality from a standpoint above them all is one of the illusions of our contemporary culture. All rationality is socially embodied, developed in human tradition and using some human language."[14]

Particularly with regard to the comparative-theology facet of this investigation — namely, engaging Jewish, Islamic, Hindu, and Buddhist beliefs of

9. Van Huyssteen, *Alone in the World?* p. 5.

10. Van Huyssteen, *Alone in the World?* p. 9.

11. Van Huyssteen, *Alone in the World?* p. 20. See further Schrag, "Transversal Rationality."

12. Van Huyssteen, *Alone in the World?* p. 12.

13. See further Van Huyssteen, *Alone in the World?* p. 45 and passim.

14. As paraphrased by Newbigin, "Religious Pluralism," p. 50; so also p. 52; the reference is to MacIntyre, *Whose Justice, Which Rationality?*

eschatology and ecclesiology — one has to be careful in following the transversality principle. The reasons are many and obvious. First of all, systematic theologians are not experts in religions — and even if we were, it would take a lifetime to learn even one tradition in any deep way. Therefore, we must do everything to avoid making "the systematic theologian into an amateur collector of religious curiosities."[15] The systematician should let the authoritative and representative voices of each tradition formulate their respective views. Second, granted the systematician knows enough to be able to dialogue meaningfully, integrating the contributions of religions in an already wide menu substantially complicates the task. Understandable is the temptation by modernistically driven theologians to give up the distinctive testimonies and "ground beliefs" of each tradition and in the name of the common core of religions try to make them speak (or at least mean) about the same. That "first-generation theological pluralism,"[16] however, is neither interesting nor useful. It also deviates from the principle of hospitality as it denies the right of the other to be *other*. As argued with some detail in the methodological introduction to *Christ and Reconciliation* (vol. 1), not only is theology confessional (rightly understood), but so also is comparative theology. It is not confessional in terms of violence and oppression but rather in a way that makes room for distinctive identities, differing testimonies — and passionate search for a common understanding even in the midst of our deepest and most deeply held differences. Confessionalism is not a denial of the pluralistic nature of theology as a discipline.

The beginning of both parts 1 and 2 will provide a detailed orientation to the topics and flow of argumentation in the following chapters.

---

15. K. Ward, *Religion and Revelation*, p. 37.
16. See further my *Trinity and Revelation*, chap. 14.

I. HOPE

1. Introduction: On the Possibility and Conditions of a Constructive Christian Eschatology

The (Omni)Presence of Eschatology

The Visions of "End" in Culture and Society

Unlike those of ancient times, contemporary cultures do not typically entertain the "myth of the eternal return,"[1] yet all living religions have a vision of the future and "end." Hence we can speak of "eschatology" as a pan-religious idea. Eschatology, however, is not limited exclusively to the religious sphere. Just think of the growing concern, at times anxiety, in secular culture over the impending "end" — either of our planet or of human life.[2] In contemporary sciences we have lately heard expressions such as "physical eschatology,"[3] which investigates the future of the cosmos and life, whether in the near or far future; similarly, questions are being raised among scientists about "evolutionary eschatology," that is, whether evolutionary process is to be considered progressive and if it ever culminates in a final goal.[4]

Indeed, even more widely, it seems obvious that "[e]very culture has an eschatology; it is part of our inescapable human attempt to make sense of the world."[5] Although these secular visions are not distinctively religious, they tend to feature structural similarities with religions, as is evident in the

---

1. As has been famously argued by Eliade, *The Myth of the Eternal Return*.
2. See Körtner, *The End of the World*, pp. 1–22.
3. A groundbreaking essay was Rees's "Collapse of the Universe."
4. Schloss, "From Evolution to Eschatology," pp. 71–79.
5. Gillman, *The Death of Death*, p. 21.

7

Marxist tripartite outline of the world's history: "A primal state of innocence, followed by a period of social tension, which is, in turn, supplanted by a new era of harmony, the communist society of the future."[6] Interestingly, it has also been argued recently that Friedrich Nietzsche, the most unlikely supporter of eschatology in either secular or religious forms, might have subscribed to a form of it. Could it be that this atheist's vision of the rescue of "the use and abuse of history" — or as he also put it, the "disease of history"[7] — may be a concealed form of a "secularized Joachimite eschatology"?[8] What if Joachim's three ages — that of the Father, Son, and Spirit — are paralleled by Nietzsche's scheme of history in three stages: premoral, moral, and ultramoral ages?[9]

Some kind of eschatological outlook can even be found in most recent predictions of the future of human civilization in sociopolitical thought. How else to think of the (in)famous proposal of Francis Fukuyama at the time of the collapse of Soviet Communism, ominously titled *The End of History and the Last Man*? With a neoconservative confidence in the final victory of free-market capitalism and its version of democracy over other political ideologies, Fukuyama took it as the most developed and final stage of evolution, finally leading into peace as democracy's supremacy is discerned by all.[10] Not surprisingly, this "right-wing" vision of the inevitable progress of history toward freedom was harshly contested by the ideological left. In the neo-Marxist manifesto of Michael Hardt and Antonio Negri, *Empire*, freedom is defeated by the empire, which replaces nation-states and even national conflicts with a new transnational global order, indeed an absolute and violent one. The new combined world rulers are international agencies and organizations from the UN to the World Bank and the alliance of rich nations, along with the "superpower" (USA). The sequel by the same authors, written after 9/11, titled *Multitude: War and Democracy in the Age of Empire* (2004), further diagnoses reasons for the failure of the dream of progress.[11] In sum: whatever one thinks of these various scenarios for the future, it appears that "eschatology" dies hard even in the secular realm.

---

6. Gillman, *The Death of Death*, p. 21, attributing the idea to Herberg, *Judaism and Modern Man*, pp. 230-31.

7. Nietzsche, *Use and Abuse of History*, p. 71.

8. Ausmus, "Nietzsche and Eschatology," p. 347.

9. Nietzsche, *Beyond Good and Evil*, p. 46, cited in Ausmus, "Nietzsche and Eschatology," p. 351.

10. Fukuyama, *The End of History and the Last Man*.

11. Hardt and Negri, *Empire* and *Multitude*.

The Eclipse of Eschatology in Christian Tradition

In distinctively Christian forms of eschatology, marked shifts have taken place in history. For the earliest followers of Christ, the intense expectation of the imminent return of their Lord was just that — *intense*; the (early) patristic church continued this focus.[12] Apocalyptic enthusiasm flourished in diverse forms. Even such intellectually oriented writers as the apologists of the second century employed urgent eschatological warnings and visions in their defense of the faith before the unbelieving world.[13] Although the eschatological hope waned some after the establishment of Christendom and its amillennialism, in no way did it die out. Indeed, more often than not, particularly in the Middle Ages and all way to the Reformation era, eschatological-apocalyptic imagination fueled spirituality.

By the time of modernity, eschatological "hope" had lost its meaning among the intelligentsia.[14] Kant's focus on religion's effect on morality undoubtedly helped the nineteenth-century liberal Protestants and others to reduce faith to the subjective and moral dimensions.[15] And even the "rediscovery" of eschatology at the turn of the twentieth century in liberal New Testament scholarship (Johannes Weiss, Albert Schweitzer, and others) hardly signaled a robust interest in the *theological* significance of the end times. Not only did these scholars not believe the content of the New Testament claims regarding eschatology, but they were more keen on apocalypticism and, most ironically, its naive but totally mistaken application by Jesus and the disciples![16]

Simultaneously, though for different reasons, dismissal — or even an aggressive disavowal — of eschatological hope was funded by other leading philosophical and cultural figures. As is well known, L. Feuerbach took the human desire for life after death as a form of egotism.[17] He completely misunderstood the essence of Christian eschatological hope, as he took it as the

---

12. Daley, "Eschatology in the Early Church Fathers," pp. 92–94. A massive resource is his *Hope of the Early Church.*

13. Just consider the influential early second-century writings the *Apocalypse of Peter* and *Epistle of the Apostles*, which discuss extensively end-time events. For the centrality of apocalypticism, see Daley, "Apocalypticism in Early Christian Theology."

14. See further Pannenberg, *ST* 3:532–45.

15. See Kant, *Religion within the Limits of Reason Alone*, p. 102.

16. For a succinct discussion with basic original sources, see J. Walls, introduction to *OHE*, pp. 7–9; even for Walls, the significance of said New Testament scholars is overrated.

17. Feuerbach, *Essence of Christianity*, pp. 170–84 particularly.

denial of true human existence, particularly physicality.[18] The Freudian rejection of (religious) imagination of the afterlife merely as a (neurotic, or at least immature) form of an illusion attracted many followers.[19]

The Freudian interpretation sticks well with the contemporary naturalist worldview. The famed early twentieth-century British atheist philosopher Bertrand Russell opined that "[a]ll the evidence goes to show that what we regard as our mental life is bound up with brain structure and organized bodily energy. Therefore it is rational to suppose that mental life ceases when body ceases."[20] Philosophers such as Anthony Flew continued their persistent critique, targeting any belief in an afterlife and personal survival after death. He found logically and rationally failing the attempts by ancient philosophers, Christians and other believers, as well as those who consider near-death experiences, to establish the possibility of personal survival.[21]

No wonder that in much of post-Enlightenment theology any talk in the line of tradition about the "end" lacked content and became marginalized. The work begun by A. Schweitzer and other liberals was picked up in the latter part of the twentieth century by the (in)famous American Jesus Seminar. The late Marcus J. Borg advocated a totally noneschatological interpretation of Jesus and took the kingdom of God as merely a this-worldly entity.[22]

Some leading systematic theologians similarly dismissed or radically revised eschatology. There is almost no mention of eschatological themes in Gordon Kaufman's *In Face of Mystery: A Constructive Theology*, with the exception of a few unnuanced, hasty rebuttals of what he considers the traditional view of the judgment of God.[23] The *Cambridge Companion to Postmodern Theology* contains no entry on eschatology — the index does not even list the term! Virtual opposition to traditional eschatology comes from many quarters of women's, particularly feminist, green, and other liberation theologians. Some analysts even consider feminist theology *qua* feminist as either "anti-" or "noneschatological."[24] While that is an overstatement, it is true that some

18. For details and sources, see Schwarz, *Eschatology*, pp. 176–77.

19. Freud, *Reflections on War and Death*, p. 19.

20. B. Russell, *Why I Am Not a Christian*, p. 45, cited in Raphael, *Jewish Views of the Afterlife*, p. 23; see also Linda Badham, who remains deeply skeptical and provides a thoughtful case for a naturalistic denial of any afterlife: "A Naturalistic Case for Extinction," pp. 158–70.

21. For an accessible account, see Flew, "The Logic of Mortality," pp. 171–87.

22. See Borg, *Jesus in Contemporary Scholarship*, pp. 47–68; Borg, *Jesus, A New Vision*. For criticism, see Witherington, *Jesus, Paul, and the End of the World*.

23. See Kaufman, *In Face of Mystery*, p. 409; I am indebted to Schwarz, *Eschatology*, p. 366.

24. Cf. Karras, "Eschatology," pp. 244–45.

leading feminist pioneers have charged the (Christian) hope for afterlife (or "personal immortality," as it is sometimes put) to be "a patriarchal concept arising predominantly from the male psyche," while others argue that it necessarily neglects the destiny of the nonhuman creation and the cosmos.[25]

Similarly, consistent opposition to all notions of the consummation of God's kingdom after the book of Revelation has come from various types of postmodern philosophers, particularly on the more deconstructionist side on the old continent. If for Derrida "eschatology" is endless postponement without any arrival of the "Messiah,"[26] for his (former) colleague Gilles Deleuze and those like-minded, eschatology signals the threat of totality and homogenization.[27]

Some Attempts at Rediscovery and Reconceiving of Eschatology

It is not that all twentieth-century theological movements are willing to ignore eschatology. There is also the desire to reconceive it. Some nuanced and creative contemporary alternatives have been put forth to construct a viable eschatological vision. One of the most sophisticated revisions comes from the soil of process theology's deeply panentheistic and in many ways immanentist conception of God: therein God (in his two "dimensions," the consequent and primordial)[28] provides the "lure" for the future events but is not the one who guarantees an eschatological solution in any certainty.[29] There is neither an *ex nihilo* beginning (as God emerges with the cosmos) nor a final eschaton. Furthermore, rather than resurrection hope for humanity, there is (in the original Whiteheadian process philosophy) an idea of "objective immortality," that is, some kind of nonpersonal recollection of us in divine memory (see chap. 6). Even the post-Whiteheadian attempts by some recent process theologians (Marjorie Hewitt Suchocki and others) to frame that "memory" in terms of

25. Karras, "Eschatology," pp. 243–44 (244); C. Keller, "Eschatology, Ecology, and a Green Ecumenacy," pp. 84–99.

26. Derrida, "Hospitality, Justice, and Responsibility," p. 70; see also his comment on the continuing "openness" of the future in Derrida, "Faith and Knowledge," p. 17.

27. Deleuze, "Nietzsche and Saint Paul," pp. 36–53.

28. Griffin, "Process Eschatology," p. 297, with the citation from Whitehead, *Process and Reality*, p. 527.

29. See Cobb, *Christ in a Pluralistic Age*, chaps. 15 and 16; for a comparison between Whitehead's (as also developed theologically by Cobb himself) and Pannenberg's (in comparison, traditional Christian) eschatology, see pp. 246–54 particularly.

"subjective immortality" are a far cry from the personal resurrection of the body of classical Christianity.[30]

Another marked reorientation of eschatology is the feminist theologian Kathryn Tanner's "Eschatology without a Future" proposal (to be engaged below), which resonates with the this-worldly approach of much of New Testament scholarship, although Tanner's reasons are theological and scientific. The main reason has to do with the obvious fact that the natural sciences' bleak picture of all life, and the cosmos itself, seems to be heading eventually toward annihilation; hence, these scientific "end-time scenarios conflict with the future-oriented, this-worldly eschatology"[31] of traditional Christianity.

Yet another highly important — as revisionist as it may be — eschatological restatement is John Hick's 1976 magnum opus, *Death and Eternal Life*. Mapping a huge domain of ideas among various religious traditions and in the tradition of Christian theology, he sets forth a creative synthesis between some living Asiatic faiths and a Judeo-Christian vision. He also staunchly opposes the prevailing naturalistic rebuttal of religious eschatologies: "In contrast to it," Hick states, "it seems to me that the claim of the religions that this life is part of a much larger existence that transcends our lifespan as animal organisms, whether through the continuation of individual consciousness or through participation in a greater transpersonal life, is very likely to be true." He further argues, "this is not ruled out by established scientific findings or by any agreed philosophical arguments."[32]

Although the current project cannot follow the material proposals of these and related revisionist eschatologies, it learns from them and constantly invites them as dialogue partners. Coming closest to the intuitions of this constructive theology are the many contemporary proposals that stay closely linked with the best of Christian tradition even when they seek to challenge and revise them. To a brief presentation of those we turn next.

"Something Old, Something New":
The Rise of Constructive Christian Eschatologies

In the midst of the dismissal and radical reworking of the doctrine of last things, some leading contemporary theologians have helped rediscover eschatology and even put it at the center of theological conversations. Barth's

---

30. See Griffin, "Process Eschatology," pp. 295-307.
31. Tanner, "Eschatology without a Future," p. 222.
32. Hick, *Death and Eternal Life*, p. 15.

classic rediscovery of eschatology is routinely mentioned as the clarion call: he claimed that without eschatology, no theology is worth its salt.[33] The publication of German Reformed theologian J. Moltmann's *Theology of Hope* in the mid-1960s launched a new movement called "theology of hope."[34] For him, eschatology is the "first" chapter of Christian theology. Another German, the Lutheran W. Pannenberg, talks about the "causal priority of the future"[35] and makes the surprising and counterintuitive claim of "the present as an effect of the future, in contrast to the conventional assumption that past and present are the cause of the future."[36] Because of that, for Pannenberg the concept of anticipation of the future became a leading theme:[37] the historical resurrection of Jesus Christ as a "proleptic" event makes Christian hope confident (albeit not yet fully determined) of the coming eschatological consummation on which ultimately hinges the truth of the Christian message.[38]

Several Americans have joined the turn to the future, including the two Lutherans, Ted Peters, with his concept of "retroactive ontology" materially repeating Pannenberg's futuristic causality,[39] and Robert W. Jenson, to whom God's true "triune identity" can be known in the course of history's unfolding toward consummation, in which process God shows his faithfulness.[40] Yet another American, the Anabaptist Thomas N. Finger, not only makes room for eschatology in his doctrinal presentation but even gives it the primary place by making it the leading theme.[41]

The British Anglican New Testament scholar N. T. Wright has labored for decades not only with issues such as resurrection but also, more recently, with the biblical basis of future hope. He has been recently joined by another senior New Testament expert, A. Thiselton.[42] Some leading science-religion

33. The most often referred to statement is in Barth, *The Epistle to the Romans*, p. 314.

34. For a brief discussion, see Kärkkäinen, "Hope, Theology of," pp. 404–5.

35. So named by R. Russell, *Time in Eternity*, pp. 117–19; Pannenberg first outlined it in *Theology and the Kingdom of God*, chaps. 1 and 4.

36. Pannenberg, *Theology and the Kingdom of God*, p. 54, cited in R. Russell, *Time in Eternity*, p. 118.

37. For a fine synopsis, see R. Russell, *Time in Eternity*, pp. 119–22.

38. See further LaBute, "The Ontological Motif of Anticipation," pp. 275–82; Harvie, "Living the Future," pp. 149–64.

39. Peters, *Anticipating Omega*.

40. Jenson, *The Triune Identity*. See also the Reformed American Donald G. Bloesch, *The Last Things*.

41. T. Finger, *Christian Theology*. For the centrality of eschatology for twentieth-century theology, see Hebblethwaite, *The Christian Hope*, pp. 131–98.

42. Thiselton, *Life after Death*.

experts, particularly the British physicist-priest John Polkinghorne and the American physicist-theologian Robert J. Russell, in collaboration with systematicians such as the German Michael Welker, have done groundbreaking work in helping rediscover the centrality of eschatology after the advent of modern science. And so forth. This is to say that with all the push toward ignoring eschatology in some theological quarters, in others it is alive and well.[43]

Not only in theology but also among the Christian communities, particularly when looked at from a global perspective, eschatology has returned. Whereas in the Global North on the old continent, eschatology rarely plays a visible role in churches' spirituality and liturgy, large sections of American Christianity still cultivate a vital hope for the return of Christ, not only among the fundamentalists but also beyond.[44] Furthermore — and this is routinely ignored and dismissed in academic theology — among majority world Christianity (Africa, Asia, Latin America), where churches are mushrooming and flourishing, eschatological proclamation still is very much a part of the daily tapestry of spirituality.

On the Conditions and Requirements of a Comprehensive Eschatology

What Is Eschatology All About?

Although the equivalent of the term "eschatology," the Latin *de novissimis* ("the last things"), was used much earlier, only at the time of Protestant orthodoxy, in the *Loci theologici* (1610–1621) of the Lutheran Johann Gerhard, did the topic receive a full-scale treatment.[45] A few decades later the term *eschatologia* itself was used in the last volume of another Lutheran scholastic, Abraham Calov's *Systema locorum theologicorum* (1655–1677).[46]

Recently, Hick has introduced the terminological distinction between "eschatology" and "pareschatology," the former relating to the ultimate consummation and the latter to everything "in-between," that is, during the "in-

---

43. For a highly useful presentation and assessment of typologies of contemporary eschatology, see Conradie, *Hope for the Earth*, chap. 13.

44. For details regarding the two continents, see Schwarz, *Eschatology*, pp. 1–2.

45. Gerhard, *Loci theologici* (1610–1621), devotes no fewer than two of nine books to the detailed discussion of eschatological topics (books 8 and 9).

46. For the historical background and contemporary role of eschatology, see Sauter, "The Concept and Task of Eschatology," pp. 499–515.

termediate" period (if any) between one's death and the consummation of everything.[47] This distinction, although not widely used (even in this project), makes the useful point that eschatology's domain is huge and comprehensive: "In its broadest sense the term 'eschatology' includes all concepts of life beyond death and everything connected with it such as heaven and hell, paradise and immortality, resurrection and transmigration of the soul, rebirth and reincarnation, and last judgment and doomsday."[48] Christian eschatology, however, is less about explorations into the sequence of events in the future and more "about a *good* future,"[49] the content of hope. For that, it must assume that "we live in a world that makes sense not just now, but totally and forever." Then, and only then, the awaited end is a "fulfillment of the history of the universe and the history of humanity."[50]

Christian theology has to try to strike a radical balance between the New Testament type of enthusiastic hope for the coming of God's righteous rule and the fact that, simply put, "we are no longer a young religion looking forward to the imminent coming of Christ, as the members of the nascent church did in the first centuries."[51] As the German Lutheran theologian Hans Schwarz puts it, "we must guard against two frequent temptations: undue restraint and a travelogue eschatology."[52] It is instructive to note that while on the one hand the Christian Bible has eschatological-apocalyptic sections, and even a whole book devoted to the topic in the New Testament, the church also wisely left out from its canon such wildly speculative and fantasy-oriented pieces of literature as the *Book of Enoch* and the *Apocalypse of Paul*.[53]

Seeking for the middle path between the two extremes, however, should not frustrate or push into the margins the radical nature of eschatological hope: "Eschatological faith has about it an undeniable defiance of common-sense appearances. In the face of suffering, violence, and seemingly hopeless injustice and tragedy, it is bold to believe that these are not the deepest and truest realities."[54] Particularly resurrection "requires of faith something even more terrible than submission before the violence of being and acceptance of fate, and forbids faith the consolations of tragic wisdom; it places all hope and

---

47. Hick, *Death and Eternal Life*, p. 399 and passim.
48. Schwarz, *Eschatology*, p. 26.
49. Watts, "Subjective and Objective Hope," p. 48, emphasis in original.
50. Polkinghorne, *God of Hope*, pp. xvii, xvi.
51. Schwarz, *Eschatology*, p. xii.
52. Schwarz, *Eschatology*, p. 247.
53. Schwarz, *Eschatology*, p. 247.
54. J. Walls, introduction to *OHE*, p. 5.

consolation upon the insane expectation that what is lost will be given back, not as heroic wisdom (death has been robbed of its tragic beauty) but as the gift it always was."[55]

But what is the "end" eschatology speaks of? A notoriously polyvalent term, "end" can mean both completion (that is, coming or bringing to an end)[56] or fulfillment (as in the Greek term *telos*). Both meanings are present in the Christian eschatological expectation.[57] P. Tillich saw this in his highly nuanced discussion of "the kingdom of God as the end of history," minding the dual nature of the term "end" as completion and fulfillment.[58] Stating that although "[p]ast and present meet in the present, and both are included in the eternal 'now,' . . . they are not swallowed by the present," he added that the future reference is not thereby ignored.[59] This sounds good and correct. Where Tillich goes astray, however, is when he argues that "the fulfillment of history lies in the permanently present end of history," leading to the disappointing thesis that, therefore, ultimately "[t]he eternal is not a future state of things; it is always present."[60] To say that the eternal is not a future state of things is of course true in one sense; eternity is "much more" than a temporal state of things; however, to say that alone (in Tillich's system) means that there is not a future in the sense that traditional eschatology intuits.[61] Tillich's abandonment of the future, final fulfillment of God's kingdom is but an example of the wide trend in the twentieth-century eclipse of future-oriented eschatology.[62]

On top of the meaningfulness of creation, three essential aspects should be integrated tightly into any constructive eschatology: first, the hope not only for the human future but also for the transformation and renewal of all creatures and the cosmos itself; second, hope for both persons and communities, including the whole of humanity; and third, hope for both the afterlife and the life-before-afterlife.

---

55. D. Hart, *The Beauty of the Infinite*, p. 392, as cited in J. Walls, introduction to *OHE*, p. 6.

56. Kant famously problematized the idea of "end" in this sense and rightly intuited that the idea of time coming to an end greatly challenges our mental powers. See Kant, "The End of All Things," pp. 221-22.

57. See Pannenberg, *ST* 3:586-87.

58. Tillich, *ST* 3:394.

59. Tillich, *ST* 3:395-96 (395).

60. Tillich, *ST* 3:396, 400.

61. So also Pannenberg, *ST* 3:587.

62. For details, see Pannenberg, *ST* 3:588-89.

The Domain and Horizon of a Constructive Eschatology

At the very center of Christian hope is "participation in the eternal life of God. . . . [And all] else that is related to it, including the resurrection of the dead and the last judgment, is a consequence of God's own coming to consummate his rule over his creation." This "future of God's kingdom," the "epitome of Christian hope,"[63] encompasses all of creation, not only humans, nor merely Earth — but the whole vast cosmos. This is the proper framework for eschatology. This widest horizon, however, has not been at the center of Christian eschatology. Indeed, what happened early in Christian theology was that personal eschatology became the focus of the Christian hope. And the concept of the kingdom of God was soon marginalized. Even worse, when employed, its meaning was reduced mainly to hope for the personal resurrection of the body. Communal and cosmic horizons were marginalized. A telling example can be found in the eighth-century (Eastern) doctrinal manual *The Orthodox Faith* by John of Damascus, in which the whole concept of the kingdom is missing and individual resurrection is made the defining theme. The same is true of Western doctrinal presentations from Lombard's *Distinctions* all the way to the Reformation and Protestant Scholasticism. Even classical liberalism's rediscovery of the kingdom of God ended in an immanentist and personalist interpretation.[64]

Only in twentieth-century theology have the centrality and comprehensive nature of eschatology been rediscovered, including not only the personal but also the communal. But even here, a key weakness can still be discerned: the lack of a cosmic orientation. Whereas Barth succeeded in helping rediscover the centrality of eschatology to theology, only in the theologies of Rahner, Moltmann, and Pannenberg, among others, have the implications of what we know of the vastness of the cosmos — in terms of size, "age," and expansion — begun to emerge as integral themes. But even in them the *cosmic* orientation is still by and large in the making.

The development of a viable constructive eschatology for the sake of the religiously pluralistic and secular culture of the globalizing world has to encompass the following spheres:

- personal and communal hope
- human and cosmic destiny
- present and future hope

63. Pannenberg, *ST* 3:527.
64. For details and sources, see Pannenberg, *ST* 3:527-30.

Personal and Communal Hope. A systematically crucial problem for constructive eschatology is negotiating personal and communal hopes (ultimately relating to the whole human race) not only as parallel with each other but also as mutually linked. Only such an eschatology that can successfully envision "the perfecting of individual life after death . . . with the consummation of humanity and world in the kingdom of God" will suffice.[65] Unless one is willing to go with the idea of physical death as an immediate entrance to God's eternity (without any "intermediate time"), a way has to be found to link one's own death and bodily resurrection with the rest of humanity. The theological options are these: "*Either* we expect full and real personal salvation at death even though this minimizes what takes place at the end, allowing for it nothing decisive for individual fulfillment and giving it the significance of an addition, since everything decisive has taken place already; *or* we expect the real decision and salvation to come only at the last day, though this is to play down death as access to Christ, as decision, as purifying, and as transformation."[66]

In the Old Testament and Jewish tradition, the communal hope lay in the forefront and the individual emerged only later gradually (see chap. 3). Even when the hope for individuals developed, it was not divorced from but rather integrated into the hope for all of humanity. The Christian church adopted this view and faced the task of even expanding it with the inclusion of Gentiles into the hope for a common destiny. In comparison, the pagan hope of the immortality of the soul (as in Plato) has no reference to the whole of humanity, only to the individual. Nor is the contemporary secular hope for the completion of human dreams in an ideal society, as expressed particularly in Marxism, successful in conceiving this utopia as for the whole of humanity; it only deals with those currently living; those who have passed away will totally miss it. The idealist philosopher Gotthold Lessing clearly understood that in his *Education of the Human Race* and was led to the idea of reincarnation for its solution.[67]

The solution of Christian tradition to this dilemma is based on the trinitarian faith, particularly on pneumatological resources. Similarly to the related locus of soteriology and ecclesiology, it is the Spirit's work to "lift us" up in filial relationship with Jesus Christ, the Savior, but not only as individuals without an integral link with others, but rather as members of the same "body" whose

65. Pannenberg, *ST* 3:546.
66. Pannenberg, *ST* 3:547, emphasis in original.
67. See Pannenberg, *ST* 3:546–50.

"head" is Christ. This "ecstatic" (as in "standing outside one's self") work of the Spirit is of course already at work in a different manner in creation, linking all creatures to the rest of creation.[68]

Human and Cosmic Destiny. Although he himself failed to carry out the program, Tillich's demand that the basic dilemma of any eschatology — the relationship between the individual and collective hope — should not be "separated from the destiny of the universe"[69] is definitely pointing in the right direction. Christian hope of the eschatological consummation includes the whole of God's creation, "the integration of the real history of human beings with the nature of the earth."[70] This holistic and "earthly" eschatological vision is masterfully expressed by the American Anabaptist theologian Thomas A. Finger: "Since the new creation arrives through God's Spirit, and since it reshapes the physical world, every theological locus is informed by the Spirit's transformation of matter-energy."[71] Christ's resurrection through the life-giving Spirit is already a foretaste of the "transformation of matter-energy" in new creation, "a transformation of the present nature beyond what emergence refers to."[72] The pneumatologically loaded eschatological openness of creation points to the final consummation in which matter and physicality — no more than time — are not so much "deleted" as transformed, made transcendent, so to speak.[73]

Present and Future Hope. The present and future are linked tightly with each other through the presence of the Spirit: "By the Spirit the eschatological future is present already in the hearts of believers. His dynamic is the basis of anticipations of eschatological salvation already in the as yet incomplete history of the world."[74] This is a corrective to merely this-worldly "eschatologies," whether those of classical liberalism and other Enlightenment-driven traditions or contemporary eco-feminist (and some liberationist) views. It is also a defeat of those fundamentalist and other otherworldly eschatological visions that end up being escapist and dismissive of work toward improving the current world. The "already" and "not yet" (of the arrival of the kingdom of God) and the "continuity" versus "discontinuity" (between new creation and this world) templates hold the present and future in dynamic tension

---

68. Pannenberg, *ST* 3:551–52.
69. Tillich, *ST* 3:418.
70. Moltmann, *God in Creation*, p. xi.
71. T. Finger, *A Contemporary Anabaptist Theology*, p. 563.
72. R. Russell, *Cosmology*, p. 37.
73. R. Russell, *Cosmology*, pp. 37–38.
74. Pannenberg, *ST* 3:552.

and mutual conditioning. R. Russell summarizes it succinctly: "Eschatologies such as these view the new creation not as a replacement of the present creation — i.e., not as a second *ex nihilo* — nor as the mere working out of the natural processes of the world. Instead eschatology involves the complete transformation of the world by a radically new act of God beginning at Easter and continuing into the future."[75]

The demand for such a comprehensive and all-embracing eschatology raises questions as to the nature of language and approach. Similar kinds of challenges can be found in other theological loci, particularly in the doctrine of creation, as it also engages not only Christian tradition and other faith traditions but also natural sciences and their particular ways of discourse. Eschatology has also its own peculiar challenges, to which we turn next, before outlining the plan of part 1.

Metaphors and Participation: On the Nature of Knowledge of Eschatology

Moltmann makes the obvious point that any claim for *logos*, "teaching," "doctrine," "principle" about eschaton, events yet-to-happen, is quite a precarious assertion![76] Rather, we could speak of "the believing hope."[77] That kind of discourse, however, is hardly analytic and doctrinal; it is rather suggestive, metaphorical, testimonial, narrative. No wonder much of the New Testament teaching on eschatology, as the late American Baptist theologian James Mc-Clendon put it, comes to us in the form of "word pictures," "words that present visual scenes."[78] Hence, he recommends "eschatological picture thinking" as a methodological guide: therein the theologian engages various biblical (and historical) pictures of God's eschatological rule to show that eschatology is both an image of the end and a directive for the church's present: eschatology is concerned "with what lasts and with what comes last."[79] Similarly, the Jewish theologian Neil Gillman says: "All eschatologies are imaginative constructs. They must be imaginative not only because they deal with events that no hu-

75. R. Russell, "Cosmology and Eschatology," in *OHE*, p. 567.

76. Moltmann, *Theology of Hope*, pp. 16-17. See also Rahner, "Hermeneutics of Eschatological Assertions," p. 343; for comments, see P. Phan, "Roman Catholic Theology," pp. 222-23.

77. Moltmann, *Theology of Hope*, pp. 19-22.

78. McClendon, *Doctrine*, pp. 75-77, 92; the latter quoted phrase is from Murphy, "The Resurrection Body and Personal Identity," p. 205.

79. McClendon, *Doctrine*, pp. 44, 75. For an insightful discussion of "the language of eschatology," see also Pannenberg, *ST* 3:621-22.

man has ever beheld, but even more because these events will inaugurate an age which is properly timeless."[80]

Add to those caveats yet another obvious one, namely, the vast size of the observed cosmos as we now know it. Speaking of its "end" and "destiny" — which we must attempt in contrast to earlier anthropocentric (and our-planet-centered) approaches — in light of its immensity should lead us into humble, tentative, and suggestive concepts.[81] Not only that, but there is yet another layer of challenges to any serious talk about eschatology, what the Italian liberationist Vítor Westhelle names as its liminality, in three interrelated senses of the term — ontologically, ethically, and epistemologically: "Eschatology is a discourse on liminality, on that which is different in an ontological, ethical and also epistemological sense. Ontologically, because it addresses the question of an Other reality, as different as the reality of God is from this world; ethically, because it pertains to a different code for morality, as different as the Sermon on the Mount is from all our ethical systems and moral prescriptions; epistemologically, because eschatology is also about the liminality of our accepted epistemic régimes, i.e., that there are other, often-suppressed 'knowledges' beyond the commonly accepted noetic realm of the academy."[82]

In light of these considerations, there is some value in Moltmann's proposal that a constructive theology of creation (and by implication, eschatology) "must try to get away from analytical thinking, with its distinctions between subject and object. . . . This means that it will have to revert to the premodern concept of reason as the organ of perception and participation (methexis)."[83] Closely related to the metaphoric orientation is participatory knowledge that seeks not to possess but rather to gratefully participate.[84] Participatory knowledge honors the relational, mutually dependent, and symbiotic nature of all created processes, including humanity as part of it.[85] While Moltmann's suggestion is useful, it also calls for some qualification and correction. First, a return to a communicative and participatory knowledge does not have to mean the return to a premodern concept of reason — how could we return, living as we are on this side of the Enlightenment? Second, participatory knowledge does not have to be antagonistic to analytical thinking; a quick look at leading

---

80. Gillman, *The Death of Death*, p. 25.

81. S. R. L. Clark, "Deep Time," p. 193; I am indebted to Wilkinson, *Christian Eschatology*, p. 25.

82. Westhelle, "Liberation Theology," pp. 312–13.

83. Moltmann, *God in Creation*, p. 2.

84. Moltmann, *God in Creation*, pp. 2–3.

85. For important comments, see Moltmann, *God in Creation*, pp. 2–4.

theologians in tradition leaves no doubt about sophisticated intellectual and analytic capacities in the service of a "premodern" doctrinal formation. Furthermore, as the evolutionary biologist Jeffrey P. Schloss reminds us, "even in their figurativeness, metaphors are metaphors of something, not nothing."[86] The use of metaphors is not funded by the desire to know "less" or more vaguely about eschatology, but rather, to try to be sensitive to the distinctive requirements of that "knowledge."

Although theologians should be quick to acknowledge the limits of human language and intellectual powers, they should also not capitulate before the bar of reason. Consider what A. McGrath, a leading expert on religion-science dialogue, states: "From a Christian perspective, the horizons defined by the parameters of our human existence merely limit what we can see; they do not define what there is to be seen."[87] Theological imagination, as much as it has to be anchored in the wider human pursuit of truth, should bravely, though also carefully, rush in where angels fear to tread. Modern and contemporary theologians have so much feared the fame of the fool that they also often lacked the rewards of the discovery of the radically new and unanticipated.

Orientation to Part 1

Chapters 2 and 3, respectively, will present the visions of the "end" of the cosmos and human life as conjectured among natural sciences and as envisioned in four living faiths. With regard to the sciences, clarifications of what is at stake theologically will be carefully considered. A number of subsequent chapters will reflect on natural sciences' implications for theological claims. Religions' eschatologies will not yet be engaged from a Christian point of view; that will happen in later chapters incrementally, in relation to topics relevant for a given faith tradition. The discussion in chapter 3 seeks to provide as coherent and representative a view of Jewish, Muslim, Buddhist, and Hindu eschatologies as possible.

As a theological prelude to the rest of the presentation of a Christian view of the "end" and the consummation, chapter 4 outlines a trinitarian theology of hope — similar to what was done with regard to, say, the doctrine of revelation (*Trinity and Revelation*, chap. 2) and of creation (*Creation and Humanity*, chap. 4). Thereafter, two long chapters (5 and 6) will seek to develop

---

86. Schloss, "From Evolution to Eschatology," p. 58.
87. McGrath, *A Brief History of Heaven*, pp. 1-7 (1).

and defend a comprehensive Christian vision of the transition from this world to new creation, paying special attention to how to conceive this transition in relation to the time-space continuum, which obviously has to be radically transformed; to the transposition from the state of decay and death to one of life in the resurrected body; and to the role of judgment and purification as necessary conditions for living in the holiness of God. A particularly complex problem of the identity-continuity between now and "then" in relation to the hope for physical resurrection will also be inspected.

Chapters 7 and 8 will take up issues only marginally (if at all) discussed in systematic/constructive eschatologies: first, the value of nature and the environment, as well as justice and equality, in relation to hope for life eternal. How should a constructive theology defeat the persistent critique of eco-feminists and other environmentally sensitive theologians to whom the Christian vision of the end represents egoism and leads to dismissal of this earthly life? Liberationists of various stripes echo the same charge by claiming that Christian eschatology lacks resources for tackling current problems in society in its hope for a better world to come. Second, a related issue, the presence of evil and suffering in a world created good, has to be carefully investigated — as does the corollary issue of violence in relation to the promise in biblical teaching of defeating all resisting powers.

In chapter 9, the difficult and complex questions related to access to eternal salvation and the possibility of eternal condemnation will be reflected on in light of Christian tradition and contemporary theological and religious plurality. The last chapter in part 1 takes up the remaining standard issues regarding final consummation, from the signs of Jesus' return, to its nature and significance, to the possibility of the earthly millennial rule of Christ, to the nature of heaven and new creation. In particular, the last topic will be carefully considered in light of dramatic intellectual, cultural, and theological shifts in the last century.

2. The "End" of the Cosmos and Life in Natural Sciences' Conjectures

The Origins of the Universe in Light of Contemporary Science

The sciences' conjectures about the future are based on our current best knowledge about the cosmos's origins, evolvement, and workings. While a detailed discussion of various aspects of scientific cosmology's views of origins and their relation to theological reflection is conducted in *Creation and Humanity* (part 1), we will summarize very briefly the key ideas as background to the current investigation.[1] Behind the contemporary cosmological theories about origins and the "end" lie radical shifts in worldview and outlook.

Rather than steady, mechanistic, and dualistic, the workings of the cosmos bespeak relationality, interdependence, dynamism, evolvement, and complexity. These are the results of the move from the Newtonian worldview to that driven by the contemporary relativity and quantum theory. What quantum theory reveals is that not only at the smallest, subatomic level (where it primarily functions), but also at the macrolevel, nature reveals surprises, irregularities, and unpredictability. This is not to say that nature acts unlawfully; the laws of nature are still in place and natural phenomena are (relatively speaking) deterministic; otherwise no scientific observations would be possible. What the unpredictability means is that determinism is not ironclad

---

1. This summary repeats the materials from my *Spirit and Salvation*, chap. 3; both that chapter and this are based on the detailed discussion in part 1 of *Creation and Humanity*. For a highly useful presentation of "the first three minutes" to nonspecialists, see chap. 3 in P. Davies, *The Last Three Minutes*. From a theological perspective, see Barr, "Modern Cosmology and Christian Theology."

and that — according to the major (Copenhagian) interpretation of quantum theory — natural processes and events are probabilistic in nature. The lack of exact results is not a matter of weakness of measurement but an inherent feature of the reality studied.[2]

This kind of world is open rather than closed in nature. In the open universe, the process of emergence is constantly at work. The basic definition of "emergence" is "that new and unpredictable phenomena are naturally produced by interactions in nature; that these new structures, organisms, and ideas are not reducible to the subsystems on which they depend; and that the newly evolved realities in turn exercise a causal influence on the parts out of which they arose."[3] A theologically and eschatologically significant observation is that "emergence at all levels of being, and not just at those of life and mind, requires that nature possess an anticipatory rather than simply a cumulative character. It must be open to a domain of potentiality that makes a quiet entrance — from the future as it were — and thus opens up the otherwise unbending fabric of things to the later-and-more."[4] In other words, there is a dynamic tension between increasing entropy and the higher structuring. "In its dependence all creaturely reality is subject to the fate of destructuring, of dissolution according to the law of entropy. Because of the openness of process structures to future events, however, new structures are constantly formed, since processes take place in open rather than closed systems."[5]

On the basis of these and related insights and discoveries, contemporary cosmology envisions the origins of the cosmos in terms of big bang cosmologies.

Big Bang Cosmologies

In the standard big bang theory, currently the basis of all scientific cosmological speculations even among those who advocate revised versions, the cosmos came into being about 13.7 billion years ago from a singularity of zero size and infinite density (usually represented as $t = 0$, in which t denotes time) and has since expanded to its current form. Supported by relativity theory and quantum physics, it has received remarkable experimental confirmation of its

2. See further McGrath, *A Scientific Theology*, 2:283–85; R. Russell, "Quantum Physics," pp. 346–48.

3. Clayton, *Mind and Emergence*, p. vi; for the history, see chap. 1.

4. Haught, *Is Nature Enough?* p. 86.

5. Pannenberg, *ST* 2:112.

basic intuitions — such as the Hubble discovery in the 1920s that galaxies are receding from us, implying that the cosmos is "expanding," and the microwave background radiation discovery in the 1960s, which is believed to be an echo from the original big bang.

The big bang theory simply looks back in time to the point when expansion began and to the "beginning point." Because of extremely complicated questions, particularly regarding the "inflation period" immediately following the big bang (the so-called Planck time, 1^{-43} second, the shortest measure of time), to which no known scientific laws apply, revisions of the standard model continue. Most well known is the Hartle/Hawkins quantum model, in which there is no "beginning" in time; the cosmos is finite with regard to its origins. Furthermore, more radical forms of quantum cosmologies are emerging all the time — including various types of "bouncing" or "oscillating" models in which big bounces, rather than one single big bang, succeed each other endlessly, as well as "multiverse" proposals, that is, ours is only one among many, perhaps infinitely many, universes. Theologically speaking, however, none of these poses a serious problem because the most foundational theistic belief (including that of other Abrahamic faiths) has to do with the contingency of the cosmos on the Creator. The world is neither self-originating nor self-sustaining. How the "logistics" might be best understood — the domain of sciences — is neither a threat nor an alternative to creation theology, but rather a necessary dialogue partner.

Scientific Predictions about the "Future" of the Universe

Dominant Options according to Current Knowledge

It is quite interesting that not only theologians — and more widely, scholars of religions[6] — until recently have for decades missed an engagement of scientific predictions of the future of the cosmos and life. Counterintuitively, even among the scientific community, the questions of the "end" have not been in the forefront at all. Notwithstanding some emerging work in the science-religion engagement of eschatology and the future of the universe, only baby steps have been taken when compared to the wide and deep interest in the question of beginnings. After massive efforts to understand clearly the origins of the universe, it took until the 1970s–1980s for the focus to include also the

---

6. See Wilkinson, *Christian Eschatology*, pp. 5–6.

far-future fate.[7] Lately, "physical eschatology" has drawn a lot of interest in cosmology and physics.[8] Unpredicted advances in science have made the task possible and urgent.[9]

In principle, the picture painted of the "future" in sciences is not complicated: it leads to eventual decay and annihilation.[10] That said, the question of "[t]he end of the Universe in scientific terms is both simple and very difficult to predict. The simplicity is that Einstein's theory of general relativity gives equations that tell us how any universe containing matter and radiation will change with time under the influence of gravity." That said, in light of current knowledge, there is no final certainty as to whether Einstein's theory is valid also at the largest cosmic scales.[11] Interestingly, John D. Barrow, himself a leading physicist who has also done groundbreaking work in physical eschatology, has recently spoken of "the speculative futures market,"[12] not to dismiss the importance of continuing speculations into the future, but rather to issue a warning to advance carefully and thoughtfully. Among other things, he reminds his fellow scientists that even "constants of nature," which by definition are supposed to be invariant, might not be so.[13]

As is well known, three basic options are available on the basis of Einstein's theory: if an open universe, then the process of expanding eventually leads to "freeze"; if "closed," the expansion will reach the culmination point and eventually "contract" until it results in "fry," the big crunch; and if a "flat" curvature, as in the first scenario, it will expand (forever) and finally reach "freeze."[14] Most all scientists in recent years have become convinced that the open universe is the correct guess and that its expansion is accelerating ever and ever more rap-

---

7. See P. Davies, *The Last Three Minutes*, pp. x–xi.

8. For a succinct account, see Barrow, "The Far, Far Future," pp. 26–28 particularly; Worthing, *God, Creation, and Contemporary Physics*, pp. 160–62. See also Rees, "Living in a Multiverse," pp. 77–82.

9. See Wilkinson, *Christian Eschatology*, p. ix. For predictions of the future fate of the cosmos among scientists, see, e.g., P. Ward and Brownlee, *The Life and Death of Planet Earth*.

10. See further P. Davies, *The Last Three Minutes*, chap. 2: "The Dying Universe."

11. Wilkinson, *Christian Eschatology*, pp. 12, 15.

12. Barrow, "The Far, Far Future," pp. 30–33; for various "scientific cosmological options" concerning the "beginning" and "end" of the universe, see the succinct statement in P. Davies, "Eternity," pp. 42–44.

13. See P. Davies, "Eternity," p. 50.

14. R. Russell, *Time in Eternity*, pp. 56–59 (and the extensive references therein, both nontechnical and technical); see also Worthing, *God, Creation, and Contemporary Physics*, pp. 162–75.

idly.[15] If so, what are the implications for the future of the universe — and for life on this earth or life elsewhere?[16] It is convenient to divide that question into three interrelated time frames: the near future (the end of life conditions on earth), the distant future (the end of earth, sun, and our solar system), and the far-distant future (the "end" of the whole cosmos).[17] Let us work our way from the far-distant end to questions related to the future of humanity on this earth.

The Far-Distant, Distant, and Near-Future Predictions concerning the Cosmos and Life Conditions

The most distant future of the cosmos, according to most current scientific predictions,[18] looks something like the following:

- In 5 billion years, the sun will become a red giant, engulfing the orbits of Earth and Mars.
- In 40–50 billion years, star formation in our galaxy will have ended.
- In 10^{12} years, all massive stars will have become neutron stars or black holes.[19]
- If the universe is closed, then in 10^{12} years, the universe will have reached its maximum size and then will recollapse back to a singularity like the original hot big bang.
- In 10^{31} years, protons and neutrons will decay into positrons, electrons, neutrinos, and photons.
- In 10^{34} years, dead planets, black dwarfs, and neutron stars will disappear, their mass completely converted into energy, leaving only black holes, electron-positron plasma, and radiation. All carbon-based life-forms will inevitably become extinct.[20]

---

15. See R. Russell, *Time in Eternity*, pp. 59–60 (59). For a nontechnical discussion, see chap. 5 in Islam, *The Ultimate Fate of the Universe*.

16. Barrow, "The Far, Far Future," pp. 36–37.

17. With minor adaptations from Boisvert, *Religion and the Physical Sciences*, pp. 229–34.

18. The predictions about the future of the cosmos did not of course begin in recent decades. A noteworthy historical precedent is the 1755 work by Immanuel Kant, *Universal Natural History*, pp. 59–70; clearly the size of the universe was dramatically smaller in the imagination of Kant and other scholars of the time. For other historical predictions, see Barrow, "The Far, Far Future," pp. 23–26.

19. The figure 10^{12} years = 10,000,000,000,000 years; and likewise for other similar figures.

20. R. Russell, "Cosmology and Eschatology," in *OHE*, p. 566; a similar, slightly more

The end result of all that is that "proton decay spells ultimate doom for life based on protons and neutrons, like *Homo sapiens* and all forms of life constructed of atoms."[21] In that light, it does not really matter which of the three above-mentioned scientific scenarios is true (open, closed, or flat); they all lead to ultimate decay. "If the predictions of scientific cosmology do indeed come to pass in the future, ours will be a barren universe devoid of any trace that life had ever existed."[22] For all forms of life, the far-distant future is bleak. It is the kind of universe we know that makes life possible — and yet, that universe is "big and old, dark and cold."[23] Life on Earth (or, if it cannot be found, on other planets) seems to be an anomaly, unique, and very much a latecomer to the scene — at least in light of our current knowledge.

But what if there are other forms of "life" or platforms other than carbon-based ones for life to continue? Not surprisingly, various alternative proposals have been set forth.[24] One of them builds on the possibility of multiverses, which might make possible endless fertility. True, this universe may come to nil, but there are many — perhaps infinitely many — other universes in which fertility in one form or another may continue. Another highly speculative and creative suggestion is that of the physicist Freeman Dyson, who joins the argument that considers the existence of life a "necessity" in the kind of universe we know. This argument believes that (at least) intelligent life never comes to an end. With unprecedentedly enhanced capacities to manipulate and engineer our environment, we may bring into existence new kinds of genetic changes that guarantee the continuation of intelligence in some form, certainly not in the form of current human life (because, as said, that seems an absolute impossibility in light of current knowledge), but in some nonpersonal form.[25] Yet another highly speculative proposal comes from an American cosmologist, Frank J. Tipler, a coauthor (with D. Barrow) of the highly acclaimed *Anthropic Cosmological Principle* in 1972. Materially similar to Dyson, Tipler's vision of "physics of immortality" intuits the continuance of intelligent life as some kind of computational process — even long after any kind of intelligent life

detailed list can be found in R. Russell, *Time in Eternity*, pp. 60–61. The main source referred to is Barrow and Tipler, *Anthropic Cosmological Principle*, pp. 653-54.

21. Barrow and Tipler, *Anthropic Cosmological Principle*, p. 684, cited in R. Russell, *Time in Eternity*, p. 61.

22. R. Russell, *Time in Eternity*, p. 61.

23. Barrow, "Cosmology," 4.8, cited in Wilkinson, *Christian Eschatology*, p. 15.

24. This paragraph is indebted to Wilkinson, *Christian Eschatology*, pp. 7–10.

25. For his early suggestion, see Dyson, "Time without End," pp. 449–50; for a recent (more) accessible account, see his "Life in the Universe," pp. 140–57.

as we know it has vanished. Indeed, he envisions that ultimately the infinite expansion of intelligence to everywhere in the universe is possible.[26] These and other proposals, as said, are highly speculative and so far have no scientific warrant, let alone "evidence."

What about the distant future prospects beyond the conditions of life on this earth and in this solar system? Well known and well documented is the possibility — as small as its probability is in a shorter time frame — of the earth being hit by a comet or asteroid.[27] A familiar example from history is the dinosaur extinction due to a hit by a comet about 65 million years ago. As recently as 1994 we observed the Shoemaker-Levy comet's damage on Jupiter. Asteroids, although smaller than comets, can also cause remarkable damage to our living conditions and can be equally deadly.[28] The conclusion is bleak: "Whether or not a comet hits, we know for certain that in 5 billion years, the Earth will be uninhabitable. The Sun will come to the end of its available hydrogen fuel and will begin to swell up, its outer layers swallowing up Mercury, Venus and the Earth. It will then lose its outer layers and the centre will become a white dwarf, an object of high density about the size of the Earth. Without the heat and light of the Sun none of the remaining planets will be habitable."[29]

For the sake of argument, let us suppose that by that time humankind would have found another habitable planet in our galaxy. In that case, a catastrophic scenario would seem to face us: "Galaxies have a local movement imposed on the general expansion of the Universe and one of our nearest neighbours, the Andromeda spiral galaxy, will crash into us." This would make an escape from the sun's death even more complicated.[30]

All the above-mentioned conditions are totally out of human control, as opposed to the relatively significant human factor concerning the near future of this earth and its life conditions. How likely are these conditions to

26. Tipler, *Physics of Immortality*; for an insightful theological engagement and critique, see R. Russell, "Cosmology and Eschatology: The Implications," pp. 195–216. Also highly useful is Worthing, *God, Creation, and Contemporary Physics*, pp. 164–75.

27. For a vivid imaginary account of comet Swift-Tuttle and other similar ones hitting the earth in the near future, see chap. 2 in P. Davies, *The Last Three Minutes*.

28. Taken from Wilkinson, *Christian Eschatology*, chap. 2; Stoeger, "Scientific Accounts of Ultimate Catastrophes," pp. 20–24; Polkinghorne, *God of Hope*, pp. 6–8. For a now-classic presentation, see Asimov, *A Choice of Catastrophes*.

29. Wilkinson, *Christian Eschatology*, p. 9.

30. Wilkinson, *Christian Eschatology*, p. 10; for details, see also Stoeger, "Scientific Accounts of Ultimate Catastrophes," pp. 24–27; Islam, *The Ultimate Fate of the Universe*, chap. 11.

remain life-sustaining? The impending catastrophes facing the future, even the near future at least in terms of conditions for human life to survive on this globe, are well known and well documented. At the top of the imminent threats for human civilization is the devastating pollution[31] of the earth and her resources, causing dramatic climate changes.[32] This pollution is considered to be "our world's most dangerous, and constant, threat."[33] Impending environmental catastrophe is linked with a matrix of more or less interrelated problems such as scarcity of food to meet the needs of the growing population, deforestation, and overuse of fossil fuels; other forms of global pollution including waste problems, global warming, and the destruction of the ozone layer; and an increase in temperature with effects on the sea level and other ecosystemic areas.[34]

These and related developments on our globe mean that "if current trends continue, we will not."[35] Not surprisingly, among the leading scientists, pessimism about the future of our globe is common: "by 2600 the world's population will be standing shoulder to shoulder, and the electricity use will make the Earth glow red hot."[36] As a result, "[the odds] are no better than fifty-fifty that our present civilisation on Earth will survive to the end of the present century."[37] Whereas the Enlightenment brought about an unprecedented optimism for the capacity of technology and science to produce ever-progressing life-sustaining and life-improving conditions, by the end of the second millennium those hopes were severely shattered and not infrequently abandoned.[38] Here religions are not mere bystanders: religiously driven attitudes help shape environmental efforts or lack thereof. Only recently have scholars come to acknowledge in a more robust manner that not only "[h]uman beliefs about the nature of ecology are the distinctive contribution of our species to the ecology

31. In this discussion "pollution" is used as an inclusive umbrella term denoting all types of harm to the environment and its processes and creatures by humans (whether directly or indirectly).

32. The famous "Gaia hypothesis" was proposed by James Lovelock; for a formative essay, see his *The Revenge of Gaia*.

33. International Conference on Environmental Pollution and Remediation, *3rd International Conference*.

34. For an up-to-date discussion, see Brunner, Butler, and Swoboda, *Introducing Evangelical Ecotheology*, pp. 49–62.

35. Maguire, *Moral Core of Judaism and Christianity*, p. 13.

36. Hawking, *The Universe in a Nutshell*, p. 158, cited in Wilkinson, *Christian Eschatology*, p. 1.

37. Rees, *Our Final Hour*, p. 8, cited in Wilkinson, *Christian Eschatology*, p. 1.

38. See Wilkinson, *Christian Eschatology*, p. 7.

itself" but that, importantly, "[r]eligious beliefs — especially those concerning the nature of powers that create and animate — become an effective part of ecological systems."[39]

Given these scientific predictions, it is no wonder various tactics either to defeat or at least escape the inevitable "end" have risen among scientists, a topic to which we turn next. Thereafter, we will consider what is at stake for theology and how theologians have reacted.

How Scientists Have Responded to the Threat of the "End"

Polkinghorne summarizes neatly the most common responses of scientists to the necessary futility of the cosmos and its processes. First, with "stoic defiance in the face of threatened reality," many consider the whole of human life (if not the rest of the cosmos) "no more than a transient episode."[40] Consider the pessimistic-realist take by the famous British philosopher Bertrand Russell: "All the labors of the ages . . . are destined to extinction in the vast death of the solar system, and the whole temple of man's achievement must inevitably be buried beneath the debris of the universe in ruins."[41] While perhaps a noble attitude, for many other scientists the "grace of tragedy," as S. Weinberg called it in his groundbreaking popular pamphlet *The First Three Minutes*, hardly suffices.[42]

Other scientists find an alternative more appealing, one that can be called "a total view": "While the universe may end badly, perhaps it is to the complete sweep of cosmic history, considered as a whole from beginning to end, that we should look if we wish to discern its significance. Meaning is to be found in the whole process and not in individual events." The total view is aligned with a certain understanding of time, probably the most common among scientists (regardless of their view of the issue under discussion), namely, "block time," that is, the denial of the commonsense flow-of-time conception. In this scenario, "meaning" is found in an "atemporally existent lifespan" of either the whole cosmos or an individual life in which distinctions

39. L. Sullivan, preface to *Hinduism and Ecology*, p. xi.
40. Polkinghorne, *God of Hope*, p. 21.
41. B. Russell, "Free Man's Worship," p. 41, quoted in R. Russell, "Cosmology and Eschatology," in *OHE*, p. 567 (which also contains several other similar statements by leading scientists and philosophers).
42. Weinberg, *The First Three Minutes*, p. 155, cited (from an earlier edition) in Polkinghorne, *God of Hope*, p. 21.

between past, present, and future are not real, any more than is the idea of progress (at least as far as it is related to time).[43] For a number of reasons, this way of responding to futility hardly satisfies all.

Yet another response is the so-called physical eschatology discussed above. In the form Dyson presented it, as the hope for the continuation of intellectual life beyond the destruction of this planet and perhaps even our galaxy, as long-term a scale as that may embrace, it is still penultimate. Only the proposal of Tipler — according to which the collapsing universe may be able to be reprogrammed, so to speak, with the help of an infinite amount of information to reach some kind of "omega" point — may carry some *almost* ultimate meaning; but that theory is the most speculative to scientists and does not have many followers.[44]

Finally, the response proposing endless fertility comes from those scientists who insist that quantum theory can be combined with general relativity theory — an enterprise totally impossible in light of current scientific knowledge and experience — to intuit "baby universes [that] are continually bubbling up from fluctuations in the primeval ur-state, which is the quantum gravitational vacuum."[45] It is believed that at least some of those "bubbles" may reach a cosmic lifetime, and hence, "[t]he cosmic pot will boil away 'for ever.'" The problem with this proposal, provided it were at all possible (which it is not in light of contemporary science), is accurately noted by John Polkinghorne: "it would only present a scene of occasional islands of transient meaningfulness erupting within an ocean of absurdity."[46]

Two short observations are in order before engaging theology. First, as all these speculations, including the naturalistic Stoicism (option 1 above), are just that, *speculations*, none of them merits any kind of scientific consensus. Second, related to the first, is the simple but often ignored point that empirical science, to be science, in principle has no answer to these kinds of philosophical and metaphysical queries. Even when scientists speak to these issues, they do not do so on the basis of science (alone) but have moved out of its own self-formulated boundaries. (Too bad most scientists hardly recognize this issue, or at least are not making it clear to their wider audience.) That is one important reason why philosophers, scholars of religion, and theologians are needed and permitted to engage the conversation about the "end."

43. Polkinghorne, *God of Hope*, pp. 22–23.

44. See Polkinghorne, *God of Hope*, pp. 23–26.

45. On "the future of the vacuum" and its implications to our topic, see Barrow, "The Far, Far Future," pp. 33–36.

46. Polkinghorne, *God of Hope*, pp. 26–27.

Sciences and Theology in Critical Mutual Dialogue about "Eschatology"

For Orientation: What Is at Stake for Theology?

Briefly and nontechnically put, the all-important and central challenge to theology from the point of view of physical cosmology's predictions about the fate of the universe is this: How can we even begin to reconcile Christian eschatology's expectation of the imminent return of Christ and the bringing about of the "new heavens and new earth" in light of the extremely, almost infinitely long horizons of sciences?[47] This was the way Pannenberg posed his last question to scientists: "Is the Christian affirmation of an imminent end of this world that in some way invades the present somehow reconcilable with scientific extrapolations of the continuing existence of the universe for at least several billions of years ahead?" The obvious dissonance comes to the fore in that "[s]cientific predictions that in some comfortably distant future the conditions for life will no longer continue on our planet are hardly comparable to biblical eschatology."[48] Wisely, Pannenberg acknowledges that "[t]o this question there are no easy solutions," and therefore, at least for the time being, theologians perhaps should just accept the tension and conflict.[49]

The mutual tension between the two disciplines is intensified by the fact that Christian theology boldly claims that although the present universe will end, it will give way to a transformed reality "to which the natural sciences provide no access, and to which our human experience gives us only obscure, but nevertheless real, intimations and indications."[50] An even greater challenge to theology is what Robert J. Russell claims: "Eschatology as necessarily including not only the resurrection of the body but also the transformation into the new creation by a new act of the Trinitarian God . . . [as] a foundational commitment"[51] is in no way limiting its vision to the "religious" or personal spheres but embraces the whole cosmic horizon.

To a great extent, the type (or even lack) of theological response and initiative depends on the wider approach to the difficult question of how these

47. For details, see Worthing, *God, Creation, and Contemporary Physics*, pp. 175-79. Note his title for chap. 5, which discusses eschatology: "Can God Survive the Consummation of the Universe?"

48. Pannenberg, "Theological Questions to Scientists," p. 48; see also his *ST* 3:589-90.

49. Pannenberg, "Theological Questions to Scientists," p. 48.

50. Stoeger, "Scientific Accounts of Ultimate Catastrophes," p. 20.

51. R. Russell, *Time in Eternity*, p. 67; for discussion of the vision of some of the said scholars, see pp. 67-70.

two disciplines can be related to each other and, should mutual dialogue be desired, under what conditions that might happen. To the clarification of these issues we turn last in this chapter.

Bridging the Gap between the Natural Sciences and Theology:
Obstacles and Opportunities

The main reason for theology (in this case, the theology of "last things") to engage science is not simply because of the "sheer magnitude of its reach"[52] (which alone should make any religion interested in the dialogue),[53] but rather because there is a solid *theological* demand for it: when "Christians confess God as the Creator of the world, it is inevitably the same world that is the object of scientific descriptions." As a result, theologians have the task of relating their statements to those of scientists.[54] While some see every scientific advancement as a step away from religion and faith, it can also be argued that "science has actually advanced to the point where what were formerly religious questions can be seriously tackled."[55]

Understandably, various ways of relating to science have emerged among the theologians and theological movements. We can condense them into two broad categories.[56] The first can be called "separation," in which science and theology are considered two separate realms. As a result, no conflict arises between sciences' predictions about the gradual, very slow decay of everything and Christian faith's expectation of the kingdom's imminent arrival. Classical liberalism's split between "nature," the domain of scientific inquiry, and "history," the area of humanist disciplines, laid the foundation for it.[57] In this reductionist outlook, the question could be raised, "Does matter really matter? It would be easy to argue that Christian faith seems to look forward only to the existence of a disembodied soul after death in a non physical spiritual

52. See Iqbal, "Islam and Modern Science," p. 3.

53. Rashed, "The End Matters," p. 37. For a current massive discussion, see McNamara and Wildman, eds., *Science and the World's Religions*.

54. Pannenberg, "Contributions from Systematic Theology," p. 359.

55. P. Davies, *God and the New Physics*, p. ix.

56. For a fourfold typology (both in Christian theology and four living faith traditions), see my *Creation and Humanity*, chap. 2. For a recent useful discussion, see also Stenmark, "How to Relate Christian Faith and Science."

57. For a highly insightful and nuanced theological reflection, see Welker, "Springing Cultural Traps"; also useful is his earlier essay "Creation."

heaven."[58] A related foundational weakness of classical liberalism has to do with the fully "futuristic-mythical" eschatology of William Wrede or Albert Schweitzer. It simply is toothless in relation to the concerns of physical cosmology, which is anchored in the material realities of the present world. Nor does the "realized eschatology" — either in the way it was first advocated by the British New Testament scholar C. H. Dodd or more recently by the American theologian Kathryn Tanner — have much to say to sciences' views of the future, even though the latter has also engaged science-religion conversation. Yet another highly important and much more nuanced example of the separation paradigm comes from a surprising scholar, namely, one of the pioneers and leading experts in the field, the late biologist-priest Arthur Peacocke. Counterintuitively to many of his colleagues, Peacocke believed that theology has little to say to sciences about the future and that sciences and theology occupy their separate venues. Indeed, he went so far as to surmise that "[a]ll speculation on detailed scenarios of this consummation, the theological exercise called 'eschatology,' surely constitutes a supreme example of attempting to formulate a theory underdetermined by the facts. As such, it seems to me a fruitless and unnecessary exercise."[59]

All these forms of a "separation" approach are in some way or another supported strongly by the prevailing (metaphysical) naturalism rampant among natural scientists. Whereas for theologians, the separation mentality is funded by the desire to avoid conflict with the dominant scientific paradigm, for naturalist scientists, the separation results from the total incredibility of theological (and other "humanistic") explanations: "According to a widespread prejudice, eschatological symbols seem to point to a realm 'totally other' than the reality we can experience."[60] Naturalist worldviews also eschew all teleological notions (other than those that in some sense can be attributed to randomness and chance, that is, evolutionary features considered to be an "improvement"). For theology, however, purposefulness is a necessary category for the simple reason that "if past history were to lack meaning, there would be no reason to anticipate future fulfillment"[61] (even when the "newness" of God's future hardly can be extrapolated in any simple manner from the past processes).

58. Wilkinson, *Christian Eschatology*, p. ix.

59. Peacocke, *Paths from Science towards God*, p. 48, cited in Wilkinson, *Christian Eschatology*, p. 48. For similar comments by others, see R. Russell, *Time in Eternity*, pp. 64-65.

60. Welker, "Theological Realism," p. 34.

61. Polkinghorne, "Eschatological Credibility," p. 43.

On the Conditions and Promise of a Mutual Critical Dialogue

As a corrective to these and related limited visions, slowly and incrementally a wider and more comprehensive outlook for theology began to emerge in the mid-twentieth century.[62] Significantly, Vatican II already hinted at it when stating that the church "will attain its full perfection only in the glory of heaven, when there will come the time of the restoration of all things [when] the entire world, which is intimately related to man and attains to its end through him, will be perfectly reestablished in Christ."[63] The same can be said of the Lutheran Paul Tillich's intuition that without the consideration of the end of the cosmos, the ultimate end of humanity cannot be properly understood.[64] That said, for him the "universe" seems to have meant less the vast, almost infinite universe of current physical cosmology and more something like the "history" of this planet.[65]

Gleaning from these and similar impulses and making a "cosmic" orientation to theology in general and eschatology in particular a defining theme, a growing number of contemporary theologians have become convinced that because humanity would not be here without the long cosmic processes, there cannot be a final and ultimate salvation of humanity and fulfillment of divine promises without the transformation of not only our earth and its creatures but also the whole cosmos.[66] Hence, the engagement of sciences is necessary. A number of science-theology experts have paved the way for this approach, including W. Pannenberg, J. Moltmann, R. Russell, D. Wilkinson, J. Polkinghorne, T. Peters, and D. Edwards, among others. Some scientists, such as the leading evolutionary paleobiologist Simon Conway Morris, have also spoken for the common interests between science and eschatology, notwithstanding radically different agendas in the main.[67]

Both sides must clearly understand the many and varied challenges to this mutual dialogue. The basic dilemma simply is that "[t]he idea of a hope after death and an end that fulfills history as a whole is as intrinsic to the

---

62. Naming it "The Method of Creative Mutual Interaction," R. Russell has refined its details with much insight and skill. For one of the latest accounts, see his *Time in Eternity*, pp. 70–83.

63. *Lumen Gentium*, #48.

64. Tillich, *ST* 3:396.

65. See also Wilkinson, *Christian Eschatology*, p. 3, for turning my attention to this particular passage.

66. See the important comments in Moltmann, *Coming of God*, pp. 259–60.

67. Morris, "Does Biology Have an Eschatology?" pp. 158–74.

Christian tradition as it is foreign to the project of science."[68] Indeed, not only for most scientists but also for the wider public, any religious claims for the consummation of eschatological hope seem not only erroneous but even fanciful and without any factual content.[69] That is fully understandable in light of current science, which tells us that "our universe is condemned to a final futility and will end either in a big crunch, or go on forever expanding in continual disintegration and decay, long after all life has vanished. To believe that Christ is risen and will come again is to insist that laws of nature, with their steady march toward disintegration, decay, and death, are not the ultimate reality."[70] In that light, it is significant what Jewish theologian Neil Gillman discerns about a major difference between the biblical/theological and the scientific cosmology, namely, that the latter "is totally predetermined. It is set in motion by the Big Bang and will run its course come what may. Whereas in the biblical account, the endtime will be determined by the will of God, either when the world will have sunk into a state of abominable evil, or, as in a different tradition, when the world will have achieved a level of sanctity."[71]

For these two inquiries to collaborate fruitfully, it has to be agreed that the dialogue between theology and science cannot be a one-way street: it must be a give-and-take conversation.[72] True, at the moment, most theologians should devote much energy to learning even the basics of scientific cosmology and integrate those basic principles into their own theological reflection. At the same time, we should follow Pannenberg, who posed "theological questions to scientists," the last five of which engage eschatology.[73] Theology's challenge to scientists is that "an unaided scientific account of the world does not succeed in making complete sense of cosmic history"[74] because "science, which can only tell the horizontal story of unfolding present process, is not in a position either to deny or confirm this 'vertical' story of divine faithfulness."[75] Christian theology boldly claims that "although the human species, life, the earth, the sun, and the universe will end, that end is not ultimate but somehow leads to a fuller, transformed reality, to which the natural sciences provide no access,

---

68. Clayton, "Eschatology as Metaphysics," p. 134.

69. See, e.g., Stoeger, "Scientific Accounts of Ultimate Catastrophes," p. 19.

70. J. Walls, introduction to OHE, p. 6.

71. Gillman, "How Will It All End?" p. 46.

72. So also Peters, "Introduction," p. xii.

73. Pannenberg, "Theological Questions to Scientists," p. 48.

74. Polkinghorne, "Eschatology," p. 38; see also Pannenberg, "Laying Theological Claim to Scientific Understandings," pp. 51–64.

75. Polkinghorne, Science and Religion in Quest of Truth, p. 102.

and to which our human experience gives us only obscure, but nevertheless real, intimations and indications."[76]

Indeed, rightly understood — and without in any way downplaying the clear demarcation lines between (natural) sciences and theology — we need to be reminded that "[b]oth science and theology have to speak about unseen realities" as they go about their investigation. Physicists deal with phenomena such as quarks and gluons (and many other, if possible, even "smaller" items of reality), which are of course totally unseen, not only because of yet-to-be-improved tools of investigation but also because of their very nature, that is, their almost infinitely small size! Their existence and workings are believed to be real because they help explain many processes and phenomena that are observable. Consider this familiar example to scientists: "When high-energy projectiles impinge on protons and neutrons in what is called a deep inelastic scattering process, they 'bounce back' in just the way that corresponds to their hitting pointlike quark constituents inside." Somewhat similarly, theologians' beliefs in doctrines such as divine action or providence may be funded at least partially by accumulated personal and communal experiences on the basis of which inferences are drawn and continuously tested, including their compatibility with texts and other testimonies of sacred tradition.[77]

Having inquired into the resources of natural sciences with regard to the "future" and "end" of the cosmos and life, we engage another preparatory task before chapter 4 delves into distinctively Christian theological resources — the investigation into four living faith traditions' eschatological intuitions.

---

76. Stoeger, "Scientific Accounts of Ultimate Catastrophes," p. 20.
77. Polkinghorne and Welker, "Introduction," pp. 3–4 (4). For thoughtful reflections on the "human" nature of science, see Coyne, "Seeking the Future," pp. 13–14.

3. Eschatological Visions and Symbols among Religions

On the Propriety and Conditions of Speaking of Religions' "Eschatologies"

Although the Christian theologian has to be careful when speaking of "eschatology" as a pan-religious theme, it is true that all world religions express a concern over mortality,[1] and all of them also envision "some form of life after death."[2] Furthermore, religions embrace beliefs not only about the origins but also about the "end" (or at least cycles of beginning and ending) of the whole of the cosmos.[3] As diverse as these beliefs and symbols may be, it is clear that some kind of common denominator exists. That said, insofar as eschatology is "the study of the final end of things, the ultimate resolution of the entire creation," then it applies much more easily to "theistic religions that hold to a doctrine of creation and a linear view of history and that believe that creation will come to a final end than to nontheistic traditions, particularly Buddhism."[4] Recall that "Buddhist scriptures regularly refer to 'beginningless *saṁsāra*,' a cycle of birth and death of the universe (as well as of the individual) for which no starting point can be discerned. Nor is there an end, for Buddhists share with members of other Indian religions (notably the Hindus and the Jains) the idea that the universe passes

---

1. See Hick, *Death and Eternal Life*, p. 21.
2. Badham and Badham, "Death and Immortality," p. 1.
3. Werblowsky, "Eschatology," pp. 2833–34.
4. J. Walls, introduction to *OHE*, p. 4. The now-classic study is Eliade, *The Myth of the Eternal Return*.

through an unending series of cycles of manifestation and nonmanifestation."[5] Add to that the general observation that "[c]ultures that view time as an endless succession of repetitive cycles . . . develop only 'relative eschatologies,' because the concept of an ultimate consummation of history is alien to them."[6] Again, Buddhism is a grand example; this principle applies also to Hinduism.[7]

This project is supported by the vision expressed by the editors of *Death and Immortality in the Religions of the World,* Paul and Linda Badham — one an atheist and the other a naturalist "atheist": "[W]e remain hopeful that a global perspective on the issues of death and immortality may indeed emerge and present a coherent and intelligible account of a possible future hope, which will draw insights from both the religious and the secular experience of the human race." An important asset in this search is the "unanimous testimony of the world religions that belief in an eternal destiny is necessary to any concept of human life serving any larger purpose than the fulfillment of the immediate aspirations we set ourselves."[8]

This investigation begins with Jewish and Islamic traditions and proceeds to study symbols and visions of the "end" in Hindu and Buddhist theologies. The discussion in this chapter refrains from making comparisons with Christian views in order to allow for authentic Jewish, Muslim, Hindu, and Buddhist eschatologies to be presented. The rest of the discussion of eschatology will engage sympathetically and critically specific beliefs and proposals of these traditions.

Jewish Eschatology

The Gradual Emergence of Eschatological Consciousness

Somewhat counterintuitively for a strictly monotheistic faith, no Old Testament books are devoted to the topic of death or afterlife; indeed, the topic is only marginally and occasionally mentioned.[9] The Old Testament worldview

5. Nattier, "Buddhist Eschatology," p. 151.

6. Werblowsky, "Eschatology," p. 2834.

7. For thoughtful constructive reflections, see R. Boyd, "The End of Eschatology?" and "In the End."

8. Badham and Badham, "Death and Immortality," p. 6; similarly, Hick (*Death and Eternal Life,* pp. 29–34) seeks to discuss "the idea of a global theology of death."

9. Segal, "Judaism," p. 13: "The authors of the Hebrew Bible, apart from its latest strata, did not teach that individuals survive death in any religiously significant way." Still a reliable guide is Gowan, *Eschatology in the Old Testament.*

is very much this-worldly (although it is deeply *theo*logical). One can hardly find incentives to look for the signs of the end in the Hebrew Bible; the rabbinic traditions have equally great reservations about that.[10] When eschatological themes appear occasionally among other key themes, they pertain less to individual and much more to national hope[11] and to Yahweh's intervention in the cosmos. This-worldly blessings from Yahweh are at the center of the Israelite religion. Both Yahweh's faithfulness in carrying out his promises[12] and Yahweh's power are manifested in this life, and his blessings are counted in terms of long life,[13] progeny, and possessions. In keeping with the focus of this-world spirituality, Yahweh's role as judge is also by and large envisioned in relation to earthly affairs, particularly with the establishment of justice and righteousness.[14] In sum: "In contrast to the elaborate myths and epics of other nations, the Israelites did not waste much thought on a life beyond."[15]

In stark contrast to neighboring lands, particularly Egypt, Israelite culture was definitely not death driven.[16] The Old Testament describes the condition of the dead as some sort of shadowy existence (Isa. 38:18).[17] The gradual rise of an eschatological consciousness in the Old Testament is just that, *gradual*. The hope for an afterlife in terms of resurrection evolves slowly toward the end of the Old Testament,[18] although intimations and anticipations appear here and there (Job 19:25–26; Pss. 49:15; 73:24; Isa. 26:19).[19] Daniel 12:2 is widely taken as the summit of that development: "And many of those who

10. Novak, "Jewish Eschatology," p. 118; as an example, he mentions *b. Sanhedrin* 92b and 97b.

11. See Goldberg, "Bound Up in the Bond of Life," p. 99.

12. See Arnold, "Old Testament Eschatology," p. 25.

13. A "good" death was one that happened in mature age (Gen. 25:8; Job 42:17), whereas death at an early age was depicted as divine judgment (1 Sam. 2:32); Schwarz, *Eschatology*, p. 37.

14. For a detailed study, see Brueggemann, *Theology of the Old Testament*, pp. 233–50. In light of its this-worldly orientation, the idea of a "good death" (as in Gen. 25:8; Deut. 34:7; and so forth) is understandable; however, that should not hinder our seeing that by and large the Old Testament sees death in deeply negative terms; see Gillman, *The Death of Death*, pp. 69–72, 79–81.

15. Schwarz, *Eschatology*, pp. 35–38 (35–36). As a result, no ethical idea was yet involved with death and afterlife. Cohn-Sherbok, "Death and Immortality," p. 24; more widely, Kohler, *Jewish Theology*, p. 279.

16. For a standard reliable source, see Morenz, *Egyptian Religion*, chap. 9; see also Schwarz, *Eschatology*, pp. 32–35; Sumegi, *Understanding Death*, pp. 51–61.

17. See chaps. 2 and 3 in Gillman, *The Death of Death*; another useful, shorter treatment is Sumegi, *Understanding Death*, pp. 80–85.

18. Brueggemann, *Theology of the Old Testament*, pp. 483–84.

19. Schwarz, *Eschatology*, pp. 39–40; Gillman, *The Death of Death*, chap. 4.

sleep in the dust of the earth shall awake, some to everlasting life, and some to shame and everlasting contempt."[20]

Only during the postexilic period can a "few inklings of otherworldliness" be found.[21] The outlook changes radically in the theology of rabbinic Judaism. The Talmud and related writings delve deeply and widely into eschatological and apocalyptic speculations.[22] Eschatology becomes a defining feature, and against that background it can be said "that no significant movement in the course of Jewish history had lacked an eschatology."[23] Whence the rise of an eschatological orientation? I am persuaded by David Novak's thesis that the major reason for the evolvement of eschatology in the Old Testament, slow as it was, has to do with the question of suffering and theodicy: Why is the believer in Yahweh suffering?[24]

With the rise of the eschatological impulse (beginning in the second century B.C.E.), the hope for the afterlife also becomes more defined, as death is no longer looked upon as "the final event" in human life.[25] In rabbinic thought, eschatological topics can be classified in three mutually related categories: "(1) the world to come (*olam ha-ba*); (2) the resurrection of the dead human body (*tehiyyat ha-metim*); (3) the Messiah (*ha-meshiah*)." Although the communal orientation still is dominant, under these categories one can see also hope for the individual — and for the whole cosmos ("the *world* to come"). The interrelatedness of these categories comes to the fore in that — particularly in early Pharisaic-rabbinic traditions — they were more or less conflated: the Messiah would bring the world renewal and promise the resurrection.[26] This kind of "eschatology is manifested in the expectation of a future eon radically discontinuous with the present." Yet this means no escapism, because in this eschatological vision "the circumstances of history will be transformed but not transcended."[27]

---

20. See further Sumegi, *Understanding Death*, pp. 86–90. Segal ("Judaism," p. 18) rightly reminds us that even with Daniel, it is not clear if bodily survival or spiritual immortality is in view.

21. Novak, "Jewish Eschatology," p. 115. The standard source is Nickelsburg, *Resurrection, Immortality, and Eternal Life in Intertestamental Judaism*.

22. Novak, "Jewish Eschatology," p. 114. Segal ("Judaism," p. 20) reminds us that rabbinic theology hardly is systematic in nature, nor uniform.

23. Gillman, *The Death of Death*, p. 12 (attributing the idea to Gerson Cohen, personal conversation).

24. Novak, "Jewish Eschatology," p. 115; materially similarly, Charles, *A Critical History of the Doctrine of a Future Life in Israel*, p. 157.

25. Gillman, *The Death of Death*, p. 18. For a massive study, see Avery-Peck and Neusner, eds., *Death, Afterlife, and the World-to-Come*.

26. Novak, "Jewish Eschatology," p. 114.

27. See further Arnold, "Old Testament Eschatology," pp. 24–25 (24). For a highly nu-

In very broad strokes, Jews came to believe that, at the end of days, the dead will be resurrected and come before God to account for their lives on earth; the righteous will be rewarded and the evil punished; Jews, free from the yoke of the exile, will return to their homeland, rebuild it, and become masters of their own destiny; they will rebuild the temple and reinstitute the temple cult; the nations of the world will flock to study Torah with the Jewish people; peace and justice will rule; the tensions that now pervade the world of nature will disappear — "the wolf shall dwell with the lamb" (Isa. 11:6); and all people will come to know and worship the God of Israel. Finally, this entire scenario will be brought to pass through the initiative of the charismatic or quasi-divine figure called Messiah (literally, "the anointed one").[28]

Like younger sister faiths, postbiblical Judaism also knows apocalypticism, which is escapist.[29] Some of these movements were also related to Christian ones.[30] The difference of this apocalypticism from the Old Testament eschatology has to do with the heightened role given to the Messiah in endtime expectations (indeed, it is quite counterintuitive that by and large the Messiah is not tightly linked to eschatology in the Old Testament).[31] Rather than Yahweh himself executing eschatological works (as even in Daniel's apocalypse), in the postbiblical apocalypticism (*1 Enoch*, *2 Esdras*, and *2 Baruch*) the Messiah is the one at the forefront of the action. Another defining feature of apocalypticism has to do with a changing understanding of history. Not only Israel's enemies (as in the Old Testament) but all powers, including cosmic and heavenly powers, would be destroyed. This leads to the apocalyptic "supranationalistic and supraworldly view of God's reign" that also assumes the unity of history — because Yahweh is the one and only ultimate power. That concept also leads to a deterministic view of history.[32]

Another development, outside the mainstream although hugely influential, is the mystical Kabbalah's visions of the end.[33] Kabbalah also tested

---

anced negotiation between this world and the world to come, see the Mishnaic tractate *m. Pirkei Avot* ("Ethics of the Fathers"), chap. 4; for comments, see Novak, "Jewish Eschatology," p. 116.

28. Gillman, *The Death of Death*, p. 22.

29. For a highly useful discussion of the sources and background, see J. Collins, "Apocalyptic Eschatology in the Ancient World," pp. 40–55. For a guide to apocalyptic literature, see J. Collins, *The Apocalyptic Imagination*. For an almost encyclopedic collection of essays on all things apocalyptic, see Amanat and Bernhardsson, eds., *Imagining the End*.

30. See Tabor, "Ancient Jewish and Early Christian Millennialism," pp. 252–53.

31. For details, see Schwarz, *Eschatology*, pp. 48–49.

32. Schwarz, *Eschatology*, pp. 51–55 (53).

33. Gillman, *The Death of Death*, p. 173; chap. 7 is devoted totally to this and related mystical eschatologies.

and at times transcended the limits of orthodoxy.[34] A particularly important case here is the doctrine of metempsychosis, or the transmigration of souls (or reincarnation).[35] Although unknown in rabbinic and Talmudic literature — and strongly opposed by the medieval philosophical masters — it has always had some following among the mystics, coupled with the doctrine of the preexistence of souls.[36]

Salvation and Condemnation — Heaven and Hell

There seem to be two kinds of attitudes in Jewish tradition concerning speculation into the nature of the world to come. As in other traditions, eschatological hermeneutics often takes its departure from the earthly scene, such as the description of David's encounter with the angel of death in the garden in the hereafter.[37] On the other hand, both Scripture and rabbinical tradition make the realities of the hereafter so incomparable with the current world that we can hardly say anything about those realities. An illustrative statement comes from Rabbi Hiyya ben Abba (speaking in the name of Rabbi Johanan): "All the prophets prophesied only for the days of the Messiah, but as for the world to come, 'Eye hath not seen, oh God, beside Thee.'"[38] Understandably, then, the Talmudic tradition often speaks of the life to come in terms of radical discontinuity.[39] Indeed, with all its this-worldly orientation, classic Jewish theology has developed quite sophisticated accounts of heaven, including several stages from the messianic age on earth to the transcendent heavenly realm.[40] Perhaps the most detailed one can be found in the Babylonian Talmud's *Eiruvin* (19a), with its sevenfold structure of hell.[41]

Who then will inherit salvation? Who will be condemned? The Jewish understanding of what is wrong with humanity is markedly different from

34. See Segal, "Judaism," pp. 25-26.

35. See Ripsman, *Reincarnation in Jewish Mysticism and Gnosticism*.

36. The standard Kabbalah source is *Sefer haBahir*, "The Book of Illumination." On the views of Kabbalah's most well-known representative, see the English translation of (and short introduction to) *Shaar HaGilgulim*, "Gates of Incarnation."

37. *b. Shabbat* 30b (for the background to the story, see first folio 30a).

38. *b. Berakot* 34b; cited in Novak, "Jewish Eschatology," p. 128 (but in a different translation).

39. See *b. Berakot* 17a and comments by Novak, "Jewish Eschatology," p. 118 (who cites it from another translation from my reference).

40. For details and sources, see Cohn-Sherbok, "Death and Immortality," pp. 26-28.

41. *b. Eiruvin* 19a (http://halakhah.com/pdf/moed/Eiruvin.pdf) for a description, see Cohn-Sherbok, "Death and Immortality," pp. 28-31.

the Christian one; hence, the way of reaching salvation is different.[42] Like the Muslim view, it insists on human freedom and responsibility.[43] Following the Torah is the key.[44] "The principle qualification for entrance to heaven (*Gan Eden*) is to lead a good life in accordance with God's law. Conversely . . . by disobeying God's law one forfeits a share in the world to come and is doomed to eternal punishment in hell (*Gehinnom*)."[45] Rabbinic theology mentions a number of types of people who might end up in hell, including those who deny resurrection or Torah's heavenly origin, or the heretic, or the one who abuses the divine name, and so forth.[46]

This much almost all Jewish traditions agree upon — keeping Torah and doing good deeds. Debated issues have to do with two topics: First, what is the balance between good and bad deeds? In other words, is there a turning point beyond which one more evil deed may tip the scales? According to Novak, it is best "to engage in constant repentance both in one's heart (faith) and in one's deeds (good works)" because it is not possible to accumulate "merit in this world so as to 'cash in' in the world to come. . . . Talmud points out that the world to come can be gained in a moment . . . or lost in a moment."[47] The second issue is whether Torah's commandments will be kept even in the world to come. These discussions centered on the interpretation of the command in Deuteronomy 16:3, "that all the days of your life you may remember the day when you came out of the land of Egypt." Put in terms of Christian theology, will the divinely sanctioned covenant-related salvation-historical commandments end or continue after the boundary of this world? Both views received authoritative support, though for the purposes of this discussion, the details do not interest us.[48]

Yet an important long-standing, unresolved issue of debate relates to the destiny of Gentiles. Not surprisingly, no canonical opinion was reached among the different rabbinical schools.[49] This much can be said: while the

---

42. For details, see my *Creation and Humanity*, pp. 413–15.

43. K. Ward, *Religion and Human Nature*, p. 175.

44. Jacobs, *Jewish Theology*, p. 245. This is not to deny that there is a deep woundedness and potential for drastic evil in humanity, but rather to understand evil in a way that does not make it innate or compromise human freedom; see pp. 246–47; Cohon, *Essays in Jewish Theology*, p. 225.

45. Cohn-Sherbok, "Death and Immortality," p. 26; Segal, "Judaism," pp. 21–22.

46. Cohn-Sherbok, "Death and Immortality," p. 26. A highly regarded list was drafted by Maimonides, *Mishneh Torah Book of Knowledge*, bk. 1: *Sefer Maddah: Hilchot Teshuvah* ("Laws of Repentance"), chap. 3.

47. Novak, "Jewish Eschatology," p. 117.

48. For details and historical sources, see Novak, "Jewish Eschatology," pp. 121–22.

49. The defining starting point for such consideration is the famous debate in the first

Christian type of *extra ecclesiam nulla salus* principle was often held as the normal opinion, there is also undoubtedly a strong prophetic tradition in the Old Testament that envisions some kind of "universal scope of salvation." Rather than leading to ultimate destruction and annihilation, Yahweh's judgment will have shalom as the final word (Amos 9:11–15; Isa. 2:2–4; 11:6–9; 65:17–25; and so forth).[50] But even then, no unanimity exists about whether "nations" (as opposed to the "people" of Yahweh) are being included in this salvation, which also encompasses nature and the whole world.

Broadly speaking, until modernity, the core rabbinic belief in two destinies stood intact (regardless of continuing debates about whom to include or exclude).[51] In contrast, the majority of modern and contemporary Jews have left it behind or at least qualified it significantly. This is possible because the Torah, as is well known, explains quite little about the nature of judgment and blessedness beyond this world. Although the opinions of rabbis and the Mishnah are formative, they are not necessarily binding in the sense that one could not be a faithful Jew while rejecting them. As for Christian theology, particularly difficult for contemporary Jewish theologians is the affirmation of hell.[52]

The Resurrection of the Body

Although "the canonization" of the doctrine happened only three centuries after Daniel,[53] according to David Novak, "the centerpiece of classical Jewish eschatology is the doctrine of the resurrection of the dead." He takes as strong evidence the prayer at the center of daily Jewish liturgy, in which we find the clause "Blessed are you, O Lord, who resurrects the dead."[54] Indeed, condemned are those who deny the centrality of this belief.[55] Briefly stated, resurrection and the authority of Torah "are the two dogmas the rabbis re-

---

century C.E. between Rabbis Eliezer and Joshua ben Hananiah (or Jehoshua); see tractate *Sanhedrin* 10:2 (p. 122). For details, see Novak, "Jewish Eschatology," pp. 120–21; Gillman, *The Death of Death*, pp. 133–34.

50. Schwarz, *Eschatology*, pp. 45–47.

51. See further Cohn-Sherbok, "Death and Immortality," p. 31.

52. For representative opinions from leading rabbis, see Cohn-Sherbok, "Death and Immortality," pp. 32–33.

53. Gillman, *The Death of Death*, chap. 5, titled "The Canonization of a Doctrine."

54. Novak, "Jewish Eschatology," pp. 122–23; Gillman, *The Death of Death*, pp. 122–25.

55. *m. Sanhedrin* 10:1: "But the following have no portion in the World to Come: He who says that resurrection is not a Torah doctrine, the Torah is not from Heaven . . ."

quired, minimally, that no Jew deny and, maximally, that every Jew affirm."[56] That is also affirmed by the medieval master Moses Maimonides.[57] That said, there were of course dissenting voices within Jewish orthodoxy: while the Pharisees fully endorsed the doctrine, the Sadducees did not.[58]

For rabbinic theology, it was not enough to merely affirm immortality (whether that be understood as an innate capacity of the soul or a divine gift);[59] a *bodily* resurrection must also be affirmed. This means a robust affirmation of the principle of embodiment and physicality as an integral part of human nature. This comports well with Jewish anthropology at large (as discussed in detail in *Creation and Humanity*, chap. 14), which is neither monist in the materialist sense nor dualist in the traditional sense. It rather approaches the Thomistic hylomorphism in which the soul is the "form" of the body; neither one can exist without the other.[60] In their attempts to imagine the nature of the bodily resurrection, the Jewish sources use various metaphors, from awakening from sleep,[61] to nature metaphors of morning dew and plants sprouting,[62] to being clothed,[63] and so forth. Some New Testament Christian images of course come to mind.

Afterlife, Resurrection, and Immortality in Contemporary Jewish Theology

By and large, modern/contemporary Jewish theologies have not paid much attention to end times.[64] Novak wonders if one of the reasons for reserva-

---

56. Novak, "Jewish Eschatology," p. 123.

57. Maimonides, *Shloshah Asar Ikkarim* (the "Thirteen Fundamental Principles"), #13 (resurrection); ##8–9 (Torah). In his later years, Maimonides penned the masterful *Treatise on the Resurrection*, in which he had to defend his orthodoxy against charges of heresy; see Gillman, *The Death of Death*, chap. 6. The standard collection of essays is edited by Dienstag, *Eschatology in Maimonidean Thought*.

58. For a detailed scrutiny of sources indicating both of these beliefs, see Gillman, *The Death of Death*, pp. 115–22 particularly. See also Segal, "Judaism," pp. 23–25.

59. While a marginal belief, there is the postrabbinical idea of the divinity of the soul that makes it immortal. See Scholem, *Major Trends in Jewish Mysticism*, pp. 239–43.

60. Materially so also Novak, "Jewish Eschatology," p. 123 (without mentioning Thomism); see also pp. 75–78, 105–12; Stern, "Afterlife," p. 152.

61. As in the above-mentioned *Amidah* (#2 in the Eighteen Benedictions) prayer: "You, O Lord, are mighty forever, you revive the dead . . . and keep faith with those who sleep in the dust"; http://www.egrc.net/articles/other/amidah.html.

62. *b. Kethubot* 111b.

63. *b. Kethubot* 111b.

64. Segal, "Judaism," p. 27; see also Adelman, "Jews, Eschatology, and Contemporary Visions."

tion has to do with the painful memories from medieval times when Jews were forced by Christians to defend their eschatological views in public.[65] Another obvious reason is the Holocaust; many Jews wonder if there is any afterlife after Auschwitz.[66] On the other end of spectrum are radical millenarian and apocalyptic expressions similar to those of other Abrahamic faiths.[67]

When contemporary theologies have touched on eschatology, quite radical reformulations have been suggested; they usually follow the ordinary lines of distinction on the continuum from most traditional/conservative to reconstructionist views. Formative early influence came from the leading modern thinker Moses Mendelssohn and his highly acclaimed *Phaedo; or, On the Immortality of the Soul, in Three Dialogues* (1767).[68] Obviously based on Plato's dialogue, it reworks his ideas into an emerging modern Jewish milieu. Making Socrates a person of the Enlightenment, Mendelssohn argues for the immortality of the soul and its indestructibility because of its noncomposite nature. Wisely, though, Mendelssohn avoids any talk about the nature of life hereafter, including silence on resurrection, although he clearly seems to believe in the continuation of life.[69]

Wide influence on modern and contemporary Jewish eschatology came also from the Reform movements' reworking of key doctrines beginning in the early nineteenth century. Deeply Jewish, they also wanted to save Judaism for modern times. Slowly and steadily resurrection as a doctrine with "no religious foundation" came to be replaced by the idea of immortality, which also continued asserting "the divine nature of the human spirit." Along with resurrection went the classic doctrines of hell and heaven; not surprisingly, Mendelssohn's legacy was appealed to.[70] Understandably, opposition arose among the conservatives. However, even Conservative Judaism of the early twentieth century did not necessarily demand a return to resurrection; rather, it insisted on a

---

65. Novak, "Jewish Eschatology," p. 126.

66. For a detailed discussion, see chap. 2 in Raphael, *Jewish Views of the Afterlife*.

67. For an overview, see Ariel, "Radical Millennial Movements," pp. 1–15. For millenarian Zionism, consult Aran, "From Religious Zionism to Zionist Religion"; for Christian fundamentalist connections, see Ariel, "Born Again in a Land of Paradox."

68. The English translation is titled *Phaedon; Or the Death of Socrates* (1789). An introduction and English translation can be found at http://www.schillerinstitute.org/transl /mend_phadn_cullen.html.

69. Gillman, *The Death of Death*, pp. 191–92 (192).

70. Gillman, *The Death of Death*, pp. 196–204 (quotation p. 202, from the Philadelphia Statement of 1869). Similar conclusions were reached by Kohler, *Jewish Theology*, pp. 296–97.

sort of spiritual immortality. In other words, by the mid-twentieth century, immortality had been adopted as the mainstream Jewish opinion.[71]

With the Reconstructionist movement headed by Mordecai Kaplan, a radically new paradigm was offered. His religious naturalism took religion as a natural phenomenon rather than as divinely revealed. As a consequence, the "Modification of Traditional Doctrines" argued that "[m]en and women brought up in the atmosphere of modern science no longer accept the doctrine that the dead will one day come to life." Beliefs in the immortality and the indestructible nature of the human spirit should be given up. Even though the revised Reconstructionist prayer books continued to mention the immortality of the soul (but not resurrection of the body), it should be understood "in terms that are in keeping with what modern-minded men can accept as true."[72] On the other end of the spectrum remained Orthodox Judaism, which firmly continued to uphold the doctrine of the resurrection of the body.[73] In sum, the core classic doctrine of the resurrection of the body became the dividing line for modern Jews in a highly ironic manner: "[C]ontemporary Orthodoxy embraces resurrection and liberal Jews reject it *for the very same reason*: They all understand it as a literal statement. All of these thinkers believe that the doctrine can only be interpreted as describing, in literal, objective terms, an event that will occur exactly as described in some future time. That is why Orthodox Jews affirm it and liberal Jews reject it."[74]

Rightly, Neil Gillman wonders why contemporary Jewish theology got stuck with this literalist understanding. Why not look for alternative ways to affirm the classic doctrine? Furthermore, why does liberal and Reconstructionist Jewish thinking seem not even interested in pursuing possible promises of a contemporary constructive doctrine of physical resurrection?[75]

Not all contemporary Jewish intellectuals are content with this conservative-liberal divide. New interest in pursuing the questions of the afterlife has emerged from surprising circles. The former Marxist Will Herberg's widely discussed *Judaism and Modern Man* (1951) tapped into not only his own religious background and those of some leading twentieth-century Jewish thinkers (particularly Franz Rozenweig) but also Christian sources in its search of eschatology beyond naturalist materialism. Whereas the Marxist "secularization of the Hebraic 'philosophy' of history . . . in which human ex-

71. Gillman, *The Death of Death*, pp. 205–8.
72. Gillman, *The Death of Death*, pp. 208–11 (210).
73. Gillman, *The Death of Death*, pp. 212–13.
74. Gillman, *The Death of Death*, p. 213, emphasis in original.
75. Gillman, *The Death of Death*, pp. 213–14.

istence is reduced to the two dimensions of nature and society and deprived of its transcendent dimension of spirit" makes history "its own redeemer," in Jewish faith "[t]he fulfilment of history is the Kingdom of Heaven (*malkut shamayim*)." This kingdom is both this-worldly and transcendent, meaning that "it is not a kingdom in a kind of superworld called 'Heaven,' but a new age in which the kingship of God is revealed in its fullness and sovereignty."[76]

Some other leading Jewish thinkers, similarly to Herberg, have been persuaded of the necessity for belief in the bodily resurrection, as difficult as that may be for the modern mind. Prominent among these is Arthur A. Cohen, whose short essay "Resurrection of the Dead" seeks to rehabilitate the doctrine as an indispensable tenet of faith for contemporary Judaism. As much as it is "scandalous to reason,"[77] resurrection is also a profound sign of divine hospitality.[78] Somewhat surprisingly, and more recently, the "liberal" Reform movement has harked back to affirming in one way or another the continuation of life beyond death. Representative is Rabbi Eugene B. Borow-itz's conclusion that "we cannot believe that having shared so intimately in God's reality in life we do not continue to share it beyond the grave."[79]

Perhaps the theologically most pregnant contemporary affirmation of the resurrection of the body comes from Neil Gillman, a leading American Jewish thinker. Honestly facing the enormous intellectual problems that belief in the resurrection creates for the modern/contemporary post-Enlightenment scientific mind, he finds two powerful reasons for refusing to let the critical mind *alone* dictate one's ultimate vision. On the one hand, with every other Jew, he is fully convinced of the omnipotence of God, even over death. Along with this theological argument, on the other hand, the anthropological argu-ment seems convincing: the biblical view of the human as a "psycho-physical unity" makes him believe that without the body his own self is not complete.[80]

What about the eschatological vision of the youngest Abrahamic tradi-tion? To the consideration of Islamic theology of the end we turn next.

---

76. Herberg, *Judaism and Modern Man*, pp. 231–32; I am indebted to Gillman, *The Death of Death*, pp. 220–25.

77. A. A. Cohen, "Resurrection of the Dead," p. 812; for a detailed discussion, see Gill-man, *The Death of Death*, pp. 225–30.

78. A. A. Cohen, "Resurrection of the Dead," p. 808; see also p. 811.

79. Borowitz, *Reform Judaism Today*, p. 48, cited in Gillman, *The Death of Death*, p. 232; see also pp. 230–36. Interestingly, Borowitz's *Renewing the Covenant* has precious little to say of afterlife and eschatology; it merely makes a few scattered references to immortality and resurrection, has nothing to say of hell, and is almost silent about heaven.

80. Gillman, *The Death of Death*, pp. 243–74 (260, 265 respectively).

Islamic Eschatology

The Significance of Eschatology in Islam

Eschatology, both personal and universal, plays an extraordinary role in Islam.[81] Recall that the Prophet's first and continuing message was about coming judgment and the need for submission to Allah to avoid the hell of judgment.[82] The lack of positive response in Mecca only intensified the prophetic warnings.[83] Both the Qur'an[84] and particularly Hadith[85] texts go to great lengths in expositing and describing (often with passionate and imaginative pictures) the events in the afterlife.[86] Consider also the prominence of eschatological beliefs in Muslim creedal statements. Take, for example, the "Hanbalī Traditionalist Creed" after the legacy of (if not even penned by) Ahmad ibn Hanbal of the ninth century. Focused on true doctrine of God and proper lifestyle of the faithful ones, it is also rich with references to eschatological events and figures, including "the one-eyed Dajjal" (a traditional description of the Antichrist), end-time trumpets, paradise, elaborate descriptions of heaven, and so forth.[87] That the densest presentation of core Islamic doctrines can be summarized under the following three headings speaks to the significance of eschatology: the unity of God, "prophecy," and "ultimate 'return' (ma'ād)."[88] The idea of "return" to God is based on Qur'an 7:29: "As He brought you into being, so return ye [unto Him]."[89] No wonder contemporary Muslims tend to take the traditional teaching on eschatology much more seriously than do most Jews

---

81. For an earlier essay, see J. Taylor, "Some Aspects of Islamic Eschatology."

82. Blankinship, "The Early Creed," p. 34.

83. For the Qur'anic rebuttal of the Meccan community's disbelief in resurrection and judgment, see, e.g., 22:1–7. For others, see 17:49, 98; 19:66; 37:16–17; 50:3; and 75:3. See J. Smith and Haddad, *The Islamic Understanding of Death and Resurrection*, p. 1 n. 1.

84. Chittick, "Muslim Eschatology," p. 132. It is claimed that nearly a third of the Qur'an is eschatological in nature; Siddiqui, "Death, Resurrection, and Human Destiny," p. 30. Useful surveys are Rahman, *Major Themes of the Qur'ān*, chap. 6; Haleem, "Life and Beyond in the Qur'an," pp. 66–79.

85. See Renard, ed., *Islamic Theological Themes*, p. 13.

86. See further J. Smith and Haddad, *The Islamic Understanding of Death and Resurrection*, pp. vii–ix, xi–xii. For the radical break from the views and rites of death of pre-Islamic times (times of "ignorance"), see Kassis, "Islam," pp. 49–50. I have also benefited from Bijlefeld, "Eschatology."

87. Translated by Watt, in Renard, ed., *Islamic Theological Themes*, pp. 104–9.

88. Hermansen, "Eschatology," p. 309.

89. See Hermansen, "Eschatology," p. 310.

and Christians.[90] The "eschatological narrative" lays claim on everything in the Muslim's faith and life.[91]

As in other Abrahamic faiths, not only is purposefulness discerned in human life and events, but also "the Qur'ān posits an understanding of meaning and significance to the flow of time and history."[92] There is a definite divinely set plan that moves history from creation to the consummation. Furthermore, similarly to Judaism and Christianity, a rich tradition of apocalypticism can be found in Islam. Not confined to one Muslim community, it is present in every denomination.[93] Understandably, some extreme forms of apocalypticism drawn to millenarian and revolutionary impulses have arisen, some of which have received a lot of publicity (particularly those of the jihadist slant).[94]

Fascination with eschatological topics is also present in the ethnic and cultural adaptations of Islam in new contexts such as China. Routinely called the "father" of Chinese-language Islam, Wang Daiyu of the seventeenth century, in his book on how to understand and define *tawhid* (the oneness of God) in relation to traditional Chinese terms, delves deeply into cosmogony, "the ten thousand things," regarding both the origins and destiny.[95]

On Discerning the Signs of the "Hour"

As in Christian tradition, in Islam the (final) hour is unknown to all but God (Q 31:34).[96] The Prophet was asked every now and then to reveal the hour of the end. Whenever that happened,[97] the Prophet responded, "Knowledge thereof lies

90. J. Smith and Haddad, *The Islamic Understanding of Death and Resurrection*, p. 2.

91. For this conception and its main features, see Chittick, "Muslim Eschatology," p. 133.

92. J. Smith and Haddad, *The Islamic Understanding of Death and Resurrection*, pp. 3–5 (3).

93. For a basic guide, see Cook, "Early Islamic and Classical Sunni and Shi'ite Apocalyptic Movements"; more widely in Cook, *Studies in Muslim Apocalyptic*. See also Bashear, "Muslim Apocalypses."

94. For a basic guide, see Kenney, "Millennialism and Radical Islamist Movements." David Cook offers a useful survey of the literature in *Contemporary Muslim Apocalyptic Literature*. See also Devji, *Landscapes of the Jihad*; G. Fuller, *The Future of Political Islam*; Moussalli, *Radical Islamic Fundamentalism*.

95. "Wang Daiyu on Translating *Tawhīd* in Chinese Traditional Terms."

96. For details about the "hour," see Stieglecker, *Die Glaubenslehren des Islam*, ##1371–72, pp. 747–48.

97. Q 7:187; 33:63; 79:42. See also *Sahir Bukhari*, bk. 3 ("Knowledge"), #56.

only with God — and what do you know, perhaps the Hour is near" (Q 33:63).[98]
Differently from Hadith and apocalyptic traditions, the Qur'an is reticent to talk
about signs — and somewhat counterintuitively seems to imply that indeed all
the signs have already happened: "Do they, then, await anything except that the
Hour should come upon them suddenly? For already its portents have come. So,
when it has come upon them, for what [benefit] will their reminder be?"[99] That
said, eschatological undergirding lies beneath a number of suras in the Qur'an.
Just think of titles such as "The Hour" (22), "The Smoke" (45), "The Darkened
Sun" (82), and "The Shattering of the Sky" (84), among others.[100]

Understandably, Muslims have not stopped looking for signs.[101] Books,
blogs, and talks on "signs of the hour" abound.[102] The search for the signs is
fueled by the presence in the Hadith of detailed lists of signs. Consider the
vivid descriptions in the famous Abu-Dawudh's "Trials and Fierce Battles"[103]
or in *Sahih Muslim*'s "Book Pertaining to the Turmoil and Portents of the Last
Hour" (Kitab Al-Fitan wa Ashrat As-Sa'ah).[104] "Geological, moral, social, and
cosmic signs . . . [as well as] the erosion of the earth, the spread of immorality,
the loss of trust among the people, and the administration of unjust rulers
[are perceived] as some signs of the Hour." In distinction from these "minor"
signs, the Hadith lists as "major" ones the "emergence of the Antichrist, the
descent of Jesus, and the rising of the sun in the west," which all point to
the imminence of the end. Quite similarly to the descriptions in the book of
Revelation, trumpets, archangels, and cataclysmic changes on earth, including earthquakes, play a role in the final consummation (Q 81:1-14; 99:1-4;
39:67-69); there will also be intense suffering by the unfaithful. The rise of the
mysterious nations of Gog and Magog also plays a role in the eschatological
scheme of Islam.[105] The descriptions of doomsday, again, are similar to those
in the two sister Abrahamic traditions. The resurrection of all will happen, of
both good and evil (Q 18:99; 36:51).[106]

98. So also Q 6:59; 31:34. This paragraph is based on Saritoprak, *Islam's Jesus*, pp. 38-40.
99. See further Saritoprak, *Islam's Jesus*, pp. 41-42.
100. As listed (and translated) in Saritoprak, *Islam's Jesus*, p. 48 n. 21.
101. See D. Peterson, "Eschatology."
102. For representative examples, see Alam, "Signs of Hour"; "The 72 Signs of Doomsday (Qayamat)."
103. *Abu-Dawud*, bk. 30, ##4228-37.
104. *Sahih Muslim*, bk. 41, ##6881-990.
105. For details, see Stieglecker, *Die Glaubenslehren des Islam*, ##1363-66, pp. 742-44;
see also Q 27:82-84 and comments in Stieglecker, #1368, pp. 745-46.
106. Saritoprak, *Islam's Jesus*, pp. 58-59.

While these eschatological sayings and traditions abound in folk Islam and popular culture in Muslim lands, contemporary Muslim theologians face similar kinds of hermeneutical challenges that Christians face. Should these "prophecies" be interpreted literally?[107] If so, then the Enlightenment-based modernist critique must be rebutted. If not, they cannot be attributed properly to the Prophet himself, in which case they can be dismissed. After all, the discussion about authenticity is an important hermeneutical task for Islam.[108]

Islam's indebtedness to Jewish-Christian tradition comes to the fore even in eschatology, as the next section will demonstrate. Therein the awaited figure of the Mahdi and his companion Jesus play a key role.

Mahdi, Jesus, and the Antichrist: The Major End-Time Figures

Although Islam is not a messianic religion in the sense that Judaism and Christianity are, Muslim eschatology widely embraces the figure of the Mahdi, who undoubtedly reflects messianic characteristics.[109] The task of the Mahdi is to defeat the Antichrist and bring justice and peace to the world and lead people to truth.[110] An ordinary human being rather than a divine figure — according to the tradition, coming from the family of the Prophet himself — the Mahdi is endowed supernaturally to accomplish his task.[111]

It is highly surprising that the Mahdi is unknown not only in the Qur'an[112] but also in the two main Hadith traditions, that of Bukhari and that of Muslim. Yet belief in the Mahdi is affirmed widely in all main denominations. Particularly important is the role of the Mahdi among the Shi'ites.[113]

Debate persists about a number of issues related to the Mahdi, not least as to whether there is one Mahdi or more than one, as well as the related

107. See Saritoprak, *Islam's Jesus*, chaps. 7 and 8.

108. Saritoprak, *Islam's Jesus*, pp. 47–48.

109. A highly nuanced and insightful discussion of Muslim "messianism" and Mahdi's place therein is Riffat Hassan, "Messianism and Islam."

110. Stieglecker, *Die Glaubenslehren des Islam*, #1362, p. 742; Saritoprak, *Islam's Jesus*, p. 85.

111. See the important book by Amini, *Al-Imam al-Mahdi*.

112. The term *muhtadun*, "the guided ones," appears in Q 3:51–56; 3:90; 6:82; and 4:175. This is taken by some as reference to the Mahdi.

113. Sachedina, *Islamic Messianism*. In terms of differences from the mainline Sunni tradition, among Shi'ites there are also groups that believe that Ali or the Prophet himself may return; see further Saritoprak, *Islam's Jesus*, pp. 91–94.

question of pseudo- (or anti-) Mahdi.[114] Not surprisingly, various Mahdist movements throughout history have tended to identify a specific person; the last significant movement was Sudanese, acclaiming as Mahdi Muhammad Ahmad ibn 'Abd Allāh (d. 1885).[115] The relationship between the Mahdi and Jesus is close — indeed, so close that, at times, particularly in early Islamic history, the two were confused to the point that the expectation of the coming of Mahdi ceased.[116]

Whatever else the Mahdi tradition may mean to Islamic eschatology, it is linked closely with the yearning for justice and righteousness in a world of evil. Hence, at times those historical figures prominent for fighting injustice have been identified as the Mahdi, including Abdullah bin al-Zubair, a companion of the Prophet himself in the struggle against some Umayyad Dynasty leaders; similarly, the famed Umayyad leader Umar II of the eight century was discerned as one.[117]

Along with the Mahdi, Jesus plays an important role in Muslim eschatology in particular. As detailed in *Christ and Reconciliation* (chaps. 10 and 15), Jesus is next to only Muhammad himself; hence, his role as the Messenger, a prophet, is an integral part of the Muslim confession of faith — although, of course, without any hint of divinity.[118] While the Qur'an itself does not directly mention Jesus' return to earth[119] — or, as it is often called, his "descent"[120] — it is widely attested in the Hadith (with about one hundred reliable references).[121] According to the standard Islamic interpretation, Jesus of Nazareth was not killed on the cross but was instead "taken up" by Allah to heaven to wait for the return. Then he will fight with the Mahdi against the Antichrist and defeat him.[122] "Then Jesus kills the pigs, destroys the crosses (since the Christians have adopted a forbidden cult by honoring the cross), tears down the Synagogues and Churches, as well as kills the Christians who are not willing to receive the true faith."[123] Importantly, the descent of Jesus is

114. Godzliher, *Introduction to Islamic Theology and Law*, pp. 197–98; see also Saritoprak, *Islam's Jesus*, chap. 6; Blichfeldt, *Early Mahdism*.

115. For other historical figures, see Hermansen, "Eschatology," p. 315.

116. Ibn Khaldun, *Muqaddimah*, 2:156, cited in Saritoprak, *Islam's Jesus*, pp. 88–89.

117. Saritoprak, *Islam's Jesus*, pp. 85, 87.

118. Saritoprak, *Islam's Jesus*, p. xii.

119. There are, however, important Hadith commentaries on passages such as Q 43:61 that mention Jesus; for details, see Stieglecker, *Die Glaubenslehren des Islam*, #1367, p. 745.

120. Saritoprak, *Islam's Jesus*, pp. 22–23.

121. Saritoprak, *Islam's Jesus*, p. xv; chap. 4.

122. Q 4:156–58; 3:55; see my *Christ and Reconciliation*, pp. 388–93.

123. See Stieglecker, *Die Glaubenslehren des Islam*, #1367, p. 745, my translation.

considered one of the surest signs of the "Hour" (*al-Sa'a*), the consummation of eschatological events in Islam.

Notwithstanding the lack of direct references to the descent of Jesus in the Qur'an, some key statements about his work and meaning have important eschatological implications, such as 3:46 ("He shall speak to mankind in the cradle, and in his manhood, and he is of the righteous"), which can be interpreted to refer to the future ("he *shall* speak") in terms of Jesus' ministry yet unfinished.[124] A very important eschatological resource for the Hadith tradition has also been Qur'an 43:61: "And indeed he is a portent of the Hour so do not doubt it but: 'Follow me. This is a straight path.'" Importantly, this passage is in the context of the people of Mecca contesting for the superiority of their gods (or angels?), in response to which the Prophet lifted up the role of Jesus as the sign of the Hour.[125]

In light of the prominence of Jesus in Muslim eschatology, it is not surprising that the picture of the Antichrist in Islam is not radically different from that in Christianity. Obviously an archenemy of Jesus, the Antichrist can be seen as the personification of evil (similarly to Satan and Iblis). Although the term itself (*al-Dajjal*) does not appear in the Qur'an, there is a wide agreement in Islamic tradition that allusions and indirect references are to be found therein, including the saying attributed to Jesus: "Nay, but verily man is [wont to be] rebellious" (96:6). That sura, even in a quick reading, is easily applied to the Antichrist. The man is "self-sufficient" (v. 7), forbids the servant to pray (vv. 9–10), and closes houses of worship; furthermore, he resists divine revelation, and so forth. Similar types of descriptions of another unknown figure in 68:10–13 and 108:3 have also been seen as allusions to the *al-Dajjal*.[126]

Understandably, the Hadith traditions greatly expand and elaborate on the description and influence of the Antichrist: "The antichrist is short, hentoed, woolly-haired, one-eyed, an eye-sightless, and neither protruding nor deep-seated. If you are confused about him, know that your Lord is not one-eyed."[127] Indeed, so seriously is the threat of the Antichrist taken that "[t]here

---

124. This view was advocated by such influential medieval interpreters as Muhammad Al-Jurjani; see Saritoprak, *Islam's Jesus*, p. 23 n. 1. A similar interpretation can be offered of Q 19:28; on the sophisticated exegetical-hermeneutical devices used by another leading medieval commentator, Fakh al-Din al-Razi, to insure the future reference, see pp. 24–25.

125. For details, see Saritoprak, *Islam's Jesus*, pp. 27–28.

126. Stieglecker, *Die Glaubenslehren des Islam*, ##1358–60, pp. 740–41; Saritoprak, *Islam's Jesus*, pp. 94–95; McGinn, *Antichrist*, p. 111.

127. *Abu Dawud*, bk. 37 ("Battles"), #4306; the same book also speaks frequently of the Antichrist in war situations.

has been no Prophet after Noah who has not warned his people about the antichrist (Dajjal), and I warn you of him."[128] The Antichrist will fight against the unbelievers until the Mahdi and Jesus come and help defeat his power. The intensity and dramatic nature of that battle have been vividly portrayed in some Hadiths.[129]

Along with cosmic and communal eschatology, Muslim theology also speaks widely of the hope for individuals. To the topics of death and resurrection we turn next.

Death and Resurrection

For the Muslim, life on this earth is but preparation for eternity,[130] at the core of which is obedience to and desire to please Allah.[131] Hence, death should be properly kept in mind (Q 23:15; 3:185).[132] As in Jewish and Christian traditions, return to earthly life after physical death is impossible (23:109-11).[133] Not only will everyone die (29:57); there is also given a "fixed" time, a stated life span (*ajal*; Q 6:2). The Qur'an makes clear that physical death forms a final and decisive boundary mark that allows for no return, not even for the repentant deceased.[134]

Although the Qur'an provides preciously few details about what happens between death and resurrection, later traditions have produced fairly detailed accounts.[135] What Christian theology traditionally has taken as the part of the human person that continues to exist in one way or another after physical death, the soul, is represented in Islamic theology as *nafs* (soul) or *ruh* (spirit). Hence, the general idea of death is that while the body decays, "God takes the souls at the time of their death" (Q 39:42). These two terms — "soul"

128. *Abu Dawud*, bk. 40 ("Tributes, Spoil and Rulership"), #4738.

129. See further Saritoprak, *Islam's Jesus*, p. 97.

130. Tug, "Death and Immortality in Islamic Thought," p. 88; see also the important statement in al-Ghazali, *Alchemy of Happiness*, p. 74.

131. Kassis, "Islam," pp. 50-51.

132. Afsaruddin, "Death, Resurrection, and Human Destiny," pp. 43-44. See the listing "Selected Passages from al-Ghazālī's *The Remembrance of Death and the Afterlife*." For comments, see Winter, "Al-Ghazālī' on Death," pp. 161-65.

133. See Q 23:98-101; J. Smith and Haddad, *The Islamic Understanding of Death and Resurrection*, pp. 7-8; Siddiqui, "Death, Resurrection, and Human Destiny," pp. 25-26.

134. For comments, see Sumegi, *Understanding Death*, p. 147.

135. See further J. Smith and Haddad, *The Islamic Understanding of Death and Resurrection*, pp. 32-33.

and "spirit" — are not clearly distinguished, and more often than not, they are confused. When a distinction is made, then it is often thought that while "the rational soul [*nafs*], which directs the activities of the body, perishes at physical death . . . the life-infusing soul or spirit [*rufs*] continues and awaits the coming of the Hour."[136] Thereafter, according to major Muslim tradition, the deceased person meets two angels — named Munkar and Nakir — who test the faith of the person and help determine the final destiny. This is likely the most traditional Islamic view of what happens at death.[137] In other words, death means the separation of soul from body. Ibn Qayyim clearly supposes the conscious state of the departed soul: "when he begins to move to another world, he sees, hears, and speaks, by some means which, we, the living, do not perceive."[138] The soul can also be recognized as the departed person by other dead.[139] In all Muslim accounts of the afterlife, there is thus an intermediate state (*barzakh*), which, according to some Muslim theologians, approaches the Roman Catholic idea of purgatory.[140]

Death, as irrevocable as it is, does not have the last word. Muslims believe in the resurrection of the body.[141] While the belief in resurrection and (eternal) retribution is firmly taught in the Qur'an (suras 75; 36:77–79; 38:27–28; 41:39; and so forth), Muslim logic also advocates several rational reasons for its necessity and meaningfulness. First, it helps one pursue a good life and avoid evil: even though the human person understands in principle the value of obeying God, one usually does so primarily to avoid punishment and gain benefits. Second, the belief in resurrection and retribution encourages human persons to take care of the poor in the hopes of an eternal reward for all good deeds. Third, the only way for the underprivileged and exploited to hope for justice is to look for resurrection and divine retribution. Fourth, without the hope in resurrection,

136. J. Smith and Haddad, *The Islamic Understanding of Death and Resurrection*, pp. 19–20 (20); see also Sumegi, *Understanding Death*, pp. 143–44.

137. For a succinct account, see Stieglecker, *Die Glaubenslehren des Islam*, #1341, pp. 730–31; on Munkar and Nakir, see #1344, pp. 732–33; for details about what happens between the grave and resurrections, see ##1351–54, pp. 736–38. For a slightly different account, see "The Soul's Journey after Death," introduction (pp. 2–3).

138. "The Soul's Journey after Death," p. 2.

139. "The Soul's Journey after Death," p. 3.

140. See further Afsaruddin, "Death, Resurrection, and Human Destiny," p. 46. Described by many, the journey of the soul in the afterlife is most vividly accounted in the seventeenth-century master Mulla Sadra's *Four Journeys*, one of the many volumes devoted to end times.

141. Stieglecker, *Die Glaubenslehren des Islam*, #1383, p. 755, my translation. For the importance of that doctrine and useful documentation, see Mahmud, *The Creed of Islam*, chap. 5.

human life would be miserable because the human person lives longer than other creatures and is capable of suffering and worrying about the future.[142]

Debates similar to those Jewish and Christian philosophers engage in concerning the nature of the resurrection can be found among Islamic scholars, particularly in medieval times.[143] Briefly put, the main question is whether resurrection entails a total annihilation of the person before re-creation or a reconstitution and renewal. The main Qur'anic word *ma'ad* means literally "to return," but that in itself does not provide a definite hermeneutical key. Indeed, one may find two kinds of directions in scripture itself. Just compare 28:88 ("Everything will perish except His Countenance"), which clearly assumes the annihilationist view, with 10:4: "To Him is the return of all of you. . . . Truly He originates creation, then recreates it," which teaches the other option. Generally speaking, the annihilationist view appeals to the Asharites, who in their occasionalism opposed some philosophers' belief in the eternity of creation: what is totally contingent for its existence is liable to annihilation before the new creation. The Asharites also by and large denied a physical resurrection in favor of a spiritual one in which the "soul" and "spirit" are integrally linked. Others, such as al-Ghazali (who of course was by and large in the Asharite camp) and many Mu'tazilites, opted for the view according to which both body and soul will be resurrected.[144] In his "Twentieth Discussion" in *The Incoherence of Philosophers*, al-Ghazali sets out to correct a number of eschatological mistakes, most prominently the denial of bodily resurrection.[145] His central argument has to do with the "philosophers' [Avicenna's] claim that anymore than it is possible for an iron to change into a garment, is the resurrection possible." Having considered various options for the possibility of one kind of material to be transformed into another (whether instantaneously or over a long period of time), al-Ghazali points to what to him is the main issue of contention in this case — divine agency.[146] In sum: belief in the resurrection of the body was and is the orthodox belief among the Muslims.

142. Stieglecker, *Die Glaubenslehren des Islam*, ##1383–87, pp. 755–57.

143. Differently from some Jewish traditions, reincarnation (metempsychosis) has never received approval among any significant Muslim movements. It is noteworthy, however, that Mulla Sadra of the seventeenth century saw it important to offer sustained critique of it in his *Four Journeys*. For details, see Rizvi, "Mulla Sadra."

144. For details, see Stieglecker, *Die Glaubenslehren des Islam*, ##1388–96, pp. 757–61.

145. He also corrects mistakes about annihilationism and resurrection in his *The Remembrance of Death and the Afterlife*, pp. 121–25.

146. Al-Ghazali, *Tahafut Al-Falasifah*, pp. 220–22; citations on #48, p. 222; help to locate the reference came from Griffel, "Al-Ghazali."

Heaven and Hell — Salvation and Judgment

Consider that a typical list of the basic beliefs of Islam includes "belief in one God, His messengers, His books, His angels, and the day of judgement."[147] Having been created from clay by Allah and appointed to the honorific status of *khalif*, vice-regent, the human being carries responsibility and accountability before Allah. This accounting happens when in the hereafter men and women "return" to their God (Q 32:7–11).[148] Almost every chapter of the Qur'an speaks of or refers to the theme of judgment.[149] Similarly to the New Testament, even the evil spirits (*jinn*) will be judged.[150]

Although the Qur'an does not specify the time of the judgment, it assures its readers that the day of judgment is near. The general picture of the day of judgment is very similar to that given in the Bible. Great earthquakes will rock the earth, setting mountains in motion (sura 99). The sky will split open and heaven will be "stripped off," rolled up like a parchment scroll. The sun will cease to shine; the stars will be scattered and fall upon the earth. The oceans will boil over. Graves will be opened, the earth bringing forth its burdens — hidden sins, lost stories, and the dead (sura 82). People will seek vainly to flee from the divine wrath. All will bow, willingly or not, before God. In traditional Islamic thought, the day of judgment is a period of great cosmic conflict when the forces of Satan — represented by a false messiah (*al-Dajjal*) and Gog and Magog — combat the forces of God, led by the Mahdi and Jesus.[151] With judgment constantly in view, life on this earth for the Muslim is preparation for eternity.[152] After resurrection, each human person is given a "book" that indicates the final destiny (18:49), either heaven or hell.[153]

The normal way in Islam to be saved (and to avoid the fires of hell) is to believe in the unity of God (*shahada*) and pursue good deeds (Q 262);[154] one should also avoid grave sins. What is debated among the Muslim schools is indeed the lot of the (gravely) sinning believer. Wide disagreements among the

147. Haleem, "Qur'an and Hadith," p. 25; for details, see pp. 29–30.

148. See further J. Smith and Haddad, *The Islamic Understanding of Death and Resurrection*, pp. 11–14.

149. See further Fromherz, "Judgment, Final"; Nyang, "The Teaching of the Quran," pp. 77–80.

150. For details, see Nyang, "The Teaching of the Quran," pp. 81–82.

151. D. Peterson, "Eschatology."

152. See Schirrmacher, "They Are Not All Martyrs," p. 251.

153. For angels' role as "bookkeepers," see Nyang, "The Teaching of the Quran," p. 81.

154. For details of Islamic soteriology, see chap. 8 in my *Spirit and Salvation*.

(medieval) schools could not be reconciled.[155] That debate relates to another: How do the person's good and bad deeds account for the final judgment received? Notwithstanding unanimity, common to all opinions is the centrality of obedience to Allah or lack thereof; furthermore, it was widely agreed that only grave sins bring about judgment.[156] On the one hand, for some (particularly among the Mu'tazilites and the conservative Kharijites [Khawārijites]), any merit accrued by good deeds can in principle be canceled out by grave sins, especially *shirk* (associating God with anything non-God) and *kufr* (unbelief, reluctance to submit under God's authority). On the other hand, Asharites and other major Sunni traditions believe in the balancing of good and evil deeds to determine the final outcome. This view is based particularly on Q 99:7-8: "So whoever does an atom's weight of good shall see it, and whoever does an atom's weight of evil shall see it." Rather than a semi-automatic process in which one grave sin deletes the value of all good deeds, it is left to Allah to balance the scales. Furthermore, human repentance and intercession count as mitigating factors in this majority (Asharite) position.[157]

What about non-Muslims? It seems like the Qur'an teaches a fairly inclusive view of salvation: "Surely those who believe, and those of Jewry, and the Christians, and the Sabaeans, whoever believes in God and the Last Day, and performs righteous deeds — their wage is with their Lord, and no fear shall befall them, neither shall they grieve" (2:62). The implications of this passage are of course widely debated among historical and contemporary Muslim scholars. Echoing the biblical view for those who have never heard the gospel, the Qur'an teaches that "we do not punish unless We send a messenger [who explains to people their obligations]" (17:15). Ultimately, the matter is to be left open.[158]

What is not debated is that there are two destinies as taught in the scripture (9:100-102; 7:37-51;[159] 75:20-25; and so forth); tradition also affirms it univocally.[160] Although understandably the Islamic tradition does not speak

155. J. Smith and Haddad, *The Islamic Understanding of Death and Resurrection*, p. 24.

156. Q 4:31: "If you avoid the grave sins that are forbidden you, We will absolve you of your evil deeds and admit you by an honourable gate." The problem is, of course, what constitutes a "grave" sin.

157. J. Smith and Haddad, *The Islamic Understanding of Death and Resurrection*, pp. 22-24.

158. Saritoprak, *Islam's Jesus*, pp. 51-53 (52).

159. Here there are three groups; the third one consists of those still waiting for the judgment and hoping to enter heaven.

160. See Haleem, "Commentary on Selected Qur'ānic Texts," pp. 148-49.

with one voice on the nature and existence of hell, there is a general under-standing:[161] it is a place of great pain and torture, as graphically described both in the Qur'an and in later tradition,[162] particularly among the Mu'tazi-lites.[163] Their views of eternal destinies were significantly guided by a semi-technical understanding of God's justice: "God, having declared Himself to be just (Qur'an 6:115; 16:90; 21:47; 57:25) . . . was constrained always to judge exactly according to the just deserts of each soul at the judgement, so that there would be no escape for the impenitent sinner."[164] Yet human freedom and responsibility were not ruled out; ultimately the final destiny is in the hands of the human person, as "God only creates in humans the power or ability to act, not the acts themselves."[165] Out of that insistence emerged the Mu'tazilite conception of "promise and threat," that is, the determination of both the blessed and the damned state by the individual himself or herself (in keeping with God's justice and fairness). The major Sunni tradition (particularly Han-bilites and Asharites) resisted this kind of notion of "security of salvation" and left the question totally up to Allah.[166]

Unlike the major view, the Mu'tazilite position thus resists the power of intercession, the idea of which has in some way or another been part of the Muslim spiritual texture from the beginning; indeed, the possibility and conditions of intercession are widely discussed in the Hadith. One such fa-mous debate has to do with whether intercession continues to be effective even on the day of resurrection. Asserting to a group of Muslim scholars that he himself will be the leader of humankind that day, the Prophet teaches that neither Adam nor Abraham nor Moses has the prerogative to intercede; only he himself can.[167]

What about heaven?[168] Often depicted in the Qur'an with garden images (3:190-99; 22:19-20; sura 37), paradise is a place of great enjoyment, peace, and reunion. The Qur'an offers sensual descriptions, including the pleasures

161. See further Afsaruddin, "Death, Resurrection, and Human Destiny," pp. 48-50.

162. Chittick, "Muslim Eschatology," p. 134.

163. See further the eleventh-century Abd al-Jabbar's "Five Principles," pp. 212-14. See also Blankinship, "The Early Creed," p. 47.

164. Blankinship, "The Early Creed," p. 49.

165. Blankinship, "The Early Creed," p. 50.

166. Hermansen, "Eschatology," pp. 318-19; Watt, *Islamic Philosophy and Theology*, pp. 51-52.

167. See *Sahih Bukhari*, vol. 9, bk. 93 ("Oneness, Uniqueness of Allah [Tawheed]"), #532A, B, C.

168. For a rich account of visions and images of the afterlife, see Rustomji, *The Garden and the Fire*.

of exquisitely delicious food and drink, as well as sexual relations with divine maidens (often interpreted metaphorically).[169] Similarly to the Bible, there are also various levels of rewards for the blessed ones, the details of which have occupied Islamic exegetes for hundreds of years.[170] Particularly splendid accounts of paradise ("Garden") can be found in the Hadith, such as its having eight gates and no less than one hundred levels, the distance between each of them being as long as that between heaven and earth.[171]

Similarly to Christian tradition, Muslim scholars have debated widely about the possibility of the "beatific vision." For the Muslim tradition, that question is even more contested because of Islam's uttermost insistence on the transcendence of God (without in any way undermining Islam's surprisingly robust account of immanence). The question also has to do with the possibility and conditions of the (bodily) resurrected person's "'ocular vision' of God who is the ultimate spiritual reality."[172] Not surprisingly, opinions vary. Whereas the Asharites (in keeping with their disgust for the highly abstract Mu'tazilite-type speculations) basically refrain from making up their minds by not delving too deeply into the details of the problem, some others, among the Shi'ites particularly, are convinced that such a vision is possible.[173]

"End-Time" Visions and Symbols in Hindu Traditions

In Search of a Distinctive Hindu Vision of the "End"

Unlike Abrahamic traditions, "Hinduism has no last day or end time, nor any completion of history, resurrection of the dead, and universal last judgment."[174] The focus lies rather on "the deliverance of the individual from the unreal realm of the empirical and temporal to the timeless realm of the

169. D. Peterson, "Eschatology."

170. See Afsaruddin, "Death, Resurrection, and Human Destiny," pp. 51–54.

171. *Sahih Bukhari*, vol. 4, bk. 54, #479; vol. 4, bk. 52, #48; see also Afsaruddin, "Death, Resurrection, and Human Destiny," p. 47. For a contemporary poetic description, see "Abū 'l-'Alā al-Mawdūdi on the Verse of Light," pp. 42–47.

172. "Bāqillāni on the Vision of God in the Next Life."

173. For a text example from an Asharite Bāqillāni of the eleventh century, see "Bāqillāni on the Vision of God in the Next Life," and from a contemporary Shi'ite, "Alī on the Vision of God," pp. 209–11. See further Watt, *Islamic Philosophy and Theology*, p. 66; Hermansen, "Eschatology," p. 320.

174. Knipe, "Hindu Eschatology," p. 171; so also Hiltebeitel, "The 'Mahābhārata,' and Hindu Eschatology," p. 95.

spirit."[175] Because of its endless-cycle worldview, Hindu eschatology can be best called an eternalistic and organic process,[176] as opposed to the linear and historical perspective in the Abrahamic faiths. Although the Lord is at times called the Creator (particularly in the Bhagavad-Gita),[177] there is neither a doctrine of creation nor a Creator in any sense similar to those of Abrahamic traditions; this corresponds to the lack of any (final) end.[178] Importantly, the role of the deities is ambiguous when it comes to end times. A number of deities undergo death and even rebirth in another form.[179]

"Cosmic eschatology" is usually described in terms of *kalpas* (a somewhat later development).[180] Each *kalpa* encompasses the life span from origination to dissolution. It equals one day in the life of Brahma (the first of the three main deities). Each *kalpa* is further divided into four ages with different religious-moral tones, from full *dharma*[181] (righteousness) to *adharma*, the worst possible condition. At the end of a *kalpa*, a great dissolution occurs, "which coincides with the end of the life of Brahma. The world will be reabsorbed into Brahma by involution and remain in that state until the hatching of a new cosmic age."[182] And so *ad finitum*. Of interest to Christian theology is that when the lack of *dharma* is at its worst, the *avatar* (incarnation) of Vishnu comes down, the beloved Krishna (or any other of the incarnations of Vishnu or even Shiva).[183]

Are there any millennial elements in various Hindu traditions? It is widely agreed that only with the rise of anticolonialist movements in the nineteenth century did millennial groups emerge. At the same time, various types of self-made gurus appeared, and in their activities millennial features

---

175. Dhavamony, "Death and Immortality in Hinduism," pp. 100–101 (100).

176. Note that the cosmos is sometimes compared to a cosmic being, a living organism, as in the famous hymn to Purusa in Rig Veda 10.90, where out of the organs of the deity everything is made.

177. Consult chap. 7 of the Gita.

178. A highly insightful "insider" account is the short pamphlet written by Maharaj, *Origin and Eschatology in Hindu Eschatology*. See also K. Ward, *Religion and Revelation*, p. 141. For the radical incompatibility with this and the Abrahamic faiths, see Zaehner, *Mysticism, Sacred and Profane*, p. 204.

179. For a useful discussion, see Doniger, *On Hinduism*, pp. 97–103.

180. Particularly interested in *kalpas* are the great epics; see *Mahabharata* 3.148; 12.231, 341; Vishnu Purana 1.3; 3.2–3; and so forth; I am indebted to Dhavamony, "Death and Immortality in Hinduism."

181. For a basic discussion, see chap. 13 in Sharma, *Classical Hindu Thought*.

182. Dhavamony, "Death and Immortality in Hinduism," pp. 100–101 (101).

183. Bhagavad-Gita 4.7–8; for details, see my *Christ and Reconciliation*, pp. 146–48.

were present. "That being said, however, the Hindu traditions do have visions of cataclysmic change, eschatological destruction, and a radical remaking of the world that have certain structural parallels to Western visions of the Millennium."[184]

Death, Rebirth, and Karmic Samsara

The last two books (ninth and tenth) of the oldest Vedic scripture, Rig Veda, speak extensively of death.[185] The Funeral Hymn (10.14), dedicated to Yama, the god of death — the first one to die and show the rest of mortals the way to go[186] — speaks of death in terms of meeting Yama and the "Fathers" (the honored ancestors).[187] Yama is assisted by two messenger dogs, the guardians of death's pathway. Yama and the "Fathers" prepare a wonderful place for the deceased, "a place to rest in adorned with days and beams of light and water" (10.14.8–11[9]).[188] The Upanishads significantly expand the theology of death. They contain the well-known legend of the Naciketas (or Nakiketas) in Katha Upanishad (1.1–3), whose main message is the possibility of two destinies, either that of pleasure and worldly enjoyment, which is nothing more than illusion, or the "good way," that of true knowledge.[189]

The most innovative and theologically significant Upanishadic development has to do with the evolvement of the doctrines of karma and transmigration of the soul (rebirth).[190] The soul continues its afterlife journey from one state to another conditioned by the deeds of one's lifetime.[191] Until one is ready to be absorbed into "Reality" (*satya*), the migration continues.[192] Known

184. Urban, "Millenarian Elements in the Hindu Religious Traditions," p. 369. A classic, still useful study is S. Fuchs, *Rebellious Prophets*.

185. For important observations, see Knipe, "Hindu Eschatology," pp. 172–74.

186. It looks to me that at times Yama is spoken of as the first *human* to ever die; at other times, Yama is named the first god to taste death.

187. See Rig Veda 10.15; for comments, see Knipe, "Hindu Eschatology," pp. 174–75.

188. For many details of what happens after death, see Rig Veda 10.15–18 (the last hymn of which is also a funeral prayer). See further Dhavamony, "Death and Immortality in Hinduism," pp. 93–94.

189. Katha Upanishad 2.1; similarly two destinies, based on one's deeds, are taught in the *Mahabharata*, bk. 11 (*Stri Parva*), #3; Bhagavad-Gita 8.24–25.

190. See Doniger, *On Hinduism*, p. 89; K. Ward, *Religion and Human Nature*, pp. 57–58.

191. Often the first destination is the sun (Rig Veda 10.16.3; Atharva Veda 18.2.7); other times the moon (Kaushitaki Upanishad 1.1–4).

192. A highly important and detailed description of the soul's transmigration can be

as karmic samsara, continuous rebirths are believed by all Hindu movements, both theistic and otherwise.[193] It is essential to note that samsara is a "universal" law concerning "the conditioned and ever changing universe as contrasted to an unconditioned, eternal, and transcendent state (*moksa* or *nirvāna*)." The liberated one is no longer under karma.[194]

Deriving from the ritual context, karma evolves from moral and immoral actions from the past lives of the individual to their consequences and one's actions in subsequent lives, finally extending to the notion that "good and bad karma may also be transferred from one person to another under certain circumstances."[195] At death, "the various component parts of . . . [the deceased person's] body unite with [his] corresponding counterparts in nature, while the sum total of his karma remains attached to his self (*atman*). The force of this karma decides the nature of his next birth where he reaps the fruit of what he merits."[196]

That teaching helps put death in a different perspective: as aversive as it may appear to human desire to cling to life,[197] it is not the ultimate reality and has only relative significance. Death is an "earthly" matter and hence belongs to the "appearance" part of reality.[198] "The knowing (Self) is not born, it dies

---

found in Brihadaranyaka Upanishad 4.3.1–4.4.2; see also Chandogya Upanishad 6.8.6. For comments, consult further Dhavamony, "Death and Immortality in Hinduism," pp. 94–95.

193. For supportive scholarly documentation, see Milner, "Hindu Eschatology and the Indian Caste System," p. 298. For a useful discussion based on the Bhagavata Purana's description of *jiva*'s (human self or living being) journey over many lives, see chap. 11 in Sharma, *Classical Hindu Thought*. On the differences between the Hindu and Buddhist notion of samsara, see Reat, "Karma and Rebirth in the *Upanisads* and Buddhism."

194. B. Smith, "*Samsāra*," p. 8098.

195. Doniger, *On Hinduism*, p. 93 (more widely, chap. 12). For the reasons Hindus give to support transmigration (rebirth), such as certain innate predilections (e.g., a baby sucking the mother's milk or the innate fear of death), see Balasubramanian, "The Advaita View of Death and Immortality," p. 123.

196. Dhavamony, "Death and Immortality in Hinduism," p. 94. A highly important and detailed description of the soul's transmigration can be found in Brihadaranyaka Upanishad 4.3.

197. Death at a mature age may also be considered a "good" death. See further A. King, "The Glorious Disappearance of Vaishnavas," p. 105.

198. On death's inevitable nature as something created by God, see the *Mahabharata*, bk. 7 (*Drona Parva*), ##52–54; Bhagavad-Gita 2.27–28. Because of its appearance (*maya*) nature, "The wise grieve neither for the living nor for the dead" (2.11). Note that the "appearance" nature of reality (as distinct from the "real" one) does not of course mean that the cosmos would not exist; even things of appearance nature do exist. It means that it is "secondary" in importance to the real one. For basics of *maya*, see chap. 14 in Sharma, *Classical Hindu Thought*.

not; it sprang from nothing, nothing sprang from it. The Ancient is unborn, eternal, everlasting; he is not killed, though the body is killed."[199] That said, however, reverence for the dead and the obligation of the relatives of the deceased are an integral part of Hindu cultures,[200] and sophisticated funeral rites have evolved to help start the journey in the afterlife.

Bhagavad-Gita, the "Bible of the common folks," affirms the basic Upanishadic teachings: the inevitability of death, its transitory nature because of transmigration, and two destinies (at least as long as one has not yet achieved the ultimate goal).[201] As is well known, the Gita pays special attention to one's last thoughts, that is, whether one is totally devoted to one's deity or to some earthly goal: "The One who leaves the body, at the hour of death, remembering Me [Krishna, an *avatara* of Vishnu] attains My abode. . . . By contemplating on Me with an unwavering mind, disciplined by the practice of meditation, one attains the Supreme divine spirit."[202] Unlike in philosophical schools (such as *advaita* of Sankara) in which true knowledge is the key to release, in all *bhakti* (devotional) schools love for the deity is at the center. In those spiritualities, "[e]very man becomes what he worships."[203] The discussion of the theistic (Vaishnavistic), particularly devotional forms of Hinduism helps us also to understand that the workings of karma can be understood less mechanistically (as in *advaita*) and more "as a soterial path leading to acceptance of the grace of Krishna." Furthermore, differently from Sankara's view, according to which there is "one non-dual self which, through the mysterious power of maya comes to see itself as many individual selves," Ramanuja's Vaishnava version "is that the material body is a reflection of a spiritual body, so that each soul has a distinct personality in the spiritual world, and liberation consists in being freed from the limitations of 'false ego,' and relating in loving devotion to the supreme personality of Godhead."[204]

199. Katha Upanishad 1.2.18; see further Dhavamony, "Death and Immortality in Hinduism," pp. 94–95. For similar teaching in the Gita, see 2.12.

200. Dhavamony, "Death and Immortality in Hinduism," p. 93.

201. A representative Upanishadic passage is Brihadaranyaka Upanishad 4.3.36; see further Rambachan, "Hinduism," pp. 74–75.

202. Bhagavad-Gita 8.

203. Dhavamony, "Death and Immortality in Hinduism," pp. 97–98 (98); see Mundaka Upanishad 3.2.9.

204. K. Ward, *Religion and Human Nature*, pp. 74, 75.

Avidya *and* Moksa: *"Ignorance" and "Salvation"*

Similarly to the doctrine of resurrection, rebirth raises the question of the constitution of human nature[205] and the corollary question of what continues beyond physical death. Although the Vedanta Hindu philosophical schools do not typically lean toward the Hellenistic type of body-soul dualism (or if they do, they frame it differently), there is a dualism of "true" (real) and "not-self."[206] As long as one does not grasp the single most important insight that "Self [*atman*] is indeed Brahman [the eternal Self],"[207] one is distanced from the real self.[208]

Hinduism knows nothing like the Christian doctrine of sin and fall. The underlying Hindu diagnosis of what human "bondage" is has to do with *avidya*, "ignorance."[209] It makes one cling to *maya*, "fiction," and thus be subject to the effects of karma, leading to rebirths over and over again.[210] Only the removal of this bondage, *moksa*, makes release or deliverance possible.[211] The key is the enlightenment insight into the true nature of reality.[212] It is safe to say that by and large Hindu movements "aim at the practical end of salvation. The systems mean by release (moksa) the recovery by the soul of its natural integrity, from which sin and error drive it."[213]

This karmic samsara template conceived of the nature of heaven and hell differently. Only vaguely intuited in the Vedic literature, a fairly clearly defined picture of heaven and hell does not appear until the great epics, particularly the *Mahabharata*.[214] Because of rebirth, their meaning is obviously different from those of Abrahamic traditions. With bad karma, one is reborn into hell

205. For basic ideas, see my *Creation and Humanity*, pp. 378–81.

206. The principle of the "appearance" nature of reality also has bearing on anthropology: "The apparent man is merely a struggle to express, to manifest this individuality which is beyond." From Vivekananda, "The Real Nature of Man," in Adiswarananda, *Vivekananda*, p. 83.

207. Brihadaranyaka Upanishad 4.4.5.

208. For accessible basic accounts, see Balasubramanian, "The Advaita View of Death and Immortality," pp. 110–17; Rambachan, "Hinduism," pp. 71–74.

209. For the *advaita* school's (Sankara) detailed analysis of the effects of *avidya*, that is, "superimposition," see Sankara, *Commentary on Vedanta Sutras*, part I, 1.1.1; *SBE* 34:4; for exposition, see my *Creation and Humanity*, pp. 422–23.

210. The Christian interpreter should not see here any kind of "Fall" or original sinfulness though. See Thatamanil, *Immanent Divine*, p. 36.

211. For a detailed discussion, see my *Creation and Humanity*, pp. 421–25.

212. See, e.g., Isa Upanishad 5.9; see further Organ, *The Hindu Quest for the Perfection of Man*, p. 5.

213. Radhakrishnan, *Indian Philosophy*, 2:26. For a lucid discussion, see also Sivaraman, "The Meaning of *Moksha*," pp. 2–11.

214. The standard discussion is Hiltebeitel, "The 'Mahābhārata,' and Hindu Eschatology."

for penalty and purification; with good karma, for a longer period of time of enjoyment in heaven. Neither one, however, is the ultimate destiny.[215] The last book of the great epic, titled "The Book of Climbing to Heaven" (*Svargarohan-ika Parva*), provides detailed descriptions of both.[216]

Buddhist Visions of End and "Release"

In Search of an Eschatological Vision after Buddhist Traditions

Although Buddhism, similarly to Hinduism, does not know any final closure — and therefore we should speak of "relative" eschatology[217] — already during the time of Gautama himself a diversity of views of the "end" of human life had emerged.[218] As is well known, Buddha showed great reticence toward speculations into the metaphysical questions of the end (and origin) because he took this to be "unbeneficial" in the pursuit of final release.[219] When entering into speculations concerning the "end," somewhat similarly to Hindu tradition, Buddhism speaks of the "history" of the cosmos in terms of exceedingly long ages — called "great eons" (*mahākalpa*) — and divides them into four periods, beginning with the destruction of the cosmos and extending to various durations of renovation when the universe again reemerges. Within each period a number of subperiods can be discerned in which the quality of human life and the level of morality vary.[220]

Rather than a doctrine of creation,[221] Buddha taught the principle of "dependent origination," also called "causal interdependence."[222] Not surpris-

---

215. Doniger, *On Hinduism*, pp. 94–95; for a highly useful analysis, see Jacobsen, "Three Functions of Hell in the Hindu Traditions."

216. For details, see Doniger, *On Hinduism*, pp. 95–98; Dhavamony, "Death and Immortality in Hinduism," pp. 104–5.

217. Werblowsky, "Eschatology," p. 2834.

218. Just see the famous discussion "IV. Speculations about the Future (*Aparantakappika*)," in *Brahmajāla Sutta: The All-Embracing Net of Views; Digha-Nikaya* 1.74–130; see also Hick, *Death and Eternal Life*, p. 21.

219. *Majjhima Nikaya Sutta* 63.8, p. 536; see de Silva, "The Buddhist Attitude towards Nature," n.p. See also the important comments by the Japanese Christian theologian Koyama, *Mount Fuji and Mount Sinai*, p. 74.

220. For details and documentation, see Nattier, "Buddhist Eschatology," pp. 152–53.

221. *Lotus Sutra* 5.80; 13.19.

222. *Saticca-samuppada-vibhanga Sutta: Analysis of Dependent Co-arising* (Samyutta Nikaya 12.2); a classic statement is in Samyutta Nikaya 12.61; for details, see Payutto, *Dependent Origination*, "Introduction," n.p.

ingly, then, "[e]verything formed is in a constant process of change."[223] Everything is fleeting and in a process[224] — everything but nirvana (which is not "conditioned").[225] The conditioned nature of all of reality is part of and makes sense against the most distinctive Buddhist concept, namely, the *dukkha*.[226] Rather than using "suffering" (or "pain" or "stress") for *dukkha*, it is best to leave the term without English translation to avoid misunderstanding. It is intentionally an ambiguous word related to the nonstatic nature of reality. All Buddhist schools consider *dukkha* to be the main challenge in life and, consequently, extinction of *dukkha* to be the main goal, the *summa* of everything in Buddhism and its scriptures.[227] Suffering is inescapable as long as one is in the circle of life and death, samsara. To be more precise, it is the craving (the second "Noble Truth") that is its real root and cause.[228]

Keeping in mind these foundational assumptions about the nature of the cosmos and life, we are prepared to begin to investigate the distinctive nature of the Buddhist analysis of how to achieve release from the "mass of suffering" and endless cycle of samsara. As is well known, Buddhism joins Indian traditions in affirming the doctrine of rebirth. That said, because of its distinctive analysis of human nature, known as *anatta*, "no-self," that doctrine is affirmed in a radically different manner from Hinduism. To that investigation we devote the bulk of this section on Buddhist eschatology.

"No-Self," Kamma, *and Rebirth*

Buddhism's most distinctive doctrine is the denial of a constitutive permanent self, persisting personhood.[229] This is but a result of the codependent orig-

---

223. de Silva, "The Buddhist Attitude towards Nature," n.p. The Pali term *anicca* is routinely used to describe this principle.

224. The authoritative statement is that of Buddhagosa, *Visuddhi Visuddhimagga* 16.71, p. 522. For a detailed account of the Buddhist view of "creation" and its relation to Christian view, see my *Creation and Humanity*, pp. 86-91.

225. For details, see Nattier, "Buddhist Eschatology," pp. 154-55.

226. Buddha's "Setting the Wheel of Dhamma in Motion" can be found, e.g., in *Dhammacakkappavattana Sutta* 11 of Samyutta Nikaya 56.11. The four noble truths are called "the teaching special to the Buddhas" in Majjhima Nikaya 56.18 (*The Middle Length Discourses*, p. 485).

227. Chandngarm, *Arriyasatsee*, pp. 9-14.

228. Similarly to the notion of *dukkha*, the term *tanhā* ("craving" or "desire") used by Buddha is a multifaceted concept. A highly useful account of *tanhā*, based on Majjhima Nikaya, is Ñānamoli and Bodhi, introduction to *The Middle Length Discourses of the Buddha*, pp. 27-29.

229. A highly important and accessible account of no-self with basic scriptural ref-

ination and impermanence as well as the *dukkha* nature of all conditioned phenomena. Calling the person a "self" is just an elusive, conventional way of referring to that fleeting combination of elements.[230] Therefore also, "[t]here is no doer of a deed."[231]

To be liberated from the illusion of being permanent and hence clinging to anything conditioned, the "salvific" insight into the true nature of reality and being is needed (release from samsara, the cycle of rebirths). Otherwise, the continuous process of rebirth continues due to *kamma*, which in the case of those who "engage in bad actions . . . generate[s] unwholesome kamma that leads them to rebirth into lower states of existence," including pain and suffering.[232] Lest one conceive of the karmic samsara cycle of rebirths along the lines of Hinduism — and common sense — that is, that the deceased self will be reborn, the doctrine of *anatta* should be remembered: "Rebirth, in the Buddhist conception, is not the transmigration of a self or soul but the continuation of a process, a flux of becoming in which successive lives are linked together by causal transmission of influence rather than by substantial identity."[233]

What, then, is the Buddhist final release, *nibbana*? What is its nature? Who will achieve it? Because the Buddha, as mentioned, was not interested in metaphysical speculations but rather in "putting an end to suffering and stress,"[234] he did not encourage speculation; rather, he set out to teach the path to liberation; doing so, he began to sketch some idea of its nature.

Nirvana and the Cessation of "Desire"

The goal of the Buddhist pursuit is to achieve the enlightening insight into the nature of the *dukkha* in order to overcome the desire to cling to it.[235] Behind the (misplaced) craving is ignorance. No wonder the very first step in the

---

erences (from the standard manual of Majjhima Nikaya) is given in Ñāṇamoli and Bodhi, introduction to *The Middle Length Discourses of the Buddha*, pp. 27–29.

230. An authoritative study is S. Collins, *Selfless Persons*.

231. *Visuddhimagga*, chap. 19, pp. 627–28 (627).

232. Ñāṇamoli and Bodhi, introduction to *The Middle Length Discourses of the Buddha*, p. 45.

233. Ñāṇamoli and Bodhi, introduction to *The Middle Length Discourses of the Buddha*, p. 45.

234. *Alagaddupama Sutta: The Water-Snake Simile* of Majjhima Nikaya 22.38 (*The Middle Length Discourses*, p. 234).

235. "Nibbana Sutta: Total Unbinding (1)" (*Udana* 8.1).

Eightfold Path of skillful means is rightful knowledge.[236] Even Buddha is not the Savior. One may only "take refuge" in Buddha. He is the one who shows the possibility of attaining such a releasing knowledge.[237] Ultimately, "one is one's own refuge, who else could be the refuge?"[238] The road to enlightenment is long and tedious.[239]

What, if anything, then can be said of the nature of *nibbana*? Recall that this is the only nonconditioned aspect of reality and therefore free from change and decay.[240] In *nibbana*, there is "neither dimension of the infinitude of space, nor dimension of the infinitude of consciousness, nor dimension of nothingness, nor dimension of neither perception nor non-perception; neither this world, nor the next world. . . . This, just this, is the end of stress."[241]

The main logical challenge to such a vision is well known among both Buddhists and its critics: If everything is nonpermanent, how can nirvana then be the "final" goal? I am not aware of satisfactory solutions.[242] How helpful is the statement in *Lankavatar Sutra* (2.1.7): "Thou dost not vanish in Nirvana, nor is Nirvana abiding in thee; for it transcends the duality of knowing and known and of being and non-being"?[243]

The end result of reaching *nibbana* in the Theravada tradition is the *arahant*, derived from the "worthy" (also rendered as "accomplished"). That

236. For standard scriptural exposition of the Eightfold Path, see Majjhina Nikaya 141 and 117; for reliable discussion, see Ñānamoli and Bodhi, introduction to *The Middle Length Discourses of the Buddha*, pp. 32–34.

237. Rahula, *What the Buddha Taught*, pp. 1–2. For the high praises of the Buddha as teacher, mentor pointing to release, see Majjhima Nikaya 108.5 (*The Middle Length Discourses*, p. 880).

238. *Dhammapada* 12.4; *SBE* 10 (in some other versions, 12.160, when verses are numbered from the beginning of the work, rather than from the beginning of each chapter). The English translation of this passage varies; I have followed here the one adopted by Rahula, *What the Buddha Taught*, p. 1. Similarly, *Dhammapada* 20.4 (20.276) puts it: "You yourselves must strive; the Buddhas only point the way."

239. For an analysis of the stages, see Ñānamoli and Bodhi, introduction to *The Middle Length Discourses of the Buddha*, pp. 41–43 (41).

240. A basic source is *A Manual of Abhidhamma* (*Abhidhammattha Sangaha*). Another authoritative statement is Buddhagosa, *Visuddhi Visuddhimagga* 16.71, p. 522.

241. "Nibbana Sutta: Total Unbinding (1)" (*Udana* 8.1). Another classic description is Majjhima Nikaya 26.13 (*The Middle Length Discourses*, p. 256). For an important contemporary discussion, see Dharmasiri, *A Buddhist Critique of the Christian Concept of God*, pp. 177–214. The discussion includes the relation to the Hindu use of the concept as well as critique of Christian responses and interpretations.

242. See also K. Ward, *Images of Eternity*, pp. 61–62.

243. *The Lankavatara Sutra: A Mahayana Text* 2.7.

enlightened one is the person, "with taints destroyed, who has lived the holy life, done what had to be done, laid down the burden, reached the true goal, destroyed the fetters of being, and is completely liberated through final knowledge."[244] At the time of the emergence of the Mahayana tradition, this original concept of *arahant* was revised into Boddhisattva, the Enlightened One who for the sake of others postpones the stepping into *nibbana*.

Is this nihilism? To merely respond to this important question in an obvious way — that it is not because there is no "self" in Buddhism[245] — misses the point and avoids the question. True, there is no "self" in that system, but there is something, how elusively and ambiguously one may wish to express it, that at least has an afterlife, if not eternally, then at least for a long period of time.

Having now outlined in some detail the visions of the "end" and "consummation" in four living faith traditions — following the inquiry into the resources of natural sciences — we will begin to develop a distinctively Christian eschatology. In the course of that process, other faith traditions as well as the sciences' insights will be critically evaluated.

244. Majjhima Nikaya 35.25 (p. 596); for other descriptions, see 22.30-35 (*The Middle Length Discourses*, pp. 233-34); 39.22-29 (pp. 37-71); for details, see Ñānamoli and Bodhi, introduction to *The Middle Length Discourses of the Buddha*, pp. 43-45.

245. So, e.g., Nattier, "Buddhist Eschatology," p. 157.

4. A Trinitarian Theology of Hope

For Orientation: Creation, Providence, and Final Consummation as the Joint Work of the Triune God

My conviction in this project is that what contemporary constructive theology requires "is a fully Trinitarian narrative of the Word and Spirit's engagement with a world of creatures, a theology of creation, incarnation and final salvation."[1] This is but to follow the honored precept of the Cappadocian Saint Basil: "And in the creation bethink thee first, I pray thee, of the original cause of all things that are made, the Father; of the creative cause, the Son; of the perfecting cause, the Spirit."[2] Having already constructed a trinitarian theology of creation and divine action (*Creation and Humanity*), of incarnation and reconciliation (*Christ and Reconciliation*), as well as of the Spirit's life-giving and life-sustaining activities (*Spirit and Salvation*), we highlight in the current discussion the works of the Father, Son, and Spirit "beginning from the end." Rather than focusing here on the "protological creation," the point of departure is "eschatological creation," which, on the basis of Christ's resurrection, looks forward to the final redemption of not only spiritual but also bodily life.[3] Doing so, I side with Pannenberg's vision according to which "[o]nly with the consummation of the world in the kingdom of God does

---

1. D. Edwards, "Where on Earth Is God?" p. 11.
2. Saint Basil, *On the Holy Spirit* 16.38; for a delightful trinitarian account of creation in Luther, see *LW* 1:9.
3. Moltmann, *God in Creation*, pp. 65–69.

God's love reach its goal. . . . Even the question of God's reality, of his existence in view of his debatability in the world as atheistic criticism in particular articulates it, can find a final answer only in the event of the eschatological world renewal."[4]

Bringing about the completion of the kingdom of God in God's eternity is the final guarantee of the faithfulness of the triune God to his creation.[5] At the same time, "[t]he eschatological salvation at which Christian hope is directed fulfills the deepest longing of humans and all creation even if there is not always a full awareness of the object of this longing."[6] Herein, creation, reconciliation, and consummation as the "action of the one God . . . is not wholly different from the action in his trinitarian life."[7]

The rest of the chapter seeks to detail the joint work of the Father, Son, and Spirit with regard to the eschatological consummation. Its modest goal is to construct a viable trinitarian theology of hope. Whereas the current chapter lays out the systematic/constructive theological vision of the hope present in Christian tradition, subsequent chapters seek to delve into the "logistics" of how that may happen — in sympathetic and critical dialogue with sciences and world religions.

God of Hope

The Loss of Hope in Our Culture

Whereas before modernity, belief in God served as the source of hope and confidence, in the post-Enlightenment world, self-confidence and trust in human resources were put in its place.[8] That led to naive optimism about progress[9] and further funded secularization and distance from God. By the latter part of the twentieth century, that confidence had encountered dramatic defeats in terms of world wars and international conflicts, impending natural catastrophes and nuclear threat, as well as other related dangers.[10]

---

4. Pannenberg, *ST* 1:447–48.
5. Pannenberg, *ST* 3:531.
6. Pannenberg, *ST* 3:527.
7. Pannenberg, *ST* 2:5.
8. For a fine analysis and comments, see Conradie, *Hope for the Earth*, chap. 12.
9. Baillie, *The Belief in Progress*, pp. 144–45, quoted in Schwarz, *Eschatology*, p. 15.
10. For a highly insightful analysis, see Bauckham and Hart, *Hope against Hope*, chaps. 1 and 3; Conradie, *Hope for the Earth*, part B (chaps. 5–8).

Rather than to theologians, many turned to philosophers and cultural spokespersons in their search for hope. Secular philosophers, however, had little to offer except for seasoned nihilism (A. Camus) or atheistic existentialism (J.-P. Sartre).[11] Not surprisingly, psychologists and psychiatrists have joined the investigation of the influence, necessity, and nature of hope.[12] Indicative of the urgency of the search is the establishment by distinguished universities of centers for the study of the psychology of hope.[13] Joint projects such as *Interdisciplinary Perspectives on Hope* (2005) have recently appeared.[14] The British psychologist Fraser Watts observes that whereas scientific examination of eschatological topics majors in propositional aspects, psychological examination focuses on what he calls attitudinal hope. Attitudinal hope oscillates between the "realized eschatology" that actually leaves very little to hope for and a totally futurist orientation that may judge the hoped-for thing unattainable.[15]

What are the theological implications of the loss of hope? How should Christian theology assess its meaning? According to the astute analysis of the German Lutheran theologian Hans Schwarz, Christian eschatology helps the confused world discern two vital truths: First, "[i]t shows that the modern idea of progress alienated itself from its Christian foundation . . . [as it] deprived history of its God-promised goal." Thereby, "we promoted ourselves from God-alienated and God-endowed actors *in history* to deified agents *of history.*" As a remedy to this dilemma, Christian eschatology, second, "provides a hope and a promise that we are unable to attain through our own efforts."[16] In other words, the "good news" of *religious* eschatology is that the bankruptcy of merely *secular* efforts is unavoidable. That acknowledgment does not lead to despair or apathy, but rather it leads to hopeful participation in the work of God in this world God has created, God has redeemed, and God will bring into final consummation. Indeed, counterintuitively "[n]ot all hopelessness is

11. For a masterful discussion and rebuttal by the Catholic convert Gabriel Marcel, see his *Homo Viator.*

12. A landmark volume in psychology of hope is Averill, Catlin, and Chon, *Rules of Hope.* For psychiatry, see Schrank, Stanghellini, and Slade, "Hope in Psychiatry."

13. For the University of Pennsylvania's Positive Psychology Center and its programs and publications, see http://www.sas.upenn.edu/psych/seligman/.

14. Eliott, ed., *Interdisciplinary Perspectives on Hope.* An excellent overview of the field is provided in the introduction by the editors. Noteworthy is also C. R. Snyder, ed., *Handbook of Hope.* Similarly to topics such as forgiveness, popular research-based literature has become a market commodity; see, e.g., C. R. Snyder, *Psychology of Hope.*

15. Watts, "Subjective and Objective Hope," p. 51.

16. Schwarz, *Eschatology,* pp. 17–21 (20; emphasis in original).

bad for us"! At times naive and empty hope may be more pathological than a realistic lack of trust in human capacities.[17]

As an alternative and challenge to either pessimism stemming from the loss of hope or optimism derived from naive confidence in human progress, Christian faith proposes a solid, historically based but also history-transcending hope based on the faithfulness of God, who raised from the dead the crucified Son in the power of the Spirit.

Hope and the Meaningfulness of History

After the end of the World War II, having just returned from exile in Japan, the German theologian Karl Löwith opined: "Historical processes as such do not bear the least evidence of a comprehensive and ultimate meaning. History as such has no outcome."[18] The current project contests that conclusion and boldly argues that, while not utopian in any sense, Christian hope intuits history as meaningful.[19] Even if its meaning may not be apparent, "grounded" hope trusts God's providence.[20] The redemption of the future is possible because "the laws and forces of the past are no longer 'compulsive' . . . [as] God's messianic future will power over the present."[21] This is the bold biblical promise vis-à-vis loss of hope in the secular cultures of the Global North.[22]

It is often said — in my understanding rightly — that whereas Asiatic faiths are "cosmic" in orientation in the sense that "true" reality stands outside or beyond this world, the Semitic religions are historical. Herein lies the wisdom of the Western mystic Aldous Huxley's critical remark against what he saw as Christian theology's "idolatrous preoccupation with events

17. Bauckham and Hart, *Hope against Hope*, p. 62.

18. Löwith, *Meaning in History*, p. 191, (partly) cited in Moltmann, *Coming of God*, p. 43.

19. See Schmemann, "Liturgy and Eschatology," pp. 9–10.

20. Moltmann (*Coming of God*, p. 43) rightly notes that "[o]nly theologians concerned to defend the secularization thesis have taken up Löwith's exposition favourably, as a way of proving that the modern philosophy of history is 'secularized theology.'"

21. Moltmann, *Coming of God*, p. 45.

22. "Hope" as a category in biblical literature has been rediscovered in contemporary biblical scholarship, both Old Testament and New Testament. However, "trajectories" of hope are diverse and varied — yet their rootedness in history and the faithfulness of Yahweh/Father of Jesus Christ are firmly established. For a highly useful survey and assessment (with regard to our topic), see Conradie, *Hope for the Earth*, chap. 9 (Old Testament), chap. 10 (New Testament).

and things in time."[23] Although not "idolatrous," the Judeo-Christian world-view is deeply oriented toward history and this world. If historical events are merely an "appearance," as the Vedic teaching has it, then rootedness with history is a great delusion. Over against this dismissal of history, the Christian theologian K. Ward asks the rhetorical question: "What if human history is the arena wherein is played out the drama of the seeking of an active personal God for persons who have become alienated from God?" He responds: "Then events in time could hardly be overevaluated, since the temporal would be the place of a real and developing set of relationships between" God and his people.[24]

In this regard such "transcendentalist" approaches to eschatology in Christian theology that divorce the coming of the kingdom of God from history — from the arena of space and time — are to be considered truncated. An example of that is the approach of C. H. Dodd, to whom Christ's return happens so much "*beyond* history" that it is not a coming in history.[25] For him and like-minded theologians, "[t]he encounter with God does not change the confines of space and time, because it occurs beyond them."[26] Gustavo Gutiér-rez corrects this view by arguing that even though "[t]he complete encounter with the Lord will mark an end to history . . . [i]t will take place in history."[27]

Historically engaged, Christian eschatology takes time seriously. Indeed, this principle becomes evident already in the Old Testament, where the people of God are a nomadic people. For them, there is the past, what was left behind, and there is the future, what is hoped for. This is linear time: from beginning, to today, to telos, the hoped-for end goal. In Asiatic religions, time is cyclical. The future is not "new"; it is a repeat. For Abrahamic religions the "future brings something new and does not repeat what is past."[28] Remembering the past invokes divine acts of deliverance that still have bearing on today and anticipate the future, "a new thing" (Isa. 43:19). Asiatic traditions stand in stark contrast in this regard.[29] The historian Arnold Toynbee goes so far as to claim that the "cyclic view of the process of history was taken so entirely for granted by Greek and Indian souls and intellects — by Aristotle, for instance, and by

23. Huxley, *The Perennial Philosophy*, p. 52. I am indebted to K. Ward, *Religion and Revelation*, p. 197, for pointing me to this phrase in the book.

24. K. Ward, *Religion and Revelation*, pp. 197-98.

25. Dodd, *The Coming of Christ*, p. 17, cited in Schwarz, *Eschatology*, p. 132.

26. A careful discussion can be found in Schwarz, *Eschatology*, pp. 129-35 (134).

27. Gutiérrez, *A Theology of Liberation*, p. 97.

28. Moltmann, *Experiences in Theology*, p. 31.

29. For details, see Badham and Badham, "Death and Immortality," p. 3.

the Buddha — that they simply assumed that it was true without thinking it necessary to prove it."[30]

A critical question is whether the orientation to the future is necessarily a "supra"-cultural value applicable to all Christian theologies. A well-known challenge has come from the senior African theologian John Mbiti, whose *New Testament Eschatology in an African Background* (1971) argues that in typical African cultures "future" as a category is missing altogether.[31] Mbiti's thesis, however, has come under severe critique both from the point of view of African religions themselves — the most obvious objection being that visions of "afterlife" abound in those cultures, indicating the presence of the category of "future" in some real sense — and from theology, namely, that were the category of future missing in a particular culture, then ways of "contextualization" would be needed to help embrace a core biblical teaching.[32]

Promise and the Faithfulness of God

Christian hope is not a utopia but is rather earth- and experience-driven: confidence in God's faithfulness arises out of doubt, despair, and hope-lessness.[33] This again brings to light the dramatic difference between the Semitic and Asiatic religions. Whereas the cosmic religions intend to bring people into harmony with the eternal laws of nature, the historical religions encounter constantly "the lack of security and the vulnerability which are the consequence of departure from the shelter of natural and social environments."[34]

In the biblical worldview, hope is expressed in terms of promise. Help-fully, Moltmann makes a distinction between the biblical "religion of promise" and the "epiphany religions of the revealed gods" of religions surrounding Israel.[35] The former is the religion of the nomadic people in search of the Land. What is remarkable about the Israelite faith is that even when it settled

---

30. Toynbee, *Civilization on Trial*, p. 14, cited in Schwarz, *Eschatology*, pp. 9-10.

31. Mbiti, *New Testament Eschatology in an African Background*.

32. For a nuanced critique with rich documentation by a South African theologian, see Conradie, *Hope for the Earth*, chap. 15 (particularly pp. 226-34).

33. For useful reflections, see also Weder, "Hope and Creation," chap. 13 (pp. 184-202); Soskice, "The Ends of Man and the Future of God."

34. Moltmann, *Experiences in Theology*, p. 30.

35. Chap. 2 of Moltmann, *Theology of Hope*, is devoted to a detailed discussion of this theme under the heading "History and Promise."

down and left behind the nomadic life, it did not leave behind the nomadic religion of promise![36]

Divine promises in the Bible often "stand in contradiction to the reality which can at present be experienced. They do not result from experiences, but are the condition for the possibility of new experiences."[37] The promise of Christ's resurrection,[38] the "anchor" of concrete hope, illustrates this best. In the biblical drama, the greatest threat is death — and the greatest promise is deliverance from under the power of death. Clearly, rising from the dead is not an event in keeping with our experiences but rather something that contradicts human experiences.[39] It calls for a faith that "takes up this contradiction [between death and life] and thus becomes itself a contradiction to the world of death."[40]

The Resurrection of the Son as the Basis of Hope

The Basis of Christian Hope

According to Saint Paul, Christ's resurrection forms the basis for the Christian hope: "If Christ has not been raised, then our preaching is in vain and your faith is in vain. We are even found to be misrepresenting God, because we testified of God that he raised Christ, whom he did not raise if it is true that the dead are not raised" (1 Cor. 15:14-15). Indeed, the apostle goes so far as to claim that "if Christ has not been raised, your faith is futile and you are still in your sins. Then those also who have fallen asleep in Christ have perished. If for this life only we have hoped in Christ, we are of all men most to be pitied" (vv. 17-19).

Although religions know myths of gods dying and rising, the biblical idea of resurrection is without parallels in religions.[41] The Christian teaching of a definite, historical act of raising the dead Messiah by God and its implication for our own future in the new creation are unknown in

36. See Moltmann, *Theology of Hope*, pp. 96-97; Vanhoozer, *Drama of Doctrine*, p. 135.

37. Moltmann, *Theology of Hope*, p. 18.

38. For a detailed discussion of the theme of "the resurrection and the future of Jesus Christ," see chap. 3 of Moltmann, *Theology of Hope*.

39. Moltmann, *Theology of Hope*, p. 18.

40. Moltmann, *Theology of Hope*, p. 21.

41. For a meticulous study of ideas about life beyond death in ancient paganism, see N. T. Wright, *The Resurrection of the Son of God*, chap. 2.

other traditions.[42] Although deeply embedded in Jewish apocalypticism and Second Temple expectations,[43] the radical revision of Jewish eschatological hope is Christians' focus on one individual before the end of this age, an idea unknown to Judaism, even with regard to the Messiah.[44]

Not surprisingly, since the advent of modernity, theologians have mounted massive attacks against the possibility of Christ's resurrection. And, although a significant number of Americans still affirm an afterlife in some form, for the majority, belief in resurrection is no longer possible.[45] In Germany the number of those who believe is much smaller still.[46] In this cultural context, the task of constructive theology is to make a viable case for the continuing relevance, indeed necessity, of the affirmation of the doctrine of resurrection. In fact, so much is theologically at stake with this doctrine that we have to speak of the possibility of falsification of Christian hope altogether. As the theologian Ted Peters puts it succinctly:

> Such a falsification would come in two forms, one looking backward and one looking forward. Looking backward, we could imagine evidence put forward to claim that Jesus hung on the cross, died, and remained dead. . . . Looking forward, we could imagine a future without a consummation, without the new creation promised by the Easter resurrection. Inextricably built into the Easter resurrection is the proleptic anticipation of the future resurrection of humanity at the arrival of the eschatological kingdom of God. The resurrection of Christ, according to Christian faith . . . was the advent of the world's transformation. Without the consummation of this transformatory promise, the Christian faith is in vain.[47]

The first task of this section is to consider whether the Christian hope necessarily entails a physical resurrection of Christ or whether that can be circumvented without giving up its theological cash value. In addition to biblical

42. See T. Torrance, *Space, Time, and Resurrection*, pp. 26, 30–31.

43. For the significance of Jewish apocalypticism as the background, see Pannenberg, *ST* 2:347–50; for a detailed treatment with massive documentation, see N. T. Wright, *The Resurrection of the Son of God*, chap. 3 on the Old Testament, and chap. 4 on postbiblical Judaism.

44. N. T. Wright, *The Resurrection of the Son of God*, p. 28; Pannenberg, *ST* 2:350–51. See also Childs, *Biblical Theology of the Old and New Testaments*.

45. Mohler, "Do Christians Still Believe in the Resurrection of the Body?"; so also Hargrove and Stempel, "Most Americans Doubt the Resurrection of the Body."

46. Schuele, "Transformed into the Image of Christ," p. 219.

47. Peters, "Introduction," p. viii.

scholars' skepticism toward maintaining a "historical," "physical" resurrection, the naturalist paradigm of contemporary "hard" sciences has to be addressed in order for the resurrection's theological validity to hold. Thereafter, an account of the cosmic significance of Christ's resurrection will be attempted, to be followed by the focus on the hope of resurrected bodily life in new creation for men and women. A growing number of theologians have made a robust link not only between Christ's resurrection and our own hope for an eternal communion with the triune God but also between Christ's resurrection and the transformation of all creation. It is what the Catholic Karl Rahner named "the beginning of the transfiguration of the world" in which the "destiny of the world is already begun"—indeed, so much so that "[a]t all events it would in reality be different if Jesus were not risen."[48] That thesis will be developed and defended in this chapter.

The Question of the Historicity of the Resurrection and Its Theological Implications

A defining feature of the New Testament narratives of Christ's resurrection[49] is a "strange tension between palpability and appearance," that is, on the one hand, they clearly assume something totally different from mere resuscitation by assuming the real physicality of the resurrected one (as when he ate fish or showed the wounds on his side), and on the other hand, they describe the disciples' reactions of not being able to recognize him or considering him to be a "ghost."[50] Theologically, it can be said that resurrection is both an event that happens in history and an event that goes beyond (but not against) history;[51] it is a *new kind of historical happening.*[52] The place of the historicity of the resurrection has become a central issue of debate since the Enlightenment. In this regard, it is convenient to divide the scholarly interpretations of

48. Rahner, "Resurrection," p. 1442, cited in R. Russell, *Cosmology*, p. 289 (from a different edition).

49. The following essays provide a detailed scrutiny of the main Lukan and Pauline materials on resurrection: Crüsemann, "Scripture and Resurrection," pp. 89–102; Lampe, "Paul's Concept of Spiritual Body," pp. 103–14; Eckstein, "Bodily Resurrection in Luke," pp. 115–24.

50. These and others are described in Luke 24 and John 21; for details, see Welker, "Theological Realism," pp. 35–37 and passim. For thoughtful reflections, see also Coakley, "The Resurrection and the 'Spiritual Senses,'" pp. 130–52.

51. See further D. Fuller, *Easter Faith and History*, pp. 145–47 particularly.

52. T. Torrance, *Space, Time, and Resurrection*, p. 88, emphasis in original.

Jesus' resurrection into "subjective" and "objective."[53] The latter means that whatever else, resurrection is more than just an idea in the minds of the early followers of Jesus, or the influence of the event on the disciples, or a temporary resuscitation as with Lazarus (these are all variations of subjective interpretation). It means to say that "something truly happened," that is, a "bodily" resurrection.[54] Since the question of the conditions and possibility of Jesus' resurrection is discussed in detail in *Christ and Reconciliation* (chap. 6), the investigation here is short (and includes minimal documentation).

The objective interpretation understandably has come under devastating criticism in post-Enlightenment biblical scholarship, so much so that N. T. Wright calls its alternative, named here the subjective, the "dominant paradigm."[55] The objections to the historicity of the resurrection usually rest on one of the three main lines of argumentation: first, that there is no access to such historical knowledge; second, that there is no analogy for such a resurrection; and third, that there is no evidence.[56] The first objection represents a typical positivistic assumption according to which things such as raising from the dead do not happen and therefore we cannot know anything about them.[57] Rightly N. T. Wright rebuts: "Ruling out as historical that to which we do not have direct access is actually a way of not doing history at all."[58] The problem with the second objection is that of course there is no analogy for a onetime event — no more than for, say, the big bang. The demand for analogy, similarly to the first objection, assumes a positivist reductionism. The third rebuttal to the objective interpretation, according to which there is no real evidence for resurrection narratives, rests on various kinds of hypothetical reconstructions of the Gospel narratives and their history. In response to these hypothetical reconstructions, it can be argued that there is a lot of historical evidence about the coherence and unity of the views of resurrection among various early Christian communities. At the core of that shared conviction was the belief in the bodily resurrection of the crucified Christ.[59]

---

53. I follow here R. Russell, *Time in Eternity*, pp. 40-42.

54. See N. T. Wright, *The Resurrection of the Son of God*, p. 8; S. Davis, *Risen Indeed*, p. 40.

55. For reasons other than exegetical, philosophers of religion such as Hick (chap. 9 in *Death and Eternal Life*) materially affirm the subjective interpretation.

56. I am following here the broad outline presented in N. T. Wright, *The Resurrection of the Son of God*, pp. 16-20. This section gleans significantly from my *Christ and Reconciliation*, pp. 125-33.

57. See Pannenberg, *ST* 2:360-63; Moltmann, *Way of Jesus Christ*, p. 244.

58. N. T. Wright, *The Resurrection of the Son of God*, p. 16.

59. Summarized succinctly by N. T. Wright, *The Resurrection of the Son of God*, pp. 209,

What about the arguments in support of the objective interpretation? Historically taken, two main supporting arguments for the historicity of the resurrection are the appearances of Jesus to a great number of eyewitnesses and the empty-tomb tradition.[60] Rather than hallucinations, there are good reasons for maintaining that the encounters with the risen One were actual. Similarly, the empty-tomb tradition was not contested by the contemporaries even though its validity as a historical claim was widely doubted by many twentieth-century biblical scholars. Had the claim to the empty tomb been a fabrication, how could the preaching about the resurrected Christ have taken place in Jerusalem, the place of execution and burial?[61] In that sense, not only the resurrection but also the empty tomb is a public event.[62]

In sum: the belief in the physical resurrection of Jesus from the dead is not necessarily a matter of faith totally apart from historical investigation and rational reasoning, and certainly not a modern fundamentalist invention, as a leading Jesus scholar recently has pejoratively labeled it![63] That said, the limits of historical inquiry alone should be acknowledged. No amount of historical evidence or logical reasoning is meant to establish indubitable certainty beyond questioning.[64]

The objective interpretation can be further divided into two subcategories — "physical" and "personal." While both of them affirm the discontinuity of the pre- and post-Easter resurrected Christ, they diverge significantly with regard to the continuity. Whereas the physical version assumes "elements of continuity . . . in *all* aspects of the person of Jesus, including what can be called the physical/material, the mental/psychological, and the spiritual," the personal denies the continuity of the physical material. The implication, then, is that the former must assume the empty tomb, that is, it is incompatible with the claim that Jesus' dead body remained in the tomb.[65] The two leading science-religion experts from the United Kingdom illustrate the difference:

476-77, based on a most detailed scrutiny of various New Testament texts and testimonies. On the centrality of the resurrection in early Christianity, see C. F. Evans, *Resurrection and the New Testament*, p. 40; I am indebted to Wright, p. 210.

60. For a detailed investigation, see Pannenberg, *Jesus — God and Man*, pp. 88-106. Materially similar arguments can be found in R. E. Brown, *The Virginal Conception and Bodily Resurrection of Jesus*, pp. 92-124.

61. Pannenberg, *ST* 2:356-59.

62. Contra Moltmann, *Way of Jesus Christ*, p. 215.

63. Strangely enough, that's what Crossan (*Birth of Christianity*, p. xviii) contends.

64. See T. Torrance, *Space, Time, and Resurrection*, p. 22.

65. R. Russell, *Time in Eternity*, pp. 42-44, emphasis in original.

while for Arthur Peacocke it might be possible to affirm Jesus' (current) existence on the right hand of God even if his body decayed like the rest of ours,[66] for John Polkinghorne, only the physical (objective) interpretation allows us the anticipation of the newness of new creation.[67] Only that would do justice to his insistence on the "new creation . . . as *ex vetere* [out of old] . . . [as] divine redemption of the old," which entails "transformation" rather than "the abolition of the old."[68] Among the leading science-theology experts, scholars such as Wolfhart Pannenberg, Ted Peters, Robert Russell, and David A. Wilkinson, among others, materially agree with that judgment.[69] It is assumed in this project.

The Possibility of Resurrection in the Science-Religion Matrix

The theologian Michael Welker reminds us of the obvious, that "[t]here is perhaps no topic that seems less suited for the dialogue between theology and the so-called exact sciences than the topic of the resurrection."[70] The reason is of course the current secular naturalist worldview that reigns among the scientific communities in the Global North, with its aversion to all notions of life after death and its "rejection of supernaturalism combined with the acceptance of a view of the mind — either materialism or epiphenomenalism — that makes the mind's existence apart from the brain seem impossible."[71] Until recently, however, theology has paid surprisingly little attention to challenges coming from physical sciences with regard to the doctrine of resurrection, even though much is at stake.[72]

Along with naturalism, the main challenge from the sciences concerning the resurrection is that it seems to violate the regularity of natural occurrences, the role of laws of nature. According to what we know of natural processes, dead people do not rise from the dead! Theologians should be reminded that

66. Peacocke, *Theology for a Scientific Age*, pp. 279-88.

67. Among others, see Polkinghorne, *The Way the World Is*, chap. 8; Polkinghorne, *The Faith of a Physicist*, chaps. 6 and 9. For details, see R. Russell, *Time in Eternity*, pp. 43-44.

68. Polkinghorne, *The Way the World Is*, p. 91, cited in R. Russell, *Time in Eternity*, p. 44.

69. See R. Russell, *Time in Eternity*, pp. 45-52.

70. Welker, "Resurrection and Eternal Life," p. 279; so also R. Russell, "Eschatology and Physical Cosmology," p. 273.

71. Griffin, "Process Eschatology," p. 300.

72. R. Russell, "Bodily Resurrection, Eschatology and Scientific Cosmology," pp. 3, 10-15; R. Russell, *Cosmology*, p. 298; Wilkinson, *Christian Eschatology*, p. 89.

science must operate with principles drawn from the workings of natural processes as we know them in order for any scientific explanations to be possible.[73] Hence, for theologians to find room, so to speak, for God to act in a world regulated by laws put in place by the same God, it has to be done in a way that does not disregard these regularities.[74]

A proper way to speak of resurrection in this context is as pointing to "a transformation of the present nature *beyond* what emergence refers to,"[75] that is, beyond what natural processes and their evolution in themselves may deliver. Rather than going against nature, the resurrection of Christ — who, himself, in biblical testimonies is the very agent of creation (Col. 1:15-17) — transcends and lifts up the natural.[76] It points to the eschatological consummation when, according to the biblical promises, creation "will be set free from its bondage to decay" (Rom. 8:21), so much so that, as a result, even death will be defeated (1 Cor. 15:55).[77] This entails that, rather than as "ironclad," laws of nature can be interpreted in a way that allows for (and even requires) the openness of the created reality and the fact that "the meaning of contingent processes which begin with a first instance in nature will only be fully clear at the end of history (that is, eschatologically)." This is in keeping with the mainstream indeterminacy interpretation of quantum theory, which allows for a "non-interventionist objective divine action," that is, divine acts that do not "interrupt" or "interfere with" naturally regular processes.[78]

Keith Ward rightly contends that the resurrection and other miracles are "law-transcending events, extraordinary events manifesting divine causality that modifies the normal regularities of nature with the purpose of manifesting

73. Note "Guideline 2" in R. Russell, *Cosmology*, p. 307.

74. This question is part of a larger theme, often referred to as divine action, that is, how to speak of the conditions and possibility of God working after creation in the world, which seems to function according to deterministic (at least relatively speaking) regularities. A detailed discussion can be found in my *Creation and Humanity*, chap. 7. For the complicated question of how to best understand laws of nature both in sciences and theology, see pp. 181–83 particularly.

75. R. Russell, *Cosmology*, p. 37, emphasis in original.

76. R. Russell has named this "first instantiation contingency" or the "first instance of a new law of nature" (for which he uses the acronym FINLON): "In a 'weak' sense, FINLON refers to first instances of phenomena within creation, such as the emergence of life on earth. . . . [I]n the context of the resurrection of Jesus [however], FINLON refers to the first instance of a radically new phenomena." R. Russell, *Cosmology*, pp. 309–10.

77. See further K. Ward, "Divine Action in an Emergent Cosmos," p. 297; Polkinghorne, *Quarks, Chaos, and Christianity*, chap. 6.

78. This is discussed in detail and defended in chap. 7 of my *Creation and Humanity*.

the basis and goal of the physical world in a wider spiritual realm."[79] Indeed, Christ's resurrection shows us "the goal of the whole physical process to be the transformation of the physical into an incorruptible vehicle of divine life."[80]

The Perfecting Work of the Spirit

While a christological event, the resurrection is of course also a trinitarian and pneumatological event, as Christ was raised to new life by the Father through the Holy Spirit (Rom. 1:4).[81] As a result, the indwelling Spirit in believers constantly reminds them of the certainty of their own resurrection by the same Spirit who raised Christ (Rom. 8:11).[82] This Spirit at work in the raising of the Son is also the life-giving "cosmic" Spirit. That observation relates to a key argument in the current project, namely, that Christian hope of the eschatological consummation, as much as it means to humanity, also includes the whole of God's creation, "the integration of the real history of human beings with the nature of the earth."[83] This holistic and "earthly" eschatological vision is masterfully expressed by the American Anabaptist theologian Thomas A. Finger: "Since the new creation arrives through God's Spirit, and since it reshapes the physical world, every theological locus is informed by the Spirit's transformation of matter-energy."[84] Christ's resurrection through the life-giving Spirit is already a foretaste of the "transformation of matter-energy" in new creation, "a transformation of the present nature *beyond* what emergence refers to."[85] The pneumatologically loaded eschatological openness of creation points to a final consummation in which matter and physicality — no more than time — are not so much "deleted" as they are transformed, made transcendent, so to speak.[86]

It is in this cosmological and nature-affirming context that the personal hope for the bodily resurrection finds its proper locus and significance. To the

79. K. Ward, "Divine Action in an Emergent Cosmos," p. 297.

80. K. Ward, "Divine Action in an Emergent Cosmos," p. 297. On the importance of the resurrection of Christ in this regard, see also Polkinghorne, *Quarks, Chaos, and Christianity*, chap. 6.

81. See Thomas, "Resurrection to New Life."

82. Pannenberg, *ST* 3:622.

83. Moltmann, *God in Creation*, p. xi.

84. T. Finger, *A Contemporary Anabaptist Theology*, p. 563.

85. R. Russell, *Cosmology*, p. 37, emphasis in original.

86. R. Russell, *Cosmology*, pp. 37–38.

rhetorical question of whether "the dead live on only in the memory of the living or, in some unimaginable way, . . . they themselves also live anew by the power of the vivifying Spirit of God,"[87] we can confidently respond "yes."[88] The hope for the future does not only relate to "spiritual" existence, although it is also that; it is a total redemption of humanity, having been created from the dust of the earth. In the words of Moltmann, "The powers of the Spirit are the powers of the new creation. They therefore possess men and women, soul and body. They are the powers of the resurrection of the dead which proceed from the risen Christ and are testified to the world through the church, which is charismatically wakened to external life."[89] Ultimately, the "work of the Spirit of God in his church and in believers serves the consummating of his work in the world of creation."[90]

Now we are ready to inquire into the ways the trinitarian theology of hope may facilitate and fund the Christian vision of the new creation. The next and the following chapter will delve into the many details of that complex issue.

87. E. Johnson, *Friends of God*, p. 181.

88. E. Johnson, *Friends of God*, p. 214; I am indebted to McCall, *The Greenie's Guide to the End of the World*, p. 224.

89. Moltmann, *God in Creation*, p. 96.

90. Pannenberg, *ST* 3:1-2, 11-12.

5. The Transition from Time to Eternity and New Creation

Introduction: The Power of Anticipation

The turn to "theology of hope," to the primacy of the future, has helped current theology grasp the significance of the future.[1] This is neither to say that therefore it is necessarily escapist, as is often uncritically claimed, nor that it dismisses history and the importance of this life. Rather, it is to say that, being future-oriented, it is anticipatory in nature, open to "new things" (Isa. 42:9; 48:6). It is "capacity to imagine otherwise, to transcend the boundaries of the present in a quest for something more, something better, than the present affords."[2] This future-directedness differs significantly from the natural sciences' "continuity" paradigm that merely presupposes the "natural" annihilation (due to entropy) of all that exists, and it necessarily entails a dynamic between continuity and discontinuity.

Understandably — but regretfully — many contemporary forms of eschatology have turned their back on the future orientation and occupy themselves merely with a this-earthly "hope." Among them, a more thoughtful turn to the historical present is K. Tanner's suggestion of an "eschatology without a future." Therein "eternal life promotes a more spatialized than temporalized eschatology" in which "eternal life is ours now as in the future . . . [and] is

1. In addition to Pannenberg and Moltmann, the Catholic Rahner has made this a critical theme in his eschatology: "Hermeneutics of Eschatological Assertions," p. 343.

2. Bauckham and Hart, *Hope against Hope*, p. 72. For an excellent reflection on "the nature of the fantastic," that is, the role of "fantasy" (as in a literary genre) in Christian eschatological imagination, see pp. 89–108.

therefore not directly associated with the world's future."[3] With all its brilliance and freshness, Tanner's proposal suffers from serious problems, the most important of which is this: along with other Abrahamic faiths — differently from Asiatic traditions — the Christian vision is historical and thus futurist, as it is based on divine promises to be fulfilled. It is impossible to even begin to imagine the redeeming of the promise of the "new creation" if entropy is not reversed and all that eschatology has to offer is only a temporary improvement of a life otherwise necessarily on the way to nothingness. This is not to make "eternal" life merely a matter of temporality, nor to relegate hope merely to the distant future. But it is to do justice to the robust theological account of eternity, which means the "swallowing up" and bringing to fulfillment of time in divine eternity.

Even though theologians' vision of the future is far more open than that of the natural scientists, this should not legitimize a dismissal of scientists' calculations and predictions. Polkinghorne makes the obvious remark that should we assume that "new creation is to be related to the present creation in a way that involves both continuity and discontinuity . . . then science may have something to say about the conditions of consonance and credibility that the continuity aspect of the relationship might be expected to fulfill."[4] That said, theologians should also expose science's main challenge with regard to the future, namely, that what happens in the future cannot be necessarily extrapolated from current processes. "New" creation is just that — something *new* that cannot be calculated on the basis of the processes we know so far.[5]

Because it is future-oriented, Christian eschatology is anticipatory in nature. Anticipation brings to the fore the important dynamic between "already" and "not yet."[6] Rather than juxtaposing the future appearance of eschatological consummation ("futurist eschatology") and the already-happened eschaton ("realized eschatology"), anticipation points to "inaugurated eschatology," that is, while already having arrived, God's kingdom has not yet appeared in fullness. Phenomenological pioneer E. Husserl's emphasis on the "internal consciousness of time" — that is, every perception of "now" — holds together these two aspects in a wonderful manner.[7]

3. Tanner, "Eschatology without a Future," p. 230.
4. Polkinghorne, "Introduction to Part 1," p. 17.
5. See Polkinghorne, "Eschatology," pp. 29-30.
6. For a profound phenomenologically oriented discussion, see Manoussakis, introduction to *Phenomenology and Eschatology*, p. 5.
7. Husserl developed this idea in a series of lectures published as *On the Phenomenology of the Consciousness of Internal Time*. For an important discussion of "anticipation," a key theo-

The establishment of the future orientation of Christian eschatology yields several important tasks for theology. Under the comprehensive umbrella term "new creation" (which could also be named the kingdom of God or simply eschatological consummation), the following topics will be clarified here in order to make sensible the Christian talk about transitioning from "here" to "beyond." First, the notions of time and space, essential coordinates of our current existence, need to be theologically investigated in terms of relationship to the transition to new creation. Only then, second, may we hope to be equipped to clarify in more detail the template of "continuity *versus* (or in) discontinuity." Finally, as a precondition for the "change" required for "this perishable nature . . . [to] put on the imperishable, and this mortal nature . . . [to] put on immortality" (1 Cor. 15:53), judgment and reconciliation have to take place.

Time-Space and Eternity

Time and Eternity: Preliminary Clarifications

A key theological issue of negotiation for properly conceiving the transition from creation to new creation has to do with time and space.[8] Having investigated carefully the topic in the doctrine of creation and having offered a constructive proposal,[9] we summarize here its main results and insights (without repeating documentation except for direct references) with a focus on issues pertinent to eschatology. The awkward expressions "time-space" and "space-time" remind us of the most radical change in the scientific understanding of time in the post-Einsteinian worldview: neither time nor space has the kind of "absolute" existence it had in classical physics (furthermore, according to the field equations of Einstein, matter and energy are integrally intertwined with space-time).

Whereas early Christian theology rightly defeated the assumption of the eternity of the world, it also mistakenly placed God "outside" time and juxtaposed time with (God's) "timeless" eternity. That led to considering God's eternity as something "timeless," as opposed to the correct view, according to

---

logical concept from the phenomenological point of view, see Lacoste, "The Phenomenality of Anticipation."

8. Rightly noted and elaborated upon by Pannenberg, *ST* 3:595-96.

9. *Creation and Humanity*, pp. 129-40.

which eternity is rather the "source of time."[10] Similarly, it thought of eternity as an unending time that would only yield endless duration, but not the kind of "newness" to be expected of God's bringing about the new creation.

For the sake of science-eschatology dialogue, the most pertinent challenge has to do with the radical difference between two notions of time, conveniently named "flowing time" and "block time" (also known as A-time and B-time, respectively). Whereas the former is the commonsense notion based on the flow of time from past to present to future, the latter argues that time and space have an equal ontological status and thus it is unnecessary to distinguish between past, present, and future. In the "block time" template, the "now" is but a human mind's construction, not a quality of nature.

In Defense of a "Flowing Time" Conception

What is at stake for theology in the debate between flowing and block time? Why bother? Indeed, much is at stake for theology in general and eschatology in particular[11]—so much so that this question may be(come) one of the defining and most critical issues in theology-science conversation for some time. Although theology does not have to insist on a too "literal" understanding of flowing time — because, as T. Peters puts it, "[t]here is a sense in which we can say the past and the future are not actual . . . [rather the] present is actual . . . [and] provides the perspective for apprehending past and future realities" — what is at stake is the Christian vision of eternity as the "boundless temporality," the source of current time and radical transformation of the cosmos. As will also be argued below, only the (rightly conceived) "temporality" (rather than tenselessness) of the new creation may secure the judgment, reconciliation, and healing of our lives and memories in new creation.[12]

Other problems result from the adoption of the block-time view. One of the most serious involves the question of authentic human freedom if the future does not mean potentialities. Furthermore, divine freedom in light of the insistence on the openness of the future to God also seems to be at stake. Finally, in terms of interfaith engagement, it seems that for Abrahamic faith traditions, a block-time model would be a major theological obstacle, whereas

10. As correctly intuited by Barth (*CD* III/1, pp. 67-71 [70]), despite some other problems in his conception of time (see my *Humanity and Creation*, p. 130). For details, see R. Russell, *Time in Eternity*, pp. 94-97.

11. See Drees, "A Case against Temporal Realism?" pp. 335-37.

12. Peters, "The Trinity in and beyond Time," p. 266.

the Asiatic faiths' cyclical worldview of eternal emergence and return points in a different direction from the Abrahamic faiths' emphasis on history and historical time.

Constructive theology's first task is to identify and assess critically the objections to block time in light of scientific and philosophical knowledge. As common as the block-time view is among natural scientists, it is far from a settled issue. What Sir Arthur S. Eddington named in 1927 "Time's Arrow,"[13] the universal intuition among men and women everywhere,[14] is of course supported by a number of indisputable scientific facts, including the second law of thermodynamics, entropy, which seems to require unidirectionality and irreversibility of time;[15] the expansion in size and increase in complexity of the universe; and the apparent cause-effect dynamic (as far as we know, the cause precedes the effects). Similarly, the majority (Copenhagen) interpretation of quantum physics with its indeterminacy principle makes much less sense (if any) if the future is not truly future and potentially open for processes to evolve in an indeterminate way.[16] To the same effect speak chaos theory and its effects on the probabilistic nature of the world. As a result, what can be said safely is that among the physicists there is no canonical opinion as to how to best reconcile the seemingly necessary idea of the arrow of time and the similarly seemingly uncontested observation of the reversibility of time at the atomic level.

In my understanding, the most promising constructive proposal in defense of the flowing-time conception comes from R. Russell's suggestion of "a modified A-theory of time with tense as relational."[17] Its main idea is that "tenses are better treated as *relations between events* than as *properties of events* and that these relationships carry an ontology in addition to the ontology of the events themselves."[18] In analogy to what is the standard separation of two basic conceptions of space (to be discussed below), Russell distinguishes the relational concept of time that "does not exist without events and their relations" and "receptacle theories of time," the latter of which means that time exists independently of events. Russell's proposal is supported theologically by the relationality of the triune God, including God's relationship to the world as

13. For a basic description, see Eddington, *The Nature of the Physical World*, p. 68.

14. W. Friedman, *About Time*, p. 92; see also Craig, *Time and Eternity*, p. 272; Heller, "Time of the Universe," 53–55 and passim.

15. See Peters, *God as Trinity*, pp. 159–63.

16. Although there are some who claim that even block time may be able to account for indeterminacy, I have a hard time seeing how.

17. R. Russell, *Time in Eternity*, pp. 129–45 particularly.

18. R. Russell, *Time in Eternity*, p. 134, emphasis in original.

God's creation. For Russell, "temporal relations between events carry some of the ontological factors normally attributed to the individual events themselves, factors typically seen as properties of the event." The crux of his proposal, then, is that "[i]nstead of viewing tenses such as past, present, or future as properties of events . . . [let us think of] a tense as relational A-theory of time, where the tenses 'past' and 'future' are relations between events and an event taken as present."[19] For the purposes of this discussion, there is no need to delve into further details of this complex conception of time; let it suffice to present it as a viable recent suggestion that has the potential of meeting the scientific and philosophical objections to flowing time.

Eternity as the "Boundless Temporality of the Trinitarian God"

Although not without merit, tradition's desire to place God "outside," with its appeal to the timelessness of God (which ironically has some resemblance with block-time theory in some real sense), has to be corrected and balanced with an equally important insistence on God's omnipresence in and engagement with creation and its time. Rather than "outside" time, on the basis of the doctrine of creation, "God should transcend space-time." Although so conceived, "God cannot be limited in space-time," this understanding also means that it is possible for God to be "in time," so to speak. Indeed, both divine omnipresence (that God is present everywhere at all times) and incarnation imply some kind of temporality in divine life. Furthermore, the openness of the future seems to require some relation to temporality.[20] Robert Russell's brilliant summary can hardly be improved: "I understand eternity to be the boundless temporality of the Trinitarian God, a lavishly rich 'supra-temporality' that is both the source and fulfillment of the temporality of creation: the temporality we experience in nature, in our lives, and in history. This is an eternity that flows out of the endless perichoretic dance of the divine persons ceaselessly taking place within the unity of Trinitarian community."[21]

In other words, eternity is neither timelessness nor lack of movement. Trinitarian doctrine alone shows the contrary: in the immanent Trinity, an eternal reciprocal loving relationship, there is movement, dynamic, receiving,

---

19. R. Russell, *Time in Eternity*, pp. 134, 135.

20. K. Ward, "God as a Principle of Cosmological Explanation," p. 250.

21. R. Russell, *Time in Eternity*, p. 5. In this section, I also glean from Pannenberg, "Eternity, Time and Space," pp. 163–74; Jackelén, *Time and Eternity*, chap. 4.

giving — let alone in the economic Trinity in its outward movement.[22] Hence, rightly conceived, we may speak of "temporalized eternity."[23] Or, as Pannenberg came to say in his later years, eternity is "omnitemporal,"[24] as the infinite source of time both transcends and incorporates it into itself. Therefore, "we find God on both sides of the fence, both as eternal and as temporal."[25] This kind of "God's own time"[26] will not divorce God from real activity and presence in the world (as timelessness would do), nor lead to the problem in which "God will be conceived by a process of abstraction from the world," as would be the case if God were placed "within" our temporality.[27]

In the dynamic trinitarian context of speaking of God's own time — and only in that context — Boethius's oft-cited definition that "[e]ternity is the simultaneous and complete possession of infinite life"[28] makes the correct point (which is neither about "block time" nor removing God from time). In God's eternity, time is transcended but not "canceled" in the sense that it never had any meaning (that would be an idea closer to the intuitions of the great Asiatic faiths). But doesn't this lead to a self-contradictory statement that in the divine life there are both timely sequence (which implies finitude) and infinite transcendence of time by eternity? Many contemporary philosophers think so.[29] Again, it seems to me that only the turn to the Trinity may help us avoid self-contradiction: the incarnation of the second person of the Trinity tells us the eternal God has entered time.[30] Why could we not apply the *hypostatic-union* template also to the eternity-time relationship?

This kind of conception of time gives us the needed resources to imagine the final eschatological redemption. Participation in God's eternity "can overcome the disintegration of human life"[31] with the "entry of eternity into time."[32] Eternity is not only the source of time, it is also the

---

22. See Pannenberg, *ST* 1:405.

23. See Peters, *God as Trinity*, pp. 146–47, 173–75.

24. Pannenberg, "Eternity, Time and Space."

25. Peters, "The Trinity in and beyond Time," pp. 263–64 (264).

26. Cf. Gunton (*The Triune Creator*, p. 92), who (rightly) rejects both God's temporality and God's timelessness but (wrongly) asks us to stop there, in an apophatic position.

27. Gunton, *The Triune Creator*, pp. 91–92 (92).

28. Boethius, *Consolation of Philosophy* 5; similarly, Augustine, *Confessions* 11.11; for comments, see Pannenberg, *ST* 1:403.

29. For debates, all the details of which are not totally transparent to me, see Stump and Kretzmann, "Eternity," and the rejoinder from Helm, *Eternal God*, chap. 2 particularly.

30. So also Peters, "The Trinity in and beyond Time," p. 269.

31. Pannenberg, *ST* 3:601.

32. Pannenberg, *ST* 3:603.

goal, the destiny. Time thus has a teleological nature.[33] This means that the "eternity of the New Creation" is the "gift of true temporality of the Trinity to our world, both as it is to be and as it is being transformed into the new creation by God's radically new act beginning with the bodily resurrection of Jesus at Easter." It is the time of healing, sanctifying, and bringing to fulfillment of God's purposes for creation; it is also the time of judgment of all that does not hold up to the standard of eternity.[34] Judgment and reconciliation call for a more nuanced understanding of the nature of God's eternity, "an eternity that holds all the events of the creation in an overarching and differentiated unity, a unity that brings together our lived experiences of the flow of fragmentary present moments without subsuming their distinctions or separations into one timeless moment."[35] To be more precise, "the *distinction* between events in time will be sustained in eternity while the *separation* between events in time will be overcome in eternity." The *distinction* allows for "the unique character of every event as present."[36] The lack of *separation* means overcoming the limitations of the earthly time in which the "present" can be had only once, the "past" is ever lost, and the "future" is not yet with us. That is the linear time. Eternal temporality overcomes it and makes it possible for events to be "re-experienced, forgiven, and savored endlessly."[37] The term "eternal temporality" thus is the current theological conception of time, rather than "timeless" eternity or endless duration. The important idea of "distinction" between events in time will make it possible for divine judgment and reconciliation to happen properly,[38] as will be discussed below.

Space-Time and New Creation

Traditionally there have been two main ways of conceiving of space, namely, as "receptacle" (or "container"), that is, space as container of all objects, and as "relational," that is, rather than having its own objective existence, space is a positional quality of material objects (i.e., how they are related to each other).

---

33. Tillich, *ST* 3:320; see also Goosen, *Spacetime and Theology*, p. 33.

34. R. Russell, *Time in Eternity*, pp. 5–6 (5). For the eschatological importance of Jesus' resurrection, see also O'Collins, *Jesus Risen*, pp. 154–57.

35. R. Russell, *Time in Eternity*, p. 6.

36. R. Russell, *Time in Eternity*, p. 14, emphasis in original.

37. R. Russell, *Time in Eternity*, p. 14.

38. R. Russell, *Time in Eternity*, p. 97.

As is well known, similarly to absolute time, the concept of absolute space was shattered, if not totally abolished, by relativity. In current understanding, "time is closely interlocked conceptually with space, matter and energy."[39] The theologian T. F. Torrance makes the surprising claim that long before that, some (Eastern) church fathers rightly saw the significance of the relational idea of space as they were explaining the meaning of creation, Trinity, and incarnation. He says: "In the light of God's creation of the world out of nothing, His interaction with nature, and the Incarnation of His Creator Word, they [Greek church fathers] developed a thoroughly relational conception of space and time in which spatial, temporal and conceptual relations were inseparable."[40] If eternity entails God's omnipresence — that is, all things are "present" to God — it also means conversely that God is present to all things in their place (space).[41] Needless to say, God's presence in the world should not be understood in any way "physically," nor as something that makes created things' presence in the same place impossible. As will be argued below, God exists in God's own space, so to speak.[42]

When speaking of the world as God's space, at the same time it is of utmost importance to speak of "the absolute priority of God over all time and space, for the latter arise only in and with created existence and must be conceived as relations within the created order."[43] The theological conclusion from all of this is — in analogy to the talk about time — that we "*should accept neither the spacelessness nor the spatiality of the being of God.*"[44] The former would separate God from the world, whereas the latter would make God yet another object among other worldly objects. God must have his own space, so to speak. God can use the space of creation, but he has his own space different from that of creatures.

Having now clarified the meaning and ramifications of time-space, we are ready to tackle the issue of continuity versus discontinuity in the transition from time to God's eternity.

---

39. Peacocke, *Theology for a Scientific Age*, p. 130.

40. T. Torrance, *Space, Time, and Incarnation*, p. 58.

41. Pannenberg, *ST* 1:410; see R. Russell, *Time in Eternity*, pp. 101-2.

42. Pannenberg, *ST* 1:411; R. Russell, *Time in Eternity*, p. 102.

43. T. Torrance, *Space, Time, and Incarnation*, p. 11.

44. C. H. Park, "Transcendence and Spatiality of the Triune Creator," p. 78, emphasis in original.

The Transition from Time to Eternity:
The Dynamic of Continuity and Discontinuity

Annihilation or Transformation? Otherworldly
or This-Worldly Locus of New Creation?

Would the transition from time to eternity imply total destruction of the world? Or is there a way to think of the transformation in other terms? There is no doubt that biblical symbols, visions, and teachings assume a dynamic tension and interrelationship between continuity and discontinuity. They fund continuous anticipation. The very term "new creation" implies this twofold dynamic: that it is "new" reflects discontinuity, and that it is "creation" bespeaks continuity. A striking juxtaposition and mutual conditioning can also be found in sayings according to which "flesh and blood" may not enter God's eternity, and yet it is *physical* resurrection that stands at the forefront of that hope![45] Polkinghorne puts it well: "the new creation does not arise from a radically novel creative act *ex nihilo*, but as a redemptive act *ex vetere*, out of old."[46]

It has taken a long time for Christian theology to reach a dynamic balance in this understanding. On the basis of 2 Peter 3:10 and related passages (Rev. 20:11; 21:1; among others), in Lutheran orthodoxy the view of the annihilation of the world established itself: "After the final judgment, the absolute end of this world will come . . . [as] everything that belongs to this world will be burnt up by fire and reduced to nothing. Not a transformation of the world, therefore, but an absolute annihilation of its substance is to be expected."[47] But if this were the case, it would not be merely destruction of all but also "a reversal of the creation out of nothing (*creatio ex nihilo*) into a reduction to nothing (*reductio ad nihilum*)."[48] An opposite position is the *transformatio mundi*, which finds support in Romans 8:19-25. Reflecting the ancient Christian prayer (also used in Catholic liturgy), *vita mutatur, non tollitur* ("Life will be changed rather than destroyed"),[49] Calvinist theology highlighted God's faithfulness as Creator to creation: "After the judgment will come the end of

---

45. So also Polkinghorne and Welker, "Introduction," p. 2.

46. Polkinghorne, *God of Hope*, p. 116; Polkinghorne, *Science and Christian Belief*, p. 167.

47. Schmid, *Doctrinal Theology of the Evangelical Lutheran Church*, §66.4, pp. 655-56, cited in Moltmann, "Cosmos and Theosis," p. 256 (from a different edition). For a recent similar statement, see the Doctrine Commission of the Church of England, *The Mystery of Salvation*, p. 199; I am indebted to Moltmann, "Cosmos and Theosis," p. 256.

48. Moltmann, "Cosmos and Theosis," p. 256.

49. Moltmann, "Cosmos and Theosis," p. 257.

this world, since God will destroy its present state by fire, i.e., not destroy the world but out of the old make a new world, a new heaven and a new earth which will not pass away."[50] Moltmann rightly concludes: "The eschatological transformation of the universe embraces both the identity of creation and its newness, that is to say both continuity and discontinuity. All the information of this world remains in eternity, but is transformed." This corresponds to the vision in Revelation (21:1): "Then I saw a new heaven and a new earth."[51]

Annihilation and transformation should not be juxtaposed, however, but rather put in a dynamic mutual conditioning. There is much in the "old creation" to be annihilated, particularly decay and effects of sin and fall. Yet, differently from the old paradigm of *annihilatio mundi*, the final cleansing and sanctification are not unrelated to the "first creation"; in all of God's works, there is continuity, even in discontinuity. This template has implications for the location of the new creation, the eschatological kingdom of God.[52] M. Volf argues that "[t]he stress on the earthly locale of the kingdom of God in the New Testament corresponds not only to the earthly hopes of the Old Testament prophets (Isa. 11:6–10; 65:17–25), but even more significantly to the Christian doctrine of the body. Theologically it makes little sense to postulate a nonearthly eschatological existence while believing in the resurrection of the body. . . . The resurrected body demands a corresponding glorified but nevertheless material environment."[53]

These two templates have to be placed in mutual dialogue. A proper negotiation of the dynamic tension between *annihilatio mundi* and *transformatio mundi* has tremendous effects on a number of lifestyle and attitudinal issues. Whereas the implications for ecology will be touched on below, let us reflect here on work and human effort to improve the conditions of earthly life.[54] If *human* work (inclusively understood) is related to the divine purpose of creation that points to new creation, then work gains its ultimate meaning from God's future; work is not only a matter of the present world. Essential to that kind of vision "is the anticipatory experience of God's new creation and a hope of its future consummation."[55] Volf argues that "[t]he assurance of the

50. Heppe, *Reformed Dogmatics*, p. 706, cited in Moltmann, "Cosmos and Theosis," p. 257 (from a different edition). Note that the section in Heppe is under the heading "Glorification."

51. Moltmann, "Cosmos and Theosis," p. 257.

52. See Gundry, "The New Jerusalem," p. 258.

53. Volf, *Work in the Spirit*, p. 95.

54. A constructive theology of work is attempted in my *Creation and Humanity*, pp. 456–64.

55. Volf, *Work in the Spirit*, p. 79; see also pp. 76–87.

continuity between the present age and the age to come (notwithstanding the abolition of all sinfulness and transitoriness that characterize the present age) is a 'strong incentive to . . . cultural involvement.' For the continuity guarantees that no noble efforts will be wasted."[56] In contrast, the annihilationist alternative stalls the valuation of human effort and work and makes it meaningless. Only in the dynamic continuity-in-discontinuity template do "the results of the cumulative work of human beings have intrinsic value and gain ultimate significance, for they are related to the eschatological new creation. . . . [T]he noble products of human ingenuity . . . will be cleansed from impurity, perfected, and transfigured to become a part of God's new creation."[57] This dynamic Christian vision stands in stark contrast to a widely held Islamic eschatological doctrine with a "focus on a sudden, even instantaneous transformation in which the earth and heaven are rent, scattered, or melted away, and each human soul stands to hear the judgment on its eternal destiny."[58] That annihilationist vision does not leave much hope for this world.

Transformed "Space" and "Time" in New Creation

What does it mean to envision time-space in the new creation (in some sense) analogously to the current world? Opinions among theologians vary. Pannenberg believes that time will not apply to eternity because "temporality is of a piece with the structural sinfulness of our life," and therefore the fulfilment requires the coming to an end of time.[59] Although he adds a helpful note — that *"God and not nothing is the end of time"*[60] — Polkinghorne disagrees with Pannenberg (as do I): the main reason for rejecting the idea that "time is no more" is that "any implication that the value of human temporal experience is ultimately a misapprehension or a deficiency" is unacceptable in light of the doctrine of creation. Rather, God is patient "who acts through temporally unfolding process in the old creation."[61] Temporality in itself cannot be something to be deleted. Indeed, we have to say even more against the idea of time literally coming to an end: if the "end" of time is understood in terms of

56. Volf, *Work in the Spirit*, pp. 91–92, citation from Lausanne Committee, *Evangelism and Social Responsibility*, p. 42.

57. Volf, *Work in the Spirit*, pp. 88–102 (91).

58. Sells, "Armageddon in Christian, Sunni, and Shia Traditions," p. 469.

59. Pannenberg, *ST* 3:561, 587.

60. Pannenberg, *ST* 3:594, emphasis in original.

61. Polkinghorne, *God of Hope*, p. 120.

literal end of time (and also, of course, of space),[62] then it means by implication the destruction of creation![63] That conclusion follows from the premise that God's giving time for creation is constitutive for creation to exist (as Augustine already saw it rightly).[64]

The idea of the "end of time" could be corrected by a more robust interpretation of the eternity bringing about the "fufilment of time,"[65] a "new" time that lacks the potentiality for sin[66] and entropy and, unlike earthly time, does not denote creaturely limitations characteristic of current space-time. This can be called "finitude beyond transience,"[67] because "transience, which human beings experience as death, is an enemy at the end of life, whose menacing and violence-including presence casts a dark shadow on the entirety of life."[68] Hence, I argue (with Polkinghorne) for a new kind of time-space environment in the new creation. It is built on the assumption that if "[i]n this universe, space, time and matter are all mutually interlinked in the single package deal of general relativity . . . [then it] seems reasonable to suppose that this linkage is a general feature of the Creator's will. If so, the new creation will also have its 'space' and 'time' and 'matter.'"[69] This means then that "the transmuted 'matter' of the new creation . . . will be the setting for human re-embodiment in the resurrection life"[70] because, on the one hand, the current form of human life is not fit for God's eternity (1 Cor. 15:50), and on the other hand, it would make no sense to speak of the resurrection of the *body* (in any sense even close to what we understand by that phrase) without some kind of time/space/matter/ energy reality, however different it may be (because of lack of entropy and so forth). As Polkinghorne brilliantly puts it: "Presently we live in a world that contains sacraments: the world to come will be wholly sacramental. In the

62. As is argued by Moltmann in the final coming of God's eternity into time (*Coming of God*, pp. 279–95); for the end of space in God's presence, see pp. 296–308.

63. Rightly noted by C. Keller (*Apocalypse Now and Then*, p. 18), who speaks of the "end of nature" if time comes to an end.

64. Volf, "Enter into Joy!" pp. 272–73.

65. I am not necessarily following Volf ("Enter into Joy!" pp. 274–75), who makes a distinction between the "fulfilment of time" and "reconciliation of times."

66. Cf. Volf ("Enter into Joy!" p. 274), who argues that rather than the lack of the "potentiality for sin," eternity is characterized by the *possibility of innocence.*

67. This would accord with the proper translation of Rev. 10:6, "that there should be no more delay" (RSV) or "There will be no more interval of time." Aune, *Revelation 6–16*, p. 567; I am indebted to Volf, "Enter into Joy!" p. 273 n. 69.

68. Volf, "Enter into Joy!" p. 273.

69. Polkinghorne, *God of Hope*, p. 117; Polkinghorne, "Eschatology," pp. 39–40.

70. Polkinghorne, *God of Hope*, p. 117.

'matter' of that world we shall see God's eschatological purpose fulfilled in the whole created order."[71] Then it is possible to intuit that what is underdeveloped in this life will be transformed, sanctified, and judged, but not left behind as if it were a failure. The ultimate fulfillment in Christian vision is, then, not a timeless "end of time" but rather renewed embodied life in the new resurrected body — totally renewed but not totally unrelated to life on this earth and the cosmos. It is embodied life in a newly conceived "time" and "space" in divine eternity in communion with the triune God.[72]

A significant part of the discontinuity between new and old creation is the overcoming of not only death and decay but also sinfulness and egoism. Only that which is compatible with God's holiness may stand face-to-face with the divine holiness. This brings us to the theme of judgment and reconciliation.

Judgment, Purification, and Reconciliation

"Eternity as Judgment": The Precondition for Transformation

For the new creation to be "new," there needs to be "redemptive purging and healing of our lives." Sins and omissions need to be confessed and forgiven, good deeds and virtues to be celebrated and honored. Eternity, the "temporality of the New Creation," as R. Russell brilliantly names it, "is not only a time of endless rejoicing in all that is true and good and beautiful, it is also a time of leaving off and destroying of all that is wrong and false and ugly in this creation through the amazing grace of justice and mercy bequeathed to all of life in the Incarnation, life, ministry, death, and Resurrection of Christ."[73] Hence, judgment is necessary to account for sinners' wrongdoings; it is nothing capricious or external, but rather "executes that which is in the nature of the case" in light of God's eternal justice and truth,[74] and for the faithful, for the sake of the gateway for forgiveness and purification.

Judgment is a frequent biblical theme, so much so that we hardly need to draft a list of passages. When it comes to the agent of judgment, the New Testament does not speak with one voice. It is clear that God the Father is

71. Polkinghorne, "Eschatological Credibility," p. 54.

72. Volf, "Enter into Joy!" p. 277; Polkinghorne has persistently and widely argued for the same kind of view, as explained in more detail below.

73. R. Russell, *Time in Eternity*, p. 6.

74. Pannenberg, *ST* 3:611. Materially similar is the Orthodox Bishop Hilarion Alfeyev, "Eschatology," pp. 112-13.

judge (Matt. 6:4; Rom. 3:6; 1 Cor. 5:13; 1 Pet. 4:5; Rev. 20:11; and so forth). Jesus' role as judge, however, is more complicated: it is said, on one hand, that Jesus judges no one (John 3:17; 8:15-16; 12:47), but on the other hand, that he serves as judge (John 5:22; so also 1 Cor. 4:5; 2 Cor. 5:10). Jesus' role as judge comes to the fore through the New Testament link with the Jewish expectation of the Son of Man who comes in the clouds of heaven (Dan. 7:13; Mark 13:26; 14:62; Luke 12:8; Acts 10:42).[75] However, at his coming Christ brings grace (1 Pet. 1:13), and even now he acts as our Advocate (1 John 2:1). Furthermore, the Spirit's role is also connected with judgment at times (John 16:8). How do we collect these various testimonies into a systematic statement concerning the agent of judgment? We can follow Pannenberg here: "Christ assigns condemnation to none. He himself is pure salvation. Those who stand with him stand in the place of deliverance and salvation. Condemnation does not come from him. It is found only where people remain aloof from him and is due to their remaining on their own. The word of Christ as the offer of salvation will then make clear that the lost drew their line themselves and separated themselves from salvation."[76]

Regarding the standard of the judgment, the New Testament speaks of it in many complementary ways, including God's will (cf. Matt. 6:10), the word of Jesus (John 12:48), or more widely, the message of Jesus (see particularly Luke 12:8-9). Indeed, "[t]he message of Jesus is the norm by which God judges even in the case of those who never meet Jesus personally," not of course in relation to the response to the gospel (which is impossible in that case), but in keeping with the direction in which Jesus' message points.[77] Theologically this can be expressed in the following way: "Eternity is judgment . . . [because it] brings the truth about earthly life to light." That, however, does not mean the annihilation or destruction of creatures, because God, the Judge, is also Creator, who holds fast to his creatures.[78] Therefore, we have to say that for creatures, "confrontation with eternity means judgment only insofar as they have made themselves autonomous in relation to God, separated themselves from him, and thus become involved also in conflict with fellow creatures."[79]

Indeed, already in this life judgment has begun, and those who submit their lives under purifying and reconciling judgment may hope to be preserved

---

75. See Pannenberg, *ST* 3:608-9, 613.

76. Pannenberg, *ST* 3:613-14 (614), on the basis of Ratzinger, *Eschatology*, pp. 205-6.

77. Pannenberg, *ST* 3:614-15 (615).

78. Moltmann (*Coming of God*, p. 236) rightly notes that ultimately the question of judgment is "the question about God" and whether he wishes to hold on to his creatures.

79. Pannenberg, *ST* 3:610.

at the last judgment.[80] Even if the faithful may suffer loss as their lifework "burns up" like wood or stubble, their lives will be saved (1 Cor. 3:12–15).[81] Unlike for those who continue to live separately from God or are merely nominal Christians, for the followers of Christ who already share in the death, judgment, and raising to new life with their Savior, judgment will be "redemptive transformation."[82] Although judgment has to bring purification from sinfulness and filth, it is not the consuming fire (1 Cor. 3:12–15).[83]

This cleansing effect of judgment is the necessary precondition for the bodily resurrection to happen in the new creation as the "perishable puts on the imperishable, and the mortal puts on immortality" (1 Cor. 15:54).[84] Herein the work of the Spirit also comes to the fore. Paul's description of the resurrected life as *sōma pneumatikon*, "spiritual body" (v. 44) — and Christ as the "life-giving spirit" (v. 45) — implies that the transformed life in new creation is made possible only by the life-giving Spirit. As a result, in the "change" (vv. 51–52) from "earthly" to resurrected body, the Spirit executes judgment as transformation. In keeping with this is the Pauline teaching that the Spirit enables the believers to judge themselves ("all things," 2:15; 11:31).[85]

Hence, the Spirit here serves a dual role in the trinitarian work of the eschaton: both as the source of salvation and as the agent of judgment. Perhaps a fitting theological concept for that dual work is glorification, which "links the new life of the resurrection to the moment of judgment that carries with it the transfiguration of this earthly life by means of the relation to God the Father and to the praise of God. The glorifying of God in this comprehensive sense is the proper and final work of the Spirit of God."[86]

Who or what will be judged? According to the New Testament teaching, it is works (1 Cor. 3:12–15), whether as affirmation of their value in God's sight or as condemnation. In that light, we have to be critical of the idea of judgment per se as our "justification." I agree with M. Volf that rather than "objects of *justification*," works are "an object of negative or positive judgment." This refutes

---

80. For judgment as a means of purification, see Isa. 1:25; Mal. 3:2–3.

81. Pannenberg, *ST* 3:610–12.

82. Pannenberg, *ST* 3:616–17 (617), following Ratzinger, *Eschatology*, p. 206.

83. Pannenberg, *ST* 3:617.

84. Pannenberg, *ST* 3:619–20.

85. Pannenberg, *ST* 3:622–23; Pannenberg (p. 623) reminds us of the significance of the Gospels' linking of the Spirit baptism of the Son of Man with fire, that is, purifying judgment (Luke 3:16; Matt. 3:11).

86. Pannenberg, *ST* 3:623–24; for further reflections on the integral link between the Spirit's work and that of the Son at his return, see pp. 626–28.

the idea that "God will justify *lived lives*, not alive persons."[87] Although fair and thoroughgoing, judgment is not an act of divine wrath or vengeance. The judge is not only the Creator, as discussed, but also the Savior.[88] This judge is fair and his judgment is in proportion to our opportunities and resources (Luke 12:48). "The judge will be none other than the Christ, who died in the place of those who sinned and suffered the fate of those who were sinned against."[89] Ultimately, we can be confident that "the final judgment is not a judgment of our merits, but of our response to God's grace which he has extended to us in Jesus Christ."[90]

Judgment is not only about the preconditions for the entrance to new creation and our standing before the holy God. It also aims at reconciliation of our lives, both at the personal and communal level.

Judgment and Reconciliation of Personal and Social Lives

Is it the case, as is often claimed, that for reconciliation to happen, all deeds and memories need to be "healed" and reconciled? Paul Tillich put forth the thesis that in "eternal memory" the negative memory is not remembered but rather "acknowledged for what it is, non being . . . [and that it] is present in the eternal memory as that which is conquered and thrown out into its naked nothingness (for example, a lie)."[91] If I correctly understand his idiosyncratic exposition, it seems to me that Tillich is mistaken in making the negative "nonexistent" in eternity. Nor do I think that (literally) all memories must be recollected in order for reconciliation to happen. A better approach is that of the Cappadocian Gregory of Nyssa, according to which "by enjoying what is more worthy," memory of inferior things is blotted out, since "at each stage the greater and superior good holds the attention of those who enjoy it and does not allow them to look at the past."[92] Gregory argues on the basis of the infinity of God that in eternity an ever-deepening knowledge of God and

87. Volf, "Enter into Joy!" p. 263, emphasis in original, in critical dialogue with Jüngel, "The Last Judgment as an Act of Grace."

88. Schwarz, *Eschatology*, p. 392.

89. Volf, "The Final Reconciliation," p. 102.

90. Schwarz, *Eschatology*, p. 391. Consider the counterintuitive essay title of Patrick Miller's: "Judgment and Joy."

91. Tillich, *ST* 3:400; see also the insightful comments by Hick, *Death and Eternal Life*, pp. 216-17.

92. Gregory of Nyssa, *Song of Songs*, p. 128, cited in Volf, "Enter into Joy!" p. 269.

divine mysteries will take place, and we may gather from that the implication that the process helps us properly deal with memories (without ever cheaply forgetting them). In the sanctifying presence of God, in eternity — to which, as argued, also belongs purifying judgment — memories of wrong deeds (as well as omissions) will be healed and lives corrected.[93]

For that to happen, we should not think of eternity in terms of static timelessness. Rather, as argued above, though not time bound, eternity is "boundless temporality," which makes possible the idea of progress. Rather than temporality — and hence the possibility of change and progress — being an obstacle to be removed, it is rather a condition for the ultimate fulfillment. Furthermore, change and progress make it possible for the attainment of reconciliation. In that sense, Pannenberg's idea of the "taking up of time into eternity" must not be understood in terms of the end of progress.[94] That is the positive meaning of Moltmann's affirmation of progress in postmortem life, in that he "believe[s] that God's history with our life will continue after our death until that perfection is attained in which we will find rest and the joy of eternal life."[95] All notions of purgatory or other "intermediate" events presuppose that.[96] Indeed, argues the Methodist theologian J. Walls, even those who reject the doctrine of purgatory have to face the challenge of negotiating "the problem of sin and moral imperfection that remains in the lives of believers at the time of death."[97]

This view is in keeping with Augustine's vision of new creation in terms "of the happiness of the eternal peace, which constitutes the end or true perfection of the saints"[98] in "peace . . . consisting as it does in the perfectly ordered and harmonious enjoyment of God and of one another in God." This peace and happiness cannot be reached alone, but rather in communion with others, because the "life of the [heavenly] city is a social life."[99] Volf rightly reminds us: "If the world to come is to be a world of love, then the eschatological

93. For the importance of "remembering rightly" for the sake of forgiveness in this world, see my *Spirit and Salvation*, chap. 10.

94. I am following here Volf ("Enter into Joy!" pp. 269–70), to whom I am indebted, though I also engage Pannenberg from a slightly different perspective.

95. Moltmann, *Coming of God*, p. 192.

96. Just consider John Calvin, in "Psychopannia," pp. 414–90, who clearly speaks of continuous progress before the final judgment day. I am indebted to Volf, "Enter into Joy!" p. 271. On the other hand, Calvin, as is well known, was adamantly opposed to the Catholic doctrine of purgatory (*Institutes of the Christian Religion* 3.5.6).

97. J. Walls, *Heaven*, pp. 53–62 (53).

98. Augustine, *City of God* 19.11 (heading); chap. 13 speaks of "universal peace."

99. Augustine, *City of God* 19.17.

transition from the present world to that world, which God will accomplish, must have an inter-human side; the work of the Spirit in the consummation includes not only the resurrection of the dead and the last judgment but also the final social reconciliation."[100] Astonishingly — against the mind-set of ancient times — Augustine envisions not the deletion of distinctive features and diversities between people groups, but rather unity-in-diversity: "This heavenly city, then, while it sojourns on earth, calls citizens out of all nations, and gathers together a society of pilgrims of all languages, not scrupling about diversities in the manners, laws, and institutions whereby earthly peace is secured and maintained, but recognizing that, however various these are, they all tend to one and the same end of earthly peace. It therefore is so far from rescinding and abolishing these diversities, that it even preserves and adopts them, so long only as no hindrance to the worship of the one supreme and true God is thus introduced."[101]

When it comes to reconciliation between peoples and groups, we have to go back to pneumatological resources, as highlighted profoundly by Pannenberg. It is the Spirit's work to "lift us" up in filial relationship with Jesus Christ, the Savior, but not as individuals without an integral link with others, but rather as members of the same "body" whose "head" is Christ. This "ecstatic" (as in "standing outside one's self") work of the Spirit both affirms the distinct personalities of each human person and binds each of them together with the "removal of the individual autonomy and separation that are part of the corporeality of earthly life."[102] This is already at work in the church, in which "[i]ndividuals become members of *one* body when they no longer have to assert themselves against one another, but mutually accept one another for what they are in their individuality, and for what in this way they are also *for others*."[103] Only then is it possible to dream of every person having "*[moved] toward one's former enemies* and *embraced them* as belonging to the same communion of love," a precondition for final reconciliation.[104]

Although not ultimately fulfilled until the arrival of the new creation, this vision urges Christians to make every effort to "maintain the unity of the Spirit in the bond of peace" (Eph. 4:3).[105] Not apathy or inactivity, but hope in reconciliation and peace is the proper attitude for those who dream of the city

---

100. Volf, "The Final Reconciliation," p. 94.
101. Augustine, *City of God* 19.17.
102. Pannenberg, *ST* 3:551–52, 628–29 (628).
103. Pannenberg, *ST* 3:629, emphasis in original.
104. Volf, "The Final Reconciliation," p. 104, emphasis in original.
105. See Volf, "The Final Reconciliation," p. 105.

of God. There and only there will we finally experience the consummation for which judgment also makes a necessary contribution:

> The divine judgment will reach its goal when, by the power of the Spirit, all eschew attempts at self-justification, acknowledge their own sin in its full magnitude, experience liberation from guilt and the power of sin, and, finally, when each recognizes that all others have done precisely that — given up on self-justification, acknowledged their sin, and experienced liberation. Having recognized that others have changed — that they have been given their true identity by being freed from sin — one will no longer condemn others but offer them the grace of forgiveness. When that happens, each will see himself or herself and all others in relation to himself or herself as does Christ, the judge who was judged in their place and suffered their fate.[106]

As discussed above (chap. 4), Christ's resurrection is the "means" by which Christians may hope for the transitioning from time to eternity, from this world to "new creation." Building on that discussion, a systematic consideration of the wider ramifications of Christ's resurrection as the gateway to the "resurrection" of the whole cosmos, and humanity as part of it, will be the theme of the following chapter.

---

106. Volf, "The Final Reconciliation," p. 103.

6. Resurrection as the Destiny of the Cosmos and Humanity

The Cosmic Significance of Jesus' Resurrection

An indication of the significance of "reclaiming the resurrection in its cosmological setting"[1] is the fact that patristic theology at large (however differently cosmology was understood at the time) widely affirmed the link between Christ's resurrection and the future of the world.[2] Highly significant is the fact that in several early theologies "the resurrection was based on a strong understanding of God as Creator, and this led to a strong sense of God's purposes for this material creation and its goodness."[3] Tertullian begins his great study *On the Resurrection of the Flesh* with these words: "The resurrection of the dead is the Christian's trust" (1.1). Resurrection is a profound statement of the continuing value of creation that is in the midst of decay and death: "God's *No* to all evil and its privation of being falls together with his *Yes* in the final affirming of the creation as that which God has made and declared to be good."[4]

Early Christian theology rightly rejected Gnosticism, which could not embrace an eschatological vision related to bodily and earthly realities because it "shared the conviction that the present, embodied condition of human consciousness is not a natural or ideal state, but is itself the sign of a fallen world."[5]

---

1. Title for chap. 5 in Wilkinson, *Christian Eschatology*, p. 89.

2. For details, see Wilkinson, *Christian Eschatology*, p. 103; C. E. Hill, *Regnum Caelorum*; Daley, "A Hope for Worms," pp. 136–64; N. T. Wright, *Resurrection of the Son of God*, pp. 480–552.

3. Wilkinson, *Christian Eschatology*, p. 103.

4. T. Torrance, *Space, Time, and Resurrection*, p. 58.

5. Daley, "Eschatology in the Early Church Fathers," p. 94.

In *Against the Heresies*, Saint Irenaeus combated these mistaken notions and affirmed not only the goodness of creation in general but also physicality and embodiment in particular, to which resurrection pointed. Rightly, avers Moltmann, "embodiment is also the end of the redemption of the world, the redemption which will make it the kingdom of glory and peace. 'The new earth' completes redemption (Rev. 21), and the new 'transfigured' embodiment is the fulfillment of the yearning of the Spirit (Rom. 8)."[6]

The emphasis on physicality and embodiment reminds us of the necessary mortality and decay not only of humans and other creatures but also of the cosmos at large. The death-life/hope-despair paradox stands at the heart of the Christian Easter message,[7] as also is evident in both continuity and discontinuity between the risen Christ and the Christ before Easter. The risen Christ is the crucified one. On the other hand, "with his resurrection from the grave something had taken place akin to the original creation, and indeed transcending it. It was not just a miracle within the creation, but a deed so decisively new that it affected the whole of creation and the whole of the future."[8] As Thomas Torrance puts it, we can speak of the "mutual involution of mortality and immortality, death and life, the crucifixion and the resurrection of Christ."[9] Consider in this light the seeming paradox related to our own hope of the future, namely, that on the one hand, "flesh and blood" may not enter God's eternity, and yet it is *physical* resurrection that stands at the forefront of eschatological hope![10] Herein the role of the Holy Spirit, the Spirit of Life, comes to the fore: based on Christ's resurrection, the Spirit is at work toward the final redemption of not only spiritual but also bodily life.[11] Here again the dynamic of continuity and discontinuity — or, as David Wilkinson puts it, the dynamic of the three interrelated themes of "continuity, discontinuity, and transformation"[12] — is again to be seen.

Recall that above we defined eternity as the "boundless temporality of the Trinitarian God,"[13] which is the source of current time and of a radical transformation of the cosmos based on Christ's resurrection and the continuing work of the triune God toward the eschatological consummation. The eschatological

6. Moltmann, *God in Creation*, p. 246.

7. Moltmann, *Theology of Hope*, p. 199.

8. T. Torrance, *Space, Time, and Resurrection*, p. 36.

9. T. Torrance, *Space, Time, and Resurrection*, p. 48; see also Moltmann, *Way of Jesus Christ*, pp. 213-14.

10. So also Polkinghorne and Welker, "Introduction," p. 2.

11. Moltmann, *God in Creation*, pp. 65-69.

12. Wilkinson, *Christian Eschatology*, pp. 111-14.

13. R. Russell, *Time in Eternity*, p. 5 and passim.

dimension of the resurrection reminds us of the integral link between creation and new creation; the redemption of space and time also bespeaks the healing and renewal of nature. The same God who in the first place created heaven and earth is going to show his faithfulness in renewing creation.[14] An important aspect of this renewal is the *"redemption of space and time,"*[15] as argued above (chap. 5). The Johannine Jesus' resurrection appearances (John 20–21) — as much as exegetical disputes should be taken into careful consideration — may be pointers to this healing of space and time. They were continuous with the premortem human life as dramatically exemplified by the eating of fish (21:13) and discontinuous in the apparent overcoming of limitations of space (20:19).[16]

In sum: Christ's resurrection, as "miraculous" as it is, is an event that belongs to this world, time, and space in order to secure not only the redemption of human life on this earth,[17] but also all created life, as well as space and time. It represents God's "new things."[18] As said, it is not a matter of violating the laws of nature but rather of pointing to the eschatological reality in which "new kinds of laws" will be put in place by the almighty God. Resurrection represents a "new" kind of happening, anticipating the coming to fulfillment of the creational project, as it were. On the basis of the hypostatic-union principle, Christian theology affirms that "in the risen Christ . . . there is involved an hypostatic union between eternity and time, eternity and redeemed and sanctified time, and therefore between eternity and new time."[19] The ascension of the resurrected Christ takes this development even further and completes the process of the "taking up of *human time* into God." As a result, in the risen and ascended Christ, "the life of human beings is wedded to eternal life."[20] That is the topic of the rest of this chapter.

Death — the "Last Enemy"

The Question of Death

It says something about our modern culture in the Global North that a best seller since the 1970s has been the anthropologist and philosopher Ernst Beck-

---

14. For a robust discussion of this theme, see Moltmann, *Way of Jesus Christ*, pp. 246–73.
15. T. Torrance, *Space, Time, and Resurrection*, p. 90, emphasis in original.
16. See further T. Torrance, *Space, Time, and Resurrection*, pp. 90–91.
17. See further T. Torrance, *Space, Time, and Resurrection*, pp. 86–87.
18. See Moltmann, *Coming of God*, pp. 27–29.
19. T. Torrance, *Space, Time, and Resurrection*, p. 98.
20. T. Torrance, *Space, Time, and Resurrection*, p. 98.

er's book *The Denial of Death*. Its main thesis is simple and profound: humanity fears death[21] and hence seeks to either ignore or overcome it. Death seems to make null and void all hopes we and our legacy may have of any lasting value. Ironically, it is so true that although humanity is the only species conscious of its mortality, it also refuses to acknowledge it![22]

But it is also true that modern society has pushed death out of its purview and does everything in its power to deny the reality of death — so much so that we can speak of the "trivialization of death."[23] Whereas in the past, even the recent past, death was an everyday experience — dead corpses frequently remained in the house while awaiting final preparations — that is no longer the case in the societies of the Global North. At the same time, the human life span has extended considerably during the past centuries, particularly in the twentieth century.[24]

That said, there is wide interest in the phenomenon of death in academia, such that a new field has emerged: thanatology.[25] Wide and deep debates about what constitutes death have been with us for some time.[26] According to the 1981 US Uniform Determination of Death Act, death is defined in terms of "either (1) irreversible cessation of circulatory and respiratory functions, or (2) irreversible cessation of all functions of the entire brain, including the brain stem" (§1).[27]

Biologists debate not only how exactly to define death but also whether death is inevitable. Opinions vary. Yet it seems that, in light of contemporary biology, "[a]t the organismal level, there are no physiological or thermody-

---

21. The title for Becker's chap. 2 says it all: "The Terror of Death."

22. See Hick, *Death and Eternal Life*, p. 13.

23. Schwarz, *Eschatology*, pp. 4–5 (4).

24. For a highly insightful discussion of "the changing sociology of death" during history, culminating in "the contemporary taboo," see Hick, *Death and Eternal Life*, chap. 4. For the difference from cultures in the Global South, e.g., in Africa, see Ogutu, "An African Perception," pp. 102–11.

25. For basic issues and methods, see *Handbook of Thanatology*. For the Association for Death Education and Counseling of the Thanatology Association, see http://www.adec.org /adec/default.aspx. A current academic journal is *Advances in Thanatology*, published by the Foundation of Thanatology, Center for Thanatology Research and Education. Degree programs and certificates in thanatology have been established in some institutions, such as Marian University (Wisconsin): http://www.marianuniversity.edu.

26. See further Bleich, "Establishing Criteria of Death," pp. 28–32; Sumegi, *Understanding Death*, pp. 9–14.

27. National Conference of Commissioners on Uniform State Laws, "Uniform Determination of Death Act," p. 3.

namic reasons why death must occur." We know of a few unicellular species that do not undergo natural death, and there is at least one advanced multicellular species without a discernible process of deterioration with age.[28] The evolutionary biologist J. P. Schloss concludes that although "death is not physiologically necessary . . . it has proven evolutionarily valuable," and that has to do with ecological matters, which are not of course infinite. As long as the resources of the cosmos are limited, its consumption and hence population cannot be ever increasing.[29] So, the precise response to the question above is: in our kind of world, death is inevitable (and, ironically, desirable from the evolutionary-ecological point of view). In the wider cosmic framework, death and decay are inevitable, as everything ultimately will come to an end.

What makes death unique to humanity is that, differently from all other creatures, we alone have an awareness of the coming to an end of life. Animals (similarly to human infants) do not have that capacity, as far as we know.[30] What can be said safely is that even if higher animals may experience an instinctual awareness of impending death in danger, only humans can make it a theme and reflect on it. In humans, that capacity is related to the conception of time with tenses.[31] In that light, it is not a surprise that hope for life after death is deeply embedded in human evolution. The custom of burials going back at least to the (Middle) Paleolithic age (300,000 to 50,000 years ago) is an indication of that hope.[32] A related, much later development (fifth/sixth centuries B.C.E.) marked a significant milestone with an emerging awareness of individuality in Greece and Israel, which meant that death came to be a threat in a way it had not been felt as long as one's own life was but part of the collective.[33]

Philosophers — particularly in the twentieth century — have devoted a lot of attention to the (existential) meaning of death.[34] In his profound

28. For information on this species, the bristlecone pine, see the article on the Blue Planet Biomes Web site: http://www.blueplanetbiomes.org/bristlecone_pine.htm.

29. Schloss, "From Evolution to Eschatology," pp. 82–84 (83).

30. Schwarz, *Eschatology*, p. 23; for his nuanced treatment of a traditional view, see pp. 16–26.

31. Pannenberg, *ST* 3:556.

32. Lieberman, *Uniquely Human*, pp. 162–63; see also Hick, *Death and Eternal Life*, pp. 55–58.

33. The philosopher Karl Jaspers took this as an important cultural shift in his *Origins and Goal of History*, pp. 18–21; see Pannenberg, *ST* 3:556–57. For a highly useful historical tracing of the emergence of beliefs about afterlife and immortality among both the Jews and surrounding cultures and religions, see Hick, *Death and Eternal Life*, pp. 60–73.

34. A useful primer is chap. 5 in Hick, *Death and Eternal Life* (including M. Heidegger,

philosophical analysis of death in *Being and Time*, the secular existentialist Martin Heidegger sets forth and develops the thesis that human life — which is "being-there" (or "being-in-the-world," *Dasein*) — is in its authentic form also a robust acknowledgment of its nature as "being-towards-death." Only then can "being-there" be understood as a "whole." This is because "being-there" is always "being-ahead-of-itself"; that directness forward, however, will find its end in death. Until then, "at each moment of its life, *Dasein* is Being-ahead-of-itself, oriented towards the realm of its possibilities, and is thus incomplete. Death completes *Dasein*'s existence."[35] Death, hence, in that special Heideggerian sense, means fulfillment of life.[36] Heidegger's final conclusion is that, on the one hand, as long as there is existence, it has not yet attained totality, which only gives it final meaning, but that, on the other hand, when that happens, "being" is not there anymore.[37] For his fellow atheist existentialist Jean-Paul Sartre, on the contrary, there is nothing noble about death (as much as he otherwise appreciated Heidegger's thought). In his *Being and Nothingness*, Sartre merely laments that we are "condemned to be free,"[38] but that freedom is worthless, as we are totally left to our own devices in a world without meaning. Finally, we all face death. "Thus we must conclude in opposition to Heidegger: death, far from being my peculiar possibility, is a contingent fact which as such on principle escapes me and originally belongs to my facticity."[39]

Among contemporary theologians, no one has provided such a nuanced theology of death as the Roman Catholic Karl Rahner. Rather than the traditional (Catholic) idea of death being the separation of soul from body, Rahner considers "death as an event concerning man as a whole"[40] because the human person is "a union of nature and person."[41] Rahner's description of death as human persons' "free, personal self-affirmation and self-realization . . . achieved

---

J.-P. Sartre, and D. Z. Phillips). Chapter 8 continues that discussion by focusing specifically on a comparison between atheistic (naturalist) humanists such as Bertrand Russell and religions' insistence on immortality.

35. M. Wheeler, "Martin Heidegger."

36. Heidegger, *Being and Time*, division 2, question 1; for concluding thoughts on death, see also pp. 304–7 particularly. An unparalleled recent discussion is Pattison, *Heidegger on Death*.

37. Heidegger, *Being and Time*, p. 280; see Pannenberg, *ST* 3:557.

38. Sartre, *Being and Nothingness*, p. 186.

39. Sartre, *Being and Nothingness*, p. 697. For details, see P. Edwards, "Heidegger and Death as 'Possibility.'"

40. Rahner, *On the Theology of Death*, chap. 1 title (p. 13).

41. Rahner, *On the Theology of Death*, p. 13.

in death definitively,"[42] clearly comes much closer to Heidegger's than to Sartre's view. Rahner's view of death as "end" (of human life) and its "fulfillment" also differs significantly from the atheist philosopher's view in that for Rahner the self-realization can happen only when the human person surrenders one's life to Christ, in "dying with Christ, the participation in, and appropriation of, his redemptive death." Otherwise the sinner excludes oneself from God.[43]

Another innovative idea of Rahner's is that at death "[t]he human spiritual soul will become . . . 'pancosmic'"; that is, in some real sense it participates in the rest of the cosmos. For Rahner, this does not mean some kind of pantheistic nonindividualized absorption of the soul by the world any more than it means the soul's omnipresence in the whole cosmos. Rather, it means that "the soul, by surrendering its limited bodily structure in death, becomes open towards the universe and, in some way, a codetermining factor of the universe precisely in the latter's character as the ground of the personal life of other spiritual corporeal beings." It is supported by faith's conviction that each personal life in some sense is coresponsible for attitudes and behavior toward other people and the world. In other words, Rahner does not wish to set up the physical/material and spiritual/"soulish" in opposition to each other, although he affirms a body-soul distinction.[44] Rahner's interpretation has not been followed at large (nor condemned as heretical).

Death = blessed (Early Christian)
Death = punishment (Augustine)
modern

Toward a Contemporary Theology of Death

John Hick makes the important observation that because of "so vivid a sense of the reality and love of God, and of Christ as having overcome death" among the earliest Christians, those who had died were considered to have reached the final blessedness ahead of others, and therefore those remaining did not necessarily consider physical death a tremendous tragedy. With the consolidation of Pauline theology, as authoritatively established later by Augustine, however, death came to be seen as an enemy and punishment for sin.[45] Regardless of the historical accuracy of that thesis, it is uncontested that until modernity physical death was attributed to original sin and the Fall in Christian tradition.[46] With the rise of

42. Rahner, *On the Theology of Death*, p. 18; on the inevitability of sin, see pp. 15–16; so also pp. 32–33 and passim.
43. Rahner, *On the Theology of Death*, p. 36.
44. Rahner, *On the Theology of Death*, pp. 20–23 (20, 21).
45. Hick, *Death and Eternal Life*, p. 207.
46. Representative examples are the Council of Trent, Session V, "Decree concerning

evolutionary theory, this belief has been replaced by the "naturalness" of death because of finitude.[47] Barth, in contrast with tradition and in agreement with liberal Protestantism, rightly saw that "finitude means mortality."[48]

The traditional position of course claimed biblical support. Even contemporary exegesis must grant, it seems to me, that for Paul "it is not possible to exclude so-called natural death as not being cointended" in passages such as Romans 5:12 and 1 Corinthians 15:44–48.[49] Be that as it may, we know that death is "natural" in the sense that all individuals of all species must die to make room for the next generation. Nor do we really find solid basis in the biblical narrative for the idea of the immortality of humanity before the Fall. In modern theology, a correct terminological distinction was made between "natural" death that is not related to sin but to finite nature and the death of "judgment" that manifests intensification of the personal feeling toward death in light of the possibility of being cut off from the life of God.[50]

The idea of death as "natural" — while true — has to be handled with care and qualified theologically. First of all, while inevitable, death is not "natural" to (at least) human persons. The Catholic catechism puts this seemingly paradoxical statement in perspective: "Even though man's nature is mortal God had destined him not to die" (#1008).[51] Second, in biblical estimation, death, while inevitable, is seen as an "enemy" (1 Cor. 15:26). In the Old Testament, death means separation from God (Ps. 88:5) and has nothing to do with the establishment of life's fulfillment. Death is not to be idealized, and basic human intuition tells us that death ends the life drive and prevents life's fulfillment.[52] As a result, even Rahner's Christianized version of Heidegger's idea of death hardly can be supported.

Original Sin," June 17, 1546; (Melanchthon's) Apology of the Augsburg Confession 2.47, p. 106. For a constructive theology of sin and the Fall in light of Christian tradition, contemporary sciences, and living faith traditions, see chap. 16 in my *Creation and Humanity*.

47. Schleiermacher (*CF* §76.2, p. 319) correctly noted the presence of death everywhere in nature and thus that it is not the result of sin.

48. Barth, *CD* III/2, p. 625; so also Jüngel, *Death*, p. 120. Schleiermacher had already made a distinction between death as "natural" and as curse (due to sin), *CF* §75, pp. 315–17.

49. Pannenberg, *Anthropology in Theological Perspective*, p. 129.

50. For details and documentation, see Pannenberg, *Anthropology in Theological Perspective*, pp. 138–39.

51. I am indebted to Schwarz, *Eschatology*, p. 259. Materially similarly, the Orthodox David Bentley Hart, "Death, Final Judgment, and the Meaning of Life," p. 477.

52. Pannenberg, *ST* 3:558; Pannenberg, *Anthropology in Theological Perspective*, p. 138. Even Phil. 1:21 is not a way to glorify death but rather an expression of Paul's intense longing to be with the Lord.

So, how should Christian theology view death? It should "understand death as a necessary companion of life, and its actual presupposition,"[53] yet as something to be defeated because it is the "last enemy" (1 Cor. 15:26). True, to the created and contingent life in this cosmos, death and decay belong as the condition of the continuation of life. In that perspective, to be born is to die. But eschatological faith visions a world in which death, as the last enemy, will be destroyed, and in which God, as the giver of life, grants as gift eternal life. Death then is "natural" only in the sense that no creature can avoid it in our kind of world.

The overcoming of mortality as a divine gift from the Creator (rather than as an innate capacity) can be only imagined in view of the "new creation." Only in new creation are resources infinite — a necessary precondition for the continuation of life forever — in contrast to this world, in which only death guarantees the availability of limited resources.[54]

In theological perspective, death as much as birth and life is ultimately only in the hands of the Creator. Cardinal Joseph Ratzinger captured it well: "Just as . . . [the human being] cannot bring forth of himself, so neither can he hurl it back into sheer nothingness."[55]

What about "after" physical death? With some overgeneralization we might say that among theologians there are two ways to intuit the relationship of each individual person's death and the resurrection of all at the eschaton. On the one hand, there is the idea according to which physical death marks a total cessation and there is no continuity in the "intermediate state." On the other hand, there is the traditional dualistic anthropology that feeds the idea that while the body decays totally, the soul more or less independently continues its existence until the two finally become united again; this latter view is shared with Jewish and Islamic traditions.

In contrast to these two, I seek to construct a radical middle position. On the one hand, we have to underline the radical coming to an end of human life at physical death: "Death denotes a demarcation between this life and the hereafter, a demarcation so radical that it could hardly sustain the idea of a continuance, unless we talk about a 'shadowy existence' in analogy to existence in Sheol."[56] On the other hand, to combat the obvious implication

53. Schwarz, *Eschatology*, p. 253.

54. For this point and related considerations (e.g., having to do with energy flow and biomass turnover, as much as those can be imagined on the basis of parallels from this world), see Schloss, "From Evolution and Eschatology," p. 84.

55. Ratzinger, *Death and Eternal Life*, p. 156, cited in Schwarz, *Eschatology*, p. 277.

56. Schwarz, *Eschatology*, p. 278.

that therefore the newly resurrected body means once again creation *ex nihilo* (because of the lack of any form of continuity), I wish to insist that the hope for a personal resurrection in new creation means that death is not the final end. Perhaps a fitting way to express this theologically is to name "death as finality and transition."[57] Even if one may no longer find compelling the traditional idea of the soul's survival without the body, there are satisfactory ways of speaking of "continuity" in God's memory or similarly (to be discussed below). Moltmann puts it succinctly: "God's relationship to people is a dimension of their existence which they do not lose even in death."[58] He reminds us of the important statement of Luther's: "Accordingly, where and with whomever God speaks, whether in anger or in grace, that person is surely immortal. The Person of God, who speaks, and the Word point out that we are the kind of creatures with whom God would want to speak eternally and in an immortal manner."[59] Moltmann names this "dialogical immortality" (in contrast with process theology's "objective immortality").[60]

However exactly the theology of death is conceived, Christian tradition agrees that the belief in the resurrection of the body is hope for defeating death in the new creation. Having clarified its meaning and conditions, we will also investigate the question of the "intermediate" state, that is, what, if anything, "happens" between my own death and the resurrection of all? Recall that the linking of personal and communal hope is one of the necessary tasks for a constructive eschatology.

Resurrection as Human Destiny

Theological Desiderata for the Hope for the Resurrection of the Body

We have argued that the resurrection of Jesus Christ on the first Easter morning provided the "first fruit," an anticipation, a prolepsis of the coming new creation in which the power of entropy, ultimate decay and death, is overcome. The whole of the cosmos anticipates the new creation in which all of creation will participate (Rom. 8:19–27).[61] In that it signals the con-

---

57. Schwarz, *Eschatology*, p. 296.
58. Moltmann, *Coming of God*, p. 76.
59. Luther, *Lectures on Genesis: Chapters 26–30*, in *LW* 5:76.
60. Moltmann, "Is There Life after Death?" p. 246. Ratzinger uses the same nomenclature, as will be discussed below.
61. See further Peters, *God — the World's Future*, p. xi.

summation of history and creation in the coming of the righteous rule of God, the Uruguayan liberationist Juan Luis Segundo sees the resurrection of Jesus as the "primordial" event that is nothing less than the recapitulation of the universe, an eschatological sign of coming consummation.[62] Humanity's hope participates in this cosmic hope. Hence, resurrection is nothing less than "healing, lifting up and projection of human being into a new order of things."[63] Furthermore, our argument has been that the hope for resurrection is not merely "spiritual" and abstract but rather an all-inclusive, personal, and "newly" embodied existence in communion with the triune God, other people, and new creation.[64]

Having set forth and clarified these theological desiderata, we now take up a complex and complicated task. It is one thing to affirm the theological significance of the bodily resurrection in the Christian eschatological vision; it is another thing to intuit how it may happen: in other words, how could we envision the transition from premortem embodied existence (via physical death as well as general resurrection and judgment) to postmortem "physical" resurrection existence in the new creation — particularly when the person we speak of has to be the same person![65] Unless one wishes merely to affirm the possibility of resurrection[66] — or stay "agnostic" about how it may happen[67] — two interrelated, complicated intellectual tasks face the constructive theologian. First, how do we think of the nature of human nature in general? (One's theological anthropology sets the parameters and conditions for the resolution of this question.) Second, based on one's conception of human nature, one has to choose from among various options in philosophical and theological traditions concerning the idea of the transition.[68]

---

62. Segundo, *An Evolutionary Approach to Jesus of Nazareth*, pp. 111–14 particularly.

63. Segundo, *An Evolutionary Approach to Jesus of Nazareth*, p. 86.

64. Dabney, "Justified by the Spirit," pp. 61–62, cited in Wilkinson, *Christian Eschatology*, p. 98.

65. On the supreme importance of this question and its corollaries, note that it also greatly concerned Ratzinger, *Eschatology*, p. 106.

66. Cf. Tertullian (*On the Flesh of Christ* 5), who said of Christ's resurrection that "the fact is certain, because it is impossible"; I am indebted to Gasser, introduction to *PIR*, p. 3.

67. Cf. Merricks, "The Resurrection of the Body," p. 481.

68. For a fairly comprehensive and accessible account, see Baker, "Persons and the Metaphysics of Resurrection," pp. 168–75.

The Dilemma of Personal Identity in New Creation

Already in early Christian theology the problem of explaining the transition from the earthly life to the life to come was clearly acknowledged. What can be conveniently called the "anthropology of composition" became a fairly standard view in patristic theology: once the body decays at death, on the last day God reassembles it from the last constitutive material particles available and rejoins it with the soul that did not die. The fathers were aware of obvious problems such as death by cannibalism or in the sea when there was no trace of the deceased person's material body available, and they sought solutions.[69] Another standard early tactic was to establish the identity on the basis of the identity of the soul, separated at death but immortal. The pagan Hellenistic idea of immortality, however, was significantly reshaped and strictly limited to one individual to avoid the (Platonic) doctrine of reincarnation. In some fathers such as Athenagoras, both composition and soul identity existed side by side.[70]

Currently we know that not only with regard to the afterlife, but even in this life, the continuity of personal identity[71] cannot be a matter of material continuity since atoms are in constant flux through wear and tear.[72] John Polkinghorne correctly notes that in itself the soul's "role as the carrier of human identity is almost as problematic within life as it is beyond death."[73] The standard philosophical distinction between "numerical" and "qualitative" identity reminds us of the obvious fact that even in this life the persistence of identity is a complex issue: although each human person stays the same person (numerically), our biological constitution because of replacement of cells is in continuous (qualitative) change.[74] There is also the time gap between my personal physical death and the final resurrection, unless one endorses some type of resurrection-in-death view. The mere time gap, however, is not necessarily a deal breaker, as will be argued below.

69. See, e.g., Athenagoras, *On the Resurrection of Flesh* 4–8; for comments, see Daley, "A Hope for Worms," pp. 147–51; S. Davis, "Resurrection, Personal Identity, and the Will of God," pp. 24–25. For Jewish tradition, see Bynum, *The Resurrection of the Body*, p. 55.

70. For Origen's profound innovation in terms of "the soul as the vital principle (*eidos*) of the body," anticipating Aquinas's hylomorphism, see Pannenberg, *ST* 3:575–76.

71. For clarification of the term "identity," see Wiggins, *Identity and Spatio-Temporal Continuity*, pp. 35–36, 50; see Murphy, "The Resurrection Body and Personal Identity," p. 208.

72. A monumental standard discussion is Parfit, *Reasons and Persons*, part 3.

73. Polkinghorne, "Anthropology in an Evolutionary Context," p. 98.

74. See Gasser, introduction to *PIR*, p. 4; Niederbacher, "The Same Body Again?" pp. 145–59.

Two standard tactics in philosophical tradition that attempt to ensure the continuation of personal identity either in this life or beyond are the "memory criterion" that, beyond mere memory, encompasses complex mental functioning, and the "bodily criterion," that is, this person can be considered to be identical with that person if and only if they have the same body throughout the life. Obviously, even if bodily sameness may be of some value in this life, it certainly cannot negotiate the transition to the next time. Regarding the former approach, perhaps more suitable nomenclature would be the "psychological continuity" view because memory itself is only part of the equation.[75] Although even that in itself hardly suffices as the guarantor of the continuity of identity because the demand that there be continuous brain activity in order to ensure the psychical structure supporting mental properties cannot be met in resurrection, a related classic version thereof points in the right direction, namely, the "consciousness continuity" — to be more precise, "self-consciousness continuity" — view. Argued already by Locke,[76] the key to identity continuity is the ability to have a first-person perspective, that is, self-reflective capacity.[77] That of course has to be assumed in order to have judgment, forgiveness, and responsibility and for it to be meaningful in the new creation. But even that alone hardly suffices.

In summative response to these proposals, we can say this much: it is obvious that minimally both physical (corporeal) and psychological (mental) criteria are required for identity continuation,[78] particularly if topped with the capacity for self-consciousness.[79] To these, "the character formation" has to be added. More than mere moral-ethical integrity, as important as that is, this component has to do with practices and virtues, and of course encompasses not only rational and praxeological but also emotional (widely understood) aspects. When placed in the wider context of communities that shape us and essential relationships, we have advanced considerably the pursuit of identity continuity in this life.[80] Without downplaying their importance, though, something more is needed when considering postmortem continuity.

75. See E. Olson, "Immanent Causation," p. 55.

76. Locke, *An Essay concerning Human Understanding*, 2.27.9.

77. So also Baker, *Persons and Bodies*, pp. 66, 91; for agreement with Locke, see p. 9. I am indebted to Quitterer, "Hylomorphism and the Constitution View," pp. 178–79. See also A. O. Cohen, *Self-Consciousness*.

78. Strawson, *Individuals*, p. 97.

79. Murphy, "The Resurrection Body and Personal Identity," pp. 208–11.

80. Murphy, "The Resurrection Body and Personal Identity," pp. 212–13. A similar kind of thick account of identity is presented in Schuele, "Transformed into the Image of Christ," pp. 224–25.

New Attempts to Resolve the Problem of Postmortem Identity Continuity

To advance the discussion beyond these and similar suggestions, a number of competing options have been proposed in philosophy (and philosophical theology).[81] One asks: Why not simply assume a "new creation" of postmortem human body identical to the one deceased? That would lead to the classical duplication problem: obviously it would not be the same body but rather a *duplicate*.[82] That is the problem facing (nonreductive) physicalism, which argues univocally for physical death as the end of everything. My problem with that is not the lack of willingness to believe that God, indeed, is able to create the person *ex nihilo* again — that shouldn't be any more difficult than the first creation (let alone creation of the cosmos!). Duplication (among other challenges) is the problem.

The philosopher Peter van Inwagen, a staunch materialist[83] and antidualist (that is, he vehemently opposes any idea of a separate soul), has suggested a disputed solution, named here the "divine snatch" model (which he believes is not against the creeds, although it of course goes way beyond them in detail): "Perhaps at the moment of each man's death, God removes his corpse and replaces it with a simulacrum which is what is burned or rots. Or perhaps God is not quite so wholesale as this: perhaps He removes for 'safekeeping' only the 'core person' — the brain and central nervous system — or even some special part of it."[84] This simply means that the dead person is only *apparently* dead (although the corpse of course is), as the person itself is revivified in God's eternity. Commentators have noted the obvious problems related to this proposal, beyond the fact that it is speculation and lacks any support in Christian tradition. It denies the finality of death and thereby diminishes the "newness" of resurrection by making it no more than a sort of reanimation. Furthermore, "it requires God systematically to deceive human beings," as others consider the dead person dead![85]

81. A formative and still useful, though of course outdated, discussion is Mavrodes, "The Life Everlasting and the Bodily Criterion of Identity."

82. It also violates Locke's principle that "one thing cannot have two beginnings of existence." Locke, *An Essay concerning Human Understanding*, 2.27.1. I am indebted to Quinn, "Personal Identity, Bodily Continuity and Resurrection," pp. 106–7 (although his reference to Locke is mistaken).

83. For details of his materialistic view according to which the human person as a "material being" cannot survive beyond the limits of the physical constituents of an organism, see his *Material Beings*, chap. 14 particularly.

84. Inwagen, "The Possibility of Resurrection," p. 121.

85. Gasser, introduction to *PIR*, p. 6.

A noted way to improve Inwagen's suggestion is Dean Zimmerman's "falling elevator model."[86] Similarly based on physicalist/materialist metaphysics, it seeks to avoid the need for the previous proposal's "clandestine" divine snatch. His model considers life to be self-maintaining and self-reproducing, "earlier stages in Life tending naturally to cause later stages that closely resemble the earlier ones in crucial ways." Thus, Zimmerman speaks of "immanent causation" in which "causal dependencies must be *direct*" rather than mediated with anything or anybody, even God.[87]

> The Falling Elevator Model is a way to allow the Life of a dying organism to go one way, while the dead matter goes another way. The trick is to posit immanent-causal connections that "jump" from the matter as it is dying, connecting the Life to some other location where the crucial organic structure of the organism [is] preserved. . . . The Falling Elevator Model affirms that, at the moment of my death, God allows each atom to continue to immanently cause later stages in the "life" or history of an atom, right where it is then located, as it normally would do; but that God *also* gives each atom the miraculous power to produce an exact duplicate at a certain distance in space or time (or both), at an unspecified location I shall call the "next world."[88]

How credible is this account? Problems are many, including that whereas in normal life processes, fission (say, nuclear fission) splits something into two parts, herein the "fission" between the "falling" and "rising" bodies brings about two complete "bodies," as it were. Furthermore, any changes in human life happen gradually, and new particles are gradually integrated in the body of the organism, unlike here. In sum: it looks like Zimmerman's solution results in a "clone of the deceased, and thus . . . provides us with no more immortality than that which comes from an identical twin surviving our death."[89] Furthermore, the in-itself useful idea of "immanent causation" has to be qualified both philosophically and theologically. If taken out of Zimmerman's "two-way"

86. Originally suggested in Zimmerman, "Compatibility of Materialism and Survival"; for a recent discussion, see Zimmerman, "Bodily Resurrection."

87. Zimmerman, "Bodily Resurrection," pp. 35–36, emphasis in original. For a programmatic essay, see Zimmerman, "Immanent Causation."

88. Zimmerman, "Bodily Resurrection," p. 36, emphasis in original.

89. These and related issues are the main concerns of Hershenov, "Van Inwagen, Zimmerman, and the Materialist Conception of Resurrection," pp. 460–63 (463); cf. Gasser, introduction to *PIR*, pp. 7–8.

model, it can be purified of the connections to the idea of "jumping" and instead connected with what I suggest below: continuity in terms of information-bearing patterns in which both continuity and discontinuity are dynamically present. From the theological point of view, talk about "immanent" causation also has to be qualified such that it does justice to the contingent nature of all creaturely life: if there is something like immanent causation, it is only so as long as the life-giving Spirit of God is at work. Hence, it is not an inherent feature of "life" per se but rather comes from the continuous relatedness to the source of divine life-giving providence.

Personal Identity in New Creation:
Divine Faithfulness and Continuity-in-Discontinuity

The starting point for all inquiries into the possibility of the resurrection of the body has to mind Paul's note of the "change" (1 Cor. 15:51) occurring in the transition, which of course signals the dynamic of continuity-in-discontinuity. Change is neither total replacement nor replication.[90] Another critical theological insight is the theology of the human being as the image of God.[91] Whatever else it might mean, at its core the *imago Dei* signals our relatedness to and contingency on God. The moment the divine life-giving Spirit is taken away, all creaturely life comes to an end (Ps. 104:29–30).[92] Referring to the basic intuition of the image of God meaning relatedness to the Divine, we have to say with Orthodox theologian John Zizioulas that "[w]hat gives us an identity that does not die is not our nature, but a personal relationship with God."[93]

In sum: the personal identity that defines me as person (as explained above) cannot be "transferred" from this earthly life to the afterlife with my own innate powers; divine faithfulness and creative power are needed. But *what* will transition from here to there: Is it the "whole package" of what has made me the kind of person I am? The judgment of my life, and its reconciliation, will be based on my capacity to recognize myself as the actor of the deeds attributed to me, on the quality of my character that has guided my choices (both what I did and failed to do) both at the personal and at

90. See Pannenberg, *ST* 3:574.
91. A detailed discussion can be found in chap. 11 of my *Creation and Humanity*.
92. S. Davis, "Resurrection, Personal Identity, and the Will of God," p. 27.
93. Zizioulas, "Doctrine of the Holy Trinity," p. 58. Materially similarly, the Catholic Ratzinger, *Eschatology*, p. 113; for useful reflections, see Tapp, "Joseph Ratzinger on Resurrection Identity," pp. 219–21.

the communal level. I believe what Keith Ward notes in this context, that memory, which is needed for me to give an account of my life, will also be "so transformed that suffering is set within a wider context of learning and development, and even earthly joy is relativized by a deeper consciousness of the presence of God." This does not mean the deletion of memories — or how else could I be held accountable for *my* choices and deeds? — but rather their transformation in a way that saves me from being overwhelmed by sadness and grief of my sinful life and so prepares me to enjoy life eternal in the infinite divine presence.[94]

What about the body in this regard? I agree with Nancey Murphy: as essential as it is for identity formation and persistence, it is "that which provides the substrate for all of the personal attributes . . . ; that which allows one to be recognized by others; that which bears one's memories." In this life, all these activities are based on and tightly linked with embodiment. But because the human being is a "person" rather than a "material object," "there is no reason *in principle* why a body that is numerically distinct but similar in all relevant aspects could not support the same personal characteristics."[95] In any case, my physical composition changes several times during my lifetime (albeit gradually rather than instantly as in resurrection).[96] Temporal interval (however that may be understood) does not in principle frustrate the continuity of identity. Indeed, for "new creation" to be *new*, as discussed already, the "matter" (body, physicality) must be different from the earthly body (notwithstanding the continuity to the point that it still makes sense to speak of "body" rather than merely "spirit").[97]

Phenomenological philosophy may help us think more properly of the nature of the "body" in resurrection. Phenomenology makes a distinction between "objects" as such and how they appear to us, their subjective meaning. In relation to the resurrection of the body, the lesson is that the subjective perception of my body as *mine* is understandably very different from a scientist's or medical doctor's analysis of a human body's behavior and composition.[98] In my own subjective perception I feel my embodiment not only as physicality but also in relation to my environment, particularly to other people and

94. K. Ward, *Religion and Human Nature*, p. 307; so also Murphy, "The Resurrection Body and Personal Identity," p. 214.

95. Murphy, "The Resurrection Body and Personal Identity," pp. 214-15, emphasis in original.

96. See Schuele, "Transformed into the Image of Christ," p. 222.

97. Similarly, Murphy, "The Resurrection Body and Personal Identity," p. 215.

98. For an enlightening discussion relevant to our topic, see K. Hart, "Without World."

my communities. Correctly understood, one phenomenologist philosopher argues that embodiment as a primary property does not necessarily require physicality or materialist aspects.[99] This observation is a needed critique of an overly materialist account of the human person (without in any way severing humanity from physicality and relation to the rest of the cosmos).

With these preliminary conclusions in mind, I find useful the Anglican Polkinghorne's way of speaking of the "how" of the continuity of identity in the transition from here to there in terms of "the almost infinitely complex, information-bearing pattern in which the matter of the body is organized at any one time." While there is no need necessarily to endorse the traditional conception of soul, it is also the case that "[t]his surely is the meaning of the soul."[100] This proposal seems to correspond to contemporary scientific understandings of information or the way complex systems could be understood — and all living beings are systems of some kind.[101] In that regard, Aquinas's hylomorphic account of human nature intuited something similar, notwithstanding his vastly different intellectual context.[102] Utilizing the concept of information, it can be stated that what the older soul theory rightly intuited was that "the faithful God will remember the pattern that is me and reembody it in the eschatological act of resurrection." I couldn't agree more with Polkinghorne, who continues: "In making this assertion, I want to affirm the intrinsically embodied character of human being, without supposing that the flesh and blood of this world represents the only possible form that embodiment might take."[103] Against hard-core materialists (and animalists),[104] to whom there is no going beyond the current constitution of the physical, it is the case that "[i]t is not necessary . . . that the 'matter' of these bodies should be the same matter as makes up the flesh of this present world. In fact, it is essential that it should not be. That is because the material bodies of this world are intrinsically subject to mortality and decay. If the resurrected life is

99. This is the main argument of Merleau-Ponty's programmatic essay, *Phenomenology of Perception*, particularly "Part I: The Body"; for comments, see Schärtl, "Bodily Resurrection," pp. 121–23 particularly. See also Gasser, introduction to *PIR*, pp. 12–13.

100. Polkinghorne, "Anthropology in an Evolutionary Context," p. 98; see also his "Eschatology," pp. 38–41; "Eschatological Credibility," pp. 50–53.

101. Polkinghorne, *God of Hope*, chap. 9 (pp. 103–12).

102. For a highly insightful and accurate investigation into the nuanced views of Thomas, see Quitterer, "Hylomorphism and the Constitution View," pp. 177–90.

103. Polkinghorne, "Anthropology in an Evolutionary Context," pp. 99–100.

104. For the basic accounts, see E. Olson, *The Human Animal*; E. Olson, *What Are We?* For a careful investigation of the animalist model's compatibility with resurrection, see H. Hudson, "Multiple Location and Single Location Resurrection," pp. 87–101.

to be a true fulfillment, and not just a repeat of an ultimate futile history, the bodies of that world-to-come must be different, for they will be everlastingly redeemed from mortality."[105]

The information-bearing pattern, it seems to me, would meet the demands of immanent causation and also receive its benefit — albeit not located within human resources but in the life-giving power of the Spirit of God. This means that as long as there is a real immanent (rather than "transeunt") causal link between the embodied personal life history most widely understood of the deceased and the resurrected person, a time gap (between physical death and general resurrection) would not frustrate it.[106] Similarly, the information-bearing pattern can be seen in agreement with the above-mentioned self-consciousness (or self-reflection) requirement: despite the time gap, the resurrected person bearing the same informational "plan" as the deceased one is able to recognize one's self as the same self.

Another way of saying this is that the time gap after the decaying of my body (and, we can say, even the information-bearing pattern, as far as innate human powers are concerned) ceases to be a problem as we bring to the equation the resources won from the discussion on the time-eternity relationship. The reason is simply that "what takes place in time can never be lost so far as God's eternity is concerned. To God all things that were are always present, and as what has been they are present in the totality of their existence." In that sense, properly understood, we can say with Pannenberg that "the duration of creatures in their own life, which we in our sense of time can grasp at least fragmentarily, is to be understood as participation in the eternity of God." Hence, the conclusion follows: "Herein the identity of creatures needs no continuity of their being on time line but is insured by the fact that their existence is not lost in God's eternal present."[107]

Having now constructed a hopefully viable solution to the thorny problem of the continuity of identity in the transition from earthly life via death to resurrection life in the new creation, we can take a closer look at the time-gap problem, no longer for the sake of identity continuation but rather for the core eschatological desideratum of linking the individual and communal destinies.

---

105. Polkinghorne, *Science and Theology*, pp. 115–16; I am indebted to Gasser, introduction to *PIR*, p. 11.

106. See E. Olson, "Immanent Causation," pp. 56–58. Similarly, Corcoran, "Physical Persons and Postmortem Survival," pp. 201–17.

107. Pannenberg, *ST* 3:606.

The "Intermediate State" and the Linking Together
of Personal and Communal Destinies

While I understand why Christian nonreductive physicalists underline the importance of death's finality to combat the obvious misconception according to which the soul possesses natural powers of immortality and independence, I also find the "gap" theory — that is, between my personal death and the final resurrection there is "nothing of me"[108] — problematic from the systematic theological point of view. Whatever one may think of the "intermediate state," the idea of physical death as literally bringing to an end all of the human person has to be qualified with the equally important thesis that "God is the future of the finite from which it again receives its existence as a whole as that which has been, and at the same time accepts all other creaturely being along with itself."[109]

A related systematic theological concern is that all talk about the completion of one's personal destiny in the eschaton has to be linked tightly with the common destiny of other human beings (and of course, the whole of creation). Rather than positing a scheme in which earthly life is followed by "nothing" (after physical death) awaiting (in the distant future) the re-creation *ex nihilo* of the human person, systematically it is far superior to think in a way that holds tightly to the following four guidelines based on the developments in this project.

First, following the continuity-in-discontinuity schema, it can be said that the earthly "body" (that is, the whole human person) has to undergo a radical change, without losing the person's identity, in the transition from "here" to "there." Second, the information-bearing pattern (or some materially similar idea) is kept in God's "memory," preserving all that makes human identity — despite the "gap" between the deceased person's entrance into eternity and the general resurrection of all at the transitioning to new creation.[110]

Third, because God in his eternity is on both sides of death whereas we are time bound,[111] it can be said that "[a]ll individuals go into eternity at the moment of death," and "yet it is only at the end of the age that all those who sleep in Christ receive in common by the Spirit of God the being-for-self of the totality of their existence that is preserved in God, and thus live with all others

---

108. See Barth, *CD* III/2, p. 632.

109. Pannenberg, *ST* 3:607; see also Volf, "Enter into Joy!" p. 268.

110. Cf. Unamuno, *Tragic Sense of Life*, p. 149; I am indebted to Hick, *Death and Eternal Life*, p. 215.

111. See Schwarz, *Eschatology*, p. 291.

before God."[112] Fourth, because we are "constituted by relation to God,"[113] even death is not able to separate us from God and God's love (Rom. 8:38–39).[114] If there is any meaning to an intermediate state, it is "God holding us fast until the resurrection."[115] As a result, we can confidently say that ultimately our life on both sides of the grave is in the hands of our Creator and Redeemer.[116]

This constructive theological work is all the more important because the Bible does not give a coherent picture of what happens after physical death.[117] Passages such as Philippians 1:20–24 seem to merely imply some type of continuation of personal life.[118] Other passages can be read as supporting immediate entrance into blessedness at death (2 Cor. 5:8; Phil. 1:23; 1 Thess. 5:10);[119] some contemporary theologians have extended this into a novel idea of "resurrection in death."[120] The biblical data also include a number of references to what became the "soul-sleep" view in tradition (Dan. 12:2; Luke 8:52; 1 Cor. 15:51; 2 Pet. 3:4).[121] Whereas "sleep" entails inactivity, some passages seem to imply conscious activity (particularly the parable in Luke 16:22–23).[122] It seems to me that the focus of all these diverse biblical testimonies and metaphors is, first, to assure us that as final and inevitable as death is, it is not the last word; God is. Similarly, they clearly seem to be saying that, second, in no way is the "intermediate" state usurping the bliss of one's eternal destiny.[123] At its best, the "gap" between personal death and general resurrection is transient, awaiting final consummation.

As long as our contemporary reflection on the nature and mode of the intermediate state is in keeping with these general biblical pointers, I believe

112. Pannenberg, *ST* 3:606–7.

113. E. Johnson, *Friends of God*, p. 194; see further McCall, *The Greenie's Guide to the End of the World*, pp. 223–25.

114. Berkouwer, *The Return of Christ*, p. 59; Grenz, *Theology for the Community of God*, p. 595.

115. Grenz, *Theology for the Community of God*, p. 597.

116. See the wise words of caution in Thielicke, *Death and Life*, pp. 216–17; I am indebted to Grenz, *Theology for the Community of God*, p. 595.

117. See Schwarz, *Eschatology*, p. 296.

118. Grenz, *Theology for the Community of God*, p. 593.

119. This view has been favored in Roman Catholic tradition, both in the past (ratified in 1336 by Benedict XII) and nowadays (*Catholic Catechism*, #1021). On the Protestant side, see Travis, *I Believe in the Second Coming*, p. 175.

120. Schärtl, "Bodily Resurrection," p. 104. See also W. D. Davies, *Paul and Rabbinic Judaism*, pp. 317–18.

121. As is well known, Luther at times subscribed to this view; see Grenz, *Theology for the Community of God*, pp. 590–91; Moltmann, *Coming of God*, pp. 101–2.

122. For detailed scrutiny, see Grenz, *Theology for the Community of God*, pp. 593–94.

123. See Grenz, *Theology for the Community of God*, pp. 595–96.

there is leeway for diverse interpretations. In the traditional body-soul view, we must remember the liability of the problematic idea of the soul continuing its life apart from the body to the extent that in resurrection — so to speak — the body and soul to be united are not the same as those of the deceased person (the soul having accumulated experiences). That said, why couldn't we think of this period as time for the beginning of healing, transformation, and change — without in any way taking away from the all-important role of resurrection? Polkinghorne puts it well: "We may expect that God's love will be at work, through the respectful but powerful operation of divine grace, purifying and transforming the souls awaiting resurrection in ways that respect their integrity."[124] Ecumenically speaking, that insight would make it easier for non–Roman Catholics to understand the possibility of the doctrine of purgatory. Could that intuition also correspond to the traditional idea of paradise (or Abraham's bosom) as the "waiting room" for the blessed?

Speculatively, one may also consider that, if we are kept by God during the intermediate state, then the biblically based intuition of some kind of connection between the living and the dead becomes meaningful. Setting aside some unhelpful — and perhaps heretical — beliefs and customs stemming from the medieval period and even before, theologically it is not only permissible but also appropriate to reserve a place, for example, for prayer for the dead. Similarly, there is no reason to exclude their prayer for us.[125]

Having outlined and defended in some detail the distinctively Christian vision of resurrection as a hope for the cosmos and humanity, we engage in the last section of this lengthy chapter a comparative exercise with competing and alternative views of life after death (or lack thereof).

Competing Views of the Afterlife

Immortality, Karma, and Rebirth: A Christian Engagement

Much older than the belief in bodily resurrection is the belief in immortality and reincarnation (rebirth) among ancient and living faith traditions. With all their differences, the Greek and Hindu versions of immortality share some common "ground beliefs" that differ significantly from the Abrahamic faiths. First, rather than the soul possessing inherent powers out of itself, in the Abra-

---

124. Polkinghorne, *God of Hope*, p. 111.
125. A similar argument can be found in Polkinghorne, *God of Hope*, p. 110.

hamic view life eternal is a gift from God, the source of life. Second, rather than the soul being the person itself, let alone the "true" person, the resurrection doctrine considers the whole human being as the human person. Flight from the material is thereby excluded. Third, rather than the soul having its endless journey and history through incarnations, the person, after once-for-all earthly life, looks forward to eternal life in communion with the Creator.[126] Finally, for Abrahamic faiths, each human life and human personality (individuality) is unique and nonrepeatable and hence cannot be "replicated."[127]

With the Abrahamic faiths' doctrine of bodily resurrection, Asiatic faiths' teaching on reincarnation/transmigration shares the problem of identity constitution, though in the latter that is of course differently framed, that is, "how to preserve the identity of the soul in the mutability of the forms which the soul assumes." The problem of identity continuation from one human life to another is a huge challenge (and has to be based on the problematic notion of the soul as the identity carrier). But it becomes hugely more challenging when we think of a sequence of lives from human to animal and back to human. Is the "soul" still the carrier of the identity?[128]

A common and persistent misunderstanding among Christian observers of Hinduism is that rebirth signifies a "second chance." That is a fatal mistake. Belief in rebirth has nothing to do with yet another potential opportunity to fix one's life. Rebirth is rather the result of the karmic law of cause and effect. Even gods cannot break the power of karma. As a result, all "major schools of Hindu (and Buddhist) philosophy strive not to be reborn . . . [but rather] strive to attain release (moksha) from ever being born again."[129] Rather than a positive offer, rebirth is more like a curse. Moltmann observes correctly that whereas "[i]n the ancient Indian world, reincarnation belongs to 'the wheel of rebirth,' and according to karmic teachings is the requital for the good and evil deeds in a life . . . [i]n the European world of today, reincarnation belongs to the modern world's principle of education and evolution."[130]

The Christian notion of grace differs significantly from the ironclad power of karma. In it God acts "contingently and historically," continuously interrupting "the chain of act and destiny," which means the repelling of karma. That is of course what forgiveness does: while not doing away with punishment — because it does not deny the "sowing and reaping" principle taught

126. Pannenberg, ST 3:571-73.
127. See also Moltmann, Coming of God, pp. 111-12.
128. Moltmann, Coming of God, pp. 112-13.
129. Doniger, On Hinduism, p. 92.
130. Moltmann, Coming of God, pp. 113-14 (114).

in the Bible (Gal. 6:7; Jer. 31:29) — it opens up the possibility of being saved without being destroyed or consumed by the consequences. That is truly a second chance in life. Even the last judgment, as argued above, aims at transformation and purification for those who are willing to be judged in light of God's holiness and offer of grace. By doing so, grace categorically distinguishes between the doer and the deed: although the latter is condemned, the person is pardoned.[131] Although grace is not unknown to theistic Hinduism,[132] it functions in a vastly different framework. Whereas in Hindu thought fortune and suffering are the result of karmic cause-and-effect logic, "[o]n a typical Christian view, I do not 'deserve' the sort of suffering I may have to endure on earth. But neither do I 'deserve' the endless bliss of a fulfilled loving relationship with God."[133]

A standard question to both Hindu and Buddhist eschatologies has to do with the assignment of this-worldly fortunes or ills to previous lives. It seems morally highly questionable to refer the sufferings of the poor, sick, handicapped, and other unfortunate people to their past deeds. Nor does it seem morally fair to count the fortunes of the rich, famous, and healthy as their own accomplishments. Equally problematic is the observation that people with good fortunes, who are supposed to be leaning toward ever-better ways and attitudes, hardly seem to do so — no more than do the ill-fortuned always cling to ever-worsening patterns of life. But that is the logic that karma assumes. Rather, in our kind of world evil and good seem to be mixed together; often the evil seem to flourish whereas the good and noble face insurmountable obstacles. "In short, it does not look as though the conditions of human life can be explained in terms of past-life activity . . . in a very plausible way." This seems to be pointing to the separation between good and evil only after death, but if that is true, then this earthly reincarnation appears to be much less meaningful than Hinduism teaches.[134]

Provided (for the sake of the argument) that the karmic cause-and-effect logic were to work, a problem arises with regard to memory. How many persons recall their former lives in order to see the logic and learn from them? That rebirth is believed to happen in any case; whether or not one is able to recall anything of one's past lives has not stopped Hindus from inquiring into the role of memory and forgetting. Merely assuming it and attempting to "locate"

---

131. While this paragraph is based on Moltmann (*Coming of God*, pp. 115-16), I also draw different conclusions about the judgment.

132. As discussed in chap. 8 of my *Spirit and Salvation*.

133. K. Ward, *Religion and Human Nature*, p. 72.

134. K. Ward, *Religion and Human Nature*, pp. 60–62 (61).

the seat of this kind of special memory in *manas*, a kind of combination of mind and heart, an organ of a sort (or, simply, in the "soul"), hardly convinces the doubter.[135] The standard Hindu response is merely that something is allegedly recalled from past lives (these are called *vasanas*, literally "perfumes"), and they are believed to guide in some way or another one's life choices. But even if those memories do not appear, the person is claimed to have lived his or her life in the "shadow" of past lives' experiences and memories.[136]

That question of memory alone is yet to be satisfactorily addressed. An even more difficult question, I fear, has to do with the capacities of the "soul" of nonhuman entities in the samsaric cycle. Rebirth (or transmigration) of course assumes some kind of "animating principle, however defined, from one more or less physical, terrestrial body to another"[137] (as in the case of humans, most often defined as the "subtle body"). Now, believing that karma may lead the human being not only upward but also downward in the evolutionary tree results in a highly problematic assumption: all souls must know and understand, make choices; in other words, they must have self-consciousness and high-level intellectual skills. While that is not a problem with most humans — unless they die as infants or are mentally impaired, a corollary problem not dealt with satisfactorily by the advocates of the belief — with subhuman entities it is a problem, beginning from even the highest animals. For example: How could the "soul" of the insect or dog (or, as assumed in some, perhaps many, forms of Hinduism, a tree) have these capacities in its way "upward" in the cycle of rebirths? It is easier to understand the downward spiral from a normal human being to an animal or lower-level entity, but the opposite movement does not seem to make sense. Keith Ward puts it well: "If an animal feels pain, but is not aware — and is not even capable of being aware — that the pain is a result of past acts which have made one such an animal, can the pain properly be considered a punishment?" That is, "to see this as punishment, one would have to remember one's relevant acts, see how they have led to this condition, and to accept that one could have chosen otherwise."[138]

To the outsider, belief in reincarnation seems highly individualistic. Obviously, it neglects the effects on each person's behavior and attitudes on environmental, social, cultural, sociopolitical, and economic factors, to name a few. However, we know that much of what we are is the result of effects from

135. See Goldman, "Karma, Guilt, and Buried Memories," p. 415.
136. Doniger, *On Hinduism*, pp. 108–11.
137. Goldman, "Karma, Guilt, and Buried Memories," p. 414.
138. K. Ward, *Religion and Human Nature*, pp. 62–63 (63).

the milieu in which we evolve and live. Often we suffer from what others are doing to us, rather than from our own "sins." Of course, the counterargument could be that we are put in this place of suffering because of our previous deeds, but even then, the effects of the community and human relatedness are not properly addressed. A corollary problem is that if another person — or even a divine being — seeks to alleviate my suffering, then it must lead to the postponement of my final release. Is that charitable act then really charitable, or rather an unintentional way of adding to my suffering?[139]

So, what is the role of the community and communal hope in a Hindu view of rebirth? There is an interesting dynamic, if not an internal contradiction, in relation to the community (of humanity) in the doctrine of reincarnation. On the one hand, it seeks to resolve every individual's fate — whether in terms of rebirth or final release — apart from the rest of humanity. No form of reincarnation envisions a communal, "universal" consummation of human destiny. On the other hand, as Moltmann notes, in some real sense every doctrine of reincarnation "sets the individual life in a wider community of generations, often in a cosmically conceived community of solidarity shared by all living beings and things."[140] Every creature's "soul" is related to the "world soul." The human person may be reborn in the form of an animal. One may even be able to say with regard to a majority of reincarnation teachings that "everyone and everything can therefore be reembodied in everything and must consequently also recognize itself in everything."[141] Be that as it may, it seems obvious that the indispensable mutual conditioning among the personal, communal, and cosmic hope that stands at the center of Christian faith points in a different direction than does the Hindu vision.

From the theological perspective, we need to raise the question of the role of embodiment in Hindu (and Buddhist) eschatology. Here is a major difference from Abrahamic faith traditions' focus on the resurrection of the body. All major philosophical schools of India, particularly the *advaita*, understand "that the Self per se is bodiless."[142] That is not to deny the temporary embodiment of the human person, but rather than ultimately the "I" (self), the body is what Sankara calls a "superimposition": "Due to ignorance [*avidya*], the characteristics of the gross body are illicitly transferred to the Self with the result that the Self is thought of as having birth and death," although the self of

---

139. So also K. Ward, *Religion and Human Nature*, pp. 66–67.
140. Moltmann, *Coming of God*, p. 111.
141. Moltmann, *Coming of God*, p. 111.
142. Balasubramanian, "The Advaita View of Death and Immortality," p. 118.

course is neither born nor will die.[143] Body and self are not inseparable; they can exist separately (to be more precise, the self is able to; the body will perish eventually).[144] *Advaita* rules out the possibility of two substances or entities of different ontological status having a real relation.[145] In this context, it becomes understandable that — somewhat counterintuitively — the *advaita* school believes that one may gain liberation even in this life when one has the final insight: "When all desires which once entered his heart are undone, then does the mortal become immortal, then he obtains Brahman. And as the slough of a snake lies on an ant-hill, dead and cast away, thus lies this body; but that disembodied immortal spirit (prâna, life) is Brahman only, is only light."[146] This is also liberation from one's body: from this person's perspective, "the body is no more, though others may see him as possessing a body and bound by it."[147] The denigration of the bodily existence undeniably points in a totally different direction from the Abrahamic faiths' hope for bodily resurrection. A related big problem is that whereas Indian traditions speak of "salvation" in terms of renunciation of one's personality ("self"), for the Abrahamic traditions eternal communion with God is the ultimate goal. They assume the persistence of the self. That hope also supports a high view of one's dignity and worth in this life.[148]

What about rebirth and our current scientific understanding of how the world functions? I fear that rebirth is at odds with the laws of physics and causality (even when they are not fully deterministic, as we now know they are not), as well as genetic-biological effects. It is generally agreed that our personal traits, bodily features, intelligence, basic socioemotional orientation, and such characteristics are by and large determined by the above-mentioned more or less deterministic factors, in collaboration with the sociocultural environment, particularly the type of nurture and training we have. Mutation and inheritance explain much of what we consider deficiencies. In sum: "The laws of the material universe do not seem to be karmic laws which the physical order simply expresses. Chance, physical necessity, and emergence" play here a crucial role.[149] Furthermore, rebirth seems to be a total denial of evolutionary theory according

143. See Balasubramanian, "The Advaita View of Death and Immortality," p. 124.

144. See Svetasvatara Upanishad 3.19; Balasubramanian, "The Advaita View of Death and Immortality," p. 120.

145. Balasubramanian, "The Advaita View of Death and Immortality," pp. 118-19 (118).

146. Brihadaranyaka Upanishad 4.4.7.

147. Balasubramanian, "The Advaita View of Death and Immortality," pp. 120-23 (120).

148. See also K. Ward, *Religion and Human Nature*, p. 73.

149. K. Ward, *Religion and Human Nature*, pp. 67-71 (68).

to which all entities emerge and evolve from the simplest to the most complex. To put it bluntly: at least theistic Hinduism simply rejects the idea that humans have evolved gradually from lower species and assumes that "eternal souls descend into matter, over millions of years," over and over again.[150]

"No-Self" and Eschatological Hope:
A Christian Engagement of the Buddhist Vision

Although the Buddhist eschatological vision has already been engaged in many ways above, a more focused theological reflection on its most distinct belief, no-self, is in order. Briefly put: with regard to Buddhism's innovative reworking of her parent religion's view of the afterlife, by far the biggest problem for Abrahamic traditions is the denial of individuality ("self"). The Christian commentator is of course deeply troubled with any kind of possibility of a "rebirth" of something that does not exist.[151] So how would a Christian response look?[152]

I have to agree with Keith Ward that "[f]rom a theistic viewpoint, it will seem to be false that there is no enduring Self and that there is no permanent and noncontingent reality — for God is precisely such a reality." In that sense, "the whole Buddhist world-view and discipline leads away from theism."[153] Indeed, in the absence of self, it is impossible — at least for the Western mind — to imagine "who" is the one who clings to life due to desire, suffers from the effects of karma, and particularly comes to the enlightening realization (if it ever happens) that the samsaric cycle is now overcome. This also has to do with what seems to me a deep and wide difference of orientation between Semitic faiths and Theravada Buddhism: the notion of individuality and the individual's relation to others. Ward nicely summarizes the Theravadin's understanding: "The goal seems to be, not a creative community of agent-subjects, but the calm of the limpid pool wherein all sense of individuality has been long transcended, and all activity has ceased in complete freedom from desire. There is no enduring individuality, and the succession of thoughts, feelings, and sensations that we call a 'self' comes to an end with the realization of pure, objectless bliss."[154]

---

150. K. Ward, *Religion and Human Nature*, pp. 71–73 (73).

151. For creative reflections, see Hick, *Death and Eternal Life*, pp. 339–41, 349–50.

152. See W. King, "No-Self, No-Mind," pp. 155–76.

153. K. Ward, *Religion and Revelation*, p. 166.

154. K. Ward, *Religion and Human Nature*, p. 106. For thoughtful reflections from a religious-studies perspective, see S. Collins, "What Are Buddhists *Doing*?"

Furthermore, I cannot think of ways to affirm the dignity of human personhood if there is nothing "permanent" (relatively speaking, because all theistic traditions consider only God to be permanent). As is often rightly noted, it is also difficult to understand what talk about rebirth may mean when there cannot be identity between the person who passed away and the one who reappears.[155] In other words, how should we conceive the principle of *kamma* when the "[a]ggregates produced in the past with kamma as condition ceased there too" and "there is no single thing that has come over from the past becoming to this becoming"?[156] How can "collections of impersonal elements"[157] ever warrant any notion of personal and moral accountability?

Although there are no major Christian movements that, strictly speaking, endorse the Asiatic faiths' idea of reincarnation (and rebirth)[158] — apart from the contemporary anthroposophic religious renewal movement founded by the German philosopher Rudolf Steiner[159] — several contemporary theologians have creatively gleaned from these resources in their desire to transcend the traditional Christian hope for the persistence of individuality in the bodily resurrection. In the spectrum of how definitely personal individuality is replaced by immersion into collective or cosmic unity, on the most robust end stand the philosopher J. Hick and feminist theologian R. R. Ruether. More complicated is the American process theology movement with somewhat varying opinions. These will be scrutinized next. Other, somewhat similar attempts to get around the belief in the resurrection of the body and the persistence of individuality in the afterlife could be mentioned, such as those of two American Anglicans, Bishop J. S. Spong's "nonreligious," "natural" view of death as bringing everything to nil,[160] and K. Tanner's "this-worldly" eschatology without an afterlife, discussed above.

155. Cf. Burns, "'Soul-Less' Christianity," pp. 93–94.

156. Buddhagosa, *Visuddhi Visuddhimagga* 19.22 (p. 628).

157. S. Collins, *Selfless Persons*, p. 160 and passim. I am not sure what K. Ward's (*Religion and Human Nature*, p. 80) statement about personal identity being "a matter of degree" may mean. Common sense tells us that one can either be a person or not be.

158. Contra Weatherhead (*The Christian Agnostic*, pp. 209–10) and in agreement with Hick (*Death and Eternal Life*, pp. 365–73); Cranston, "Reincarnation," pp. 143–60.

159. See further, "Reincarnation" on the Waldorf Watch Web site, https://sites.google.com/site/waldorfwatch/reincarnation, and "Reincarnation and Karma" on the Anthromedia Web site, http://www.anthromedia.net/en/themes/anthroposophy/reincarnation-and-karma/.

160. The subtitle of Spong's *Eternal Life* says it all: *Beyond Religion, Beyond Theism, Beyond Heaven and Hell*; for an insightful discussion, see Simut, "Understanding Death beyond Religion."

Transcendence of Individuality and
Dissolution into "the Matrix of the Whole"

Ruether bluntly states that "the notion of personal immortality is discredited as a real possibility."[161] One of her reasons has to do with her conviction that immortality is usually sought by males who "are primarily concerned about their own self-perpetuation" while for women that is not important — and if women think of it, it is mainly with regard to relationships with others.[162] Furthermore, Ruether opines, hope for immortality — particularly as far as it is based on Greek heritage — fosters dualism of the body and the spirit, of this world versus the world to come, making the former without value.[163] Even worse, female sexuality and giving birth are conceived as representing this lower domain of bodily (and even sinful) existence as opposed to the "spiritual body" in eternal life.[164]

> [Ruether] believes that we need to start by acknowledging our mortality, not as something evil, but as an acceptance of our place as finite organisms among other finite organisms. Our consciousness, our life breath, is the interiority and vitality of our finite organism and dies with it. At the same time, we are upheld and sustained by a larger matrix of life and renewal of life. Everything that lives and dies goes back into this matrix and is reborn in and through it. Our dreams and accomplishments live on through the collective memory of our communities through which insurgent hope is continually reborn. In ways that we can neither understand nor guarantee, this matrix of life and the renewal of life are also God for us and with us.[165]

For her ultimate eschatological vision of "relinquish[ing] our small self back into the great Self," Ruether claims to find support from "new physics," in which everything in the cosmos is irreducibly intertwined, interrelated. The final dissolution of each being into the "ongoing matrix of the whole" is impermanence and lack of life after death writ large.[166] The obvious critical question to Ruether is, by what logic can it be maintained that hope for an afterlife per se is a particularly male characteristic?

161. See Ruether, "Eschatology in Christian Feminist Theologies," p. 335.
162. Ruether, *Sexism and God-Talk*, pp. 235–37 (235).
163. Ruether, *Sexism and God-Talk*, pp. 239–40.
164. Ruether, *Sexism and God-Talk*, pp. 245–49.
165. Ruether, "Eschatology in Christian Feminist Theologies," p. 339.
166. Ruether, *Gaia and God*, pp. 248–53 (253).

Although American process theology at large does not speak with one voice on the question of the afterlife,[167] mainstream process thought stands "against any subjective immortality, holding that as objectively experienced by God our lives are wholly preserved and cherished forever."[168] According to Charles Hartshorne, the reason for the denial of "immortality as a career after death . . . in which our individual consciousnesses will have *new* experiences not enjoyed or suffered while on earth" is the fear that belief in personal survival after physical death runs the danger of "mak[ing] God a mere means for our everlasting happiness."[169] Even the concept of "subjective immortality" coined by some process theologians (as a development from and revision of Whitehead's "objective immortality") does not match the mainstream biblical-Christian idea of personal physical resurrection.[170] The same can be said of John Cobb's highly revisionist view: instead of the "resurrection of body," Cobb advocates the hope for the "resurrection of the soul,"[171] which "implies that the power to survive death is now inherent in the soul, so that no supernatural intervention is needed" because humans would not be here without billions and billions of years of divine creative activity and provision of meaning and "lure." Differently from scientific naturalism, this (Whiteheadian "naturalism") relegates the possibility and power to survive to divine influence.[172] While noting process theology's recognition of divine influence, there is no need to elaborate the differences of all the process visions of the afterlife from the personal bodily resurrection hope of mainstream Christianity.

Perhaps the most sophisticated challenge to the Christian view comes from Hick. In his earlier work on theodicy, *Evil and the God of Love*, he advocated the possibility of progress and development in the afterlife for the simple

167. For an excellent source on diverse views (including some nonprocess interlocutors such as Moltmann), see Bracken, ed., *World without End*; its focus is the leading process female eschatologist, Suchocki. For a comprehensive account of various options, see Müller, *Gott, Welt, Kreativität*, pp. 269-94; I am indebted to Brüntrup, "3.5-Dimensionalism and Survival," p. 67 n. 1.

168. Ford, *The Lure of God*, p. 114, cited in Schwarz, *Eschatology*, p. 168. For details, see Pittenger, *After Death — Life in God*.

169. Hartshorne, *Omnipotence and Other Theological Mistakes*, pp. 4, 117; for a highly informative discussion, see Griffin, "Process Eschatology," pp. 297-98; Hick, *Death and Eternal Life*, pp. 217-21.

170. A classic essay is Whitehead, "Immortality." See further, Suchocki, *God, Christ, Church*, p. 198; Suchocki, *The End of Evil*, chap. 5. For the marked difference between personal resurrection of the body and "subjective immortality," see Griffin, "Process Eschatology," pp. 298-300, to which I am indebted here.

171. Cobb, "The Resurrection of the Soul," pp. 213-27.

172. Griffin, "Process Eschatology," p. 305.

reason that one life hardly is long enough for the attainment of the goal of perfection set by God.[173] In his later eschatological monograph, *Death and Eternal Life* (1976), Hick rejected both the traditional Abrahamic faiths' belief in resurrection (including two destinies) and Asiatic faiths' doctrine of repeated reincarnations on earth. Instead, he chose "a third possibility . . . , namely that of a series of lives, each bounded by something analogous to birth and death, lived in other worlds in spaces other than that in which we now are,"[174] ultimately leading to the transcending of individuality in corporeality in which persons will "no longer be separate in . . . [the] sense of having boundaries closed to one another . . . [but rather will] be wholly open to another." In that final sense, even embodiment will be transcended and "the individuals' series of lives culminates in a last life beyond which there is no further embodiment but instead entry into the common Vision of God, or nirvana, or the eternal consciousness of the atman in its relation to Ultimate Reality."[175] While acknowledging deep discrepancy between the eschatologies of the West and those of the East, Hick also believes it "holds only on the surface" and that Hindu, Buddhist, and Christian views are "open-ended" in their look for a human destiny that can at its best be described in general terms.[176] Although Hick's hybrid construct of the afterlife is highly ingenious, its main challenge from the Christian perspective is its radical deviation from both biblical and traditional contours. From the religious studies' point of view, this kind of invention is representative of no known religious tradition and thus probably will not attract much lasting following.

The final group of contenders consists of rapidly proliferating emerging speculations into immortality in a way that clearly transcends humanity as we now know it.

Beyond Humanity: Emerging Speculative Proposals of "Immortality"

Titles such as *Posthuman Bodies*[177] signal an imagination of — and to many also a hope for[178] — the possibility of transcending not only human embodiment but also the borders of humanity. The first generation of posthuman

173. Hick, *Evil and the God of Love*, pp. 337–41.

174. Hick, *Death and Eternal Life*, p. 456; for details, see pp. 414–22 (titled "Many Lives in Many Worlds").

175. Hick, *Death and Eternal Life*, pp. 459–64 (461, 463–64).

176. Hick, *Death and Eternal Life*, pp. 425–28 (427, 428).

177. Halberstam and Livingston, eds., *Posthuman Bodies*.

178. See, e.g., More, "On Becoming Posthuman."

intuitions opened a way for thinking of new projects such as the cloning of men and women.[179] Closely related to this project is genetic manipulation, which raises the question, "what are we *becoming* with our technology?"[180] A somewhat elusive term, the "posthuman condition" refers to "a world in which humans are mixtures of machine and organism, where nature has been modified by technology, and technology has become assimilated to form a functioning component of organic bodies." From a theological and ethical point of view, dangers are obvious and include not only dehumanization but also "creation out of control," the tendency to "play God," and technocracy in its various forms.[181]

A new generation of hopes for significantly longer life comes from the advocates of "evolutionary immortality"[182] and "biological immortality."[183] Their vision is the overcoming of the limits of senescence of finite human life.[184] The challenges to such an endeavor, however, are many, namely, "to prevent the shortening of the telomeres, and to ensure that degenerative mutations do not occur in cellar replication and rejuvenation . . . [and that] the immune system will be genetically enhanced and deleterious genetic defects will be removed or corrected to protect individuals from life-threatening and chronic diseases or disabilities."[185]

Whereas these and related posthuman imaginations were funded mostly by the desire to enhance well-being and lengthen life on this earth,[186] the new generation of post- and transhuman thought experiments are robustly future-oriented, and in that sense are eschatological alternatives to the Christian hope for resurrection. The physicist F. Tipler's dream of "physical immortality" (discussed above in chap. 1) has some affinities with what is now called "cybernetic immortality"[187] (or "bionic immortality").[188] Under that umbrella concept are a number of related fields, all of which employ emerging developments in nano-

179. Graham, "Liberation or Enslavement."
180. Hefner, *Technology and Human Becoming*, p. 9, emphasis in original.
181. Graham, "Liberation or Enslavement," n.p.
182. Miconi, "Evolution and Complexity."
183. For a thoughtful discussion, see Carnes and Olshansky, "Evolutionary Perspectives on Human Senescence"; see also Kurzweil, *The Singularity Is Near.*
184. A near-future hope is to live at least from 150 to 200 years. See Grey, "The War on Aging"; see also Rose, "Biological Immortality."
185. Waters, "Whose Salvation? Which Eschatology?" p. 166.
186. For details and theological assessment, see my *Creation and Humanity*, pp. 437–39.
187. For the basic ideas and plentiful resources, see Dubrovsky, "Cybernetic Immortality."
188. See the Immortality Project Organization Web site: http://www.immortality
-project.org/.

technology, AI, and computer technologies. The project Extreme Lifespans through Perpetual-equalising Interventions (or ELPIs, from the Greek word meaning "hope")[189] also belongs to this matrix, as does the neologism "digital immortality."[190] The basic idea is to try to transfer "life" from the decaying physical bodily level to another level of "brain" functioning assumed able to be self-preserving (and perhaps self-correcting). The distinction between the "human" and "computer" (robot or artificial being) gets diminished, perhaps even eliminated.[191] Common to these speculations is the continuation of life in virtual cyberspace without any kind of embodiment.[192] These attempts express strong confidence in the superiority of AI — computer-based intellectual powers — over human resources, although they are devised by humans.[193]

The basic question to all of these thought experiments, including Tipler's, is simply this: How "human" could such a life be (if, for the sake of argument, its possibility were granted)? N. Herzfeld summarizes succinctly: "Cybernetic immortality is based on the assumption that thoughts, memories, feelings, and action define the human person. These are products of consciousness, which is an emergent property of the complexity of our brains. In other words, human beings are basically biological machines whose unique identity is found in the informational patterns that arise and are stored in the neuronal structures of the brain. If these patterns could be replicated, as in sophisticated computer technology, the defining characteristics of the person would be preserved."[194]

Abrahamic theism's teachings about the creation of humans as moral persons after the image of God and ensuing responsibility to the Creator intensify the force of these questions.[195] Furthermore, what about emotions or relationality? While ironically the view of the human person in these thought experiments is biological/naturalist, it is dismissive of the body and embodiment![196] Finally, there is a category mistake — or at least a difference — from the belief in resurrection: whereas for the cybernetic vision, immortality is

189. See http://www.elpisfil.org/index.htm. Another useful site is that of the Cryonics Institute: Technology for Life, and its page "The Prospect of Immortality," at http://www.cryonics.org/resources/the-prospect-of-immortality. "Cryonics" means simply preservation of corpses in low temperatures.

190. See Woollaston, "We'll Be Uploading Our Entire MINDS to Computers."

191. See, e.g., Moravec, *Mind Children.*

192. A pioneering discussion was Benedikt, *Cyperspace,* chap. 2.

193. See Kurzweil, *The Age of Spiritual Machines;* Moravec, *Robot.*

194. Herzfeld, "Cybernetic Immortality," p. 194.

195. This section (including some key sources) is deeply indebted to Herzfeld, "Cybernetic Immortality," p. 193.

196. See also Herzfeld, "Cybernetic Immortality," pp. 198-99.

merely more time, for the Christian vision it is time's transition to eternity.[197] To summarize: although a few AI experts have suggested that there is not necessarily inconsistency between the two hopes of the afterlife, Christian and "virtual,"[198] for the reasons given, that opinion cannot be supported.[199]

We have clarified in some detail the cosmic and personal significance of Christ's resurrection as the hope for overcoming death and decay in terms of the bodily resurrection in new creation. But a lingering question involves whether that vision ultimately is so otherworldly that concerns for the well-being of this world — with regard to both the flourishing of nature and the pursuit of justice and equality among men and women — are marginalized. To these pertinent issues we turn next.

197. Herzfeld, "Cybernetic Immortality," with indebtedness to R. Niebuhr, *Nature and Destiny of Man*, 2:291, and conversation with R. Russell.

198. Crevier, *AI*, p. 278; I am indebted to Herzfeld, "Cybernetic Immortality," pp. 193–94. An up-to-date discussion and survey of views can be found in Geraci, *Apocalyptic AI*.

199. For a thoughtful reflection, see Waters, "Whose Salvation? Which Eschatology?"

7. The Flourishing of Nature and Humanity in the Perspective of New Creation

Liberating Eschatology[1]

For Orientation

There is word out that, among many doctrinal loci, eschatology may be the most suspicious one for liberationists and eco-theologians of various stripes. How helpful is it for the well-being and flourishing of nature to await the final judgment and establishment of a new heaven and new earth? How useful for the sake of liberation and reconciliation of people is the expectation of God's coming shalom?

A quick look at some representative works by liberationists easily reveals the marginal role, at times even omission, of the doctrine of last things. Consider the senior American black theologian J. Deotis Roberts's essay in the *Cambridge Companion to Black Theology* (2012): "Dignity and Destiny: Black Reflections on Eschatology." Notwithstanding the title, the writing speaks of anything but eschatology![2] Another senior black liberationist, J. Cone, devotes but five pages to eschatology in his programmatic *Black Theology of Liberation*.[3] A promising collection of essays titled *Liberating Eschatology* (1999), in honor of the leading American feminist theologian L. M. Russell, has very little to say of eschatology — except for the essay by Moltmann! And so forth.

---

1. I have borrowed the heading from the book title *Liberating Eschatology: Essays in Honor of Letty M. Russell*, edited by Farley and Jones.
2. J. D. Roberts, "Dignity and Destiny."
3. Cone, *Black Theology of Liberation*, pp. 144–51.

This chapter takes up the challenge of integrating a robust future-oriented hope for God's new creation with a deep involvement of Christians and churches in the advancement of ecological and human flourishing.

Eschatological Hope under Suspicion

A few decades ago liberationists, having "revived utopian hopes for the over-coming of social evils and the establishment of the 'reign of God' on earth," faced the "disappointing realities of a world that is largely getting worse rather than better, socially and ecologically."[4] That did not lead to resignation or apathy but rather to a more nuanced analysis of what is wrong with the world. Some current liberationists have followed the Italian philosopher Antonio Gramsci in speaking of "hegemony" as a major challenge to tackle. "Hegemony" here means "the supremacy of a social group [that] manifests itself in two ways, as 'dominion' [*dominio*] and as 'intellectual and moral leadership' [*direzione*]."[5] What makes this kind of hegemony so subtle and subversive is that it "designates a situation in which power can be exercised without the need for overt use of force; it creates an uncontested régime of truth." Many contemporary liberationists argue that it also includes "the hegemonic canons of Western theology."[6] Furthermore, feminists and other female theologians seek to expose severe "gender and class biases" in Judeo-Christian eschatological traditions (including their ancient sources in surrounding cultures).[7] In that analysis, the biases have to do with the pejorative and dehumanizing apprehension of the female, building up of the masculine and patriarchal ego with the hope of immortality,[8] adoption of Platonic body-soul dualism,[9] and severing of the human destiny from that of the rest of creation, among others.

Not only assigning eschatology a marginal role but also treating it with deep suspicion is typical of much of liberationism. Particularly apprehensive about eschatology has been feminist theology, which by and large can be said

4. Ruether, "Eschatology in Christian Feminist Theologies," p. 335.

5. Frogacs, ed., *The Antonio Gramsci Reader*, p. 249, cited in Westhelle, "Liberation Theology," p. 311.

6. Westhelle, "Liberation Theology," pp. 311–12.

7. Ruether, "Eschatology in Christian Feminist Theologies," p. 328.

8. Karras, "Eschatology," p. 244. For an example of obsession with the threat of the masculine and a sort of millennial vision of its overcoming, see E. Davis, *The First Sex*, pp. 338–39.

9. Ruether, "Eschatology in Christian Feminist Theologies," pp. 331–32.

to have left behind traditional future-oriented hope of eschatological consummation (with the exception of important scholars such as E. Johnson, who embraces a fairly traditional Catholic doctrine of last things).[10] As discussed in the previous chapter, R. Ruether and some other leading feminists have totally rejected the idea of personal survival in the resurrected body because of its alleged egoistic male motifs and have turned to an elusive hope for dissolution into the cosmic matrix.

If eschatology is included in the theological menu, most liberationists seek to revise quite radically its canons and orientations. Again, feminist theologians have been among the pioneers, as they "have refocused eschatology from the distant future ('unrealised eschatology') to the here-and-now ('realised eschatology'). Simultaneously, these feminist thinkers have shifted the thematic centre from humanity, as the apex of creation, to creation itself, with humanity removed from centre stage to a supporting position as an interwoven, interdependent component of that creation. In short, realised eschatology has become the ethical culmination of ecofeminism."[11] This means a marked shift away from spiritual hopes to concern for the earth and other human beings.[12] The Brazilian American liberation theologian Vítor Westhelle echoes similar sentiments as he argues that "eschatology is no longer 'the last things' but 'those things in our midst.' The stress is on a God acting in history and on the need to discover God's direction for abundant life in the midst of our ambiguous and conflict ridden history." In keeping with this is the claim that "[p]rophecy, then, so intimately connected to eschatological vision and hope, does not involve predicting the future or mapping out the end times, but discerning God's activity in the world now, the meaning of that activity for the community of faith, and the appropriate response."[13]

So deeply suspicious are some liberationists toward holding on to the future-directed eschatological hope that they are willing to replace that not only with the present but even with the past. Theologically I find it disturbing to hear a feminist theologian announce that "[t]he future is envisioned as a return to the pristine past, before human degradation of nature, but with humanity fulfilling its symbiotic potential."[14] Whatever that statement may

10. Cf. Karras, "Eschatology," pp. 244–45.

11. Karras, "Eschatology," p. 243.

12. Ruether, *Sexism and God-Talk*, pp. 254–56 and passim. See also her *New Woman, New Earth*, pp. 186–211.

13. Engel and Thistlethwaite, "Introduction," pp. 14–15, cited in Westhelle, "Liberation Theology," p. 319.

14. Karras, "Eschatology," pp. 243–44.

mean in details, seeking to rediscover the "lost paradise" sounds like an odd goal, particularly for liberative purposes.

In response to these rebuttals and rejections of the Christian eschatological hope for the coming of God's kingdom and hope for personal resurrection life in new creation, a liberationist-sensitive vision will be attempted.

Eschatological Hope as the Catalyst for Liberation and Reconciliation

This project argues that "only in the kingdom of God will human society find the consummation that is freed from all self-seeking and mutual oppression."[15] Ultimately, reconciliation of peoples and societies requires the reconciliation of the basic relationship between the individual and society. Although efforts toward that should be pursued persistently, it may only happen finally at the eschaton: "The rule of God's righteous will means that to each of us will be given our own and that none of us can arrogate to ourselves any more. Strife regarding the amount that is specifically due to each will thus be ended, and with it the suffering caused by the feeling that others and the social 'system' have unjustly deprived us."[16]

This is the vision and dream of countless earthly societies, most recently that of atheist Marxism-Leninism, which has never even nearly materialized. And even if it were to happen by earthly means, it would only relate to that particular generation — never to countless generations that have passed away. Hence — again — the need for a future orientation of eschatological hopes. Only with the tying of the fulfillment of human society's destiny of equality, peace, and reconciliation with the coming of God's righteous kingdom can the "reconciliation of the individual and society in the concept of fulfillment of human destiny" happen.[17]

Knowing that the ultimate reconciliation of peoples and groups can only happen in new creation does not lead the church into passivity, let alone apathy. The church is joining the work for liberation and justice exactly because it knows that thereby it participates in the work of the trinitarian God. I endorse the vision of the Brazilian Catholic liberationist L. Boff: "The historical process anticipates and paves the way for definitive liberation in the kingdom. Thus human forms of liberation acquire a sacramental function: They have a weight

15. Pannenberg, *ST* 3:523.
16. Pannenberg, *ST* 3:584.
17. Pannenberg, *ST* 3:585–86 (585).

of their own, but they also point toward, and embody in anticipation, what God has definitively prepared for human beings."[18] Deeply involved in the liberative work in anticipation of the consummation, the church is living out her missionary way of existence as "[a]mid the strife of world history God's people is called on to offer a model of his kingdom"[19] based on love, fairness, and compassion.

The missionary church participates in the liberative work for its own sake; that is, helping people in need is a Christian "thing." At the same time, "being aware that all of its efforts are at best patchwork, bandages on the wounds of a hurting world, the church also witnesses with its action to a world that will be without anguish and suffering. Similarly to the miracles of its Lord which were both a help for people in need and signs of a new creation, the church is the symbol of God's future."[20]

Rather than fostering passivity and apathy, Christian hope for the future, God's future, inspires commitment to liberation. The Uruguayan Catholic liberationist Juan Segundo reminds us that believers, having been delivered from under the power of fear of death, are thereby liberated for service and solidarity with others.[21] Sadly, the church knows how often it not only fails to live up to the lofty calling but also even conducts her life in deep contradiction to it; thereby, the church — similarly to the world — lives under God's redeeming judgment and needs constant renewal.[22]

Liberation in the present age and the coming of God's kingdom belong integrally together, but they should not be confused with each other or one subsumed under the other. The late Argentinean Methodist liberationist José Míguez Bonino's warning is spot-on: "When the cause of Jesus Christ . . . is totally and without rest equated with the cause of social and political revolution, either the Church and Jesus Christ are made redundant or the political and social revolution is clothed in a sacred or semi-sacred gown."[23] Under the heading "Eschatological Hope and the Commitment for Temporal Liberation," the Sacred Congregation for the Doctrine of the Faith in its *Instruction on Christian Freedom and Liberation* (1986) boldly announced that although a careful distinction — but not separation — be made "between earthly progress

---

18. Boff, *Liberating Grace*, p. 152. I am indebted to Schwarz, *Eschatology*, p. 156.

19. Pannenberg, *ST* 3:524.

20. Schwarz, *Eschatology*, p. 371.

21. Segundo, *An Evolutionary Approach to Jesus of Nazareth*, pp. 111–14 particularly.

22. Pannenberg, *ST* 3:525.

23. Bonino, *Doing Theology in a Revolutionary Situation*, p. 163. I am indebted to Ross, "Christian Mission and the End of Poverty," p. 89.

and the growth of the kingdom, which do not belong to the same order," the eschatological "hope does not weaken commitment to the progress of the earthly city, but rather gives it meaning and strength . . . for man's vocation to eternal life does not suppress but confirms his task of using the energies and means which he has received from the Creator for developing his temporal life."[24]

In keeping with the Thomistic fulfillment theory, in which the grace of God does not destroy but rather brings to fulfillment what is there in nature on the basis of God's creative work, Vatican II's *Gaudium et Spes* (#39) puts it succinctly: "On this earth that Kingdom is already present in mystery. When the Lord returns it will be brought into full flower." A radical balance should be sought between two extremes, which can be expressed in the following slogans: "Why invest on the earth when only heaven counts?" and "Why do we need heaven when only earthly matters count?"[25] This attitude "allows the Christian to bring both hope and realism to engagement with contemporary social challenges. An ultimate eschatological horizon that inspires and provokes engagement with current challenges is combined with recognition that whatever is achieved will be partial, provisional, and penultimate."[26] While human work and efforts to improve the world have their intrinsic value, theology's task is also to issue a self-critical note to the effect that "all human activity, constantly imperiled by man's pride and deranged self-love, must be purified and perfected by the power of Christ's cross and resurrection."[27] Only in the eschaton does liberating eschatology achieve its ultimate goal.

The Flourishing of Nature and Eschatological Hope

A Theological Acknowledgment and Assessment of Eco-Feminist Critique

According to the leading American eco-feminist, R. R. Ruether, "[e]cofeminism seeks to dismantle the basic paradigm of male over female, mind over body, heaven over earth, transcendent over immanent, the male God outside of and ruling over the created world — and to imagine an alternative to it."[28]

24. Sacred Congregation, *Instruction on Christian Freedom and Liberation*, #60; so also Gutiérrez, *A Theology of Liberation*, p. 104.

25. Boff, *Was kommt nachher?* pp. 26–28 (I have translated freely from German these phrases that appear as subheadings).

26. Ross, "Christian Mission and the End of Poverty," p. 91; see also *Gaudium et Spes*, #39.

27. *Gaudium et Spes*, #37.

28. Ruether, "Eschatology in Christian Feminist Theologies," p. 337, with reference par-

She and others have relentlessly critiqued Christian (and by implication, any such theistic) eschatology for wrongful tendencies like these in its dismissal of the destiny and well-being of nature and, by implication, for the disastrous effects on the current lifestyle of Christians. Feminists have also critiqued harshly the alleged "universal" subordination of women — due to the linking of the female with "nature" and physicality, the lower realm of reality, in contrast to the male connection with culture, the higher realm — which has contributed to the subordination of and "dominion" over the environment.[29]

In the context of her "chaos"-based creation theology,[30] Catherine Keller has joined the critics for the escapist view of nature in Christian eschatology.[31] A particularly sharp criticism is targeted against all notions of apocalypticism.[32] Along with secular exploitation of nature's resources, religious apocalyptic escapism is the other major culprit for the eco-catastrophe, she opines.[33] Gleaning from process thought, Keller categorically rejects *ex nihilo* (by favoring gradual becoming), believing it leads to God-world hierarchic dualism.[34] Throughout, she strongly advocates nondualistic and immanentist explanations against what she thinks is tradition's emphasis on God's distance and hierarchic difference from the world, with implications for binaries such as male/female, human/natural, soul/body, and so forth. Zooming in on the beginning verses of the first creation narrative in Genesis, she accuses traditional theology of "tehomophobia," which is built on Jewish-Babylonian mythical "identification of the sea with the primordial; with the female, chaos, the Tehom."[35] Along with the subordination and "demonization" of femininity, "order" is placed on a pedestal and indeterminacy and

---

ticularly (but in no way exclusively) to the vision of the Brazilian Catholic Ivone Gebara; see her *Out of the Depths*.

29. A programmatic early essay is Ortner, "Is Female to Male as Nature Is to Culture?" For a critique of this white feminist universalizing tendency and essentialization of the female across cultures, see Pui-lan, "Mending of Creation."

30. C. Keller, *Face of the Deep*. For a recent assessment of various uses of "chaos" in biblical, systematic, and science-religion creation theologies, see Vail, "Using 'Chaos' in Articulating the Relationship of God and Creation."

31. See also C. Keller, "Eschatology, Ecology, and a Green Ecumenacy."

32. See, e.g., C. Keller, "Women against Wasting the World," p. 251. A comprehensive and insightful engagement of Keller's views to which my discussion is indebted here is McCall, *The Greenie's Guide to the End of the World*, chap. 1.

33. See, e.g., C. Keller, "Women against Wasting the World," pp. 255-56.

34. See, e.g., C. Keller, *Face of the Deep*, p. 117.

35. C. Keller, "Women against Wasting the World"; C. Keller, *Face of the Deep*, pp. 15, 26, and passim.

uncertainty are rejected. As a result, nature's complexity and transience are being reduced to simplicity and coherence.[36] All these negative features in traditional theology lead to escapism that justifies the unashamed utilitarian rape of nature, as hope is relegated merely to the future divine intervention, including desire for immortality. Even worse, the traditional eschatological myth includes the total destruction of this world and its replacement with a totally new world. Instead of future-oriented, God-driven "apocalyptic" (as she routinely names it),[37] Keller recommends an immanentist, this-worldly solution to the impending eco-crisis. The burden and hopes are placed on humanity's capacity to deliver the promise.

While the current project agrees with Keller's critique of certain ways Christian tradition has abused the category of the apocalyptic (and its resultant dismissal of nature's integrity and its value), her uncritical (and, I fear, uninformed) rejection of mainline Christian eschatology's account of nature is liable to devastating critique.[38] Not only is it one-sided, but it is also dismissive not only of a number of nature-embracing theologies of Christian tradition but also of a large number of contemporary constructive theological proposals from the "left" and the "right" (many of which had already been available at the time of her writing).[39] Furthermore, it is highly suspicious to claim that building a this-worldly, human-made hope for the future of creation would *necessarily* deliver a nature-affirming lifestyle (as Keller's passionate and often-obscure prose seems to suggest).

As a counterargument, we should remember the most obvious viewpoint: in all scientific accounts, not only the earth and her life but also the whole cosmos will come to an end; and in terms of near-future prospects, even

36. C. Keller, "No More Sea," pp. 183–98. This essay is an extended critique and rejection of the book of Revelation; for details, see McCall, *The Greenie's Guide to the End of the World*, pp. 41–44.

37. See C. Keller, *Apocalypse Now and Then*.

38. Here I leave aside a number of problems in her analysis and proposal not necessary for the purposes of this discussion, such as the interpretation of *ex nihilo*.

39. In addition to several monographs by Moltmann engaged in this project, see the following (in chronological order): Birch, Eaking, and McDaniel, eds., *Liberating Life*; Berry, *Befriending the Earth*; Hesse, ed., *After Nature's Revolt*; Haught, *The Promise of Nature*; Boff, *Ecology and Liberation*; Daneel, *African Earthkeepers*, vol. 2, *Environmental Mission and Liberation in Christian Perspective*; Conradie, *Hope for the Earth*; Deane-Drummond, *Eco-Theology*; Nürnberger, *Regaining Sanity for the Earth*; Conradie, ed., *Creation and Salvation*. See also other recent titles listed below in this section. A useful recent essay (with rich bibliography to which this discussion is also indebted) is Conradie, "What Is the Place of the Earth in God's Economy?" pp. 65–96.

if human-made threats such as pollution, waste, and nuclear disaster could be avoided, sooner or later "super"-human asteroid collisions or something similar may totally wipe us out. In that light, how appealing and realistic is Keller's this-worldly (and, I fear, this-earth-focused) vision?[40] Even worse, Keller fails to provide any hope for individual life beyond physical death because in her estimation physical death means the absolute end. Therefore, this project argues — in sync with another eco-feminist, the Catholic Elizabeth Johnson (who of course joins with much of the criticism of Keller and those like-minded against escapism) — that "a solely immanentist end is not the only conceivable possibility, even within an ecological and feminist perspective." Indeed, Johnson goes so far as to argue (in agreement with feminist theologians from the Global South) that "hope for life with God after death for human persons and the whole earth not only does not cut the nerve for action on behalf of justice but actually sustains it, especially in violent situations. Furthermore, such transcendent hope, when cast into a nondualistic framework, functions critically and creatively to promote care for the earth precisely because it sees that this world has eternal value."[41]

This statement is in keeping with the "core intuition" of much of contemporary mainline eschatology as well as eco-theologies: "it is hardly possible to motivate people to care for the earth unless they are convinced that there is indeed some future for themselves on earth." Indeed, it is the case that despair before the impending eco-crisis most likely elicits resignation and apathy.[42]

In light of these criticisms of Keller's position, I find equally disappointing Ruether's own constructive proposal. Of course, I wholeheartedly support her view that "we need to dismantle the system of distortion that gives a privileged class overweening wealth and power at the expense of most humans and which is destroying the life-sustaining balances of the earth." But I also strongly disagree that in order for that to happen, "we will not expect a paradise free from tragedy and death, but rather a community of mutual life-giving where we can hold one another in the celebrative as well as the tragic moments of our common life as earth creatures."[43] Similarly, I am not convinced at all that her "vision of an ecological hope freed from false escapism and content to make common joys abundant and available to us all" should cast off all dreams

40. Similarly, McCall, *The Greenie's Guide to the End of the World*, pp. 46–50 (49).

41. E. Johnson, *Friends of God*, p. 197; I am indebted to McCall, *The Greenie's Guide to the End of the World*, p. 223.

42. Conradie, "What Is the Place of the Earth in God's Economy?" p. 75; similarly Haught, *The Promise of Nature*, p. 24.

43. Ruether, "Ecofeminism," pp. 29–30.

of an eschatological coming of the kingdom because of its selfish and egoistic implications due to hope for immortality.[44] While I also do not subscribe to a hope based on "an assurance of continuing progress in history," I definitely do cast my hope on "divine intervention to defeat God's enemies" (when appropriately understood, as detailed in the following chapter). For me that eschatological hope is not an obstacle but rather an incentive to join Ruether and others in the work of resistance, resulting in "a refusal to accept the dehumanizing oppression of ourselves or others and the counter-dehumanization of others, including those who are dehumanizing us and others."[45] Without repeating other criticisms against Ruether's proposal, similar to those of Keller's, it will suffice to repeat this question: How can it be that the lack of hope for the afterlife necessarily leads to concern for the earth; why not "destructive nihilism" instead?[46] And the other side of the coin: Why should we ultimately care about the cultivation of moral and ethical life if no postlife consequences are to be expected? I fear that for most people a "faceless" dream of immersion into the "matrix" of everything and a fatalistic assurance of lack of hope may not sound like empowering and inspiring good news.

An Eschatologically Funded Ecological Theology of Creation

As a constructive alternative, this project proposes boldly that genuine hope for the earth is supported by the hope for personal life beyond death[47] and a future for the whole cosmos in new creation.[48] In its widest horizon, a Christian eschatological vision includes not only human and cosmic hope but also hope for nature, the environment.[49] As Moltmann puts it succinctly, Christian eschatology awaits "the redemption *of* the world . . . [rather than] *from* the world" and the "redemption *of* the body . . . [rather than] a deliverance of the soul from the body" because "[t]heir eschatological future is a human *and* earthly future."[50] Christian eschatological vision values embodiment exactly

---

44. Ruether, "Ecofeminism," p. 30; in this context she is approvingly referencing both Ivone Gebara (see her *Out of the Depths*, pp. 109–44 particularly) and "The Women's Creed."

45. Ruether, "Eschatology in Christian Feminist Theologies," p. 339.

46. McCall, *The Greenie's Guide to the End of the World*, p. 71.

47. See also Brunner, Butler, and Swoboda, *Introducing Evangelical Ecotheology*, chap. 10.

48. For several important ecumenical projects with similar goals related to (but not limited to) the World Council of Churches, see Conradie, *Hope for the Earth*, pp. 249–58.

49. So also Horvath, *Eternity and Eternal Life*, p. 148.

50. Moltmann, *Coming of God*, pp. 259, emphasis added.

because of its hope for future life in a resurrected body, in communion with the triune God and other human persons, in the renewed cosmos. Indeed, it can be argued that to the "communion of saints" inclusively understood belong also animals and the whole of creation.[51] This vision is funded by the conviction that — against naturalism and reductionist-immanentist accounts — the universe "must make sense everlastingly, and so ultimately be redeemed from transience and decay."[52] It is confident that this kind of hope-filled expectation may provide a superior incentive for working toward preservation of the earth in anticipation of the "new heaven and new earth." Rather than wishing to be relinquished into the matrix of all things, created and sustained by the life-giving Spirit of God, we are destined for the attainment of the bodily resurrection based on Christ's resurrection. Having been created for the divine destiny, as Vatican II's *Gaudium et Spes* puts it (#22), human persons cannot achieve their fulfillment and goal if physical death and decay are the last word.[53] No mere this-worldly vision can satisfy that yearning; nor is the Christian hope to be seen as in any way antagonistic to the renewal of nature, but rather — as Paul teaches in Romans 8:18–22 — it joins the "groanings" of nature currently subjected under death and decay.

This nature-affirming eschatological approach to ecology joins in the critique of escapist and other destructive approaches. The South African eco-theologian Ernst M. Conradie has recently outlined a number of approaches to eschatological fulfillment that have varying ecological implications:[54]

- A "replacement" model ends up being more or less escapist and dismissive of the fate of the earth and the cosmos.
- The "recycling" model's vision (Keller, Ruether, and like-minded) is that our remains be "taken up in the great matrix of being and thus becom[ing] food for new beings to emerge," ultimately leading up to "a pantheistic omnipresence of the everlasting matrix of life" overlooking the need for the earth to be redeemed.[55]
- The "restoration" model, widely represented by traditional Protestant tradition, is anthropocentric in a dual sense: on the one hand, it takes human sin as the root problem of the world and hence requires the

51. See E. Johnson, *Friends of God*, p. 242 and passim.
52. Polkinghorne, *God of Hope*, p. 148.
53. So also Pannenberg, *ST* 3:523.
54. Conradie, "What Is the Place of the Earth in God's Economy?" pp. 82–92.
55. First citation from Conradie, "What Is the Place of the Earth in God's Economy?" p. 84, and second (cited therein) from Moltmann, *Coming of God*, p. 266.

incarnation for atonement; on the other hand, it envisions redemption only in relation to human destiny.

- An "elevation" model, in contrast to all the others, "allow[s] room for eschatological completion, fulfillment and consummation. Accordingly, salvation makes the ennobling, and not merely the restoration, of creation possible."[56] In that template Christ's incarnation, while the remedy for human sin, relates to wider cosmic purposes as well.

There is no need to elaborate the supremacy of the last model, the one in keeping with the current theological project.[57] I could not agree more with His Holiness the Patriarchate Bartholomew's remark that regarding ecological concerns "we should turn our attention to the future, to the age to come, toward the heavenly kingdom" with which "we do not imply a sense of escapism or other-worldliness . . . [but rather] a way of envisioning this world in light of the next."[58]

How might this Christian eco-sensitive and liberation-fostering trinitarian eschatological vision relate to views of other faiths? That will be the focus of the last section of this chapter.

Ecological Sensibilities and Obstacles in Religions' Visions of the "End"

Two deeply held opinions about religions' relation to nature and the environment are as persistent as they are noncritical and unnuanced. According to the first, Abrahamic traditions are inherently nonconservationist, if not even destructive toward nature. The complaints are well known since they are often repeated: God's transcendence does not cultivate an intimate relationship with nature; the Creator as "male" represents hierarchy, tyranny, and abuse; to humanity has been given the task of dominion rather than cultivation; and — for the sake of this discussion most importantly — the transcendent eschatological vision fosters escapism, neglect, and instrumental use of nature's resources (soon to be "burned" to ashes). According to the second widely held view, things are very different in Asiatic traditions, as they cultivate harmony, intimacy with nature, and the peaceful coexistence of all creatures.

Both beliefs are wrong at their worst and only half-truths at their best. Having discussed this matter with much detail concerning all four faith tra-

56. Conradie, "What Is the Place of the Earth in God's Economy?" p. 88.
57. Another such useful typology is provided by Haught, *The Promise of Nature*.
58. Bartholomew I, "Called to Be One Church."

ditions engaged in this project in *Creation and Humanity* (chap. 8), here we will repeat only the results of the investigation (without documentation) and relate them to eschatological hope. Since the first prejudice, as far as Christian faith is concerned, has been defeated above (and I will leave for Jewish and Muslim scholars to work out the details of their ecological sensitivities), let us focus here only on the second one.

The question of the ecological resources of Buddhism — widely lifted up as the most "green" philosophy — is highly complex and nuanced. Consider this: some leading Buddhologists and scholars who know Buddhism beyond superficialities warn us of appearances and often end up with a negative assessment of that tradition's alleged eco-friendly attitude.[59] Potential features in support of its green vision often include its alleged nonanthropocentrism, its focus on this-worldly ethical pursuit rather than centering on transcendental salvation, and Buddha's compassion toward all beings, among others. Let us focus here only on aspects relevant to eschatology. Unlike in Abrahamic traditions, in which nature has intrinsic value as the handiwork of a personal Deity, in Buddhism (deriving from classical Hinduism) and its cyclical view of time/history, nature is doomed to a repeated cycle of arising–maintenance–annihilation–return to "nothingness"–arising again — *ad infinitum.* "If this universe, which includes our Earth . . . is ultimately going to be annihilated, there is no motivation to take any steps to preserve it from inevitable destruction. In this context, the ecological deterioration of our Earth can be taken as an indication of the oncoming stage of annihilation, seen as an inevitable order of things, and therefore not as a cause for concern calling for action to try to stem it."[60] In light of this repeated annihilationist cycle, it is difficult for me to see how even the most foundational principle of interdependence (of everything on everything) would provide an environmental impetus. Similarly, the Buddhist soteriological-eschatological vision, against appearances, seems to be deeply anthropocentric and individualistic rather than cosmic and nature-embracing in its pursuit of liberation from *dukkha.* At the heart of the individual Buddhist's future "hope" is the coming to an end of one's life, the dissolution into nirvana — of a "person" who possesses "no-self." How would that vision necessarily cultivate either communal or cosmic sensibilities (outside some Christian eco-feminists' overly idealistic imagination, as discussed above)?

What about her parent religion, Hinduism? Obviously, similarly to

59. A prime example is R. Habito, "Environment or Earth Sangha"; my discussion is deeply indebted to his.

60. R. Habito, "Environment or Earth Sangha," p. 134.

Buddhism, the cyclical worldview potentially leans toward oblivion for the conservation of the earth. Furthermore, Hinduism's "appearance nature"[61] of reality and the cosmos as *līlā* ("play," that is, an unintended "by-product") similarly easily lead to considering this earth a secondary, temporary dwelling place. Other potential obstacles include the following: Can the strongly ascetic Hindu outlook (in pursuit of one's own deliverance) contribute to the communal (most widely understood, including nature) good? What is the role of karma, the bondage to the world because of deeds in the past and present, with regard to environmental care? What about the deeply *theologically* based and (originally) divinely sanctioned hierarchic nature of society (caste system) when it comes to ecological concern? Isn't that a prime manifestation of dualism and hierarchy, features harshly critiqued by Christian and secular eco-feminists? These kinds of considerations make me highly suspicious of popular promotional literature's claims for the inherently nature-affirming tendency of Hinduism.

Lest my observations coming from the Christian perspective be judged one-sided and ideological, I hasten to add two caveats. First, I am not denying *potential* eco-affirming, "green" resources in either Asiatic tradition (and I have highlighted some of them in the above-mentioned writing). I am rather seeking to dismantle the myth according to which Asiatic faiths and their "eschatological vision" *by nature* are eco-sensitive whereas Abrahamic faiths are the opposite. Second, I have lamented above the potential abuses and misuses of the environment in "Christian" lands; that is deplorable and unfortunate. Having said that, regretfully, I have to mention India (as the home of Hinduism) as one of the most environmentally catastrophic places in the whole world. I leave it to Hindu experts to reflect on the reasons. Moreover, Buddhist lands are doing no better. Without denying the reality of colonialist powers, just blaming "Western" or Christian influences does not suffice.

61. This does not mean that the world/cosmos does not exist; of course it does (even appearances are existents, albeit differently). What this complex term means (when overly simplified) is that what we think is truly "solid" and lasting, namely, the (physical) world as it appears to us, is just that: *appearance*. Beyond this appearance is the truly lasting "world."

8. Overcoming Evil and Defeating Violence

Theodicy in Christian Theology: A Need for Revision and Reassessment

Two Defining Traditions: Augustinian and Irenaean

The mystery of evil is not only a pressing philosophical-ethical conundrum; it is also a profound challenge to all theistic faiths, particularly Abrahamic traditions that insist on God's fairness, love, and goodness. Even Barth — who sought to avoid the task of justifying God's goodness in light of the presence of evil by pronouncing "creation as justification,"[1] that is, creation is good solely by virtue of that divine declaration — had to deal with theodicy.[2]

Named "the argument from neglect," the challenge to advocates of a personal God is this: Doesn't the lack of apparent divine intervention make belief in God a nonsensical posture?[3] Early modern atheists saw this clearly and spared no ammunition against Christianity — failing to see at the same time that evil and suffering are also a problem for atheists, albeit differently.[4]

---

1. Barth, *CD* III/1, §42.3.

2. See also Pannenberg, *ST* 2:163-64. Another telling example is N. T. Wright, who, throughout his *Evil and the Justice of God*, seeks to ignore (and more than that, somewhat pejoratively dismiss) all attempts by philosophers (and theologians) to construct a theodicy — and who then goes ahead and develops a biblically based defense of God in light of evil and suffering!

3. The term was coined by Wesley Wildman, himself a naturalist (nonpersonal) theist; see his "Incongruous Goodness, Perilous Beauty, Disconcerting Truth," pp. 277-78. For an important discussion, see Clayton and Knapp, "Divine Action," pp. 179-94.

4. Hick's note that for the atheist (*Evil and the God of Love*, p. 11) the theodicy question

The atheistic challenge has intensified considerably in the post-Enlightenment world with its shift from a theo-centric perspective, in which the highest good was identified with God, toward an anthropocentric perspective that assesses beliefs (including belief in God) in terms of humanity's benefits and concerns.[5] On a related theme, leading Enlightenment thinkers and cultural figures such as Voltaire, Hume, and Kant came to question the idea of the goodness of the world and the justification of the theodicy project at large.[6]

Theodicy is a highly complex issue, and the basic theological question about it is the negotiation among three kinds of claims: (1) God is perfectly good, (2) God is omnipotent, and (3) evil exists.[7] Negotiating among these three claims can result in vastly different solutions; that is the classic dilemma of theodicy. Unless one is willing to pay the price for compromising any of the three — almost universally assumed to be givens in classical theistic (at least Abrahamic) traditions — a dynamic tension between them must be tolerated.[8]

To make sense and provide a "big picture" of the complex theodicy reflections in Christian theology, John Hick famously suggested two traditions, or "orientations,"[9] namely, the Augustinian and the Irenaean.[10] For the Augustinian tradition — which heuristically means the whole Western Church's tradition through Thomas and the Protestant Reformers all the way to Barth — evil is merely a "privation," a lack of goodness. This does not undermine the reality of the empirical *experience* of suffering and pain; it is an ontological statement. Ultimately only good exists.[11] Indeed, not only is the world

---

is no problem is only a half-truth and as such quite mistaken: although technically the atheist does not have to account for the *theo*dicy part of the question, it is not true that the atheist "is not obliged to explain the universe." The atheist's explanation of the universe, including its suffering, just takes another form. See also Rowe, "The Problem of Evil and Some Varieties of Atheism."

5. Hvidt, "Historical Developments," pp. 21–22; for the oft-cited quotation, see C. S. Lewis, *God in the Dock*, p. 244.

6. Kant, *On the Failure of All Philosophical Attempts at a Theodicy*; for a reliable exposition of Kant, Hegel, and Nietzsche, see chaps. 2 and 3 in Suchocki, *The End of Evil*.

7. A classical formulation is Mackie, "Evil and Omnipotence," pp. 25–37. For the distinction between a "defense" and "theodicy," see Tilley, "The Problems of Theodicy," pp. 35–51; Hasker, *Triumph of God*, pp. 16–21.

8. For the negating of evil, as in Christian Science, see Hick, *Evil and the God of Love*, pp. 23–25. A radical version of limiting the power of God is represented by process theologians. A mildly promising new process theodicy is suggested by J. A. Keller, *Problems of Evil and the Power of God*.

9. Hvidt, "Historical Developments," p. 2.

10. Hick, *Evil and the God of Love*.

11. Augustine, *Enchiridion* 13; see also, e.g., *City of God* 11.9; so also Aquinas, *ST* 1.48.1.

very good because of God's creation, but the principle of plenitude even helps explain the presence of evil (maximizing its plenitude, the so-called aesthetic principle).[12] Along with privation, the key claim of the Augustinian view is that evil's origin is linked tightly with the human abuse of the God-given (in itself good) capacity for making choices. Even nature's suffering can be traced to the human Fall (and ultimately to the precosmic angelic fall),[13] the ultimate "whence" of all evil.[14] With the Fall came not only spiritual but also physical death (based on a certain reading of Rom. 5:12).[15]

The major alternative is the Irenaean-originated "the world as a vale of soul-making" tradition. This Eastern Church view of humanity leans more easily toward what Hick calls a "teleological" or "developmental" idea; rather than being perfected beings, humanity begins a long path of development toward maturity. In that process, evil, suffering, and other troubles help cultivate character. Thus, negative experiences serve the higher teleological purposes. An important — albeit historically unrelated — modern development is that of Schleiermacher, who similarly rejected the idea of original perfection and did not attribute all evil and suffering to human sin. According to Hick, perhaps the most revolutionary contribution of Schleiermacher was that he was "the first great theologian" to affirm openly that God is "ultimately ordaining sin and suffering," and hence, bears the ultimate responsibility.[16] Evil is instrumental for testing and maturity to take place.[17]

Hick himself takes up the Irenaean-Schleiermachian scheme in order to forge a contemporary version of a teleological, developmental theodicy.[18] On the one hand, he critiques the standard features of the Augustinian theodicy tradition, including its outdated mythical features (a literalist understanding of the Fall, a precosmic angelic fall, and so forth), its focus in the past, its abstract nature, its desire to absolve the Creator from responsibility, and its making evil

---

Augustine did not of course invent the notion; it can also be found earlier among the Eastern fathers: Origen, *De principiis* 2.9.2; Athanasius, *Against the Gentiles* 7; Gregory of Nyssa, *The Great Catechism* 7.

12. Augustine, *City of God* 12.4; 11.23.1.

13. See Hick, *Evil and the God of Love*, p. 85; Munday, "Animal Pain," pp. 435-68.

14. Augustine, *City of God* 14.27.

15. For details on Augustine and subsequent tradition, see Hick, *Evil and the God of Love*, part 2.

16. Hick, *Evil and the God of Love*, p. 228.

17. For details on Irenaeus and subsequent tradition, see Hick, *Evil and the God of Love*, part 3.

18. For comparison between the two traditions and Hick's reasons to opt for the Irenaean, see Hick, *Evil and the God of Love*, chap. 11.

merely a matter of human disobedience.[19] Thereby Hick advances significantly the discussion. A number of his moves are commendable: first, his teleological view is of course in keeping with current cosmic and anthropological evolutionary understanding; second, the refusal to relieve God of responsibility for evil and sin helps avoid dualism; and third, the loosening of the link between human sin and evil, particularly natural evil, is to be affirmed. At the same time, Hick's approach calls for significant qualifications and clarifications (on top of the fact that theologically I am not willing to follow his soteriological universalism). First, Hick's program's making *all* evil a matter of maturity can only be taken as a partial explanation. Undoubtedly, there is (much?) evil that has little to do with the maturity of any being. Consequently, this leads to what is obviously "the major challenge to Hick's theodicy: the existence of dysteleological evil, that is, evil ruthlessly destructive and damaging to persons, evil that seems disproportionate as punishment for wrongdoing and that obstructs the soul-making process."[20] Furthermore — and this is something Hick shares with the rest of the Christian tradition — what is still lacking in his theodicy is a cosmic, "evolutionary theodicy" in the sense of a robust account of natural evil[21] — although it takes important steps in the right direction. In other words, even Hick's theodicy is still hopelessly human centered and, hence, focused on this globe of ours. Suffering, pain, and evil in nature have received remarkably little attention — let alone physical natural evil such as earthquakes, hurricanes, the impact of asteroids, and so forth (apart from the immediate damage caused to humanity).[22] All in all, it lacks the vast cosmic dimensions appropriate for a comprehensive theodicy.

To combat and correct the merely human-centered tendency, a detailed "evolutionary theodicy," that is, a negotiation between the goodness of creation and Creator vis-à-vis rampant suffering and (natural) evil in nature, was constructed in the doctrine of creation.[23] Although that discussion will not be repeated here, it will be assumed and its implications will be carefully consid-

19. A useful summative comparison between the two traditions is chap. 12 of Hick, *Evil and the God of Love*.

20. S. Pinnock, *Beyond Theodicy*, p. 6.

21. Linzey, "Is Christianity Irredeemably Speciesist?" pp. xi–xx. Roughly similar to natural evil is "evolutionary evil," a term coined by Southgate, "God and Evolutionary Evil," pp. 803–21. For the term "cosmic theodicy," see R. Russell, "Physics, Cosmology, and the Challenge," p. 110.

22. For the inevitability of suffering and death in nature, see, e.g., Peacocke, *Theology for a Scientific Age*, pp. 63, 221.

23. My *Creation and Humanity*, chap. 8. Other such contemporary accounts include Linzey, *Animal Theology*; see also M. Murray, *Nature Red in Tooth and Claw*.

ered. What strikes me about the most well-known biblical account of evil — Job's narrative — is that it puts human suffering in the wider context of nature's beauty and wonder, as well as its suffering (chaps. 38-39). Indeed, Job's laments culminate and find resolution in "natural theodicy."[24] The close linking of human destiny — including evil and suffering — to that of nature and the cosmos helps us correct yet another major liability in tradition: the linking of evil and suffering to human sin, indeed, making the Fall the main culprit, as Augustine famously established it. Whatever connection there might be between sin and suffering, it seems to me nonsensical to make that in any way the main explanation for earthquakes, floods, and other "natural" catastrophes, as well as animal suffering. The four-billion-year evolutionary history of our planet alone would disqualify any proposal that leaves the reason for suffering until the last seconds of the timeline, as it were, until the appearance of humankind and its sinfulness.

Yet another reorientation is needed in order for a robustly theological[25] account of theodicy to function. That has to do with its location. Traditionally, theodicy has been placed in the context of creation (and providence). Although that choice is not mistaken in principle, theodicy ultimately belongs to eschatology, to the consummation of God's creational and providential purposes. Hence, its location not only belongs in the doctrine of creation (providence) but first and foremost in eschatology.[26] The only theologically sustainable hope for defeating evil is the turn to eschatological hope.[27] Otherwise, any purely theoretical, abstract theodicy reasoning is liable to the charge of Barth against Leibniz that ultimately his effort minimizes and trivializes the seriousness of evil and suffering.[28] Pannenberg describes the eschatological hope succinctly: "Hence it is only the union of creation and redemption against the background of eschatology that makes possible a tenable answer to the question of theodicy, the question of the righteousness of God in his work." Until then, "the world looks only at its uncompleted and unredeemed present," and the presence of evil remains but "an insoluble riddle and offense."[29] Indeed, the whole

---

24. See Bauckham, *Living with Other Creatures*, pp. 7-9.

25. Indeed, philosophers (of religion) have labored with this topic far more industriously than have theologians. Philosophers as early as the ancient Greeks attended to the theme; see Hvidt, "Historical Developments," pp. 14-16.

26. Similarly also Pannenberg, *ST* 2:161-74 (providence) and *ST* 3:632-42 (eschatology); see also chap. 8 in Hasker, *Triumph of God*.

27. For an important discussion highlighting the importance of Christ's suffering and eschatological hope for theodicy, see D. Edwards, "Why Is God Doing This?"

28. Barth, *CD* III/1, pp. 388-95 particularly.

29. Pannenberg, *ST* 2:164.

question of God is at stake since "only the eschatological consummation of the world will bring definitive proof of God's existence and final clarification of the character of his nature and works. Up to then the world in its autonomy vis-à-vis God and the absurdity of its suffering and wickedness will always provide material enough for . . . atheism."[30]

Beyond Theodicy: No Resolution but Resistance

Not surprisingly, not only some philosophers[31] but also many theologians, both Jewish and Christian, have rejected the whole project of theodicy in the post-Holocaust world[32] — or they have attempted a theistic "protest theodicy."[33] To these theologians the focus of theodicy should be shifted to practical ways of tackling suffering and evil rather than continuing philosophical-theological reflection.[34] In this turn, many are taking a lesson from Kant's refusal to speculate about the ways evil might relate to God and instead turn to "practical" responses.[35] Indebted to the Jewish atheist Ernst Bloch and his *Principle of Hope*,[36] Moltmann's *Theology of Hope* refuses to pursue an intellectual theodicy and rather seeks to ground the Christian response to suffering in concrete hope that is located in the suffering, death, and resurrection of Jesus Christ. His subsequent writings further develop the meaning of the suffering of the crucified, trinitarian God in the history of Jesus the Christ.[37] Rather than Job's friends who pursue the "why" question, Moltmann advises, we should seek company with the only "theological friend" Job had, the crucified Jesus.[38] The problem of suffering is not a theodicy question as much as it is "*the open wound of life* in this

30. Pannenberg, *ST* 3:631.

31. For an extended and harsh critique of the whole theodicy project from an analytic philosophical perspective, see D. Z. Phillips, *The Problem of Evil and the Problem of God*, pp. 49-94; for critical comments, see Hasker, *Triumph of God*, pp. 40-54.

32. S. Pinnock, *Beyond Theodicy*, p. xi.

33. Roth, "A Theodicy of Protest"; for comments and engagement, see Hasker, *Triumph of God*, chap. 2.

34. See Swinton, *Raging with Compassion*.

35. Kant, "On the Miscarriage of All Philosophical Trials in Theodicy" (1791), pp. 24-37. For a fine exposition of Kant's theodicy, see S. Pinnock, *Beyond Theodicy*, pp. 12-17.

36. For a detailed discussion of Bloch's relation to theodicy, see chap. 5 in S. Pinnock, *Beyond Theodicy*.

37. See further Bauckham, "Theodicy from Ivan Karamazov to Moltmann."

38. Moltmann, *Trinity and the Kingdom*, p. 47.

world" waiting for divine help.[39] If there is any theodicy left for Christian theology, Moltmann surmises, it is the hopeful and humble questioning with the dying Christ, "My God, my God, why hast thou forsaken me?"[40] Rather than trying to "justify" God, that questioning turns to the cross and "the theodicy trial on Golgotha."[41]

Similarly to Moltmann, several liberationists have found in Job a paragon not only of suffering but also of protest and rejection of theodicy explanations. Job takes on the role of advocate for those who suffer rather than seeking an abstract intellectual resolution.[42] The Roman Catholic liberationist Johann Baptist Metz's sociopolitically oriented theology echoes many of Moltmann's orientations (including deep engagement with the post-Auschwitz Jewish questioning) with its hopeful and patient tackling of suffering in society and positing its final resolution at the eschaton.[43] His approach has been appropriately named a "'theodicy-sensitive' religious response to suffering," in which faith and suffering, rather than being opposites, presuppose and shape each other.[44] Consider also the senior American black theologian James Cone, who seeks to go beyond the abstract turn to practical theodicy in his locating the experience of evil in "the struggle of an oppressed community for justice."[45] And so forth.

In response, let me mention the obvious: although suffering is an existential problem, it is not only that. It is a deep *theological* question as well. The turn to praxis should be welcomed — but not as an alternative to continuing sophisticated and careful "theoretical" thinking. In critique of (at times) naive calls for abandoning theodicies in favor of practical approaches, Michael Stoebe argues convincingly that it is rather a question about how to think of suffering and in what ways that may fund the work of helping those who suffer. He is in search of a theology of "transformative suffering" without in any way naively making suffering necessary.[46] Deepening of analysis and reasoning can go hand in hand with a more robust tackling of issues and cultivation of a pa-

39. Moltmann, *Trinity and the Kingdom*, p. 49, emphasis in original.

40. Moltmann, *The Crucified God*, p. 4; so also Moltmann, *Way of Jesus Christ*, p. 152.

41. Moltmann, *Way of Jesus Christ*, p. 171.

42. Gutiérrez, *On Job*, pp. 32-37. Sölle, *Suffering*, pp. 110-19. See also the masterful treatment of Job in chap. 4 of Tilley, *The Evils of Theodicy*.

43. Metz, *Faith in History and Society*.

44. S. Pinnock, *Beyond Theodicy*, p. 81; chap. 6 is an excellent discussion of Metz's "theodicy."

45. Cone, *God of the Oppressed*, p. 168 and passim; see p. x for rejection of theoretical theodicy.

46. Stoebe, "Transformative Suffering."

tient and hopeful attitude. Even more importantly: as soon as "posttheodicists" announce the rejection of the theodicy project, they begin to offer reasons about why and whence suffering, evil, and painful experiences. It would be utterly naive to think that "theory" and "praxis" — thinking and acting — could be separated from each other (as a modernist dualistic mind-set often implies). Hence, a "theodicy-sensitive" religious response to suffering (with or without a link with Metz) might be as good a nomenclature as any.

A distinct and novel current attempt to go beyond theodicy comes from American evangelicalism's progressive open-theism movement. Gregory Boyd's "trinitarian warfare" theodicy represents the more extreme forms of that orientation.[47] In his view, it is not that "God always has a specific reason for allowing evil deeds to occur" for the simple reasons that "at least sometimes God is *unable* to prevent them."[48] That is not only because there is this cosmic "warfare" going on but also because — given that God has granted irrevocable freedom to creatures — the world processes (with regard to their future possibilities particularly) are so complex that the future is open. Hence, God has no choice but to "genuinely battle if he is to accomplish his will."[49] It simply is not possible for God to create a world with free subjects without assuming risk. Indeed, God has "placed an irrevocable limitation on himself with his decision to create beings who have the capacity to love and who are therefore free."[50] Astonishingly, Boyd ultimately rejects even "natural" evil: "*All* evil ultimately derives from the wills of free agents" (human or spiritual beings).[51] Briefly stated: the warfare theodicy is beset with a number of challenges and unresolved problems. Having critiqued it in detail elsewhere,[52] I will mention in this context these problems: the denial of "natural evil"; the overestimation of human agency to suffering and evil; and the compromising of divine omniscience and omnipotence.

As much as there is value in the "practical" approaches to the problem of suffering, they should not lead to an abandonment of theological reflection

---

47. A moderate, "mainstream" open-theist theodicy building on the free-will defense is Hasker, *Triumph of God*; see particularly chaps. 6–8 for the constructive proposal. Indicative of the diversity within the movement is Hasker's total lack of engagement of Gregory Boyd (although Hasker wrote much later)!

48. G. Boyd, *Satan and the Problem of Evil*, pp. 13, 16.

49. G. Boyd, *Satan and the Problem of Evil*, p. 16.

50. G. Boyd, *Satan and the Problem of Evil*, p. 24; for a summary of six theses, see pp. 22–25; for details, see part 1.

51. G. Boyd, *Satan and the Problem of Evil*, p. 24, emphasis in original.

52. In *Spirit and Salvation*, chap. 4.

on theodicy. The reasons are many: first, because — as the discussion above shows — any "practical" tackling of suffering and work for liberation has to assume a theological framework; second, because theological reflection and resistance to evil do not have to be alternatives; and third, because failing to attempt theological reflection may lead one into highly problematic and counterproductive views of evil and suffering. Hence, below we attempt a constructive proposal in two parts.

Overcoming Evil as the Ultimate Eschatological Hope

On the Conditions and Parameters of a Theological Theodicy

Before anything else, this topic calls for a word on the approach to and "method" of the discussion of theodicy. First, when speaking of suffering and evil in relation to God, we must resist abstract, "nonpersonal" accounts. Second, we have to see the centrality of the "marginal" theodicies, that is, discussions that represent particular situations, victims, and questions, such as women, African Americans, the poor, rape victims, children, and so forth.[53] That is the lasting lesson of liberationist and other praxis-oriented approaches to suffering and evil. Finally, all suffering, whether human or nature's, has to be located in its ultimate cosmic context (if we believe that God is the creator of *all* that there is).

We should follow Augustine in that "metaphysical evil," namely, the finitude and "natural" limitations of the created reality in itself, is not sinful, as Leibniz mistakenly assumed;[54] indeed, creation is good even as something finite, including the material world.[55] Similarly correct is Augustine's denial of evil's ontological existence.[56] (That affirmation, however, should not lead us into the obscure and semimythical theory of Barth's about evil as *Das Nichtige,* "[the] Nothing.")[57] Evil is a later intrusion into God's world. Although evil and

---

53. Scott, "Theodicy at the Margins"; on "theodicy" from the perspective of suffering among women, see S. Jones, *Feminist Theory and Christian Theology,* pp. 69–93.

54. For an enlightening analysis of Leibniz's view and its checkered relationship to Augustine's, see Suchocki, *The End of Evil,* chap. 1.

55. See Hick, *Evil and the God of Love,* pp. 13–14, 45. The sinner's misuse of good things makes them sinful, that is, abandoning that which is ultimate good (God) for the created things (which, in themselves, are of course good). Augustine, *City of God* 12.6.

56. Similarly, for the *dis*order to be, there needs to be order. Tillich, *ST* 2:60. (However, I am not sure what to think of Tillich's idea of the "order" even in chaos.)

57. Barth, *CD* III/3, §50, "God and Nothing."

wickedness must have come with God's permission, "they are not objects of his will in the sense of reflecting his creative pleasure."[58] That said, Augustine's incapacity to provide any credible rationale for the rampant presence of evil, suffering, and pain in nature is untenable.[59] Even worse, it seems like his idea of plenitude makes nonhuman creatures and beings merely instrumental to the perfection of the universe.[60]

Although neither the exercise of human will nor human corruption can be made solely responsible for evil and suffering — not even in human life (as illustrated in rampant innocent suffering), let alone in the life of nature[61] — a carefully nuanced free will defense (FWD), such as that of the American analytic philosopher Alvin Plantinga (based on the Augustinian tradition), is useful. It is designed to rebut the atheistic charge that it is impossible for God and evil to coexist in any possible world. Simply put, the critics say, a good, omnipotent, omniscient God would want to prevent evil and be able to do so. To counter this objection to theism, Plantinga's defense aims to show that the existence of evil and the existence of God are logically compatible.[62] At least on a formal basis,[63] Plantinga is quite successful in establishing the minimum thesis that it is not impossible to think that God allows evil for a good and honorable purpose, in this case, for bringing about truly (relatively speaking) independent conscious beings endowed with freedom of choice. Free choice of course entails its misuse.[64] Where Plantinga errs is that (materially similarly to Augustine) he seeks to absolve God of responsibility, assuming that free, independent creatures rather than the Creator are to be held ultimately responsible.

Indeed, we have to reject the Augustinian (and Plantingan) reluctance to make God responsible for the entrance of evil in the world (as much as it

58. Pannenberg, ST 2:169.

59. While Augustine does not of course deny the existence of pain and suffering in animals, its description also follows that of his privation theory (Enchiridion 3.11).

60. Augustine, City of God 12.4.

61. So correctly already Schleiermacher; although he did not deny a connection between sin and suffering, neither did he attribute all (perhaps even most) evil to it (see CF §71.1, p. 315; §75.3, p. 317; and §59 postscript, pp. 243–44). He intuited correctly that with regard to natural evils, connection to human sin is only indirect (§76.2, p. 319).

62. Nontechnical, accessible discussions are Plantinga, "God, Evil and the Metaphysics of Freedom," pp. 83–109; Plantinga, God, Freedom, and Evil, part Ia.

63. In his earlier works, Plantinga focused so much on formal logic that his proposal stayed at a highly abstract level.

64. For insightful comments and cautious affirmation of Plantinga, see Hasker, Triumph of God, chap. 3 and passim.

was occasioned by legitimate opposition to Manicheism).[65] Although Judeo-Christian tradition never directly blamed God for evil, in the final analysis God is to be held responsible for allowing its presence in God's world.[66] Otherwise dualism follows and will not be resolved even eschatologically. Having decided to create this kind of world and independent creatures, God assumed (at least the indirect) responsibility for suffering and the misuse of freedom. The kind of evolutionary world we know entails growth and decay, pain and joy, birth and death, justice and injustice, ecstasy and pain.[67] Whether or not this is the "best possible world" of the Leibnizian theory,[68] it is a world filled with death and decay, suffering and pain, as well as violence and cruelty. Happily, we know from the biblical testimonies that God, the Creator, did not shirk responsibility for evil and suffering. According to the biblical testimony, God rather, in the suffering of his Son, embraced evil and made sin his own.[69] This shows that the God of the Bible is not a disinterested, deistic "Unmoved Mover," but a loving Father who shares in and helps overcome the suffering of the world.[70] With his creatures' joys, God rejoices; with their tears, he sympathizes. Under the neologism "classical panentheism," such a view of the trinitarian God was attempted in *Trinity and Revelation* (chaps. 10–12).[71]

Furthermore, the biblical promise includes the eschatological overcoming of both death and decay. Making God responsible for sin, however, should not lead theology to the conclusion of Schleiermacher, according to which God was "ultimately ordaining sin and suffering" and hence bears the ultimate responsibility.[72] Nor should we say that God wills sin — any more than, say, a medical doctor wishes a car accident in order to have a surgery. On the contrary, in a world like ours, car accidents — negative and bad events in themselves — happen, and surgery is a way to "redeem" many.[73]

65. G. Evans, *Augustine on Evil*, p. 98. More widely, Hvidt, "Historical Developments," pp. 16–20.

66. In that sense, it is wrong to say: "The purpose of theodicy is to propose reasons why God is not responsible for evil in the world." Hvidt, "Historical Development," p. 1.

67. See K. Ward, *Religion and Human Nature*, p. 248.

68. Leibniz, "Theodicy," pp. 194–204. For a succinct exposition, see Hvidt, "Historical Developments," pp. 23–26; Hick, *Evil and the God of Love*, pp. 154–68. For insightful discussion of the whole concept of the "best possible world(s)," see Hasker, *Triumph of God*, chap. 4.

69. Pannenberg, *ST* 2:165–66.

70. For an important application of *kenosis* to the God-world relationship, see Coakley, "Kenosis," pp. 192–210.

71. See also McFague, *Body of God*, p. 160.

72. As paraphrased by Hick, *Evil and the God of Love*, p. 228.

73. Cf. Hick, *Evil and the God of Love*, p. 232.

At the same time, we also have to handle with great care the Irenaean-Hickian insistence on the pedagogical and sanctifying role of suffering. Although no one contests the occasional redemptive value of suffering and pain, the limitations of that argument are severe and well known. First of all, it seems that much less (and much less random) suffering and pain would deliver the same results. Furthermore, this reasoning hardly helps explain natural catastrophes and much violence and pain.

"Cosmic Theodicy": The Final Resolution[74]

As mentioned, the foundational question to any theistic theology is the dual affirmation of the world created good and its existence in a state of dissipation, decay, and destruction as well as with the presence of evil and suffering. Only with confidence in the final overcoming of evil and entropy can the theodicy question be handled. Although cosmic theodicy (including natural theodicy) and human theodicy can be discussed separately (if not for other reasons, then for the limitations of the human mind), they are deeply and widely interrelated. A leading theme in this constructive project is to link them tightly together, as Christian eschatological hope encompasses the whole of creation, not only the destiny of humans. The overcoming of evil and death for humanity is intertwined with the destiny of the cosmos. It requires the redemption of time and space, as discussed above, as well as the transformation of embodiment as reflected in the bodily resurrection of Christ.

Reference to eschatological consummation raises the question of the redemption of *individuals*. Although the Christian eschatological vision includes not only the renewal of the cosmos but also of all creatures, realistically it is not justifiable to expect recompense in this life, either for humans or for other creatures. That is one of the reasons why dissolution into the matrix of everything and other similar nonpersonal end-time visions should be rejected. Only the hope for a personal physical resurrection in the renewed cosmos can deliver on the promise of individual recompense and fulfillment.

A related question has to do with the destiny of nonhuman creatures. Neither biblical nor theological tradition gives much guidance on this, other than the delightful pictures of the messianic peace and shalom, including the flourishing of nature, both in the shared portion of Jewish-Christian Scripture and at the end of the New Testament. Although this is not to expect similar

74. This section comes from my *Creation and Humanity*, pp. 205-7.

kinds of "religious ends" for humans and nonhumans, that is, the same kind of hope of the afterlife for nonhuman creatures as for men and women,[75] it is to envision an end according to each creature's kind. I couldn't agree more with Polkinghorne, who argues that "all creation must matter to the Creator in ways that are appropriate to its nature," for the simple reason that God, the Creator, has in the first place made every creature "according to its kind" (as repeated in Gen. 1). As a result: "The form that fulfillment will take will surely vary with the kind of creature involved." Hence, one does not have to believe that every bacterium, as he puts it brilliantly, has to await resurrection and eternal destiny![76]

Ultimately, the eschatological coming of the kingdom of God also brings about the needed monistic resolution: Abrahamic faiths can only have one ultimate reality, although prior to that, depending on one's theology, it seems like two powers are in place.[77]

Christian theodicy also raises questions about how this vision of the overcoming of evil may relate to hopes in other faith traditions. To that topic we turn next.

Evil and Suffering among Religions: The Challenge to Abrahamic Traditions

All religions are bound to offer some explanations for the presence of suffering and evil in relation to Ultimate Reality.[78] That said, each religious tradition has its own specific kinds of evils to account for.[79] Particularly pertinent is the challenge of theodicy among the three Abrahamic traditions. Hence, for the purposes of this constructive theological consideration, only Jewish and Islamic views are being engaged, whereas Buddhist and Hindu views are not (without in any way implying the immunity of either one to this issue).[80] The

---

75. Therefore I find mistaken the "pelican heaven," an afterlife hope for animals, of McDaniel, *Of God and Pelicans*, p. 45.

76. Polkinghorne, "Eschatological Credibility," pp. 48–49; see also Wilkinson, *Christian Eschatology*, pp. 159–70.

77. For details, see Hick, *Evil and the God of Love*, chap. 2.

78. See P. Berger, *The Sacred Canopy*, chap. 3. For a classic sociology-of-religion discussion of theodicy, see M. Weber, *Economy and Society*, pp. 518–26. An up-to-date overview is M. Peterson, "Religious Diversity, Evil," pp. 154–68.

79. See the important work of Bowker, *Problems of Suffering in Religions of the World*.

80. For theodicies in the Indian context, see Doniger, *The Origins of Evil in Hindu Mythology*; Herman, *The Problem of Evil and Indian Thought*.

reason for not engaging them is that neither Buddhism nor Hinduism (at large) traces evil and suffering to God. It is rather karma that functions as the main reference point.[81] In comparison to the deeply theo-centric Christian theodicy, Jewish and Islamic theodicies provide reasonable counterparts.

Jewish Theodicies — and Antitheodicies

As discussed, the rise of Jewish eschatology is widely attributed to the theodicy question, as the conviction arose that final resolution of innocent suffering can only be had in the life to come. The urgency of the theodicy question to Judaism is unsurpassable for several reasons.[82] First, unlike in the Asiatic religions, its turn to history — locating God's deeds in the historical arena — naturally raises the question of God's responsibility for evil. Second, its theology of election, based on the covenant, elicits the painful question of why this people has suffered so much.[83] The covenant points to a deeply personal relationship to God: "A Jew loyal to the covenant perceives every aspect of reality as expressive of the personal will of God."[84] Third, the sheer amount and absurdity of suffering, not only at Auschwitz but also throughout Israel's existence, make the issue a burning one.[85] Those painful and horrific experiences did not elicit the philosophers' fairly abstract and theoretical approach so much as it did existential anguish and questioning: "How is it logically possible to claim that God is the just Lord of history in view of the senseless evil manifest in the world?" Rather than trying to "justify" God, the focus is on how the people of God can maintain their trust in Yahweh. With Job they ask: "Why do you hide your face and treat me like an enemy?"[86]

Not surprisingly, Jewish tradition does not speak with one voice when it comes to relating evil to God.[87] In light of Israel's covenant theology, questions such as the following beg for a response: Could Yahweh be put on trial? Or is suffering merely a matter of the chosen nation's lack of faithfulness? Although the Deuteronomic tradition more or less unequivocally sees evil as the result of disobedience, in some later Old Testament traditions in the Writings and

---

81. Green, "Theodicy," p. 9112.

82. For an up-to-date standard discussion, see Neusner, "Theodicy in Classical Judaism."

83. For a construction of a Jewish theology of election, see my *Spirit and Salvation*, chap. 9.

84. Hartman, "Suffering," p. 939.

85. Braiterman, *(God) after Auschwitz*, pp. 5-6 and chap. 2.

86. Hartman, "Suffering," pp. 940–41.

87. See Schwartz, "The Meaning of Suffering," pp. 444–51.

the Prophets, final retribution and vindication are relegated to the eschato-logical future and "new covenant." The testimony of Job also offers a decisive rebuttal to the Deuteronomic direct cause-and-effect link between suffering and human behavior.[88] In the final analysis, the Old Testament contains several perspectives on the question of suffering, and no neat solution is available on a scriptural basis alone.[89] This much can be said: there is a marked shift between the pre- and postexilic teachings on suffering and evil. Whereas in the former, God is seen as the sovereign source of both good and evil, after the catastrophe a more dualistic understanding begins to emerge in which God's power and human disobedience each play their roles. At the same time, confidence in the capacity of God to bring good out of evil — as is evident in the life testimonies of Joseph and Job — is maintained.

Later Jewish literature includes voices that tell us "everything God does is for the good" (*b. Berakhot* 60b) and "nothing evil dwells with God" (mid-rash on Ps. 5:7).[90] Hence, evil must have come through some other interme-diary, most prominently human freedom to sin (as attested in Lev. 26:14–20 and Deut. 11:13–17). This is the theory of divine retribution, which does not deny but presupposes divine mercy, but not without punishment (in order to maintain God's holy nature). In Jewish liturgy this theme appears frequently. Similarly to the Christian tradition, divine retribution is often linked with messianic redemption and eschatological fulfillment.[91]

At some point, the divine-retribution template turns out to be unsatis-factory to those who suffer too much and too long, without seeing any sign of retribution (see Jer. 12:1–2; Job 9:24). Not surprisingly, by the time of the Holocaust, retribution theology came under radical shaking and revision — to the point that many Jewish theologians saw it as completely useless for the post-Holocaust world.[92] B. L. Sherwin rightly notes that while retribution theodicy may be able to explain *some* suffering, it is not able to do so for *all* or even most of it, particularly innocent suffering. It attempts to absolve God from evil and lay the burden on humanity. In contrast, some strands of scriptural theology dare to attribute both evil and good to God (Lam. 3:38; Isa. 45:7; Job 2:10; Eccles. 7:14). This is what some contemporary Jewish scholars name "dysteleological surd."[93] Indeed, "in a monotheistic faith evil as well as

---

88. M. Peterson, "Religious Diversity, Evil," pp. 156–57.
89. See further J. McDermott, *The Bible on Human Suffering*.
90. Both cited in Sherwin, "Theodicy," p. 960.
91. Sherwin, "Theodicy," pp. 960–63.
92. See, e.g., Berkovits, *Faith after the Holocaust*, p. 89.
93. Sherwin, "Theodicy," pp. 963–65.

good must ultimately be referred back to God";[94] this is similar to the way this project argues.

As mentioned, a number of leading theologians, both Jewish and Christian, in the second half of the twentieth century have rejected a theodicy project for the simple reason that "[t]o speak the name of Auschwitz in the same sentence as the word 'theodicy' seems unconscionable."[95] To be more precise, different types of responses have emerged in the post-Shoah era, from protest atheism, to nontheistic responses, to Deism, to reaffirmation of traditional Jewish theism.[96] Although not totally rejecting theodicy, Martin Buber gleans widely from the Hebrew Bible and Hasidic literature to outline "a narrative faith response to suffering."[97] For Eliezer Berkovitz, Job's example speaks of the necessity to hold on to faith even when one cannot understand why things are the way they are; holding on to faith is still greatly to be preferred over the "humbug of disbelief."[98] God's hiddenness in Auschwitz does not mean God's absence. Clearly, this is not a theodicy in the traditional sense. It is a call for the patience of faith and trust.[99] Dan Cohn-Sherbok makes the very important remark that there is one consistent defect in all these different attempts to cope with the Shoah, namely, the lack of eschatological vision. Although it is true that in general Jewish tradition does not assign to the afterlife the kind of significance present in the two other Abrahamic faiths, the virtual lack of reference to the afterlife is stunning indeed from a Christian point of view. Jewish tradition could take a lesson from its own history, from the rise of the hope for an afterlife in the Maccabean period, amidst great suffering.[100]

While contemporary Jewish theologians continue pursuing different paths for tackling suffering and evil, Christian theologians should acknowledge in a repentant spirit that "Christianity has failed to grasp the crucial nature of the questions raised by the Holocaust for its own theology and fu-

94. Sherwin, "Theodicy," p. 966.

95. See Rubenstein, *After Auschwitz*, p. 153; Wiesel, "A Plea for the Dead," p. 71.

96. For a survey, see Cohn-Sherbok, "Jewish Faith and the Holocaust"; for important discussions, see the collection of essays by leading scholars: Katz, ed., *The Impact of the Holocaust on Jewish Theology*.

97. So described in S. Pinnock, *Beyond Theodicy*, p. 46; chap. 3 is an excellent discussion of Buber's scattered writings relevant to theodicy and suffering.

98. Berkovitz, *Faith after the Holocaust*, p. 6.

99. A materially similar kind of view is that of Maybaum, *The Face of God after Auschwitz*.

100. Cohn-Sherbok, "Jewish Faith and the Holocaust," pp. 289–91.

ture, just as it generally has refused to admit any responsibility for the death camps."[101] Happily, some Christian theologians have recently begun to engage the theodicy question in a more intentional manner from the perspective of the Jewish experience.[102] Along with the Protestants Moltmann and Dorothee Sölle, the Roman Catholic Johann Baptist Metz has pursued a "theodicy question in the face of Auschwitz."[103] Rather than trying to defend God, he is seeking ways to help those who suffer reach salvation.[104] He is not totally rejecting the classical theodicy project but recommends "theodicy-sensitive" work on behalf of the victims and those who suffer.[105]

Obviously theodicy — or antitheodicy — reflection stands at the heart of Jewish faith. Based (partially) on the same scriptural traditions as Christianity, Israel's theodicy is similar in many ways to that of her younger sister faith while also challenging it, boldly ascribing suffering to Israel's God. In the pluralistic world of ours, a joint venture toward a more coherent "theodicy-sensitive" collaboration is necessary and useful for both faith traditions.

Suffering and Evil in Light of Allah's Sovereignty and Justice

What should we think of Kenneth Cragg's claim that the theodicy project is not important for Islam because of its extreme emphasis on divine transcendence and desire to submit to Allah's will?[106] It certainly is true that at the center of Islamic tradition is God's unqualified power rather than divine vindication, as it is in Judeo-Christian theodicies.[107] As a result, the urgency of theodicy in Islam is far less intense than in Judaism. That said, there is also a long tradition of reflection on suffering and evil. Just think of the narrative of Job — "Ayyub" (one of the prophets!) — scattered over several places (Q 4:163; 6:84; 21:83; 38:41–44).[108] In keeping with Islam's stress on Allah's sovereignty,

---

101. Eckardt, "The Holocaust," p. 453.

102. For a representative survey and assessment across the ecumenical spectrum, see Willis, "Christian Theology after Auschwitz"; Hawk, "Recent Perspectives on the Holocaust"; David, "The Holocaust and the Problem of Theodicy."

103. Metz, "Facing the Jews," p. 31; for an insightful engagement, see S. Pinnock, *Beyond Theodicy*, chap. 8.

104. Metz, "Theology as Theodicy?" p. 55.

105. See S. Pinnock, *Beyond Theodicy*, pp. 93–96.

106. Cragg, *The House of Islam*, p. 16; I am indebted to Green, "Theodicy," p. 9118.

107. For the absolute omnipotence in Islam, see Ormsby, *Theodicy in Islamic Thought*, pp. 17–18. For the Qur'an, consult, e.g., 2:20, 215; 21:23; 35:1.

108. Muslim commentators seem to adopt many missing details (in the short Qur'anic

it is understandable that the role of Satan ("the evil one") is more marginal in the Qur'anic account than in the Old Testament. This is also in keeping with the Qur'anic teaching that Satan has no other power over humans than that of suggestion (15:42; 58:10). Although Ayyub stands out as the paragon of patience in the midst of calamities,[109] the focus overall is less on theodicy and more on the instructions God gives Ayyub for him to settle the problems. Significantly also, there is no hint of the biblical wager between Satan and God to test the loyalty of Ayyub.[110]

In light of the divine sovereignty, almost an antitheodicy results. This is not to deny the equally strong insistence in the Qur'an of the compassion of Allah, but rather to indicate the main focus of discussion in this arena. Nor is it to ignore the fact that, somewhat similarly to Judaism (although less vocally expressed), at times suffering may be taken as punishment for sin. The Qur'an cites many examples of this, including Moses and the killing of Pharaoh's army in the Red Sea or the battle in which Meccans defeated the Muslims at Uhud.[111] That said, in light of divine omnipotence, the idea of suffering as the test of character and faithfulness is more prominent a theme in the Qur'an. One example is this widely used saying among Islamic scholars: "O my son! Gold and silver are to be examined by fire and the believer is to be examined by affliction."[112] Furthermore, similarly to Judaism and Christianity, Islam also invokes the final eschatological resolution.[113]

The first philosophically oriented theodicy projects were attempted by the Mu'tazilite school. Unqualified omnipotence with a rationalistic notion of divine justice, including belief in freedom of will, appeared to many to lead not only to an overemphasis on reason but also to an abstract, nonpersonal account of the omnipotence of God. The Ash'arites, soon the main "orthodox" school (beginning from the tenth century C.E.), sought a more scripturally based account of divine omnipotence that, however, left little room for free will. Whereas for the Ash'arites the belief in divine justice was ultimately just

---

narrative) found in the Old Testament. See Yazicioglu, "Affliction, Patience and Prayer." Thematic similarities between the Old Testament and Qur'anic depictions of Job are highlighted extensively in the little study of Maqsood, *The Problem of Evil*.

109. See Yazicioglu, "Affliction, Patience and Prayer."

110. For a fine discussion, see Mukhtar, "A Comparative and Critical Analysis of the Story of Job."

111. M. Peterson, "Religious Diversity, Evil," p. 162.

112. M. Peterson, "Religious Diversity, Evil," p. 163.

113. For an important recent analysis of both philosophical and practical approaches to theodicy in Islam, see Ghaly, *Islam and Disability*, chaps. 2 and 3.

that, *belief,* the Mu'tazilites assumed that divine justice can be both understood and defended on the basis of rational reasoning. Hence, it led to a quite strict notion of justice, including that God always has to reward good works and punish evil.[114] The strict affirmation of divine omnipotence also raised an important problem with regard to the presence of faith (or lack thereof) in God: How is it that even disbelief is not attributed to Allah if no freedom of will exists? Not surprisingly, similarly to Augustine,[115] a suggestion was made that indeed free will is needed to help absolve God from responsibility.[116]

With their strict, rationally based stress on divine justice, the Mu'tazilites not only wished to separate God from all evil but also, importantly, reasoned that God is obliged to provide "the optimum" (that is, "the most salutary/beneficial" option) for his creatures, an idea that raised the question among their opponents (including some within the school) of the obvious danger of limiting absolute divine freedom.[117] No wonder the concept stayed highly contested. An important insight on the Ash'arite side, with the emphasis on divine volition,[118] was to make God the author of both good and evil. This leads of course to an "extreme predestinarian position, according to which not only suffering or blessedness but the acts and volitions that lead to them are totally in the hands of God."[119] This determinism, however, does not lead to questioning, let alone blaming, Allah for lack of justice or fairness, as it was firmly believed that divine justice and human justice operate according to different criteria.[120] At the same time, it leads to a kind of privation theory of evil, as it was believed that "good and evil were determined by divine fiat."[121] The privation view indeed became the standard position in later tradition. Notwithstanding many internal debates, Ormsby succinctly summarizes the leading intuitions of Islamic theodicy shared by most classical movements: "The frank ascription to God of evil as well as of good, the strict reliance on the sovereign efficacy of the divine will, the belief that everything that occurs is the direct and inevitable result of the divine decree — these elements, which do

114. A highly useful short primer is Robinson, "Ash'ariyya and Mu'tazila."

115. For a useful and knowledgeable engagement of Augustine in the context of Islamic theodicy, see Adeel, "Divine Justice and the Problem of Evil."

116. Ormsby, *Theodicy in Islamic Thought,* pp. 198–217.

117. See Heemskerk, *Suffering in the Mu'tazilite Theology,* p. 24.

118. Note this oft-cited dictum on divine volition: "What He wills, is; what He does not will, is not." Ormsby, *Theodicy in Islamic Thought,* p. 24.

119. Green, "Theodicy," p. 9118.

120. See further Green, "Theodicy," pp. 9118–19.

121. Ormsby, *Theodicy in Islamic Thought,* p. 24.

represent a severe form of fatalism, are also, however, the very elements upon which a distinctive Islamic version of theodicy would be erected. 'Fatalism,' after all, may itself be a response to the dilemma of theodicy."[122]

As on most other topics, no scholar surpasses in significance the leading Islamic (Ash'arite) thinker al-Ghazali. His most well-known dictum is: "There is not in possibility anything more wonderful than what is."[123] This is of course another version of Leibniz's interpretation of the "best possible world." Unknown to Westerners until recently, this one sentence of the master was a center of intense internal Muslim debate from the twelfth century to the nineteenth century. Al-Ghazali's statement means that for both the natural and the social orders, what actually is, is the best possible way for things to be. He also reminds us that while perfect (for its God-given goal), the world is totally and always contingent on the Creator. It is not self-sustained.[124] Ibn Taymiyya follows suit.[125] In that sense, both of the masters are "optimists"[126] — Leibnizians before Leibniz himself![127]

At the same time, Ibn Taymiyya expands and elaborates the concept of justice and theodicy. He is fond of a three-tiered typology of divine justice: the Mu'tazilite "retributive" (in the sense that God strictly metes out rewards for good and punishments for evil), the Ash'arite volitional, and a third type of his own in which he defines God's justice as putting things in their proper places.[128] Ibn Taymiyya rightly critiques the Mu'tazilites for applying the strict rational template as a limit on and definition for God's justice. His problem with the Ash'arites is that their template would make any notion of injustice impossible: How could God really will bad or evil? His own approach defines "injustice" in terms of putting something in a place other than its own proper place, and he defines "justice" as putting a thing in its own right place. While not explicitly mentioning it, he must have had al-Ghazali's "best possible world" template in mind; although that opinion does not have to expect a perfect world, it assumes perfection in relation to

122. Ormsby, *Theodicy in Islamic Thought*, p. 25.

123. In Ormsby, *Theodicy in Islamic Thought*, p. 32; for a detailed analysis of this idea in al-Ghazali, see chap. 1 in Ormsby, *Theodicy in Islamic Thought*.

124. See Ormsby, *Theodicy in Islamic Thought*, pp. 259–65.

125. Hoover, "Justice of God," p. 75; for a whole monograph, see Hoover, *Ibn Taymiyya's Theodicy of Perpetual Optimism*.

126. It is ironic that in many other respects Ibn Taymiyya harshly critiques the other two!

127. For an important discussion of Mulla Sadra's relation to optimistic theodicy, see Kalin, "Mulla Sadra on Theodicy and the Best of All Possible Worlds."

128. Hoover, "Justice of God," pp. 57–71.

the highest goal.[129] Of course, materially this opinion is not too far from retributive justice either because the assumption is that to the evil belongs punishment and to the good, reward. The difference is subtle but important: here there is no semi-automatic compulsion put over divine justice, but rather, a faith-based expectation of the architect of justice acting justly. God's mercy and goodness accompany justice more robustly than in the Mu'tazilite rigorous view of God's omnipotence and justice. But in order to counter the obvious critique that thereby he is beginning to compromise God's power, Ibn Taymiyya hastens to note that in principle God *could* do injustice even though he is not doing it.[130]

This brief consideration of approaches to suffering and God's justice in Islam evinces deep diversity between different schools, not unlike among its older sister traditions. Noteworthy is the material similarity in the conception of evil as privation with the classic Christian (Augustinian) notion. An important "global" difference from Christian theodicies is Islam's strict focus on divine determinism rather than vindication of Allah. The most radical difference, however, has to do with the role of the suffering Messiah of Christian tradition. It is rejected completely as a way to explain suffering, because "paragons of success and vindication" such as Abraham, Noah, Moses, and David are much more appealing to Islam; indeed, "the Passion would imply in its eyes that God had failed."[131] A related reason for the rejection is that the diametrically different idea of atonement does not know any kind of substitutionary act.

The remaining question with regard to evil has to do with violence. There is wide suspicion out there that a theistic imagination of the overcoming of evil necessarily entails violence. To that problematic we turn last in this chapter.

Defeating Violence and Establishing Peace in the Eschaton

Violence is part of all religions' texture and history, whether Christian or others.[132] Therefore, for any credible constructive theology in the beginning of the third millennium, a careful consideration of the theme is urgent (particularly because of its rampant omission in most systematic theologies). *Christ*

129. See Hoover, "Justice of God," p. 71.
130. Hoover, "Justice of God," pp. 71-72.
131. Merad, "Christ according to the Qur'an," pp. 14, 15, quoted in Leirvik, *Images of Jesus Christ in Islam*, p. 4.
132. Nelson-Pallmeyer, *Is Religion Killing Us?*

and Reconciliation (chap. 12) attempted a careful assessment and combating of charges concerning the alleged necessary violence-laden nature of Christian theology of atonement focused on Christ's suffering and death. In *Trinity and Revelation* (chap. 13), a detailed response to the widely held prejudice according to which belief in God/gods in itself leads to violence and exclusive "tribalism" is offered. While those lengthy discussions will not be repeated here, their results are assumed (including a careful assessment of the presence of violence and resources for peace among four other faith traditions). The present discussion will focus solely on the question of the alleged violence in relation to the coming of the new creation, execution of justice, and establishment of divine rule over the cosmos.

Before anything else, one important reminder: having acknowledged the potential for violence among religions, in the name of fairness we hasten to add that violence is also part of atheist and other secular ideologies' record. Just think of those 70 million people claimed to have died at the hands of communists, among them of course a large number of believers of various faiths. Rightly, then, the Radical Orthodox thinker John Milbank argues that even secularism and late modernity cannot save us from violence. On the contrary, associating secularism with "paganism," he contends that such systems are ultimately about the worship of sheer power and thus foster violence. That ideology also accepts the basic forces of the world as brute givens of fate, fortune, and chance.[133] In light of these impending challenges, we can only hope that atheists would labor more intensely in constructing a program of hospitality and nonviolence.

Christian theology of creation is based on the goodness of creation (Gen. 1:31) and cultivates graceful hospitality. As a result, it refuses to ontologize violence, war, and conflict. In that respect, its vision differs from those theories of religion that assume an ontology of violence. Regretfully, that is the case even in the most ambitious attempt to defeat violence, namely, the French anthropologist René Girard's mimetic theory. We engaged Girard extensively in Christology (*Christ and Reconciliation*, chap. 12), so it suffices here to say that because of its fixation on a certain interpretation of religion's link with the scapegoat (sacrifice), it is unable to ultimately defeat violence (other than by naively assuming that by exposing the cycle of violence due to the scapegoat mechanism people suddenly refrain from violence!).[134] In the Christian vision

---

133. Shakespeare, *Radical Orthodoxy*, K ##312–15.

134. See further Boersma, *Violence, Hospitality, and the Cross*, pp. 134, 138, and passim; Milbank, *Theology and Social Theory*, p. 395.

of peace and reconciliation, diversified unity linked with loving and inclusive embrace of the other is ontologically founded in the triune God. Covenant love stands at its heart. As a result, its celebration of (rather than opposition to) diversity-in-unity is far superior to establishing peace and reconciliation over the secular ontology of immanence, which is nothing less than an "ontology of violence" and therefore inherently "conflictual."[135]

Although violent death stands at the center of Christian theology of reconciliation, that violent death is for the ending of all violence — and for the atonement of sins. As Miroslav Volf puts it, "the Crucified Messiah" absorbs aggression as it challenges violence by unearthing scapegoating and struggling actively against it. Ultimately, then, Christ's cross is an act of embrace of his opponents. It also makes it possible for human beings to embrace the enemies.[136]

I agree with Volf's argument that while humans have no right to violence, God does, as divine use of force is free from perversion and self-serving motives. Taking his cue from the vision of Revelation 19, Volf concludes: "The end of the world is not violence, but a nonviolent embrace without end," which leads to the conflation rather than separation of the images of the "victorious rider on the white horse" and the "sacrificial lamb": "The world to come is ruled by the one who on the cross took violence upon himself in order to conquer the enmity and embrace the enemy. The Lamb's rule is legitimized not by the 'sword' but by its 'wounds.' . . . With the Lamb at the center of the throne, the distance between the 'throne' and the 'subjects' has collapsed in the embrace of the triune God."[137] It is clear that humans have no right whatsoever to imitate violence; humans are not gods.[138] The key here — to repeat the statements above — lies in the nature of the triune God as the God who embraces rather than excludes:

> The starting point is the primacy of the will to embrace the other, even the offender. Since the God Christians worship is the God of unconditional and indiscriminate love, the will to embrace the other is the most fundamental obligation of Christians. The claim is radical, and precisely in its radicality, so socially significant. The will to give ourselves to others and to welcome them, to readjust our identities to make space for them,

---

135. Milbank, *Theology and Social Theory*, pp. 376, 296 (quote in the latter).

136. Volf, *Exclusion and Embrace*, pp. 291-95.

137. Volf, *Exclusion and Embrace*, pp. 300-301. See also Boersma, "Irenaeus, Derrida and Hospitality."

138. Volf, *Exclusion and Embrace*, pp. 301-2.

is prior to any judgment about others, except that of identifying them in their humanity. The will to embrace precedes any "truth" about others and any reading of their action with respect to justice. This will is absolutely indiscriminate and strictly immutable; it transcends the moral mapping of the social world into "good" and "evil."[139]

The questions of theodicy and violence also are interrelated with the problem of religious ends, the topic of the following chapter. It asks whether God has the "right" to determine every human person's eternal destiny.

---

139. Volf, "Forgiveness, Reconciliation," p. 872. For details, see Volf, *Exclusion and Embrace.*

9. A Christian Theology of Religious Ends in the Pluralistic World

The Traditional Theology of Two Destinies and Its Rebuttals

The Dilemma of Hell

All Abrahamic traditions and Asiatic faiths engaged in this project endorse the doctrine of hell as an unparalleled eschatological suffering and penalty. Although there are diverse views in Judaism, the mainline belief is that those who do not obey Yahweh, along with heretics and the like, should prepare for eternal judgment. The destiny of Gentiles is disputed. Similarly to modern Christian tradition, among Jews there are diametrically opposed beliefs about the reality of hell — for and against. Islamic tradition has unusually rich traditions about hell.[1] Regarding Asiatic faiths, a persistent misunderstanding among those who do not know either Buddhist or Hindu traditions is that neither one includes hell; particularly with the former, nothing could be more wrong — the notion of *kamma* alone makes hell necessary.[2] The many uses of hell in Hinduism are also well known to experts.[3]

Both advocates and opponents freely grant a strong biblical support for what became the Christian doctrine of hell, whether one thinks of the Old Testament (Isa. 66:15-16; Jer. 7:30-34; 19:6; Dan. 12:2; Joel 3:1-2)[4] or the New

---

1. Thomassen, "Islamic Hell," pp. 401-16.
2. For a recent useful study, see Braarvig, "The Buddhist Hell."
3. Jacobsen, "Three Functions of Hell in the Hindu Traditions."
4. The Greek transliteration *gehenna* comes from the Hebrew *ge hinnom*, a valley south

Testament, both in relation to Jesus traditions (Matt. 13:42, 49–50; 22:13; 24:51; 25:10–46; and Synoptic parallels)[5] and apostolic teachings (2 Thess. 1:9; Heb. 6:2; Jude 7; Rev. 14:10–14).[6] That said, despite its wide, almost universal attestation in Christian tradition until modernity, there is no single understanding of hell.[7] What might be called the "traditional" understanding (in the sense that it has occupied the majority position throughout history) includes the following arguments (or something close to them): hell is for punishment for sins in earthly life and refusal to receive forgiveness from God; it is a final judgment from which there is no escape once executed;[8] at least part of humanity will end up there (against soteriological universalism); and it invokes the "eternal existence thesis: hell is a place of conscious existence."[9] Although this traditional model continued throughout history, particularly in the medieval and pre-Reformation times, a close relation to the sacrament of penance was established, to the point that rightly conducted penance helps save one from the torments of hell.[10] An important alternative model is that which denies the eternity of hell (in terms of unending existence).[11] That version fits both universalism, according to which after one has suffered for a period of time in hell, all will be saved, and annihilationism, which teaches the ultimate destruction (coming to an end) of those who are not believers. Yet another revision of the traditional interpretation — which can be called the "punishment model" — considers hell rather the outcome of one's own

of Jerusalem where garbage was brought and children were sacrificed to Molech in fire (2 Kings 16:3; 2 Chron. 28:3; 33:6). Details are readily available in standard biblical encyclopedias.

5. See Geach, *Providence and Evil*, pp. 123–24.

6. Grenz, *Theology for the Community of God*, p. 641. In addition to standard biblical encyclopedias, useful is the recent detailed study of New Testament perspectives by Clark-Soles, "The Afterlife," pp. 65–74; more widely: Clark-Soles, *Death and Afterlife in the New Testament*, pp. 9–59. Also highly informative is Kyrtatas, "The Origins of Christian Hell," pp. 282–97.

7. No fewer than six different variations are identified in J. Walls, *Hell*, pp. 10–15 (throughout this section, my discussion is indebted to Walls); see also Crockett, ed., *Four Views on Hell*.

8. Academically and scientifically worthless is the speculation that the traditional view of judgment can be attributed to the perverted human mind and desire for vengeance, as suggested by Barnhart, *Religion and the Challenge of Philosophy*, pp. 126–27. The role of human belief in relation to hell is insightfully analyzed in chap. 1 of J. Walls, *Hell*.

9. Kvanvig, "Hell," p. 414. The sermon of "America's preacher," Jonathan Edwards, "Sinners in the Hands of an Angry God," is routinely lifted up as a template for a traditional model; see further J. Walls, *Hell*, pp. 1–2; for critical scrutiny of the biblical basis of the sermon, see Pauley, "Soundly Gathered Out of the Text?"

10. For details, see Rasmussen, "Hell Disarmed?"

11. E.g., the Dutch Reformed theologian Hendrikus Berkhof, *Well Founded Hope*, p. 62.

choices. In other words, hell means the honoring of the human person's choice to live separately from God.[12]

That hell is not a favorite topic among contemporary theologians — let alone in wider culture[13] — may have some historical and theological justification to it.[14] Unlike frequent depictions in popular Christian imagination, hell was not in any way the focus of early Christians' hope for the future. Rather, they "portrayed an optimistic certainty concerning salvation and focused much more on heaven as a desirable state to reach." While belief in the resurrection of the body and eternal life is affirmed in the early creeds, they contain no mention of hell. Only after the establishment of Christianity as a state religion with unprecedented mass conversions and a rapid increase of nominalism did the need to highlight the reality of perdition give the topic increasing significance. By the Middle Ages, occupation with hell had become an intensive affair.[15]

It is curious that while no major works on the doctrine of hell were produced for over one hundred years before the 1960s, interest has picked up since.[16] Both rebuttals and revisionist attempts have emerged as a result. I find the following revisions to the traditional model theologically rightly guided and useful: First, physical punishment and suffering are not an integral or necessary part of the doctrine. Metaphors such as "gnashing of teeth" and similar in the Bible are just that, *metaphors*. Second, punishment does not have to be the leading motif (although it is certainly an aspect in biblical testimonies): the logic of hell may be supported by other forms of justice (such as restorative), the integrity of the divine nature, the irrevocability of human freedom, and so forth. Third, the position that hell will be "densely populated" should not be the default position; rather, our desire and prayer should be that as few as possible would be found there. Fourth, making hell an absolutely unending form of damnation to all that may end up there does not necessarily follow (even if, as discussed below, that is the normal meaning of "eternal"). And finally: although normally one's eternal destiny is sealed at the moment of death, one could also imagine some kind of possibility of purification and preparation before final consummation.[17]

12. For details, see Kvanvig, "Hell," pp. 416–21.

13. See B. Russell, *Why I Am Not a Christian*, p. 195.

14. For the statement on moratorium on hell, see Camporesi, *The Fear of Hell*, p. vi; see also Albert Mohler's article, "Modern Theology: The Disappearance of Hell."

15. Schwarz, *Eschatology*, pp. 399–404 (399–400).

16. Walker, *The Decline of Hell*, p. 3; see Kvanvig, *The Problem of Hell*. For a recent collection of essays, see Buenting, ed., *The Problem of Hell*.

17. See further J. Walls, *Hell*, pp. 10–11; Kvanvig, "Hell," p. 422.

Understandably, the rise of universalism(s) has seriously challenged the whole existence of hell, at least as the final solution. Similarly, conditional immortality has provided a partial alternative. Let us take a brief look at the latter before assessing typical objections to hell, since these two topics are obviously interrelated.

Annihilation and Conditional Immortality as an Alternative

Particularly among evangelicals in the UK and North America, a view of religious ends called annihilationism has in recent decades garnered interest.[18] It "designates the views of those who hold that the finally impenitent wicked will cease to exist after (or soon after) the last judgment." It is usually coupled with conditional immortality, according to which believers may live forever as the gift of God (because no human person is immortal on one's own account).[19] Annihilationists believe that their view is in keeping with human persons' freedom: "The choices which they have made in life will be respected, which means that they will have no part in the kingdom of God and, being severed from the source of life, they will exist no more as persons."[20] The biblical support for annihilationism comes from the numerous allusions in the Bible, both Old and New Testaments, to the effect that the "wicked" face destruction at the end (Ps. 37:2, 9–10, 20; Mal. 4:1; Matt. 3:10–12; 10:28; 13:30; Phil. 3:19; 2 Thess. 1:9; 2 Pet. 3:7; Rev. 20:14–15; among others).[21] Opponents are quick to resort to other biblical texts that seem to support the idea of the ultimate finality of hell (Matt. 25:46; Rev. 14:9–11; 20:10; among others).[22]

Annihilationists readily acknowledge that theirs has been a minority view in tradition. But perhaps the unambiguous support for the traditional view of hell is less convincing among some teachers than is usually assumed. The late Canadian Baptist Clark Pinnock, a leading advocate of annihilationism, reminds us that although the *Didache* speaks of "the way of life and the way of death" (1.1; 5.1), it makes no mention of the nature of the latter. "This was true also of Barnabas, Clement of Rome, Ignatius of Antioch, and the

---

18. Fudge, *The Fire That Consumes*; C. Pinnock, "The Conditional View"; Travis, *I Believe in the Second Coming*, pp. 198–99.

19. C. Pinnock, "Annihilationism," p. 462.

20. C. Pinnock, "Annihilationism," p. 464.

21. See C. Pinnock, "Annihilationism," pp. 464–65; Fudge and Peterson, *Two Views of Hell*.

22. See C. Pinnock, "Annihilationism," pp. 465–66; and more widely in Fudge and Peterson, *Two Views of Hell*.

Epistle to Diognetus," Pinnock adds. He also opines that some sayings of Irenaeus such as that "it is the Father who imparts continuance forever on those who are saved" (*Against Heresies* 2.34.3) could be seen as supportive of his view. Seemingly clear support comes from Arnobius of Sicca's statement: "The wicked are cast into hell and, being annihilated, pass away vain in everlasting destruction which is man's real death" (*Adversus Nationes* 2.14).[23] Be that as it may, annihilationism still is to be considered a minority view, as most all leading teachers of the church throughout its history and all major Christian traditions have not endorsed it.

Much is at stake with conditionalism and the interpretation of the term "eternal," a challenge shared with universalists. Well-known difficulties in excluding the idea of "unending" from the meaning of "eternal" result from the way the biblical testimonies use the term with heaven in parallel with hell (Matt. 25:46). Furthermore, it is often noted that the idea of just passing out of existence is not necessarily a greatly comforting idea to many, and it also raises the question: Can we so easily escape the consequences of choosing alienation from God rather than reconciliation and fellowship with God?[24]

The Logic of Hell and Its Objections

Typical objections to hell are concisely listed by the universalist John Hick:

> [F]or a conscious creature to undergo physical and mental torture through unending time . . . is horrible and disturbing beyond words; and the thought of such torment being deliberately inflicted by divine decree is totally incompatible with the idea of God as infinite love; the absolute contrast of heaven and hell, entered immediately after death, does not correspond to the innumerable gradations of human good and evil; justice could never demand for finite human sins the infinite penalty of eternal pain; such unending torment could never serve any positive or reformative purpose precisely because it never ends; and it renders any coherent Christian theodicy impossible by giving the evils of sin and suffering an eternal lodgment within God's creation.[25]

23. C. Pinnock, "Annihilationism," p. 467. For a major study, see Froom, *The Conditionalist Faith of Our Fathers*.

24. See Grenz, *Theology for the Community of God*, pp. 640–41; see also Schwarz, *On the Way to the Future*, p. 262.

25. Hick, *Death and Eternal Life*, pp. 200–201.

The opponents of hell claim that many of these objections are supported by exegetical considerations. Three classes can be discerned in that respect: First, some scholars believe that the New Testament texts understood as teaching the existence of hell mean something other than what appears on the surface, such as the "fire of God's love" (Origen). A related version of that tactic is Emil Brunner's reasoning that the texts talking about two destinations for sinners are not intended to give theoretical information but are existential invitations to sinners to come out of a state of perdition.[26] Second, another opinion argues that those biblical authors who taught eternal punishment were simply mistaken.[27] The third tactic sees two different themes in Scripture and regards them as paradoxical. So Barth taught that "Scripture teaches both that God elected all in Christ and that some reject that election, which is the greatest mystery of all."[28] Although all these hermeneutical tactics have some value, none of them is satisfactory per se. A more integral and coherent way to look at the New Testament complexity is just to acknowledge it: there is no denying that the possibility of two destinies is grounded in the dynamics of the New Testament witness itself. One can easily find passages that warn us of the possibility of eternal damnation (Matt. 18:8-9; 25:41; Mark 9:43-48; Luke 16:26) and passages that carry a "universalist" orientation (Rom. 5:18; 11:32; 1 Cor. 15:22, 28; 1 Tim. 2:4).[29] Rather than pitting them against each other, both types of passages have to be maintained. I agree with the German Lutheran Hans Schwarz that in the New Testament "we notice that the tenor is not one of universal homecoming but of a twofold outcome of human history, namely acceptance and rejection," as illustrated most dramatically in Jesus' parable of the bridesmaids (Matt. 25:1-13), as well as in his parable of Lazarus and the rich man (Luke 16:19-31). The New Testament seems to make the human response a condition: consider the harsh saying in Mark 9:43 of cutting off one's hand, if need be. Hence, the "universalistic message would contradict the New Testament's insistence that our response to the gospel determines our final destiny."[30]

Among the exegetical debates since the nineteenth century, probably none has been as controversial as the one surrounding the exact meaning of the term "eternal" (*aionios*) judgment. Although there used to be a strong case for making it mean less than final,[31] in recent years the tide has turned. The

26. E. Brunner, *The Christian Doctrine of the Church*, pp. 421-24.
27. This seems to be the conclusion of Schleiermacher, *CF*, p. 720 (#163).
28. G. McDermott, "Will All Be Saved?" p. 236.
29. Ware, "Dare We Hope," pp. 195-97.
30. Schwarz, *Eschatology*, p. 346.
31. For details, see Blanchard, "Universalism," pp. 131-35 and passim.

general scholarly consensus does not support the idea that "eternal" means only "temporary."[32] Importantly, the British New Testament scholar C. F. D. Moule bluntly acknowledges the presence of two destinies in the New Testament, even if he himself supports the universalistic interpretation.[33]

Recently, it has been claimed that rather than eternal damnation of the human person, hell is something this-worldly, a "hellish" suffering and torment men and women undergo,[34] or the "hell" of forsakenness and judgment of Christ on the cross.[35] What to think of the revision? Although there is no reason to prohibit metaphorical usage of hell — no more than metaphorical understandings of other theological topics should be forbidden — its problem lies in making hell mean *merely* that. Linguistic acrobatics is hardly a solid theological way to deal with this difficult and complex issue.[36]

Assuming two destinies poses severe philosophical and theological challenges, the most serious of which is perhaps the seeming conflict between hell and divine love.[37] To negotiate that dilemma, I find convincing the argument of the Eastern fathers that "God did not create hell: it was created by humans for themselves. The source of eschatological torment is the will of those humans who are unable to partake in God's love, to feel God's love as a source of joy and blessedness."[38] This line of argument disagrees with Moltmann's argument that "[i]f I can damn myself, I am my own God and judge. Taken to a logical conclusion this is atheistic."[39] Moltmann ignores the value — the gift — of human independence: as limited as it is, it is also true, and the Creator honors it. At the same time, "God does everything he can to save all persons, short of destroying their freedom."[40] The Orthodox bishop Kallistos Ware rightly reminds us of the importance of holding tightly to the tension between God's love and human freedom. That God is love means God is "generous, inexhaustible, infinitely patient." That, however, does not mean overruling the freedom of choice by human beings whom God has created

32. Bauckham, "Universalism," p. 52; so also Ware, "Dare We Hope," p. 196.

33. See Moule, *The Meaning of Hope*, p. 46 particularly.

34. Berdyaev, *Truth and Revelation*, p. 138.

35. Moltmann, *Coming of God*, p. 251.

36. See also Bloesch, *The Last Things*, p. 219.

37. Closely related is the relation of hell to divine goodness; for a useful discussion and argument, see J. Walls, *Hell*, chap. 4.

38. Alfeyev, "Eschatology," pp. 113–14; he refers to Isaac the Syrian, *Homily 28* (English numbering).

39. Moltmann, *Coming of God*, p. 109.

40. J. Walls, *Hell*, pp. 87–88; see also Swinburne, "A Theodicy of Heaven and Hell," p. 49.

with certain independence.[41] The current project agrees materially with the Orthodox position.

I find useful the Catholic liberationist Leonardo Boff's claim that the "human person has absolute value: he can say *no* to God. He can decide alone for his future which centers around himself and his navel."[42] Along similar lines, Polkinghorne adds that although "God's offer of mercy and forgiveness is not withdrawn at death" because God's love lasts forever, it is also the case that "no one will be carried into the kingdom of heaven against their will by an empowering act of divine power."[43] In that regard, with Orthodox theology, we can speak of the self-imposed kenotic "self-limitation" of God. Having created the human person endowed with free will as the "other," God suffers the implications of the human person's choices even when they lead to the horrible separation of the person from the Creator.[44] Orthodox theology also teaches that perhaps the great suffering in hell for men and women "consists in being tormented by sorrow for the sin against love." However, this deep sorrow is "a fruitless and belated remorse, to be distinguished from the repentance that one can bring forth during one's life."[45]

Tension exists not only between divine love and hell but also between divine knowledge (particularly foreknowledge) and damnation. It was classically formulated by John Stuart Mill, who advised us to think of a God to prepare a hell and then "create the human race with the infallible foreknowledge, and therefore with the intention, that the great majority of them were to be consigned to horrible and everlasting torment."[46] As intuitive as that reasoning sounds to common sense, however, it is far from convincing in light of the standard philosophical distinction between intentional harm and harmful side effects.[47] Wishing to create persons with freedom of choice may have as its side effect the implications for choosing wrongly; those implications (damnation), however, cannot be taken as intentional harm.[48] Only such accounts of divine foreknowledge that assume omniscience on the basis of predestination (that

---

41. Ware, "Dare We Hope," p. 194.

42. Boff, *Was kommt nacher?* p. 75, emphasis in original, my translation.

43. Polkinghorne, *God of Hope*, p. 136.

44. Florovsky, "The Last Things and the Last Events," pp. 245-46.

45. Alfeyev, "Eschatology," p. 114.

46. Cited in J. Walls, *Hell*, p. 33.

47. Originally formulated by Aquinas (*ST* 2/2.64.7), this principle is known as "double effect" reasoning; for details, see McIntyre, "Doctrine of Double Effect"; Boyle, "Toward Understanding the Principle of Double Effect."

48. See J. Walls, *Hell*, pp. 33-35; more widely, all of chap. 2.

is, God knows all events because God has determined all events) may be liable to the charge of Mill's type of reasoning. This project advocates a view of divine foreknowledge that heuristically is called "pneumatological-trinitarian Molinism" (as detailed in *Creation and Humanity*, chap. 13). Like any form of Molinism, it claims to be able to keep together God's omniscience and true human freedom with the help of God's "middle knowledge," that is, God creates the circumstances under which true human choice may take place according to God's knowledge.[49] This view is further supported by a theology of election that rejects Augustinian-Calvinist determinism (without necessarily landing on the side of its alternative, Arminianism) by affirming the irrevocability of authentic and "graced" human choice (as discussed in *Spirit and Salvation*, chap. 9).

What about the oft-repeated argument that it is impossible for God to experience happiness when knowing of the damnation of many, or even some? Rather than appealing to divine impassibility — a traditional view rejected in this project in favor of the sympathetic cosuffering of God — we first have to state the minimum: an almighty and all-wise God can hardly be made hostage to human manipulation of emotions. Furthermore, although God is capable of suffering (which is another way of saying God is love), it does not mean that God is in need of human response of love. Indeed, says R. E. Creel: "Were God to pine away over those who reject his kingdom, he would be as immature as a jilted lover who pines over what could have been if only the beloved had chosen differently." Similarly to a loving parent, God is sorrowful for wayward children and does everything to pursue them. That said, "God's suffering is not a feeling which could dominate the divine consciousness. It is rather a moral attitude, a certain way of thinking about loved ones who have experienced great loss. . . . This means that God's perfect happiness, like his perfect goodness, does not depend in any way upon human choice. God views rejection with an attitude of regret because he *wants* human beings to be happy for *their own* sake. But he does not *need* them to be happy for *his sake*."[50] Finally, mind that we have to be very careful in not making God's *perfect* happiness equate with our human understanding in our always-less-than-perfect state.[51]

Before moving to the biggest challenge to the idea of two destinies — universalism — we can summarize this much: as noted above, this project finds the five revisions common in contemporary theological-philosophical

---

49. A form of Molinism (in criticism of the Augustinian-Calvinist view) is advocated in J. Walls, *Hell*, chap. 2. My view of the relationship between hell and divine power is materially similar to that of Walls as discussed in chap. 3.

50. Creel, *Divine Impassibility*, pp. 141-43 (142), emphasis in original.

51. J. Walls, *Hell*, p. 109.

discussion (among those who affirm two destinies) useful. The discussion so far has already established the particular kind of logic of hell advocated here, to be deepened in what follows.

The Appeal and Problems of Universalisms

The Evolvement of Universalism in Christian Tradition

Universalism — a.k.a. universal salvation or the restoration of all things (*apokatastasis panton*)[52] — is undoubtedly the most vividly and widely disputed concept in Christian eschatology. Although "[t]here was not a hint of universalism in the first two centuries of Christianity,"[53] the third century brought about significant developments.[54] Despite well-known inconsistency (even to the point of apparent contradictions),[55] Origen is undoubtedly the major pioneering architect of *apokatastasis panton*, "universal salvation of all (things),"[56] including all people.[57] His main argument is twofold: that at the end, all things will be restored to their original state and all things will be subjected under the lordship of Christ; his most often-cited biblical passage in support is 1 Corinthians 15:22–28.[58] At the end, even hell will be destroyed. Importantly, *apokatastasis*, "restoration" of all creation, is a more comprehensive term than soteriological universalism in itself.[59]

52. Behind *apokatastasis* is the idea of returning/restoring to an original perfect state; Bauer, *Greek English Lexicon*, pp. 91–92. The noun itself occurs only once in the New Testament: Acts 3:21 (and the verbal form fewer than ten times, meaning restoring and healing). For details, see Blanchard, "Universalism," pp. 13–17. I am indebted to his detailed discussion, including several sources, throughout this section.

53. G. McDermott, "Will All Be Saved?" p. 232.

54. For earlier emerging universalist tendencies, see Blanchard, "Universalism," pp. 36–60.

55. See further Norris, "Universal Salvation in Origen and Maximus," p. 56. The essay by Scott, "Guarding the Mysteries of Salvation," highlights — perhaps somewhat one-sidedly — the anti-universalist elements of Origen's thought. In the midst of scholarly disputes, it is a consensus that *De principiis*, his main theological opus, advances universalism; so, e.g., Greggs, "Exclusivist or Universalist?" p. 317.

56. See Origen, *De principiis* 1 and 3; Blanchard, "Universalism," pp. 60–69; Daley, *Hope of the Early Church*, pp. 47–64.

57. See Alfeyev, "Eschatology," pp. 115–16. The ultimate fate of Satan in Origen's *apokatastasis* vision is disputed; see Holliday, "Will Satan Be Saved?"

58. Both of these key arguments come together particularly in Origen, *De principiis* 1.6.1–2; 3.6.8. For the destruction of death as the last enemy, see 3.6.5–6.

59. See Blanchard, "Universalism," pp. 16–17.

Origen was not the only early advocate of *apokatastasis* and universalism; in some form or another, noted proponents included such central figures as Gregory of Nyssa,[60] Evagrius of Pontus, Saint Isaac of Nineveh,[61] and later Maximus the Confessor,[62] among others.[63] Despite these influential figures, universalism encountered strong opposition, even condemnation, from the start[64] — notwithstanding early theology's great interest in and hope for post-mortem salvation[65] (in some cases, even of "noble" pagans).[66] Augustine's strict doctrine of predestination led him to firmly assure two destinies, the other one being the condemnation of masses.[67] No wonder he adamantly opposed all notions of universalism.[68] Universalism was also officially condemned at the Second Council of Constantinople (552).[69] Most creeds and confessions all the way through Reformation times ruled against universalism and in favor of two destinies.[70] As a result, *apokatastasis* and universalism were relegated to the margins.[71]

Theology had to wait until the time of the Enlightenment and modernity to have another generation of fully developed universalisms.[72] Schleiermacher's extended theology of universalism, based on the theology of election, was an important trailblazer. Behind his universalism is his foundational turn to religious "experience" ("feeling" of absolute depen-

60. Tsirpanlis, "Concept of Universal Salvation in Saint Gregory of Nyssa."

61. See Ware, "Dare We Hope," pp. 205–10.

62. Daley, "Apokatastasis and 'Honorable Silence,'" pp. 309–39.

63. See, e.g., Clement of Alexandria, *Stromata*, or *Miscellanies* 7.2.

64. See Bauckham, "Universalism." This is to reject the older thesis, according to which the first Christian centuries were universalism-friendly (and that opposition arose only later), as argued in Hanson, *Universalism*.

65. The biblical passages invoked included 1 Cor. 15:29; 1 Pet. 3:19–20; 4:6; among others. For details, see Trumbower, *Rescue for the Dead*.

66. See Justin Martyr, *First Apology* 1.46.

67. See further Wetzel, "Predestination, Pelagianism, and Foreknowledge," pp. 49–58.

68. Just look at Augustine, *City of God* 21 (for denouncement of Origen, see 21.17).

69. Attached to the council documents: "The Anathematisms of the Emperor Justinian Against Origen," XI, *NPNF*[2] 14:465.

70. G. McDermott, "Will All Be Saved?" lists the following, among others: Athanasian Creed (early sixth century); the Fourth Lateran Council, Canon 1 (1215 C.E.); the Augsburg Confession, chap. 17; the Second Helvetic Confession, chap. 26; the Dordrecht Confession, art. 18; and the Westminster Confession of Faith, chap. 33.

71. For a detailed history of universalism from the post-Origen period to the medieval and Reformation periods, see Blanchard, "Universalism," pp. 69–110.

72. For the effect and implications of the Enlightenment to the rediscovery of universalism, see chap. 3 in Blanchard, "Universalism."

dence) as a universal phenomenon.[73] Related is Schleiermacher's revised understanding of the Reformed doctrines of election and predestination.[74] Notwithstanding the acceptance of two types of elections, both positive and negative, he refused to see that as an occasion for *eternal* damnation. From the fact that in the reprobates the election "has not attained its aim — that is, the initiation of blessedness in Christ," one should not conclude that they are eternally lost because their nonelect state applies only to the present life. Reprobation, while true in this life, does not mean eternal judgment.[75] The main reason for his not approving the traditional teaching of eternal damnation is its blocking of "the consummation of the Church."[76] Furthermore, Schleiermacher surmised that the traditional separation between two destinies is a function of misunderstanding the distinction between the invisible and visible church, which, in his theology, applies only to the present but not to eschatology.[77]

One of the ironies of theology is that as deeply critical as Barth was of liberal theology, for reasons other than Schleiermacher's universalist motivations, Barth ended up embracing a form of universalism deeply anchored in Christocentrism. Behind Barth's universalism (whose roots go back to the dialectics of the divine "Yes" and "No" elaborated in the revised *Romans* commentary)[78] is his radically reworked Reformed doctrine of election, in which Jesus Christ rather than the human person (or even humanity at large) is in focus.[79] Christ is both the "Elected Man" and "Electing God."[80] The traditional "double predestination" is strictly rejected and a radically revised doctrine of predestination in terms of the dual role of Christ and his "dual treatment" — rejection (crucifixion) and vindication (resurrection) — is put in its place.[81] The logical conclusion from Christ's rejection on the cross and his resurrection on the day of Easter is that no one else will be rejected, as

73. Blanchard, "Universalism," p. 118; the main sections relevant for this discussion in Schleiermacher, *CF*, are pp. 548-51, 720-22.

74. See DeVries, "Providence and Grace," pp. 189-208.

75. Schleiermacher, *CF* §119, pp. 546-51; quotation p. 548.

76. Schleiermacher, *CF* §162.1, p. 714; for a concluding statement, see §163 Appendix (p. 722).

77. Schleiermacher, *CF* §162.1, p. 714.

78. For details, see Blanchard, "Universalism," pp. 136-37.

79. Barth, *CD* II/2, p. 116.

80. Barth, *CD* II/2, p. 103. A succinct discussion can be found in O'Neill, "Karl Barth's Doctrine of Election," pp. 313-16.

81. For a detailed discussion and criticism in the wider context of traditional and contemporary doctrines of election, see chap. 9 in my *Spirit and Salvation*.

"God has ascribed to man the former, election, salvation and life; and to Himself He has ascribed the latter, reprobation, perdition and death."[82] I have a hard time understanding why his view should not be labeled universalism (of a sort).[83]

Though he is in some ways linked with neo-orthodoxy, the Lutheran Paul Tillich's deep sympathies with universalistic orientations, gleaning also from Schleiermacher, are more complex and nuanced. In line with an idiosyncratic ontology, Tillich opines that the only way to resolve the main human challenge, namely, the "ambiguity of life," is "[p]articipation in the eternal life [which] depends on a creative synthesis of a being's essential nature with what it has made of it in its temporal existence." Whatever negative there is in life has to be totally "excluded from eternal memory" since "the state of final perfection is the norm."[84] This means simply that "we are not accepted or rejected in our entirety. Part of us will participate in eternal life and part will be excluded from it. The decisive factor for participation is to what extent essentialization has taken place in our existence."[85] As to what exactly this "partly"/"partly" proposal means in terms of each human person's final destiny is left unclear (to me, at least). Yet its main idea strongly points toward a form of universal resolution.

Among the contemporary systematic theologians, Moltmann's tightly argued and carefully nuanced universalism makes a major statement in favor of reconciliation of everything. His main arguments in favor of universalism include these: that divine grace is more powerful than human sinfulness; that divine judgment "serves the universal establishment of the divine righteousness and justice"; that God's desire to save as power of love and compassion is able to convince even the sinner; that at stake is "confidence in God: what God wants to do he can do, and will do," that is, salvation rather than condemnation — or else the human decision to believe or not to believe has such eternal significance that ultimately human destiny is left in the hands of the human person himself or herself;[86] and finally, "If *the double outcome of judgment* is proclaimed, the question is then: why did God create human

---

82. Barth, *CD* II/2, p. 163. On the other hand, Barth tried hard to rebut *apokatastasis* (*CD* II/2, p. 417; IV/3, pp. 477-78). For his defense, see Colwell, "Proclamation as Event."

83. Blanchard ("Universalism," p. 139) agrees. Also important is the judgment of E. Brunner, *Dogmatics*, 1:348.

84. Tillich, *ST* 3:401; the section in which this discussion occurs is titled "4. The End of History and the Final Conquest of the Ambiguities of Life."

85. As paraphrased by Schwarz, *Eschatology*, p. 344.

86. Moltmann, *Coming of God*, pp. 243-46 (243, 244).

beings if he is going to damn most of them in the end, and will only redeem the least part of them?"[87] No need to mention that thereby Moltmann strongly opposes his own Reformed tradition's double-predestination doctrine, which he sees as categorically opposite universalism.[88] His version of universalism, however, does not deny damnation or hell — although both are radically reinterpreted: "damnation" and "hell" symbolize the uttermost suffering and God-forsakenness Christ underwent when he as the condemned one reconciled the world in the crucifixion and descent into hell.[89]

Although mostly a phenomenon of the post-Enlightenment Global North, nowadays universalism can also be found among some theologians in the Global South, including theologians from Africa[90] and Asia.[91] Furthermore, against common intuitions, universalisms have also emerged lately among some American and British evangelicals, despite evangelicalism's significant opposition to that kind of theology.[92] Theologically and philosophically, the most sophisticated representative is Thomas Talbott.[93] His main motive for universalism has to do with the prominence of divine love, which he sees as utterly incompatible with the idea of eternal judgment.[94] Talbott is firmly convinced of "love's final victory."[95] He believes in the destruction of (temporary) hell at the end.[96] The final salvation of all is not to deny but rather to affirm human freedom, as he believes that a fully informed embrace of God — if not earlier, then at the latest in the postmortem state — is inevitable for a rational person.[97] Finally, somewhat counterintuitively, Talbott attempts to make the case that Saint Paul himself was a universalist.[98] It is easy to see how similar in essence Talbott's proposal is to that of Schleiermacher: both believe

87. Moltmann, *Coming of God*, pp. 239–40, emphasis in original.

88. Moltmann, *Coming of God*, pp. 246–49.

89. Moltmann, *Coming of God*, pp. 250–55 (251).

90. Igenoza, "Universalism and New Testament Christianity."

91. D. Adams, "Universal Salvation?"

92. McDonald [Parry], *The Evangelical Universalist*; Bell, *Love Wins*.

93. The basic argument is presented in three opening essays by Talbott in part 1 of Parry and Partridge, eds., *Universal Salvation?* The rest of the book consists of responses to his proposal. See also Talbott, "Universalism."

94. Talbott, *The Inescapable Love of God*, pp. 5–10, 113–14; Talbott, "Punishment, Forgiveness, and Divine Justice," p. 152.

95. The title of chap. 12 in Talbott, *The Inescapable Love of God*.

96. So, e.g., in Talbott, "Christus Victorious," p. 28.

97. For detailed argumentation, see Talbott, "Freedom, Damnation, and the Power to Sin with Impunity."

98. Talbott, *The Inescapable Love of God*, chap. 5.

that love is the primary and essential attribute of God; that (at the latest) in a postmortem state God's redemptive purposes are fulfilled; that the leading metaphor for Christ's atoning work is *Christus Victor*; and that the "eternity" of hell is to be understood figuratively.[99] Regarding the biblical basis of Talbott's position, fellow evangelical critics have rightly pointed not only to his controversial position of Paul's universalism but also to the virtual neglect of Jesus' teachings on two destinies and his somewhat uncritical acceptance of the older view of "eternal" (hell) as merely figurative.[100]

Universalisms among Religious Pluralists

The latest wave of pluralisms beyond the ones discussed above is in one way or another related to the robust rise of religious pluralisms — in itself a diverse constellation of movements and orientations. The "first generation" of theological[101] and christological[102] pluralisms gleans from the Enlightenment ideals of the common essence of religions (despite differences in outer manifestations — or even deep structures), the history-of-religions school's relativization of the "uniqueness" of any religion or ideology, the quest of the historical Jesus movements' immanentist "Jesusologies," and a certain type of understanding of tolerance (in terms of no ideology having the right to instill its own values and claims on others), among others.[103] The "second generation" of pluralisms, often deeply critical of them, drinks from the postmodern and late modern wells of diversity, alterity, and otherness (of which more below).

John Hick's pluralistic universalism is most well known in the former category. In his earlier work on theodicy, *Evil and the God of Love* (1966), Hick makes theodicy and hell alternatives, opting for the former.[104] This obviously leads him to a sort of universalism.[105] After his decisive turn to pluralism, a universalistic orientation was placed in the context of interfaith issues. Appealing to the "metaphorical" or "mythical" nature of religious language,

99. For details and sources, see Blanchard, "Universalism," pp. 155–56.

100. For details and ample sources, see Blanchard, "Universalism," pp. 156–66.

101. For a detailed discussion and assessment, see my *Trinity and Revelation*, chap. 14.

102. For a detailed discussion and assessment, see my *Christ and Reconciliation*, chap. 9.

103. For a brief discussion, see also Blanchard, "Universalism," pp. 141–44.

104. Hick, *Evil and the God of Love*, pp. 341–45.

105. A materially similar solution is that of M. Adams, *Horrendous Evils and the Goodness of God*. For a comparative study of the traditional view and Hick's, see L. Hall, *Swinburne's Hell and Hick's Universalism*.

which he believes makes it possible to divorce Christology from the strictures of Chalcedonian "exclusivistic" claims (such as that the incarnation is a statement about a onetime historical event rather than a general principle of divine embodiment after Strauss and Hegel), the impossibility of negotiating deep theological/religious claims in any final manner, and a reworked, allegedly pan-religious soteriological vision in which "salvation" simply means a return from a "me-centered" to an "other-centered" lifestyle, he advocates the typical first-generation pluralistic idea of the rough parity of religions. In that template, claims about heaven and hell — however they might be framed and named in any religious tradition — can be stripped off from their "truth" claims and put on par with each other.[106]

The final and highly novel universalistic vision came to full fruition in Hick's monumental *Death and Eternal Life*. It bases "universal salvation"[107] on the idea that "since man has been created by God for God, and is basically oriented towards him, there is no final opposition between God's saving will and our human nature acting in freedom; and that accordingly the universalist argument is not after all undermined by the fact of human freedom."[108] Acknowledging a multiplicity of ideas of religious ends in the New Testament, he ends up choosing the universalistic option on the basis of human freedom and God's love and desire to have all of his creatures be saved.[109] Hick ultimately ends up supporting "a third possibility, other than eternal-heaven-or-hell or repeated earthly reincarnations, namely that of a series of lives, each bounded by something analogous to birth and death, lived in other worlds in spaces other than that in which we now are,"[110] ultimately leading to the transcending of individuality in corporeality in which persons will "no longer be separate in . . . [the] sense of having boundaries closed to one another . . . [but rather will] be wholly open to another."[111] The most severe critique against Hick's form of universalism comes from the simple observation that world religions hardly even come close to sharing a common "soteriological" vision.[112]

106. See Blanchard, "Universalism," p. 251.

107. Title of chap. 13 in Hick, *Death and Eternal Life*, p. 242.

108. Hick, *Death and Eternal Life*, p. 254.

109. Hick, *Death and Eternal Life*, pp. 243–59.

110. Hick, *Death and Eternal Life*, p. 456.

111. Hick, *Death and Eternal Life*, pp. 459–64 (461, 463–64).

112. As argued in DiNoia, "Varieties of Religious Aims." For a detailed discussion of "salvific" visions among religions, see my *Spirit and Salvation*, chap. 8.

Against Universalisms and in Support of "Optimism of Salvation"

Universalisms come in many forms and versions, as the previous discussion has indicated.[113] In addition to negative objections to hell and eternal punishment, universalisms also enjoy support from the following kinds of viewpoints: the power of divine love to accomplish its salvific purposes, even when the human person resists (cf. 2 Tim. 2:13), and the nonreality of evil, which means that only God, the goodness, lasts, whereas everything evil does not. (This argument can be used by annihilationists as well.)[114] Furthermore, general human feelings of resistance to the whole idea of eternal punishment and compassion for all humans are often invoked.

On the other hand, reasons against universalisms include these: the argument from free will cannot imagine that God, the giver of freedom, will overrule it if the human person wishes to choose otherwise; "the point of no return" argument opines that although God is patiently waiting for repentance, physical death constitutes a final boundary mark; the argument from justice simply means that if everybody ends up in the same eternal destiny, all demands of justice and fairness may be in danger of being compromised; the pastoral and missiological argument opposes universalism for the obvious reason that it has the potential of making Christian outreach and discipline meaningless.[115]

Universalism as a stated, dogmatic position is not a coherent Christian resolution. I find reasonable and useful the statement of the Orthodox bishop Hilarion Alfeyev. According to him, the "Orthodox Church is far from the excessive optimism of those who maintain that all people will necessarily be saved." There are several factors that speak against universalism: First of all, that view "contradicts the vision of the historical process as a path to the final transfiguration and change into a better state . . . [rather than] as a return to the starting point." (Origen, as mentioned, taught *apokatastasis panton* as a return to the original primordial state.) Furthermore, the bishop reminds us that an unreserved universalism also ignores the importance of human freedom to choose to live with God. Finally, universalism raises grave questions about "the moral sense of the entire drama of human history, if good and evil are ultimately irrelevant before divine mercy and justice."[116] This much has to

---

113. For a useful rough typology, see M. Murray, "Three Versions of Universalism."
114. Ware, "Dare We Hope," pp. 210-12 (without necessarily endorsing them himself).
115. Ware, "Dare We Hope," pp. 212-14 (without necessarily endorsing them himself).
116. Alfeyev, "Eschatology," p. 116.

be said clearly and loudly (and of course, the previous section on the defense of two destinies already implies it).

As soon as we state these rebuttals, however, we hasten to add the comment by the Orthodox bishop Kallistos Ware: "There are some questions which, at any rate in our present state of knowledge, we cannot answer; and yet, unanswerable though these questions may be, we cannot avoid raising them." Tackling the issue is all the more important as we realize that "[u]nanswerable or not, it is a question that decisively affects our entire understanding of God's relationship to the world."[117] In light of these sobering words, constructive theology for the sake of the religiously pluralistic world should equally loudly pronounce that rejection of dogmatic universalism and affirmation of the possibility of eternal damnation does not have to mean exclusivism in relation to other religions or people in the "Christian" lands. Just think of the Catholic Karl Rahner's theology of religions: his denial of universalism[118] was situated in the wider context of his church's inclusivism and — going beyond that — in the (in)famous idea of anonymous Christians.[119] Christocentrisms rather than pluralism and inclusivism emerged as a result.

All Christians, notwithstanding their denominational affiliation, could gladly acknowledge the radical widening in the offer of salvation in the New Testament. Although the "New Testament is still concerned with the promises that are given by the same God to the same ethnic community in the same geographical area of our earth, . . . it shows that only the sameness of God is decisive while the ethnic and geographical boundaries are no longer valid. Everyone and everything will participate in the new future."[120] This means taking up and significantly transforming the incipient universalistic scope of salvation present in the Old Testament. Important in this light is the passage in Matthew 8:11-12 in which Jesus says: "I tell you, many will come from east and west and sit at table with Abraham, Isaac, and Jacob in the kingdom of heaven, while the sons of the kingdom will be thrown into the outer darkness; there men will weep and gnash their teeth." The passage seems to be saying that those who take for granted their entrance into God's kingdom — be it Israelites or Christians — may face condemnation, whereas pagans (non-Jews) or non-Christians may be included. Pannenberg correctly notes that whereas "such sayings were perhaps handed down because they were later

117. Ware, "Dare We Hope," p. 193.

118. Rahner, "Hell," p. 8.

119. Rahner, "Anonymous Christians." For details, see my *Introduction to the Theology of Religions*, chap. 19.

120. Schwarz, *Eschatology*, p. 61.

viewed as promises that Gentile Christians would come in as a result of global Christian mission . . . they have a greater breadth than that . . . [namely] a universal perspective."[121] In light of these considerations, it is useful to follow the distinction between "strong" and "hopeful" universalism: whereas the former assumes "universal salvation," the latter concedes to hope that as few as possible find themselves in eternal punishment.[122] Notwithstanding terminological confusion (that is, only the first option represents universalism in its literal sense), soteriological hopefulness should be adopted as the main Christian attitude. The late Canadian Baptist Clark Pinnock coined it "optimism of salvation." It is based on one's understanding of God as "unbounded generosity." Says Pinnock: "The God we love and trust is not One to be satisfied until there is a healing of the nations and an innumerable host of redeemed people around his throne (Rev. 7:9; 21:24-26; 22:2-6)." This attitude speaks of hospitality, a "hermeneutic of hopefulness,"[123] as opposed to the "fewness doctrine," according to which it is certain that only a small number of people will be saved.[124]

On the basis of biblical teaching and Christian tradition, not much more can be conclusively claimed. Ware puts it well: "Our belief in human freedom means that we have no right to categorically affirm, 'All *must* be saved.' But our faith in God's love makes us dare to *hope* that all will be saved. . . . Hell exists as a possibility because free will exists. Yet, trusting in the inexhaustible attractiveness of God's love, we venture to express the hope — it is no more than a hope — that in the end . . . we shall find that there is nobody there."[125] As a result, Ware concludes: "For the time being we cannot do more than hold fast with equal firmness to both principles at once, while admitting that the manner of their ultimate harmonization remains a mystery beyond our present comprehension."[126] That said, along with a Lutheran theologian, the late Paul Althaus, we can assert "that until eternity commences, faith is always on the way from the fear of a possible twofold outcome to a prayerful hoping for a universal homecoming. Dogmatics . . . can neither take a stand for or

121. Pannenberg, *ST* 3:616; he draws a parallel between this passage and 1 Pet. 3:19-20 in this regard.

122. Parry and Partridge, eds., *Universal Salvation?* pp. xx-xxii.

123. C. Pinnock, *Wideness in God's Mercy*, pp. 18-24, 99.

124. C. Pinnock, *Wideness in God's Mercy*, pp. 13-14. For a useful distinction between "limited" and "preferential" hospitality of God, see the argumentation of the Canadian Reformed theologian H. Boersma, *Violence, Hospitality, and the Cross*, chap. 3.

125. Ware, "Dare We Hope," p. 215, emphasis in original.

126. Ware, "Dare We Hope," p. 214.

against *apokatastasis*, nor for or against a twofold outcome."[127] At the same time, Christians (who know that at the final judgment the knowledge of Jesus serves as the standard of entrance into eternal life and of judgment) may possess grateful confidence, though no presumption: "By relating their lives to Jesus Christ in baptism and faith they can also be sure already of future participation in salvation."[128]

Positing the possibility of two destinies does not mean that the "lost" are lost to God. This was already affirmed early in Christian tradition: according to Isaac the Syrian, "it is not right to say that the sinners in hell are deprived of the love of God," although the blessed experience the divine love as blessing and the "reproved" experience it as suffering.[129] Much later, Barth put it similarly: "Therefore even in hell we shall be in His hands. Even in its torments we shall be shielded with Him. We shall not be alone in death. We shall be with God who is the Lord of death."[130] In that sense, the mystic Jakob Boehme's statement can be rightly conceived: that "Hell is in Heaven and Heaven is in Hell."[131]

There is also a further reason to link heaven ("salvation") and hell closely together, one that has to do with the ancient biblical and creedal doctrine of Christ's descent into hell. What are its implications for the teaching on the final destiny of men and women?

The Soteriological Implications of Christ's Descent into Hell

Although the biblical basis is scanty[132] — which may be one reason contemporary theology has relegated the ancient doctrine of the descent into hell to the margins[133] — it became a vibrant topic in patristic theology[134] and Christian

---

127. As paraphrased by Schwarz, *Eschatology*, p. 347, with reference to Althaus, *Die christiliche Wahrheit*, p. 671.

128. Pannenberg, *ST* 3:616-17 (616), following Ratzinger, *Eschatology*, p. 206.

129. Cited in V. Lossky, *Mystical Theology of the Eastern Church*, p. 234; I am indebted to Bloesch, *The Last Things*, p. 219; Bloesch himself agrees.

130. Barth, *CD* III/2, p. 609.

131. Cited in Bloesch, *The Last Things*, p. 223 (without original source).

132. Interestingly, extracanonical literature is pregnant with explicit references to the descent, including *Gospel of Nicodemus* and *Odes of Solomon*. For a survey of apocryphal literature, see Alfeyev, *Christ the Conqueror of Hell*, pp. 20-34.

133. For details, see Schwarz, *Christology*, p. 290.

134. For a basic listing of important patristic references, see Pannenberg, *ST* 3:616 n. 275; more detailed discussion can be found in J. N. D. Kelly, *Early Christian Creeds*, pp. 378-83. An almost encyclopedic study is Alfeyev, *Christ the Conqueror of Hell*.

spirituality.[135] Except for the two references in 1 Peter (3:18–20; 4:6),[136] which in themselves have stirred a lot of exegetical debate,[137] the New Testament leaves us with fairly little.[138] In that light, it is surprising that the descent of Christ into hell is part of the Apostles' Creed. Jaroslav Pelikan offers an important interpretation of its function in the creed: "The descent into hell then assumed the function that the Greek fathers had assigned to the death and resurrection, the triumph celebrated by Christ over the devil and his legion."[139]

Both in Catholic and in Orthodox traditions, the descent into hell was originally related mainly to the deliverance of the Old Testament righteous ones, but it soon became "an expression of the universal significance of Christ's death for salvation," encompassing all deceased before the coming of Christ.[140] It is hard to contest the fact that "the natural reading of 1 Peter . . . is that Jesus' preaching is to the disobedient, and that preaching is meant to lead to penitence."[141] The late Reformed theologian D. Bloesch coined the term "divine perseverance," which expresses this hope in contemporary theology. The view "holds that God in his love does not abandon any of his people to perdition but pursues them into the darkness of sheol or hell, thereby keeping open the opportunity for salvation. . . . God's grace penetrates the barrier of death, thus kindling the hope of conversions beyond the pale of death."[142] Similarly to others who have materially held this kind of view both in tradition and contemporary theology,[143] Bloesch is not advocating universalism (or the

135. Consider that, in ancient Byzantine and Russian icons depicting the resurrected Lord, his coming out of the grave is never present, whereas as a rule they show the descent into hell. Alfeyev, *Christ the Conqueror of Hell*, p. 9. For accounts of the descent in early Christian poetry, see pp. 34–42.

136. Early in Christian tradition, the descent was connected with the story of the prophet Jonah in the Old Testament. See Alfeyev, *Christ the Conqueror of Hell*, p. 17.

137. The debate was already acknowledged by Luther (*LW* 30:113) in his commentary on 1 Peter. Exegetical disputes include the diversity of opinions about items such as the identity of the "spirits in prison," ranging from the sons of God in Gen. 6:4 to the souls of the preflood generation.

138. Important allusions in Paul include Eph. 4:9 and 1 Cor. 15:54–57; also relevant may be Rom. 10:7 and Col. 2:14–15. See Alfeyev, *Christ the Conqueror of Hell*, p. 19.

139. Pelikan, *CT* 1:151.

140. Pannenberg, *ST* 3:616; see also Schwarz, *Christology*, p. 294.

141. K. Ward, *Religion and Human Nature*, p. 273; so also Alfeyev, *Christ the Conqueror of Hell*, p. 10.

142. Bloesch, *The Last Things*, p. 40.

143. Bloesch, *The Last Things* (p. 40), gives this list (without any further discussion or documentation): Cyril of Alexandria, Ambrose, Hilary of Poitiers, George MacDonald, P. T. Forsyth, George Lindbeck, Stephen Davis, and Gabriel Fackre.

"harrowing of hell" to the point of making it empty) but acknowledges that various kinds of hopeful expectations can be based on this template. As he pointedly puts it: "God loves all and pursues all into the darkness of sin and hell. The paradox is that God's grace accomplishes its goal but in and through human determination. This goal is never fully realized while there are some who live in defiance of grace. Yet even this defiance of grace could not take place without God's inscrutable sanction. God's love will not let us go — even when we use our freedom to resist this love." That said, "[w]hen we resist and defy God's plan of salvation, it is God who is withholding his grace, thereby preventing us from faith and obedience." With this "mystery" — though not "a total conundrum" — we are left,[144] never able to read "God's mind." It must suffice to hold in tension the width and depth of divine love, holiness, and justice, as well as to acknowledge the role given to (limited, though authentic) human freedom graciously granted by the same God.

Theologically, Christ's proclamation and releasing work can be seen as dramatic expressions of the victory over death and the underworld after the Pauline statement: "death is swallowed up in victory" (1 Cor. 15:54).[145] With the inclusion of this statement in the creed, the church meant "not only to indicate that Christ has triumphed over all possible dimensions, even over that dimension where death usually reigns, but also to express something of the divine compassion."[146]

The last chapter of part 1 seeks to inquire into the final consummation of all things: What will be the nature of "heaven," the new creation? What, if anything, happens prior to that?

---

144. Bloesch, *The Last Things*, p. 240.

145. In that light, I do not see justified Calvin's and the wider Reformed tradition's (including Barth's) interpretation of the descent into hell in terms of the culmination point of Christ's sufferings in the grave. The Lutheran tradition's view of the descent being linked with resurrection, hence, commends itself to me. For references and details, see Lauber, *Barth on the Descent into Hell*, pp. 10–12.

146. Schwarz, *Christology*, p. 294. For the "triumph of hell," see Barth, *CD* II/2, p. 496.

10. The Consummation: "New Heavens and New Earth"

"The End Is Nigh": The Ambivalence and Dynamic of the Imminent Return of Christ[1]

Having discussed widely a number of topics related to eschatology, including the visions of both natural sciences and other faith traditions, we now gather together many threads and attempt a "summative" statement about the consummation as understood in mainstream Christian tradition. Topics most closely related to that discussion include the "signs" of Christ's return and its nature (as well as "delay"), the possible "interim" in the process of the establishment of the "new heavens and new earth" (known under the umbrella concept of the millennium), as well as intimations of the nature and "newness" of the symbol of heaven. Finally, as with other topics, a comparison with other faith traditions' intimations of the end and fulfillment will be attempted.

The Problem of the Interim

When it comes to the role of eschatology in Jesus of Nazareth's proclamation, two internally dynamic features were present.[2] On the one hand, Jesus' proc-

---

1. The first part of the heading borrows from vol. 1 in *The Apocalypse Triptych*, ed. John Joseph Adams and Hugh Howey, 2016, http://www.johnjosephadams.com/apocalypse-triptych /the-end-is-nigh/.

2. A highly useful and accessible account of the New Testament Gospels' eschatology

lamation was thoroughly eschatological,[3] but on the other hand, Jesus did not provide any kind of prophetic timetable for future events. "He did not spell out certain eschatological doctrines, but confronted the people with a radical decision for or against God."[4] This entails a radical departure from apocalypticism, which is prone to setting dates.[5] This is not to undermine the eschatological orientation of Jesus' proclamation — as has happened in diverse forms of "this-worldly eschatologies," whether of C. D. Dodd's "realized" ("consistent") or Rudolf Bultmann's "existentialist" or Marcus J. Borg's "noneschatological" interpretations — but rather to argue that "Jesus pointed to the present in which the kingdom of God had been realized as well as also announcing the future dimension of the kingdom. Yet that future was neither far off into the distance nor seen as immediately near."[6] The classic title of the late American New Testament scholar G. E. Ladd puts it in focus: in the ministry and proclamation of Jesus was *The Presence of the Future.*[7]

What about the problem in the Gospel traditions, so widely debated among generations of biblical scholars, regarding an interim? Is it the case that the original followers of Jesus, including the Gospel writers and Paul (who was not a follower in person), were simply and sadly mistaken in expecting the coming of God's kingdom during their lifetime, which did not happen (as Johannes Weiss and Albert Schweitzer in their own distinctive ways famously claimed)? The data in the Synoptic Gospels is far more complex. Notwithstanding their internal differences, all sought to combat the apocalyptic enthusiasm that set dates, which would first have led to disenchantment and then to final disappointment with the overly long delay in meeting the intense expectation. All three Synoptics seem to balance statements that can be interpreted to propose an immediate eschatological consummation within their lifetime (Mark 9:1; 13:10) with those that postpone its coming to the future (if not necessarily to the distant future, at least to a later period of time).[8] Highly illustrative is

---

and its various interpretations by New Testament scholarship is Viviano, "Eschatology and the Quest for the Historical Jesus," pp. 73–90.

3. Notwithstanding his deeply existentialist bias, still informative is the now-classic discussion of Bultmann, *Theology of the New Testament,* pp. 4–11.

4. Schwarz, *Eschatology,* p. 69; so also p. 79. It is common knowledge that Q (the hypothetical source of Jesus' sayings) includes hardly any indication of the prophecy of the imminent end.

5. For basic categories and emphases of apocalypticism, see J. Collins, "Apocalyptic Eschatology in the Ancient World," pp. 40–51. More widely, J. Collins, *The Apocalyptic Imagination.* A massive resource is Amanat and Bernhardsson, eds., *Imagining the End.*

6. Schwarz, *Eschatology,* p. 71.

7. Ladd, *The Presence of the Future.*

8. This thesis is clearly presented in Hoekema, *The Bible and the Future,* chap. 10.

the intentional dynamic contained within one and the same saying preserved in all three: "Truly, I say to you, this generation will not pass away before all these things take place. Heaven and earth will pass away, but my words will not pass away. But of that day or that hour no one knows, not even the angels in heaven, nor the Son, but only the Father" (Mark 13:30–32; par. Matt. 24:34–36; Luke 21:32–33). Clearly, the first part is speaking of the imminent end, whereas the latter leaves it open, perhaps even to the distant future.

Whereas Mark, as the earliest account, is closest to the enthusiasm of the imminent expectation, he also importantly makes the interim period the time of mission to the world, as is most clearly evident in the longer ending of his Gospel (16:9–20). For Matthew it is important to highlight the continuity in Jesus' ministry with the old covenant and the fulfillment in him of the divine promises. Matthew is also the only one to speak explicitly of the *ekklesia* (the church; 16:18), including its structures and how to cope with practical problems (18:15–17), thus implying a significant interim. Finally, it was given to Luke to move "beyond the notion of a strict interim period by introducing a salvation-historical understanding of history" and place Jesus in the wider context of the history of the whole world (1:5–6; also 2:1–4). Indeed, it looks like he does not even seek to engage the challenge of impending eschatology. Most striking in this respect is the Lukan Jesus saying that "when you hear of wars and tumults, do not be terrified; for this must first take place, but the end will not be at once" (21:9). As is well known, in the Gospel of John, a "realized eschatology" seems to take the upper hand, although not exclusively, as C. H. Dodd and others have claimed.[9] Similarly, Saint Paul, the chronologically earliest writer of the New Testament, clearly intuits the Christian's and church's life between two ages, this age and the age to come, which had already arrived, but not yet in its fullness. Hence, mission and labor in the service of Christ's gospel were the call to Christians. In this way the apostle "saved Christian eschatology from two blind alleys: unhistorical spiritualism and overanxious disappointment."[10]

Signs of the Return of Christ

Despite the repeated reservation of Jesus, beginning from the New Testament times the interest in discerning, and more often than not determining with some accuracy, the signs of the end has been quite popular among Christians

9. This long paragraph is based on Schwarz, *Eschatology*, pp. 83–90 (86).
10. Schwarz, *Eschatology*, pp. 91–96 (95).

(Matt. 12:38–39; 24:36; Luke 11:16; John 4:48; Acts 1:7). At every critical juncture of historical events the "end" has been proclaimed, not least during the time of establishing Christendom in the fourth century and at the time of the Reformation.[11] The same is true of Islam — if not more true (as discussed above): an intense expectation of the end events, the return of the Mahdi, and subsequent events is rampant among the faithful.[12]

That said, a cautious and discerning scrutiny of signs is not discouraged in the New Testament. Among the expected signs, the New Testament mentions a heightened excitement over the occult, "the fascination with extraterrestrial powers (1 Tim. 4:1) and the desire to uncover the secrets of the universe," coupled with self-appointed prophets eager to lead astray the faithful (Matt. 24:24; 2 Thess. 2:3, 9–11; among others).[13] The gathering back to their homeland of the Jews and their restoration is an abiding mark of the coming end in both Testaments (Isa. 11:11; Luke 21:24; Acts 15:14–17; Rom. 9–11). Dramatic cosmic changes and portents in nature and the heavens (Isa. 13:13; Joel 2:30; 3:14–16; Matt. 24:29; Luke 21:26; Acts 2:20), including seismic events and famines (Luke 21:10–11; Rev. 6:12), as well as intensified wars and conflicts (Mark 13:7; Matt. 24:6; Luke 21:9), signal the parousia of the Lord. To the end-time signs belongs also the proclamation of the gospel unto the whole world (Matt. 24:14).[14] A sure sign of the impending end is the appearance of the Antichrist, indeed antichrists — christ counterfeits.

Indeed, a prominent figure in the Christian (and Islamic) imagination of the end times is the Antichrist, a human opponent of Christ. As discussed above, Islam has the richest imagination concerning the Antichrist, his nature and activities. In light of the prominence of Jesus in Muslim eschatology, it is not surprising that the picture of the Antichrist in Islam is not radically different from that of Christianity.

In the biblical testimonies (2 Thess. 2:3–12), he is depicted as "a universal ruler whose reign of unprecedented evil . . . Christ will defeat at his parousia."[15]

11. See the sixteenth-century (in)famous *Prophecies of Nostradamus*, Internet Sacred Text Archive, 2010, http://www.sacred-texts.com/nos/. For examples from Luther, the seventeenth-century American Millerites (Seventh-day Adventists), and several twentieth-century American "end-time prophets" of various sorts, see Schwarz, *Eschatology*, pp. 310–21.

12. In this light I find misguided the argument according to which the emphasis on the sovereignty of Allah to determine the hour avoided the problem of the "delay of parousia," as argued in Sharma, "Apostolic Islam and Apostolic Christianity," pp. 39–46.

13. Bloesch, *The Last Things*, p. 74.

14. Bloesch, *The Last Things*, pp. 74–75.

15. Bauckham and Hart, *Hope against Hope*, pp. 110–11. In John's Epistles, the Antichrist represents heretical doctrine about Christ (1 John 2:18, 22; 4:2–3; 2 John 7).

Clearly, there are here echoes from the Fall narrative's mention of the desire to "be like God" (Gen. 3:5). We glean from the Jewish apocalyptic prophecy concerning the Syrian ruler Antiochus Epiphanes, who defiled the temple (Dan. 11:29–45), that he is not only a religious but also a political figure — Antichrist simply seeks to usurp universal power. His rule "is the evil antithesis of the kingdom of God . . . [and a] counterfeit theocracy."[16]

Jewish apocalypticism also provided cues for corollary adversaries with its depiction of the enticing false prophet (Deut. 13:1–5), which lies behind the Christian Apocalypse's (book of Revelation) account of two monsters, the sea beast and land beast (Rev. 13:1–18), the former a blasphemous ruler and the latter a false prophet (16:13; 19:20).[17] Similarly to the false prophet of old, these antagonists in the New Testament perform miracles and seek to entice people away from worship of the true God to idols. Chapter 17 of Revelation adds yet another evil figure, the harlot of Babylon, likely representing economic enticement.[18]

Fascination with the figure of Antichrist has been intense throughout history. Although the appearance of such an evil figure has been assigned to the future, there has also been constant attention to identifying his appearance in contemporary life. For the Reformers, it was the pope; for twentieth-century Christians, Hitler or Stalin or the European Union.[19]

Although modern and contemporary academic theology has virtually dismissed the topic as something mythical without any content, the expectation of the Antichrist persists vividly in apocalypticism, particularly in Christian and Islamic forms. Ironically, much of recent Islamic apocalyptic shows dependence on Christian sources, some of which have been translated into other languages from English.[20] Somewhat counterintuitively, the role of the Antichrist in these apocalyptic and millennial movements is related to the destruction of the unfaithful and unbelievers both inside and outside. "[Whereas] Apocalyptic Christians foresee the destruction of nominal Christians as part of the ushering in of the drama of the final days, . . . Muslims look to a period of deep devastation of the Muslim community as one of the signs of the end."[21] Furthermore, in Muslim imagination, Israel and America are often depicted as the Antichrist, and therefore as enemies.

---

16. Bauckham and Hart, *Hope against Hope*, pp. 111–12 (111).

17. For false prophets, see also Mark 13:22; Matt. 24:24.

18. See Bauckham and Hart, *Hope against Hope*, pp. 112–13.

19. For a massive study, see McGinn, *Antichrist*. Useful is also Jenks, *The Origin and Development of the Antichrist Myth*.

20. Haddad and Smith, "The Anti-Christ and the End of Time," pp. 521–26.

21. Haddad and Smith, "The Anti-Christ and the End of Time," p. 505.

On the other hand, fundamentalist Christians tend to see the United States as a "divinely guided" actor in the end-time events, particularly in its support of Israel. In their imagination, particularly as a result of intensifying anti-Muslim polemic, a Muslim figure now seems the most likely candidate for the Antichrist![22] No wonder contemporary Muslims "are specifically concerned with what they see as the humiliation of Muslims through Western imperialism and support of Israel, and with Christian dispensationalist triumphalism that seeks the eradication of Islam."[23] In the fight against the West and godless nations, as discussed above, Islamic apocalyptic imagination also centers on the figure of Mahdi.[24]

In light of the long history of failed attempts by Christians to identify the Antichrist, we should consider carefully the hermeneutical question of whether it is "an imaginative narrative about the final part of human history or an imaginative portrayal of what human history may be like at any time." Theologically, we have to say that, on the one hand, the God-opposing "mystery of lawlessness is already at work" (2 Thess. 2:7) in any given historical time, and that, on the other hand, the final culmination of the growth of evil will happen on the eve of the final consummation when the "restraint" is taken away (vv. 6, 8–12).[25]

Rather than fear, however, the biblical and theological depiction of the Antichrist reminds Christians of two demands. The first is the need for prophetic and spiritual discernment, as the "Antichrist is above all plausible and impressive . . . [and] offers what everyone wants: security, peace, prosperity."[26] The better the counterfeit offer for the kingdom of God, the more seductive and appealing it is to the masses, including Christian folks. It is the power of the lie. This huge potential of the Antichrist at the same time serves as a warning against its misuse, that is, a too-quick identification of someone or something as the Antichrist. Second, there is the demand that believers be willing to suffer, resist evil, and even lay down their lives for Christ. It is the demand of martyrdom. It is no coincidence that it is the martyrs under the altar, faithful witnesses of Jesus Christ, who triumph over the beast in Revelation.

---

22. See Haddad and Smith, "The Anti-Christ and the End of Time," pp. 506–7. For example, Richardson, *The Islamic Antichrist.*

23. Haddad and Smith, "The Anti-Christ and the End of Time," p. 512.

24. Haddad and Smith, "The Anti-Christ and the End of Time," pp. 526–28.

25. So also Bauckham and Hart, *Hope against Hope,* p. 117.

26. Bauckham and Hart, *Hope against Hope,* p. 115.

Parousia: The Presence and Appearance of Christ

An important and significant difference among the three Abrahamic traditions comes to the fore in relation to the Christian expectation of Jesus' return. According to Jewish expectations, the Messiah is yet to appear. In Islamic eschatology, the one to return is the Mahdi — accompanied by Jesus. For Christian theology, Christ's return clearly is the central image of hope in Christian eschatology. All else depends on it.[27] Ultimately Christian eschatological hope is about "Jesus Christ and *his* future,"[28] in which we and the whole cosmos have been graciously invited to participate. Hence, we can speak of the future as "Christ-shaped."[29]

The term "parousia," as is well known, has the dual meaning of both "appearance" (as in "coming") and "presence."[30] Barth saw this clearly in his extended reflections on the meaning of the term as he distinguished not only the "first" coming at Easter and the "final" coming at the eschaton but also the third coming at Pentecost.[31] Recall that according to biblical testimonies, this Coming One is the agent of creation (John 1:3; Col. 1:16–17; Heb. 1:2), providence (Heb. 1:3), and reconciliation (2 Cor. 5:19; Col. 1:20). He embodies the fullness of God (Col. 1:19; 2:9). His "return" is not a return (as in going back or coming again) but rather a cosmic "re-turn" (as in making a turn): finally and ultimately, God's eternal purposes of creation and reconciliation of the world (*kosmos*) will be redeemed and the power of entropy be reversed in the eternity of God.

Rather than a "private" meeting with a tiny flock of the faithful, Christ's return will be an establishment of God's righteous rule and renewal of cosmic dimensions. A critical aspect of the biblical and Christian understanding of the parousia is that it is not the final event in history (although, in one sense, it is of course that) but rather the *end* of history (and time). "It cannot be an event in time and space like the other events of history, since it is the event that happens to all time and space and transforms them into eternity." But because human imagination is unable to envision an event "outside" of time-space, the only way the New Testament can speak of it is like an occurrence in time-space, as in descent from heaven, accompanied by the angels, seated on the clouds, and so forth (1 Thess. 4:16; Jude 14–15).[32]

---

27. Bauckham and Hart, *Hope against Hope*, pp. 117–18.
28. Moltmann, *Theology of Hope*, p. 17, emphasis in original.
29. Bauckham and Hart, *Hope against Hope*, p. 118.
30. For details, see N. T. Wright, *Surprised by Hope*, pp. 128–32 (and chap. 8 at large).
31. Barth, *CD* IV/3, pp. 292–96; I am indebted to Bloesch, *The Last Things*, p. 63.
32. Bauckham and Hart, *Hope against Hope*, pp. 118–19 (118).

An essential part of the parousia is Christ's assumption of universal rule and execution of righteous judgment over the whole cosmos and all people (Matt. 25:31–36; Acts 10:42; 2 Thess. 1:9–10; Heb. 9:28; 1 Pet. 4:5). This is no whimsical vengeance and illegal usurping of power by a tyrant but rather the "revelation" or "appearance" of the faithful Creator, Sustainer, Reconciler, and Consummator. The two aspects of lordship and revelation belong together: "The revelation of his lordship will also be its final implementation." Up to this point hidden, Christ's rule will now become evident, and all knees will bow before him to the glory of the Father (Phil. 2:9–11). In sum: "the parousia is the event which concludes history by making the final truth of all things manifest to all."[33]

The biblical vision of Christ's return and cosmic renewal, as dramatically new as that is vis-à-vis expectations based on the normal course of history, differs significantly from apocalypticism. Thus, a careful assessment and critique of contemporary forms of apocalypticism is a necessary theological task.

Contemporary Neo-Apocalypticism and Its Liabilities

Tapping into the long and rich tradition of apocalypticism with its deeply dualistic view of the world and expectation of the imminent catastrophic end of history, contemporary neo-apocalypticism is gaining strongholds not only in conservative and fundamentalist Christian but also in Jewish[34] and Islamic movements,[35] among others.[36] Although it is easy to dismiss these kinds of movements as harmless or excessive, their importance both to the faithful themselves[37] — and American politics susceptible to an anti-environmentalist and prowar mentality[38] — should not be underestimated.[39] Globally, the best-known demonstrators of heightened love for one's nation are the American Christian Right advocates[40] — who also lend uncritical support for the nation of Israel[41] and whose counterparts can be found among the Iranian Muslim

---

33. Bauckham and Hart, *Hope against Hope*, pp. 120–22 (121).
34. Gorenberg, *The End of Days*.
35. Cook, *Studies in Muslim Apocalyptic*.
36. Sells, "Armageddon in Christian, Sunni, and Shia Traditions," p. 468.
37. See further Frykholm, *Rapture Culture*; Price, *The Paperback Apocalypse*.
38. Guyatt, *Have a Nice Doomsday*.
39. See also Wilkinson, *Christian Eschatology*, p. 5.
40. Tuveson, *Redeemer Nation*.
41. For an assessment, see T. Weber, *On the Road to Armageddon*; Sizer, *Christian Zion-*

rulers.[42] From the ranks of Christian fundamentalist neo-apocalypticism come best-selling titles such as *The Late, Great Planet Earth* (1972) by Hal Lindsey[43] and the Left Behind series by Tim LaHaye (and Jerry B. Jenkins).[44]

The neo-apocalyptic vision of the world is deeply dualistic; it "divides the world into the good and the evil, demonizes all who are considered enemies, is absolutely convinced of the righteousness of its own cause, and calls for holy warfare."[45] Notwithstanding great diversity and creativity, a common hallmark of the fundamentalist movements in all Abrahamic traditions is the expectation of the terror of Armageddon.[46] Often the advocates of neo-apocalypticism also consider themselves agents of God's righteous judgment. That has too often led to violence — or at least catered to militarism.[47]

The theological and ethical liabilities of neo-apocalypticism are obvious given its deep dualism and built-in potential violence. It reads Scripture ideologically in its attempt to justify its own cause and show the falsehood of the other. The neo-apocalyptic eschatological timetable is deterministic and may lead to fatalism. Furthermore, work for the peace of the world, cleaning and caring for the environment, erasing poverty and injustice, and similar good efforts for the improvement of the world are pushed away as efforts that impede the coming of the Day. Each new international conflict and impending nuclear catastrophe, however, is hailed as a sign of the end. In specifically Christian fundamentalist versions of neo-apocalypticism, the focus of the eschatological hope is the rapture of a small number of the chosen ones to meet the Lord "in the air" while the world rapidly descends into terror and chaos.[48]

Although the dangers and liabilities of neo-apocalypticism should be theologically exposed, academic theology and established churches should

---

ism. Love for Israel is funded also by dispensationalism, a view teaching a strict separation of the church and Israel with different eschatological goals; for basics, see Clouse, "Fundamentalist Eschatology," pp. 263–77.

42. Sells, "Armageddon in Christian, Sunni, and Shia Traditions," pp. 467–68; M. Evans and Corsi, *Showdown with Nuclear Iran*.

43. For details, see Clouse, "Fundamentalist Eschatology," pp. 263–77.

44. See the Left Behind Web site, http://www.leftbehind.com/. For a critical analysis, see Stevenson, "Revelation's Warning to Evangelicals."

45. Migliore, *Faith Seeking Understanding*, p. 334.

46. For a broad overview, see Sells, "Armageddon in Christian, Sunni, and Shia Traditions." See also V. Clark, *Allies for Armageddon*.

47. Migliore, *Faith Seeking Understanding*, pp. 334–35.

48. See further Migliore, *Faith Seeking Understanding*, p. 337; see also Beker, *Paul's Apocalyptic Gospel*, pp. 26–27.

also take a self-critical look and ask why apocalypticism garners such an appeal among the faithful, particularly when it is not limited to one religion but encompasses at least all Abrahamic traditions. Are liveliness and intensity of eschatological hope missing among professional theologians and church leaders? Furthermore, the observer of neo-apocalypticism has to be reminded that with regard to the Christian church, not all evangelicals, not even a majority, support the extreme features described above. Even among fundamentalists, that is most probably the case.

Although closely related to fundamentalist and neo-apocalyptic eschatological sensibilities, millennial hopes are in no way limited to those movements. Indeed, the types of visions of Christ's earthly rule in the process of ushering in the fullness of the kingdom also require careful scrutiny in our constructive task.

The Critical and Inspiring Role of the Millennium as the Penultimate Earthly Hope

Disputes about Millennial Hopes

Although there is only one explicit statement in the New Testament regarding what became the hope for the millennium in Christian theology — Revelation 20:1-15 — a number of other biblical references in both Testaments have been linked to it.[49] The idea also appears in the Jewish apocalyptic tradition.[50] While in early theology some opted for an allegorical interpretation,[51] the majority went with a more-or-less literal expectation of a thousand-year rule. Leading early theologians such as Justin Martyr, Tertullian, Hippolytus of Rome, and Lactantius were among the advocates of the earthly rule of Christ.[52] Named in hindsight premillennialism, this doctrine teaches that following Christ's return to earth, the millennium will be set up for a thousand-year period, after which the new heaven and new earth will be established. That was the

---

49. 1 Cor. 15:23-25; Dan. 7:18, 27; and numerous passages in the book of Revelation, among others. In the Old Testament, typical passages invoked include Isa. 2 and 11; Jer. 31-33; Ezek. 36-37; and Mic. 4.

50. See 2 *Baruch* 40:1-3. Similarly to Christian tradition, in Judaism millennial expectations are also allied with apocalyptic literature, which flourished during the "intertestamental period," including *Enoch, 4 Ezra, Assumption of Moses, Apocalypse of Baruch,* and so forth.

51. See Eusebius of Caesarea, *Church History* 3.39.

52. For details, see T. Weber, "Millennialism," pp. 369-71.

default option in earliest theology.[53] In a great eschatological passage toward the end of *Against Heresies*, Irenaeus links the hope for the millennium with the doctrine of creation and recompense for the sufferings of the saints: "For it is just that in that very creation in which they toiled or were afflicted, being proved in every way by suffering, they should receive the reward of their suffering; and that in the creation in which they were slain because of their love to God, in that they should be revived again; and that in the creation in which they endured servitude, in that they should reign. For God is rich in all things, and all things are His. It is fitting, therefore, that the creation itself, being restored to its primeval condition, should without restraint be under the dominion of the righteous."[54]

Beginning from Augustine, the enthusiasm for an earthly rule of Christ began to wane, undoubtedly also because of the new status of the Christian religion. Instead, the church became the locus and embodiment of God's kingdom.[55] Usually named amillennialism, this view soon established itself as the normative one. It believes that there is no other "reign" of Christ but that which already happens in the church.[56] Significantly, the Council of Ephesus condemned outright the millennial hope (a gesture followed by later confessions among the Protestant churches, both Lutheran and Reformed).[57]

Earthly millennial hopes did not, however, die out. Not surprisingly, various types of mystical and spiritualist movements took up the importance of the millennial hope.[58] Similarly, premillennialism did not disappear, notwithstanding a steady and strong resistance from the establishment. Beginning from various types of revival movements during the Protestant Reformation, such as the Anabaptists, many other free churches, including Pentecostal/charismatic groups, adopted it as a favorite expectation.[59] Expecting the return

53. See, e.g., Tertullian, *The Five Books against Marcion* 3.24; Lactantius, *The Divine Institutes* 7.14.

54. Irenaeus, *Against Heresies* 5.32.1.

55. Augustine, *City of God* 20.9.

56. For reasons other than Augustine's, Origen rejected any vision of an earthly reign of Christ as a discredited Jewish speculation and instead offered a highly spiritualized view of Christ's rule; see *On First Principles* 2.11.

57. For historical details and documentation, see Moltmann, *Coming of God*, pp. 153–56; for the Protestant denial, see the Lutheran Augsburg Confession, #17.

58. For an account of Joachim of Fiore's vision of the millennium, see Schwarz, *Eschatology*, pp. 325–27, and for related medieval manifestations of apocalyptic millennialism, see T. Weber, "Millennialism," pp. 371–72; for Thomas Münster and other militant millennialists, see pp. 373–75; and Schwarz, *Eschatology*, p. 328.

59. For a succinct account, see T. Weber, "Millennialism," pp. 375–79.

of the Lord to take place before the establishment of the earthly reign, they also believe that

> [a]t the end of the present age will be "signs of the times" — wars and rumors of wars, famines and natural disasters, the decline of morality, the prevalence of religious apostasy, the preaching of the gospel throughout the world, the rise of the Antichrist, and the great tribulation. Christ's coming will be dramatic and sudden: he will break out of the clouds with his warrior saints to defeat his enemies at the Battle of Armageddon, then establish his own kingdom, which will endure for a thousand years. Most modern premillennialists expect the Jews to regather in the holy land and convert to Christ. The millennium itself will be a golden age of peace, righteousness, and justice. Premillennialists equate the millennium and the messianic kingdom predicted by the Jewish prophets.[60]

The third form of millennialism, which emerged later in history, is named postmillennialism, according to which Christ's reign is progressing in history with the presence and proclamation of the church and will culminate in a "Christianized" world. Postmillennialists "locate the Second Coming after a long period of gradual and incremental 'gospel success' in which the vast majority of humanity is converted to Christ and human society is radically reformed."[61] Their understanding of the golden era of Christ's rule on earth is consequently less literal than that of the premillennialists; yet, interestingly, both views believe that by the end of the millennium Satan will be released for a short while and then the final consummation will take place. This belief of course fits well the optimism related to missions movements as expressed particularly in the modern missionary movements.[62]

Whereas in twentieth-century theology the millennium became marginalized and virtually forgotten[63] — except for conservative Protestant traditions — a striking exception to the omission is Moltmann. He relentlessly critiques the established church and theological academia for totally ignoring the importance of the earthly reign of Christ: "By excluding the future hope for Christ's

---

60. T. Weber, "Millennialism," p. 367.

61. T. Weber, "Millennialism," p. 368.

62. For details, see Moltmann, *Coming of God*, pp. 156–59. For biblical, historical, and systematic theological details of all things millennium, see the following sources: *OHM*; Hunt, ed., *Christian Millennialism*; Clouse, ed., *The Meaning of Millennium*; Erikson, *A Basic Guide to Eschatology*; Grenz, *Millennial Maze*.

63. Pannenberg is a telling example: he is virtually totally silent about the whole issue.

coming kingdom in history, the established Christian churches condemned part of their own hope too, so that all that was left to them was hope for souls in the heaven of a world beyond this one." An important reason for the denial of the millennium had to do with power: considering the present church (age) as the custodian of Christ's reign, Christendom opposed Christ's millennial kingdom, as that was seen "as subversive criticism of their own authority."[64] Although I find Moltmann's critique too harsh and one-sided (on both accounts of his criticism), his plea for the rediscovery of the millennium should be heeded even if not necessarily formulated similarly. Linking the millennium with the "future" of history, Moltmann places the millennium hope between personal and cosmic expectations.[65] He makes a distinction between "apocalyptic eschatology" that focuses on history's "end" and "millenarian eschatology" that thinks of history's goal. The latter is divided into either "historical millennialism," which envisions the present (in various forms) as the "golden era," or "eschatological millennialism," which "hopes for the kingdom of Christ as the future which will be an alternative to the present, and links this future with the end of 'this world' and the new creation of all things." This eschatological millennialism, a sort of "bridge" from history to cosmic renewal, is Moltmann's recommendation.[66] His main target of criticism is what he calls, somewhat obscurely, "historical millennialism," of which he discerns three forms:

- In *political millennialism*, "the holy empire" — whether that based in Rome, Byzantium, Moscow, or Washington, D.C. — becomes the focus of "messianic" hopes. Built on violence and "colonialism," it cherishes "the chosen people" mentality. In the contemporary world Moltmann is particularly critical of the "American experiment" along these lines.
- *Ecclesiastical millennialism* invests the church and its head with millennial expectations and earthly power. The papal authority beginning from Leo I in the fifth century has been its most visible global expression.
- *Epochal millennialism* considers the power of human development as the tool for fulfilling all dreams. While the Enlightenment legacy with its naive confidence in scientific-technological advancement is its most dramatic manifestation, human history knows such "epochs" also from earlier times.[67]

64. Moltmann, *Coming of God*, p. 147; see also p. 197.
65. Moltmann, *Coming of God*, pp. 131–34.
66. For a brief statement of the typology, see Moltmann, *Coming of God*, p. 146.
67. Moltmann, *Coming of God*, pp. 159–92.

All these forms of historic millennialism are based on "messianic violence," and they legitimate earthly power in the service of reaching the desired dream. Their opposite, what Moltmann names "eschatological millennialism," "is a necessary picture of hope in resistance, in suffering, and in the exiles of this world." It is open to God's new creation and the coming to an end of these illegitimate human edifices. It is a millennialism that "must be firmly incorporated into eschatology" or else "it leads to the catastrophes of history" and to disillusionment.[68] Eschatological millennialism, argues Moltmann, is thoroughly christological, and it sees "Christ's resurrection *from* the dead . . . [as] his exaltation to be lord of the divine rule, and his transformation into the Spirit who is 'the giver of life' (1 Cor. 15:45)."[69] Whereas millenarian eschatology (in its eschatological millenarian form, as opposed to historical millennialism) fosters hope and work in anticipation of God's new creation, apocalyptic eschatology occupies itself merely with the coming to an end of history — exterminism, whether in terms of nuclear threat, ecological disaster, impoverishment, or other "apocalypses."[70]

I draw two lessons from the history and the contemporary forms of millennial developments: First, its omission is a theological lacuna. Second, the confusion about what the millennium might mean calls for a fresh proposal.

"The Realizing Millennium"

It is surprising how little the Bible, and particularly the book of Revelation, speaks of the millennium — that alone would make any dogmatic statements suspicious. Similarly, "[w]e must not view the millennium as the core of the Christian hope," which is directed to the final consummation of the triune God's eternal purposes.[71] An important reason here is the cosmic reach of the ultimate eschatological hope: were Christians too occupied with millennial hopes — which are this-world and this-globe centered — they would commit a sin of reductionism[72] (sadly, this is too common among theologies of the past and also the present).

68. Moltmann, *Coming of God*, p. 192.
69. Moltmann, *Coming of God*, pp. 194–96 (195).
70. Moltmann, *Coming of God*, pp. 202–35.
71. Bloesch, *The Last Things*, p. 112.
72. So also Grenz, *Millennial Maze*, p. 214, approvingly cited by Bloesch, *The Last Things*, p. 112.

There is much to commend in the argument that the main reason for the millennium in the narrative of Revelation is the vindication of the martyrs. Those who have laid down their lives because of the testimony of Christ appear to be victorious, whereas the haughty earthly rulers are not.[73] For the sake of contemporary constructive theology, there are also other reasons for being open to the significance of the millennial hopes.

Moltmann's analysis of the critical role of millennial theology in exposing false earthly hopes makes a valuable contribution. There is no denying the constant temptation of the church to fall into perverted this-worldly hope liable to violence and oppression. That said, rightly understood, the true significance of the millennial hope nevertheless has to do with its "earthly" orientation. It represents the this-worldly part of the eschatological hope.[74] While it can be argued that Christ's earthly rule as a transition from history to eternity is needless because the hope for the consummation in new creation delivers the same motivation[75] (in material agreement with Moltmann), I see the relevance of the millennial hopes (however they may be framed exactly) for liberative and redemptive work. There is no reason this transition should detract from the fullness of consummation. That is not an attempt to make the millennium too human-centered, but is rather to link the eschatological hope tightly with the issues of righteousness and justice in this world.[76] That said, it is equally important, if not more so, that thereby the eschatological horizon not be reduced to serving human needs or that its cosmic ramifications are ignored.

One way of speaking of the millennial hope in a manner that seeks to keep in a dynamic tension the human-initiative *and* God-centered activity as well as this-globe-centered *and* cosmic expectations is to use the nomenclature "realizing or unfolding millennium."[77] This language seeks to combine "elements of apocalyptic, realized eschatology, and millenarian eschatology." Therein, "the kingdom of God bursts into history and advances in history as an invading force of righteousness." In order for that expression not to be understood too much like a typical postmillennial optimism concerning

73. Bauckham and Hart, *Hope against Hope*, pp. 134–36; Bauckham, *Theology of the Book of Revelation*, pp. 106–8.

74. See also Bauckham and Hart, *Hope against Hope*, pp. 137–38.

75. So Bauckham, "The Millennium," pp. 135–36. Volf ("After Moltmann," p. 243) goes even further and takes Moltmann's millennialism as "detrimenta," as it is liable to falling back into historical millennialism.

76. See also Morgan, "Eschatology for the Oppressed."

77. Bloesch, *The Last Things*, p. 110.

the power of human efforts to bring about the consummation, it has to be complemented by this specification: "The focus is not on the progressive realization of the kingdom in history but on the invasion of history by a heavenly city whose goal is to bring history into submission to eternity."[78] In that dynamic, "[t]he millennium belongs to both history and superhistory," to use the somewhat obscure terminology of D. Bloesch.[79] This kind of template has the promise of holding together (and at the same time defeating the one-sidedness of) the optimism of postmillennialism in its reliance on the role of the church in advancing the kingdom and the pessimism of premillennialism in its apocalyptic expectation of the divine intervention at the expense of human initiative.[80]

As emphasized, millennial hopes are penultimate hopes — to use Hick's language, they belong to par-eschatology. The consummation in its fullness in Christian theology has to do with the establishment of a new heavens and new earth. That will be the focus of the rest of the chapter and conclude the discussion of eschatology in this volume.

A Theological Rediscovery of "Heaven"

The Eclipse and "Immanentization" of Heavenly Hopes in Modern Theology

As widely and deeply as the imagination and spirituality of heaven occupied the minds of patristic and medieval theologians,[81] so theological reflection on heaven is ominously missing in contemporary academic theology; even hell is given passing treatment (if for no other reason than to deny its existence). Curiously, this glaring omission does not apply merely to the usual suspects such as the noneschatological American Jesus Seminar[82] or the earlier "realized eschatology" advocates (particularly among the students of John's Gospel)[83] or the revisionist-immanentist systematician G. Kaufman, who gave

78. Bloesch, *The Last Things*, p. 32.

79. Bloesch, *The Last Things*, p. 110.

80. For the template of optimism (postmillennialism), pessimism (premillennialism), and realism (amillennialism), see chap. 7 in Grenz, *Millennial Maze*.

81. Saward, *Sweet and Blessed Country*; J. Walls, *Heaven*.

82. A thoughtful critique is Hays, "Why Do You Stand Looking Up toward Heaven?" pp. 118-20.

83. For a critique, see Hays, "Why Do You Stand Looking Up toward Heaven?" pp. 116-18.

notice that Christians "are now in a position to dispose rather quickly of such symbols as . . . 'heaven.'"[84] The omission is so frequent in almost all biblical and systematic theologies that — embarrassingly! — the world's largest and most prestigious theological encyclopedia, *Theologische Realenzyklopädie*, in thirty-six volumes, has no entry on "heaven"![85] Curiously, the topic of heaven is also missing in the otherwise more traditional treatment of eschatology by the German Lutheran Pannenberg. In the index to the third volume of his *Systematic Theology*, "heaven" is listed only once (along with the generic term "new heaven and new earth" a few times), and there is no section devoted to it, not even a short one![86]

A delightful exception to contemporary theology's lack of discussion about heaven is Moltmann. His *Coming of God* devotes a whole section to the topic of heaven, under the weighty heading "Cosmic Temple: The Heavenly Jerusalem."[87] That said, Moltmann's discussion of cosmic eschatology under the wider rubric of "New Heaven — New Earth"[88] is so strongly focused on the hope for the "new earth" that at times one is left wondering how much newness he dares to hope for. The readers are constantly warned not to be too otherworldly minded. While it is useful to keep on repeating that "men and women are not aspirants for angelic status, whose home is in heaven and who feel that on this earth they are in exile" and insist that because "[t]hey are creatures of flesh and blood . . . [their] eschatological future is a human and earthly future," if that is all theologians have to say of the new creation, it is not enough. Nor is it legitimate to artificially juxtapose God's role as Creator with God's role as Redeemer as if to imply that redemption could not also include something truly *transcendent* in its hope regarding what the metaphor of heaven means in Christian imagination.[89]

A highly important and thoughtful challenge to the traditional notion of future-driven hope for heaven comes from the Scottish New Testament scholar N. T. Wright. Although not denying the future hope per se, he also reinterprets the Gospels' teachings in a quite radical manner. Although Wright, a fairly traditional scholar, deviates radically from those "liberal" scholars who major in rejecting the authenticity of eschatological sayings attributed to Jesus

---

84. Kaufman, *Systematic Theology*, p. 471; I am indebted to J. Walls, *Heaven*, p. 4.

85. I am indebted for this observation to Schwarz, *Eschatology*, p. 398.

86. For other similar examples coming from various theological agendas, see J. Walls, *Heaven*, pp. 4–7.

87. Moltmann, *Coming of God*, pp. 308–19.

88. Moltmann, *Coming of God*, part 4.

89. Moltmann, *Coming of God*, p. 259.

or in demythologizing them, he takes the "Small Apocalypse" of Mark 13 (and parallels in other Synoptics) almost exclusively as a description of the return of Israel's Yahweh to his people having been announced and embodied in his own person. These sayings are thus not prophetic in the sense of a future orientation. Apocalyptic sayings were fulfilled in Jesus' highly symbolic journey to Jerusalem and the subsequent events of the cross, resurrection, and destruction of Jerusalem (70 C.E.).[90] The novelty of Wright's approach, however, is that he still acknowledges the future orientation (of Christ's return, judgment, and resurrection of the body) elsewhere in the New Testament, although still quite minimally.[91]

That said, Wright's insistence on the future consummation leans strongly in a direction that robustly undermines its (in any way) transcendent, "otherworldly" nature. Just take this programmatic statement in his more recent, widely acclaimed eschatological presentation, *Surprised by Hope* (2008): "Heaven, in the Bible, is not a future destiny but the other, hidden, dimension of our ordinary life — God's dimension, if you like." While I of course agree with Wright that in the Bible (he mentions Rev. 21–22) "we find not ransomed souls making their way to a disembodied heaven," I challenge the claims that therefore heaven has nothing (much) to do with the future, or that heaven as "God's dimension" excludes its being also a future destiny with fuller (fullest) consummation, or that passages such as Revelation 4–5 depict *only* the present reality. Furthermore, I fear that Wright's vision of "the new Jerusalem coming down from heaven to earth, uniting the two in a lasting embrace"[92] (an idea I of course wholeheartedly endorse), leads to what seems to me a hopelessly reductionist, this-worldly and this-globe-centered enhancement of God's presence with us rather than a radical working out of divine purposes that renew the whole cosmos. With all its continuity with the present order of life, heaven in my vision also represents something that "no eye has seen, nor ear heard, nor the heart of man conceived."[93]

Another traditional biblical scholar who follows the former Scottish bishop is the Jamaican-Canadian evangelical J. Richard Middleton. The

---

90. See particularly N. T. Wright, *Jesus and the Victory of God*, pp. 339–68, 612–53. A highly useful engagement of Wright is Newman, ed., *Jesus and the Restoration of Israel*.

91. That idea is present in N. T. Wright, *New Testament and the People of God*, pp. 459–61 particularly. In this paragraph I am following closely Hays's argumentation ("Why Do You Stand Looking Up toward Heaven?" pp. 120–23).

92. Citations in N. T. Wright, *Surprised by Hope*, p. 19.

93. 1 Cor. 2:9; I acknowledge that the context of that passage is not eschatological, so it is used heuristically here.

main message of his recent *New Heaven and New Earth: Reclaiming Biblical Eschatology* (2014) — which the author somewhat curiously describes as a "worldview shift" — is that so far the church has misunderstood the nature of heaven, making it an otherworldly, transcendent spiritual "final destiny." Instead, Middleton has finally grasped that "redemption of creation" simply means a this-worldly new creation in which "salvation includes not just moral transformation and the renewal of community . . . but also the renewal of all things, including our bodies and the earth itself."[94] The argument is supported by what the author takes as a corrective reading of biblical texts that speak of annihilation and destruction as well as an exposing of "the problems of otherworldly hope."[95]

Is that so? Would only a this-worldly "holistic salvation" (as it is repeatedly named) support a truly cosmic and comprehensive vision of God's making "all things new"? Is the vision of the "new Jerusalem" coming down from heaven to be equated with this small, tiny planet? How would a fixing of our globe's life conditions be a lasting solution to the problems of entropy and decay? In other words, how *cosmic* (in light of our current scientific knowledge) is a vision of a "new earth" if "cosmic" (by and large) is understood as our globe? As the detailed discussion above on the continuity-in-discontinuity template between this world and the world to come as well as the importance of eco-liberationist work at the horizon of the new creation clearly indicates, the current project has no affinity with eschatological escapism that seeks to get around all the work for the improvement of this world and the combating of its problems. Nor does it support a one-sided "total destruction before it gets better" mentality. However, the more I encounter one-sided and (at least in my reading) somewhat uncritical accounts of the dangers of embracing the vision of "heaven" in its rightly conceived "traditional" manner, the more concerned I become about its reductionism.

Hence, counterculturally (as far as the theological milieu is concerned) — although totally in keeping with both the wide and deep Christian spiritual tradition of the past and much of Christian sentiment outside the "critical" academia — this project dares to envision the future not only of humanity and our globe but also of the (almost) infinitely large cosmos following the intuitions of "heavenly city."[96] While it clearly acknowledges the many pit-

94. Middleton, *New Heaven and New Earth*, pp. 11–19 (18) and passim.
95. Middleton, *New Heaven and New Earth*, chaps. 9 and 10, and chap. 1, respectively.
96. I fully endorse the American biblical scholar R. B. Hays's ("Why Do You Stand Looking Up toward Heaven?" pp. 123–29) similar kind of vision of what he calls (somewhat inaccurately) "apocalyptic eschatology" and his critique of this-worldly visions. Where there

falls of overly spiritual, overly otherworldly, overly human projection-driven dreams of the future, the current project is confident that the continuity-in-discontinuity template should have equal emphasis on both sides. That is, whereas contemporary theology has so one-sidedly opted for the idea of continuity between the eschatological future and this life, and traditional theology has too often hopelessly erred on the opposite side, a robust account of the radically new future with the consummation of God's kingdom is badly needed. Consider the astute assertion of the Christian philosopher J. L. Walls, who has probed into the theology of heaven more than most other scholars: "Theism raises the ceiling on our hopes for happiness for the simple reason that God provides resources for joy that immeasurably outstrip whatever the natural order can offer."[97]

Heaven as Communion and Consummation

As is routinely mentioned, the biblical narrative provides a meager account of the nature of heaven — and when it engages the theme, the chosen genre is imaginative and poetic. Pictures, images, and metaphors rather than definitions, statements, or analyses are provided. It is also noteworthy that none of the classical creeds rule on the nature of heaven and eternal life; they are merely assumed.[98]

The biblical symbols and metaphors of heaven could be conveniently classified under three linguistic forms: space-language, person-language, and time-language.[99] Space-language-driven metaphors abound, including the "city" and "garden," gleaning from the rich traditions of Jerusalem, the holy city, and the paradise of Genesis 3 (often, but not exclusively, named Eden).[100] The garden stands as a symbol "of innocence and harmony, a place of peace, rest, and fertility."[101] The classic imagery of heaven as a city can be found in Revelation 21–22.[102] In biblical testimonies, the city speaks of the security and

---

is need to expand Hays's vision is the robust inclusion of the truly *cosmic* ramifications of eschatology.

97. J. Walls, "Heaven," p. 399.

98. See further J. Walls, *Heaven*, pp. 7–8.

99. Horvath, *Eternity and Eternal Life*, pp. 124–32.

100. For details, see Bauckham and Hart, *Hope against Hope*, pp. 147–53.

101. McGrath, *A Brief History of Heaven*, p. 41; chap. 2 is a survey of biblical and historical accounts of garden imagery related to heaven.

102. For the rich imagery of "city" in Christian spirituality throughout the ages, see McGrath, *A Brief History of Heaven*, pp. 13–38.

community of people, as well as settlement (for a nomadic, wandering people). The new Jerusalem of Revelation is a walled city, denoting protection, but also a city with permanently open gates, implying constant access.[103] Mixing metaphors, the city itself becomes a temple, as the separate temple is not needed anymore because all are priests. Examples of person-language are expressions such as "being with Christ" (Phil. 1:22–23), "seeing God face-to-face" (Matt. 5:8; 1 Cor. 13:12), and related metaphors such as glorification (John 17:4–5, 22–26). Time-language relates to expressions such as "eternal life" and corollary terms. All these and other images and pictures should be appreciated as such — *images and pictures* — without taking them literally, yet still taking them quite seriously. They seek to express something of a reality beyond our language.

The cartographers of the images and ideas of heaven in Christian tradition Colleen McDannell and Bernhard Lang have conveniently distinguished two main approaches: anthropocentric and theo-centric. Whereas the former envisions heaven in terms of rectifying all ills and fallenness of the current human life in terms of a paradisiac return to harmony, reunion, and happiness, the latter puts the main focus on the "vision" and love of God as the center of eschatological hopes. Aquinas's pursuit of the beatific vision manifests this search: "Since we are rational creatures, our happiness consists in activity of the intellect, and since knowledge of God is the final end of our intellectual quest, our perfect happiness consists in contemplation of God."[104] These two of course overlap and are not in any way to be taken as mutually exclusive.[105] At the same time, these two orientations can also be better integrated in order to reach a "holistic" vision of heaven.

Highlighting the theo-centric orientation, the feminist Catholic theologian Elizabeth Johnson reminds us that "[at its] root, heaven is the symbol of a community of love sharing the life of God."[106] This is what the human person, having been created in the image of God, desires. Indeed, Christian tradition from the beginning has believed that the insatiable human yearning for fulfillment and happiness can only be met by the ultimate encounter with God and the "vision" of God.[107] Augustine put it memorably: "He shall be the end of our desires who shall be seen without end, loved without cloy, praised with-

---

103. For details, see McGrath, *A Brief History of Heaven*, pp. 7–12.

104. J. Walls, "Heaven," p. 402.

105. McDannell and Lang, *Heaven*. The other two standard scholarly historical accounts are J. Russell, *A History of Heaven*, and J. E. Wright, *The Early History of Heaven*. Also highly useful is A. O. Roberts, *Exploring Heaven*.

106. E. Johnson, *Friends of God*, p. 190.

107. For an early testimony, see Irenaeus, *Against Heresies* 4.20.6.

out weariness."[108] As Moltmann pointedly says, "men and women are erotic beings, driven by hungry hearts which can find fulfilment only in God."[109] Mystical experiences already embrace "an anticipation of the eschatological, immediate and direct seeing of God 'face to face,'"[110] but those experiences also always hunger for a deeper and lasting union with God.

While all Christian traditions materially share this ultimate desire, it is envisioned in different ways. The Orthodox D. Bradshaw helpfully discerns three differences between the Western and Eastern Christian spiritualities. First, whereas the Catholic tradition[111] and Aquinas intuited that the beatific vision is made possible by God to human "eyes" in new creation (though not yet in this life),[112] in Eastern imagination that is not possible because of inherent limitations of the created human being.[113] Aquinas goes so far as to claim the possibility of seeing the "essence" of God based on the scriptural promise in 1 John 3:2 ("we shall see him as he is").[114] However, this vision cannot be had with physical eyes, and even in the beatific vision itself after resurrection, the glorified humans' knowledge of God is not exhaustive.[115] Second, whereas for Aquinas the vision of God is an intellectual experience[116] (as much as it is also spiritual), in the Eastern Church's *theosis* (deification) the whole human being, including embodiment, participates in transformation. The third difference between the two Christian families relates to the fact that whereas for Aquinas the vision of God means the satisfaction (and hence, coming to an end) of all desires and needs, in the East even the deified faithful are in constant progress toward further perfection.[117]

Constructive theology may take a lesson from these differences between orientations. First, it is reasonable to assume that the beatific vision is pos-

---

108. Augustine, *City of God* 22.30; I am indebted to J. Walls, *Heaven*, p. 37.

109. Moltmann, *Spirit of Life*, p. 199.

110. Moltmann, *Spirit of Life*, p. 205.

111. For the classic Roman Catholic statement on the vision of God, see the 1336 encyclical by Pope Benedict XII, *Benedictus Dei* (On the beatific vision of God), at Papal Encyclicals Online, http://www.papalencyclicals.net/Ben12/B12bdeus.html. Although less technically defined, even Protestant tradition has materially the same kind of vision. Said Melanchthon: "Eternal life will be perpetual adoration," cited in Jenson, *Systematic Theology*, 2:340.

112. Aquinas, *ST* 2a.2.

113. See further Jenson, *Systematic Theology*, 2:342–43.

114. Aquinas, *Summa contra Gentiles* 3.1.53.6.

115. Aquinas, *ST* 3 suppl. 92.1–3.

116. Note the heading ("That the Created Intellect Needs an Influx of Divine Light in Order to See God through His Essence") in Aquinas, *Summa contra Gentiles* 3.53.6.

117. Bradshaw, *Aristotle East and West*, pp. 255–57; I am indebted to J. Walls, "Heaven," pp. 402–3.

sible to the measure that God, the infinite Giver, grants that gift to men and women. Second, the vision of God is at the same time not only "the absolute fulfillment of human person" but also represents something that at its core is "most deeply 'human'" (*zutiefst menschlich*). Heaven "brings into fulfillment the human [aspirations] in all of their dimensions," whether in relation to the world at large, or other people, or God. Of that fulfillment we can dream in this life, but we can never realize it.[118] As we have been created in the image of God, life eternal in communion with the Creator then represents "our homeland and the location of our identity."[119] Rather than a return to an idyllic innocence of paradise, communion with God is reaching the future destiny of the human being.

Third, even though one has "arrived" in eternity, progress and evolvement do not have to stop. "The life of heaven will be lived in the presence of the divine reality, but the exploration by finite creatures of the infinite riches of that reality will be unending."[120] That is because God "has ever new aspects of himself to reveal, and the bringing of others into an ever-developing relationship with God, would provide a life worth living forever."[121] This is an idea deeply embedded in Christian tradition.[122] And with it, the contemporary complaint about the "boredom" of heaven — a challenge noticed by traditional theologians but not felt as something to be rebutted — loses whatever force it may have.[123] In response to the boredom challenge, a distinction between self-exhausting pleasures and repeatable ones is useful. Whereas the former ones will ultimately be exhausted once fully experienced, the latter ones — such as meaningful work, giving or receiving love, or an artistic work — are capable of being repeated time after time (and may even become more desirable).[124]

Fourth, life in heaven is embodied life as long as one holds on to the hope of the resurrection of the body. Indeed, here we come to one of the most distinguishing features of the Christian view of consummation. Heaven

---

118. Boff, *Was kommt nacher?* p. 59.

119. Boff, *Was kommt nacher?* pp. 61–63 (61), my translation.

120. Polkinghorne, *God of Hope*, pp. 132–33.

121. Swinburne, *Faith and Reason*, p. 135, cited in J. Walls, "Heaven," p. 7.

122. For details and sources, see Hick, *Death and Eternal Life*, p. 422.

123. For typical, oft-cited challenges to heaven, see B. Williams, "The Makropulos Case," pp. 73–92. Zaleski ("In Defense of Immortality," p. 42) puts it memorably: "Our ancestors were afraid of Hell; we are afraid of Heaven. We think it will be boring."

124. Fischer, "Why Immortality Is Not So Bad," pp. 262–67; I am indebted to J. Walls, "Heaven," p. 406. See also Hallett, "The Tedium of Immortality." This paragraph is indebted to J. Walls, *Heaven*, pp. 196–97.

comes not by an ascent (of individuals, as in Jewish traditions) but rather by a descent: "And I saw the holy city, new Jerusalem, coming down out of heaven from God" (Rev. 21:2).[125] Having critiqued N. T. Wright above for making the hope of heaven too this-worldly, I also wish to endorse his earth-driven view as long as it is stripped of its "consummation-as-our-globe" liability and connected to a truly cosmic vision. When we read it against the vast cosmic ramifications of the "coming of God" to renew all of creation, we note that "the ultimate future, as chapters 21 and 22 [of Revelation] make clear is not about people leaving 'earth' and going to 'heaven,' but rather about the life of 'heaven,' more specifically the New Jerusalem, coming down from heaven to earth — exactly in line with the Lord's Prayer."[126] Here is the clue to the tight linking of theological imagination of heaven with the embodied and "earthly driven" orientation of the hope for the resurrection of the body.

Fifth, as implied throughout this discussion, the "new heaven" must be imagined as cosmos-wide: the mere fixing of life conditions in one part of the cosmos would only be a temporary solution. Human knowledge at the moment has very few resources at its disposal for imagining such a cosmic renewal (somewhat similarly to the question of the ultimate origins of the cosmos in the first place). What can be said safely is this: if Christian theology — along with that of sister Abrahamic traditions — believes in God as the creator of the whole vast cosmos, confidence in the same God's capacity to bring to fulfillment the promises of renewal is no more difficult a challenge in principle.

Finally, heaven signifies full freedom. Although Christian tradition has negotiated the challenge of freedom in heaven in more than one way — in response to the simple question of whether it makes sense to speak of freedom of the will when it appears that it must be "predetermined" that no wrong choices will take place — it seems to me something like the following could be argued:[127] while, strictly speaking, in heaven there is no longer any possibility to sin (or else heaven would not be heaven), that does not have to mean total determinism if the person's character formation and insight into the true and good as a result of the transformation in eternity make all wrong choices impossible.[128]

125. See McGrath, *A Brief History of Heaven*, p. 75.

126. N. T. Wright, *For All the Saints*, p. 59, cited in J. Walls, "Heaven," pp. 2-3.

127. Various tactics are masterfully surveyed and assessed in Gaine's *Will There Be Free Will in Heaven?*

128. I follow here materially the argument in J. Walls, "Heaven," pp. 404-5, which in turn agrees in the main with Sennett, "Is There Freedom in Heaven?"

Implied in our discussion has been the claim that the Christian vision of heaven is distinctive not only among the Abrahamic faiths but also among other faith traditions. It is appropriate to end this chapter on the final consummation by once again placing Christian hope in relation to that of other faiths.

Visions of Consummation among Religions: A Brief Statement

We constructed the eschatology of four living faith traditions above (chap. 3), so this comparative exercise can be brief (such that documentation is not repeated). The Jewish tradition has not spent much ink trying to describe the final consummation because of its this-worldly orientation; similarly to Christian tradition, a virtual omission of heaven occurs in post-Enlightenment nontraditional Jewish movements. Even in the rabbinic writings, reservation in speaking about the future is the norm. Similarly to Christian tradition, symbols and metaphors are taken from our world, although radical discontinuities with the present realities can also be occasionally found. Somewhat similarly to the Christian vision, various stages on the way to the final messianic consummation can be seen in Judaism; the Christian counterparts are the intermediate state and the millennium. A defining feature in modern Jewish visions (those that have not abandoned transcendent consummation) is very much a "Christian" type of "new earth" vision, an orientation totally at home with Jewish religion. Although the cosmic eschatological vision is not totally foreign to Judaism — recall "the world to come" aspect of future hopes, which may have cosmic ramifications — neither is it at the heart of that tradition.

Among the Abrahamic traditions, Islam's vision of heaven is the most transcendent and has the least correspondence with this world. Islamic tradition is rich with elaborate descriptions of the final consummation, which of course — in order to make sense — take their departure from the beauties and enjoyment of this world but also develop them into highly sophisticated accounts of otherworldly bliss. The connection between this world and the world to come is not a theme in Islamic tradition; this is a significant difference from her older sister faiths. In that sense, the danger of escapism looms large in many forms of Muslim spirituality, not least in Sufi traditions.

A radical difference concerning consummation can be found between Asiatic and Abrahamic faiths. The Asiatic traditions reject final resolution in their cyclical and ever-repeating cosmologies (even if the individual person's cycle may come to an end in nirvana). A major difference also has to do with the decidedly theo-centric vision of Abrahamic faiths in their expectations of consummation. Even in theistic Hinduism as well as Buddhism's Mahayana traditions, which freely acknowledge deities, their role is ambiguous or at least marginal. Particularly for Buddhism, any talk about "eschatology" in reference to a doctrine of "last things" or "consummation" with any meaning of "closure" is highly problematic in principle. For the sake of interfaith hospitality, these dramatic differences have to be highlighted and appreciated.

The second part of this book will take up and further develop the question of the ways different religious traditions are envisioning "good life" on earth and its consummation in "the end" as we delve into the many details of the theology of community, known as "ecclesiology" in Christian tradition. That discussion will also further clarify — in the spirit of hospitality and mutual learning — the basis for the Christian confidence in the triune God as the source of hope for this life and the life to come.

II. COMMUNITY

11. Introduction: The Christian Church and Ecclesiology in the Matrix of Secularism(s) and Religious Pluralism(s)

How to Do Ecclesiology in the Beginning of the Third Millennium

Meeting the Subject

The senior Catholic ecclesiologist Hans Küng opens his now-classic *The Church* (ET 1967) observing that "[t]hough there is much talk nowadays about the Church in the secular world, there is not a corresponding awareness of what the Church is."[1] I fear that after the turn of the new millennium, that lack of awareness may now be even greater. Not only in the world, but also within the church, questioning is going on, particularly about her relevance in the secular and religiously pluralistic world. Sentiments and attitudes have been transformed radically since the first centuries.[2]

The contemporary ecclesiologist should hold in dynamic tension the honorable heritage of the past centuries and the cynical criticism of contemporary people. At the same time, the ecclesiologist should heed the wise advice of Küng: "Clinging tenaciously to the past . . . is no less dangerous than a misdirected adaptation to the present."[3] Ecclesiology as a theological discipline has to exercise constantly critical judgment, lest it "turn into the ideology of

---

1. Küng, *The Church*, p. 11.
2. See G. Evans, "The Church in the Early Christian Centuries," p. 29; a useful discussion is also S. Hall, "The Early Idea of the Church," pp. 41–57.
3. Küng, *The Church*, p. 12; see also Moltmann, *The Church in the Power of the Spirit*, p. xv.

the church in its existing form."[4] This criticism does not have to be destructive or "antichurchly," since its ultimate goal is to help the church be renewed; yet, as the representatives of the theologians' guild, critique we must.

As important a role as ecclesiology is playing in contemporary theology, we should recall that as a fully developed separate locus, the doctrine of the church did not emerge until the time of the Reformation. This is of course not to ignore the many church-related themes discussed already in the patristic and later doctrinal manuals, particularly sacramentology. It is rather to remind us of the polemical setting of the Reformation theology out of which a full-orbed ecclesiology, an understanding of the "true" church, emerged.[5] Not surprisingly, the first full-scale ecclesiologies at the time advanced slowly and had a somewhat haphazard tone due to circumstances.[6] That situation has happily changed. The constructive theologian writing in the first decade of the third millennium is fortunate to be able to tap into unprecedented resources due to the resurgence of and enthusiasm over the doctrine of the church over many decades.[7] Indeed, the flow of new publications is overwhelming. The theologian has to be selective if one wants to say something worthwhile.

Some Methodological Desiderata

The constructive theologian should resist the widespread misconception that there once was a unified and fixed master plan for the church.[8] Diversity and plurality have characterized churches' lives beginning from the New Testament. Consequently, the ebb and flow of the historical developments have to be sifted critically at all times to discern the quality and value of the growth of tradition. A seasoned theologian should be wary of both a "progressive" view of history, according to which the last is always the best, and a "primitivist" view, in which the earliest is always the best.[9]

In shaping and clarifying the methodological approach to doing constructive ecclesiology (as part of the wider methodology adopted in this five-

---

4. Moltmann, *The Church in the Power of the Spirit*, p. 7.

5. A brief detailed outline of the emergence and history of ecclesiology can be found in Pannenberg, *ST* 3:21-27, on which this section is based.

6. For Melanchthon, Calvin, and others, see Pannenberg, *ST* 3:22-23; see also Ocker, "Ecclesiology and the Religious Controversy" (with excellent documentation).

7. Mannion and Mudge, "Introduction," p. 1.

8. Volf, *After Our Likeness*, pp. 21-22 (21).

9. Volf, *After Our Likeness*, p. 22.

volume series), I am critically and sympathetically appropriating lessons from contemporary work in the doctrine of the church across the ecumenical and theological spectrum. A constant companion during the writing process has been the American Roman Catholic R. Haight's trilogy *Christian Community in History*, which follows ecclesiology "From Below" (analogous to christological method). Its focus is on "concrete, existential, and historical," as opposed to "abstract, idealist, and a-historical,"[10] which is happily a widening trend in contemporary ecclesiology.[11] I also follow Haight's diachronic approach in which "critical theology must keep theological assertions attached to the historical symbols that mediate the experiences on which they depend."[12] Yet another shared methodological feature is careful attention to sociohistorical, ideological, and political factors, including liberation as well as globalization, which shape the context of the development of ecclesiology. To those I add a careful consideration of gender issues and questions related to power, among others.

Again like Haight, my study is not limited to nor does it come from a particular denominational perspective but rather is widely and definitively ecumenical in orientation — like the German Reformed theologian Jürgen Moltmann's now-classic *The Church in the Power of the Spirit* (ET 1977), or the Lutheran Wolfhart Pannenberg's massive ecclesiological discussion in the third volume of the *Systematic Theology* (ET 1998), or the earlier Catholic classic by Küng, *The Church*. This does not mean that I either seek to hide my particular location in the Christian world or pretend not to be limited by my own perspective; it is rather an attempt to glean from various ecclesiastical traditions and sources and make a modest contribution to the international and ecumenical — that is, catholic — ecclesiology. Even when I write as a Protestant theologian, here, as elsewhere, I engage deeply and widely Roman Catholic and Orthodox sources as well.

Furthermore, as much as I am tutored by the great contemporary "mainline" masters (including those mentioned above), my constant dialogue partners are also feminists and other female theologians, other liberationists of various sorts, postcolonialists, as well as theologians from the Global South (Africa, Asia, and Latin America). Finally, similarly to Moltmann, I adopt as equal conversation partners not only the established churches but also younger churches, including free churches of various types, Pentecostal/charismatic

10. Haight, *CCH*, 1:4-5; more extensively in chap. 1.
11. Küng, *The Church*, pp. 411-12, 46-52. See also Schillebeeckx, *Church*.
12. Haight, *CCH*, 1:ix-x; see also pp. 1-2.

groups, and others. I also consult and learn from a diverse group of what is now called either "fresh expressions of the church" (mostly in the UK) or "emerging/emergent churches" (in the United States). Another similarity to Moltmann — and now a commonplace in most ecclesiological and ecumenical writings — is a deep missional orientation. Rather than the church having a mission, in this new paradigm the church exists as mission. Following Moltmann, Küng, and Pentecostals/charismatics, I also envision the church not only as a sacramental communion, which it truly is, but also as a charismatic community in the service of God's mission. It is a grave liability in most all earlier works on ecclesiology (and too many recent ones, including the magisterial ecclesiology in Pannenberg's third volume of systematics) to simply be silent about anything smacking of "enthusiasticism"!

In keeping with the comparative theological methodology of this five-volume series, my investigation distinguishes itself from all others with its wide and detailed engagement of not only religious plurality,[13] but also specific teachings and insights of four living faiths concerning the community, liturgy, and worship. The only existing study that resembles mine in this regard is the British Anglican K. Ward's *Religion and Community*.

The context and conditions of doing ecclesiology in the beginning of the third millennium have been radically transformed because of changes both within the global church itself and in the world around it. The rest of the introduction seeks to locate the doctrine of God in this wider global and ecclesiastical context.[14]

The Many Facets of the "Globalization" of the Christian Church

The Christian Church Goes Global

From what is estimated to have been fewer than ten thousand Christians in 100 C.E.,[15] Christianity has grown to be the world's largest religion, with over 2.4 billion adherents. Nothing less than a "macroreformation"[16] is taking place, as

13. Moltmann, in *The Church in the Power of the Spirit*, is to my knowledge the first systematician in a major presentation of Christian ecclesiology to open up a window to Jewish faith (pp. 133-50) and to world religions (pp. 150-63), though he does so only briefly and at a formal level without any consideration of specifics of religions' teachings (even of Judaism).

14. For a thoughtful reflection, see Cox, "Thinking Globally about Christianity."

15. Stark, *Rise of Christianity*, pp. 57-61; see also pp. 3-21.

16. González, *Mañana*, p. 49.

Christianity is moving from the Global North (Europe and North America) to the Global South (Africa, Asia, Latin America); by 2050, only about one-fifth of the world's Christians will be non-Hispanic whites. "If we want to visualize a 'typical' contemporary Christian, we should think of a woman living in a village in Nigeria or in a Brazilian *favela*."[17] At the same time, the composition of the church worldwide is changing dramatically; as of now, one-half of all Christians are Roman Catholics, another quarter comprises Pentecostals/charismatics (in three subgroups, as outlined below), and the rest are Eastern Orthodox Christians, as well as Anglicans, mainline Protestants, and members of free churches.[18] This means that Roman Catholics and Pentecostals/charismatics together constitute three-fourths of the global membership. As a result, conservative and traditional mind-sets will be strengthened even when theological liberalism and pluralism reign in Western academia. The "Pentecostalization" of the Christian church in terms of Pentecostal/charismatic spirituality and worship patterns infiltrating all churches is yet another implication of the transformation.[19]

Globalization: A Threat or a Promise to the Church?

The meaning and implications of "globalization" are widely debated both inside and outside the church.[20] Briefly put, some of the main opinions and "schools" in this continuing complex set of issues are the following.[21] First, the predominantly negative assessment of globalization focuses on the effects of global-culture phenomena such as advertising, mass media, and particularly consumption, which are a means of taking over, as it were, the whole culture

17. Jenkins, *The Next Christendom*, p. 2. For Asia, see P. Phan, ed., *Christianities in Asia*; Poon, ed., *Christian Movements in Southeast Asia*; for Africa and the Caribbean, see Sundkler and Steed, *A History of the Church in Africa*; Sanneh and Carpenter, eds., *The Changing Face of Christianity*; for Latin America, see Cleary and Steigenga, eds., *Conversion of a Continent*; Schwaller, *History of the Catholic Church in Latin America*.

18. The basic statistical sources are Barrett, Kurian, and Johnson, *World Christian Encyclopedia* (pp. 12–15 contain a useful global summary), and the more recent T. Johnson and Grim, *The World's Religions in Figures*. Furthermore, the January edition of *International Bulletin of Missionary Research* continues providing annual updated data.

19. For important contributions, see Ormerod and Clifton, eds., *Globalization and the Mission of the Church*.

20. See Huntington and Berger, eds., *Many Globalizations*.

21. My analysis owes to the highly insightful theological reflection and assessment of these positions in Muthiah, *Priesthood of All Believers*, pp. 91–103.

and people's values.[22] Second, on the opposite end, there is the mainly positive (or at least, not primarily negative) view represented by the sociologist Anthony Giddens and like-minded thinkers. He believes that despite potential liabilities, globalization's threats can be thwarted and its positive contributions released for good, such as cosmopolitan values and increase of democracy, which may foster tolerance and peace.[23] Third, not surprisingly, there is the middle position that discerns both positive and negative assessments of globalization and (at least, at the moment) leaves it open as to whether negative and destructive values such as hegemony and domination or positive influences like freedom and flourishing emerge out of the mill of globalization.[24] Constructive ecclesiology has to follow carefully these discussions and exercise caution in assessing globalization's meaning.

Particularly significant to the future of the Christian church is the rapid and steady growth of Christianity in Africa — which also has become an important exporter of migrant and diaspora Christianity to the Global North.[25] Against common misconceptions, the American-based Sierra Leonean missiologist Jehu J. Hanciles debunks the myth that African Christianity is by and large a result of Western mission work. Rather, he argues: "In the final analysis, the story of African Christianity and the growth of the modern African church has been a decidedly African production in which foreign agents have made dramatic entrances and exits."[26]

A defining feature of current globalization has to do with massive moves of peoples and people groups around the globe. For ecclesiologists, the phenomena of migration and diaspora are highly meaningful.

Diaspora and Migration: New Ways for the Church to Be Global

After the term "globalization" had caught the eye of ecclesiologists and missiologists, the focus then shifted to "migration studies," and most recently to the phenomenon of "diaspora"[27] and, correspondingly, to "diaspora missiol-

22. Budde, *The (Magic) Kingdom of God*; Ritzer, *The McDonaldization of Society*.

23. Giddens, *Runaway World*.

24. Goudzwaard, *Globalization and the Kingdom of God*; see also Csordas, ed., *Transnational Transcendence*.

25. Adogame, *African Christian Diaspora*; Adogame, Gerloff, and Hock, eds., *Christianity in Africa and the African Diaspora*; Manning, *African Diaspora*.

26. Hanciles, "Africa Is Our Fatherland," p. 220.

27. For basics, see Dufoix, *Diasporas*.

ogy."[28] This includes the continuing debate about migration's and diaspora's implications for religion.[29]

According to 2013 Pew Research Center data, of over two hundred million migrants (roughly 3 percent of the world's population), about one-half are Christians; the United States houses most of them. The next largest group is Muslims (about one-fourth), followed by smaller groupings of other religious affiliations.[30] In terms of origins, migrants globally come (in ranking by size) from the Asia-Pacific region, Europe (and migrate mostly within Europe), Latin America and the Caribbean, as well as sub-Saharan Africa, the Middle East, and North Africa. The destinations from most to least are the United States, Europe, Australia, and the Arab states of the Persian Gulf.[31]

Due to massive intake of migrants, American Christianity diversifies unprecedentedly fast. As is well known, Christianity of Hispanic backgrounds is becoming a major form of Catholic, Protestant, and Pentecostal/charismatic expressions. Significant also are the emerging Asian-descent communities. Combined with an already-diverse and plural population, migration and diaspora make the United States a new kind of "laboratory" for diverse expressions of ecclesial existence.[32]

The majority of new migrants in Europe live in the western part of the continent. Although Muslims are the largest migrant group in the old continent (differently from the USA), Christian migrants in Europe have already left their mark on and continue to challenge the old bulwarks of Christendom.[33] Particularly visible is the presence of Pentecostal/charismatic immigrant and diaspora communities both in the United States and in Europe, a significant number of those being of African descent.[34] As could be expected, the impact of migrants and diaspora folks on and within churches is a continuously debated issue.[35]

28. The basic guide (even among those who are critical of some of its methodological and material claims) is Wan, ed., *Diaspora Missiology*.

29. See Krabill and Norton, "New Wine in Old Wineskins."

30. A standard reference work is Castles and Miller, *The Age of Migration*. A standard missiological analysis is Hanciles, *Beyond Christendom*.

31. General migration data can be found in the continuously updated database of the Pew Research Center: http://www.pewresearch.org/topics/migration/; for religious migration data, see Pew Research Center, "Faith on the Move."

32. Levitt, *God Needs No Passport*; Howell, "Multiculturalism, Immigration."

33. Jongeneel, "Mission of Migrant Churches in Europe"; see also Gerloff, "Significance of the African Christian Diaspora."

34. F. Ludwig and Asamoah-Gyadu, eds., *African Christian Presence in the West*.

35. See Doyle, Furry, and Bazzell, eds., *Ecclesiology and Exclusion*.

Should they be considered either a new catalyst for mission and energy for the church life or a burden and threat?[36]

Related to these dramatic shifts in the epicenter of global Christianity, from north to south, are also unprecedented transformations, changes, and hybrid identities of various ecclesial forms.

Continuing Transformations and Changes in Ecclesial Life and Structures in the Global Church

New Forms of Ecclesial Existence

Reading typical systematic theological discussions of ecclesiology, one often wonders if the theologian and the reader live in different worlds.[37] By and large, doctrines of the church — similarly to ecumenical documents — are still written as if a Christendom model were in place and "mainline" churches were the only players on the field. Similarly, denominational markers stay intact for theologians and ecumenists although they have become fluid and at times almost nonexistent among a growing number of church members. Yet, by and large, traditional churches have lost their former status both in society and in the Christian imagination — even if the Roman Catholic Church, differently from all counterparts, continues to constitute a majority. At the same time, new forms of the Christian church are mushrooming and flourishing.

Many specialists hold the opinion that the free church congregational model might well be the major paradigm in the third millennium, alongside the Catholic one.[38] Owing to the heritage of the Radical Reformation, Christian communities such as the Anabaptists and (later) Mennonites, Baptists, Congregationalists, Quakers, Pentecostals, some Methodist and Holiness movements, as well as a growing number of independent movements, are usually included under the somewhat elusive concept of "free churches." Another self-designation used by many among these Christians is "believers' church."[39]

---

36. For basic issues and debates, see E. Phan and Padilla, eds., *Contemporary Issues of Migration and Theology*; J. D. Payne, *Strangers Next Door*. An important ecumenical statement is *The 'Other' Is My Neighbor*.

37. For insightful observations about the context of ecclesiology in the current world, see Mannion and Mudge, "Introduction," pp. 4-5.

38. Volf, *After Our Likeness*, p. 12.

39. See further Little, "Concept of the Believers' Church."

Yet another term is sometimes used: the "gathered church," over against the "given church" of the older traditions.[40]

Surprisingly, the free church type of ecclesiality and congregationalism is also infiltrating traditional churches, including Roman Catholicism,[41] as evident in the rise of base communities in Latin America. As a result, ecclesiological values such as voluntarism, egalitarianism, and independence at the cost of clericalism, hierarchic structure, and collective regulations are being embraced.[42] In his highly acclaimed *Ecclesiogenesis*, Leonardo Boff of Brazil summarizes key features: "Slowly, but with ever-increasing intensity, we have witnessed the creation of communities in which persons actually know and recognize one another, where they can be themselves in their individuality, where they can 'have their say,' where they can be welcomed by name. And so, we see, groups and little communities have sprung up everywhere."[43] Understandably, the theological claim for the ecclesial nature of these communities has also placed them in tension with Catholic ecclesiology and hierarchy.[44]

A radical challenge and inspiration to the global church have come from the rapidly growing Pentecostal/charismatic phenomenon. While nothing like a uniform definition of Pentecostalism(s) exists, a helpful scholarly typology divides into three categories:

- (classical) Pentecostal denominations such as the Assemblies of God and Foursquare Gospel, which owe their existence to the famous Azusa Street Revival in 1906
- charismatic movements, Pentecostal-type spiritual movements within the established churches beginning in the 1960s (the largest of which is the Roman Catholic Charismatic Renewal)
- neocharismatic movements, including Vineyard Fellowship in the USA, African Initiated Churches, as well as countless independent churches and groups all over the world; usually even China's rapidly growing house-church movements are included herein[45]

---

40. G. Williams, "The Believers' Church and the Given Church."

41. Cf. Ratzinger, in *The Ratzinger Report*, pp. 45-46.

42. See further Volf, *After Our Likeness*, pp. 11-18.

43. Boff, *Ecclesiogenesis*, p. 1.

44. See Dulles, "The Church as Communion," p. 133.

45. Burgess and van der Maas, eds., *New International Dictionary of Charismatic and Pentecostal Movements*, promotes this typology.

The American "Ecclesiological" Laboratory:
Theological Challenges — and Promises

The American ecclesiastical environment is characterized by unprecedented denominational diversity, originally going back to the pilgrimage of European immigrants from the old continent and now fostered by immigration and diaspora. Although the Catholic Church is nowadays the biggest ecclesiastical player, large numbers of the first generations of new settlers also came from various types of Protestant and Anglican constituencies in which particularly the nonconformists often felt marginalized and were even occasionally oppressed. As a result, what Europeans would name free church ecclesiality forms the "mainline" American church reality. Among the Protestants, Baptists of various stripes are the largest group.[46]

Alongside the historically unheard-of denominational plurality, the American experiment is also characterized by a deepening and widening multiculturalism.[47] To express this intensifying hybrid ethnic composition of America, a new term — "postethnic" — has been coined, which "promotes multiple identities, emphasizes the dynamic and changing character of many groups, and is responsive to the potential for creating new cultural combinations."[48]

Among the several major American-based ethnic group families, none grows as fast and proliferates as widely as the Hispanic American churches.[49] The special challenge and asset of Hispanic communities in the United States is their ecumenical background in both Catholicism and Protestantism, lately also in Pentecostal/charismatic spiritualities.[50] As in other ethnic communities, Latino churches possess a feeling of "in-betweenness," as they live in two cultures, both ecclesiastically (Catholic, Protestant) and nationally (USA and the country of origin).[51]

Most recently, Asian-descent churches and movements have been gaining significance.[52] Predominantly evangelical in theological orientation, Asian

46. Statistics of the National Council of Churches (USA) for 2011 are available at https://theosophical.wordpress.com/2011/02/16/top-10-largest-christian-denominations-in-the-usa/.

47. See Chaplin, *Multiculturalism.*

48. Hollinger, *Postethnic America*, pp. 3–4.

49. See "Rise of Hispanic Evangelical Church."

50. González, *Mañana*, chap. 4 (part of chapter title and a heading). See further Martínez, *Los Protestantes.*

51. See further Martínez, "Historical Reflections on the 'In-Betweenness.'"

52. For the difficulty and complexity in defining "Asian American" (whether using a cultural, marginality, or postcolonial approach), see D. Lee, "Karl Barth, Contextuality, and Asian-American Context." See also Cha, "Ethnic Identity Formation."

American churches have mushroomed in many US contexts and in the near future will constitute a significant ecclesiological force.[53] Similarly to Hispanic American Christianity, that of Asian Americans reflects amazing diversity and plurality; we should speak, as a result, of "multiple Asian American ecclesiologies present in the form of ethnic churches, pan-Asian churches, and multiracial churches."[54]

Before the Hispanics and Asians, African American Christianity had already established its significant place in American religiosity. Black churches continue to grow, whether one speaks of Episcopal or evangelical or Pentecostal communities.[55] One single black Pentecostal denomination, the Church of God in Christ, is one of the largest non-Catholic church expressions in the United States.[56]

The newest and most complex set of ecclesiastical developments is linked with late modern/postmodern cultures, virtual connections, and new "tribalism." Those trends will be highlighted in the following.

Churches for Postmodern Times: Emerging Churches and "Fresh Expressions"

What would the church look like in the "post-world," whether postmodern, postliberal, postfoundationalist, postcolonial, postmetaphysical, postconservative, postsecular, post-Christian, or post-?[57] Titles such as *Church-Next* (2000)[58] and *The Liquid Church* (2002)[59] testify to this ecclesial "postexistence." A few decades ago, ecclesiologists spoke of the baby boomer generation. It was served with the so-called seeker-friendly suburban-based churches that catered to all kinds of needs of individuals and families.[60] Thereafter, "purpose-driven" churches and similar expressions caught our

53. Chuang, "9 Things about Asian American Christianity."

54. D. Lee, "Karl Barth, Contextuality, and Asian American Context," pp. 184–85; see also Park, Rah, and Tizon, eds., *Honoring the Generations*; Jeung, *Faithful Generations*.

55. J. Evans, *We Have Been Believers*, pp. 119–20; for details, see J. Wright, "Protestant Ecclesiology," and C. Davis, "Roman Catholic Ecclesiology."

56. See the Church of God in Christ's official Web site at http://www.cogic.org.

57. See chap. 10 of Bosch, *Transforming Mission*; Mannion, "Postmodern Ecclesiologies," pp. 127–52; more widely in Mannion, *Ecclesiology and Postmodernity*. Also highly useful is Lakeland, *Postmodernity*; Sivalon, *God's Mission and Postmodern Culture*.

58. Gibbs, *ChurchNext*.

59. P. Ward, *Liquid Church*.

60. For the Willow Creek Community Church (Barrington, Ill.), see http://www.willow creek.org/.

attention.[61] Most recently, these kinds of models, while still having an appeal with their own generation, are giving way to Gen X and other postmodern generations.[62] Among them, a most exciting phenomenon ecclesiologically is known under the rubric of "emerging church" (USA) and "fresh expressions of the church" (UK). Highly active in virtual networks and ways of connecting, their ecclesiologies are fluid.[63] Nor do they always meet in sanctuaries but may instead rent comedy clubs or pubs. Deeply missional in orientation with a focus on practices and everyday Christian service, they do not typically bother to delve into theological debates about ecclesiology, although many of their leaders may have a solid academic training in religion.

So far the most thorough study — ethnographic as well as theological — on both sides of the Atlantic Ocean, *The Emerging Churches*, by American missiologists Eddie Gibbs and Ryan Bolger, suggests that emerging churches (1) identify with the life of Jesus, (2) transform the secular realm, and (3) live highly communal lives. Because of these three activities, they (4) welcome the stranger, (5) serve with generosity, (6) participate as producers, (7) create as created beings, (8) lead as a body, and (9) take part in spiritual activities.[64] The church life and the emerging theological activity among these communities are an interesting mix of old and new. On the one hand, they harken back to some aspects of sacramentality and mysticism, as well as neomonasticism, and on the other hand, they desire to connect with the latest moves and techniques in postmodern culture and ways of communication.

The basic difference between the US-based emerging churches and UK fresh expressions is that whereas the former is usually separatist, forming their own communities, in the latter category most communities are birthed by and stay within the Church of England (and other mainline denominations).[65] As the name "emerging" suggests, it is yet to be seen — both by its critics[66] and by its supporters[67] — what the future holds for these new ecclesiological expressions.

61. The concept was launched by Warren, *Purpose-Driven Church.*

62. See Ritzer, *McDonaldization of Society.*

63. See T. Jones, *The Church Is Flat.*

64. Gibbs and Bolger, *The Emerging Churches*, p. 45. An important recent theological study is P. Oden, *Transformative Church.*

65. See the Fresh Expressions Web site: https://www.freshexpressions.org.uk/about /introduction. The definitive source is the Church of England report *Mission-Shaped Church.*

66. See, e.g., Carson, *Becoming Conversant with the Emerging Church*; for an assessment of and response to the critique, see McKnight, "Five Streams of the Emerging Church."

67. See Pagitt and Jones, eds., *An Emergent Manifesto of Hope.*

Having now briefly outlined and highlighted some radical transformations and changes within the global Christian church, we will scrutinize two more formative features of the third millennium's "global village," namely, secularisms and religious pluralisms.

Religious Pluralism(s) and Secularism(s) as Ecclesiological Challenges

Religious Plurality and Diversity

What had been expected to become a "secular" world with the progress of modernity has become even more religious. At the global level, religions are not only holding their own but are also flourishing and (in some cases) growing in numbers. Religious plurality is no longer a matter of certain locations and continents, but is now a reality over the whole globe, including the Global North.[68]

Currently about a third of the world's population belongs to the Christian church (2.4 billion) and about a quarter is comprised of Muslims (1.6 billion). The 1 billion Hindus make about 15 percent, followed by Buddhists at half that number. Jews number fewer than 15 million, and over 400 million belong to various kinds of "folk religions." Only about 15 percent (1 billion) label themselves religiously unaffiliated (even though the majority of them entertain some kind of religious-type beliefs and practices).[69]

Whereas Hinduism and Buddhism are mainly regional (Asian) religions, Christians are by far the most evenly distributed around the globe. Roughly equal numbers of Christians live in Europe (26 percent), Latin America and the Caribbean (24 percent), and sub-Saharan Africa (24 percent). Muslims are also fairly evenly spread out, although a majority (over 60 percent) live in Pacific Asia, and the rest in Africa and the Middle East. Theologically, three-quarters of adherents of the world's religions live in a majority position in their own context — Hindus in India most consistently so.[70]

The statistical analysis itself should be a clarion call for Christian theology at large and ecclesiology in particular to seriously engage other religions' views, teachings, and doctrines.[71] That they seem not to be interested in that

68. See C. Cohen and Numbers, eds., *Gods in America*.

69. Pew Research Center, *The Global Religious Landscape*, p. 9 (executive summary); see also the massive resource of Brunn, ed., *The Changing World Religion Map*.

70. Pew Research Center, *The Global Religious Landscape*, pp. 10–11 (10).

71. See the important reflections and suggestions in D. Hall, *Thinking the Faith*, pp. 208-9.

should not be made a pretext for Christian oblivion. Although a growing number of comparative theological explorations come from the publishing pipeline, they are still disconnected from the major presentation of Christian doctrine. There are of course reasons for that oblivion, beyond the lack of awareness, such as that the task of acquiring enough learning even in the basics of other faiths is daunting for the theologian.[72] That, however, should not be an excuse but rather an invitation for expanding scholarship.

Because of the overwhelming continuing presence and force of religious plurality and forms of religious pluralisms (ideologies and interpretations of how to deal with the fact of plurality), the ambitious and noble call for all Christian theologians writing on ecclesiology would be to work toward a truly comparative doctrine of the church in an authentic dialogue with visions of community of other traditions.[73] Willingness to do that takes the theologian out of the safe zone of one's own tradition and makes him or her vulnerable,[74] but at the same time it opens up whole new ways of engaging the complex world around us. To that complexity also belongs the phenomenon of secularisms of various forms.

The Forces of (Post)Secularism

Due to the sweeping removal of God-consciousness from the minds of modern people and the public realm,[75] combined with the loss of institutional power of churches (first) in Europe and (then) in North America, particularly in Canada, the (in)famous "secularization" thesis of the 1960s predicted that religions would soon die out and secularism be the default position.[76] Although reports of the progress of secular forces are heard from Christian and other religious traditions,[77] the critical question to be raised is simply this:

---

72. Tennent, *Theology in the Context of World Christianity*, p. 55.

73. Clooney, *Hindu God, Christian God*, p. 7.

74. Clooney, *Comparative Theology*, p. 7.

75. Pannenberg, *ST* 1:63. For details, see my *Trinity and Revelation*, pp. 182–86.

76. Schultz, "Secularization," p. 171. Representative are P. Berger, *The Sacred Canopy*; Luckmann, *Invisible Religion*; Martin, *A General Theory of Secularization*; among theologians, Cox, *Secular City*.

77. For Islam, see Sachedina, *Islamic Roots of Democratic Pluralism*, p. 3; see also his *Role of Islam in the Public Square*; for Buddhism, see Abe, "Kenotic God"; for Hinduism, see Selvanayagam, "Indian Secularism"; atheism and secularism are so common among Jews that no documentation is needed.

Will secularism win over? How reliable and accurate is the prediction of the secularization thesis? The response is twofold and a bit ambiguous.

On the one hand, current statistics and analyses seem to support the secularization thesis at least in the Global North. A Pew Research Center (2014) report revealed that the share of US adults belonging to mainline Protestant churches (United Methodist, Evangelical Lutheran Church in America, Episcopal Church) dropped from 18.1 percent in 2007 to 14.7 percent in 2014. Among Catholics, the drop in membership went from 23.9 percent to 20.8 percent. In contrast, evangelicals and historically black Protestant traditions now make up the majority (55 percent) of all Protestants in the United States; that figure was 51 percent in 2007.[78] The membership losses and passivity of churchgoers in many western European countries are even more dramatic, so much so that headlines such as "Europe's Empty Churches Go on Sale" are a commonplace in the media.[79] Secularism in the Global North, particularly among academics and the intelligentsia, is allied with the philosophical position known as naturalism, "the philosophy that everything that exists is a part of nature and that there is no reality beyond or outside of nature."[80] Although there are various types of naturalisms, from totally religion-opposed to religion-friendly, all of them either remove God from their calculations or radically reinterpret belief in God as the "ground" of everything.[81] In the popular imagination, the (hard) sciences have by and large replaced the church with the scientific academy as the source of wisdom.

On the other hand, notwithstanding secularism's powerful presence in the Global North, the original prediction of the death of religions has been shown to be embarrassingly misguided, or at least in need of serious nuancing and revising. As said, the thesis is pretty accurate when it comes to the loss of power of religions over secular institutions such as, say, the universities[82] — with the exception of Islamic contexts and India at large. Furthermore, when

---

78. Pew Research Center, "America's Changing Religious Landscape." The neologism "nones" has been coined to speak of the decline of church alignment, a particularly common trend among (well-educated) young adults, as documented by Pew Research Center, "'Nones' on the Rise"; Gallup and Lindsey, *Surveying the Religious Landscape*.

79. Bendavid, "Europe's Empty Churches Go on Sale." See also McLeod and Ustorf, eds., *Decline of Christendom*; See also Brierly, *The Tide Is Running Out*.

80. Goetz and Taliaferro, *Naturalism*, p. 6; a similar definition is that of Clayton, *Mind and Emergence*, p. 164.

81. A fourfold typology of naturalisms was developed and defended in *Creation and Humanity*, chap. 1.

82. See Marsden, *The Soul of the American University*.

it comes to the (public) role of religion in the Global North, particularly in Europe and Canada, the thesis is not far off the target.[83] But even there, as the Italian philosopher Gianni Vattimo's *After Christianity* notes, religion has not necessarily been left behind in Europe (and the USA), as what he calls "secular transcendence" is gaining momentum.[84] Where the secularization thesis has embarrassingly failed is in its prophecy of the disappearance of religions globally.[85] Says Peter L. Berger, once a spokesman for the death of religions in modern society: "[T]he assumption that we live in a secularized world is false. The world today, with some exceptions . . . , is as furiously religious as it ever was, and in some places more so than ever."[86] In keeping with this assessment — counterintuitively to the proponents of the secularization argument — fundamentalist[87] and other traditional forms of religion, within both Christian and other faith traditions, are growing rather than disappearing.[88] Just consult the growth statistics of Christianity in the Global South, mentioned above. Whereas ironically the "assimilationist" or "liberal" expressions of religions are losing momentum, the traditional ones are strengthening.

As already mentioned, similarly to religious pluralisms, secularisms come in many forms. Those will be investigated in more detail in the last chapter, along with what might be proper missional responses by the Christian church.

Brief Orientation to Part 2

The next immediate task regards the exposition of visions of community among Jewish, Muslim, Hindu, and Buddhist traditions (chap. 12). As mentioned, in that context no intentional Christian engagement will be attempted. Rather, as accurate as possible a profile of each tradition's "ecclesiology" is the aim.

Thereafter, the construction of the distinctively Christian doctrine of the church will begin. Throughout that constructive work, relevant insights

---

83. See further Carter, *Culture of Disbelief*; Chadwick, *The Secularization of the European Mind*; Jacoby, *Freethinkers*.

84. Vattimo, *After Christianity*.

85. See Schultz, "Secularization," p. 174.

86. P. Berger, "Desecularization of the World," p. 2.

87. See the massive five-volume series edited by Marty and Appleby, *The Fundamentalism Project*.

88. P. Berger, "Desecularization of the World," p. 6.

and teachings from other religions will be kept in mind, although only in the very last chapter (20) will a full-scale dialogue and mutual engagement be the main task. The first step in the development of ecclesiology — following the template employed throughout the five-volume project — is to link the church with the Trinity, the distinctively Christian understanding of God (chap. 13). The trinitarian unfolding of the nature and mission of the church will then be subsequently executed throughout the project.

Chapters 14 and 15 belong together. The former seeks tentatively to clarify the question of "ecclesiality," that is, the conditions of what makes the church, church (in contrast to all other human institutions and societies), by putting forth an ecumenical proposal with the hope that Christian communities could move away from exclusive nonrecognition of each other to mutual recognition. The latter chapter then continues the task of inquiring into the nature and life of the Christian church by tapping into the rich resources of a trinitarian communion theology.

Clarifying the nature of the Christian communion through the resources of trinitarian communion theology also brings to the fore the essentially missional nature of the church. Linked with and derived from the life of the triune God, the church is graciously drawn into the "missionary" movement of the Son, sent by the Father, in the power of the Spirit for the salvation of the world. Mission, rather than being a task given to the church, among other duties, belongs to the very nature of the church. It is not so much that the church has the mission; it is rather that mission has the church, as it were (chap. 16). Thereafter, the following two chapters, 17 and 18, envision the missional existence of the church in the world in terms of the liturgical and sacramental and what is called here the "charismatic-diaconal" ministry, respectively.

Although the concern for the unity of the one church of Christ characterizes the whole ecclesiological task in this project, the many complex details about ecumenisms will be the focus of chapter 19. Fittingly for the postmodern/late modern and pluralistic world, the ecumenical vision of the project can be described as "the diversified and plural unity of the church."

The last challenging and demanding task (chap. 20) is to concentrate on a deep engagement of visions and teachings of religious community in Jewish, Muslim, Hindu, and Buddhist traditions. That relates to the domain of comparative theology. As a way into the comparative task, a lengthier constructive proposal concerning a distinctively trinitarian Christian theology of hospitality in terms of dialogue and interfaith engagement will be set forth. The bulk of the last chapter, then, delves into a comparing and contrasting of Christian visions of community with those of Judaism, Islam, Hinduism, and Buddhism.

Throughout this comparative exercise, insights and results from similar work with all other (Christian) doctrinal topics in the other four volumes will be referred to and utilized. Along with the four faith traditions, the church's missional response to forms of (post)secularisms will also be included.

The epilogue then takes a brief look at the comprehensive vision behind this innovative and novel presentation of Christian constructive theology and once again raises the question of its credibility and appeal in the religiously pluralist and (post)secular world.

12. Visions of Community among Religions

Religions' grip on the lives, beliefs, and lifestyles of the global community of peoples is wide and deep.[1] As argued above, even with the rise of secularism, religions are flourishing and doing well.[2] An important contribution to religions' flourishing comes from religions themselves, namely, the missional vision and activity of Buddhist, Muslim, and Christian communities.[3]

Although it would make only little sense to speak of "ecclesiology," the doctrine of the church, in pan-religious terms, "it is part of the belief-structure of most religions that there should be a particular society which protects and sustains their basic values and beliefs, within which one may pursue the ideal human goal, as defined within the society"[4] and religion itself.[5] That said, the importance and role of the community vary greatly from religion to religion; similarly, the community's relation to the Divine differs among traditions. In terms of orientation, it is useful to highlight three broad theologically/ecclesiologically significant differences.

1. Juergensmeyer, "Thinking Globally about Religion"; see also Banchoff, ed., *Religious Pluralism, Globalization, and World Politics.*

2. Religions are far from static and frozen; they are constantly under change and transformation; see further Netland, *Christianity and Religious Diversity,* p. 71.

3. See Chanda, *Bound Together,* p. xiii; Netland, *Christianity and Religious Diversity,* pp. 44-46.

4. K. Ward, *Religion and Community,* p. 1.

5. Here it is not possible to delve into the continuing complex scholarly debates about the concept of "religion" itself (and cognate terms such as "world religions"), which is a modern Western invention. An up-to-date, highly useful discussion for theologians is Netland, *Christianity and Religious Diversity,* chap. 1 (with rich, diverse literature), which also clarifies the meaning of "worldview" and "culture" in relation to religion.

First, whereas the Abrahamic (Jewish, Muslim, and Christian) traditions are integrally and deeply communal in orientation, neither of the Asiatic faiths engaged here is; commensurately, the Asiatic faiths' visions of "salvation" focus neither on the whole of humanity nor on the reconciliation of the cosmos as in the Abrahamic faiths, particularly Jewish-Christian traditions. In Buddhism, the communion involves basically the religious "professionals," monks, and only indirectly, through their contact with them, laypeople. Hinduism is basically individualistic and its communal structure highly diverse — and to the outsider, endlessly complex and elusive.

Second, whereas for Abrahamic traditions the religious community is deeply rooted in a "personal" God and divine election (notwithstanding differences in election theologies), in Asiatic faiths that is not the case. In Buddhism, particularly in its original Theravada form, the community is about ethico-religious pursuit, and in Hinduism, even theistic forms (which constitute the majority of popular religiosity throughout India), the communities' relation to the Divine (however diversely understood) is complex and ambiguous.

Third, with little exaggeration it can be said that whereas the Asiatic faiths major in the renunciation of society in pursuit of final release, particularly the Christian faith (with many variations, of course) seeks to both renounce "the world" and penetrate it for the sake of its flourishing in this age and salvation (of many) in the eschaton. With Judaism and Islam, that issue is a bit more complex, although essentially different from that of Asiatic faiths.[6]

The plan of the current chapter is straightforward. With each of the four religious traditions, three tasks are attempted: first, to describe the religious community; second, to outline her liturgical and ritual life; and, third, to examine the self-understanding of the community in relation to other traditions' communities (religious plurality). As said, intentionally, no attempt is made to engage them comparatively — that task is for chapter 20.

Synagogue — the Jewish Community

The Emergence of the Jewish People and Community

Similarly to her Abrahamic sister faiths, Judaism is communally oriented and community centered. This comes to expression in the prayers alone: although personal prayers have their place, the main focus is on the communal prayer

---

6. See the somewhat similar kind of reflection in K. Ward, *Religion and Community*, pp. 1–4.

life.[7] Although a close relation to ethnicity and a particular nation hardly is unique among religions — just think of Hinduism in India — Judaism is the only religion that originally was purely tribal and still continues to be ethnic. While beliefs, particularly uncompromising monotheism (Deut. 6:4), came to be part of Jewishness from early times, the basis of the Jewish identity "is not a creed but a history: a strong sense of a common origin, a shared past and a shared destiny."[8] Indeed, one's Jewishness is not cast away by the lack of faith or even a pronounced atheism — an unthinkable situation for a Muslim or Christian. One either is a Jew, by birth (of a Jewish mother), or one is not. Belonging is hereditary, unlike in any other religion.[9]

So far I have used the term "Jewish" in the established contemporary sense. However, totally differently from sister Abrahamic faiths (and Buddhism), the emergence and birth of the religion of Judaism is unique in that it happened in two distinct phases and over a millennium-long time span. Indeed, technically we should speak of two religions and communities — Israel and Judaism. Israelite religion and community have Moses' legacy as the defining origin, as recounted in the *Tanakh* (which Christians call the Old Testament). Judaism emerged beginning from the renewals led by Ezra following the Babylonian exile in the sixth century; that story begins in Ezra-Nehemiah, and the defining identity is shaped by the rabbinic tradition's Talmud.[10] The emergence of the synagogue as the religious community in that phase is an important event. In the following discussion, we will follow the established custom of regarding these two streams, Israel and Judaism, as one Jewish religion with the synagogue as its community.

Israel's distinctive identity is based on Yahweh's election of her as a "chosen people," even "holy people" (Deut. 7:6).[11] Election came to be understood in terms of covenant and its call for total devotion to Yahweh. Basically, separatism follows from this status and at the same time a claim for a specific territory, the Holy Land, ideally to be lived in under a theocracy (Num. 34, among others).[12] Due to separatism, intermarriage has not been encouraged (as common as that has been in various eras), nor are conversions sought,

---

7. Langer, "Worship and Devotional Life," pp. 9805-6.

8. De Lange, *Introduction to Judaism*, p. 26. For details and opinions, see the massive recent discussion in Poorthuis and Schwartz, eds., *A Holy People*.

9. See also K. Ward, *Religion and Community*, pp. 12-14.

10. For details, see Ludwig, *Sacred Paths*, pp. 347-58.

11. See further Novak, *The Election of Israel*; my *Spirit and Salvation*, chap. 9.

12. On the complicated questions of the land and its occupation, see K. Ward, *Religion and Community*, pp. 13-15, 18-19.

although proselytism is possible under certain conditions.[13] Separatism and ethnic orientation, however, are only one part of the Jewish identity.[14] A strong trend in the Old Testament has to do with a missionary calling to help other nations of the world to know the name of Yahweh and be a vehicle of divine blessings (Gen. 12:1–3). Although Israel's missional vocation is not similar to that of Islam and Christianity in terms of making concentrated efforts to reach nonbelievers, it still is embedded in Israel's identity in terms of expecting a universal end-time pilgrimage to Jerusalem to worship God (Isa. 2:1–4; Mic. 4:1–4).[15]

A further defining feature of Jewish identity and her community is the continuing diaspora status beginning from the fall of Jerusalem in the sixth century B.C.E. and continuing all the way until the founding of Israel in 1948.[16] But even since then, the large majority live in diaspora outside the Holy Land, with a majority of that in the United States. When it comes to Israel's current existence as a nation among others, it is a secular state, even if deeply and widely linked with Jewishness as its religio-cultural matrix. As a result, deeply diverse and conflicting interpretations of the role of religion in the contemporary world characterize daily life.[17]

Liturgy and Religious Cycle

Although the origin of Jewish religious community, the synagogue, is widely debated, it is safe to relate it to the sixth-century B.C.E. national and religious crisis of losing the land and the temple, the beginning of (what became) rabbinic Judaism. The first synagogues were probably structures like ordinary houses, but the perception of holiness later led to fairly elaborate sacred building structures; that said, they are varied, often sensitive to the local context.

---

13. See Shatz, "A Jewish Perspective," pp. 369–71; for details, see chap. 10 in *Spirit and Salvation*. Highly useful is also D. Berger, "Reflections on Conversion and Proselytizing."

14. On the changing notion of separatism related to historical-political events, see Coward, *Pluralism in the World Religions*, pp. 3–4.

15. K. Ward, *Religion and Community*, pp. 15–17; for a short description of the main contemporary movements — Reform, Orthodox, Conservative, and Reconstructionist — see Ludwig, *Sacred Paths*, pp. 363–65; for a more detailed account, see Neusner, *Judaism in Modern Times*.

16. For the history of its existence in diaspora beginning from the rise of Islam all the way to the twentieth century, see Ludwig, *Sacred Paths*, pp. 358–66.

17. For details, see K. Ward, *Religion and Community*, pp. 18–23.

Ten men are usually needed to establish the synagogue (called *minyan*);[18] in later liberal modern settings, women could be counted among the ten. Traditionally women have been separated from men into a different space in the synagogue; in modern and contemporary times that varies.[19]

Similarly to the Christian church, the synagogue is the "visible side of the Jewish community," and the word may refer to either the community or the building. A further similarity is its close connection with the Jewish home, as evident, for example, in weekly and annual sacred meals. Usually led by an elected council or official, synagogues are autonomous, without any authoritative superstructure (notwithstanding organizational associations).[20]

Unlike in most Christian churches (but similar to Islam), no professional clergy is needed to lead prayers and worship in the synagogue, even if cantors and wardens are often designated to help the process. That said, in practice the rabbi, the religious leader and teacher since the founding of (rabbinic) Judaism, presides over the liturgy. Although theologically there is no basis for a lay-clergy distinction, similarly to Christianity, such a consciousness is typical among Jews. That said, the rabbi is not a "priest" in any technical sense, and those two categories should not be confused. The rabbi is a religious scholar and expert.[21] As in other religions, rabbis used to be only men; nowadays, in diaspora Judaism, many Reform movements endorse a gender-inclusive view.[22]

Although a number of issues concerning liturgy, prayers, and worship are a matter of continuous historical debate,[23] it is safe to say that "Rabbinic liturgy was built around the recitation of the 'Shema' (Deut. 6:4-9; 11:13-21; Num. 15:37-40) and its 'blessings' together with the Eighteen Benedictions (also known as

18. For the significance of the rule of "ten" in the life of the synagogue beyond the "founding," see de Lange, *Introduction to Judaism*, pp. 119-20.

19. For details and sources, see Gurmann and Fine, "Synagogue"; de Lange, *Introduction to Judaism*, pp. 125-27. The standard scholarly monograph (until the rise of Islam) is L. I. Levine, *The Ancient Synagogue*. On women, see Grossman and Haut, eds., *Daughters of the King*.

20. The Greek-derived word "synagogue," similarly to the Hebrew *bet kneset*, basically means "gathering together," that is, community, and thus resembles *ekklesia*; de Lange, *Introduction to Judaism*, pp. 120-21, 125 (120).

21. De Lange, *Introduction to Judaism*, pp. 121-22. Technically, a priestly status is inherited in Judaism, claiming origin in the Aaronic priesthood. For the distinction between the rabbi and the priest and the question of ordination of the rabbi, see pp. 122-23.

22. See de Lange, *Introduction to Judaism*, pp. 123-24.

23. For two comprehensive reviews of scholarly debates about all aspects of liturgy and worship, including its development, see Langer, "Revisiting Early Rabbinic Liturgy"; Fleischer and Langer, "Controversy."

the 'Standing prayer', the *Amidah*) morning and evening, and the Eighteen Benedictions with accompanying liturgy in afternoon prayers."[24] Another ancient habit is the encouragement to recite one hundred prayers per day, covering all aspects of life and faith, from the mundane to the heavenly.[25] There is no need to mention that the reading of Torah is an essential part of the worship.[26]

The question of sacred language, not unlike in Islam (Arabic) and Christianity (Latin), has also been a matter of debate over the centuries. Furthermore, similarly to Christianity, the role of sacred music and its place in worship have also divided minds.[27] Needless to say, the contemporary diaspora, particularly in the United States, has produced a wide variety of liturgical patterns and orientations.[28]

Not unlike other religions, there is a religiously ordered pattern for both the Jewish person's life cycle[29] and the life of the community following the sacred calendar.[30] What is unique is the centrality of weekly Sabbath, even more so than Christianity's Sunday. The weekly religious ritual is totally centered around Sabbath (the common Friday evening pre-Sabbath service is an integral part of it, rather than something separate), the only ritual determined already in the Decalogue.

Perceptions of the Religious Other

The Canadian comparativist H. Cowan makes the brilliant observation concerning the covenant Yahweh made with Israel that as much as that calls for unreserved commitment, it also implies that the same God who did this with Israel could also covenant with other nations. That observation echoes the kind

24. Gurmann and Fine, "Synagogue," p. 8922.

25. See Langer, "Worship and Devotional Life," p. 9806.

26. Langer, "Worship and Devotional Life," p. 9806. For details concerning the different kinds of sacred texts and readings in synagogue worship, see de Lange, *Introduction to Judaism*, pp. 134-37, and for a typical structure of the service, see pp. 138-41.

27. De Lange, *Introduction to Judaism*, pp. 127-29.

28. See Caplan, *From Ideology to Liturgy*.

29. For the meaning and ritual of the important life-cycle rites, circumcision, and bar mitzvah (or bat mitzvah), see de Lange, *Introduction to Judaism*, pp. 110-12 and 147-50, respectively.

30. For the details of the ritual and celebration of High Holy Days (a.k.a. Days of Awe), namely, Rosh Hashanah (New Year) and Yom Kippur (Day of Atonement), as well as others, including the Passover and Sukkot (Tabernacles), see de Lange, *Introduction to Judaism*, pp. 141-47.

of dynamic mutuality between particularity (separatism) and universalism (missionary calling) discussed above. That dynamic seems to be implied in passages such as Deuteronomy 32:8–9, an interesting mixture of particularity[31] and universality (also present in the Qur'an, as will be studied below):

> When the Most High gave to the nations their inheritance,
>   when he separated the sons of men,
> he fixed the bounds of the peoples
>   according to the number of the sons of God.
> For the LORD's portion is his people,
>   Jacob his allotted heritage.

As with any other tradition, Israel's relation to other religions has fluctuated over the centuries between exclusivism and inclusivism.[32] Throughout history there have been formative progressive thinkers who have championed openness, from the first-century (C.E.) Hellenistic Philo; to the ninth-century Saadiah Gaon, the "first" Jewish philosopher; to the twelfth-century Moses Maimonides, the Jewish counterpart in fame to Christianity's Thomas Aquinas; all the way to the nineteenth-century liberal modernist "European" Moses Mendelssohn; not to mention a number of contemporary thinkers.[33] Indeed, with the proliferation and diversification of views of Jewish movements in the twentieth century, a further polarization of views of religions and religious pluralism has only intensified.[34] In sum: Jewish diversity of views is not unlike in Christian tradition.

In a comprehensive historical scrutiny of Jewish views of other religions and their adherents, David Shatz argues convincingly that there are important theological reasons behind the wide-openness projected toward the religious other. A main reason for the "Talmudic position that embracing Judaism is not necessary for a Gentile's entering the world to come is that God wants to

---

31. Coward, *Pluralism in the World Religions*, pp. 2–3.

32. For a recent comprehensive survey of the diversity of views, see Brill, *Judaism and Other Religions*.

33. For details and sources, see Coward, *Pluralism in the World Religions*, pp. 4–8. For Maimonides, see Blidstein, "Maimonides and Mei'iri on the Legitimacy of Non-Judaic Religion," pp. 27–35.

34. For Emil L. Fackenheim, Franz Rosenzweig, Abraham Heschel, Robert Gordis, and Jacob Agus, see Coward, *Pluralism in the World Religions*, pp. 8–13. For a thoughtful current pluralist proposal, see Cohn-Sherbok, "Jewish Religious Pluralism." For different views, see Soloveitchik, "On Interfaith Relationships"; Brill, "Judaism and Other Religions."

give all people just rewards. He would not consign most of the world to hell or nihility without giving them opportunities for salvation." This position is firmly supported by the Mishnah and other rabbinic literature, authoritative to (most) Jews.[35] This is not to deny that this gracious openness has not always been the hallmark of the Jewish perception of the religious other, particularly with regard to Christians. But it is to appreciate the fact that despite horrible and inhumane treatment of Jews throughout the centuries and particularly in the twentieth, there is this robust inclusivist impulse.[36]

Ummah — the Islamic Community

The Birth and Meaning of the Ummah

Islam as a religion shares with Judaism and Christianity a deep communal orientation anchored in one God: "It is integral to this vision that human fulfilment should be achieved in a communal life of fellowship, loyalty, and trust, and that all human life should be related to God, who is the final goal."[37]

Originally (in pre-Islamic usage) the *ummah* was deeply ethnic and tribal,[38] but the term *ummah* appears in the Qur'an over sixty times with diverse and varying meanings.[39] The incipient universal vision of early Islam is evident in Qur'an 10:19, which states: "Mankind was but one community; then they differed," a statement that, according to "several early exegetes, . . . refers to the primordial existence of all humanity as a single *ummah* with a single religion, a state that was ruined by sin as exemplified by the murder of Abel by Cain."[40]

When it comes to its specific religious-community meaning, there is a marked development. Passages from the Meccan (and early Medinan) period are inclusive in nature, including in their widest meaning not only Muslims but also Jews and Christians.[41] Belief in (one) God was the criterion for inclu-

35. Shatz, "A Jewish Perspective," p. 367.

36. For details, see Shatz, "A Jewish Perspective," pp. 365–66, and summary statement on p. 376.

37. K. Ward, *Religion and Community*, p. 33.

38. Saeed, "Nature and Purpose of the Community (Ummah)," p. 16.

39. Saeed, "Nature and Purpose of the Community (Ummah)," pp. 15–16. See also Karamustafa, "Community," pp. 93–103; still highly useful is Denny, "Meaning of Ummah."

40. B. Wheeler, "Ummah," p. 9446.

41. For the famous Medina Constitution (or Charter), see Watt, *Muhammad in Medina*, pp. 221–28.

sion. Roughly speaking, beginning from the mid-Medinan period, a narrower understanding emerged: only the followers of the Prophet were included. A further dramatic shift happened after the death of the Prophet: whereas during his lifetime the *ummah* was primarily a religious community, thereafter the sociopolitical and juridical aspects were introduced, including determined expansion into new areas.[42] That said, "[i]n many Qur'ānic commentaries this community is seen as being based primarily on faith in God. It is described as fair and just, and a community that seeks to promote good and forbid evil."[43]

Muslim theologians debate what the saying concerning the exemplary community in Qur'an (Al Imran) 3:110 might mean: "You are the best community brought forth to men, enjoining decency, and forbidding indecency, and believing in God."[44] An ideological interpretation makes the Islamic community superior to all. A more hospitable view pays attention to the virtues mentioned in the verse, perhaps implying that other God-fearing communities may also excel. Another widely disputed passage speaks of the "midmost community" (or "middle nation") (Q 2:143). An appealing interpretation takes the term in the meaning of "just" and "moderate," that is, between two negative extremes.[45]

The Divisions of the Ummah: *The Emergence of the Sunnis and Shi'ites*

The *ummah* did not stay intact for long after it was founding. The major division, between the Sunnis and Shi'is, arose over the issue of the Prophet's successor after his death (632 C.E.). The Prophet's beloved wife Aisha's father, Abu Bakr, was made the first leader (*amīr*, "commander") by the majority, but that did not settle the matter, as the minority of the community preferred Ali, Muhammad's daughter Fatima's husband, as leader. Both theological and political issues were involved. Whereas for the majority, the leadership choice after the passing of the Prophet belonged to the *ummah* at large, for the rest it was a divine choice falling on Ali — with the ambiguous claim that he had divine endorsement as well as the Prophet's. The majority wanted to stay in the line of Mecca's dominant tribe, the Prophet's own tribe, Quraysh, whereas a minority received support from Medina. Full separation of the *ummah*, however, did not come about until after the brief leadership of Umar I and the longer office of

---

42. See Saeed, "Nature and Purpose of the Community (Ummah)," pp. 16–17.

43. Saeed, "Nature and Purpose of the Community (Ummah)," p. 17.

44. Saeed, "Nature and Purpose of the Community (Ummah)," pp. 18–19.

45. Asad, *Message of the Qur'ān*, on Q 2:143, cited in Saeed, "Nature and Purpose of the Community (Ummah)," p. 21.

the caliph Uthman, whose assassination in 656 brought Ali to power for half a decade, during which virtual civil war was fought. At the end, the community's separation was final, between the majority Sunnis with the powerful, almost century-long rule of Umayyad,[46] and a small minority of Shi'is following Ali's legacy. Both sides further continued splitting internally,[47] leading to the kind of complex denominationalism characteristic of most religions.

All Shi'is share the belief in the divinely ordered status of Ali as the successor to the Prophet (Q 2:124; 21:72–73), "guaranteeing that the community would not be led astray and providing divinely inspired leadership."[48] By far the largest and most important Shi'ite denomination, "the Twelvers" has developed a highly sophisticated genetic line of succession from Ali through his two sons (Hasan and Husayn) all the way to the Twelfth one. The most distinctive claim therein has to do with the last imam (after Hasan ibn Ali al-Askari of the ninth century), titled Muhammad b. Hasan, who allegedly went into "occultation" (that is, concealment) and whose return they await. All imams in this interpretation possess inerrancy in order to be able to prevent the community from being led astray. That said, there are a number of fiercely debated issues among the three main Shi'i traditions (the Twelvers, the Ishmaelites, and the Zaydis, the first two sharing much more in common concerning the imamate) about the line of succession and related issues. Even among the Twelvers, no unanimity exists about the nature and scope of inerrancy and the identity of the returning "al-Mahdi," as also discussed in part 1.[49]

Although this well-known broad outline of the emergence of the main factions of the *ummah* forms a common story in Islam, its many historical and particularly theological issues are a matter of continuing debate between the Sunnis and the Shi'is.[50] What is amazing and confusing to the outsider about the global Muslim community is that, despite how extremely much they share in tradition and doctrine, their mutual relationships are so antagonistic and

46. During the Umayyad rule, the name "God's Deputy" (*khalīfat Allāh fī al-arḍ*) was adopted. On the caliphate, see Nagel, "Some Considerations."

47. On the early emergence of major movements on both sides that are also formative for understanding later philosophical and theological positions, see Blankinship, "The Early Creed," pp. 38–54.

48. Haider, *Shī'ī Islam*, p. 31.

49. An accessible, basic introduction to the imamate is Haider, *Shī'ī Islam*, chap. 2; for a wider discussion, see Crone, *God's Rule*, particularly chaps. 6, 9, 10, and 15. For Twelvers, see also Haider, *Shī'ī Islam*, pp. 41–45, 94–98.

50. For an up-to-date, accessible (to nonspecialists) discussion, see Haider's (*Shī'ī Islam*, pp. 3–4) summary of the main issues; more widely, see Donner, *Muhammed and the Believers*.

condemnatory. Both parties share the same Qur'an, the same prophethood, and the five pillars, including prayers, fasting, and other rituals (albeit somewhat differently nuanced and practiced). Internal divisions among both the Sunnis and Shi'is seem to the outsider at times more profound than the main separation.[51] Yet, as the noted Islamic scholar Feras Hamza opines, "Notwithstanding twentieth-century *taqrīb* ('bringing closer together') initiatives to bridge the divide between Sunni and Shi'i, sectarianism had been ingrained so early on in Islamic history that it could never really transcend its divisions into a pan-Islamic ecumenical project."[52]

The effects of and reactions to the Enlightenment and modernity have further helped split and diversify contemporary global Islam.[53] On top of all this, particularly challenging the attainment of unity is the diverse and pluralistic globalized world.[54] Be that as it may, the work for the unity of the *ummah*, similarly to the Christian tradition, is a scriptural mandate for all Muslims, and its future fruit is yet to be seen: "And hold fast to God's bond, together, and do not scatter. . . . He brought your hearts together so that by His grace you became brothers. . . . Let there be one community of you calling to good. . . . Be not as those who scattered and disputed" (Q 3:103–5).

Spiritual Life and Worship

Obedience, submission to Allah, and honoring *tahwid*, the absolute unity/oneness of God, shape Muslim life in all aspects, including what we call devotion and liturgy: "The necessity of obedience to God's will is thus the foundation for all devotion in Islam. Every human being should aspire to live as a servant ('*abd*) of God. For this reason, the required ritual acts of worship are referred to collectively as '*ibādah*, which can be translated as either 'worship' or 'service.'"[55] It consists of "five pillars"—confession, ritual prayer, fasting, pilgrimage, and alms—routinely preceded by the important rites of purification, both physical and spiritual.[56]

---

51. For a brief, useful account, see Haider, *Shī'ī Islam*, pp. 1–3. In addition to standard textbooks, some useful recent resources (accessible to nonspecialists) include Bar, "Sunnis and Shiites"; R. Brunner, "Shi'ite Doctrine."

52. Hamza, "Unity and Disunity," p. 74; see also K. Ward, *Religion and Community*, pp. 36–37.

53. See K. Ward, *Religion and Community*, pp. 48–52; Watt, *Muslim-Christian Encounters*, chaps. 7 and 8; Arjomand, "Thinking Globally about Islam."

54. Riaz Hassan, "Globalisation's Challenge to the Islamic 'Ummah,'" n.p.

55. Schubel, "Worship and Devotional Life," pp. 9816–18 (9816).

56. For a highly useful, detailed discussion, see Denny, *Introduction to Islam*, chap. 7.

The ritual prayer is the most visible form of piety. Muslims ought to pray five times a day at designated times, regardless of their location. Prayer is preceded by ablution and employs a prescribed form and content. Prayer is also the main activity in the mosque;[57] nowadays the Friday afternoon gathering there includes a sermon. Since there is no clergy and no theologically trained priesthood, any male in principle is qualified to lead; he is usually chosen from among those most deeply knowledgeable in the tradition.

As in many other traditions, holy scripture is highly honored and venerated. Although the Prophet Muhammad was but a human being, particularly in folk Islam and forms of Sufism his status gets elevated to a (semi)divine object of veneration. Sufi mysticism also knows a number of saints similarly highly elevated. Alongside the Prophet, Ali is highly honored not only in the Shi'i spirituality but also in a modified way among the Sunnis. Depending on the tradition to which one belongs, other key figures in Islam, particularly imams, former and current, receive high treatment.[58]

As in other religions, the annual life cycle follows the religious calendar, starting from the honoring of the date when Muhammad migrated from Mecca to Medina (called *Hegira*). Friday is not considered a holy day, although it is the day of congregation. Instead, a number of other holy days commemorate significant days in the life of the Prophet and early *ummah*.[59] Although rites of passage and other ritual acts and events order and shape personal and family life, they are unusually diverse in global Islam, showing evidence of great contextual flexibility. This is a notable fact for a faith that in doctrine and prayer life is so unified.[60]

Mission to Nonbelievers and Perception of the Religious Other

Like Christianity's, Islam's outlook is universal. Echoing biblical theology, the Qur'an teaches that "'to God belongs the kingdom (*mulk*) of the heavens and earth' (e.g., 2:107)" and God is the "'Master (*malik*) of the kingdom' (3:26)."[61]

57. Mahmutcehagic, *The Mosque*.

58. Schubel, "Worship and Devotional Life," pp. 9817–20; for Sufi mysticism and other forms of esoteric worship common in folk Islam, see chap. 12 in Denny, *Introduction to Islam*.

59. See Braswell, *Islam*, pp. 77–80.

60. For details, see Eickelman, "Rites of Passage"; Denny, *Introduction to Islam*, chap. 14.

61. Woodberry, "Kingdom of God in Islam and the Gospel," p. 49.

Similarly, echoing the Deuteronomic passage cited above (32:8–9), the Qur'an instructs us that "had God willed, He would have made them one community; but He admits whomever He will into His mercy, and the evildoers have neither guardian nor helper" (42:8). Furthermore, "whatever you may differ in, the verdict therein belongs to God" (42:10). The conclusion then is: "God is our Lord and your Lord. Our deeds concern us and your deeds concern you. There is no argument between us and you. God will bring us together, and to Him is the [final] destination" (42:15).

In this light it is understandable that the earliest Qur'anic passages were not calling people to convert to a new religion; rather, the Meccans were called to "worship the Lord of this House [Ka'ba]" (106:3). Only later, with the rising opposition from the worshipers of local deities, a decisive break was announced (106:9) and the confession became "There is no god except God" (37:35). We know that in Medina the Prophet with his companions lived among the Jews, and we may safely infer that he obviously assumed that the new faith was in keeping with theirs as well as Christian faith (2:40–41).[62] Recall also that at that time the term *muslim* could also be applied to non-Muslims such as Solomon (27:45) and disciples of Jesus (3:52). Only when the Jews rejected the Prophet was the direction of prayer changed from Jerusalem to Mecca (2:142).[63]

In keeping with this is the special status assigned to Abrahamic sister faiths. Between what Muslims call "the Abode of Peace and the Abode of War," a third region was acknowledged, "the Abode of the People of the Book," that is, Jews and Christians.[64] These two traditions enjoy a unique relation to Islam (2:135–36 and 5:12).[65] "Surely those who believe and those of Jewry, and the Sabaeans, and the Christians: whoever believes in God and the Last Day and behaves righteously — no fear shall befall them, neither shall they grieve" (5:69; repeated almost verbatim in 2:62).[66]

These kinds of scriptural passages seem to imply that in some real sense the diversity of religions is not only tolerated by Allah but even planned and

62. Woodberry, "Conversion in Islam," p. 24.

63. See further Donner, *Muhammad and the Believers*, pp. 68–74.

64. Fakhry, "An Islamic Perspective," p. 395; see also Watt, *Muslim-Christian Encounters*, pp. 26–27.

65. Along with inclusive statements about the Jews, there are also negative statements, as in 5:82–86; for details, see Watt, *Muslim-Christian Encounters*, pp. 12–14.

66. The Sabaeans (or Sabeans, Sabians; also in 5:69) are an obscure, little-known (Old) Arabic-speaking tribe, also mentioned in the Old Testament (Joel 3:8; Isa. 45:14); see Gündüz, "Problems on the Muslim Understanding of the Mandaeans."

endorsed, at least when it comes to those who are the "people of the book" (48:29; 5:48; 3:114).[67]

This inclusive tendency notwithstanding, Islam retains a unique place in God's eyes. The inclusion is similar to Catholic inclusivism: while other nations might have known God, only Muslims know Allah intimately and are rightly related to God. That is most probably the meaning of the Qur'anic statements that Muslims, in distinction from others, are "God's sincere servants" (37:40), and "they are of the elect, the excellent" (38:40).[68] Therefore, ultimately even Jewish and Christian traditions suffer from corruption and misunderstanding of the final revelation.[69]

Whatever the nuances regarding Islam's perception of religious diversity and tolerance may be,[70] at its core — similarly to Christianity but unlike Judaism — Islam is an active missionary community. Not unlike in the Bible, Qu'ranic passages urge the faithful to reach out to nonbelievers and spread the true message (16:125–26). This is often expressed with the Arabic term da'wah, literally "call, invocation, or summoning." It is "used especially in the sense of the religious outreach or mission to exhort people to embrace Islam as the true religion. . . . In the modern period, da'wah most often refers to Islamic missionary activities, which are increasingly characterized by long-range planning, skillful exploitation of the media, establishment of study centers and mosques, and earnest, urgent preaching and efforts at persuasion."[71] Combining a universalizing tendency and fervent missionary mandate, Islam's goal of outreach is comprehensive, including ideally social, economic, cultural, and religious spheres. Ideally it would result in the establishment of Shari'a law and the gathering of all peoples under one ummah.[72]

During various historical eras, da'wah has been exercised with the help of military and political means, as Christianity was as well, although the

---

67. So also K. Ward, *Religion and Community*, p. 34. For a comprehensive listing of relevant passages, see Rahman, "Appendix II."

68. Umansky, "Election," p. 2748.

69. Blankinship, "The Early Creed," pp. 33–34.

70. For highly useful resources, see Y. Friedman, *Tolerance and Coercion in Islam*; Legenhausen, *Islam and Religious Pluralism*; Jackson, *On the Boundaries of Theological Tolerance in Islam*. For an attempt by a Christian scholar to construct a typology of Islamic theologies of religions, see Winkler, *Contemporary Muslim and Christian Responses to Religious Plurality*, chap. 1.

71. W. Miller, "Da'wah." See also Ammar, "Principles of Dawah"; Ahmad and Kerr, eds., *Christian Mission and Islamic Da'wah*.

72. Kateregga and Shenk, *Islam and Christianity*, pp. 79–81; I am indebted to Muktar, "Response," p. 59; so also K. Ward, *Religion and Community*, p. 31.

Qur'an prohibits evangelism by force (2:256).[73] Alliance with earthly powers, militarism, and economic interests were all employed to spread Islam with force and brutality. Although it is unknown by some observers, not only does Christianity bear the heavy burden of colonialism, it is also very much part of the Muslim legacy, from the time of the second caliph Umar (633–634), to the Umayyad Dynasty, all the way to the Ottoman rule to the end of the nineteenth century.[74]

Hindu Spiritual Life and Community

In Search of Hindu Identity and Religious Community

Judaism and Hinduism have some commonality concerning their rise as religions.[75] Both emerged over a long period of time, and they evolved gradually. Furthermore, neither one has a human founder. They are also similar in that while one can be a Jew only by birth (through a Jewish mother), the assumption is that to have been born as an Indian, one is Hindu (unless the family subscribes to another religion, in which case one's "Indianness" may be questioned). Similarly, doctrine does not determine belonging in either tradition, although holy scriptures are honored in both. While one is not usually considered a Hindu unless one endorses the Vedas as sacred scriptures, Jews acknowledge the *Tanakh* as divine revelation, or at least as formative to Jewish identity. The role of believing and doctrine in relation to belonging is so marginal that one is a Jew totally apart from one's beliefs, and likewise, most Indians born into a Hindu family are taken as Hindus even if they do not follow the religious rites and beliefs.

Community does not play an essential role in Hinduism, as the religion's main goal is the spiritual release of the individual rather than either reform of the society or communal (let alone cosmic) eschatological renewal. This does not mean in any way to undermine the deeply and widely communal orientation of Indian culture and, as part of that, the celebration of religious rites in communal settings in family, village, or temple. Rather, it means that

73. W. Miller, "Da'wah," p. 2225.

74. For details, see Watt, *Muslim-Christian Encounters*, chap. 5 and pp. 89–94.

75. We continue to use the designation "religion" for Hinduism although, as is well known, that is a nineteenth-century Western invention and has to be understood most loosely. A useful guide and discussion for theological purposes is Lipner, "Ancient Banyan." For a thoughtful essay, see Clooney, "Restoring 'Hindu Theology,'" pp. 447–77.

the basic orientation of Hinduism lacks an internal and ultimate communal goal. In keeping with this, there is no single term to describe the communal side of Hindu spirituality. Perhaps closest in intention comes the term *sampradaya*, which, however, is not universally nor even very widely used. It "refers to a tradition focused on a deity, often regional in character, into which a disciple is initiated by a guru. Furthermore, each guru is seen to be within a line of gurus, a *santana* or *parampara*, originating with the founding father." Originating in Vaishnavism (the followers of the Vishnu deity and his many *avataras*, particularly the most famous, Krishna), *sampradayas* differ in orientations and ethos: some may require celibacy; others include whole households; most of them express local contextuality.[76] At times, terms such as "sects" or "movements" may be used more or less synonymously — even the term "religion" is so used.[77]

The plurality of *sampradayas* and similar movements brings to light another defining feature of Hindu religion and spirituality: diversity and plurality. Indeed, Hindu religious life allows for much more diversity, locality, and plurality than any other living tradition. This includes local deities (and incarnations of deities) to be worshiped. That said, the existing diversity does not translate into personal choice of the deity, as might be misunderstood in the manner of the hyperindividualism of the Global North. It is, rather, the family and wider community's religion and rites that are followed. Furthermore, the allowance for diversity of rites and beliefs does not have the same meaning as modernity-driven "first-generation" pluralism that alleges the equality of all paths.[78] On the contrary, even within Hinduism fierce debates and not infrequently mutual condemnations similar to those in Abrahamic and other faiths take place between different sects,[79] and it is reasonable to assume that typically the follower of any Hindu sect intuitively considers one's own the true(est) way.[80]

76. Flood, *An Introduction to Hinduism*, p. 134; for which see also the main Vaishnava *sampradayas*. In his treatment of Hinduism, Keith Ward takes *sampradaya* as the main concept of community (*Religion and Community*, chap. 4).

77. See Nesbitt and Arweck, "Retrospect and Prospect," pp. 52–54; see also Geaves, "Community of the Many Names of God."

78. For a thoughtful reflection, see Madan, "Thinking Globally about Hinduism."

79. For fierce debates about God, including the God-world relationship, the key concern between various kinds of *advaita* schools, see my *Trinity and Revelation*, pp. 394–401, and *Creation and Humanity*, pp. 95–97.

80. Materially similarly is K. Ward, *Religion and Community*, pp. 79–81. Particularly narrow-minded and at times hostile to the religious (and even national) other are the followers of Hindutva movements, promoting a "Hindu India" (see pp. 81–82; more extensively, Sathianathan, "Hindutva, Religious and Ethnocultural Minorities").

Hindu "Sacraments" and Ways of Spirituality

Without any claim for material similarity between Christian sacraments and Hindu life-cycle-related *samskāras*, through which one becomes a full member of the community and society, the Christian interpreter may duly identify them as "Hindu sacraments." Similarly to rites of passage in most all religions, they cover all life from birth to death. Guidelines for *samskāras* are found throughout the sacred literature.[81]

Highly important is one called "the second birth," which occurs at eight to twelve years of age, depending on the status of the family's son. The exact time of this rite of initiation (*upanayana*) is routinely determined by an astrologer, and it helps make a shift from childhood to the first of the four ashrams, which is studenthood, including religious education.[82]

A central role is also played by the last sacrament, that of death, universally practiced by all Hindus, even secular ones. The funeral, in which the body is burned, includes elaborate rites and rituals.[83] Following the funeral, ancestor rites typically continue over the years: "These rites establish the deceased harmoniously within their appropriate worlds and prevent them from becoming hungry and haunting their living descendants."[84]

As explained in detail in the context of soteriology (*Spirit and Salvation*, chap. 8), Hinduism at-large knows three paths (*margās*) to liberation, one focused on devotion (*bhakti*), another on knowledge (*jnana*), and yet another on effort (or work, karma).[85] By far the most typical at the grassroots level is the middle path, and for the large majority, this *bhakti* devotion comes in the form of theistic Vaishnavism (with endless denominational and geographic diversity).[86]

---

81. For the meaning and number of *samskāras*, see Pandey, *Hindu Saṁskāras*, pp. 15–24 (the monograph itself is almost an encyclopedic treatment of all aspects); see also chap. 10 in Klostermaier, *A Survey of Hinduism*.

82. Klostermaier, *A Survey of Hinduism*, pp. 149–50.

83. Klostermaier, *A Survey of Hinduism*, pp. 152–55.

84. Courtright, "Worship and Devotional Life," p. 9821.

85. For a reliable, accessible account, see Klostermaier, *A Survey of Hinduism*, chap. 8 (karma), chap. 11 (*jnana*), and chap. 14 (*bhakti*). The rest of part 2 of the book includes details on each of those.

86. Majumdar, *Bhakti Renaissance*, p. 159; for the importance of *bhakti*, see also Klostermaier, *Survey of Hinduism*, pp. 181–82; chap. 14 contains a succinct introduction to forms and practice of *bhaktimargā*; chap. 15 contains further details on the devotion to the Vishnu deity (the main god of Vaishnavism). As practical tools for devotion, Bhagavad-Gita (2.23, 39) suggests yoga techniques. The ancient yoga guide widely used in *bhakti* devotion is Patanjali's *Yoga Sutras*, written about 200 C.E.

Based on the Bhagavad-Gita, this loving, intimate devotion is often focused on Krishna, the most important *avatara* of Vishnu (discussed in chap. 10 of *Christ and Reconciliation*).[87]

Not limited to *bhakti* devotion, though certainly part of it, a defining feature of India's worship life is that "space and time are permeated with the presence of the supreme." According to K. Klostermaier, "[c]ountless temples, many of impressive dimensions, manifest the presence and power of Hinduism in all towns and villages. The intensity of devotion of the Hindus is revealed in numberless images: artistic creations in stone, metal, and wood, and cheap prints on colored paper."[88] Among them, the most profound is *mūrti*, or image, which can also be called "embodiment." It is the highest form of spatiotemporal manifestation of the divine.[89] In temples, the devout Hindus are surrounded and embraced by this divine presence. Consequently, a temple is not primarily an assembly room for the faithful, as in all Abrahamic traditions, but rather "the palace of . . . the embodied lord." In that presence masses of devotees may experience *darśana*, the special kind of spiritual "seeing" or insight.[90] Indeed, this "auspicious seeing" is mutual as, on the one hand, the deity makes herself or himself to be seen, and, on the other, the god is "seen" by the devotee.[91] Regular *pujas*, acts of worship to the deities, open to all Hindus, take place from day to day to celebrate the divine presence.[92] Closely related to the centrality of divine presence is a special kind of prayer rite, originating in Vedic religion,[93] the mantra "OM," which "represents all of reality and Brahman itself" to the Hindu. It is typical to have the head of the household utter this word first thing in the morning after purification rituals.

Similarly to other religious traditions, along with rites of passage, a rich and diverse annual festival menu is an essential part of Hindu devotion and worship life. Although the basic structure of festivals may be simple, to outsiders these festivals look extremely complex. They may last several days and exhibit unusually rich local and denominational diversity. As with rites of passage, determination of the exact time is linked with astrology, claimed to be connected with the special theology of divine grace, namely, "the Vaisnava theory that Visnu's grace waxes and wanes like the moon," bringing about set times of "at-

87. Just consult Bhagavad-Gita 12.6–8.

88. Klostermaier, *Survey of Hinduism*, p. 263.

89. Klostermaier, *Survey of Hinduism*, pp. 263–69 (264).

90. For details, see Klostermaier, *Survey of Hinduism*, pp. 268–77 (268).

91. Courtright, "Worship and Devotional Life," p. 9823.

92. For details, see Ludwig, *Sacred Paths*, pp. 109–10; Courtright, "Worship and Devotional Life," p. 9823.

93. The classic passage is Rig Veda 3.62.10.

traction" and "rejection."[94] To the annual devotional calendar also belongs *tīrtha*, pilgrimage, whose local and denominational diversity looks exhaustive to the outsider; in practice, part of the Hindu population is always on a pilgrimage.[95]

So far we have spoken of religious and devotional life, which is basically open to all Hindus who wish to participate. Not unlike in other faiths, there is also the "professional" religious class, the Brahmins, related to the ancient class system of India, formerly a caste society.[96] Whereas ordinary devotees have Puranas, the rich narrative and epic literature, as their holy scripture, only the Brahmins are experts in Vedic literature. Another related structure of Indian society and culture has to do with the four ashrams. Ideally one reaches at the end of life the final stage of the "renouncer" (*samnyāsa*), after studenthood, family life, and the period of forest hermit. Only a tiny minority of Hindus belong to the Brahmin class or reach the stage of renouncer. Indeed, at first only one born into the Brahmin caste could reach the renouncer stage; during the course of history, the fourth stage was gradually opened to others as well.[97] Along with these two classes, there is an innumerable group of gurus of various sorts, many highly respected, others less so. Around the guru, a *sampradaya* is formed, a main community concept for masses of Hindus.

The Perception of Religious Diversity Both within and in Relation to the Other

Hinduism embraces diversity in a way no other major living tradition does.[98] This diversity, however, differs from the modernist Western pluralism in many respects. First of all, Hindus, even in their tolerance of other rites and deities,

94. Klostermaier, *Survey of Hinduism*, p. 280.

95. Klostermaier, *Survey of Hinduism*, pp. 280-81; more extensively, Bhardwaj, *Hindu Places of Pilgrimage*.

96. The four classes are Brahmins, Kshatriyas, Vaishyas, and Shudras. Technically, one should use here the term *varna*, which does not change, whereas "caste" does, having produced over three thousand different subcategories, maybe more. A most detailed and careful discussion is chap. 19 in Sharma, *Classical Hindu Thought*; useful is also chap. 20 in Klostermaier, *Survey of Hinduism*. The Brahmins' special status also comes to the fore in the important purity rules of Vedic Hinduism; in Vedic rituals, only the Brahmins may do worship, and they have to avoid being polluted by contact with lower classes. See Ludwig, *Sacred Paths*, pp. 108-9.

97. See chap. 20 in Klostermaier, *Survey of Hinduism*.

98. Sharma, "A Hindu Perspective," p. 312, with reference to the classic Vedic dictum "the truth is one, sages call it variously" (for the longer literal version, see Rig Veda 1.164.46). For similar kinds of sayings in scriptures, see pp. 315-16. For a thorough scriptural scrutiny of Hinduism's perception of pluralism, see Daniel, *Hindu Response to Religious Pluralism*, chap. 2.

typically take their own beliefs as true, as opposed to typical critical Christian "demythologizer" or atheist or agnostic views. Second, Hindu tolerance has much to do with the idea that since God is bigger than any other concept of ours, various ways of approaching God are complementary in that, beyond and transcending any particular path, there is the infinite God (an idea that has parallels in the original version of J. Hick's pluralist interpretation).[99]

What about mission and desire to convert others? It is clear that Hinduism is not a missional religion after Buddhism, Christianity, and Islam. Considering itself the "original" religion, it tends to assimilate others under its own purview, not necessarily inviting them to change. Understandably, Hinduism faces grave difficulties when encountering Christian and Islamic types of claims for the finality of revelation and uniqueness of God.[100] In keeping with the assimilationist principle, Hindus resist, and not infrequently actively oppose, any efforts at evangelization by other traditions. In that light it appears inhospitable that some movements, such as Arya Samaj, opposed the conversion of Hindus to Islam and Christianity while at the same time strongly advocating reconversion of recent converts to Christianity back to Hinduism.[101] All in all, notwithstanding the hesitancy about conversion, Hinduism not only knows the reconversion of lapsed faithful but also engages in active missionary efforts to convert "pagans." This was certainly the case in the third to fifth centuries during the establishment of Hindu rajas in South India to replace Buddhism. Itinerant "evangelists" played a critical role in this enterprise. More recently, Hare Krishna and a number of less well-known revival movements in the West have sought new converts.[102]

The Buddhist *Sangha* and Spiritual Pursuit

The Rise of Sangha *and Rapid Proliferation of* Dhamma

Not only with Hinduism but even more so with Buddhism, the whole idea of naming it a religion is highly contested. Reasons are many and well known,

---

99. See further K. Ward, *Religion and Community*, pp. 82–84, 96–99. For the role of the stratification of Indian society in terms of caste-like differences (notwithstanding the absolving of the official caste system decades ago) in religious pluralism, see pp. 86–93. On the appeal of Western pluralisms to some intellectual Hindus, see Hospital, "The Contribution of Keshub Chunder Sen."

100. See also Sharma, "A Hindu Perspective," pp. 317–19.

101. Ahluwalia, "Shudhi Movement."

102. Hiebert, "Conversion in Hinduism and Buddhism," pp. 15–16.

beginning from its nontheistic foundational structure. Although not atheist in any modern Western sense, a main impetus behind the original Buddhist vision is to turn away from deities — whose existence, including a highly spirited cosmos, was of course never denied — to ethical pursuit of release from attachment.[103] Consequently, no Buddhist school acknowledges a creator, as do Abrahamic faiths, or a "beginning" (but rather the idea of "codependent origination").[104] That said, after the mid-nineteenth century, when Buddhism was "discovered" by Western scholarship, it has been routinely counted among world religions;[105] that custom will be followed here, as well as in the rest of comparative theology.[106]

Differently from the parent religion of Hinduism,[107] Buddhism has a founder, Siddhartha Gautama. Although the historical details of Gautama's life are very scarce, including the lack of precise dating of his birth,[108] the religion- and community-forming narrative is based on the enlightenment experience of this former noble prince and renouncer.[109] The teaching of the emerging new religion, as first expounded in Gautama's first sermon, "First Turning of the Wheel of *Dhamma*,"[110] similarly to Hinduism, is not centered on faith as much as on commitment to pursuing release from attachment to the world of impermanence and resulting *dukkha*.[111] Although the Buddha discouraged metaphysical speculations as useless and counterproductive, later traditions have produced very sophisticated and complex technical discussions of truth, being, and ethics.

The enlightened Sakyamuni (Gautama) established the *sangha*, community, with five initial disciples.[112] Originally it was an inclusive community,

---

103. Cf. the somewhat hasty denial in W. D. Hudson, *A Philosophical Approach*, p. 16. A more balanced discussion can be found in Steinkellner, "Buddhismus," pp. 251–62.

104. For a detailed discussion, see chap. 5 in my *Creation and Humanity*.

105. See further Netland, *Christianity and Religious Diversity*, pp. 80–83.

106. The strong Buddhist areas include China, Tibet, Japan, Thailand, Vietnam, and other areas of that part of Asia. Buddhism engaged the religions of the area, including Confucianism, Taoism, and Shintoism.

107. On its separation from Hinduism, see Ludwig, *Sacred Paths*, p. 127.

108. For a concise and useful historiographical and material discussion, see Nagao, "Life of the Buddha"; more widely, Nakamura, *Gotama Buddha*.

109. The authoritative narrative by Asvaghosa can be found in *The Buddha-Carita or The Life of Buddha*; the last chapter (14) recounts the actual enlightenment experience.

110. *Dhammacakkappavattana Sutta* of Samyutta Nikaya 56.11.

111. Rahula, *What the Buddha Taught*, p. 3. The translation "suffering" for *dukkha* is misleading; it is best left untranslated and conceived as an elusive term to denote "why things are wrong" due to clinging to something that is not permanent because of misguided desire.

112. For a basic succinct account, see Bechert, "Samgha." Still defining essays are Young, "The Sangha in Buddhist History"; Bechert, "Theravada Buddhist Sangha."

open to both male monks and female nuns (in Pali: *bikkhus* and *bikkhunis*, respectively).[113] The nuns lived separately from the men but belonged to the community. That inclusive vision, however, came to be limited through the centuries, and it is normal (particularly in Theravada contexts) to have only male monks.

Soon after the founding of *sangha*, Buddha began to send the enlightened monks (*arhats*, "worthy ones") out on missionary trips to preach the *dhamma*, the Buddha's teachings. So, unlike Hinduism, but like Christian and Muslim traditions, Buddhism is a missionary religion,[114] and one can find scriptural commissioning for it.[115] Indeed, it seems to me that it was even more so in the founding centuries.[116] Similarly to Christianity, the new religion also proliferated through merchants and other travelers.[117] Furthermore, not unlike in Christian history, every now and then royal protection and even promotion took place, of which the most celebrated is the great expansion of religion under the auspices of the convert king Asoka of the third century.[118]

Following Buddha's *parinirvana* (complete liberation at death), the First Ecumenical Council was summoned, gathering together five hundred *arhats* to whom Buddha's *dhamma* was entrusted, comprising Tipitaka, the "Three Baskets" of teachings, the middle one of which (Vinaya Pitaka) contains all instructions and teachings for the life of the *sangha*. Subsequently, the Second Council, one hundred years later, brought to the surface disagreements and strife (although, at this early stage, allegedly about fairly trivial issues). A number of other councils followed, along with deep disagreements and splits.[119]

Around the beginning of the Common Era, the most significant split occurred, giving birth to the Mahayana school.[120] Significantly, the Ma-

---

113. Indeed, the first nun was Gautama's aunt (who also served as foster mother), Mahapajapati Gotami.

114. See J. Walter, "Missions."

115. For the Buddhist "Great Commission," see *Mahavagga* (of *Vinya*) 1.11.1; *SBE* 13:112.

116. An example of the rapid divisions and proliferation of Buddhism from its beginnings onward is the rise of about eighteen different schools (*nikaya*) during the first century after the death of Gautama. Of those, the only one surviving is Theravada. Hence, its scriptural canon is defining for all later developments. The Theravada tradition is concentrated in Cambodia, Laos, Myanmar, Sri Lanka, and Thailand.

117. See Netland, *Christianity and Religious Diversity*, pp. 74–75. A recent major treatment is Learman, ed., *Buddhist Missionaries in the Era of Globalization*.

118. Mitchell, *Buddhism*, pp. 70–72.

119. See Prebish, "Councils."

120. Mahayana is currently present in India, Vietnam, Tibet (mainly in the form of

hayana tradition claimed to build on Buddha's own teaching and thus allegedly represented the "Second Turning of the Wheel of *Dhamma.*" This sermon was believed to be hidden for a while and then rediscovered by this renewal movement. Mahayana advocates a much more open access to the pursuit of nirvana for all men and women, not only to a few religious.[121] It also adopted a more theistically oriented cosmology and highlighted the importance of notions of grace and mercy, particularly in its later developments having to do with the Pure Land and related movements. Mahayana has also developed a growing tradition of spiritual exercises in pursuit of liberative insight.[122] The third major strand is commonly called Vajrayana ("Diamond Vehicle") or Tantrism and can be found in Tibet. Broadly related to Mahayana, it has also contextualized itself in rich Tibetan folk religiosity and mysticism with a focus on "many rituals, mantras (sacred words), mandalas (sacred diagrams), ritual sexual intercourse, and the like, to achieve realization of Buddhahood."[123]

Devotion and Liturgy

Differently from Jewish-Christian tradition, but in keeping with Hindu traditions, becoming a Buddhist does not usually entail any initiatory rite (whereas joining the *sangha* takes a long period of discipline and teaching, culminating in "ordination" by a legitimate leader). Instead of an initiatory act, it is (almost) universally taught among Buddhists that taking refuge in Buddha, *dhamma,* and *sangha* constitutes becoming a Buddhist. It normally entails adhering to the five precepts of abstaining from killing, stealing, adultery, lying, and drinking. At the same time, one commits oneself to the pursuit of liberation from *dukkha* following the Noble Eightfold Path.[124]

Although in Theravada the releasing enlightenment is typically thought to be attained only by the monks, and even among them, by few, Gautama

---

Tantric Buddhism or Vajrayana), China, Taiwan, Korea, and Japan, among other locations. That tradition is also the most familiar form of Buddhism in the Global North.

121. Whereas in Theravada the *arhat,* enlightened one, wishes to "cross the river" and extinguish in nirvana all desires, thus reaching personal salvation, in Mahayana, the enlightened Boddhisattvas postpone their own final bliss for the sake of helping others. See J. R. Davis, *Poles Apart,* pp. 98-104.

122. See Largen, *What Christians Can Learn from Buddhism,* pp. 108-29.

123. Ludwig, *Sacred Paths,* p. 137.

124. For details, see Rahula, *What the Buddha Taught,* p. 80.

included in the sphere of the *sangha* also laypersons, regardless of their profession.[125] The religious were tasked to teach these adherents. *Sanghas* are
supposed to be located near the rest of the society, distinct from but not so
separated as to be isolated. Monks go out every morning to collect gifts and
donations, and they also serve the people in the temples and homes in religious rituals.

While in principle (at least in the original form of Buddhism) there are
no mandatory rituals or rites to perform — as Buddhism is more a way of
life than a religious system — Buddhist lands are filled with most elaborate
devotional and worship acts and patterns,[126] and it is true that "[l]iturgy lies
at the heart of Buddhist practice."[127] Furthermore, unbeknownst to strangers
to Buddhist countries, all denominations, astonishingly even Theravada, are
highly "animistic":[128] in everyday religiosity spirits and spirituality are alive
and well.

Furthermore, not unlike most religions, "[m]any Buddhists believe that
ritual and devotion are also instrumental in bringing about blessings in life and
even inner spiritual transformation." These devotional rituals are looked upon
as beneficial to solving everyday life problems, big and small. Worship may
also help toward good rebirth, particularly if earning merits through making
offerings to Buddha is involved.[129] Indeed, notwithstanding wide and deep
variety in the Buddhist world, rites related to giving or offering in worship
form the basic structure. Giving with the right attitude is the key, and only
then meritorious. To the honoring posture toward Buddha belong the use of
candles, water, food, flowers, and so forth.[130] The presence of images of deities
further helps honor the Buddha and countless deities.[131]

Yet another defining feature across the varied Buddhist world is meditation, whose aim is to bring about "a state of perfect mental health, equilibrium

125. Buddha's inclusive and, in that sense, less world-renouncing vision is evident in
his teaching laypeople about the six directions of the "noble discipline" in family, school, and
workplace; *Sigālaka Sutta*, pp. 461–69.

126. See Rahula, *What the Buddha Taught*, pp. 80–81. Reliable succinct accounts include
Skilling, "Worship and Devotional Life"; R. Payne, "Worship and Devotional Life."

127. Skilling, "Worship and Devotional Life," p. 9827.

128. I am well aware of the caution of scholars, particularly scholars of religion and anthropology, toward continuing to use the term "animism." While other concepts such as "folk
religion" adequately convey much of the meaning, probably no other term so appropriately
highlights the importance of the spirits/spiritual at the core (Lat. *anima*).

129. Ludwig, *Sacred Paths*, p. 158.

130. See Ludwig, *Sacred Paths*, pp. 158–59.

131. See Skilling, "Worship and Devotional Life," pp. 9828–30.

and tranquility." Unlike in many other contexts, Buddhist meditation is not an exit from ordinary life but, on the contrary, is deeply embedded in it. Its core has to do with mindfulness, an aptitude and skill to be developed throughout one's life.[132] Indeed, the main (Pali) term *bhāvanā* literally means "culture" or "development" and so denotes "mental culture," aiming at cleansing from filthy and inappropriate attitudes and instead cultivating virtues and positive qualities, ultimately hopefully helping reach *nibbana*.[133]

Because of the nontheistic orientation and nondivine status of Buddha, strictly speaking there is no prayer in original Buddhist devotion; "it is only a way of paying homage to the memory of the Master who showed the way."[134] Similarly, the scriptures — as much as they are honored and venerated in many forms of (particularly Mahayana) liturgy — are not looked upon as divine revelation but rather as guides to human effort. That said, just consider *Lotus Sutra*, the bible of many Mahayana faithful, and one is struck by its way of speaking of Buddha in divine terms, of the authority of his sayings, and of his "salvific" works.[135] Furthermore, Buddhist devotion, similarly to Islamic religious life, particularly in folk spirituality, has elevated the founder to a (semi)divine status.[136]

Similarly to all other religions, Buddhism embraces daily rituals and worship patterns as well as holy days and festivals. There are rites of passage from birth to initiation into (young) adulthood to death.[137] All this is to say that, for an outsider, the nontheistic and mainly ethical orientation of (original) Buddhism is neither hardly visible nor a defining feature. All over the Buddhist world, the worship patterns, rituals, and rites seem to be similar to those of theistic faiths, with a strong focus on devotion.[138]

132. See M. Batchelor, "Meditation and Mindfulness."

133. Rahula, *What the Buddha Taught*, pp. 67–68; see the whole of chap. 7 for details.

134. Rahula, *What the Buddha Taught*, p. 81. See also Gross, "Meditation and Prayer."

135. Read, for example, *Saddharmapundarika (Lotus Sutra)*, chap. 24 (a few pages in English)—which strongly echoes not only the Vedic teaching but also teachings of many theistic religions concerning the divinely given revelation—as an authoritative message, which leads to salvation. Here the savior Buddha is named Avalokitesvara, known as Amitabha in the Japanese (and some Chinese) Pure Land traditions.

136. Behind this divinization is Mahayana's theological interpretation of Buddha in terms of the notion of trikaya, "three bodies," for which see *Christ and Reconciliation*, p. 270.

137. For details, see Ludwig, *Sacred Paths*, pp. 159–63.

138. Skilling, "Worship and Devotional Life," p. 9827.

The Religious Other

Similarly to Hinduism, the proper perspective on investigating the discerning of the religious other among Buddhists embraces both intra- and interfaith dimensions.[139] Also similarly to the parent tradition, the internal diversity within the Buddhist world is breathtaking. Yet another shared feature is that it is typical for Buddhist movements to consider other Buddhist movements through the lens of "hierarchical inclusivism." Here is also a resemblance to Catholicism. All of these three traditions consider their own movement as the "fulfillment," while others are at a lower level and yet belong to the same family. An aspect of that tolerance of sectarian diversity is to lift up one's own scriptures as superior to the other sister movements' ones.[140] At the heart of Buddhist teaching lies the concept of skillful means (*upaya kausalya*), which turns out to be an excellent aid in the intra-Buddhist engagement of diversity as well: "Just as a kindly and experienced doctor prescribes medicines in accordance with the malady, so the Buddha has the skill and compassion to adapt his teachings to the capacity of those he teaches. The methods employed to advance people on the path to enlightenment will vary depending on their needs and ability to understand. So the views of other Buddhist sects can be accommodated as appropriate for those who are not yet ready for or do not have access to the highest teaching as expressed by one's own group."[141]

Encounter with the non-Buddhist religious other is not new to the tradition; on the contrary, during Buddhism's rise in India, along with emerging Jainism, it had to negotiate its identity not only in relation to Hinduism and other local religions but also (when moving outside India) in relation to Taoism, Confucianism, Shintoism, and others.[142] Although Buddhism's past — or present life — is not without conflicts with the other, occasional campaigns of coercion, and other forms of religious colonialism, by and large Buddhism has sought a peaceful coexistence. The inclusivist paradigm has also applied at times at least to its closest cousin faiths.[143] That said, as can be said of Hinduism, "one would be hard pressed to find many examples in traditional Buddhism of interreligious pluralism, in the sense of an outlook that would grant

139. Burton, "A Buddhist Perspective," p. 321.
140. Burton, "A Buddhist Perspective," p. 322; Lamotte, "Assessment of Textual Interpretation in Buddhism," pp. 16–23.
141. Burton, "A Buddhist Perspective," p. 323.
142. See further Abe, *Buddhism and Interfaith Dialogue*; Chappell, "Buddhist Interreligious Dialogue"; Hayes, "Gotama Buddhism and Religious Pluralism."
143. See Kiblinger, *Buddhist Inclusivism*.

that the teachings of other religions are as able as Buddhism to communicate truth and bring about salvation." Buddhists tend to believe in the truthfulness and thus superiority of their own beliefs. Well known are also the harsh criticisms against the Vedic religion by the Buddha himself.[144] Only recently have a growing number of Buddhists, many of them scholars from or residing in the Global North, begun more systematic work toward Buddhist comparative theology and interfaith engagement,[145] including a more systematic drafting of typologies.[146] Christian-Buddhist engagement will be discussed in the last chapter of this book.

Having now briefly and tentatively presented the visions of community as well as the devotional and liturgical life of Judaism, Islam, Buddhism, and Hinduism, we will delve into distinctively Christian ecclesiology. Throughout the discussion relevant minor comparisons will be attempted until a full-scale comparative theological exercise will be conducted in the last chapter of the book.

---

144. Burton, "A Buddhist Perspective," pp. 324–26 (325).

145. See R. Habito, "Japanese Buddhist Perspectives"; M. Habito, "The Notion of Buddha-Nature"; Berzin, "A Buddhist View of Islam."

146. Vélez de Cea, "A Cross-Cultural and Buddhist-Friendly Interpretation"; Ives, "Liberating Truth."

13. Community after the Trinity

The Trinitarian "Foundation" of the Church

The Church and the Trinity: A Distinctively Christian Vision of the Community

Similarly to her Abrahamic sister faiths, Christian tradition anchors the religious community in (the doctrine of) God and divine election. Herein is a radical difference from the Asiatic faiths; neither the Buddhist *sangha* nor Hindu communities claim any divine origin or purpose. The internal difference within the Abrahamic family has to do with the distinctive Christian confession of faith in the trinitarian God. Whereas both Jewish and Muslim communities are guardians of strict monotheism, the Christian church's understanding of monotheism is trinitarian; hence, the church is linked with and shaped by belief in one God as Father, Son, and Spirit.

Among numerous metaphors and symbols of the church in the New Testament,[1] the following three have gained particular importance in Christian parlance, reflecting the Trinity: people of God (1 Pet. 2:9; Rev. 5:9-10); body of Christ (Eph. 1:22-23; 1 Cor. 12:27; Col. 1:18); and temple of the Spirit (Eph. 2:19-22; 1 Pet. 2:5).[2] Ecumenically it is of utmost importance that virtually all Christian churches are currently in agreement about the trinitarian basis

---

1. Minear, *Images of the Church*; see also E. Ferguson, *The Church of Christ.*
2. See further Grenz, *Theology for the Community of God*, pp. 465-67. A massive study of biblical materials is E. Ferguson, *The Church of Christ.*

and nature of the church[3] and the anchoring of communion (*koinonia*) in the shared divine life itself.[4]

Since the trinitarian confession of faith, and, derivatively, the trinitarian basis of the church, is never an abstract, formal statement but rather a particular and specific narrative about the creative, redemptive, and perfecting work of Father, Son, and Spirit in the world, let us delve in more detail into the mystery of the trinitarian structure and basis of the church. Let us begin from the end, as it were — or from the last — that is, from the work of the Spirit, and then proceed to the Son and Father, although the *taxis* (order) is usually the other way. We begin with the Spirit in order to follow the order of economy: it is through the Spirit-inspired testimony and Word, as well as Spirit-energized works and manifestations, that men and women first come into contact with the church.[5] Through the Spirit, human beings are led to submit their lives to Jesus the Savior and Lord, to the glory of God, the Father.

Beginning from the last trinitarian member, as it were, we consider first the least-often-invoked image — the church as the temple of the Spirit. From there we will proceed to the meaning of the body of Christ and the people of God. This is to correct and balance Western Christianity's too often merely christological founding of the church. Recall that in the creedal intuitions the church is linked primarily with the Holy Spirit. Christological and pneumatological grounding should not of course be pitted against each other; it is a matter of a dynamic balance.[6]

Church as Temple of the Spirit

The Spirit's work in the New Testament is not only present in the individual believer's life. There is also a robust community direction.[7] As Pannenberg puts it, "The gift of the Spirit is not just for individual believers but aims at the building up of the fellowship of believers, at the founding and constant giving

---

3. For a summary of major ecumenical dialogues on topic, see Kasper, *HTF*, ##26–31.

4. A profound trinitarian anchoring of the church can be found in *LG*, ##1–4. For rich theological reflections on the church-Trinity relationship, see Moltmann's section "The Church in the Trinitarian History of God" in *The Church in the Power of the Spirit*, pp. 50–65; Harper and Metzger, *Exploring Ecclesiology*, p. 19 (and chap. 1 at large).

5. See Barth, "The Holy Spirit and the Gathering of the Christian Community," *CD* IV/1, par. 62, p. 643.

6. See chap. 4 in C. Pinnock, *Flame of Love*.

7. See McDonnell, "The Determinative Doctrine of the Holy Spirit," p. 142.

of new life to the church." This was evident on the day of Pentecost, when a *koinonia* of believers was brought into existence.[8]

This is not to contend that Pentecost in itself is the "birthday" of the church — it is rather Easter, because without the raising to new life of the crucified Messiah, the church would not have emerged — but to highlight the importance of the Spirit, along with the Son, as the "dual foundation" of the Christian community.[9] The balance between the christological and pneumatological basis of the church honors the deep and wide "Spirit Christology" of the New Testament. In the Gospels and beyond, this "Spirit Christology" comes to the fore in that from the beginning of the history of Jesus Christ to his glorious resurrection there are references to the work of the Spirit, and conversely, the Spirit's work is everywhere associated with that of the Son.[10]

This is where the ecclesiologies constructed in the Christian West need to take a self-critical look. Whereas Western ecclesiologies are predominantly built on christological categories, the Eastern doctrine of the church seeks a balance between Christology and pneumatology. Eastern theologians speak about the church as the body of Christ and the fullness of the Holy Spirit.[11] John Zizioulas expresses this principle with the help of two concepts: the church is *instituted* by Christ and *constituted* by the Holy Spirit.[12] To follow the East's intuitions is not to downplay the significance of the metaphor of the body of Christ, but rather, to hold on to that important metaphor and couple it with the equally important pneumatological orientation.[13] That kind of trinitarian balance would help us avoid the liability that the leading American Roman Catholic pneumatologist, Fr. Kilian McDonnell, OSB, laments: "[w]e build up our large theological constructs in constitutive christological categories, and then, in a second, nonconstitutive moment, we decorate the already constructed system with pneumatological baubles, a little Spirit tinsel."[14]

8. Pannenberg, *ST* 3:12-13; see also p. 624. The classic passage from Luther is *Small Catechism*, Creed, art. 3.

9. See Küng, *The Church*, p. 219; so also Pannenberg, *ST* 3:15-19 particularly.

10. See my *Christ and Reconciliation*, chap. 8, for the Spirit's role in Christology, and my *Spirit and Salvation*, chap. 2, for Christ's role in pneumatology. In Luke's Gospel and Acts, the "dual foundation" comes to fullest expression in the NT. See Twelftree, *People of the Spirit*, chap. 3.

11. V. Lossky, *Mystical Theology of the Eastern Church*, pp. 157, 174.

12. Zizioulas, *Being as Communion*, p. 22; see also Ware, *The Orthodox Church*, pp. 249-50; V. Lossky, *Mystical Theology of the Eastern Church*, pp. 190-92.

13. See Volf and Lee, "The Spirit and the Church"; *NMC*, ##22-23.

14. McDonnell, "The Determinative Doctrine of the Holy Spirit," p. 142.

It is important to note that this work of the Spirit is not isolated from the wider divine economy but integrally linked with it.[15] The Spirit that is "at work in creation as God's mighty breath, the origin . . . of all life" is the same Spirit who raised Jesus from the dead and who also helps bring about the final consummation. For believers, this Spirit has been given as a special "gift," as tradition puts it (Rom. 5:5; 1 Cor. 3:16), and in the church, there is "the special mode of the presence of the divine Spirit in the gospel."[16] In this comprehensive pneumatological framework, the Spirit's eschatological work merits special highlighting as the Christian community is an anticipation of the final advent of the kingdom of God and the gathering of all people under one God in the new Jerusalem, as detailed below.[17]

Church as Body of Christ

Although the precise expression "body of Christ" appears only once in Paul's authentic letters (1 Cor. 12:27),[18] body terminology abounds, particularly in the form of "one body" or "one body in Christ."[19] Whereas in 1 Corinthians and Romans the individual community is depicted as a body, in Ephesians and Colossians it is the whole church.[20] The main point of employing the body metaphor for individual communities in Pauline teaching has to do with interrelated virtues and qualities of love, unity, and working for the common good; just study 1 Corinthians 12–14 to that effect.[21] In the context of the whole church as the body, at the fore is a cosmological Christology and the cosmic work of the triune God working out eternal purposes toward the reconciliation of all peoples and all of creation.[22]

15. See Hinze, "Releasing the Power of the Spirit."

16. Pannenberg, *ST* 3:1-2.

17. See further Küng, *The Church*, pp. 216-24.

18. Oddly enough, Pannenberg (*ST* 3:102) claims that the "body of Christ is no mere metaphor nor is it just one of the biblical ways of depicting the nature of the church." Of course it is a metaphor — but its power and significance are in no way lessened by that acknowledgment.

19. What is noteworthy is that rather than appearing in christological or soteriological contexts, almost exclusively the body metaphor is employed in admonition, paraenesis; Küng, *The Church*, pp. 296, 97.

20. Küng, *The Church*, p. 299.

21. See also Küng, *The Church*, pp. 186-89.

22. Küng, *The Church*, pp. 298-304 particularly; see also pp. 304-13 for a careful discussion of the relation of Christ to the church.

Early in Christian tradition, the body metaphor (in reference to the whole church) began to be developed in primarily institutional and hierarchic terms. This development reached its zenith in medieval Catholic ecclesiology and was fine-tuned in the nineteenth-century Vatican I conception of the Catholic Church as the divinely instituted true church. It led to the identification of Christ's body with that earthly community and was often expressed in terms of the church "as the continuation of Christ's incarnation" (J. A. Möhler). As recently as 1943, in the encyclical *Mystici Corporis Christi* (1943) by Pope Pius XII, this conception was authoritatively pronounced.[23] If not exactly saying it, behind that body ecclesiology was the idea of the church as the "perfect society."[24] Vatican II's *Lumen Gentium* provided the needed corrective in describing the church in a dynamic, organic manner and returning to the biblical narrative rather than abstract formulations (#7, among others).

For a proper and balanced ecclesiology, the whole history of Jesus the Christ is determinative, not only, say, his teachings and ethics, as in classical liberalism, or his suffering and cross, as in some forms of traditional theology.[25] To that ecclesiologically constitutive and supportive history belong the earthly life of Jesus with teachings, miraculous acts and works, as well as the pronouncement of forgiveness and inclusion of even "outsiders"; his suffering, cross, and death; his glorious resurrection in the newness of life; as well as his ascension, the Pentecost pouring out of the Spirit, and his current cosmic rule.[26] With this kind of wide and comprehensive christological grounding, the church's mission can be framed in a dynamic and multilayered manner, which will be attempted in the chapter on mission (16). To that task also belongs the reminder that an important biblical emphasis in the body analogy of the church has to do with reconciliation and peace not only between God and humanity but also within humanity, including even cosmic dimensions, as is evident particularly in the employment of the analogy in Ephesians and Colossians. This theme, similarly, will be developed below.

23. Important influences on this conception come from the church as the "continuation of Christ's incarnation" theology represented by Johann Adam Möhler and others, for which see Himes, *Ongoing Incarnation*; further, Riga, "The Ecclesiology of Johann Adam Möhler."

24. For comments, see Bosch, *Transforming Mission*, pp. 368-69.

25. See *NMC*, ##20-21.

26. For an attempt to construct a Christology (and theology of reconciliation) in keeping with this "whole history of Jesus Christ" ideal, see my *Christ and Reconciliation*.

Church as People of God

Peoplehood is based on divine election,[27] as first presented in the Bible with regard to Yahweh's choosing of Israel as his people. That election, however, should not lead to separation (as happened at times with Israel, as discussed above); rather, membership in the community is toward the goal of the gathering of the people of God in the new Jerusalem.[28]

Whereas in the theology of the early church the concept of the people of God played a significant role, it receded into the background subsequently, particularly with the entrance of Christendom and Christianity's official status as the civic religion.[29] The peoplehood of the church was somewhat rediscovered in the Reformation with the rejection of Rome's claim to the headship of all Christendom and consolidation of highly hierarchic structures.[30] Happily, in recent ecumenical ecclesiology,[31] tutored particularly by Vatican II's *Lumen Gentium* (chap. 2), the depiction of the church as the people of God has been rediscovered.[32] Another significant contribution of *Lumen Gentium* is the depiction of the people of God as a *pilgrim* church, which, markedly different from Vatican I's "perfect society" mentality, envisioned the ecclesial community on the way and hence in need of growth and holiness.[33] Conceiving the church as the pilgrim people highlights her eschatological, future-driven nature.[34]

The people of God is the most comprehensive among the three main metaphors considered here. It not only means everything that the "church" denotes but also, importantly, includes Israel, the "first" people of God.[35] Vati-

27. Pannenberg, *ST* 3:431-34, 437.

28. See the extended discussion of the individual-communal dialectic in election in Pannenberg, *ST* 3:455-62; for the tight link between election and the people of God, see pp. 463-65 and passim.

29. That new status of course raised difficult and complex questions as to the ways the sacerdotal and secular powers were to relate to each other; for a brief discussion, see Pannenberg, *ST* 3:466-67.

30. See Luther, *On the Councils and the Church* (1539), WA 50:625.16-30; *LW* 41:143. See also Pannenberg, *ST* 3:465-67.

31. See *NMC*, ##18-19.

32. For a highly informative and insightful discussion, see Küng, *The Church*, pp. 147-200.

33. *LG*, chap. 7; for comments, see Garijo-Guembe, *Communion of the Saints*, pp. 124-30.

34. *LG*, #48.

35. Rightly noted in the Catholic-Lutheran dialogue *Church and Justification* (1993), #19 (in Kasper, *HTF*, #27).

can II's talk about the church as the *new* people of God linked to the old people of God in the same covenant[36] correctly intuited this indissoluble link between the two (although it also made itself liable to a potential misunderstanding of the "new" replacing the "old," to be clarified in chapter 20 below). Not only is the people metaphor comprehensive in the sense of also encompassing Israel; it also highlights the inclusiveness and equality of all Christians: "The Church is always and in all cases the *whole* people of God, the *whole* ecclesia, the *whole* fellowship of the faithful. Everyone belongs to the chosen race, the royal priesthood, the holy nation."[37]

Having now reflected briefly on the implications of the church of the triune God as the Spirit's temple, Christ's body, and God's people, we deepen this consideration of the trinitarian basis by clarifying first what the expression in the chapter title "Community after the Trinity" may mean. We will inquire about the implications for the nature and life of the church in the community shaped after and birthed by the triune God. That discussion brings to surface closely related theological considerations stemming from the trinitarian nature of Christian communion, particularly its relation to the kingdom of God, the Father's righteous rule dawning and embodied in the Son, who came in the power of the Spirit.

The Church as the Image of the Trinity

Correspondence and Limitations of the Trinitarian Analogy

The most foundational ecclesiological statement in the Eastern tradition is that the church is an image of the Trinity.[38] Just as each person is made according to the image of the Trinity, so the church as a whole is an icon of the Trinity, "reproducing on earth the mystery of unity in diversity."[39] This ancient ecclesiological conviction of an analogy between the triune God as a community and the church of Christ on earth as a human-divine community has become an ecumenical commonplace, and it is embraced widely also by the Christian West.[40] The triune God is the eternal communion of Father, Son, and Spirit.

36. *LG*, #9.
37. Küng, *The Church*, p. 169.
38. See further V. Lossky, *Mystical Theology of the Eastern Church*, pp. 176-77; Ware, *The Orthodox Church*, pp. 240-45.
39. Ware, *The Orthodox Church*, p. 240.
40. Even among free church–oriented traditions this is nowadays being rediscovered,

Consequently, the church as the communion of human persons may be said to echo that communal, relational existence.[41]

That said, before delving deeper into the search for potential correspondence between the divine communion (Trinity) and the ecclesial community, an important question has to be raised: Provided that Trinity gives guidance to the formation of human community, how should we imagine the correspondence? In other words, how much can we claim to learn from the "divine society" for the sake of human societies? Both continuities and discontinuities between the divine and ecclesial communion should be acknowledged. The continuity is based on the creation of men and women in God's image. That image will be renewed and sanctified in the new life as Christians and in the power of the Spirit's continuing enlivening energy. The discontinuity is obvious: whereas divine life is uncreated and infinite, the human is not; whereas divine life is perfect, the human is not; and so forth.[42]

The Brazilian Catholic liberationist Leonardo Boff saw clearly the continuity-in-discontinuity, as in his *Trinity and Society* he warned theologians of the danger of approaching the question from a "utilitarian" perspective, that is, by asking how the Trinity might help inform our conceptions of the nature of the community. Instead, he wishes to start "From Above," that is, from a cautious and humble inquiry into the life of the triune God as revealed in Holy Scriptures, spiritual traditions, prayer, and liturgies. Only thereafter is it appropriate to reflect on lessons toward developing a socially and politically relevant liberation program drawing from the Trinity as the template of loving, equalitarian, and inclusive community. "Trinity is not something thought out to explain human problems. It is the revelation of God as God is, as Father, Son, and Holy Spirit."[43] In doing otherwise, trinitarian theology in search of "relevance" may fall into projections onto God of the shallow democratic sentiments that emerged when modern, "functionally-differentiated societies replaced traditional, hierarchically-segmented societies."[44] Should that happen, theologians simply end up constructing "an image of the Trinity that justifies the views we already hold regarding the nature of the church."[45]

---

as in Harper and Metzger, *Exploring Ecclesiology*, chap. 1. See also G. Hill, *Salt, Light, and a City*, chap. 17.

41. See Grenz, *Social God*, pp. 3–14.

42. For an important discussion of the limitations of the correspondence, see Volf, "Trinity Is Our Social Program," and his *After Our Likeness*, pp. 191–200.

43. Boff, *Trinity and Society*, p. 3.

44. Volf, "Trinity Is Our Social Program," p. 407.

45. Muthiah, *Priesthood of All Believers*, p. 50.

Boff's warnings are spot-on and should be carefully minded. That said, it is possible and appropriate to consider the implications of the church as the image of the Trinity.[46]

The Nature and Life of the Church in the Trinitarian Analogy

A recent theologically pregnant proposal that gleans from the riches of contemporary trinitarian ecclesiology comes from a somewhat surprising direction, from an American free church theologian, the Anabaptist Robert Muthiah.[47] He suggests the following connecting points between the triune God as community and the church as community on earth:

- relationality
- presence-for-the-other
- equality
- nondomination
- unity
- difference

Relationality. Relationality is based on the communion of Father, Son, and Spirit in mutual relations to each other,[48] traditionally named *perichoresis*, mutual interpenetration. Never a "closed" circle, the divine relationality encompasses and invites the church and humanity to participate. Moltmann lays out programmatically the wider and complex ecclesiological implications of the Trinity's relationality: "Through the sending of the creative Spirit, the trinitarian history of God becomes a history that is open to the world, open to men and women, and open to the future. Through the experience of the life-giving Spirit in faith, in baptism, and in the fellowship of believers, people are integrated into the history of the Trinity. Through the Spirit of Christ they not only become participants in the eschatological history of the new creation, but

46. It seems to me the Lutheran Ted Peters (*God as Trinity*, p. 185) overstates the danger when he seems to think that any use of the analogy eventually leads to negative kinds of projections.

47. Muthiah, *Priesthood of All Believers*, pp. 57-68. The rest of this section follows the outline of his exposition, including employment of a number of sources.

48. Grenz, *Rediscovering the Triune God*, pp. 117-18. For biblical grounding of the Trinity's relationality, see Muthiah, *Priesthood of All Believers*, pp. 54-55. On the importance of the ancient concept of *perichoresis*, see pp. 55-57.

through the Spirit of the Son they also become at the same time participants in the trinitarian history of God himself."[49]

Speaking of the relationality in terms of the participation in and union with God (John 17:21: "that they may all be one; even as thou, Father, art in me, and I in thee, that they also may be in us") again brings to light the continuity-in-discontinuity between heavenly and ecclesial communion. Our union with the triune God, though based on the *perichoresis*, the mutual indwelling of Father, Son, and Spirit, is qualitatively different because, as created beings, we can form a unity only in a certain measure.[50]

Relationality implies that the church is more than an institution — "*people* are essential to the church"; in other words, "its institutional existence is dependent on the presence of believers gathered in Christ's name. The relationships between Christians are crucial to the existence of the church."[51] We will expand the meaning of that statement when delving deeper into the communion ecclesiology and the idea of the gathered church.

Presence-for-the-Other. "The relational nature of the Trinity means that each Person of the Trinity is present with and for the others. Being present with another means assuming an inviting posture that hears and receives the other, and involves a movement toward the other."[52] Another way to speak of this kind of turning to others is "self-donation."[53] Of old, the term *ek-stasis*, literally "to stand outside one's self," was used to explain the possibility of relating to the other in a way that one is not trapped within one's own boundaries. For John Zizioulas, that is an important concept in relation to both intratrinitarian communion and relations among church members. It can be said that "ecstatic" means "a movement toward communion,"[54] and although most profoundly expressed in the life of the triune God,[55] it is reflected in the church as well. Its important implication is succinctly explained by Miroslav Volf: "This movement [toward communion] itself attests the person's freedom. The person is free because it transcends the boundaries of the self and because it is not determined causally by the given natural or historical reality."

49. Moltmann, *Trinity and the Kingdom*, p. 90.

50. Similarly Volf, *After Our Likeness*, p. 211; Muthiah, *Priesthood of All Believers*, pp. 58-59.

51. Muthiah, *Priesthood of All Believers*, p. 59, emphasis in original.

52. Muthiah, *Priesthood of All Believers*, pp. 59-60.

53. For an extended discussion, see Volf, "Trinity Is Our Social Program," pp. 412-17.

54. Zizioulas, "Human Capacity and Human Incapacity," p. 408; for the necessity of relationality for personhood, see also Zizioulas, *Being as Communion*, p. 236.

55. Zizioulas, *Being as Communion*, pp. 44-46 and passim.

This kind of "catholic" personality (as both Zizioulas and Volf name it) "bears within itself human nature in its entirety, which . . . includes all other persons within itself and is thus a unique reflection of them all."[56]

This "bearing" and "including" others in one's own person, however, are not to be confused with subsuming the other under one's own personhood. On the contrary, as Zizioulas tell us, in true personhood "otherness and communion are not in contradiction but coincide." Importantly, this kind of relation "does not lead to the dissolving of the diversity of beings into one vast ocean of being, but to the affirmation of otherness."[57] Volf says the same with regard to how to understand an authentic identity: "[I]dentity is not self-enclosed. The other is always already in the self and therefore the identity of the self cannot be defined simply oppositionally."[58] This kind of authentic personhood (or identity), which I name here *ecstatic communion*, is possible only for the one who is born of God and thus has been linked with the divine communion.[59]

Equality. Among the advocates of the "social Trinity" analogy,[60] full equality among the trinitarian members has become such a canonical statement that for most it is no longer a matter of argument but is simply assumed.[61] On the other side, both in Roman Catholic and Orthodox theologies, the hierarchical nature of the Trinity is an axiom, and as a result, the conception of the church is hierarchical.[62] Learning from both opinions but also correcting and transcending them, the current project argues that while Trinity reflects authentic mutuality and equality, it is not necessarily exactly the way social trinitarians announce it, namely, without any differing roles of authority. Instead, I build on Pannenberg's idea of mutuality ("mutual dependence") of Father, Son, and Spirit, which means that none of the trinitarian members could be what that person is without the others. That said, there is what Pannenberg calls the "monarchy" of the Father, but even that monarchy,

56. Volf, *After Our Likeness*, p. 82, italics removed, on the basis of Zizioulas, "Human Capacity and Human Incapacity," pp. 408, 418; Zizioulas, *Being as Communion*, p. 106.

57. Zizioulas, *Being as Communion*, p. 106.

58. Volf, "Trinity Is Our Social Program," p. 410, italics removed.

59. Zizioulas, *Being as Communion*, pp. 106-7.

60. Named "a social doctrine of the Trinity" in Moltmann, *Trinity and the Kingdom*, p. viii.

61. E.g., Moltmann, *Trinity and the Kingdom*, p. 176; Volf, "Trinity Is Our Social Program," p. 407.

62. For a representative Catholic position, see (the then) Cardinal Ratzinger's theology (as exposited in Volf, *After Our Likeness*, chap. 1) and *LG*, chap. 3, on the hierarchical nature of the church; and for the Orthodox, see the theology of Metropolitan Zizioulas (in *Being as Communion*, chap. 2).

while in some sense a place of primacy, is not a matter of hierarchy, as it also is dependent on the other two trinitarian members.[63] The conclusion, then, simply is that although there might be in the church different levels of leadership and authority, say, related to the office of "senior pastor" or bishop, there is no such hierarchy that would make some stand above others or use power for any other purpose than advancing common mission.

Nondomination. Although critical of some of the ways mainstream social trinitarians simply reject all notions of authority, I fully endorse their conception of the Trinity as free of all forms of domination and oppressive hierarchy. Muthiah puts it well: "The trinitarian relations are characterized by nondomination. The relations are consensual and free. No one Person in the Trinity dictates what the other Persons must do. No one Person of the Trinity forces the others to participate in the relationships or to act in certain ways."[64] Too often, forms of hierarchical church structures, often echoing hierarchies of secular governmental institutions, have caused domination, even abuse. They have to be rejected.[65] Particularly harshly treated have been women in this respect; not only has their access to forms of ministry been blocked, but they have also been left out of leadership positions.

Unity. Even with the starting point in the threeness rather than the oneness of God, contemporary trinitarian theology — following in the footsteps of the Cappadocians and other Eastern fathers of old — is not thereby ignoring the centrality of unity in the Trinity. Indeed, Christian belief in the triune God is belief in one God; even its trinitarian doctrine is "concrete monotheism."[66] Yet that unity is relational, as it is the unity of the Father, Son, and Spirit. In keeping with these intuitions is Moltmann's social notion of "personhood," which he discerns in the distinction and unity of Father, Son, and Spirit. In that kind of diversified unity, "personal character and social character are only two aspects of the same thing. The concept of person must therefore in itself contain the concept of unitedness or at-oneness."[67] Not surprisingly, Moltmann employs the concept of *perichoresis*.[68]

---

63. For details, see my *Trinity and Revelation*, pp. 323-24.

64. Muthiah, *Priesthood of All Believers*, p. 63.

65. See Moltmann, *Trinity and the Kingdom*, pp. 192-200 and passim.

66. Pannenberg, *ST* 1:335-36; see also Augustine, *On the Trinity* 6.10.12. To endorse unity in my robustly trinitarian depiction of the Christian God, I affirmed the existence of divine "essence" but, following Pannenberg (*ST* 1:334-35, 366-67), defined it relationally (*Trinity and Revelation*, chap. 11).

67. Moltmann, *Trinity and the Kingdom*, p. 150.

68. Moltmann, *Trinity and the Kingdom*, p. 175.

Similarly to relationality and other shared features in the analogy, the kind of unity spoken of in relation to the divine life can only be approximated in created human life. Yet, as discussed above, Jesus' statements (John 17:21–23) about true and real unity of believers both with God and among themselves should be taken with full seriousness. Pannenberg's linking of the term "ecstatic," explained above, with the special work of the Spirit helps us understand the diversified unity among the believers. The same Spirit who unites the believer with Christ and thereby Christ's body and "releases and reconciles the tension between the fellowship and the individual in the concept of the church" also is the principle of believers' unity with others: "The work of the Holy Spirit lifts individuals ecstatically above their own particularity not only to participation in the sonship of Christ but at the same time also to experience of the fellowship in the body of Christ that unites individual Christians to all other Christians."[69]

Difference. The simple reason why unity alone can never be affirmed, based on either the Trinity or commonsense logic, is this: "Unity presupposes differentiation; if no differences exist, we have nothing to unite."[70] With regard to the Trinity, the basic axiom agreed on by all is that "each of the Persons possesses the divine nature in a non-interchangeable way; each presents it in his own way."[71] This was one of the points Augustine belabored in his trinitarian doctrine, namely, that the Father is not the Son and the Son is not the Father (although one has never been without the other), and the same with regard to the Spirit.[72] The currently oft-used expressions of "unity-in-diversity" and "diversity-in-unity" illustrate well the Trinity-driven differentiation in the one God.

The Christian church of old saw unity-in-diversity/diversity-in-unity illustrated wonderfully in the many tongues of the day of Pentecost (Acts 2). "The diversity which marked the people of God at Pentecost stands in stark contrast to the homogenizing forces at work in Babel (Gen. 11) and prefigures the diversity to be found in the eschatological kingdom of God (Rev. 7:9; 14:6). The people of God are united in Christ through the Spirit, and at the same time these people are marked by great diversity."[73] Along with Pentecost, the many and diverse gifts of the one and same Spirit illustrate the diversification (1 Cor. 12).

69. Pannenberg, *ST* 3:130; see also pp. 133–34.
70. Muthiah, *Priesthood of All Believers*, p. 67.
71. Moltmann, *Trinity and the Kingdom*, p. 171.
72. See, e.g., Augustine, *On the Trinity* 6 ("Linguistic and Logical: The Problem of Appropriation").
73. Muthiah, *Priesthood of All Believers*, pp. 67–68.

Having now established a limited but significant analogy between the triune God and the church as communion, and before, in the following chapter, delving into the nature, meaning, and significance of *koinonia*, we take up an important task in the last section of this chapter, namely, looking more closely at the place and task of the church in the trinitarian economy of God, that is, the church as an eschatological anticipation of the coming of God's kingdom in the person of Christ in the power of the Spirit.

The Church of the Triune God as an Eschatological Anticipation of the Kingdom

Church as Anticipation

An essential aspect of the church's nature and status in the trinitarian economy is its reference to the future, the consummation in the coming of God's kingdom. Following Volf, we can put this foundational statement in this way: "According to the message of Jesus, the gathering of the people of God is grounded in the coming of the Kingdom of God in his person. Commensurately, New Testament authors portray the church, which emerged after Christ's resurrection and the sending of the Spirit, as the anticipation of the eschatological gathering of the entire people of God."[74]

Although thoroughly an earthly community, the church is not only that. Its future "in God's new creation is the mutual personal indwelling of the triune God and of his glorified people," as described in Revelation 21:1–22:5 and pleaded for in Jesus' high priestly prayer (John 17:21).[75] The scope of the church's anticipation is wide and comprehensive, as the ultimate goal "as a provisional manifestation and significatory anticipation of the eschatological people of God" is to gather men and women "from every tribe and tongue and people and nation" (Rev. 5:9) before the one God in the new Jerusalem.[76] Not only that: in this consummation awaited by the church, there is also the consummation of God's eternal plans regarding the whole cosmos,[77] as argued

---

74. Volf, *After Our Likeness*, p. 128; materially similarly, Pannenberg, *ST* 3:28. See also Moltmann, *The Church in the Power of the Spirit*, p. 13; *The Uppsala Report 1968*, pp. 16–17; *LG*, #48.

75. Volf, *After Our Likeness*, pp. 128–29 (128).

76. Pannenberg, *ST* 3:478.

77. Duly noted also in "The Church as Community of Common Witness to the Kingdom of God," p. 180.

in part 1 of this volume. "The all-embracing framework for an appropriate understanding of the church is God's eschatological new creation."[78]

The anticipation of God's future links the church integrally with the coming of the kingdom, which it serves as sign and instrument and which makes the church missional by nature (chap. 16). Because of many misunderstandings throughout history, the kingdom-church relation calls for careful systematic clarification.

The Church as the Sign of the Coming Reign of God

It is clear theologically — and absolutely important to realize — that the church in herself is not to be equated with God's rule. God's reign, his kingdom, is much wider than the church or even human society. What the church is, is a preceding sign pointing to the coming righteous rule of God in the eschaton, an anticipation of the coming consummation and gathering of all God's people under one God (Rev. 21:3-4).[79] The distinction between the sign and the "thing" sets the church and her function in relation to God's rule in the proper place:

> A sign points beyond itself to the thing signified. It is thus essential to the function of the sign that we should distinguish them. We must not equate the thing with the sign in its weakness. Only by this distinction can the thing signified be, in a certain sense, present by way of the sign. . . . If the church fails to make this distinction clearly, then it arrogates to itself the finality and glory of the kingdom, but by the poverty and all too human character of its own life it also makes the Christian hope incredible. . . . Only as it renounces exclusive claims for its own specific form can it plainly be a sign of the universality of the kingdom of God and an instrument of the reconciliation of human beings with one another and with God, transcending all the differences that separate people from one another and from the God of Israel.[80]

Herein Pannenberg sees a parallel between the self-differentiation of the church from the consummated kingdom of God, of which she is a sign, and

---

78. Volf, *After Our Likeness*, p. 128.
79. See also Pannenberg, *ST* 3:27-32; Bloesch, *The Church*, chap. 4.
80. Pannenberg, *ST* 3:32.

the self-differentiation of the Son within the eternal Godhead.[81] "Just as her Lord, in whom she grounds herself by the power of the divine Spirit, is unified with the Godhead of God through self-differentiation, the church is the present signifier of the Kingdom of God not through a self-equating, but through the resolute differentiation of her own presence from the future of the coming Kingdom."[82] That this has not often been the case is sadly witnessed in various historical periods of the church's existence.[83]

Acknowledging the anticipatory and preparatory nature of the church's existence helps avoid uncritical alignment with any political or ideological order.[84] This awareness puts all earthly commitment and bonds in proper perspective. As Barth put it succinctly: "Christians will always be Christians first, and only then members of a specific culture or state or class or the like. . . . Christianity exists in Germany and Switzerland and Africa, but there is no such thing as a German or Swiss or African Christianity."[85]

The nature of the church as sign and instrument with a view toward kingdom-related missional existence and task was wonderfully formulated in the beginning of *Lumen Gentium*. It introduces the church "in Christ . . . as a sign and instrument both of a very closely knit union with God and of the unity of the whole human race" tasked with "universal mission" (#1). At the same time, we should acknowledge humbly and openly the weaknesses and liabilities of the church in this lofty calling. We are painfully aware of the fact that as the instrument of hoped-for unity of all people, the church itself is deeply and widely divided; hence, its sign function as an anticipation is "broken manifestation."[86] The same can be said of the church as a "sign of reconciliation"; as much as the church anticipates the final eschatological gathering of the renewed humanity in God's kingdom, within the church are strife, competition, and conflict.[87] As far as the church faithfully functions as the sign, it "has its end not in itself but in the future of a humanity that is

81. Pannenberg, *ST* 3:32–33.

82. Wenz, *Introduction*, p. 169. Cf. Pannenberg, *ST* 3:45.

83. For details and sources, see Pannenberg, *ST* 3:33–37, covering the whole history from the fathers to the rediscovery of the distinction in twentieth-century ecclesiology.

84. Pannenberg, *ST* 3:482.

85. Barth, *CD* IV/1, p. 703; see Moseley, *Nations and Nationalism*.

86. Pannenberg, *ST* 3:42–43; this is also affirmed by the WCC's 1968 Uppsala statement, although there the emphasis on social-political involvement as the means of realizing unity is much stronger when compared to Vatican II (*The Uppsala Report 1968*); for comments, see Pannenberg, *ST* 3:47–48.

87. Pannenberg, *ST* 3:44. This vision also lies behind the important Faith and Order document from 1970, *Church and World*.

reconciled to God and united by common praise of God in his kingdom."[88] Exactly as an imperfect, often-failing sign and instrument, the church shows to the world that it points to something more perfect and permanent.

Anchoring the church in the life of the triune God, as a communion shaped after God's own life, is the first theological task for Christian ecclesiology. That completed, it leads to the question of what exactly makes the church, church. Would any kind of gathering of believers be *church* in the true sense of the word? That is the question of ecclesiality to which we turn next.

---

88. Pannenberg, *ST* 3:45–46 (45). Similarly *NMC*, #8: "In God's providence the Church exists, not for itself alone, but to serve in God's work of reconciliation and for the praise and glory of God."

14. The Ecclesiality of the Church: An Ecumenical Proposal and Appeal

What Is at Stake in the Discussion of Ecclesiality?

The Twofold Ecclesiological-Ecumenical Dilemma

The leading theological impetus behind the current constructive proposal concerning the ecclesiality of the church — that is, what makes the church, church[1] — has to do with two unresolved issues. The first of the two relates to the continuing impossibility of mutual recognition of the ecclesiality (the "churchliness") of other Christian communities. In other words, some churches do not consider others as churches but as something "less" or "defective." This wound is particularly deep between the "older" (Roman Catholic and Orthodox) and "younger" churches (free churches and various types of independent churches), but it also relates to Protestant and Anglican communities, which in this respect stand somewhere in the middle of the debate. The second impasse has to do with the disconnect between what the church is claimed to be — call it ecclesiality "proper" — and what the church does, that is, the church's "mission" or "ministry." This has led to the disconnect between two kinds of discourse: while some continue probing the basic problems of ecclesiality per se, as if mission were a secondary moment to be "added" to the churchliness once the foundational theological clarification is finished,[2] others engage the

---

1. See also Volf, *After Our Likeness*, p. 127.
2. I fear that liability relates even to the in-many-ways groundbreaking ecumenical proposal of Volf, *After Our Likeness*; see p. 7.

missional paradigm as if that could bypass or ignore the remaining deep gulf between various notions of ecclesiality. My ecumenical proposal seeks to bring those separated discussions to the same table.

The first unresolved problem of ecclesiality ("proper") has to do with the radically different ways of conceiving what makes the church, church. The key debate has to do with the role of sacraments, episcopacy, and personal confession of faith. There are three main positions. First, for Orthodox and Catholic ecclesiology, not only does the church carry out the sacraments, but the sacraments first and foremost make the church. This means that only where there is the celebration of the sacrament of the Eucharist (whose attendance requires water baptism), there is the Christian church. And for that celebration to be ecclesiologically valid, there needs to be a bishop whose standing is considered to be linked with the first apostles (somewhat differently defined in those two traditions, a topic into whose details there is no need to delve here). In sum: this is the "sacramental" and "episcopal"[3] (lowercase) rule of ecclesiality. Second, for the youngest Christian family, the free churches, decisive is the presence of personal confession of faith of men and women who then gather together as the church. That faith is mediated directly, as it were, and does not necessarily require mediation by the sacraments or office. The celebration of the sacraments of water baptism and the Lord's Supper is an important part of the church's life, but they are not considered ecclesiologically constitutive and, where personal faith is missing, might even be taken as something formal and useless. Furthermore, among those free churches that have an ecclesiastical office by the name of "bishop,"[4] it does not have any ecclesiologically determinative function. Third, there is the Protestant mainline definition of the church's "foundation" in terms of the administration of the sacraments (baptism and Eucharist) and the preaching of the gospel. Although for Anglicans and many Protestants (all Lutherans and some Reformed) the theology (of salvation) is sacramental in the sense that one comes to the faith and is sustained in it by the sacraments (when integrally linked with the Word), neither sacraments nor ministerial patterns are considered ecclesiologically constitutive after the manner of Orthodox and Catholic theology. As a result, even if they have a bishop (as a large

---

3. Hence, in the following the word "episcopal" (as distinct from the proper name of the Episcopal, i.e., Anglican, Church) is used in that technical theological sense.

4. This is common among most African American churches in the United States, as well as in a large number of Pentecostal and other free churches all over the world, particularly in Africa but also in the former Soviet Union, and so forth.

number of Lutherans do), that office is not constitutive for the being of the church and can also be otherwise.[5]

Now, the ecumenical and ecclesiastical implications are simply these: for Orthodox and Catholics, neither Protestant/Anglican communities, regardless of their sacramentality, nor free churches qualify as churches because they lack episcopal and sacramental validity for the reasons explained above. Even the Anglican and Protestant celebration of the sacraments (particularly the Eucharist) is invalid because of the episcopal deficit. On the other hand, for free churches, particularly in the beginning years of the movements, no amount of appeal to episcopacy or sacraments had any church-constitutive meaning; indeed, putting them in the forefront often elicited a response against mere formal religion! The mainline Protestants (and Anglicans, I suppose) come closest to not having binding reasons for nonrecognition of either free churches, as long as they also honor the sacraments (and they do appreciate the preaching of Word, after all), or Orthodox and Catholics (without endorsing their exclusive appeal to episcopal succession).

This impasse of the mutual recognition is an open wound for ecclesiology and ecumenism. If we were not so used to it, it would appear to be unbearable, excruciating. And it is! Neither theologically nor in terms of common sense — let alone Christian love! — can it be tolerated anymore. It simply means that Christian churches who claim the presence of one and the same Lord continue refusing to grant the same to other Christian communities with similar claims![6] Taken seriously, the implications of nonrecognition lead to conclusions and implications that simply are absurd and bizarre. Just listen to Volf's illustrations:

> Should, for example, a Catholic or Orthodox diocese whose members are inclined more to superstition than to faith and who identify with the church more for nationalistic reasons — should such a diocese be viewed as a church, while a Baptist congregation that has preserved its faith through the crucible of persecution *not* be considered such? . . . Equally untenable is the early, though still widespread Free Church position that denies ecclesiality to the episcopal churches. Smyth's [the British founder

---

5. A materially similar presentation (limited to Orthodox/Catholics and free churches) can be found in Volf, *After Our Likeness*, pp. 130-35. For details, see my "Unity, Diversity, and Apostolicity."

6. Similarly Volf, *After Our Likeness*, pp. 133-34 and passim.

of the Baptist movement] conviction that during his age there was no true church is doubtless an expression of sectarian narrow-mindedness and arrogance.[7]

The second problem, namely, the disconnect between the "being" (ecclesiality proper) and "doing" (mission) of the church, is simply that, a *disconnect*. Mission is then considered a second moment, as it were, auxiliary to the being of the church, or as most often happens in practice, one of the many "tasks" of the church. In other words, missional existence is something separate from the ecclesial existence. Instead, in keeping with an emerging ecumenical consensus, this project defines the church as mission. The implication is to link the classic "marks of the church" — oneness, holiness, apostolicity, and catholicity — tightly and integrally with the dynamic missional nature of the church. Chapter 16 further deepens and widens the many implications of that paradigm, and the rest of the discussion in part 2 on the tasks and role of the church in the world derives from that missional ecclesiality.

Having now outlined the twofold ecclesiological-ecumenical impasse, we can outline the plan for the remainder of the chapter. First of all, there will be a critical assessment of attempts to argue and defend these positions, and a way out of the impasse will be looked for. Thereafter, a constructive ecumenical proposal for ecclesiality proper will be tentatively set up. Third, that ecumenical proposal will be complemented and completed by the linking of ecclesiality proper with the argument for the missional nature of the church (to be further developed and deepened in subsequent chapters). Finally, as a topic linking both ecclesiality proper and missional nature, a brief look at the four marks of the church as a church-defining perspective will be scrutinized.

The State of the Art of the Ecclesiality Discourse: A Critical Assessment

There is an ecumenical consensus about the presence of Christ (and therefore, of the Spirit or the triune God) as ecclesiologically constitutive. This rule goes back to the fathers and is solidly based in the New Testament witness. The theologically pregnant Matthean passage affirms: "For where two or three are gathered in my name, there am I in the midst of them" (18:20).[8] Ignatius

---

7. Volf, *After Our Likeness*, p. 134; reference is to Smyth, *Works*, p. 757.
8. Tertullian's oft-cited maxim states: "But where three are, [there] a church is" (*On Exhortation to Chastity* 7).

taught that "wherever Jesus Christ is, there is the Catholic Church," and Irenaeus expressed the same with reference to Christ's presence.[9] This issue is not contested. What is debated has to do with the way Christ's (and the Spirit's) presence can be determined, as it is hardly self-evident.[10] It is widely agreed that whatever instruments one may employ in trying to determine Christ's ecclesiologically constitutive presence, they cannot be so external to the task that they fail to disclose something essential about the church. If they fail to do that, they are arbitrary at best. Yet, obviously, they have to be externally perceivable.[11]

It is here that Miroslav Volf takes up the task in an important ecclesiological proposal searching for a minimalist, yet significant, principle of ecclesiality, seeking to develop a theology of the church based on the best and "redeemable" elements of congregationalist–free church traditions, in dialogue with Catholic and Orthodox ecclesiologies.[12] Building on the above-mentioned programmatic passage from Matthew 18:20, Volf puts forth his tentative description of what makes the church, church: "Where two or three are gathered in Christ's name, not only is Christ present among them, but a Christian church is there as well, perhaps bad church, a church that may well transgress against love and truth, but a church nonetheless." Volf claims that this definition expresses what Ignatius, Irenaeus, Tertullian, and others argued, and that it is also in keeping with the rule of ecclesiality propounded by the seventeenth-century English founder of the Baptist movement, John Smyth:[13] "A visible communion of Saincts is of two, three, or more Saincts joyned together by covenant with God & themselves, freely to use al the holy things of God, according to the word, for their mutual edification, & Gods glory. Mat. 18 20 Deut. 29, 12. &c Psal. 147, 19 & 149, 6–9. Rev. 1. 6."[14]

Volf takes several steps toward an ecumenically fruitful and promising position in suggesting that even the free church traditions join the consensus across the ecumenical spectrum according to which the two sacraments, water baptism and Eucharist, serve the task of identifying Christ's presence. That is a tentative but also important response to the question of how to discern Christ's (and the Spirit's) church-constitutive presence. Second, important particularly to the mainline Reformation churches, the sacraments are tightly integrated

---

9. Ignatius, *To the Smyrnaeans* 8; Irenaeus, *Against Heresies* 3.24.1, respectively.

10. So also Volf, *After Our Likeness*, p. 129.

11. Volf, *After Our Likeness*, pp. 129–30.

12. For an exposition and useful comments, see G. Hill, *Salt, Light, and a City*, chap. 12.

13. Volf, *After Our Likeness*, pp. 135–37 and passim (136; emphasis removed).

14. Smyth, *Principles and Inferences*, p. 252.

with the Word of God, the gospel, as the sacraments left alone can hardly mediate Christ's presence.[15] As much as the Baptist Smyth underscored the unmediated presence of Christ in the church, even he considered necessary the use of "the holy things of God," namely, "the meanes of salvation . . . : the word, Sacraments, prayers."[16]

So far all churches are most likely to follow my argumentation, even if for Orthodox and Catholics this is not yet enough. Indeed, where Volf's free church–driven (but mainline Protestant church–sympathetic) proposal differs strongly from the Roman Catholic and Orthodox ecclesiologies is that it does not accept their claims for the necessity of a specific kind of office, namely, episcopacy, for the validity of the sacraments.[17] As a Protestant theologian, I agree with Volf's refusal to make a bishop the absolute requirement for the sacraments' validity.[18] But instead of leaving the issue there and so living with the impasse, I wish to bring to the discussion table the ecumenically pregnant definition of ecclesiality from the mainline Protestant traditions, particularly from Lutheran ecclesiology, with the hope that several important steps toward rapprochement could be had in relation to Orthodox and Catholics.

Toward a Mutual Recognition of the Ecclesiality of the Church: A Constructive Proposal

Locating the Proposal

Betraying my own Protestant location — situated in and deeply indebted to both Lutheran "mainstream" Protestantism and Pentecostal "free church" congregationalism — I wish to propose a new way of conceiving the ecclesiality of the church that hopefully helps advance the ecumenical conversation across

---

15. Volf, *After Our Likeness*, pp. 152–54.

16. Smyth, *Principles and Inferences*, p. 254. For a highly useful discussion, see Haight, *CCH*, 2:251–53 particularly.

17. Volf, *After Our Likeness*, pp. 133–34, 152, and passim. I will not go into the details of differences as to how Orthodox ecclesiology distinctively expresses this condition; see Volf, *After Our Likeness*, pp. 130–31.

18. In my material agreement with Volf's position in this regard, I hasten to mention that it is not convincing that he supports it, among other patristic witnesses, by Ignatius, who binds his rule of ecclesiality as the presence of Christ to the presence of the bishop as the presider of the Eucharist; Ignatius, *To the Smyrnaeans* 8. This same deficit in Volf's argumentation is also noted, e.g., by Erb in his "Responses to 'The Spirit and the Church,'" pp. 61–62.

the spectrum, from Orthodox and Catholic sacramental-episcopal orientations of ecclesiality, to those driven by mainstream Protestant Word-sacrament beliefs, to those based on free church personal faith commitments. No serious ecumenical proposal can — or should — pretend to come "from nowhere"; each and every one is particular and perspectival. But they do not have to be exclusively so: one may also build on one's tradition self-critically and attempt to transcend it for the sake of inclusivity and unity-in-diversity of the whole church. If I have learned anything during more than two decades of intense ecumenical work at regional, national, and international forums, it is that only proposals that are specific and particular further the effort to resolve ecumenical problems, but those proposals have to be specific and particular with a view toward inclusivity rather than cementing already existing hard walls.

I will take as a starting point the description of the ecclesiality of the church from the "middle" of the ecclesiality debate spectrum, between the oldest and youngest churches, namely, mainstream Protestantism. According to the Lutheran Augsburg Confession (article 7), the church "is the assembly of all believers among whom the gospel is preached in its purity and the holy sacraments are administered according to the gospel. For it is sufficient for the true unity of the Christian church that the gospel be preached in conformity with a pure understanding of it and that the sacraments be administered in accordance with the divine Word." In other words, as long as the gospel and sacraments are there, it "is not necessary for the true unity of the Christian church that ceremonies, instituted by men, should be observed uniformly in all places."[19] Clearly, the theological and ecumenical cash value of CA 7 lies in that as long as the gospel and sacraments are there, most everything else can be named a matter of *adiaphora*, including church structures and ministerial patterns.[20]

Hence, the ecumenical potential of CA 7 runs wide and deep. Even when adding "discipline," that is, obedience, as a necessary condition[21] and insisting on divinely sanctioned structures and offices,[22] the Reformed tradition firmly agreed with Lutherans. Even the first and formative free church tradition,

---

19. CA 7; *BC*, p. 32.

20. For useful comments, see Saarinen, "Lutheran Ecclesiology," pp. 171–73.

21. Calvin, *Institutes of the Christian Religion* 4.1.9. Note that even the current Presbyterian Church of the USA's *Book of Order* devotes the largest section to discipline (rather than, say, to worship or government).

22. Calvin (*Institutes of the Christian Religion* 4.3.1) begins his consideration of offices: "We are now to speak of the order in which the Lord has been pleased that his Church should be governed." For Reformed orthodoxy's fixation on a certain order, following the fourfold office based on Eph. 4:11, namely, pastors, teachers, presbyters, and deacons, see Pannenberg, *ST* 3:385.

the Baptist movement, materially agreed with the Lutheran definition, even though it added, similarly to the Reformed, fixed structures and obedience.[23] It also seems to me that the CA 7 definition of ecclesiality can be seen in line with the Radical Reformation, although the latter would also wish to add other points. While the 1527 Swiss Brethren's Schleitheim collection of Seven Articles contains more than CA — although, importantly, it lists baptism and the Lord's Supper — undoubtedly these early Anabaptists meant to stick very carefully with the preached Word; indeed, the rest of the articles, namely, the ban, separation from the world, pacifism, and refusal to take an oath, were based on a most literal reading of the Bible.[24]

Before proceeding, let me raise this self-critical question after listing examples from free churches and the Reformed to whom CA 7 has to be complemented by adding office- and structure-related elements. On what basis is it not self-contradictory on my part to reject the Catholic and Orthodox requirement of episcopacy for ecclesiality (because of its ecclesiality-defeating implications in relation to others) while seeming to overlook the other kinds of additions by Baptists, Anabaptists, and the Reformed? My response is that the additional requirements by the Reformed and the free churches are *additions* and are not meant to necessarily discredit or reject the claim for ecclesiality by the Lutherans; if they were forced, I assume, not only the Reformed but also (at least, most of) the free churches would be willing to negotiate the additions and live with the CA 7 definition. That is markedly different from the categorical rejection of the ecclesiality of all other churches (but the Orthodox) by Roman Catholics.[25]

The Ecumenical Promise of the Gospel and Sacraments as Ecclesial Rule

Ecumenically, it is of utmost importance that notwithstanding serious challenges to the acknowledgment of full ecclesiality to Protestant (and Anglican communities), "Catholic theology has never had any positive objection to raise

23. Smyth, *Principles and Inferences*, pp. 252, 253, respectively.

24. The articles (also called the Schleitheim Confession) can be found, e.g., at Anabaptists, http://www.anabaptists.org/history/the-schleitheim-confession.html. Menno Simons's marks of the true church include pure doctrine, baptism, the Lord's Supper, obedience to the Word, love, confession of Christ, and suffering for God (Simons, *Reply to Gellius Faber*, p. 752; for similar kinds of descriptions, see also pp. 744, 755).

25. Even according to the Vatican (*LG*, ##15 and 26), Protestants, Anglicans, and free churches are not "churches" but rather ecclesial communities.

against the two classic Protestant signs: without the preaching of the gospel in accordance with Scripture and the administering of the sacraments as divinely ordained there can be no true Church according to the Catholic view either; both are absolute prerequisites for the Catholic Church too."[26] This robust statement by the Catholic Küng is definitively endorsed by Vatican II's *Lumen Gentium*: "This Church of Christ is truly present in all legitimate local congregations . . . [in] which the faithful are gathered together by the preaching of the Gospel of Christ, and the mystery of the Lord's Supper is celebrated." So, what is the problem from the Roman side? It has to do with placing the preaching and sacraments in the context of episcopal ministry, as only a "bishop [is] marked with the fullness of the sacrament of Orders," and therefore, "[e]very legitimate celebration of the Eucharist is regulated by the bishop."[27] As long as that claim is taken as a final statement from the Catholics, I see little hope for rapprochement. But what if it could be placed in a bit different context?

I find useful Küng's note that at the core of the Catholic objection to the sufficiency of the CA 7 principle of ecclesiality lies the fear that "these two characteristics of the true Church are not truly distinguishing features" and hence do not fulfill the required task of identifying where the true church really is.[28] If that is the case, I think there is some hope of bringing the divergent viewpoints closer together if we consider the issue in light of the marks of the church, classically taken as the distinguishing distinctives of or pointers to the true church. I think it is fair to claim an ecumenical consensus for the stance that the two defining features of the ecclesiality of CA 7 are integrally and irreconcilably linked with the four marks (to be discussed in more detail below): unity, holiness, catholicity, and apostolicity. Indeed, Küng himself, as a Catholic theologian, contends that the marks "do not mean anything if they are not based on the pure Gospel message, valid baptism, and the proper celebration of the Lord's Supper. Always and every case the Church must be certain it is in essential agreement with the original New Testament message."[29] Isn't there some kind of real mutuality between the two "marks" of CA 7 and the four "marks" of the creed? Neither one alone is specific and concrete enough to help us discern where the presence of the triune God may lie in an ecclesiologically constitutive manner. When linked together, they help us be more confident. Rather than a vicious circle of trying to prove what one

26. Küng, *The Church*, p. 346; materially similarly Moltmann, *The Church in the Power of the Spirit*, p. 341.

27. *LG*, #26.

28. Küng, *The Church*, p. 346.

29. Küng, *The Church*, p. 347.

presupposes, this mutuality can be seen as just that: a *mutuality* of enrichment, information, and specification.

The legitimate fear among the Catholics and Orthodox concerning the challenge of being able to discern Christ's community-forming presence may also be eased by the observation that as much as Protestant Reformers emphasized the immediacy of believers to Christ (to defeat what they saw as the destructive human-made hierarchy-related and institutional obstacles), in no way could CA 7 be made a matter of a "community of believers" merely coming together as individuals to be the church. That would of course make the claim for ecclesiality random and release it from all contours of traditional safeguards. (Indeed, that liability should be carefully minded by free churches, as they at times tend to emphasize problematically the mere unmediated access to Christ by all.) The community's ecclesiality depends on the preaching and sacraments, which both represent apostolicity as they go back to Jesus and the institution by the apostles. Recall the *Large Catechism* (on the third article of the creed): "It is the mother that begets and bears every Christian through the Word of God,"[30] and by implication, in connection with the sacraments. Pannenberg rightly notes that the idea of the church among the Reformers as a "mother" begetting and nurturing believers alone would defeat the mistaken interpretation of Christian gathering as arbitrary. Here at the center of Reformation ecclesiology appears to be a materially similar kind of principle at work to set parameters and indicators to help discern God's presence as the (somewhat) technically defined Catholic interpretation of apostolic succession and (what seems to the outsider) the more or less taken-for-granted claim by the Orthodox as allegedly the oldest and hence "original" church community. For a Protestant theologian, it seems that a mere claim to the apostolicity of the episcopacy in Catholic theology — now that even Catholic exegetes and historians admit that no kind of "historical" argument can be made — may not be stronger (and perhaps is indeed weaker) than a broad appeal to the apostolicity on the basis of the Word and sacraments.

Furthermore, it seems to me that sticking with the two foundational standards, *pure* gospel and *right* administration of sacraments — as much as it is true and routinely noted that the Protestant Reformation at large failed to provide any specific criteria for their ascertainment — also functions toward the unity in faith and love for all communities committed to them. Whatever

---

30. Luther, *Large Catechism* 2.42; *BC*, p. 416; Calvin, *Institutes of the Christian Religion* 4.1.4; see Pannenberg, *ST* 3:100-101. For the rediscovery of the idea in contemporary evangelical ecclesiology, see Harper and Metzger, *Exploring Ecclesiology*, pp. 11-12.

else purity and correctness may mean, they must stand in continuity with the apostolic Scriptures and creeds (again, as much room as there may be for differences in details of formulations). Rather than pushing toward exclusivity, isn't their embrace rather compelling the Christian community to consider as true church any community bound by and committed to the same ecclesiastical criteria? Pannenberg succinctly argues that, on that basis, "the universal unity of the church across the ages finds manifestation in the worship of the local congregation that exists in virtue of its apostolic basis, having fellowship with past saints and martyrs. For the pure teaching of the apostolic gospel and administration of the sacraments that is faithful to their institution constitute the church's unity across the centuries and at the same time characterize each local congregation of believers as the church of Christ."[31] As Küng helpfully reminds us, believing the church to be one, holy, catholic, and apostolic for ourselves, we "want to believe and hope for others too."[32]

Having now considered the criteria for the "observable" ecclesiologically constitutive forms of Christ's presence — with hope for an ecumenical rapprochement — we note that Christ's presence is not of course limited to that function alone. Moltmann importantly reminds us that on the basis of the New Testament texts we should expect Christ's presence in many forms and places. "Christ is present in the apostolate, in the sacraments, and in the fellowship of the brethren." The term "apostolate" here denotes "the medium of the proclamation through word and sacrament, as well as the persons and community of the proclaimers." There are a number of New Testament assurances, such as "he who hears you hears me" (Luke 10:16) and "I am with you always, to the close of the age" (Matt. 28:20), to those going out to share the gospel by preaching and baptizing. Similar promises of Christ's presence are attached to the celebration of the Eucharist (1 Cor. 11:23-27). The baptized will be sharing death and life with Christ (Rom. 6:1-12). Second, Christ has pledged his presence in the children, the poor, and other "little ones." Matthew 25:31-36 is an extended exposition of that theme. Third, Christ is present in his parousia, which, as discussed in part 1, means both "presence" and "appearance." The One who has come and is present in Spirit will also appear to the church.[33]

The Protestant Reformation–originated ecumenical proposal toward a mutual recognition of the churchly nature of other Christian communities

---

31. Pannenberg, *ST* 3:101.

32. Küng, *The Church*, pp. 53-59 (53); so also Moltmann, *The Church in the Power of the Spirit*, pp. 337-38.

33. Moltmann, *The Church in the Power of the Spirit*, pp. 121-32.

is necessary but not yet sufficient for this constructive proposal. It has to be tweaked and reoriented by the insistence on church as mission, a paradigm enthusiastically adopted not only by free churches and Reformation communities but also by Catholics (and to some extent by the Orthodox, who, however, have not widely engaged the discourse).

The Missional Reorientation of the Ecclesiality of the Church

As will be investigated in more detail in the chapter on mission below (16), for various reasons the dynamic and missionary-charismatic conception of the church present in the New Testament and early Christianity began to be lost with the advent of Christendom. This led to a fairly static and at times abstract and lifeless vision of the nature of the true church, as is evident also in the traditional conception of the four marks of the church (to be discussed below).

A highly promising, *theologically* grounded (that is, grounded in the doctrine of God, the triune God) rediscovery of the dynamic, missional nature of the church in recent decades helps us reframe the ecclesiality (and the ancient marks of the church) in an authentically missional context and ethos. The argument of this section is that in the CA 7–driven, ecumenically aspiring understanding of the church as a kerygmatic-sacramental communion, the church is missional by her very nature. That is because the triune God, who has called the church, is a sending God: "Mission begins in the heart of the Triune God and the love which binds together the Holy Trinity overflows to all humanity and creation."[34] Importantly, this statement also reestablishes the term's original meaning with the link of the church's "sent-ness" with "sending" in the triune God.[35] While the many implications of the church's missional nature will be the focus of chapter 16, let us focus here on the connection with the ecclesiality question as seen through the "marks" of the church.[36]

---

34. *TTL*, #2. See also WCC, "Mission and Evangelism in Unity Today," ##11–13 (pp. 65–66).

35. For details and sources, see Bosch, *Transforming Mission*, pp. 1–2, 8–11. See also Chung, *Reclaiming Mission*.

36. Promisingly, this orientation was adopted in the most recent version of *NMC*; see ##43–47. For an important similar Orthodox affirmation, see Meyendorff, "The Orthodox Church and Mission."

The Four Marks of the Church in Action[37]

What Do the "Marks" of the Church Mark?

Unlike too often in later tradition, the four classical marks of the church (also called "notes" or "signs" in tradition)[38] — unity, holiness, apostolicity, and catholicity — were not used first in any apologetic sense. Rather than carefully formulated, fixed definitions, the marks were most probably added to the creed somewhat haphazardly.[39] Indeed, rather than abstract definitions of the church, the marks are first and foremost the object of faith. Whereas in the creeds we believe *in* the triune God as Father, Son, and Spirit, when it comes to the third article, an accurate rendering of the original text states that we believe the church.[40] As a result, they are as much also "statements of hope." Eventually, they also become "statements of action," because they urge us to realize what is believed and hoped for.[41]

It is usual and useful to consider the marks as "gifts" and "tasks." Indeed, the twofold sense is already implied in the above. On the one hand, they are gifts from God. We do not make the church one, holy, apostolic, and catholic; only God can. On the other hand, we see only too clearly that any church in the world, including our own, is far from those markers. Hence, each description is also a matter of hope, which leads to action to more closely attain their realization.

To underline the dynamic and missional orientation of the marks — and to save them from the abstract and formal — the leading American Reformed mission theologian Charles Van Engen's naming them "adverbs" points in the right direction. Rather than static adjectives, the adverbial conception is a call for the church to be "the unifying, sanctifying, reconciling, and proclaiming presence of Jesus Christ in the world," thereby "challenging local congregations to a transformed, purpose-driven life of mission in the world, locally and globally."[42] Building on this dynamic conception of the marks, the

---

37. This heading modifies "The Four Attributes in Action" in Van Engen, *God's Missionary People*, p. 66.

38. For other lists of marks, see Bloesch, *The Church*, pp. 103-9.

39. See Küng, *The Church*, p. 344; Moltmann, *The Church in the Power of the Spirit*, p. 337.

40. See Garijo-Guembe, *Communion of the Saints*, pp. 1-6.

41. Moltmann, *The Church in the Power of the Spirit*, pp. 339-40.

42. Van Engen, "Church," p. 193. See Van Engen, *God's Missionary People*, pp. 59-71. For supporting comments, see Hastings, *Missional God, Missional Church*, p. 48.

leading American Catholic mission theologian Stephen Bevans, SVD, further develops these classic descriptions of the church in a way I think best helps the self-understanding of Christian community in the beginning of the third millennium.[43] In his description, both the twofold nature of the marks as gifts and tasks as well as their originally and ultimately missional orientation come to expression in a new kind of "threefold identity of each mark":

> Thus the church is apostolic as a gift; it is called to be apostolic in fidelity to its missionary nature and let that apostolicity shape the church's entire thinking about itself; and it is to act apostolically in mission in terms of its zeal and its fidelity to apostolic truth. Similarly, the church is catholic but called to be catholic in its appreciation of local identity and diversity-in-unity, and it is commissioned to work for the catholicity of the world by protecting and fostering diversity (in terms of culture, theology, gender, and generational identity) in a constant dialogue for unity. Such unity is already a gift and yet calls the church to work for unity among Christians and to work as well for unity among all religions and peoples. Finally, the church is holy as God's special people and therefore called to be holy as a sign of God's presence in the world. The church is called as well to point out the holiness beyond its boundaries and invite people into the explicit relationship with God that it already enjoys.[44]

In keeping with this multidimensionality of the "distinctives,"[45] the free church (Wesleyan) theologian H. Snyder importantly suggests that the marks be understood dynamically and in a way that attends to their elusive nature: the church is not only one but also many, the church is not only holy but also charismatic, the church is not only catholic but also local, and the church is not only apostolic but also prophetic. Whereas the older churches have tended to think of these marks as indicating "organized institution" in terms of uniformity, sacredness, universality, and authority — as Snyder claims, obviously an (intentional?) overstatement, yet worth hearing — younger churches focus on diversity, the charismatic, locality, and the prophetic word.[46]

43. Bevans, "Beyond the New Evangelization," p. 18.

44. The citation is from Bevans's (yet) unpublished paper, "What Does Rome Have to Do with Pasadena?" p. 11.

45. Named so by Van Engen, *God's Missionary People*, pp. 59–71.

46. H. Snyder, "The Marks of an Evangelical Ecclesiology," pp. 85–89. See also Conniry, "Identifying Apostolic Christianity."

In sum: all these constructive refinements of the marks point to their dynamic, missional, and concrete meaning. As such, they are deeply interconnected, as is proper for a living organism, the community of God. Take, for example, apostolicity: only that church which is also one, holy, and catholic can claim it.[47] Only because of the limitations of human language must the marks be taken one at a time.[48]

Church as One — and Many: Unity in Diversity or the Scandal of Division?

The most striking and dramatic plague of Christianity is not the diversity and plurality of churches (and denominations) but that these churches do not recognize each other and even actively contribute to deepening of divisions.[49] The divisions and lack of love should cause all churches to repent and turn to each other in order to build unity, in obedience to the numerous exhortations and warnings in the New Testament (John 10:16; 17:20–26; Acts 2:42; Rom. 12:3–8; 1 Cor. 1:10–30; 12:12–27; Gal. 3:27–28; Eph. 4:1–6).[50] Although the unity of the church has been a spiritual and theological conviction from the beginning of history,[51] we should not idealize the early church. As is evident already in the New Testament, divisions and strife emerged as soon as new communities mushroomed. Importantly, early in patristic theology deep concern for restoring unity emerged, as is evident in ecumenical tracts such as the early third-century *On the Unity of the Church* by Cyprian.[52]

That said, for Christian living in postmodern times and pluralist settings, talk about unity might not be good news.[53] In the words of *In One Body through the Cross: The Princeton Proposal for Christian Unity*, "In late modernity we fear unity, often with good reason. We cherish our particularity — our family and ethnic heritage, our established patterns of life and thought. We look with suspicion on the political and economic forces that impose homogeneity. We celebrate diversity and pluralism, sometimes as a good in its own

---

47. Pannenberg, *ST* 3:405; T. Oden, *Life in the Spirit*, p. 349; V. Lossky, "Concerning the Third Mark," p. 171.

48. In the headings of the four sections to follow, I am employing (with significant modification) Howard Snyder's and Küng's ideas mentioned above.

49. See *UR*, #1.

50. Küng, *The Church*, pp. 352–53.

51. For examples, see J. N. D. Kelly, *Early Christian Doctrines*, pp. 200–201.

52. See J. N. D. Kelly, *Early Christian Doctrines*, pp. 204–7.

53. So also Haight, *CCH*, 3:91.

right, because we fear the constraints of single sets of ideals."[54] Would that "turn" to diversity frustrate the vision of unity? No, it would not. Along with diversity — and not antagonistic to it — the same drafters also affirmed visible Christian unity as "not a modern dream, but a permanent and central aspect of Christian life." By the same token — in keeping with current ecumenical consciousness — they saw the unity as not eliminating diversity.[55]

Rightly the Catholic Roger Haight reminds us that "not only historical consciousness but also the apostolic witness and the apostolic church show that the unity among the churches does not necessarily involve uniformity but has to be pluralistic";[56] it can also be, as another Catholic, Hans Küng, puts it, a "unity in diversity."[57] Indeed, he makes the brilliant observation that the multiplicity of churches, rather than being a barrier to unity, might indeed be a key to it as long as plurality is not conceived in self-contained and isolated terms but rather as an asset and way of enrichment.[58]

The Church as Catholic — and Local: Oppressing Universality or Flourishing Contextuality?

In keeping with the nonapologetic employment of the marks of the church in early Christianity, the term "catholic" — literally in Greek, "directed toward the whole" — in Ignatius of Antioch, in whom we find it for the first time, simply meant the "whole" church in distinction from local communities.[59] There is no indication yet of the later meaning attached to catholicity of "fullness" and "perfection," that is, lacking in anything; nor is that meaning present in secular Greek. The linking of "catholic" with the *pleroma* (fullness) of Ephesians 1:23 came later, in the third century, due to polemics and apologetics. Then the term's meaning first comes to match materially with "orthodox," and by derivation mean something like "valid." This came to its zenith with the establishment of Christianity as the only legitimate state religion in Christendom.

---

54. Braaten and Jenson, eds., *In One Body through the Cross*, #2 (p. 12).

55. Braaten and Jenson, eds., *In One Body through the Cross*, ##3, 4, respectively (pp. 12–13).

56. Haight, *CCH*, 3:92; similarly Harper and Metzger, *Exploring Ecclesiology*, pp. 32–35.

57. Küng, *The Church*, p. 349.

58. Küng, *The Church*, p. 355; see also Moltmann, *The Church in the Power of the Spirit*, p. 343.

59. Ignatius, *To the Smyrnaeans* 8. For this and other early testimonies to the same effect, see Küng, *The Church*, p. 384.

Quite naturally, the additional layers of the term also took on geographical and numerical connotations as the church extended to new territories and grew in membership. By the fifth century, Vincent of Lérins's celebrated formula speaks of "that faith which has been believed everywhere, always, by all."[60]

Although the 1054 split between the Christian East and Christian West, oddly enough, did not call into question catholicity, the Protestant Reformation did. How could one continue affirming catholicity now that unity had been lost? That said, all the time the Reformers claimed to belong to the Catholic Church (as is evident, for example, in the inclusion of the ancient creeds in the preamble of Lutheran confessional books). Whereas for the Reformers the accent naturally fell on the meaning of catholicity as "orthodox," for Catholic polemicists it was about "catholicity of space and time and numbers," that is, membership in the Catholic Church.[61]

The contemporary understanding has to remember the original New Testament meaning of the term "catholic" (notwithstanding the lack of the term therein): it simply means the whole church as that consists of all local churches, which in themselves are full churches insofar as they are in communion with other similar communities. "While the individual local Church is *an* entire Church, it is not *the* entire Church." By derivation, each such local church is truly catholic. In other words, the plurality of local churches does not make either them or the whole church uncatholic; what only strips the church(es) off from catholicity is separation from others, self-sufficiency, and isolation.[62] Furthermore, although spatial extension, numerical quantity, and temporal continuity are not irrelevant to catholicity, they do not alone — or even primarily — constitute it. As Küng pointedly puts it, "The most international, the largest, the most varied, the oldest Church can in fact become a stranger to itself, can become something different, can lose touch with its own innermost nature, can deviate from its true and original course."[63]

It is often noted — rightly — that the term "catholic" comes close to "ecumenical," whose basic meaning, "pertaining to the whole inhabited world," came to mean (the search for) the wholeness, that is, oneness and unity, of the Christian church. Its early use, in the *Martyrdom of Polycarp* (8.1), links the two in speaking of "the whole Catholic Church throughout the world [*oikoumene*]." Summary wise we may now state: "The catholicity of the Church,

60. Vincent of Lérins, *A Commonitory* 2.6. For details of this development, see Küng, *The Church*, pp. 385–86.

61. Küng, *The Church*, pp. 386–87.

62. Küng, *The Church*, pp. 387–88.

63. Küng, *The Church*, pp. 388–89 (389).

therefore, consists in a notion of entirety, based on identity and resulting in universality. From this it is clear that unity and catholicity go together; if the Church is one, it must be universal, if it is universal it must be one. Unity and catholicity are two interwoven dimensions of one and the same Church."[64]

When speaking of unity and "universality" in connection with catholicity, one has to mind two liabilities. First is the Enlightenment-driven idea of homogeneity, as if differences and peculiarities were to be deleted for the sake of the common good. On the contrary, catholicity connotes the openness of the church to the entire world[65] and hence resists exclusivity, limitations, and oppressing universality. Catholicity, instead, fosters "contextuality" and allows for inclusive locality.[66] Second is the need to make a concentrated effort within the one catholicity of the church to attend in a particular manner to certain groups often found at the margins: children, the poor, the handicapped, the underprivileged, the tortured — and at times, unfortunately, also women deprived of ministry opportunities and "voting rights." To true catholicity also belongs, as Moltmann creatively puts it, "partisanship." Not the rich but the poor, not the powerful but the weak, not the glamorous but the despised were favored by Jesus. Even more than that: at times "Jesus turned to the sinners, tax-collectors and lepers in order to save the Pharisees and the healthy as well. Paul turned to the Gentiles in order to save Israel too. Christian partisan support for the oppressed is intentional and its goal is to save the oppressor also."[67]

The Church as Holy — and Sinful:
Sainthood by Separation or Pursuit of Holiness by Patient Love?

The ecumenical document *The Nature and Mission of the Church* reminds us of the obvious dilemma facing each and every church: "The essential holiness of the Church stands in contrast to sin, individual as well as communal."[68] Not surprisingly, various tactics have been tried to ensure the church's holiness.[69] One of them is isolating the "holy members" from the rest. This goes back all the way to the (in)famous Donatist controversy.[70] Whereas the rigorist Do-

64. Küng, *The Church*, pp. 391-92.
65. Haight, *CCH*, 3:93.
66. Haight, *CCH*, 3:93.
67. Moltmann, *The Church in the Power of the Spirit*, pp. 347-52 (352).
68. *NMC*, #54; see also #51.
69. These tactics are outlined and assessed in Küng, *The Church*, pp. 415-17.
70. A reliable, succinct guide with meticulous documentation to Donatism's basic theo-

natists started off from the premise of the purity of the church, Augustine's point of departure, based on the legacy of Cyprian (and others), was the unity of the body of Christ and the principle of love.[71] For the Donatists, the validity of the sacraments depended on the level of spirituality of the minister; similarly, the church's status as Christ's body was compromised by the tolerance of the *traditor* (a lapsed leader). For them, the true church consisted only of saints. The "catholic" party (headed by the bishops Optatus and Augustine) refuted all these claims and found the sacraments' validity in the trinitarian God rather than in God's people. Similarly, they conceived of the church as "a mixed body," including sinners and saints — even the Donatists, should they wish to be included. The holiness of the church was seen as the function of the church's Lord: only at the end would God sort out the saints from the sinners.[72] Augustine anchored the unity in love: without loving God and neighbors one cannot be part of the church; severing the bond of love, as schismatics did, broke the principle of love.[73] Yet another tactic makes a distinction between a church that is holy in herself and her sinful members; that is, it considers the *church* holy and her membership sinning. The obvious question arises, however: What is a church without Christians? Is it an abstract concept? An "invisible" nonearthly reality?

What, then, would be a theologically and pastorally appropriate way to envision a "holy" church of the creed despite the necessary sinfulness of all her members? The starting point is the honest and bold acknowledgment of the sinfulness of the church.[74] Even in her holiness, the church is "sinful and yet holy."[75] This is true as much as the confession of the unity of the church in the midst of rampant divisions — or else we are not speaking of a real, concrete church composed of human beings! This means that the church does not derive her holiness from the members — as free church ecclesiologies too often tend to imply — but from her Lord, nor does the church lose her holiness because of the presence of sin in the lives of men and women.[76]

---

logical claims is J. N. D. Kelly, *Early Christian Doctrines*, pp. 409-12; Augustine's response is pp. 412-17; highly useful is also Pelikan, *CT* 1:308-13.

71. Detailed sources for Cyprian can be found in J. N. D. Kelly, *Early Christian Doctrines*, pp. 203-7; for Ambrose, p. 409; and Hilary, pp. 409-10.

72. J. N. D. Kelly, *Early Christian Doctrines*, pp. 410-13 (411).

73. For details and sources, see J. N. D. Kelly, *Early Christian Doctrines*, pp. 414-15.

74. The American Reformed feminist Amy Plantinga Pauw puts it delightfully in her title: "The Graced Infirmity of the Church."

75. Küng, *The Church*, p. 411; so also Moltmann, *The Church in the Power of the Spirit*, pp. 21-24; Harper and Metzger, *Exploring Ecclesiology*, pp. 30-31. See also Rahner, *Foundations*, pp. 418-19.

76. So also Küng, *The Church*, pp. 416-17.

Yes, the idea of separation is at the core of the biblical notion of holiness (both in the OT *qadosh* and in the NT *hagios*). Holiness simply means turning away from all that is un- and anti-God(ly) and turning to things of God. But notwithstanding the human act of turning (away and toward), ultimately holiness is the work of the triune God. According to the New Testament, God made our sanctification, and "God chose you from the beginning to be saved, through sanctification by the Spirit" (2 Thess. 2:13). What God has started, God will finish in the eschaton. While the New Testament frequently calls people in local churches "saints" and holy whose lives displayed all kinds of attitudes and acts of sin — just think of 1 Corinthians — never does the expression "holy church" appear in the New Testament; only "holy nation" (1 Pet. 2:9) and "holy temple" (Eph. 2:21) do. Importantly, the New Testament also never calls any materials or acts such as baptism or the Eucharist holy. Dramatically different from the Old Testament, the New Testament "knows nothing of institutional sanctity, or a sacred 'it.'"[77] The New Testament only knows of "personal" sanctity. This leads us to the following conclusion: "The Church is holy by being called by God in Christ [in the power of the Spirit] to be the communion of the faithful, by accepting the call to his service, by being separated from the world and at the same time embraced and supported by his grace."[78]

The Church as Apostolic — and Charismatic:
A Conserving Institution or an Expanding Organism?

An elusive and pluriform concept both in the New Testament[79] and in later ecclesiastical usage,[80] beginning from the early fathers, "apostolicity" became a commonplace in Christian usage, whether in relation to the church, a bishop, or Christ.[81] Although the adjective "apostolic" never occurs in the Bible (and

77. The designation (holy) "temple" referred to above is not a reference to "it" but to the people (of God).
78. Küng, *The Church*, pp. 417-20 (418-19).
79. See further Schnackenburg, "Apostolizität," pp. 51-73; and Garijo-Guembe, *Communion of the Saints*, pp. 29-36.
80. An up-to-date survey of apostolicity as it is explicated in several international ecumenical documents can be found in O'Gara, "Apostolicity in Ecumenical Dialogue."
81. Similarly to the term "catholic," "apostolic" also appears for the first time in Ignatius of Antioch (inscription to his *Epistle to the Trallians*), where the reference is to Jesus Christ rather than to the church. In *Martyrdom of Polycarp* (16.2) the reference is to Polycarp, the "apostolic and prophetic teacher."

hardly anywhere outside it), the term "apostle" occurs frequently in the New Testament, most often in Luke and Paul, where its meaning resembles that of "ambassador" (for Christ). The term is not limited to the Twelve, as is often popularly assumed. It can also refer to various persons and groups; Paul himself is of course often its object, and he also mentions "false apostles."[82]

Despite complex debates in later history, it is undisputed that the original meaning of the term simply had to do with the linkage to apostles.[83] Apostolicity, then, essentially involves continuity[84] with the life and faith of the apostles and the apostolic church of the New Testament.[85] In other words, "the church is at all times *referred to its apostolic origin*."[86] This linkage with the apostolic church should not be understood too narrowly or too technically. It is a matter of the church of every generation living in dynamic continuity with the whole life and mission of the whole apostolic church.

That raises the question about the kind of characteristics and emphases present in the apostolic church. No doubt, deep missional orientation was her defining feature as the church expanded from "Jerusalem" to "Samaria" to "the end of the earth" (Acts 1:8).[87] Alongside the integral missionary existence, the apostolic church's life was charismatic.[88] Indeed, the ecclesial-missional existence of the churches in the Acts of the Apostles was energized, guided, and inspired by charisms, including many kinds of spiritual gifts, from healings and exorcisms to prophecy and words of wisdom. In that light — in referring the church back to her apostolic roots — the claim to apostolicity by the youngest Christian family, Pentecostalism, gains a new credibility and significance. Unbeknownst to uninformed observers of Pentecostalism, the notion

---

82. For details and references, see Küng, *The Church*, pp. 443-55 particularly.

83. That holds even if we know that soon thereafter another meaning was added, namely, "ascetic," meaning total devotion to God and renouncement of the world; see Küng, *The Church*, pp. 443-44.

84. I prefer here the term "continuity" rather than "succession," since the latter term has such heavy connotations of a specific kind of succession, e.g., episcopal succession in terms of a continual chain of bishops.

85. So, e.g., *NMC*, #56.

86. Joint Lutheran–Roman Catholic Study Commission, *Malta Report*, #57, emphases added. So also *BEM*, #34.

87. Wainwright, *Doxology*, p. 135. So also Anglican-Lutheran International Continuation Committee, *The Niagara Report, 1987*, #21; Braaten and Jenson, eds., *In One Body through the Cross*, chap. 3 (pp. 26-37).

88. Congar, *I Believe in the Holy Spirit*, 2:39-44; F. A. Sullivan, *The Church We Believe In*, pp. 185-97; V. Lossky, "Concerning the Third Mark," p. 172; Schlink, *Ökumenische Dogmatik*, pp. 591-98 especially.

of apostolicity is located in the very roots of the movement.[89] Claiming to be linked with the charismatic spirituality of the churches in the New Testament, a significant number of Pentecostal churches, organizations, and publications carry the nomenclature "apostolic."[90] This claim does not have to be taken as ideological, meaning that only Pentecostals were apostolic, but rather as an essential link to what apostolicity meant in the New Testament. Not surprisingly, missionary enthusiasm is also a hallmark of Pentecostal/charismatic Christianity[91] and is another feature strengthening the appeal to apostolicity.[92]

Clearly, the "apostolicity" of the church should be understood theologically in two dynamically conditioned ways — and that simultaneously. On the one hand, the church of every age has to ensure its deep and integral connection with the living legacy, that is, "tradition," of the founding apostles. On the other hand, when doing so the church is harking back not to antiquated relics or frozen formulae but rather to a living, dynamic, charismatic, and expanding life of the apostolic church as described in the book of Acts and the rest of the New Testament. Even if securing this link with the living past can be done in differing ways — whether through an episcopal succession (Orthodox and Roman Catholics) or through an appeal to the Bible as the apostolic Word (Reformation churches) or through the charismatic experience similar to that of the first church (Pentecostals/charismatics) — this twofold dynamic of both past-rootedness and living-in-the-now should be the main concern. Too often in history and contemporary ecclesiology, debates on apostolicity have focused on fairly narrowly and at times (semi)technically conceived "logistics" of how to best secure the link to the past. Rather, as *The Nature and Mission of the Church* contends, apostolicity characterizes the whole church, not only some Christian churches.[93] In a word, it means continuity with the apostolic life(style) and tradition.

89. Robeck, "A Pentecostal Perspective on Apostolicity"; Yong, *The Spirit Poured Out on All Flesh*, pp. 146-51.

90. See further my "Pentecostalism and the Claim for Apostolicity" and "The Apostolicity of Free Churches."

91. See my "Pentecostal Mission and Encounter with Religions."

92. The global Pentecostal movement's legitimate claim to apostolicity should not be linked in any way with a very dubious and theologically/pastorally highly problematic "new apostolic" movement represented by some independent charismatics. For their views, see Wagner, *Churchquake!* and *The New Apostolic Churches*. For an analysis, see Shiver, "Ken Sumrall and Church Foundational Network."

93. *NMC*, #70. So also Küng, *The Church*, pp. 355-56.

15. Church as Communion of Communions

Trinitarian Communion as the Source of Ecclesial Communion

Orientation to the Discussion

Having anchored the Christian community in the life of the triune God and in the missionary ("sending") movement of the coming kingdom for the salvation and reconciliation of the world (chap. 13), as well as tentatively establishing the criteria for where and how the ecclesially constitutive presence of Christ and Spirit may be discerned (chap. 14), we focus in this chapter on the life of the church as communion. By picking up from where the discussion was left in chapter 13, the investigation here begins by expanding on the many dimensions and facets of *koinonia* springing forth from the triune God. Thereafter, before a more specific look is taken at the implications of *koinonia* with regard to the local church and then the ways local churches are in communion with other local churches, a brief but important consideration of the communal or ecclesial nature of Christian personhood is attempted. Thereafter, the discussion on the one church of Christ as the communion of communions also brings to light the ancient problems of "visibility" and "invisibility," topics to be carefully nuanced for the sake of our pluralistic world.

Writing to the global and ecumenical church, I cannot dismiss topics that are routinely ignored in systematic ecclesiological presentations, although their importance is evident among the faithful. What I mean are these two interrelated topics: first, whether the "communion of saints" also includes those believers who are deceased, a conviction firmly shared particularly by

Orthodox and Roman Catholics; and second — particularly with reference to many Africans, Asians, and others in the Global South — whether Christian *koinonia* has any relation to the ancestors. After these themes have been dealt with, I end the chapter by seeking *koinonia* resources for engaging some urgent needs and themes prevalent in the postmodern cultures of the Global North — issues of identity, belonging, and difference.

The Rich and Multidimensional Nature of Koinonia

On the basis of the rediscovery of the Trinity as the structuring principle of theology and thus also of ecclesiology, a wide ecumenical consensus has grown about the church as "communion," *koinonia*.[1] Communion is nothing "added" to Christian existence, as if it were optional, but rather, living in communion with God and other Christians is an essential part of Christian life.[2] This, nontechnically and briefly put, is the main thesis of the celebrated Orthodox theologian John Zizioulas's *Being as Communion* (1985).[3] Its argument is simple and profound: God is not first "one substance" and only then exists as "trinity"; rather, the "Holy Trinity is a *primordial* ontological concept and not a notion which is added to the divine substance."[4] In other words, "the substance of God, 'God,' has no ontological content, no true being, apart from communion."[5] *Lumen Gentium* says the same, speaking of God who "does not make men holy and save them merely as individuals, without bond or link between one another. Rather has it pleased Him to bring men together as one people."[6]

The focus on church as communion is not a new idea in itself nor a mere theological construction. *Koinonia* language is deeply embedded in the biblical witness, particularly in Acts and the Pauline literature.[7] Deriving from the root

1. *NMC*, ##24, 32. For important agreements in four defining ecumenical dialogues, namely, Catholics with Lutherans, Anglicans, Reformed, and Methodists, see Kasper, *HTF*, ##37-40; and between Catholics and Pentecostals, see *Perspectives on Koinonia*. See WCC, *Towards Koinonia in Faith, Life, and Witness*; for useful reflections, see Moore, "Towards Koinonia in Faith, Life and Witness."

2. A useful essay is Wood, "Ecclesial *Koinonia* in Ecumenical Dialogues"; see also Wood, "Baptism and the Foundations of Communion," pp. 38-43.

3. See also Zizioulas, "Human Capacity."

4. Cf. "In the Beginning Is Communion," chapter title in Boff, *Trinity and Society*, p. 9.

5. Zizioulas, *Being as Communion*, p. 17.

6. *LG*, #9. See also the important remarks by the Catholic ecclesiologist Doyle, *Communion Ecclesiology*, pp. 12-13.

7. A massive recent study of all aspects of *koinonia* is L. Fuchs, *Koinonia and the*

meaning "common" and "communal," *koinonia* also "carries the overarching meanings of 'association,' 'communion,' 'fellowship,' and 'close relationships,'" as well as "sharing" and "participation."[8] It is used in various and diverse contexts in the New Testament, including the following:

- fellowship with the triune God (1 Cor. 1:9; 2 Cor. 13:13; Phil. 2:1; 1 John 1:3, 6)
- sharing in faith and the gospel (Rom. 15:27; 1 Cor. 9:23; Phil. 1:5, 7; Titus 1:4; Philem. 6; 1 John 1:3, 7)
- sharing in the Eucharist (Acts 2:42; 1 Cor. 10:16)
- participation in (co)sufferings (2 Cor. 1:7; Phil. 3:10; Heb. 10:33)
- partnering in common ministry (2 Cor. 8:23; Gal. 2:9; Philem. 17)
- sharing in and contributing to economic and financial needs (Acts 2:44; 4:32; Rom. 12:13; 15:26; 2 Cor. 12:13; Gal. 6:6; Phil. 4:14–15; 1 Tim. 6:18; Heb. 13:16)[9]

This multiplicity of biblical perspectives on *koinonia* is aptly illustrated in the Lutheran document *The Church as Communion*, which speaks of "the unity of the church across all time and space, the nature of life together in the local church, and the relationship between local churches in a regional and global context."[10] Most profoundly, the many interrelated facets of *koinonia* include the time dimension, the inner life of the church, as well as interecclesial relations at all levels. The same document also reminds us of the all-important missionary dimension inherent in the concept of *koinonia*: "The church as communion does not exist for itself. It has received a commission; it is sent into the world to proclaim and praise God."[11] Through this mission the church serves the world as a sign of "God's creative, transforming and final intention for humanity and creation."[12]

Quest. Other standard sources are Panikulam, *Koinōnia in the New Testament*; Reumann, "Koinonia in Scripture."

8. L. Fuchs, *Koinonia and the Quest*, pp. 6–8; see also McDonnell, "Communion Ecclesiology and Baptism in the Spirit," p. 674.

9. L. Fuchs, *Koinonia and the Quest*, appendix 1 (pp. 519–25); see also Rossing, "Models of Koinonia."

10. "Toward a Lutheran Understanding of Communion," section 2 in *CC-LCE*, p. 13; for the background and context, see Root, "Communion Statement in Its Context."

11. "Toward a Lutheran Understanding of Communion," section 16 in *CC-LCE*, p. 20; see also section 4, p. 14.

12. "Toward a Lutheran Understanding of Communion," section 17 in *CC-LCE*, p. 21; see also section 27, p. 27.

Before we delve into the implications of this multifaceted category of *koinonia* for our understanding of the local church as communion and, thereafter, the communion among all local communions, we discuss the importance of *koinonia* to personal faith and Christian existence.

The Ecclesial Mediation of Personal Faith

If prior to the Enlightenment, before the full emergence of individual personhood in the modern sense, Christian faith (like any other religion or ideology) was often imposed by the community on the individual without giving the individual an opportunity to embrace it, in the post-Enlightenment Global North the opposite liability arose. Particularly among Protestants and free church Christians, hyperindividualism has too often not only taken over communal commitment but even blurred the meaning of faith as a communal event.[13] The task of a balanced communion ecclesiology is to keep in dynamic mutual conditioning both personal embrace of faith and its communal mediation by the Word, sacraments, and significant Christian persons in family and at church. Rightly understood, every believer receives his or her faith from the church, but then that faith must be personally embraced and owned for it to be more than an external religious or cultural feature.[14]

Particularly free church communities need to be constantly reminded that the gathering of Christians together around the gospel and sacraments is more than an arbitrary social get-together; they are bound and ruled by something that has existed before them and will continue thereafter. Call it the "objective basis" of the fellowship. The "subjective basis" is called forth by a personal appropriation and embrace of the received gospel message and sacramental celebration. This subjective side, based on personal faith, is more than just a human person's faith as a disposition, as an isolated capacity. If it were only that, the church would not be needed; one could believe in God "directly," as it were. "Only by the common content of faith are individuals aware of belonging to the fellowship of believers over and above mere external church membership." This sharing in the common content of faith comes to the fore

13. Instructive in this sense are the well-meaning but misleading words of the first Baptist, J. Smyth (*Works*, p. 743), of the claim for "direct" reception of faith; for comments, see Volf, *After Our Likeness*, pp. 161-62.

14. The materially same argument is developed in Volf, *After Our Likeness*, pp. 160-71; see also his nuanced reflections on the "ecclesial character of salvation," pp. 172-81. Also useful is chap. 3 in Bloesch, *The Church*.

in public confession of faith, commitment to biblical doctrine as a faithful exposition of what the triune God has done and is doing for the salvation of the world; it also comes to the fore in partaking in the church's liturgical and missional life rather than creating one's own religious rites. So, confession of faith is both a personal matter and a receiving of it from the community that preexists and remains after the individual.[15]

This is not to undermine the importance of the individual's right — and in case of a mature person: responsibility — to think through one's faith critically and carefully. In fact, even when the person, often a young person or a person young in faith, receives the Christian message by the church's authority, personal appropriation and assessment are essential in due course. What the emphasis on the ecclesial mediation of personal faith seeks to ascertain is that even the personal testing and critique, rather than meaning a move away from mediation, is its confirmation.[16] So, the conclusion is that the relationship between the individual person and the church community is not either individual driven or community driven but rather both-and. "On the one hand, it would seem to be meaningless to think of the church apart from people, the individuals. On the other hand, for each individual to be a member of the *church* with its faith, liturgy, institutional characters, and so forth would not be possible in case the church did not precede him or her."[17]

Furthermore, as will be detailed below (chap. 19 on ecumenism), the common confession of faith has also wider ecumenical ramifications. By sharing in confession with the same content and object, namely, the triune God, we participate in the common confession of all churches and Christians.[18] After all, there is only one Christ. Miroslav Volf speaks of the importance of the "*openness* of every church toward all other churches as an indispensable condition of ecclesiality." This is so because by "isolating itself from other churches, a church attests either that it is professing faith in 'a different Christ' than do the latter, or is denying in practices the *common* Jesus Christ to whom it professes faith, the Christ who is, after all, the Savior and Lord of *all* churches, indeed,

15. Pannenberg, *ST* 3:110–14 particularly (110); see also Volf, *After Our Likeness*, pp. 148–51.

16. Pannenberg, *ST* 3:122–24.

17. Pannenberg, *ST* 3:97, emphasis in original; so also p. 102; Küng, *The Church*, p. 123. For the (in)famous characterization of Schleiermacher concerning the alleged community orientation in Catholicism and individualism orientation in Protestantism, see §24 epithet (p. 103).

18. Volf, *After Our Likeness*, pp. 154–58.

of all the world." This can be named the "*interecclesial minimum*" through which "a church necessarily sets out on the *path* to its future, a path on which it is to express and deepen its communion, that is, its differentiated unity, with all other churches through the common confessions of faith and appropriate structures of communion (see Eph. 4:2, 13–16)."[19]

Having anchored the ecclesial communion in the life of the triune God and God's "mission" in the world, and having established the coexistence and mutuality of personal and communal/ecclesial faith, we next look at the meaning of *koinonia* to the local communion and its relation to all other local communions, the communion of communions.

The Communion of Communions

Church as Local Communion

The New Testament does not clarify the relationship between what later tradition calls the "local" and the "universal" church; it speaks of both, sometimes in the same context.[20] Theologically speaking, it is clear that the basic unit is the particular, concrete, local gathering of people in Jesus' name around the gospel and sacraments, as well as missional ministry. Indeed, the church, concretely speaking, is the "visible assembly of visible persons at a specific place for specific action." The implication of this statement is that the church does not exist, as it were, "*above* the locally assembled congregation, but rather 'in, with, and beneath' it."[21]

Rightly conceived, to cite the late Reformed theologian Emil Brunner, "[t]he Body of Christ is nothing other than a fellowship of persons. It is 'the fellowship of Jesus Christ' [1 Cor. 1:9] or 'fellowship of the Holy Ghost' [2 Cor. 13:14; Phil. 2:1] where fellowship or koinonia signifies a common participation, a togetherness, a community life. The faithful are bound to each other through their common sharing in Christ and in the Holy Ghost, but that which they have in common is precisely no 'thing,' no 'it,' but a 'he,' Christ and His Holy

---

19. Volf, *After Our Likeness*, pp. 156–57, emphasis in original.

20. For the most well-known (though, of course, not the only) designation, namely, *ekklesia*, see Gooder, "In Search of the 'Early Church,'" pp. 10–15; Garijo-Guembe, *Communion of the Saints*, pp. 9–11; Haight, *CCH*, vol. 1, chap. 2.

21. Cited in Volf, *After Our Likeness*, pp. 137–38, from O. Weber, *Versammelte Gemeinde*, pp. 32, 33, respectively.

Spirit."[22] This principle of "fellowship of persons" gathered in a local communion is robustly present in the description of the life and nature of the first Christian church following the day of Pentecost in Luke's summary statement in Acts 2:42–47.

The local gathering, fellowship, *koinonia* around the Word, sacraments, and common sharing, is the church in the full sense of the term. As a result, "[a]t each local liturgical celebration where Jesus Christ is himself present the whole global fellowship of Christians find manifestation . . . [and] all Christianity is present."[23] This is the ecclesiologically all-important starting point for speaking of the church in her concrete existence. But that is not everything that should be said of the local church.[24] Equally important is to insist that the *communion* of local congregations among themselves is "essential to the integrity of each congregation as a form and manifestation of the one universal church of Christ."[25] The obvious conclusion, then, is that the church is a communion of many (local) communions[26] rather than a universal institution (as forms of Catholic theology claim) and also rather than an aggregate of more or less isolated individual communities (the liability of forms of free church ecclesiologies). In other words, the universal church is but the communion of (local) communions.[27] The clarification of the relation of the local communion to other communions, and thus to the universal church, is an important theological task attempted below. But before that, an important deepening of the ecclesial nature of faith is in order to underline the mutual conditioning of the individual and community, a key insistence of communion theology.

Local Church, "Universal Church," and Eschatological Consummation

Defining the "essence" of the church as a local communion in communion with all other churches in one body of Christ calls for a careful systematic clarification of three interrelated yet clearly distinct relationships:

22. E. Brunner, *Misunderstanding of the Church*, pp. 10–11.

23. Pannenberg, *ST* 3:103.

24. See Volf, *After Our Likeness*, p. 3.

25. Pannenberg, *ST* 3:103. See J. N. D. Kelly, *Early Christian Doctrines*, p. 189 (with examples from early fathers).

26. Pannenberg, *ST* 3:103; materially similarly the noted Catholic J. M. R. Tillard, *Church of Churches*.

27. For Cyprian's legacy and implications, see further Uzukwu, *A Listening Church*, pp. 51–56.

- What is the relationship between the local and the "universal" church?[28]
- What is the relationship between the local church and the eschatological consummation?
- What is the relationship between the visible and the invisible church?

The Local and the Universal Church. Early in the Christian West, this relationship was conceived in terms of the local churches being "parts" of the universal. Hence, a schism was envisioned as a fragmentation of the one body, as it were.[29] Another view, more akin to Eastern sensibilities, was the microcosm/macrocosm scheme. Both views are not so much wrong as inadequate and somewhat unhelpful. Minding the full ecclesiality of each local gathering, we are not helped by thinking of the local church merely as a part of the universal. Rather, each local church is a full church, and conversely, the whole church "comes to realization in a local church."[30] At the same time, this local church, as a "full" church, is necessarily part of the one universal body of Christ. Hence, to speak of the local and universal is to speak dialectically of "two distinct perspectives on the church which always mutually interact and influence each other."[31] We see already in the New Testament the association and mutual engagement of local communions with each other.[32]

This much was established above. To expand the last statement, we should add that although each local church is a full church, each is also linked with other churches, as they all "receive one and the same Gospel . . . the same mission and the same promise" under the one and the same Lord.[33] *The Nature and Mission of the Church* summarized this well: "The communion of the Church is expressed in the communion between local churches, in each of which the fullness of the Church resides. The communion of the Church embraces local churches in each place and all places at all times. Local churches are held in the communion of the Church by the one Gospel, the one baptism

---

28. The reason that "universal" is in quotation marks has to do with the term's potentially liable connotations, particularly stemming from an Enlightenment epistemology in which it may represent an oppressive "concept" (Derrida and others) and postcolonial power play (Foucault and others). My use of the term has nothing to do with those; in the following, the quotation marks are dropped.

29. For details and early sources, see G. Evans, "The Church in the Early Christian Centuries," pp. 36–37.

30. Haight, *CCH*, 1:41. So also *LG*, #26.

31. Haight, *CCH*, 1:41–42; similarly, Küng, *The Church*, p. 121. See also Komonchak, "The Church Universal," pp. 30–35.

32. *NMC*, #64.

33. Küng, *The Church*, p. 122.

and the one Lord's Supper, served by a common ministry. This communion of local churches is thus not an optional extra, but is an essential aspect of what it means to be the Church."[34]

While the relationship between the local and the universal church is routinely discussed in ecclesiological presentations, a related relationship, that of the local church to the eschatological consummation, is usually missing. Let us clarify it. Doing so also gives us an opportunity to deepen the understanding of the relationship between the local and the universal.

The Local Church and the Eschatological Consummation. We placed the church in the context of the coming kingdom in chapter 13. The question here has to do with the relation of the local church to "the totality of the eschatological people of God" gathered under one God in the eschaton.[35] Following uncritically the free church template would suggest that the eschatological totality is but the composition or sum of all local churches. But that raises the question of how a local church could be a full church. It couldn't in that logic. Hence, it looks like the Orthodox idea of identifying the local with the universal church would help negotiate the dilemma: if the whole Christ is fully present in all eucharistic gatherings, then in each local communion the whole church is present (and of course in the eschatological gathering as well).[36] The problem here is what Volf rightly calls "overrealized eschatology" and the accompanying problem of equating the church with Christ.[37] What, then, about the Roman Catholic view in which, so to speak, the local church receives its ecclesiality from the universal church or, to put it another way: "[T]he local church participates in the reality of the larger church; the larger church is actualized in the local church"?[38] The problem with this has to do with the neglect of the still-eschatological and thus anticipatory nature of the universal church prior to consummation. In other words, in the Catholic conception the local church is not seen as an anticipation of the totality of the eschatological people of God but rather as a realization of the now-existing church on earth.

Only by minding the eschatologically oriented and therefore provisional nature of the church communion do we arrive at a proper understanding of

---

34. *NMC*, #65.

35. Volf, *After Our Likeness*, p. 139; here I am following closely his argumentation on pp. 139-45.

36. For a detailed exposition of the Orthodox position (through Zizioulas's ecclesiology), see Volf, *After Our Likeness*, pp. 97-102.

37. For this important critique, see Volf, *After Our Likeness*, pp. 99-101 particularly.

38. Volf, *After Our Likeness*, p. 140; for the details of the Catholic position (through Ratzinger's ecclesiology), see pp. 42-47, particularly pp. 46-47.

the relation of the local to the eschatological communion. The theologically satisfactory solution to the relationship between these two is something like this: "The local church is not a concrete realization of the existing universal church, but rather real anticipation or proleptic realization of the eschatological gathering of the entire people of God." Therefore, while not an identification, there is a relationship of overlapping between the local and the universal church "insofar as the universal church includes all local churches, and every local church is a part of the universal church understood in this way."[39]

Finally, the thorny question of the relation of the "visible" to the "invisible" communion should be taken up. Even there, communion ecclesiology serves as the guide.

The Visible and the Invisible Church. Although the New Testament speaks of the church most often in concrete local terms, as a visible fellowship in a particular location, also implied is the idea of what came to be known in tradition as the invisible church.[40] Quite early, particularly in the Christian East (Alexandria), the emphasis began to shift to the invisible church, the "true" church, the company of the elect. Along with Platonizing influences, rigorism and concern for purity contributed to that tendency.[41] The Western counterpart, guided by Tertullian and later Augustine, stuck more firmly with the importance of the visible, empirical congregation.[42] At the same time, Augustine (building on the work of Cyprian, among others) also brought about a classic understanding of what the invisible church may mean: over against many who had been baptized, only a minority were truly Christians, and those only God knew.[43]

A quite different understanding of the relationship between the visible and the invisible church emerged out of the controversies arising from the existence of competing, simultaneous popes in the medieval church; there the distinction had to do with the difference between the externally divided church and the "true" invisible church in which "the great body of Christians remained the same they always were, united in the same faith in God through

---

39. Volf, *After Our Likeness*, pp. 140-41 (140).

40. A useful survey and discussion is Bloesch, *The Church*, pp. 70-75.

41. For examples in Clement of Alexandria, see J. N. D. Kelly, *Early Christian Doctrines*, pp. 201-3; see also pp. 401-6, "Christ's Mystical Body," which includes discussion of the Cappadocians in the East.

42. For details and sources, see J. N. D. Kelly, *Early Christian Doctrines*, pp. 203-7; pp. 412-17 (Augustine).

43. Augustine, *On Baptism, against the Donatists* 4.3.5; for finding this reference, I am indebted to Haight, *CCH*, 3:186.

Jesus Christ."[44] Yet another way of conceiving the difference between the two aspects of the church arose at the time of the Protestant Reformation: rather than limiting the "true" (invisible) church within their own community, Luther (and Calvin) believed that wherever the gospel is purely preached and the sacraments rightly celebrated, the church is there. "The meaning of the invisible church in this context varied: sometimes it referred to the communion of saints wherever it gathered united in one authentic faith around gospel and sacrament; sometimes it referred to the whole Christian movement united in one faith as distinct from the Roman institutional superstructure; sometimes it referred to Augustine's inner core of those truly regenerated and united with God." The Roman Catholic Church, on the contrary, denied this Protestant distinction between the empirical and the invisible church.[45]

Without unduly simplifying a complex question, it seems that contemporary ecclesiology may be in a place to resolve this debate and suggest a constructive proposal. The first statement is so obvious as to be easily missed: "There has never been such a thing as a completely invisible Church, neither at the time of its founding, nor in the time of the Fathers, nor at the time of the Reformation. . . . A real Church made up of real people cannot possibly be invisible."[46] This claim was not of course contested by the Reformers, although the Roman polemic sometimes seemed to undermine it.[47] The Catholic resistance to the distinction between visible and invisible intuited rightly had to do with the unfounded "spiritualist" claims for the sole invisibility of the true church, which Karl Barth called "ecclesiastical Docetism . . . which paradoxically tries to overlook the visibility of the Church, explaining away its earthly and historical form as something indifferent, or angrily negating it, or treating it only as a necessary evil, in order to magnify an invisible fellowship of the Spirit and of spirits."[48]

That said, it is also true that — in critique of the mainline Catholic position — the denial of the distinction between these two aspects has to be rejected. My position is supported here by a Catholic, namely, Küng: "In as far as the Church is recognizable *fide solum* [by faith alone] it is hidden and invisible";[49] otherwise, why would believing be required! In that sense, the

44. Haight, *CCH*, 3:186-87.

45. Haight, *CCH*, 3:187.

46. Küng, *The Church*, p. 59.

47. For a strong statement in Luther, see WA 39.2:161.8: "Propter confessionem coetus Ecclesiae est visibilis" (not available in *LW*); for Roman Catholic comments in agreement with my interpretations, see Küng, *The Church*, p. 60.

48. Barth, *CD* IV/1, p. 653.

49. Küng, *The Church*, p. 62.

"Church is essentially more than what it appears to be." Thus, rather than the two aspects of the church being alternatives, they are mutually conditioned and integrated: "The real Church is the Church we believe, and yet is visible; it is at once visible and invisible."[50] Schleiermacher got it right (albeit with his usual idiosyncratic way of formulation): "Thus the *invisible* church is the totality of the effects of the Spirit as a connected whole; but these effects, as connected with those lingering influences of the collective life of universal sinfulness which are never absent from any life that has been taken possession of by the divine Spirit, constitute the *visible* church."[51] In other words, there never are two churches, as it were, visible and invisible, but rather the church of Christ is simultaneously both visible and invisible. "The *credo* does not remove the existence of the ecclesia, but gives it its foundation. The ecclesia does not give the lie to the *credo*, but supports it."[52]

Linked with the question of the invisible church is the relation of the communion of saints still on earth to that communion binding it together with the deceased. That question will be investigated briefly next. Furthermore, the question of Christian communion's relation to ancestors — another kind of "invisible" community — will be taken up thereafter.

The Wider Context of the "Communion of Saints" in Relation to the Deceased and Ancestors

Communion of the Faithful between "Below" and "Above"

According to the New Testament testimonies, communion between believers in God stretches beyond the boundary of physical death. The author of Hebrews describes that communion in terms of being "surrounded by so great a cloud of witnesses" (12:1). In early Christian theology and in Eastern Orthodox and Roman Catholic traditions throughout church history, this extension of the communion of saints beyond the faithful living in the same age has also led to certain prayer and ritual practices not embraced by Protestant communities. It has to be minded, though, that the vehement Protestant opposition during the time of the Reformation was not so much against the concept itself

---

50. Küng, *The Church*, p. 62.
51. Schleiermacher, *CF*, §148, p. 677, emphasis in original; I am indebted to Haight, *CCH*, 3:188.
52. Küng, *The Church*, p. 64.

as against its alleged abuses in folk spirituality; yet, subsequently, in Protestant traditions at large, ways of honoring the faithful dead were virtually lost.

So, what is the theological meaning of the communion of saints in this wider context? Following the Catholic feminist E. Johnson, we can say this: "The creedal symbol of the communion of saints expresses the understanding that a community of faithful God-seekers exists around the earth and across time itself, through the life-giving communion of Spirit-Sophia who forever weaves links of kinship throughout the world."[53] As such, at its core it is a "most relational symbol," in keeping with the relationality of the triune God, who stands, so to speak, on both sides of (what appears to humans as) physical death.[54] Communion links our lives to the lives of those who have gone before and sets before us the hopeful future to which we aspire.[55] An important part of the memory is oriented toward those who sacrificed their lives for Christ,[56] for victims of violence, war, and disasters, as well those whose death went unnoticed.[57]

On the way toward a shared ecumenical understanding and embrace of the communion of saints on both sides of death — without a need to come to a unified theology of saints departed — we can benefit from the recent project of the WCC titled "A Cloud of Witnesses: Opportunities for Ecumenical Commemoration." Notwithstanding significant differences in ways of commemorating (or even virtually not commemorating at all), there is a unanimous conviction that "[i]n the communion of saints, all the faithful of every age and of all places are united by the Spirit in one fellowship."[58] Churches also have much to learn from each other in terms of how to best incorporate that aspect of communion of saints in their life and liturgies.[59] In recent years, ecumenical commemorations have been developed, testifying to common faith amid differences of practices and traditions.[60]

An important part of the said WCC project is to work toward a common "ecumenical martyrology,"[61] a continuing pressing need for the global church. Recall the reminder of the late John Paul II in his encyclical *Tertio Millennio*

---

53. E. Johnson, *Friends of God*, p. 163.

54. E. Johnson, *Friends of God*, p. 219; for fascinating reflections in this respect on the triune God "beyond" (Father), "with" (Son), and "within" (Spirit), see pp. 223–29.

55. E. Johnson, *Friends of God*, chap. 12 and passim.

56. E. Johnson, *Friends of God*, chap. 4.

57. E. Johnson, *Friends of God*, pp. 233–36 and passim.

58. WCC, "A Cloud of Witnesses," 4.1; for a fuller account, see *A Cloud of Witnesses*.

59. WCC, "A Cloud of Witnesses," 4.2.

60. WCC, "A Cloud of Witnesses," 5.2.

61. Dotti, "Bose Monastery's Ecumenical Martyrology."

Adveniente (2000): "The Church of the first millennium [which] was born of the blood of the martyrs . . . [a]t the end of the second millennium . . . has once again become a Church of martyrs." The pope appealed for the global church not to forget that the "persecutions of believers — priests, Religious and laity — has caused a great sowing of martyrdom in different parts of the world. The witness to Christ borne even to the shedding of blood has become a common inheritance of Catholics, Orthodox, Anglicans and Protestants" (#37).[62]

A theological question distinct from but not necessarily separate from this has to do with the attitude toward the ancestors, an important feature of the religio-cultural milieu in many parts of the world where the Christian church is growing rapidly — and a common and long-standing phenomenon in the history of religions.[63] By and large, Christian missionaries have rejected or seriously critiqued attempts by their "national" brothers and sisters to incorporate those elements into Christian worship. This has been especially typical of conservative Protestants.[64] An alternative minority view of dismissing their importance has been "nonconcern," in which "the ontological basis for the existence of ancestors' spirits is simply denied" on the basis of science and "civilization."[65]

Should We Have a Communion with the Ancestors? A Theological Reflection

Particularly important is the link between generations in contexts where honoring ancestral relations is an essential part of the culture, particularly, but not limited to, various African and Asian cultural locations.[66] Roman Catholic theology and the Roman Catholic Church have stood at the forefront in seeking ways to critically "baptize" these cultural elements into the Christian liturgy in Asia,[67] Africa,[68] and elsewhere; more recently, Protestant churches have also engaged the topic,[69] including even evangelicals.[70]

62. See further Cunningham, "Saints and Martyrs."

63. See Bae, *Ancestor Worship*, chap. 2.

64. For a representative account from Africa, see Staples, "Christianity and the Cult of the Ancestors," pp. 273–75; for Asia (Korea), see Myung Hyuk Kim, "Ancestor Worship."

65. Staples, "Christianity and the Cult of the Ancestors," pp. 275–77.

66. Hardacre, "Ancestor Worship"; Bae, *Ancestor Worship*.

67. For Korea, see Ki-bok Ch'oe, "Ancestor Worship."

68. For some examples, see Staples, "Christianity and the Cult of the Ancestors," pp. 277–91; for critical assessment of various types of approaches to contextualization, see pp. 291–305.

69. For Japan, see Berentsen, *Grave and Gospel*. For the Cameroon Republic, see Ndingwan, "Ancestor Veneration among the Mankon."

70. Bong Rin Ro's collection of essays *Christian Alternatives to Ancestor Practices* dis-

The Catholic Church's contextualization has been part of the wider effort for a creative recasting of Christology[71] and the Trinity[72] along the ancestral cultural matrix. In a chapter wittily titled "Our Fathers and Mothers Who Art in Heaven," the Nigerian Jesuit priest Agonkhianmeghe E. Orobator reminds us that although belief in ancestors is not a universal phenomenon in the complex cultural texture of Africa, it is significant enough to be theologically engaged.[73] The same can be said of many Asian locations, including Korea with its Confucian ancestral background.[74]

What makes ancestors particularly important for Africans is the blood-relative status, whether based on common parentage or in terms of a more inclusive concept of sharing in ancestry. Importantly, Orobator speaks of "warm communion with the ancestors" as a way to underline the intimacy of the connection.[75] The Roman Catholic Bénézet Bujo of the Democratic Republic of the Congo pays special attention to the Eucharist in the connection between Jesus as the main Ancestor, ancestors, and the church. He names the Eucharist "the proto-ancestral meal" and considers it "the foundation-stone of a Church which is truly African." The Eucharist in this context is not only the celebration of the crucified and risen Christ but also a communion with the ancestors.[76]

A point Christians commonly fail to understand is that the ancestor cult places the afterlife at the forefront, which is a strong commonality with Christian faith. While atheistic and naturalistic worldviews can hardly be found in locations (Africa and Asia) where ancestors play a central role, generally speaking, the interest in ancestors is much more guided by their influence on living peoples' lives before death. Russell Lynn Staples, who has studied ancestors among the Bantu in southern Africa, goes so far as to claim: "Almost everything about the ancestor cult can be measured in terms of its reciprocal benefit to the living."[77]

cusses from a moderate evangelical perspective the topic from Japanese, Chinese (both mainland and Taiwan), Malaysian, Thai, and Korean perspectives.

71. See my *Christ and Reconciliation*, pp. 74-78.

72. See my *The Trinity*, chaps. 21, 24, 25. The first and only attempt to my knowledge to forge a wider connection between the theology of ancestors and ecclesiology, including the Eucharist, comes from the Democratic Republic of the Congo Catholic Bénézet Bujo, *African Theology in Its Social Context*, chaps. 11-12; see also 13, 14.

73. Chapter 9 title in Orobator, *Theology Brewed in an African Pot*.

74. See Young-chan Ro, "Ancestor Worship."

75. Heading in Orobator, *Theology Brewed in an African Pot*, p. 115.

76. Bujo, *African Theology in Its Social Context*, pp. 85-88 (85).

77. Staples, "Christianity and the Cult of the Ancestors," p. 272.

Theologically, the defining question is the avoidance of idol worship, which is strictly prohibited in the Bible and thus applicable to both Jewish and Christian faiths (Exod. 20:3-5). Before delving into that question, a terminological clarification is in order. Because the term "worship" is widely used, it is best to follow the theologically useful distinction between "worship" of God and "veneration" or paying homage to or honoring ancestors.[78] Now, in relation to the biblical warning against idol worship,[79] what constitutes the making of "another god," that is, an idol, of any object? No object in itself is an idol. Humans make idols by their worship. Worship in this sense has to be understood as a qualitatively unique way of honoring and giving allegiance to the object. Should that happen, idolatry follows, which is totally forbidden for all Abrahamic faiths. As long as the religio-cultural understanding does not consider the ancestors in terms of idols — divine-like beings — to be worshiped, but rather as images or symbols that recall the dead ancestors, honoring that memory would constitute something closer to a Christian memorial service than illegitimate idol worship. Particularly in folk religiosity, whether in African or Asian folk religions or Christianity's folk version, this border is easily transgressed, and therefore, should ancestral honoring be practiced, most careful continuous catechesis is required.[80]

The last section of this communion-ecclesiology investigation takes us from the Global South to a very different ecclesiastical context, late modern and postmodern cultures (predominantly) in the Global North. What would a trinitarian communion ecclesiology speak into that context?

Identity, Alienation, and Belonging: Communion Ecclesiology as "Contextual Theology" for the Postmodern World

As already indicated, one of the "turns" of late modernity (or postmodernity) is the turn to relationality and community[81] in reaction to modernity's hyperindividualism and autonomy.[82] Coupled with similar interdisciplinary

78. See also Bae, *Ancestor Worship*, pp. 252-57.

79. For a careful, detailed study, see Bae, *Ancestor Worship*, chap. 6.

80. I was much helped by and follow some basic guidelines in J. Y. Lee, "Ancestor Worship," pp. 83-85; Bae, *Ancestor Worship*, pp. 248-52.

81. I am indebted in this section (including several bibliographic details) to the extended ecclesiological reflection on the effects of postmodernity through the lens of relationality and communion by Grenz, "Ecclesiology."

82. For the well-known analysis of the loss of "social capital," that is, networks and

interest in fields such as (personal, social, and developmental) psychology, sociology, (personalist) philosophy,[83] social ethics, cultural studies, and (social) anthropology,[84] the category of community has come to the center of attention.[85] In keeping with late modernism's dynamic and nondualistic ways of explanation, the turn to community does not mean the neglect of the individual person; importantly, there is talk about the "person-focus" in communitarianism as well.[86] A best seller in academia for some time has been the late sociologist (of religion) Robert N. Bellah and colleagues' *Habits of the Heart: Individualism and Commitment in American Life*, which is a critique of destructive individualism in American society, including religious communities, and a manifesto for a new kind of communitarianism in which persons may flourish.[87]

Consider these postmodern developments in light of the powerful programmatic statement of the late Catholic theologian Karl Rahner. Speaking of Christian religion as "necessarily ecclesial religion," he calls passionately for the indispensability of communion for all of Christian life and vision: "If man is a being of interpersonal communication . . . [in] the whole breadth and depth of his existence, and if salvation touches the whole person and places him as a whole and with all of the dimensions of his existence in relationship to God . . . [with the implication that religion] concerns the whole of human existence in its relationship to the all-encompassing God by whom all things are borne and towards whom all things are directed, then this implies that *the reality of interpersonal relationship belongs to the religion of Christianity*."[88]

With these needs and desiderata in mind, one wonders — with another Catholic theologian, Brian P. Flanagan — about the potential of "communion ecclesiologies as *contextual* theologies."[89] On top of theological reasons, he

---

relationships lost in the hyperindividualized world of ours, see Putnam, *Bowling Alone*; for a constructive proposal to heal the problem, see Putnam and Feldstein, *Better Together*. Important contributions also come from the sociologist Bauman, *The Individualized Society* and *Liquid Modernity*. For an insightful ecclesiological reflection, see Muthiah, *Priesthood of All Believers*, pp. 103–19.

83. Still influential is the work of the late nineteenth-century idealist philosopher Josiah Royce, whose classic is *The World and the Individual* (1899–1901).

84. Mead, *Mind, Self, and Society*.

85. For defining discussions, see further D. L. Phillips, *Looking Backward*; Nisbet and Perrin, *The Social Bond*.

86. Grenz, "Ecclesiology," pp. 253–54.

87. Bellah et al., *Habits of the Heart*.

88. Rahner, *Foundations*, pp. 322–23, emphasis added.

89. Flanagan, "Communion Ecclesiologies as Contextual Theologies."

is convinced that communion ecclesiologies might also be a response to the "contextual" need for belonging in (post)modern society. He also notes the importance of the category of community in cultures of the Global South, particularly in Africa and Latin America. It seems to me Flanagan is spot-on with this intuition. Drawing from the trinitarian communion theology, we may address pertinent questions of late modernity such as difference and identity or belonging and alienation in a theologically solid manner. In my *Spirit and Salvation* (chap. 6), the late-modern questions of difference, identity, belonging, and solidarity were cast in a pneumatological framework, gleaning from the pneumatological resources of the Spirit of *koinonia*. Without repeating that discussion, let us briefly continue the work from the perspective of the trinitarian communion ecclesiology developed here.

Healthy relationships in the current world and church require a balance between embracing differences and finding a common place in order to embrace. Particularly pertinent is this task for the highly complex pluralistic and diverse world of the third millennium, as aptly described by the Korean American Anselm Min: "The globalization of the world brings together different groups into common space and produces a twofold dialectic, the dialectic of *differentiation*, in which we are made increasingly aware of differences in nationality, culture, religion, ethnicity, gender, class, language; and the dialectic of *interdependence*, in which we are compelled to find a way of living together despite our differences. The central challenge of the globalizing world is how to manage and transform this twofold, antithetical dialectic of simultaneous differentiation and interdependence into a solidarity of others, the mutual solidarity of those who are different."[90]

Without unduly attempting to oversimplify a highly complicated challenge, constructive theology can confidently tap into the heart of trinitarian theology in which unity and difference, identity and mutual belonging between the Father, Son, and Spirit serve as the template for community formation. With justification, the Orthodox Zizioulas summarizes thus: "There is no other model for the proper relation between communion and otherness either for the Church or for the human being than the trinitarian God. If the Church wants to be faithful to her true self, she must try to mirror the communion and otherness that exists in the Triune God . . . [in whom] otherness is constitutive of unity. . . . God's oneness or unity [is] expressed through the unbreakable koinonia (community) that exists between the three Persons,

90. Min, *Solidarity of Others*, p. 1, emphasis in original. See also Caron, "Towards an Inclusive Communion Ecclesiology."

which means that otherness is not a threat to unity, but the *sine qua non* of unity."[91]

This insight was well captured in the recent report of the WCC's International Network Forum on Multicultural Ministry among migrants: "In God's grace, the love which enables the unity of the different persons of the Trinity also enables us to live in the differences of our cultural and individual particularity."[92] This is not to exaggerate difference in an absolutist sense — a liability among some leading postmodern thinkers such as the late French thinker Jacques Derrida.[93] What *koinonia* facilitates is not "the absolutization of difference but its sublation into the solidarity of the different precisely for the sake of justice and liberation."[94] The Trinity testifies to the irreducible difference as well as the complete sharing, perichoretic mutuality of the three. "The Holy Spirit brings about this communion and solidarity by unifying the divided, reconciling the alienated, and incorporating them into the body of the Son."[95]

The next task in this constructive ecclesiology will be to delve into many details of the claim for the missionary nature of the Christian communion, tentatively established so far. That discussion will then lead into various aspects of the missional existence in sacramental life, liturgy, and the manifold ministries of the church.

91. Zizioulas, "Communion and Otherness," n.p.; I found this citation in Summers, *Friendship*, pp. 159-60.

92. "Multicultural Ministry," pp. 12-13, cited in Stromberg, "Responding to the Challenge of Migration," p. 46.

93. Derrida's motto ("the wholly other is every other") celebrates alterity — indeed, infinite alterity — to the point that not only every other human person but also God remains the other. For a highly insightful theological critique of Derrida's position, see Min, *Solidarity of Others*, chap. 2.

94. Min, *Solidarity of Others*, p. 47; see chap. 4, "From Difference to the Solidarity of Others."

95. Min, *Solidarity of Others*, p. 83; see also chap. 6, "Solidarity of Others in the Movement of the Holy Spirit."

16. The Church as Mission

Mission in the New Context(s)

The Many Meanings — and Challenges — of "Mission(s)"

The meaning of few other terms in the theological thesaurus has undergone and still embraces so many meanings as "mission." Whereas until the Reformation it denoted simply the "sending" (*missio*) of the Son (and in the Christian West, also of the Spirit) by the Father in the trinitarian logic, thereafter its meaning became related to the work for the conversion by Catholics (spearheaded by the Jesuits) of non-Catholics (mainly Protestants rather than non-Christians), until in modern times it adopted the meaning virtually synonymous to "foreign" mission. Only in recent decades has its basic meaning in theology and missiology become comprehensive and inclusive, referring to the basic nature of the church as a "sent" community, as Vatican II's missionary document *Ad Gentes* famously put it: "The pilgrim Church is missionary by her very nature."[1] The missionary nature of the church is a leading idea for this project, to be further developed in what follows.

In keeping with the pluriform meanings of the term, what one can call paradigms of mission, that is, ways of understanding its meaning, focus, and goal, have also understandably dramatically changed over church history.[2]

---

1. *AG*, #2.
2. Two standard works are Bosch, *Transforming Mission* (1991), and Bevans and Schroeder, *Constants in Context* (2004).

Noteworthy is that Catholics and Protestants have done mission differently. In the Protestant spread of the church, mission societies and entrepreneurial individuals were the key. In Catholic missions, monastic and other religious orders took the forefront. Furthermore, while the Catholic Church virtually withstood the influence of the Enlightenment until Vatican II, Protestant churches flung their doors wide open to modernity.[3] While much smaller in scale, the missionary enterprise of the Eastern Orthodox Church, particularly in the eighteenth century, should not be dismissed. Orthodox priests and monks traveled to Russia, Siberia, Alaska, and other places to establish significant Orthodox constituencies.[4]

A serious contemporary challenge to Christian mission is the growing questioning of mission's legitimacy in the first place. Beginning from the "secular" 1960s, calls for a moratorium or even total end have been issued, not only by outsiders of the church but also by many of her own missiologists and leaders. Just recall titles such as *Missionary, Go Home! A Reappraisal of the Christian World Mission* (1964)[5] and many others.[6] Although acknowledging the liabilities of Christian mission such as proselytism and the colonial legacy, this project seeks to promote a healthy and balanced concept of mission as an indispensable part of the nature of the church.

To clarify the location and context of the church's mission in the contemporary secular and religiously pluralistic world of ours, before deepening the foundational argument about the missionary nature of the church we will take a brief look at the implications of the move away from the Christendom status of the church and of the renouncing of the alliance with the colonialist enterprise.

The Mission of the Church in the Post-Christendom World

What was the Christianity of Christendom like? What were its problems?[7] M. W. Goheen puts it succinctly: "The church moved from a marginal position

3. See Bevans and Schroeder, *Constants in Context*, chap. 7. For the wide influence among Protestantism of "voluntarism" out of which missionary organizations and initiatives emerged, see Bosch, *Transforming Mission*, pp. 327–34.

4. Bevans and Schroeder, *Constants in Context*, pp. 227–28.

5. Scherer, *Missionary, Go Home!*

6. Bosch, *Transforming Mission*, pp. 2–4. A highly informative recent discussion and assessment is Reese, "John Gatu and the Moratorium on Missionaries."

7. For a standard source, see Herrin, *The Formation of Christendom*; see also S. Murray, *Post-Christendom*, chap. 4.

to a dominant institution in society; from being socially, politically, and intellectually inferior to being in a position of power and superiority; from being economically weak and poor to being in a position of immense wealth; from being an oppressed minority to being the oppressive majority; from being a religio illicita to becoming the only religion in the civic community; from being resident aliens in a pagan environment to being an established church in a professedly Christian state."[8]

In sum: Christendom's great liability at its core has to do with the self-understanding of the church herself.[9] Rather than a missionary community dispersed among the nations in the service of the coming kingdom of God, the church's status was identified with a stable earthly institution. Rather than a witness to the reconciling work of the triune God for the salvation of the world, ministry was at times confused with delivering privileged services to insiders.[10] Although it is not of course literally true that "[t]he Christendom model of church may be characterized as *church without mission*"[11] — just recall the numerous missionaries and mission agencies particularly of the various Catholic orders throughout the medieval and later church — it is regrettable that the idea of the church as mission was virtually lost with the establishment of the church as the custodian of the religion of the empire.[12] At the same time, Christendom's — and later, colonialism's — spirit tried "to impose the Gospel on others without the vulnerability of witness."[13] This means that "[p]rior to Constantine, it took courage to be a Christian. After Constantine, it took courage to be a pagan. Before Constantine, no one doubted that Christians were different. After Constantine, it became increasingly unclear what difference being a Christian made."[14]

---

8. Goheen, *As the Father Has Sent Me*, pp. 2–3, cited in Nikojlasen, *Distinctive Identity of the Church*, p. 6.

9. For worldly standards as the criteria, see Hauerwas, *With the Grain of the Universe*, p. 221. Also worth recalling is the sharp criticism of Christendom's truncated understanding of the church and its membership in Kierkegaard, *Attack upon "Christendom."*

10. See Guder, "Missional Hermeneutics."

11. Shenk, *Write the Vision*, p. 35, emphasis in original.

12. So also Guder, "Nicene Marks in a Post-Christendom Church," p. 5; for the lack of missionary orientation in Reformation Christendom, see Newbigin, *Household of God*, pp. 1–2. See also the essay by the late untiring critic of Christendom, Yoder, "Meaning of the Constantinian Shift."

13. Hauerwas, *The State of the University*, p. 103; I am indebted to Tolonen, *Witness Is Presence*, p. 90.

14. Hauerwas and Wells, "How the Church Managed Before," p. 42, cited in Tolonen, *Witness Is Presence*, p. 90.

Having acknowledged those serious and fatal theological-ecclesiological liabilities of the Christendom era, the constructive theologian should also exercise critical judgment regarding the all-too-common and reckless "Christendom bashing." It simply is not the case that by the fifth century the church had lost her ecclesiality and mission. Had that really happened, it would have meant that "the Holy Spirit left the earth around the 4th century, when Constantine came to power, only to reappear in the modern group or movement with which we may now be affiliated." As D. Guder, himself an incisive critic of Constantinianism, correctly observes: "If God is faithful to his purpose and calling, then God has been present and at work through this very ambiguous history that we call Christendom, just as God was present and at work through one thousand years of kings in Israel, most of whom the ancient Chronicler found wanting."[15] This is not an attempt to whitewash Christendom's facade, but rather to help us more soberly think of the ecclesiological implications of the final transition from the remains of Christendom to the third millennium's pluralistic and secular environment.

To the task of reappraisal of the church's self-understanding and identity also belongs the continuing reflection on the relationship between church and power structures. That brings to surface the sad history of modern colonialism, which is in many ways related to Christendom mentality.

Christian Mission Meets Colonialism(s) — Past and Present

Similarly to the term "post-Christendom," the nomenclature "postcolonial" (when it means moving away from the colonial era) has to be handled with care. Even if old forms of colonialism of the nineteenth century may have been left behind in a significant way,[16] new and subtle forms are still with us.[17] These include the power of entertainment, culture, language, education, and so forth.[18]

At the heart of colonialism is the will to subjugate the other by the dominant group or culture. Just think of the massive occupation of land and resources in the majority world by the Western powers beginning from the end of the eighteenth century. Colonialism includes but is not limited to racial

15. Guder, "Nicene Marks in a Post-Christendom Church," p. 4.

16. See also Bosch, *Transforming Mission*, pp. 302–13 (for modern colonialism) and pp. 226–30 (for medieval "colonialism" in terms of crusades and similar uses of coercion).

17. D. Gregory, *The Colonial Present*; Harvey, *The New Imperialism*.

18. See Ritzer, *McDonaldization of Society*.

discrimination, economic poverty, and political marginalization. The more subtle manifestations of colonialism encompass ideological, cultural, epistemological, and other means of violence and oppression; even the terminology used, such as "expansion" or "inferior" or "authority," betrays this defeat of the other.[19] In its extreme form, namely, slavery, as happened with blacks and the first nations of America,[20] it means making human beings a commodity.[21] Lest it be mistakenly assumed that this only happened from the West to the "rest" (as dominant as that was), the same hegemonic abuse of power was also in play, for example, in the subjugation of Korea by Japan in the early twentieth century[22] and in the expansion of China and the Ottoman Empire over some of their neighboring territories.

Although it is crystal clear that the Christian church at large was involved with the colonial expansion of modern times and bears guilt for it, that should not lead to the kind of uncritical and unnuanced debunking of the whole project of modern missions prevalent among both secular and Christian analysts. Without in any way trying to whitewash deplorable associations between mission and colonial powers, the newest missions history has been able to provide a much fairer and more accurate picture.[23] Similarly, the accusation of missionaries serving as agents of "cultural imperialism" has been rightly critiqued.[24] Indeed, it has been discovered that some missionaries in Africa and elsewhere were often used against their own will by local leaders as tools to further their local political or economic interests. Furthermore, on the positive side, it is now uncontested that missionaries have advanced local empowerment, cultural development, ethnic affirmation, and other forms of inclusivity and liberation.[25] A powerful example of that is what Lamin Sanneh names "mission as translation": the translation of the Bible helped the vernacular, local languages become important factors in culture and played a crucial role not only in the spread of Christian mission

---

19. Said, *Culture and Imperialism*, pp. 6-8.

20. For the cruel treatment of the first nations, see D. Brown, *Bury My Heart at Wounded Knee*.

21. Cone, *The Spirituals and the Blues*, p. 22.

22. For commentary, see Seo, *Critique of Western Theological Anthropology*, pp. 72-73.

23. Stanley, "Conversion to Christianity."

24. Porter, "Cultural Imperialism," pp. 367-91. For example, the British missions historian Brian Stanley has demonstrated a lack of evidence for the claim that the British churches' support for mission and the peak of British imperialism were correlated (Stanley, *Bible and the Flag*).

25. See further WCC, "Treasure in Earthen Vessels," #41; see also Johann-Albrecht, "Ecclesiology as Doing Theology."

but also in the liberation of the indigenous people.[26] That same missionary translation also empowered indigenous resistance to colonialism. While the colonial system represented a worldwide economic and military order, mission represented vindication for the vernacular.[27] On the basis of these and related results of current research, Sanneh discredits the view that mission was little more than "imperialism at prayer." On the contrary, he wonders whether colonialism could have been an *obstacle* rather than a facilitator of the spread of Christianity.[28]

We have located the mission of the church in the complex context of our world, and now a deeper probing into the implications of the thesis that the church exists as mission is in order. Thereafter, a detailed discussion of the many facets and dimensions of the church's mission will occupy us for the rest of the chapter.

The Missional Nature of the Church

"Missionary by Nature"

As emphasized in this project, there is a consensus across the ecumenical spectrum concerning the essentially missionary nature of the church: "The pilgrim church is missionary by its very nature."[29] To this missional existence is related also the pregnant statement in *Lumen Gentium* that sets the framework for the mission of the church in the widest possible terms as it explains "its own inner nature and universal mission" in terms of being "in Christ . . . as a sign and instrument both of a very closely knit union with God and of the unity of the whole human race."[30] Nothing less than the gathering of the whole humanity as one community before God in the new Jerusalem is the Christian vision of the church and future.

Importantly, several streams of missiological thinking coalesced in this new acknowledgment of the church's missionary nature. Highly influential was the untiring call from the late United Reformed bishop Lesslie Newbigin, a long-term missionary to India, to consider the West (Europe and USA) as

26. Sanneh, *Translating the Message*, pp. 31, 82.

27. Sanneh, *Translating the Message*, p. 123. For another important work, see A. Walls, *Missionary Movement*.

28. Sanneh, *Whose Religion Is Christianity?* p. 18.

29. *AG*, #2.

30. *LG*, #1; for comments, see Bosch, *Transforming Mission*, pp. 374-76.

a "mission field" and that all churches everywhere should adopt a missional approach and existence.[31] One of the offshoots from that call was the establishment of an ecumenical network and research initiative by the name Gospel and Culture;[32] soon it was followed by similar networks in the United States[33] and beyond. In the American context, the 1998 book titled *Missional Church: A Vision for the Sending of the Church in North America*,[34] a collection of essays by representatives of the Gospel and Our Culture Network, made an effort to bring World Council of Churches' discussions of *missio Dei* ("the mission of God") and Newbigin's missionary insights to bear on North America. The book urges the church to move away from a Christendom model that focuses on maintenance to a missional way of life based on outreach and expansion.[35]

That understanding is a needed corrective to what the American Presbyterian theologian Darrell Guder calls "mission-less theology and confession."[36] Embracing the missional understanding of the church helps conceive of ecclesiality and the marks of the church in the same dynamic manner, he further argues (in keeping with our discussion above in chap. 14): "By 'apostolicity,' we do not merely mean 'the church descended from the apostles,' as important as that is. We mean 'apostolicity' in the active sense of the New Testament verb, meaning 'to be sent out,' and the noun 'apostle' as the 'sent-out' one. The community formed by the Holy Spirit through the initial apostolic witness is called to be sent." The second mark, catholicity, would remind the church of "the message . . . to be made known to the ends of the earth, . . . [to be] translatable into the life and experience of every ethnicity, as concretely demonstrated at the first Pentecost."[37]

A key theological insight that lies behind the affirmation of the missionary nature of the church came to be known already decades ago as the *missio Dei*.[38] Let us take a closer look at this important concept.

---

31. The best resource to get into basic ideas is Newbigin, *Gospel in a Pluralist Society*.

32. Introduction, activities, and resources can be found at the Gospel and Our Culture Web site, http://www.gospel-culture.org.uk/index.htm.

33. See, e.g., the Gospel and Our Culture Network at http://www.gocn.org/.

34. Guder, ed., *Missional Church*.

35. See Frost and Hirsch, *The Shaping of Things to Come*; Van Gelder and Zscheile, *Missional Church in Perspective*.

36. Guder, "Nicene Marks in a Post-Christendom Church," p. 7.

37. Guder, "Nicene Marks in a Post-Christendom Church," pp. 9–10.

38. The following paragraph is gleaned from Bosch, *Transforming Mission*, pp. 389–93; Bevans and Schroeder, *Constants in Context*, pp. 286–95.

Missio Dei

All theologians and traditions are currently in agreement about the phrase's basic meaning, which simply is that mission is God's mission — and therefore, the church, as repeatedly explained above, is drawn graciously into the movement of the coming kingdom. In other words, the church does not *have* or possess mission because it is not hers; God is the source and "owner" of mission.[39] This foundational conviction rules out notions of mission as cultural, ethnic, "civilizing," or any similar concepts.[40]

Soon after the emergence and wide embrace of *missio Dei*, the church's existence and mission in the world became a matter of debate.[41] The debate relates to the place and role of the "agenda" provided by the world in relation to God's mission. This has to do with whether the mission of the church continues flowing, as in tradition, from the Trinity's mission and the preaching of the gospel, or whether it should begin from the realities, problems, and programs of the hurting world, aiming at "humanization" rather than traditionally conceived "salvation." Whereas Barth, evangelicals, and most Catholics and Orthodox, in keeping with the church's tradition, looked at *missio Dei* primarily through the lens of the Trinity's mission and gospel preaching through the church, on the other end of the spectrum there was the desire not only to make mission much larger than the church but also to effectively push away traditional ways of doing mission through proclamation and service with a view toward conversion to Christianity. The 1966 WCC document "The Missionary Structure of the Congregation" advocated quite strongly this nontraditional orientation with its lead idea that "the world provides the agenda."[42] Some leading Protestant missiologists similarly advocated this "secular" approach to living out *missio Dei* in which all talk about the church's mission in any traditional terms came to be virtually banned.[43]

Eventually, a loosely defined and still-under-continuous-debate middle stance has emerged in Catholic, Protestant, and WCC circles in which a holistic task of mission was set as the aim, firmly anchored in the Trinity and with a proper place reserved for gospel proclamation and sacramental-liturgical life. That vision is masterfully explicated in *Gaudium et Spes* (*The Pastoral*

---

39. See also Moltmann, *The Church in the Power of the Spirit*, p. 64.

40. For a comprehensive account, see Flett, *The Witness of God*.

41. Still a standard basic discussion is Rosin, *Missio Dei*; for more recent discussion, see Flett, *The Witness of God*.

42. In Kinnamon and Cope, eds., *The Ecumenical Movement*, pp. 347–50.

43. For details and sources, see Bosch, *Transforming Mission*, pp. 381–89.

Constitution on the Church in the Modern World).[44] While liberationists have untiringly — and rightly — reminded the church of the perils of focusing merely on the "salvation of souls," that orientation toward a holistic mission has not been seen as a pretext for ignoring proclamation and personal spiritual life.[45] The often-cited multidimensional vision of Christian salvation by the Peruvian Catholic Gustavo Gutiérrez illustrates well that mainstream orientation, which is also supported in this project: Christian salvation has three interrelated facets:

1. Personal transformation and freedom from sin
2. Liberation from social and political oppression
3. Liberation from marginalization (which may take several forms, such as unjust treatment of women and minorities)[46]

Defining the church as mission, with a holistic and comprehensive vision of salvation, is to say that everything the church does — proclamation and service, pursuit of unity, as well as dialogue with other faiths — derives from mission; the spiritual power and energy come from continuous liturgical and sacramental life (chap. 17).[47] The rest of this chapter will outline in some detail the many dimensions of the holistic mission as the master plan for the ministry of the church (chap. 18).

Multidimensional Mission in the Service of the Coming of God's Kingdom

The Interrelated "Layers" of the Mission of the Church

As has been repeatedly mentioned, the church's existence as a missional communion derives from and is integrally linked with the life of the triune God, the sending God, in whose sending the church may graciously participate for the sake of the coming of God's kingdom. Even though there is no identity between the coming rule of the triune God and what the church

---

44. For a recent discussion, see Bergant, "Does the Church Have a Mission?"

45. For debates and issues, see Bosch, *Transforming Mission*, pp. 400–408.

46. Gutiérrez, *A Theology of Liberation*, pp. 43–44, 83–105, passim.

47. On the other side, the British missionary bishop Stephen Neill (*Creative Tension*, p. 81) reminds us of the obvious liability: "When everything is mission, then nothing" is; so also Bosch, *Transforming Mission*, pp. 511–12.

is doing in the world, neither can they be separated. The kind of missional existence and life appropriate for the missional community consists of a number of dimensions and facets. For the sake of managing the complex and wide discussion, let us sketch the mission of the church under six inter-related layers or spheres:

- mission as evangelism and common witness
- mission as healing and restoration
- mission as social justice and equality
- mission as integrity and flourishing of nature
- mission as reconciliation and peace building
- mission as dialogue and interfaith engagement

In what follows, we will discuss the theological basis and significance of each of these six layers, gleaning also (but not unduly) repeating themes already investigated above in part 1 (related to social justice and equality as well as integrity and flourishing of nature). Similarly, the discussion will also connect with and take advantage of relevant investigations carried out in other volumes of the project (particularly with regard to restoration and healing as well as reconciliation and peace in volume 4, *Spirit and Salvation*). The last aspect, interfaith engagement, will be discussed in much detail in the last chapter of this book.

Mission as Evangelism and Common Witness

Toward Comprehensive Evangelism. Although a widely attested biblical term (*euangelion* and related words), "evangelism" (or "evangelization") in normal church usage was not rediscovered until the nineteenth century.[48] An important recent call for evangelization came from Pope Paul VI's *Evangelii Nuntiandi*. A few years later, the WCC's *Mission and Evangelism — an Ecumenical Affirmation* (1982) attempted a programmatic statement about evangelism that included some theologically and pastorally significant statements, which by and large can be seen as a matter of ecumenical consensus currently.[49] Acknowledging that "[i]t is at the heart of Christian mission to

---

48. For the many meanings of the term(s), see Bosch, *Transforming Mission*, pp. 409-11.

49. A highly informative and ecumenically widely representative (including evangelical and Pentecostal voices) discussion is Bevans and Schroeder, *Constants in Context*, pp. 323-40.

foster the multiplication of local congregations in every human community [as the] planting of the seed of the Gospel will bring forward a people gathered around the Word and sacraments and called to announce God's revealed purpose" (#25),[50] the statement indicated that the following guidelines should be minded:

- Evangelism, as part of the wider mission, should be done in "Christ's Way" (sec. 4).
- Each person has the right to hear the call to repentance and conversion.[51] Related to that is "a call to repentance and obedience . . . addressed to nations, groups, and families" (#12).[52]
- The call of the gospel relates to all realms of life, in keeping with Jesus' all-embracing proclamation of the kingdom of God (sec. 2). Part of that holistic aim is that the gospel is "good news to the poor" (sec. 5).
- A most sincere concern for the unity of the church should be minded at all times when evangelizing, with the attempt to engage common witness as well (sec. 3).
- The work of evangelism belongs to all churches in all locations in the spirit of "mission in and to six continents" (sec. 6). This also includes "witness among people of living faiths" (sec. 7).[53]

To these principles and recommendations can be added Bosch's suggestions about the meaning of evangelism, including clarifying and correcting its misuses.[54] An essential aspect of evangelism "involves witnessing to what God has done, is doing, and will do" in keeping with Jesus' announcement of the advent of the kingdom as an occasion to repent (Mark 1:15);[55] hence, it calls for a definite response from the hearer, including repentance and conversion — topics curiously avoided, at times even resisted, in many current ecumenical discussions around evangelism. "To dispense with the centrality of repentance and faith is to divest the gospel of its significance." That said, all notions of proselytism should of course be avoided, and the evangelist should never assume the posture of a "judge," but should rather be

---

50. So also *EPCW*, ##11, 12, 13.
51. Similarly also WCC, *Mission and Unity*.
52. See Bosch, *Transforming Mission*, pp. 416–17.
53. In Kinnamon and Cope, eds., *The Ecumenical Movement*, pp. 372–83.
54. Bosch, *Transforming Mission*, pp. 409–20.
55. Bosch, *Transforming Mission*, p. 412.

a witness.[56] Although the first goal of evangelism is not church extension, the growth of the membership of the evangelizing church cannot be dismissed either (as was also affirmed above in *Mission and Evangelism*, #25). Finally, Bosch reminds us, credible evangelism is contingent on credible Christian and ecclesial life.[57]

A number of pertinent, interrelated issues routinely arise when the church considers the work of evangelism: particularly proselytism, common witness, and social concern. In other words: What are the role and justification of conversion and repentance — or does evangelism with that goal represent a perverted power play? What, if anything, is the difference between evangelistic persuasion with the aim of initiating a response and proselytism? Under what conditions could Christians from various churches collaborate in giving a common witness? And what about the role and meaning of social justice, inclusivity, and equality in evangelization? Since the first topic — conversion — is discussed widely and in much detail in the context of the *ordo salutis* in volume 4, *Spirit and Salvation* (chap. 10), that conversation will not be repeated here. Instead, the twin themes of proselytism and common witness will now be taken up.

Proselytism and Common Witness. Ironically, there are two opposing trends in modern mission ethos. On the one hand, there is a widespread resurgence of evangelism, not only in younger churches but also in older churches, especially in the Catholic Church.[58] There is also a new awareness of the possibility of giving a joint testimony to Christ, usually called "common witness." On the other hand, the issue of proselytism has emerged as one of the most hotly debated topics. It is, understandably, a concern of older, more established historic churches. The evangelizing activities of many free churches and their numerous outreach organizations have been effective to the point of raising concern among older churches about the danger of losing a substantial number of their members.[59] Indeed, until recently, younger churches — those regarded by others as "proselytizers" — have not been invited to participate in discussions on the subject; regretfully, it is also not readily apparent that they are particularly concerned to address the subject themselves.[60]

---

56. Bosch, *Transforming Mission*, p. 413.

57. Bosch, *Transforming Mission*, p. 420.

58. See, e.g., Martin and Williamson, eds., *John Paul II and the New Evangelization*.

59. Particularly painful has been the question after the dismantling of the Soviet Union across Eastern Europe. See further Szabolcs, "Proselytism and Religious Freedom."

60. See the balanced and wise words in Best and Gassmann, eds., *On the Way to Fuller Koinonia*, p. 257.

Concerning proselytism, the most important first task is to clarify its meaning — and also to dispel some notions routinely attached to it.[61] Particularly the Roman Catholic Church has actively discussed this delicate topic in mutual dialogues with the Orthodox Church[62] and younger Christian families such as evangelicals,[63] Baptists,[64] and Pentecostals.[65] In 1995 the joint document between the WCC and the Vatican, "The Challenge of Proselytism and the Calling to Common Witness," took careful stock of the earlier joint work, the 1982 "Common Witness" and the 1970 "Common Witness and Proselytism." As a result, in 1997 a highly significant statement by Catholics and the WCC titled "Towards Common Witness: A Call to Adopt Responsible Relationships in Mission and to Renounce Proselytism" (TCW) was prepared, with even a wider participation on that work invited. Building on these formative contributions and being sensitive to the complexities of the discussion in the context of a globalized[66] and multireligious environment,[67] as well as amid "competitive missionary activities" in various parts of the world often carried out by independent groups from outside the area, we are in a good place to work toward a shared understanding.

Although "proselyte" originally meant a convert to Judaism and later, by derivation, a convert to any other religion, "'[p]roselytism' is now used to mean the encouragement of Christians who belong to a church to change their denominational allegiance, through ways and means that 'contradict the spirit of Christian love, violate the freedom of the human person and diminish trust in the Christian witness of the church,'" and it is "the corruption of witness."[68] Some of the features of proselytism in contrast to authentic evangelism include the following:

61. *Christian Witness, Proselytism and Religious Liberty* was drafted and recommended to member churches in the 1961 WCC meeting. Earlier, the Toronto declaration *The Church, the Churches, and the World Council of Churches* (1950) was one of the first ecumenical attempts to define proselytism among the WCC member churches and in relation to the Roman Catholic Church. In the 1960s, the Roman Catholic Church drafted the Vatican II document *Dignitatis Humanae*, which addresses, among other topics, religious freedom and proselytism. In 1970, the WCC produced another joint document, *Common Witness and Proselytism*.

62. "Uniatism, Method of Union," pp. 95-99.

63. "Evangelical and Roman Catholic Dialogue on Mission, 1977-1984."

64. "Summons to Witness to Christ in Today's World."

65. *EPCW*; for an analysis, see my *Ad ultimum terrae*.

66. Freston, "Globalization, Southern Christianity, and Proselytism."

67. Hackett, ed., *Proselytization Revisited*.

68. TCW, II (citations from earlier mentioned documents).

- unfair criticism or caricaturing of the doctrines, beliefs, and practices of another church without attempting to understand or enter into dialogue on those issues
- presenting one's church or confession as "the *true* church" and its teachings as "the *right* faith" and the only way to salvation
- taking advantage of and using unfaithfully the problems that may arise in another church for winning new members for one's own church
- offering humanitarian aid or educational opportunities as an inducement to join another church
- using political, economic, cultural, and ethnic pressure or historical arguments to win others to one's own church
- using physical violence or moral and psychological pressure to induce people to change their church affiliation
- exploiting people's loneliness, illness, distress, or even disillusionment with their own church in order to "convert" them[69]

Now, while all churches should condemn and reject these kinds of proselytizing activities and attitudes,[70] it is equally important not to confuse authentic evangelism and common witness with proselytism nor with the change of one's church per se.[71] Indeed, failure to distinguish (legitimate) evangelism from (illegitimate) proselytism may have fatal consequences, as has indeed happened in some locations in which "antiproselytism" laws by the government have effectively prohibited any evangelistic work and proclamation of the gospel.[72]

Most helpfully, TCW clearly distinguishes between rightful and wrongful activities: authentic Christian witness, including common witness, "is constructive: it enriches, challenges, strengthens and builds up solid Christian relationships and fellowship" instead of the proselytizing "counterwitness," which "brings about tensions, scandal and division, and is thus a destabilizing factor for the witness of the church of Christ in the world." Furthermore, as long as the person decides to move from one Christian community to another out of one's own volition and freedom, charges of proselytism should not be leveled.[73] A related ecumenical consensus is that "[a]ll Christians have the

69. TCW, II; similarly, e.g., *EPCW*, #93.
70. See the important Pentecostal contribution by Robeck, "Mission and the Issue of Proselytism."
71. Thiessen, *The Ethics of Evangelism.*
72. See *EPCW*, #97.
73. TCW, II.

right to bear witness to the Gospel before all people, including other Christians. Such witness may legitimately involve the persuasive proclamation of the Gospel in such a way as to bring people to faith in Jesus Christ or to commit themselves more deeply to Him within the context of their own church," and as long as that happens in love, it is not proselytism — and it may lead to a transfer into another church, although that should not be the suggestion or encouragement of the evangelizer.[74] Instead of competition, dialogue and mutual conversations are needed.[75] It is particularly important to continue working toward a shared conception of the church, as difficult as that may be.[76] To that challenge belongs a careful assessment of the other tradition's perceptions of the nature of the church.[77]

An important goal for all Christian churches is to work toward new initiatives in engaging common witness, which "means standing together and sharing together in witness to our common faith. Common witness can be experienced through joint participation in worship, in prayer, in the performance of good works in Jesus' name and especially in evangelization."[78] This is not a call "to compromise. Common witness is not a call to indifference or to uniformity," but rather a rich and diverse testimony to God's grace holding on to the common treasure embraced by both or all parties as Christian churches. It requires much prayer together, and more often than not, forgiveness, both asking for it and receiving it. Such a witness done in the spirit of humility is credible.[79]

Mission as Healing and Restoration

Unlike proclamation and evangelism, healing — whether physical or mental — has not been the hallmark of Christian mission for a long time, nor does healing occupy any place in standard theological discussions.[80] That is astonishing, because Jesus was not merely a gospel preacher but was first and foremost an

---

74. *EPCW*, ##94-95 (94).
75. TCW, III.A.2; see also *EPCW*, #79. A related theme has to do with differences in understanding conversion; see Kankanamalage, "Conversion and Proselytism."
76. See *EPCW*, #69.
77. See *EPCW*, #91.
78. *EPCW*, #118.
79. *EPCW*, ##122-23.
80. A delightful exception is Moltmann, *Spirit of Life*, chap. 9. For a full-scale systematic discussion, see chap. 12 in my *Spirit and Salvation*. For a distinctively Pentecostal discussion, see Yong, *The Spirit Poured Out on All Flesh*, chap. 2.

itinerant healer and exorcist in whose proclamation of the kingdom of God healings and deliverances — alongside the pronouncement of sins — were enacted as "signs" of the approaching righteous rule of God.[81] That work was continued by the early church. In the book of Acts, healings (and exorcisms) were a regular activity alongside prayer, liturgy, sacraments, and missionary outreach (5:16; 8:7; 13:6–12; 16:19; among others).[82] Importantly, the same focus continues in current church life in the Global South, the epicenter of world Christianity.[83]

While marginal, healing was of course never totally ignored in the history of the church's missional existence. Indeed, there is a great diversity of ways it has been done:

- In the "confrontational" model, the emphasis is on liberty and defeat of powers of evil, as represented by Irenaeus, Tertullian, Origen, and, in later history, figures such as the Reformed theologian J. C. Blumhardt of the nineteenth century.
- The "intercessory" model calls upon the saints to intervene on behalf of the sick and suffering; this model is widespread throughout Orthodox and Catholic traditions.
- Closely related is the "reliquarial" model, in which relics are believed to have curative powers; this practice goes back to healing handkerchiefs and aprons touched by the apostles. The famous miracles at St. Medard attributed to the remains of the eighteenth-century Frenchman François de Paris represent the Western version.
- The "incubational" model is related to the long history of establishing sanitariums, hospitals, and other "healing rooms" for patients for a longer period of restoration.[84]

Focusing on the contemporary scene, the Czech Reformed theologian Pavel Hejzler has discerned "two paradigms for divine healing." The "healing evangelists" expect an instantaneous recovery to normally take place, and often the charismatically endowed healer is the instrument. The "pastoral healers" equally believe in a rapid restoration of health, but they are open to both gradual and instantaneous work by God; the healer's role is less pronounced

---

81. Porterfield, *Healing in the History of Christianity*, p. 21.
82. Porterfield, *Healing in the History of Christianity*, p. 3.
83. See further Asamoah-Gyadu, "Mission to 'Set the Captives Free.'"
84. Kydd, *Healing through the Centuries*. With all the emphasis on various types of divine healing, beginning from early Christianity medical sciences and hospitals have been dear to Christian tradition. Porterfield, *Healing in the History of Christianity*, pp. 51–53.

and may also include a group of Christians over a period of time.[85] A predominantly sacrament-oriented approach to healing is placed in the forefront by some Christian traditions, particularly Eastern Orthodoxy, Roman Catholicism, and Anglicanism;[86] in others, the charismatic gifts and hope for instantaneous healing are more typical, as in Pentecostal/charismatic movements.[87] With the global expansion of Christianity to the Global South beginning from the early twentieth century, healing practices, approaches, and theological interpretations are further diversifying.[88] The continuing interest in healing and restoration in the work of the WCC and other ecumenical actors, engaging also the professional medical communities, is promising for the proliferation of the vision to all Christian churches.[89]

In engaging healing and restoration, the church needs careful discernment. Wisely the recent WCC document advises that while as "an integral part of their witness to the gospel, Christians exercise ministries of healing ... [t]hey are called to exercise discernment as they carry out these ministries, fully respecting human dignity and ensuring that the vulnerability of people and their need for healing are not exploited."[90] A proper theological understanding is needed to ensure that. First, although faith and healing are correlated in the biblical testimonies, there is no fixed formula like a "name it and claim it" technique in which the believing person is supposed to merely "claim" healing by virtue of true faith. In contrast, in the New Testament cases of healings, at times the faith (of the healed) is mentioned, at other times it is friends' faith that counts, and every now and then faith is not mentioned at all. Second, although "atonement," the reconciliation achieved by the triune God through the incarnation, cross, resurrection, and ascension of Christ, lays the foundation for healing and restoration, there is no kind of automatic "healing-in-atonement" formula that assumes every ailment is cured for every believing person. Rather, the processes of decay and death are at work with every generation of men and women, whether Christians or not, until the work of reconciliation finds fulfillment in the eschaton.

85. Hejzlar, *Two Paradigms for Divine Healing*.

86. For the importance of sacraments in healing, see the Orthodox George Mathew Nalunnakkal, "Come Holy Spirit, Heal and Reconcile," p. 18.

87. Alexander, *Pentecostal Healing*.

88. See further Porterfield, *Healing in the History of Christianity*, chap. 5; Healey and Sybertz, *Towards an African Narrative Theology*, chap. 2, "Jesus as Healer"; chap. 7, "Healing in Church"; Jenkins, *New Faces of Christianity*, chap. 5 (including also exorcisms).

89. *Healing and Wholeness*; "The Healing Mission of the Church," pp. 127-62.

90. CWMRW, "Principles," #5.

In correction to both of these misconceptions, the healings (and exorcisms) in the New Testament serve as "signs" of the coming kingdom of God in the eschaton, pointing to the era when death and decay will be removed and all sicknesses and bondages defeated. An essential part of the "sign" function, healings and deliverances in this age are temporary, as every cured person will eventually die of a sickness; even Lazarus, a resuscitated person, eventually died. Thus, getting sick again after the cure or dying after the resuscitation does not imply the failure of divine work but rather the necessity of keeping the eschatological perspective at all times. Only with the eschatological consummation will signs give way to fullness and completion.

Notwithstanding these correctives, churches that fail to include healing in their mission (either because of negligence or for fear of these and other mistakes) need to be reminded of a foundational failure: the omission of this integral aspect of the church's mandate as missional communion. Not to engage healing certainly eliminates mistakes related to healing beliefs and practices. But it also reduces the church's mission in an unacceptable manner and may prevent many from receiving a cure.

Finally, as much as the church should work for healing and restoration, Christians should also be prepared to undergo sufferings, failures, disappointments, and other setbacks. Often good and faithful Christians do not get healed. At other times, people we would not assume to be cured may receive cures. And, as said, eventually decay, sickness, and death will catch every one of us. It is always good to remember that no more than preaching for conversion follows human expectations, let alone dictations, does prayer for healing take place according to human stipulations.[91]

Mission as Social Justice and Equality

The church's sociopolitical mandate was carefully considered in part 1 (chap. 7) in the context of eschatology, in response to the common charge that the expectation of the coming kingdom causes Christians to be oblivious to the responsibility for alleviating injustice and oppression in this world. Hence, a brief reaffirmation for the sake of mission suffices here.[92] The recent WCC statement on mission and evangelism, *Together towards Life* (2012), reminds us

91. For a detailed discussion, see my *Spirit and Salvation*, chap. 12.
92. For highly useful reflections, see Chung, *Christian Mission and a Diakonia of Reconciliation,* and his "Engaging God's Mission and Diakonia."

that a particularly important duty for the church is attending to the "margins" of the globalized and hurting world. There are two important tasks of discernment here. First is this: "Mission from the margins calls for an understanding of the complexities of power dynamics, global systems and structures, and local contextual realities." And the second is "to recognize God's alignment with those consistently pushed to the margins," a duty the church has too often failed to do. Only then is the church in a place to "reimagine mission as a vocation from God's Spirit who works for a world where the fullness of life is available for all."[93] But that is not all that the "turn" to the margins means; in complete reversal of the values of the competitive world spirit, mission is also to be entrusted to Christians at the margins: "It seeks to be an alternative missional movement against the perception that mission can only be done by the powerful to the powerless, by the rich to the poor, or by the privileged to the marginalized. . . . People on the margins have agency, and can often see what, from the centre, is out of view."[94]

Often, particularly in the past, traditional churches have stood at the opposite extreme from younger churches, including a majority of evangelicals, when it comes to social concern.[95] It used to be that the latter communities were routinely blamed for focusing primarily on the "salvation of souls" at the cost of communal, sociopolitical, and creational concerns. Without unduly whitewashing the still continuing differences of emphasis, undoubtedly a rapprochement is in view, as a growing number of theologians among the evangelicals and younger churches hold a comprehensive, holistic vision of the church's mission and ministry. The late Canadian Baptist Stanley J. Grenz was one of the pioneers when he claimed that in order to "set forth a proper ecclesiology, we must view the church from the perspective of God's wider purposes" to discern and highlight "the wider purposes of God in his activity in history from creation to consummation." That is because "[i]n history God is at work in bringing to pass his intention for all creation."[96] Similar theological convictions emerged among the Pentecostals in their long-standing dialogue with the Catholic Church on social justice: "Pentecostals have a great concern for the eternal salvation of the soul, but also for the present welfare of the body as is readily apparent in the high priority they give to the doctrine of divine healing. In addition, they have

93. *TTL*, #37.
94. *TTL*, #38.
95. For a background and key issues, see Bosch, *Transforming Mission*, pp. 432–47; Bevans and Schroeder, *Constants in Context*, pp. 305–17.
96. Grenz, *Theology for the Community of God*, p. 487.

had a real concern for the social as well as for the spiritual welfare of their members, especially in the third world."[97]

Mission as Integrity and Flourishing of Nature

The theological basis of healing, flourishing, and integrity of creation is first developed in this project in the context of the doctrine of creation (*Creation and Humanity*, chaps. 3 and 8) and thereafter deepened and widened in the discussion of pneumatology, particularly concerning the Spirit's role in creation (*Spirit and Salvation*, chap. 3). Furthermore, the topic of the flourishing of and care for nature and the environment was discussed in detail above in part 1 (chap. 7) in response to the common suspicion that eschatological hope makes the church ignore this-worldly affairs. In order not to repeat those extensive discussions, a brief statement suffices here.

Ecologically sensitive Christians and communities keep in a dynamic tension an attitude of reverent admiration for the beauty of creation in its endless diversity and creativity and a deepening concern for nature's vulnerability and suffering at the hands of the current global economic-industrial rape. Honoring and caring for the environment does not take divinizing it, as is a common tendency in some eco-feminist and other green theologies and neopagan movements. I also argue that it does not take making nature a sacrament, as has been suggested every now and then by theologians from various persuasions. Although nature may display some "sacramental" features — similarly to so many others things in the world, in terms of reflecting the divine presence in the mundane — calling nature a sacrament is a category mistake, and I do not see its cash value. Nature as creation, God's artifact, has an inherent value, after all. Christian churches should seek ways of collaborating with secular communities and with other religious communities in caring for nature. Those relationships may also be an opportunity for mutual learning. Particularly beneficial in this respect is the give-and-take with Asiatic traditions, which, contrary to popular opinion, face serious "theological" challenges with regard to motivation and energy for preserving nature in this world.[98]

As to the ways Christian communities may incorporate green aspects into their regular life and ministry, we have far fewer historical precedents and

97. *EPCW*, #40.
98. For interfaith engagement with regard to environmental care, see *Creation and Humanity*, chap. 8.

templates than we do with regard to prayer, liturgy, preaching, and sacraments. In diverse global contexts and locations, those practices undoubtedly differ widely. It is one thing to conserve the environment in the affluent Global North and quite another in the poorest parts of the world.[99]

Mission as Reconciliation and Peace Building

Following the intuitions of current ecumenical missiology, we adopt reconciliation in this project as the widest and most inclusive concept denoting the various dimensions and aspects of salvation, God's gift of shalom. Reconciliation is the work of the triune God bringing fulfillment to God's eternal purposes of creation and salvation through Jesus Christ (Col. 1:19–20; 2:9).[100] In the discussion on Christology (*Christ and Reconciliation*, chap. 14), reconciliation as the church's mission was first developed as a theological theme, encompassing "spiritual" and sociopolitical aspects at the personal, communal, and "global" levels. The discussion of the doctrine of the Trinity, under the rubric of "divine hospitality" (*Trinity and Revelation*, chap. 13), further widened the multidimensional nature of salvation, encompassing inclusivity, equality, and peace.

At its core, reconciliation is about restoring broken relationships and effecting a new covenant-based relationship of mutual love and commitment.[101] Originally a secular concept, it was used particularly in international diplomacy in antiquity and subsequently adopted by Christians as a theological theme grounded in Christ.[102] To the vision of reconciliation also belongs the church's missional mandate in working toward peace and easing conflicts. That missional task requires the church to take another critical look at the history of violence deeply embedded in her history,[103] as illustrated by the Crusades and similar anti-evangelical enterprises. Promisingly, there have also been those such as the Quakers[104] and the Menno-

---

99. Inspiration and ideas can be gleaned from Ayre, "Where on Earth Is the Church?"

100. Langmead, "Transformed Relationships," p. 6; see WCC, "Mission as Ministry of Reconciliation," pp. 90–126; Schreiter, "Reconciliation and Healing."

101. See further Gunton, *Actuality of Atonement*, p. 143.

102. See Aletti, "God Made Christ to Be Sin," p. 104.

103. Langmead, "Transformed Relationships," p. 12.

104. See "Quaker United Nations Office — Specific Peacebuilding Activities," Geneva Peacebuilding Platform, http://www.gpplatform.ch/content/quaker-united -nations-office-specific-peacebuilding-activities.

nites[105] (Anabaptists) who have adopted peace building and the renouncing of violence as a key value in mission and ecclesial existence.

The mandate to further peace and conciliation is a task uniting all religions and women and men of good will. Recall the untiring clarion call of the Catholic Hans Küng:

> No peace among the nations without peace among the religions.
> No peace among the religions without dialogue between the religions.
> No dialogue between the religions without investigation of the foundations of the religions.[106]

Another way of expressing the widest possible vision of salvation — what David Bosch also calls "comprehensive salvation"[107] — is to speak of creation as the first salvific act, political liberation as "self-creation of man," and "salvation . . . [as] re-creation and complete fulfillment."[108] This does not mean, the liberationist Gutiérrez reminds us, making the church serve a short-term worldly cause of good will, but rather, it means linking God's work in history with the redemption and renewal brought about by the coming of the new creation.[109] Indeed, in its widest and most comprehensive sense, *missio Dei* reaches to the whole of creation, as *Together towards Life*, from the WCC's Commission on World Mission and Evangelism, put it: "God did not send the Son for the salvation of humanity alone or give us a partial salvation. Rather the gospel is the good news for every part of creation and every aspect of our life and society. It is therefore vital to recognize God's mission in a cosmic sense and to affirm all life, the whole *oikoumene*, as being interconnected in God's web of life."[110]

Having now established the nature of the church as mission and having outlined in some detail the many dimensions of the missional task in the world, based on the trinitarian sending of the community by Father, Son, and

---

105. See, e.g., the US Mennonites' Peace and Justice Support Network Web site: http://www.pjsn.org/Pages/default.aspx.

106. This can be found, e.g., in Küng, *Islam*, p. xxiii.

107. Bosch, *Transforming Mission*, pp. 399-400; for debates about "salvation" in mission, see also pp. 393-99.

108. Gutiérrez, *A Theology of Liberation*, pp. 153-60.

109. Gutiérrez, *A Theology of Liberation*, pp. 160-68; quotes pp. 158, 165.

110. *TTL*, #4. For further details about the missionary vision of the flourishing of nature, see ##19-23 of *TTL*. See also the comprehensive vision of salvation in Yong, *The Spirit Poured Out on All Flesh*, pp. 91-98.

Spirit for the shalom of the world, we will engage three important tasks. First, we will consider theologically the life of the missional communion around the preaching of the gospel and sacraments in liturgy and worship (chap. 17). No missional existence is possible without the constant nourishment, corrective, and empowerment of the sacramental-liturgical life of the community. Thereafter, a theology of ministry and church structures appropriate for being constantly involved in God's mission in the world will be attempted (chap. 18). The whole people of God serve as the minister(s) of the church, even if some are appointed into more visible roles. Finally, before placing again the Christian community in relation to other faith traditions and the secular society of the Global North, the all-important task of working toward the unity of the church will be scrutinized (chap. 19).

17. Missional Existence as the Sacramental and Liturgical Celebration

Liturgy and Worship at the Heart of the Church's Missional Existence

The Spiritual Source of Mission

Recall that the "rule" of ecclesiality recommended in this project is the gathered communion around the gospel and sacraments. That communion, fashioned after and derived from the trinitarian communion, is missionary by nature, as it has been graciously drawn into the sending process of Father, Son, and Spirit for the salvation of the world. That communion is anticipatory, awaiting the eschatological consummation of the triune God's eternal purposes for the world, the cosmos. Now, moving from the previous chapter, "The Church as Mission," to the current one with a focus on liturgy, worship, and sacraments is to leave behind neither mission nor missional existence. On the contrary, the missional communion gathered around the gospel and sacraments constantly feeds, renews, and reinvigorates her spiritual life and missional fervency in regular prayer, reading of Scripture, and sacramental and liturgical participation.

The recent WCC missionary document *Together towards Life* highlights spirituality as the energy of mission: "Authentic Christian witness is not only in *what* we do in mission but *how* we live out our mission. The church in mission can only be sustained by spiritualities deeply rooted in the Trinity's communion of love."[1] Recall also the ancient missional rule of the Eastern

---

1. *TTL*, #29. For the whole section titled "Transformative Spirituality," see *TTL*, ##29–35.

Church, "mission as liturgy after liturgy." Although all aspects of worship, as long as their source and goal are the triune God, can be said to be missional, that is particularly true of the Eucharist, in which "all the facets of the *Missio Dei* find expression: God's continuing love for the world that He created; His self-identification with the fallen world by the incarnation; His redemption of the world through Christ's death and resurrection; His gift of new life in the Holy Spirit; His promise of the new creation at the end of time."[2]

Nowhere else is this deep and wide connection between liturgy, sacramental life, and missionary orientation as evident as in the life of the first church in the Acts of the Apostles (2:42–47):

> And they devoted themselves to the apostles' teaching and fellowship, to the breaking of bread and the prayers. And fear came upon every soul; and many wonders and signs were done through the apostles. And all who believed were together and had all things in common; and they sold their possessions and goods and distributed them to all, as any had need. And day by day, attending the temple together and breaking bread in their homes, they partook of food with glad and generous hearts, praising God and having favor with all the people. And the Lord added to their number day by day those who were being saved.

The liturgical-sacramental life, filled with prayer and Bible study, helped launch this world-transforming movement to the ends of the earth.

Liturgy and Worship Fashioned after the Trinity

The Eastern Orthodox theologian G. Florovsky reminds us that the "Church is first of all a worshipping community. Worship comes first, doctrine and discipline second."[3] In keeping with the triune nature of the church as the image of the triune God, it is appropriate to conceive of the church's worship and liturgy in trinitarian terms as well. Just think of the great liturgical hymn in Revelation 5 in which "the Lamb receives the very same kind of worship as the Almighty YHWH does in chapter 4."[4] The first chapter of the book of

---

2. Maynard, "Worship Is Mission Seeing the Eucharist," p. 83.

3. Florovsky, "The Elements of Liturgy," p. 24; as cited by Ware, *The Orthodox Church* (1963), p. 266.

4. Harper and Metzger, *Exploring Ecclesiology*, pp. 86–87; see also J. Torrance, *Worship, Community, and the Triune God*, chap. 1. For profound theological-liturgical reflec-

Ephesians is an important template of worship to the triune God: the Father is blessed through the blessings stemming from the sending of the Son, whose work of reconciliation and redemption is communicated to us via the sealing and work of the Holy Spirit.[5] Rightly we speak of Christians worshiping the Trinity and with the Trinity.[6]

Stemming from the church's anticipatory nature, Christian worship is deeply eschatological, anticipatory at its core: "If worship is the activity of the church in which it proclaims and celebrates God's person and redemptive work, then worship must be eschatological. For, in worship, especially in the liturgy of the Eucharist, God comes to us in the person of the resurrected Christ, through the Spirit, engaging us as the One on the last days." Recall that the eschatological direction is present in the texts of institution both in the Gospels (Matt. 26:29) and in Paul (1 Cor. 11:26).[7]

Having now briefly clarified the theological grounding and dimensions of worship and liturgy for the existence of the missional communion, we organize the rest of the chapter into two unequally sized portions. The first concentrates on theological aspects of worship, liturgy, and proclamation; the second, on sacraments. The immediately following section seeks to establish the nature of worship liturgy as an embodied corporate action. Thereafter, liturgy's public, "political" role will be taken up. The final section of the first major part delves into the theology of proclamation.

One of the important topics about which I am passionate — the use of inclusive language in liturgy and everywhere in church life — will not be taken up in this chapter because I have dealt with that in much detail in *Trinity and Revelation* (chap. 14). Let it suffice to summarize that discussion's main conclusion: My strong recommendation is that, on the one hand, the traditional naming of God as Father, Son, and Spirit be retained because there are no credible theological reasons not to. On the other hand, to insure inclusivity from women's perspective, complementary ways of naming God need to be creatively employed with a view to contextual appropriateness as well.

---

tions, including a detailed study of Rev. 4 and 5, see Uzukwu, *Worship as Body Language*, pp. 69-78.

5. See further Harper and Metzger, *Exploring Ecclesiology*, p. 87.

6. Parry, in *Worshiping the Trinity*, importantly titles chap. 5 "Worshiping with the Trinity" and chap. 6 "Worshiping the Trinity."

7. Harper and Metzger, *Exploring Ecclesiology*, pp. 88-91 (88).

"Worship as Body Language"

My (un)educated guess is that should a poll be taken among ordinary church-goers, irrespective of church or denomination, responses to the following two questions could be easily predicted. To the question "Should we consider liturgy 'spiritual' or 'bodily' in nature?" the responses would be on the spiritual side. To the question "Is liturgy a 'religious' or a 'political' event?" the answers most probably would fall on the side of "religious." The current project argues that these responses are not so much wrong as they are only partially true — and as any half-truth, they are as misleading as they are enlightening. Indeed, liturgy and worship is a spiritual act, but it is done very much "as body language," as the American-based Nigerian Catholic Elochukwu W. Uzukwu's book title has it.[8] And as religious an act as liturgy is, it also has political connotations and expresses the core values of the missional community. Let us take up these two issues in succession.

After the long dominance of body-soul dualism in Western culture, embodiment has had a hard time in Christian theology. Well known are the antibodily dualisms that culminated in the modern Cartesian juxtaposition of the "mind" (soul) and body. Although body-soul dualism still reigns among all religions (less so in Judaism, though) and is prevalent among the Christian faithful as well, particularly in more traditional and conservative traditions, during the last century or so significant steps have been taken toward a more balanced and dynamic view. In Christian theology, it has been a joint effort of biblical students, psychologists and neuroscientists, Christian philosophers, and systematicians, among others. Notwithstanding continuing debates and differences, it is safe to say that in the mainstream theological understanding of the image of God and personhood, embodiment plays an essential role in the dynamic and complex account of the human person.[9]

Importantly, a first attempt has been made by two American neuropsy-chologists to see the life and ministry of the church through the lens of the category of embodiment, in other words, to see the implications for our understanding of the church through the lens of "the physical nature of Christian life."[10] Commensurately, some theologians from the Global South, particularly from African contexts, are reminding us of the significant place given to the body in the traditional cultures in the contexts of nonanalytic, holistic views

8. Uzukwu, *Worship as Body Language*.
9. For a detailed argumentation and sources, see chap. 12 in my *Creation and Humanity*.
10. W. Brown and Strawn, *The Physical Nature of Christian Life*.

of humanity.[11] Indeed, while spiritual, worship is an act that "involves motion . . . [in which] humans move toward God in response to God's movement toward humans"; it also engages the whole human being for the simple reason that "[t]he total human person (embodied spirit) makes this gesture toward God and toward other humans."[12] In this light, it is ironic that in the church, shaped by the Greco-Roman classical cultures, bodily gestures, movement, and enthusiasm have been eschewed in favor of "the ideal of godlike immobility . . . [as that] was understood as the gesture of 'spirit' as opposed to the motions of 'body.'" Even worse, not only Stoicism and Platonism, but also the doctrine of original sin as developed in the Christian West beginning from the end of the fourth century, further consolidated the repulsive attitude toward everything bodily, which was often mistaken for the biblical concept of "flesh."[13]

If not totally thwarted, bodily movements in liturgy came to be strictly regulated in order to eliminate the individuality of gestures and ensure that body motions remain at "levels considered acceptable — the reasonable proportion." As a result, "[g]estures classified as excessive (gesticulation) were denounced." There is no need to mention that by the Middle Ages widely attested biblical forms of worship such as dance were totally rejected.[14] So persistent has this "ascetic embodiment" style been that even with the spread of the church (back) to Africa and other locations in the Global South, resistance in traditional churches, whether Catholic or Anglican or Protestant, toward body language in the liturgy has sought to defeat the cultures' expressive nature. A routine object of ridicule in the African Instituted Churches, in African American churches, and among Pentecostal/charismatic communities[15] everywhere has been their enthusiastic worship style with movements, shouts, and emotional expressions. Interestingly enough, those kinds of enthusiastic expressions are well regarded in other societal gatherings, from sports to politics to arts.[16]

One benefit of highlighting the embodied nature of liturgical life is to save it from a narrow "spiritual" reductionism and thus make space for a holistic participation of men and women. This is in no way to undermine the

---

11. In addition to Uzukwu, *Worship as Body Language*, see also Bujo, *African Theology*, pp. 18–21.

12. Uzukwu, *Worship as Body Language*, p. ix.

13. Uzukwu, *Worship as Body Language*, pp. 5–6.

14. Uzukwu, *Worship as Body Language*, pp. 7–8 (8).

15. For the Pentecostal type of worship and its theological and spiritual significance, see further Hollenweger, "From Azusa Street to Toronto Phenomenon."

16. Uzukwu, *Worship as Body Language*, pp. 10–14; see also pp. 26–34.

importance of the liturgy also as ritual, an ordered and planned event. It is rather to help — for the sake of the global church with many colors, sounds, movements, and tastes — open up diverse and dynamic ways of expressing the "heavenly liturgy." This is not to undermine in any way the power of the ritual correctly understood. Any regular and repeated human action organizes itself into ritual. A wonderful example of the coexistence of "enthusiasm" and ritual ordering comes to the fore in the following observation of Pentecostal worship: "[Pentecostal] churches are designed to provide a context for a mystical *encounter*, an experience with the divine. This encounter is mediated by the sense of the immediate divine presence. The primary rites of worship and altar/response are particularly structured to sensitize the congregants to the presence of the divine and to stimulate conscious experience of God. . . . The gestures, ritual actions, and symbols all function within this context to speak of the manifest presence."[17]

This observation is in keeping with the American anthropologist Monica Wilson's insight, based on cross-cultural fieldwork, that human persons "express in ritual what moves them most."[18] Coupled with that — and important for ecclesiological considerations — is that a meaningful religious ritual has community-forming and re-creating power.[19] The American ethicist S. Hauerwas is spot-on with these reflections: "The sacraments enact the story of Jesus and, thus, form a community in his image. We could not be the church without them. For the story of Jesus is not simply one that is told: it must be enacted. The sacraments are means crucial to shaping and preparing us to tell and hear that story. Thus baptism is that rite of initiation necessary for us to become part of Jesus' death and resurrection. Through baptism we do not simply learn the story, but we become part of that story."[20]

A robust linking of embodiment, dynamic enthusiasm, and ritual has the promise of yielding an experience of the "heavenly liturgy" that is grounded in earthly realities of Christian life and is spiritually enriching. This dynamic is vividly expressed in the vision for the Eucharist of two American-based

17. Albrecht, "Pentecostal Spirituality," p. 21, emphasis in original; more extensively, Albrecht, *Rites in the Spirit*.

18. Wilson, "Nyakyusa Ritual and Symbolism," p. 241, cited in V. Turner, *Ritual Process*, p. 6; I am indebted to Uzukwu, *Worship as Body Language*, p. 41. Another way of saying this is to talk about "participatory knowledge" in religious ritual — or "indwelling" the ritual; see Wood, "The Liturgy"; Polanyi, *Personal Knowledge*, p. 198, respectively. I am indebted to Vanhoozer, *Drama of Doctrine*, pp. 79-83.

19. Uzukwu, *Worship as Body Language*, pp. 42-44 particularly.

20. Hauerwas, *The Peacable Kingdom*, pp. 107-8.

feminist theologians, Andrea Bieler and Luise Schottroff — which, for me, could apply to everything in worship:

> We seek to develop a theology of the Eucharist that holds together the materiality of bodies and ordinary things as they are lifted up and shared in liturgical practice *and* the eschatological horizon of the holy meal in which we celebrate the Eucharist as resurrection meal and await with eager longing God's coming. The material work is lifted up in God's promise to be present in the very ordinary things of bread and wine and in the bodies of ordinary people. . . . The created world in its ordinary physicality is cherished in the breaking and sharing of bread, in bodies eating and drinking, chewing and swallowing.[21]

The last comment helps link liturgy deeply and solidly with this-worldly, earthly experiences. That is the reminder of the public role of liturgies.

"Cultural Liturgies"

In his provocative and innovative "Cultural Liturgies" project, the American Reformed philosopher J. K. A. Smith advances the claim that whatever else the human being is, she or he is *homo liturgicus*, a worshiping animal. Or to put it in another way, following Augustine: "We are what we love." We are not only rational, thinking beings, although we are also that; for Smith, we are basically imaginative and desiring (loving) creatures who express their desires and love in "liturgies."[22] We are not even primarily believing beings, as opposed to rationalist beings, although faith obviously is not to be dismissed for a Christian person. Mere focus on beliefs may yield a picture of the human person in quite abstract and disembodied terms.

In sum: instead of imagining the person primarily "as thinker" or "as believer," Smith is after "persons as embodied agents of desire and love."[23] "Rather than being pushed by beliefs, we are pulled by a *telos* that we desire."[24] By looking at our cultural liturgies, whether in the shopping mall or at school or on the football field or as a citizen of the nation, others can determine what

21. Bieler and Schottroff, *The Eucharist*, p. 3, emphasis in original.
22. J. K. A. Smith, *Desiring the Kingdom*.
23. J. K. A. Smith, *Desiring the Kingdom*, pp. 46-47.
24. J. K. A. Smith, *Desiring the Kingdom*, p. 54.

we vision as the good life. Indeed, all the time, we are bombarded by visions of the good life, which replace love of God, the highest value, with lesser loves. This leads to worship of idols rather than God and his kingdom. Rather than worshiping idols, Christians are meant to practice true worship that is guided by the love of God, "creational desire for God." True worship also corrects misguided cultural liturgical directions as it "functions as a counter-formation to the mis-formation of secular liturgies into which we are 'thrown' from an early age."[25] To follow "ultimate liturgies," as Smith names them, a continuous and critical cultural exegesis is a given task of theology and the church. That helps unmask the failures of secular liturgies.[26]

In this light the Catholic W. T. Cavanaugh's provocative claim becomes understandable: in his study of the relationship between torture and the Eucharist, he says that torture can be regarded not merely or primarily as an "attack on individual bodies" but first and foremost as an attack on "social bodies."[27] It represents the power of the state and demands its worship over other institutions.[28] In that sense, it represents another form of "secular" liturgy, to use Smith's terminology. It is, as the original sense of *leitourgia* (from Greek roots for "people" and "work") means, "an action by which a group of people become something corporately which they had not been as a mere collection of individuals."[29] Torture can be taken as a "a kind of perverted liturgy, a ritual which organizes bodies in the society in to a collective performance, not of true community, but of an atomized aggregate of mutually suspicious individuals."[30]

Before considering the details of the church's sacramental life, we take a focused look at the theological significance and conditions of proclamation as an integral part of worship experience.

Proclamation as a "Dramatic Event"

"Why is it . . . that Christian doctrine so often appears strikingly dull," K. Vanhoozer wonders in the beginning of his programmatic work *The Drama of*

---

25. J. K. A. Smith, *Desiring the Kingdom*, p. 88.

26. J. K. A. Smith, *Desiring the Kingdom*, chap. 3; see also his *Imagining the Kingdom*.

27. Cavanaugh, *Torture and Eucharist*, p. 12.

28. Cavanaugh, *Torture and Eucharist*, p. 30; see also pp. 23–34 particularly.

29. Schmemann, *For the Life of the World*, p. 25, cited in Cavanaugh, *Torture and Eucharist*, p. 12.

30. Cavanaugh, *Torture and Eucharist*, p. 12.

Doctrine, if "[a]t the heart of Christianity lies a series of vividly striking events that together make up the gospel of Jesus Christ," an "intrinsically dramatic" event?[31] Following in the honored footsteps of the late Catholic thinker Hans Urs von Balthasar[32] and joining some other contemporary theologians,[33] Vanhoozer is seeking to (re)discover the "dramatic" nature of Scripture and — they are related — of preaching and doctrine. This idea goes deeply into the biblical idea of "promise" that Luther called *Tat-Wort* (rather than *Deute-Wort*), referring to something "done" rather than only "meaning."[34] Another way of talking about the "making" or "doing" aspect of the Word is to employ the well-known "speech-act" terminology of the linguistic philosopher J. L. Austin. In distinction from the "locutionary," the simple enunciation of a sentence, and the "illocutionary," expressing the speaker's intention, the "perlocutionary" refers to what was achieved by the speaker. In other words, speech-act theory describes, to follow the title of one of his most well-known books, *How to Do Things with Words*.

In light of this integral connection between words and deeds — or action and speech — they should not be differentiated in a way that the modernist epistemology and intuitions particularly tend to do. Rather, to follow Vanhoozer, "theo-drama" is both "divine speech and action." From the beginning of the Bible, God "does" many things with speech. "And God said, 'Let there be light'; and there was light" (Gen. 1:3). The word of God is "living and active" (Heb. 4:12). Hence, theology needs to rediscover the nature of the word of God "as something God both says and does."[35] Or, as Vanhoozer wittily puts it: "The gospel is something *said* about something *done*. . . . *Speaking is one of God's mighty acts*."[36] Preaching that misses this is liable to the same fallacy that merely propositional theology is: "*dedramatizing* Scripture."[37] Instead, theology's task, Vanhoozer argues — and, I add, proclamation's task, similarly — "is to enable hearers and doers of the gospel to respond and to correspond to the prior Word and Act of God, and thus to be drawn into the action."[38]

---

31. Vanhoozer, *Drama of Doctrine*, p. xi; see also his recent less scholarly, more pastorally oriented *Faith Speaking Understanding*. See also Horton, *A Better Way*, chap. 2.

32. Balthasar, *Theo-Drama*.

33. Horton, *A Better Way*; see also Dyrness, *Poetic Theology*.

34. See further Moltmann, *Experiences in Theology*, p. 94.

35. Vanhoozer, *Drama of Doctrine*, pp. 44-45, emphasis removed.

36. Vanhoozer, *Drama of Doctrine*, p. 46, emphasis in original.

37. Vanhoozer, *Drama of Doctrine*, p. 87, emphasis in original. For useful reflections on preaching, see also Bloesch, *The Church*, chap. 9.

38. Vanhoozer, *Drama of Doctrine*, p. 44, emphasis removed.

Along with liturgical life and worship, the missional existence of the Christian communion is sustained and cultivated by sacramental participation. That will be the focus of the latter part of this lengthy chapter.

The Sacramental Life of the Missional Communion in a Theological Outlook

Sacraments as "Signs": A Theological Clarification

Although "sacramental" or sacrament-type phenomena and gestures — call them "doors to the sacred" — can be found in the wider history of religions[39] (as chap. 12 indicated), doctrinally/theologically defined ecclesial acts, sacraments, at the center of ecclesial existence, are a uniquely Christian thing.[40] While in Orthodox theology, beginning from the seventeenth century, the number of sacraments (usually named "mysteries") is usually seven, throughout history there has been no defined number.[41] The Roman Catholic Church acknowledges seven sacraments: baptism, confirmation, Eucharist, penance, anointing the sick, ordination, and matrimony.[42] For Protestants, the number is two (although the Lutheran confessions also know "confession" as the third).

With the exception of the (original) Quakers, even free churches, following Protestantism, practice sacraments — some Pentecostals and members of other churches also practice foot washing.[43] Often, instead of "sacrament," these communities speak of "ordinances."[44] Reacting vehemently against gross misuses of sacraments in the Catholic Church, Radical Reformers and their Baptist

---

39. For some general observations, see Martos, *Doors to the Sacred*, chap. 1.

40. Making the church itself "sacrament" — or, to be more precise, "like a sacrament," as *Lumen Gentium* (#1) does—further complicates and confuses the matter. Nor is it advisable to follow Barth (*CD* IV/2, p. 55) and relate it to Christ (even if the NT speaks of "mystery" in relation to Christ).

41. See further Meyendorff, *Byzantine Theology*, pp. 191–92; Ware, *The Orthodox Church*, chap. 14 (particularly p. 275 for the number of sacraments).

42. *LG*, #11. The number seven established itself definitively at the Council of Lyons in 1274 and since has been the norm for Rome.

43. Most ironically — and this is yet another indication of the complexity and fluidity of the term "sacrament" — foot washing certainly seems to meet the basic requirements of sacraments, namely, divine command (John 13:14–15), and so "institution" by Christ, even his own example, and "material" element. Yet the church at large never adopted foot washing as a sacrament; see Hunter, "Ordinances," pp. 948–49.

44. For "ordinances," see Grenz, *Theology for the Community of God*, pp. 512–18.

forebears went to the other extreme, away from the *ex opere operato* type of (semi)magical effectuality, as they saw it, to emphasize obedience: baptism and the Lord's Supper were to be celebrated because they had been "ordained" by the Lord in the Bible. Rather than divine acts bringing about what they symbolized, ordinances were primarily a means of human response to God's command.[45]

Although sacraments carry a fixed meaning (notwithstanding their number), in principle we could list a number of other acts that, if not sacraments, certainly carry a strong sacramental ring. As Pannenberg puts it, "wherever we can discern in the church's life a relation to the person and work of Jesus in such a way that Jesus himself may be said to be present in it . . . [then we] might think of the works of mercy mentioned in Matthew 25:35-37, or of evangelization and healings along the lines of what in Mark 11:4-5 are called signs of the presence of salvation characterizing the ministry of Jesus." Furthermore, proclamation of the Word also certainly "belongs to the dimension of the 'sacramental' presence of Christ's salvation."[46]

Notwithstanding differences with regard to the meaning and scope of the sacraments, all (Western) Christian traditions build on Augustine's teaching on the sacraments as signs.[47] With reference to Christ's sacrifice, Augustine speaks of "the visible sacrament or sacred sign of an invisible sacrifice."[48] Augustine bases this on a thematic distinction between the "sign" and the thing signified.[49] While not equated, they are closely and intimately related. Signs point to the thing, and sacramental sign and the thing are always combined with the Word. Speaking of baptism, the bishop puts it succinctly: "Take away the word, and the water is neither more nor less than water. The word is added to the element, and there results the Sacrament, as if itself also a kind of visible word."[50]

From early on, to the sacrament was attached divine command; that theme was picked up strongly by the Lutheran Reformation: "This means that those who by the proclamation of the gospel have not reached the point of accepting baptism have not yet fully understood the meaning of the message

45. Grenz, *Theology for the Community of God*, pp. 514-15.

46. Pannenberg, *ST* 3:355-56; for a fascinating theological reflection on "marriage as reminder of a broader sacramental understanding," see pp. 358-64.

47. For background, see J. N. D. Kelly, *Early Christian Doctrines*, pp. 422-24.

48. Augustine, *City of God* 10.5.

49. Augustine, *On the Christian Doctrine* 1 and 2; for the nature and variety of signs, see 2.1. Still a masterful theological commentary on signs in the context of sacraments is Ebeling, *Word of God and Tradition*, pp. 227-29 and passim.

50. Augustine, *Lectures or Tractates on the Gospel according to St. John* 80.3; see also Pannenberg, *ST* 3:349.

concerning Christ as promise and appropriated it in faith."[51] With the tight linking of the sacrament with the Word of promise, we can say that "Christ's own presence at the Supper fulfills the promise contained in the words of institution."[52] With the Word and promise in mind — but only so doing — it is justified to maintain what Saint Thomas defined as the core of sacraments, namely, that "they effect what they signify."[53] So much can be — and should be — said even if the Protestant tradition at large eschews the (semi-)automatic and technical *ex opere operato*.

To arrive at a proper theological understanding of the sacrament, the intimate link between sign and thing should be kept in mind and, at the same time, the distinction affirmed — but in a way that allows for the thing signified to already be present in a true anticipatory manner in the sign. Put it this way: "[i]n biblical thought . . . a sign actually *was*, in some measure, the thing which it signified."[54] We hasten to add that in all effects of the sacraments, it is Christ's presence that makes it what it is.[55] The reference to anticipation reminds us of the ultimate eschatological context of the sacraments, in keeping with the church's nature as anticipation. Ultimately the sacrament as sign points to final fulfillment, "like the Eucharist, [which] grants a share in Jesus Christ, in whom God's promises are already fulfilled even though we still await the final demonstration and consummation of the event of incarnational fulfillment by the future of the returning Christ."[56]

Baptism

Baptism and Christian Initiation

Baptism has been part of Christian initiation and thus church life from the very beginning.[57] This is affirmed by all churches, notwithstanding the diversity of interpretations of its meaning and significance. Orthodox, Catholic, Anglican,

---

51. Pannenberg, *ST* 3:351.
52. Pannenberg, *ST* 3:352.
53. Aquinas, *ST* 3.62.1.
54. W. Ward, "Baptism in a Theological Perspective," p. 44; I am indebted to Grenz, *Theology for the Community of God*, p. 516.
55. Materially similarly Pannenberg, *ST* 3:353-54. For an interesting typology of the power and efficacy of sacraments, see van Dyk, "The Gifts of God for the People of God," pp. 205-6.
56. Pannenberg, *ST* 3:352-53 (353).
57. Küng, *The Church*, pp. 267-68; so also *BEM*-B, #1.

and Lutheran traditions uniformly understand it sacramentally in the sense of the baptismal act, linked with the faith (of the church) and Word of God, bringing about what it promises, that is, new birth. In the Reformed family, there are well-known internal differences. For the Zwinglian covenant theology, baptism indicates belonging to the people of God (somewhat similarly to the Old Testament rite of circumcision). The Calvinist majority oscillates between Lutheran and Zwinglian understandings in the sense that while it does not consider the rite regenerative in the sense the sacramental traditions do, it does consider it a "seal" of the covenant with God. As such, it is done with a view to forthcoming faith.[58] Baptists, Anabaptists, and most all other free churches understand water baptism as an "ordinance," in other words, as an act ordained by Christ. Rather than sacramental, it is a public response of a believer.[59] Rather than infant baptism as in Catholic, Orthodox, Anglican, and Lutheran churches, free churches practice believers' ("adult") baptism by immersion.[60]

On the way toward a constructive ecumenical proposal, a careful theological reading and assessment of both biblical and patristic perspectives on baptism are in order. This is not done for historical purposes but for theological reasons: by the end of the patristic era the main contours of baptismal theology and practice were hammered out.

The Diversity of New Testament Perspectives: A Brief Assessment

Although baptism is not without pagan and Jewish antecedents,[61] the New Testament establishes a distinctively Christian view of baptism with close links not only to the preparatory work of John the Baptist[62] but also, more

58. See, e.g., C. Hodge, *Systematic Theology*, 3:582. For a useful discussion of Calvin, see Haitch, *From Exorcism to Ecstasy*, chap. 5.

59. For a useful ecumenical discussion, see *OBTMR*, ##26–31. That said, there can also be thick accounts of baptism's effect, as in the Anabaptist John Howard Yoder, for whose views see chap. 2 in Haitch, *From Exorcism to Ecstasy*.

60. For a careful, ecumenically sensitive Baptist view, see Grenz, *Theology for the Community of God*, pp. 529–31; for a similar Anabaptist treatment, see T. Finger, *A Contemporary Anabaptist Theology*, pp. 160–84.

61. For details, see E. Ferguson, *Baptism in the Early Church*, chap. 2 (Greco-Roman pagan washings), chap. 4 (Jewish), and chap. 5 (John the Baptist). A meticulous terminological study of all important *bapt*-rooted terms and their meaning is chap. 3, which concludes that "baptize" "meant to dip, usually a thorough submerging" (p. 59). Useful is also the liturgist Spinks, *Early and Medieval Rituals*, chap. 1, "The New Testament Foundations."

62. Spinks, *Early and Medieval Rituals*, p. 5.

importantly, to Jesus' own baptism (recorded in all four Gospels).[63] That said, as is well known, there hardly is a single baptismal theology in the New Testament. The Acts of the Apostles of course provides the most baptismal data and examples of the first Christian baptisms (chaps. 2, 8, 9, 10, 11, 16, 18–19, 22). Ordinarily conversion stories mention baptism, which followed immediately upon becoming Christian. All the baptized were in the age of responsibility.[64] No information is given as to what kind of person performed baptism. The initiation included hearing the gospel, repentance, faith, and the reception of the Holy Spirit (at times with charismatic manifestations); forgiveness of sins is promised to the baptized. Immersion was the normal baptismal mode. Baptism was done in the name of Jesus (although the church adopted soon the trinitarian formula present in Matthew and elsewhere). Baptism was done by another and constituted the door to the congregation. "Baptism was viewed as both a human act and an act in which God was at work."[65]

In the Pauline and other New Testament epistles,[66] a number of diverse images and metaphors are attached to baptism, without any attempt for harmonizing, including the following: "Baptism is participation in Christ's death and resurrection (Rom. 6:3–5; Col. 2:12); a washing away of sin (I Cor. 6:11); a new birth (John 3:5); an enlightenment by Christ (Eph. 5:14); a re-clothing in Christ (Gal. 3:27); a renewal by the Spirit (Titus 3:5); the experience of salvation from the flood (I Peter 3:20–21); an exodus from bondage (I Cor. 10:1–2) and a liberation into a new humanity in which barriers of division whether of sex or race or social status are transcended (Gal. 3:27–28; I Cor. 12:13)."[67]

When it comes to the spiritual effects of baptism, there are three types of orientations. Important passages link regeneration with baptism (John 3:5; 1 Pet. 3:21; 1 Cor. 12:13[68]). Others seem to imply that what is decisive are repentance and faith, to be followed by baptism (Mark 16:16; Acts 2:38; 8:12, 13, 36; 10:45–48; etc.).[69] And finally, there are sayings in which repentance and faith without sacraments are linked with regeneration and new birth (Luke 24:47; Acts 4:4; 5:14; 11:21; etc.). Two broad conclusions seem warranted: First, in a

63. E. Ferguson, *Baptism in the Early Church*, chaps. 6 and 7.

64. This is the rule, whatever one may make of the case of the jailor's household in Acts 16.

65. This paragraph is based directly on E. Ferguson, *Baptism in the Early Church*, chap. 11 (citation on p. 185).

66. For details, see E. Ferguson, *Baptism in the Early Church*, chap. 9 (Paul); chap. 11 (the rest of the NT).

67. *BEM-B*, #2.

68. Note that this passage mainly speaks of "Spirit baptism" rather than water baptism.

69. Matt. 28:19-20 may belong to either the first or second group of sayings above.

number of passages baptism is seen as effecting or "causing" salvation.[70] That said, second, baptism happens in the context of hearing the gospel, repentance, and faith. That speaks of the importance of human response to God's doing. This dynamic divine-human aspect of baptism should be kept in mind when weighing out the ways to define how a person becomes a Christian in relation to baptism. Constructive theology has the task of negotiating these diverse perspectives, minding the two broad principles mentioned above, namely, baptism as divine work and the need for active human response.

The Emergence and Establishment of Baptismal Theologies in Postbiblical Early Christianity

The (early) second-century *Didache* offers the first known description of baptismal practice (chap. 7): it is done in the triune name in "living" (or running) water (where available), and the candidates were expected to have fasted — fasting was a regular feature in early Christianity. Before baptism, preparatory teaching was obviously given. Eucharistic participation followed (chap. 9), as well as instructions for ethics and Christian life.[71] Ignatius is the first to determine who administrates baptism: the bishop.[72]

A fairly informative source is the mid-second-century *The Pastor [Shepherd] of Hermas* (perhaps multiauthored), which, echoing (but not citing) 1 Peter 3:20-21 imagery and baptismal theology, comparing the church to a tower, states: "It is because your life has been, and will be, saved through water."[73] That salvation through baptism also calls for faith and commitment is emphasized.[74] The fullest baptismal account from the second century comes from Justin Martyr's *First Apology* (chap. 61). It follows the earlier records in describing that having been persuaded of the truth and demands of the gospel, people are baptized for the forgiveness of sins and experience regeneration, followed by joining the congregation. Only the baptized may partake in the Eucharist (66.1).[75]

---

70. See the Baptist NT scholar Beasley-Murray, *Baptism in the New Testament*, pp. 263-305.

71. For details, see E. Ferguson, *Baptism in the Early Church*, pp. 201-6; see also Stander and Louw, *Baptism in the Early Church*, pp. 31-34. For the liturgical perspective, consult Spinks, *Early and Medieval Rituals*, pp. 14-16.

72. Ignatius, *To the Smyrnaeans* 8.2; E. Ferguson, *Baptism in the Early Church*, p. 209.

73. *Shepherd of Hermas* 1.3.3.

74. *Shepherd of Hermas* 1.3.7; see also 1.3.5; see E. Ferguson, *Baptism in the Early Church*, pp. 214-20; Stander and Louw, *Baptism in the Early Church*, pp. 38-42.

75. See further E. Ferguson, *Baptism in the Early Church*, pp. 327-44; Stander and Louw,

In the leading second-century teacher Irenaeus's theology, faith, forgiveness of sins, and reception of the Spirit are closely linked.[76] The regenerating and cleansing power of baptism necessitates faith.[77] Clement of Alexandria teaches similarly.[78] In keeping with this, the important third-century source about baptism, *Apostolic Tradition* (routinely assigned to Hippolytus), following earlier traditions, helps establish the three-year catechumenate for the sake of a thorough instruction in faith before baptism. New components that seem to be established patterns in the West by that time include anointing with oil and exorcism.[79]

It is interesting that not until the third century was the first baptismal manual, Tertullian's *On Baptism*, written. Notwithstanding well-known historical uncertainties about the possible influence of Montanism on him at that point of his life, the manual is universally regarded as a milestone and treasure. Following earlier witnesses, Tertullian links water baptism, faith, and repentance with the reception of the Spirit.[80] On the one hand, everywhere Tertullian emphasizes the importance of hearing the gospel and faith as a requirement for baptism.[81] On the other hand, he would be the last one to undermine the importance of baptism as a requisite for salvation for believers.[82]

As is well known, Augustine's influence towers over the theology of baptism in the Latin Church. On the one hand, he follows keenly the received tradition in highlighting the importance of faith and repentance and the effects of baptism in terms of forgiveness and regeneration.[83] Innovative teachings, on the other hand, emerged out of his painful encounters with the Donatists and

---

Baptism in the Early Church, chap. 4. For the liturgical perspective, consult also Spinks, *Early and Medieval Rituals*, pp. 25–28.

76. Irenaeus, *Against Heresies* 5.11.2; similarly, *Demonstration of the Apostolic Preaching* 3; for the link with forgiveness, see also *Against Heresies* 3.12.7.

77. See, e.g., Irenaeus, *Demonstration of the Apostolic Preaching* 3. For a detailed study of Irenaeus, see E. Ferguson, *Baptism in the Early Church*, chap. 18.

78. Clement of Alexandria, *Instruction* 1.6 (p. 217); see E. Ferguson, *Baptism in the Early Church*, pp. 214–15 for other such examples.

79. See E. Ferguson, *Baptism in the Early Church*, pp. 327–33, chap. 20; also chap. 8 in Stander and Louw, *Baptism in the Early Church*.

80. Tertullian, *On Baptism* 10.6; so also *Prescription against Heretics* 36 (baptism seals faith, to be followed by the Spirit).

81. Tertullian, *On Repentance* 6.

82. Tertullian, *On Baptism* 12; this paragraph draws from the detailed investigation of Tertullian in E. Ferguson, *Baptism in the Early Church*, chap. 21.

83. See chap. 51 in E. Ferguson, *Baptism in the Early Church*. From the liturgical perspective, consult Spinks, *Early and Medieval Rituals*, pp. 63–67.

Pelagians, and those contributions became his legacy to the Western Church. Against the former, he leveled the charge of rejecting Christian baptism — a somewhat ironic claim in light of the importance of that sacrament to the Donatists! He developed a thick theology of the sacrament in terms of its "indelible character"; its efficacy is immune to the quality of the administrator or the recipient, as its validity lies in the triune God;[84] hence, rebaptisms administered by the opponents are both useless and wrong. Augustine also comes to endorse strongly infant baptism, which of course fits this framework. For that, Augustine claims to have support in tradition[85] (a precarious claim at the time, to say the least!). The fight with the Pelagians further helped consolidate this innovative baptismal theology and practice. There the link was not to the validity of heretics' baptism but to the emerging doctrine of original sin — another innovation against the whole patristic tradition in both West and East.[86] If even the babies of Christian parents are born guilty and, hence, deserving of the judgment of God, baptism's cleansing from original sin — on top of the sins of the past, as in tradition — was necessary.[87]

The Rise of Infant Baptism

In light of current research, it is indisputable that infant baptism is a new development in relation to the New Testament and the earliest patristic theology. Infant baptism emerged slowly and sporadically in various Christian locations, and its legitimacy had to be demonstrated (Origen) and was sometimes outright rejected (Tertullian). This momentous shift began slowly from the end of the second century, and not earlier than the end of the fourth and beginning of the fifth, infant baptism established itself as the main mode of baptism.[88]

The first reliable and documented evidence for the beginning of infant

---

84. The main source is of course the highly polemical treatise of Augustine, *On Baptism, against the Donatists*; for a detailed discussion, see E. Ferguson, *Baptism in the Early Church*, pp. 795–803.

85. See particularly Augustine, *On Baptism* 4.23.31; 4.24.32.

86. For details, see my *Creation and Humanity*, chap. 15.

87. The main source is Augustine, *A Treatise on the Merits and Forgiveness of Sins, and on the Baptism of Infants*; see also Letter 98 (to Boniface); for detailed discussion, see E. Ferguson, *Baptism in the Early Church*, pp. 803–16.

88. In addition to sources cited frequently below, I have benefited greatly from D. F. Wright, *What Has Infant Baptism Done?*; D. F. Wright, *Infant Baptism in Historical Perspective*; Stander and Louw, *Baptism in the Early Church*, chap. 1.

baptism at the end of the second century comes from Tertullian's strict opposition to it. Resisting infant baptism, he strongly recommended delaying baptism in order to ensure proper instruction in faith (except for some exceptional cases of impending death).[89] Like the early fathers (almost universally), he regarded children as innocent, as the later Western Augustinian doctrine of original sin was not yet in place. Instrumental in the slow rise of infant baptism were the debates in the latter part of the third century guided by Cyprian (who was of course baptized as an adult). The debates had to do with baptism by heretics/schismatics and "clinical" or deathbed baptisms (deemed legitimate notwithstanding the impossibility of immersion). Disputes about infant baptism's legitimacy continued for a long time.[90] The first authoritative pronouncement in favor of infant baptism — along with, but not as an alternative to, adult baptism — is the statement from the council presided over by Cyprian about the middle of the third century.[91] The main theological justification is that "there is the same equality of the divine gift" to young and old.[92]

Earlier forced efforts to read infant baptism into some well-known passages such as Justin Martyr's *First Apology* (15.6) or the *Martyrdom of Polycarp* (9.3), among others, are just that: forced.[93] Even the passage in *Apostolic Tradition* (21.4-5) that speaks of small children being baptized along with others requires them to publicly profess faith, and only for those unable to do so is the promoter to step in. In other words, even that document assumes the traditional adult baptism but makes concessions to younger persons (and scholars remind us that "children" has a whole range of meanings in that culture).[94] As a conclusion from the massive survey of available evidence from the first

---

89. Tertullian, *On Baptism* 18.

90. See chap. 23 in E. Ferguson, *Baptism in the Early Church*.

91. Cyprian, *Epistle 58: To Fidus, on the Baptism of Infants*. The (first) Council of Carthage's exact date is not known, but is usually determined somewhere between 251 and 257 C.E.

92. Cyprian, *Epistle 58: To Fidus, on the Baptism of Infants* 3; see E. Ferguson, *Baptism in the Early Church*, pp. 370-72; Stander and Louw, *Baptism in the Early Church*, chap. 13.

93. Sadly, as recently as 2009 (incidentally, the same year E. Ferguson's massive work *Baptism in the Early Church* was released), an uncritical and highly selective use of these and related incidents in support of infant baptism — astonishingly claimed to have been "practiced in the Latin church before the end of the second century" — was published: S. Ferguson, "Infant Baptism View," pp. 77-112 (82).

94. For a careful scrutiny of the three well-known passages in which Origen ends up defending infant baptism not on the basis of original sin (nor forgiveness of sins because innocent infants do not need it) but on the basis of "apostolic tradition" — in itself an ambiguous and somewhat biased argument — see E. Ferguson, *Baptism in the Early Church*, chap. 23; Stander and Louw, *Baptism in the Early Church*, chaps. 1 and 9.

five centuries, E. Ferguson states that, apart from emergency baptisms of infants (which began at the latest at the turn of the third century), with healthy children "there is no evidence that their parents presented them for baptism. The instruction to parents to baptize their children begins in the late fourth century . . . and the routine baptism of babies belongs to the fifth century and after, when evidence for accommodations of the baptism ceremony to the presence of infants begins to appear." Only with Augustine at the turn of the fifth century did infant baptism become the norm, although believers' baptism of course did not thereby disappear at once.[95]

Notwithstanding the rise of infant baptism, believers' baptism as the dominant form of Christian baptism survived at least until the fourth century and continued as an alternative, legitimate form at least until the fifth (or even sixth) century. Instructive in this regard is the (perhaps) most important and extensive teaching manual on baptism and for baptismal candidates, *Catechetical Lectures*, authored by Cyril of Jerusalem in the mid-fourth century. The first part prepares the candidates, and the second part is for the newly baptized, covering also the Eucharist and confirmation. Everywhere adult baptism is assumed.[96] The same can be said of *On Baptism* and *Exhortation to the Holy Baptism* by the fourth-century Cappadocian Basil the Great[97] as well as scattered remarks on baptism by his contemporary, Athanasius, the leading Alexandrian theologian.[98] Importantly, in works such as the Antiochean John Chrysostom's twelve *Baptismal Instructions* (or *Catechetical Instructions*), baptisms administered at any age are considered appropriate in order for the persons, young and old, to receive all possible blessings (he numbers ten in his list).[99] Note, however, in keeping with the title (specifically the term *Catechetical*), the manual emphasizes throughout the necessary link between baptism, faith, and repentance, making forgiveness and regeneration its effects.[100] In this light it is somewhat ironic that Chrysostom's influence helped the church to transition to a stronger infant-baptism ethos. The same applies to the Cappadocian Gregory of Nazianzus, another theologian instrumental toward the

95. E. Ferguson, *Baptism in the Early Church*, pp. 627–28 (627).

96. For details and sources, see Stander and Louw, *Baptism in the Early Church*, chap. 15; E. Ferguson, *Baptism in the Early Church*, pp. 473–87.

97. Stander and Louw, *Baptism in the Early Church*, chap. 17; E. Ferguson, *Baptism in the Early Church*, chap. 36. The original source is Basil the Great, *A Treatise on Baptism*.

98. See E. Ferguson, *Baptism in the Early Church*, pp. 455–60.

99. John Chrysostom, *Baptismal Instructions* 3.6 (in *Ancient Christian Writers*, p. 57); for details, see E. Ferguson, *Baptism in the Early Church*, chap. 33.

100. For details and sources, see E. Ferguson, *Baptism in the Early Church*, chap. 34.

same effect, who expressed some objections to the practice of infant baptism because of the incapacity of infants to account for their faith (hence, his recommendation that baptism not be offered to those younger than age three).[101]

At the end of this brief historical examination, we have to raise the question, why infant baptism? Scholarship does not speak unanimously here,[102] and for the sake of doctrinal theology it is best not to claim too much. It seems reasonable to assume that in addition to historical reasons, such as the shift to Christendom with Christianity as the "religion of the land," the practice of "clinical" baptism, that is, sickbed baptism, somewhat ironically, made a contribution: if the child or infant was seen in danger of premature death, baptism was considered to be necessary.[103] Furthermore, there is no doubt that — at least in terms of infant baptism's consolidation as the dominant pattern in the Christian West — the rise of the traditional Augustinian doctrine of original sin from the fourth century onward made infant baptism mandatory.[104] (In terms of later history, whereas the Lutheran and Roman Catholic traditions followed Augustine consistently,[105] in Reformed tradition, with its concept of baptism as sign of grace, cleansing could be had without the sacrament through the Word,[106] although Reformed churches for other reasons retained infant baptism.[107] Whatever the ultimate reason(s) for this momentous shift from believers' to infant baptism, in light of current scholarship and the brief survey above, the standard claim of the "missionary situation" as the main justification for adult baptism is not valid at all; believers' baptism continued as a normal mode even in territories and during the age of Christendom.[108]

---

101. Gregory of Nazianzus, *Oration 150: The Oration on Holy Baptism* 40.28; see also 40.16. For a detailed study, see E. Ferguson, *Baptism in the Early Church*, chap. 37; consult also Stander and Louw, *Baptism in the Early Church*, chap. 18.

102. For a succinct survey of opinions, see E. Ferguson, *Baptism in the Early Church*, pp. 377-79.

103. Convincingly argued in E. Ferguson, *Baptism in the Early Church*, chaps. 23, 39, and passim. Chapter 22 includes discussion of sickbed baptism.

104. See Canon 110 of the Council of Carthage (418), *NPNF*² 14:496-97; see Aland, *Did the Early Church Baptize Infants?* pp. 100-111. For an exposition and critical analysis of traditional original sin, see my *Creation and Humanity*, chap. 15. In this sense, as D. F. Wright (*Infant Baptism in Historical Perspective*, p. 28) surmises, it was the case that baptism was a "practice in search of a theology."

105. See CA 9 (*BC*, p. 33) for the Lutheran tradition.

106. *Heidelberg Catechism* (1563), Q. 66 (Schaff, *Creeds*, 3:328; at www.ccel.org).

107. *Heidelberg Catechism* (1563), Q. 74 (Schaff, *Creeds*, 3:331); for details, see Pannenberg, *ST* 3:258-59.

108. So also Stander and Louw, *Baptism in the Early Church*, pp. 185-86.

Having now tentatively clarified the origins and theological shifts in the practice and theology of baptism during the formative centuries, we begin work toward a constructive theological proposal.

Baptism as Divine-Human Act

As argued on the basis of the New Testament data, baptism has both a human and a divine aspect. From the latter point of view, baptism "is the visible sign of grace . . . and the guarantee and presentation of God's justifying grace proclaimed and given to the believer." From the human side, it is "the individual, spiritual and corporeal visible expression of faith," a confession of faith before the community.[109] Building on images, metaphors, and teachings of the New Testament, the *Baptism, Eucharist and Ministry* document elaborates the many theological meanings of this divine-human act in the following manner:

- participation in Christ's death and resurrection (Rom. 6:3–11; Eph. 2:5–6; Col. 2:13; 3:1)
- conversion, pardoning, and cleansing (Acts 22:16; 1 Cor. 6:11; Heb. 10:22; 1 Pet. 3:21)
- the gift of the Holy Spirit (2 Cor. 1:21–22; Eph. 1:13–14)
- incorporation into the body of Christ: the New Testament consistently testifies to the pattern of baptism after one becomes a Christian and thereby after one becomes a member of the local community
- sign of the kingdom of God and of the life of the world to come[110]

Through baptism and faith the Christian is given a new identity; this insight was behind the patristic idea of Christians as the "third" race.[111] New identity is indicated by being baptized in the "name" of Jesus, which implies his lordship and human commitment and submission.[112] So carefully was this idea of baptism placing a total claim taken in the early church

109. Küng, *The Church*, p. 272.

110. *BEM*-B, ##3–7.

111. *Apology of Aristedes* 2.2 (in this passage there are four races, as "Barbarians" and "Greeks" — as Gentiles — and Jews and Christians are distinguished from each other); see also 1 Pet. 2:9; 1 Cor. 10:32; 12:2; Gal. 3:28; Col. 3:11.

112. Whereas at first baptism in Jesus' name seemed to have been more common, soon the adoption of the triune name became standard and the rule. See Pannenberg, *ST* 3:239–40.

that preparation for baptism normally included no fewer than three years of catechism.[113]

While related to a lifelong process, baptism is a onetime event (Eph. 4:5).[114] The New Testament knows nothing of repeated baptisms of Christians (differently from repetitions of lustrations and washings in Judaism).[115] Even if a person ignores one's baptism — or renounces it — baptism does not need to be repeated, but rather reappropriated. Luther's way of making Christian life a continuous return to the baptismal grace and power in daily repentance illustrates both the unrepeatability of the baptism and its lifelong effects and pledge.[116] He said, "you have been once baptized in the sacrament, but you need continually to be baptized by faith, continually to die and continually to live."[117]

Incorporation into the body of Christ, baptism, is a communal event; one can never baptize oneself; rather, one submits oneself to the community to be baptized.[118] Baptism and the baptized person cannot be divorced from the community.

An essential biblical aspect of water baptism, too often ignored or minimized in the Christian West, has to do with its pneumatological dimension: "In God's work of salvation, the paschal mystery of Christ's death and resurrection is inseparably linked with the pentecostal gift of the Holy Spirit. Similarly, participation in Christ's death and resurrection is inseparably linked with the receiving of the Spirit."[119] While theologically there is no disagreement ecumenically about this, there are various ways of linking the Spirit with baptism, either with water itself or with anointing — as was common in patristic times and still is in the Eastern Church, in which confirmation as the prayer for the Spirit is an integral part of the baptismal ritual.

---

113. For a detailed description, see Hippolytus, *The Apostolic Tradition of Hippolytus*, ##16-19.

114. *BEM-B*, #13.

115. The baptism by Paul of John the Baptist's disciples in Acts 19:3-5 does not constitute a rebaptism, as these disciples had not yet been baptized in the context of Christian faith.

116. Luther, *The Babylonian Captivity of the Church* (1520), *LW* 36:69; WA 6:534.30-35.

117. *LW* 36:69; WA 6:535.10-11; for a detailed discussion, see Pannenberg, *ST* 3:248-50.

118. *BEM-B*, #12; Küng, *The Church*, pp. 272-73.

119. *BEM-B*, #14.

Faith, Baptism, and Lifelong Commitment

In keeping with the New Testament teaching in which faith normally precedes baptism and the act of baptism is a personal choice, all churches agree that baptism and faith belong together irreversibly.[120] "Not the sacrament, but the faith of the sacrament, justifies," declared Luther.[121] He further explained that sacraments' "whole efficacy, therefore, consists in faith itself, not in the doing of a work."[122] The key is that "a word of promise which requires faith"[123] is attached to sacraments, and thereby they are effective. The Catholic Küng agrees, and on the basis of the New Testament teaching (Mark 16:16; Acts 4:12) states that "baptism by itself is of no value . . . [as] baptism and faith go together."[124]

Faith commitment should follow the baptized throughout life. Christian initiation is just that — *initiation* — rather than completion of the Christian life.[125] It is particularly important for parents and mentors of baptized infants to be reminded that "[p]ersonal commitment is necessary for responsible membership in the body of Christ,"[126] or else the goal and fruit of the sacrament may very well be lost.[127] Indeed, baptism places a lifelong claim on the whole life of the Christian as a responsible member of the community. It "has ethical implications which not only call for personal sanctification, but also motivate Christians to strive for the realization of the will of God in all realms of life (Rom. 6:9ff; Gal. 3:27–28; I Peter 2:21–4:6)."[128]

That said, the relationship between baptism and human response is dynamic and mutual: the irreducible link with faith should be connected with the equally important link in the New Testament between seeing baptism as "both God's gift and our human response to that gift."[129] In contrast to *wrongly* conceived, extreme ideas of the sacrament as a semimechanical *ex opere operato* or a merely human act, the divine-human/human-divine nature of baptism helps steer a radical middle road. In this light — and only in this light — we should argue: "Faith alone is not the basis of baptism; baptism is more than

120. *BEM*-B, #8; see also Pannenberg, *ST* 3:257.

121. WA 6:532.29; *LW* 36:66.

122. WA 6:532.26–27; *LW* 36:65–66.

123. WA 5:532.25; *LW* 36:65.

124. Küng, *The Church*, p. 271. So also Luther in *Large Catechism* (IV.34; *BC*, p. 440).

125. *BEM*-B, #8; see also #12.

126. *BEM*-B, #8.

127. *BEM*-B, #12.

128. *BEM*-B, #10.

129. *BEM*-B, #9, #8, respectively.

a sign of faith and confession, designed merely to confirm faith. Conversely, baptism alone is not the basis of faith; faith is not the natural consequence or the automatic fruit of baptism. The New Testament does not allow us to take either view." The reason is that baptism and faith do not "have their bases in themselves, but alike in the saving act of God in Christ," in the eschatological act of salvation. Küng succinctly summarizes: "baptism comes from faith, and faith leads to baptism."[130]

The emphasis on the close link between personal faith and baptism brings to light the problems and liabilities related to infant baptism. These were already recognized early on in Christian theology, as the discussion above indicated.

Believers' Baptism as the Theological Norm

In light of biblical and patristic scholarship, briefly reviewed above, the first foundational guideline leading toward an ecumenical proposal for a baptismal theology and practice is this: believers' baptism should be adopted as the theological norm and standard when assessing various baptismal practices in the contemporary global church. The term "believers' baptism" refers not to the age of the candidate (although it of course is related to it) but rather to the baptismal act in which a candidate with personal faith requests to be baptized in accordance with the New Testament command and promises. This principle follows and is in keeping with *Baptism, Eucharist and Ministry*: "While the possibility that infant baptism was also practised in the apostolic age cannot be excluded, baptism upon personal profession of faith is the most clearly attested pattern in the New Testament documents."[131] Adopting believers' baptism as the theological standard does not have to lead — and in this project will not lead — to discrediting infant baptism, but rather helps those churches that continue this practice to constantly evaluate its theological value and hopefully reconsider the adoption of both believers'- and infant-baptism models as legitimate. Efforts toward consistent adoption of baptismal theology and practice in keeping with the New Testament and patristic standard could be made a long-term ecumenical program, which even at its best would take generations to be realized.

What concerns and even amazes me is how slow traditional churches are to fully embrace and support that theological commonplace, even when

130. Küng, *The Church*, p. 271.
131. *BEM*-B, #11; see also Giblet, "Baptism."

one has a hard time imagining weighty biblical or patristic theological reasons for that attitude. The discussion over baptismal practice and theology is also sadly frustrated by the continuing fruitless — and often pointless — disputes focused on arguments for or against infant or believers' baptism without the needed theological framework.

Intentionally narrow and polemic arguments have not in any way furthered the search for Christian unity, but have rather bolstered its opposite, church divisions.[132] While criticism of the established practice of infant baptism by Baptists (including Anabaptists and most free churches) has certainly not always been courteous or theologically flawless, it is also regrettable how skewed and at times theologically thin have been the counterattacks of traditional churches, with clergy and the theological academy far better formally trained than their "opponents."

The adoption of believers' baptism as the theological norm raises the question of how to negotiate the presence of faith in the context of infant baptism, which was the main reason for Tertullian[133] and more recently for Barth[134] to reject that practice altogether. In support of infant baptism in the absence of faith, ingenious tactics have been devised, but none of them sounds theologically — and *logically* — very convincing. Augustine's justification of vicarious faith of the infant (that is, parents or other believing adults believe for the child) with the reasoning that, similarly to original sin, which comes from outside the child (from parents), the family members and the church bring faith on behalf of the yet-to-mature infant[135] falters on more than one account. First of all, as will be argued below, this project does not endorse the Augustinian doctrine of original sin — it is another innovation and deviation from the New Testament and early patristic theology of sin.[136] Second, nowhere in the New Testament is the sinfulness of humanity (which the Bible of course teaches, albeit not necessarily after the later doctrine of original sin) linked with baptism. In one sense, Luther's idea of *fides infantium* (infant faith) — notwithstanding other problems and questions related to it[137] — is on a firmer foundation, as (at least in the *Large Catechism*) he does not make

---

132. *BEM-B*, #6 (Commentary).

133. Tertullian, *On Baptism* 18.

134. See particularly Barth, *CD* IV/4, p. 2.

135. Augustine, *Against Two Letters of the Pelagians* 1.40.

136. See my *Creation and Humanity*, pp. 389-96.

137. For that complicated and debated issue, see Boomgaarden, "Können Säuglinge glauben?"; Huovinen, "Fides infantium — fides infusa?"; more widely, Huovinen, *Fides Infantium*. Still useful is also Grönvik, *Die Taufe in der Theologie Luthers*.

the child's faith a precondition of and justification for baptism but merely assumes its presence.[138]

That said, the general effort to find a "substitute" faith for that of the infant baptized — whether Augustine's vicarious faith or Luther's "infant faith" or related proposals ("seed of faith," for instance) — is not convincing theologically. The reasons are many, not the least of which is lack of biblical support. It is clear that the normal view of faith in the New Testament, as much as it is divine gift communicated through the Holy Spirit, is a personal choice and leads to commitment ("faithfulness," from the Greek term *pistis*, following the Old Testament *emunah*). A related observation is that in the New Testament no one is baptized without the person's request or consent. In that sense, it seems to me confusing at best that Saint Thomas affirms the necessity of "intention" to be baptized by the candidate and yet, in the same context, refuses to make the faith of the candidate a precondition![139] This is not to deny the importance of either the Christian family or the church in cultivating the child's spiritual life, nor is there any reason to expect an infant to display cognitive and volitional features of faith similar to those of a mature person. Those concessions, however, have very little to do with baptismal practice. My advice thus is that practitioners of infant baptism simply drop these faltering efforts to appeal to either vicarious or "infant" faith and instead follow the Reformed (Calvinist) principle of baptizing with the view toward the emergence of future faith.[140] Although even that principle is hardly in keeping with the New Testament faith-preceding-baptism order, it is at least more coherent and unambiguous.

In contemporary culture a further question arises as to whether baptizing infants may at least implicitly fail to honor each human person's integrity and inviolability. What I mean is this: While it is clear to everybody that baptism could — and should — never be administered against the will of people able to decide on it, how can it be taken for granted that baptism can be done for an infant? In secular society this has led to "unbaptisms" by atheists and other nonchurch folks.[141] That many things are done for infants by their parents and guardians without their permission or initiative, such as clothing, feeding, and protecting from harm, belongs to a different category than making them members of the Christian church — or any other religion, like, say, Islam — without any input from the children. Wouldn't Christian education

138. *Large Catechism*, IV.57 (*BC*, p. 444); I am indebted to Pannenberg, *ST* 3:263-64.
139. Aquinas, *ST* 3.68.7, 8, respectively.
140. C. Hodge, *Systematic Theology*, 3:584; for Calvin himself, see Haitch, *From Exorcism to Ecstasy*, chap. 5.
141. Denison, "100,000 Atheists Are 'Unbaptized.'"

with the hope for the child to willingly embrace faith later in life fit much better the principle of honoring each human person's right and responsibility?[142]

I also advise that another typical argument set forth in the hope of supporting infant baptism — appeal to the unconditionality of God's mercy — be renounced. As Moltmann pointedly says, the "defenselessness of new-born babies" has little to do with "a creative receptivity" of God's grace by mature men and women. Furthermore — and this I consider an important point — were the unconditionality really the theological basis for infant baptism, then it would necessarily lead to the conclusion that *all* infants, whether those of Christians or of non-Christians, should be baptized indiscriminately, which is a procedure all churches condemn.[143] Indeed, nowhere in the New Testament is the connection between unconditional grace and baptism established; rather, where unconditionality comes to the fore is in Jesus' blessing of children — but that is totally unrelated to baptism (notwithstanding its uncritical use in its support).

My further piece of advice to practitioners of infant baptism is that, following the New Testament and early patristic baptismal theology, the attempt to ground infant baptism and its necessity on original sin be abandoned. Although the sinfulness of men and women is an integral Christian doctrine, the traditional Augustinian-driven account endorsed (although somewhat differently) by the main Western churches — but not by the Eastern Church or many free churches — is not credible anymore (see the detailed argumentation in *Creation and Humanity*, chap. 15). Be that as it may, let me just endorse what Pannenberg as a Lutheran theologian categorically puts out: "The idea of exclusion of unbaptized children from eternal salvation on the basis of the doctrine of original sin is not in keeping with the total witness of the NT."[144] Should original sin have been the reason for baptizing infants, surely the early church would have adopted that practice immediately; recall that the basing of infant baptism on original sin was not formulated as a doctrine until the fourth and fifth centuries.

In light of making believers' baptism the standard, I also find dubious and problematic yet another common way of supporting infant baptism: with appeal to Israelite circumcision as finding its Christian counterpart. Problems in this reasoning are many and well known. The origins of baptism in the New Testament of course point in completely different directions. John's baptism has absolutely no relation to circumcision, but rather differs greatly given both

---

142. Cf. different kinds of conclusions in Pannenberg, *ST* 3:262–63.
143. Moltmann, *The Church in the Power of the Spirit*, pp. 229–30 (230).
144. Pannenberg, *ST* 3:264.

its location, the desert rather than a religious site, and its purpose, repentance rather than belonging to community. Neither Jesus nor the apostles invoke circumcision in any way as a precedent for baptism. Finally, circumcision is part of Jewish religion, which is based on birthright, whereas Christian baptism is a public commitment of both Jews and Gentiles willing to commit their lives for Christ and the church.[145]

The last observation relates to the important link between baptismal practice and the idea of the church's mission. Unlike the early church, which spread through calling men and women into personal faith commitment, infant baptism–practicing communities ensure continuity of faith from generation to generation by means of sacraments and hope that a personal embrace of faith at some point emerges. Over the centuries this has led to, or at least was an integral part of, the Christendom-type "state church" model, which still persists in the Global North even after the dismantling of Christendom.[146] The Reformed theologian Moltmann goes so far as to deplore this as "an open theological problem" for churches in need of critical scrutiny.[147]

To follow up these conclusions and observations based on the criteriological function of believers' baptism, let us conclude the discussion of baptism with a set of ecumenical suggestions and proposals. My aim is no less ambitious than to make a contribution to a hoped-for mutual recognition of baptismal practices among the churches and, ultimately, to work toward a unified practice.

Ecumenical Suggestions for a Renewed Baptismal Theology and Practice

First of all — and this is ecumenically of prime importance — all churches should make concentrated efforts to learn to recognize the baptismal practices of other churches. The Lutheran Pannenberg importantly asserts that sacramental churches ought to give up the misguided insistence on infant baptism as the only legitimate mode of baptism. It simply is biblically and theologically unfounded. That would help churches strive toward considering both infant and believers' baptism as parallel and legitimate practices.[148] This task is theologically supported by the conviction that the "differences between infant and believers' baptism become less sharp when it is recognized that both forms of baptism

---

145. Materially similarly, Moltmann, *The Church in the Power of the Spirit*, pp. 230–32.
146. Moltmann, *The Church in the Power of the Spirit*, pp. 228–29 (229).
147. Moltmann, *The Church in the Power of the Spirit*, pp. 226, 228.
148. Pannenberg, *ST* 3:264–65.

embody God's own initiative in Christ and express a response of faith made within the believing community."[149] Herein lies also a practical challenge — and an asset — to both baptismal traditions: whereas believer baptizers should seek to highlight more robustly that already before baptism all children are put under the care and grace of God, infant baptizers should make every effort to stay away from indiscriminate baptisms and continuously encourage parents and guardians to work toward helping the growing person to find personal faith.[150] Here much can be learned from the experiences of those churches that are practicing both forms of baptism.[151] The end goal of this learning and acknowledging process is no less than what *Baptism, Eucharist and Ministry* sets before us: "Churches are increasingly recognizing one another's baptism as the one baptism into Christ when Jesus Christ has been confessed as Lord by the candidate or, in the case of infant baptism, when confession has been made by the church (parents, guardians, godparents and congregation) and affirmed later by personal faith and commitment. Mutual recognition of baptism is acknowledged as an important sign and means of expressing the baptismal unity given in Christ. Wherever possible, mutual recognition should be expressed explicitly by the churches."[152]

As already established, believers' baptism should be lifted up as the theological norm. At least indirectly this is reflected in the 2011 WCC/Faith and Order document *One Baptism: Towards Mutual Recognition*: "Churches baptize those who make a personal profession of faith. Some, agreeing that faith is a condition for being baptized, also baptize infants 'brought by parents or guardians who are ready, in and with the church, to bring up the children in the Christian faith.'"[153] The long-term ecumenical goal should be, on the one hand, a full mutual acknowledgment of both modes of baptism and, on the other hand, gradual transition toward believers' baptism as the normal mode of the beginning of Christian initiation. Even if that goal may not be materialized, the goal would keep its criteriological function before churches. As a result, the least that can be done — and as soon as possible — is to lift up the condemnations of opponents of infant baptism, as the Lutheran Pannenberg demands.[154]

The timing of baptism should be left to the parents. Consequently, those churches whose bylaws require the bringing of infants for baptism (such as

---

149. *BEM-B*, #12.

150. *BEM-B*, ##16, 21 (Commentary).

151. *BEM-B*, #12 (Commentary).

152. *BEM-B*, #15; see also *OBTMR*, ##93–95.

153. *OBTMR*, #97 (citation from *BEM-B*, #11).

154. Pannenberg, *ST* 3:264; a harsh condemnation of Anabaptists can be found, among other places, in CA 9.3; *BC*, p. 33.

the Lutheran church) should change this ruling. It is somewhat ironic that in many secularized contexts of the Global North, particularly on the old continent (including my homeland, Finland), an increasing number of parents already do not baptize their children (even without any theological reason for or against); in some exceptional dioceses as many as half of "Christian parents" — in strict violation of current church bylaws — do not bring their infants to be baptized. Fortunately, many of those children later in life find their way to the church and receive baptism.

Furthermore, minding the criteriological role of believers' baptism also means that all churches should consider carefully rediscovering the original mode of immersion, as that "can vividly express the reality that in baptism the Christian participates in the death, burial and resurrection of Christ."[155] That practice is of course used widely in Eastern Christianity and as a norm by most churches practicing believers' baptism.

In the absence of and in place of infant baptism, a rite of blessing for infants and young children, ideally in the worship service setting, could be adopted as a standard act, as is already the case for most believers' baptism communities. That would match the New Testament example of Jesus' blessing of children. Naming — "christening" — of the child could be related to the event, if so desired, but is not necessary. If name giving is attached, two critical considerations are in order: First, through teaching and preaching, it should be made clear to the community witnessing the baptism that the act is much more than a mere cultural event. Second, in the choice of a child's name, cultural considerations should be kept in mind and encouraged in order to avoid giving the impression that Christianity is a Western religion, as has often happened in Africa, Asia, and elsewhere.[156]

Churches practicing infant baptism should do everything in their power to help the baptized embrace the baptism later in his or her life: "The sacramental sign of baptism and the lasting effect that rests on it aim at the personal faith of the baptized. Only then do the regeneration and justification that take place in the event of baptism come to full actualization."[157] All of this requires a lot of concentrated teaching and reflection among the churches about the meaning and significance of baptism.

Finally, what about confirmation, an important rite linked to baptism (whether a sacrament, as in Catholic and Orthodox churches, or merely a "sacramental" act, as in Protestantism)? Ironically, there is hardly any New Testa-

---

155. *BEM*-B, #18.
156. See further *BEM*-B, #21 (Commentary); *OBTMR*, #40.
157. Pannenberg, *ST* 3:265–66.

ment evidence for what confirmation means today. Instead, the reception of the Spirit both in the Bible and in early Christianity was linked with baptism itself. Unless one keeps baptism and confirmation together, as the Eastern Church has always done — the unity of the two acts is also nowadays acknowledged in principle by Catholic theologians[158] — the delegating of the reception of the Spirit to a future rite is not justifiable.[159] This is not to deny the important practical and pastoral function confirmation has served over the centuries among Western churches, as it has provided an occasion for both catechesis for the baptized and public confession of faith. The focus here is its theological basis — which is questionable.[160] Instead of confirmation classes, churches should make a focused effort for Christian teaching of the youth, and the content of that teaching can glean much from hundreds of years of confirmation classes.[161]

Eucharist

The Shared Meal at the Center of the Church's Gathering

Historically, it can be established that the celebration of the Lord's Supper has stood at the center of Christian worship from the beginning (Acts 2:44-46). "The meals which Jesus is recorded as sharing during his earthly ministry proclaim and enact the nearness of the kingdom, of which the feeding of the multitudes is a sign." It is of no little importance that two Evangelists tell about the risen Christ sharing meals with his disciples (Luke 24:30-31; John 21:13). These meals look forward to the final eschatological banquet (Rev. 19:9) while also holding on to the crucial salvation-historical covenant meals of the Old Testament (such as that in Exod. 23).[162]

Regardless of long-standing scholarly debates about the details of the role of Jesus in "founding" this meal, it is uncontested that it is all about the gathering of disciples to commemorate and celebrate the death, resurrection, and return of their ascended Lord; indeed, the whole saving history of Jesus is its source and foundation. In that derivative sense — and only there — the "in-

158. Rahner, *Foundations*, pp. 416-17.

159. So also Pannenberg, *ST* 3:267-68.

160. I am following here some of the key insights and reflections of Pannenberg, *ST* 3:268-71.

161. I am following here and expanding suggestions made by Moltmann, *The Church in the Power of the Spirit*, pp. 240-42.

162. *BEM*-E, #1.

stitution" by Jesus of the Eucharist is also church forming;[163] the (semi)technical Orthodox and Catholic insistence on the "Eucharist making the church" is not necessarily helpful. Pannenberg puts it well: "What is thus constitutive for the being of the church is not its organization form but the significatory action of Jesus' Supper, which the church celebrates with the assurance based on the gift of the Spirit. As the fellowship that celebrates the Lord's Supper the church is the sign and instrument of humanity's eschatological ordination for fellowship in God's kingdom."[164] That perspective should be in the forefront rather than the ecumenically highly frustrating insistence (by the Orthodox and Catholic traditions) on a strictly defined episcopal (as in having to do with the bishop) legitimation of the celebration.

Theological and Spiritual Dimensions of the Eucharist

Apart from long-standing and ongoing differences in the interpretation of the meaning of the Eucharist in various Christian traditions,[165] ecumenically we have come to a place where it is possible to discern and highlight a significant consensus about the basic dimensions and aspects of the meal. Before anything else, the Lord's Supper is a profound embodiment of divine hospitality, a gift of God to the church par excellence.[166] As with any other works of God, the Eucharist is trinitarian in its nature and form: "the sacrament of the gift which God makes to us in Christ through the power of the Holy Spirit."[167] In the sacred meal, none other than the Lord and Savior hosts and presides.[168]

Based on this *theological*-trinitarian grounding of the sacred meal, *Baptism, Eucharist and Ministry* expresses the significance and manifold meanings of this divine act of hospitality in a most comprehensive manner:

- thanksgiving to the Father (as the term *eucharisteo* literally means)
- *anamnesis*, the memorial of Christ's passion and resurrection as the resurrected Christ himself has instituted (1 Cor. 11:23–25)[169]

163. Cf. Pannenberg, *ST* 3:290.
164. Pannenberg, *ST* 3:292; see also pp. 283–85.
165. For a critical overview, see G. Smith, *The Lord's Supper*. For an overview of the Orthodox view, see, e.g., Ware, *The Orthodox Church*, chap. 14.
166. *BEM*-E, #1.
167. *BEM*-E, #2.
168. *BEM*-E, #29.
169. For a detailed, insightful discussion, see Pannenberg, *ST* 3:305–11. No wonder the

- invocation of the Spirit[170]
- communion of the faithful[171]
- meal of the kingdom, pointing to the return of Christ (1 Cor. 11:26; Matt. 26:29)[172]

Furthermore, related to a number of these dimensions is proclamation, which has been integrally linked with the celebration of the Supper from the beginning; just observe the accounts of the early church in Acts 2–4 and beyond, as well as Pauline teachings about the Eucharist (1 Cor. 11:26). Proclamation is of course most closely linked with the *anamnesis* and memorial.[173]

Anamnesis means "representation and anticipation."[174] It re-presents to the gathered community the significance and meaning of Christ's suffering and victory over death and thus anticipates the final consummation when all decay and death are conquered. The continuing challenge for Roman Catholic sacramentology is to negotiate *anamnesis* in relation to the sacrifice of the Mass. Trent's view of the Eucharist as a re-presentation of Christ's sacrifice is not acceptable either theologically or ecumenically, if for no other reason than it potentially obscures the completed nature of the work of the cross (Heb. 10:14); it could also easily imply tendencies toward "works righteousness."[175] A satisfactory way to conceive the remembrance of Christ's sacrifice is to consider the whole liturgical celebration as *anamnesis*.

Although *anamnesis* in itself does not bring about Christ's presence but rather the Word (of promise), remembrance is a clear biblical command. Even the Word pronounced should not be understood in any (semi)mechanical way but rather — as in all Christian life — in terms of inviting believing human response. We can be confident that when Christians recall Christ's suffering and glorious resurrection and the words of institution are pronounced and embraced in faith, the Holy Spirit effects Christ's presence among the gathered people.[176] This remembering is always a communal event that, in the words of the Catholic

---

Lutheran Reformation reacted vehemently against it; see, e.g., Luther's critique in the Smalcald Articles, chap. 2 (in *BC*). For historical details, see Pannenberg, *ST* 3:308–11.

170. For insightful notes, see Pannenberg, *ST* 3:320–24.

171. See also Pannenberg, *ST* 3:325–32.

172. *BEM-E*, part II.

173. See Pannenberg, *ST* 3:332–36.

174. *BEM-E*, #7.

175. "[I]n the mass there is offered to God a true, proper, and propitiatory sacrifice for the living and the dead." *Profession of the Tridentine Faith, A.D. 1564,* #5; Schaff, *Creeds,* 2:208.

176. Materially similarly, Pannenberg, *ST* 3:311.

W. Cavanaugh, is a "literal re-membering of Christ's body, a knitting together of the body of Christ by the participation of many in His sacrifice."[177]

Considering the Eucharist as the invocation of the Spirit should not be understood to "spiritualize" the presence of Christ, but rather to "affirm the indissoluble union between the Son and the Spirit." The Spirit's role is to bring Christ's memory and presence to the church.[178] This is in keeping with the integral link between Easter and Pentecost. The readoption of the *epiclesis*, the prayer for the descent of the Spirit, has helped Western Christianity to rediscover the pneumatological dimension of the Lord's Supper. Even more than that: "The whole action of the eucharist has an 'epikletic' character because it depends upon the work of the Holy Spirit."[179]

As the recipient of the gracious gift of hospitality, the gathered community is not merely giving thanks for her own sake; the "eucharist is [also] the great sacrifice of praise by which the Church speaks on behalf of the whole creation" of God.[180] In doing so, the church is pointing to the final consummation and hope for the cosmos: "The eucharist thus signifies what the world is to become: an offering and hymn of praise to the Creator, a universal communion in the body of Christ, a kingdom of justice, love and peace in the Holy Spirit."[181] To the eschatological direction also belongs the universal missional zeal of the church as, on the basis of the promise of her Lord, she awaits the day when women and "men will come from east and west, and from north and south, and sit at table in the kingdom of God" (Luke 13:29; cf. Matt. 8:11).[182] Appropriately, in the Eucharist the limitations of "earthly" time are transcended, as is evident in the Pauline words of institution: "For as often as you eat this bread and drink the cup, you proclaim the Lord's death until he comes" (1 Cor. 11:26). Present (eating), past (death), and future (coming) are held together in one transcending moment, awaiting the "newness" of the kingdom (Matt. 26:29).[183] Every time the church gets comfortable in this world and loses sight of her destiny as the pilgrim people, the eschatological orientation gets blurred.[184]

---

177. Cavanaugh, *Torture and Eucharist*, p. 229.

178. *BEM-E*, #14 (including commentary).

179. *BEM-E*, #16.

180. See further Cavanaugh, *Torture and Eucharist*, pp. 222-29. For an important monographic discussion, see Wainwright, *Eucharist and Eschatology*.

181. *BEM-E*, #4.

182. See also Cavanaugh, *Torture and Eucharist*, p. 225.

183. See further Marion, *God without Being*, pp. 161-82 particularly.

184. See Cavanaugh, *Torture and Eucharist*, p. 225.

Similarly to water baptism, which issues a claim on the whole life of the baptized person, the Eucharist also binds the celebrant to the values of the Lord of the Supper; it is no "cheap" communion but touches every aspect of our lives: "The eucharistic celebration demands reconciliation and sharing among all those regarded as brothers and sisters in the one family of God and is a constant challenge in the search for appropriate relationships in social, economic and political life (Matt. 5:23f; I Cor. 10:16f; I Cor. 11:20–22; Gal. 3:28). All kinds of injustice, racism, separation and lack of freedom are radically challenged when we share in the body and blood of Christ."[185] This brings to light the liberative aspects of the Eucharist, to be discussed below. Before that, in order to continue the inquiry into the theological-spiritual meaning of this sacred meal, the question of how to best conceive of Christ's presence therein will be the focus.

Christ's Presence in the Eucharist

Instead of endless abstract speculations into technically formulated ways of defining the mode of the presence of Christ in the eucharistic elements, contemporary biblical scholarship (currently also followed by systematicians) correctly sees that what is primary about this question is "the personal and full presence of Jesus Christ" in the celebration.[186] It is in this light that a critical scrutiny of the heated controversy at the time of the Reformation should be undertaken. It is clear now that Luther's rejection of transubstantiation was in no way an attempt to undermine the full and robust presence of Christ in the Eucharist, notwithstanding persistent critique and condemnation by Rome to that effect. Rome also ignored Luther's concessions in the Smalcald Articles, where he is not so much opposing the doctrine of transubstantiation per se as emphasizing its voluntary, thus nonbinding, status.[187] Even Trent's authoritative formulations of 1551 are deeply controversial and nondiscerning concerning the Reformers' sacramental theologies.[188]

It is not that it is useless or mistaken to inquire into the relationship between the elements and Christ, if for no other reason than to recognize

185. *BEM-E*, #20.

186. Pannenberg, *ST* 3:293. It is quite instructive that in his main (albeit fairly short) treatment of the Eucharist in *Foundations of Christian Faith* (pp. 424–47), Rahner invokes not once the term "transubstantiation," even in his talk about Christ's presence therein.

187. Smalcald Articles, *BC*, I.6.5, p. 311.

188. For details, see Pannenberg, *ST* 3:297–98.

and understand the biblical sayings that "this is my body" and "my blood." The problem emerges when these sayings' symbolic nature is not honored.[189] Recall the wise comment by Karl Rahner that "no theology can be complete without also being a theology of the symbol."[190] Certainly, in the eucharistic celebration there is an intimate relationship between the "sign" (bread and wine) and the "thing" (Christ's presence) — unlike typically when the sign indicates the clear distinction between it and the thing (as in a signpost that points to the destination away from it). At the Eucharist, "sign and thing are together, as when the sign indicates the presence of the things signified." That is similar to, say, the presence of the dawn in the sunrise's red sky or, to use a theological illustration, "the rule of God that Jesus proclaimed . . . present already in his message and ministry." If so, then we have to say that "Christ's bread denotes the presence of the thing signified in the sign," not as a "super-natural substance (impanation)" but rather in "a way that what is signified is there in the sign as an indication of its presence."[191] Terms such as "trans-signification," invoked by both Catholic and Protestant theologians, might be useful here: it means a change in the "meaning" of an act, such as when a sheet of paper is "changed" into a letter, but not in any kind of literal or technical manner. Furthermore, and very importantly, Hans Küng underscored that "Christ becomes present not through the power of the bread or the wine, but through the word which is proclaimed at the Lord's Supper, the word which is an efficacious act."[192] As far as the contemporary Roman Catholic ecclesiology is moving in this direction, an ecumenical convergence may be dawning.[193]

My ecumenical recommendation and hope are that Rome would be willing to consider transubstantiation a *theolougemon*, a traditional way of affirming the real presence but not binding on other traditions who materially affirm the real presence in their own respective ways. The Orthodox, Anglicans, Lutherans, and others should be able to affirm the real presence of Christ in the Eucharist without requiring a certain kind of semitechnical

189. Although invoking the term "symbol" may also imply a "nonrealist" (Zwinglian) type of interpretation, it is not justifiable nor useful to ban the whole term, as seems to have happened in the encyclical *Mysterium Fidei* (1965) of Paul VI; under "False and Disturbing Opinions," he lists symbolic approaches to the Eucharist (#11).

190. Rahner, "The Theology of the Symbol," p. 235; see also the Lutheran Gustav Aulén, *The Drama and the Symbols*, pp. 116-17.

191. Pannenberg, *ST* 3:299-300.

192. Küng, *The Church*, p. 287. Similarly, Rahner, "Word and Eucharist," pp. 253-86.

193. Pannenberg, *ST* 3:300-301; Schillebeeckx, *The Eucharist*, part 2, particularly pp. 144-52. For a helpful discussion, see Duffy, "Sacraments in General," pp. 201-5 particularly.

apparatus.[194] The technical Lutheran term "consubstantiation" (Christ "under," "in," and "above" the elements), in my understanding, says materially the same and claims no exclusivity.[195]

Similarly, the intra-Protestant disputes should be put under critical scrutiny. The seeming impasse between the Zwinglian incapacity to intuit how the ascended heavenly Christ could have his body present at the table and the ingenious Lutheran solution of the "omnipresence" (ubiquity) of Christ's body due to *communicatio idiomatum* can now be resolved with the help of the idea of the whole of Christ being present in the celebration, rather than the "body." Already pointing in that direction was Calvin's middle position that, in critique of Luther (and Catholics), contested the "real presence" in the elements and, in critique of Zwingli, still insisted on a "real *spiritual* presence" through the Holy Spirit.[196] As long as Christ's presence is conceived personally, the abstract and forced options among the Protestant Reformers can be healed and overcome.[197] To that also points Calvin's "representational" understanding, according to which — in contrast to Zwingli's anti-Catholic "memorial" or symbolic understanding — the elements "point beyond themselves to bring to heart and mind the reality of salvation."[198] It seems to me this might be a fruitful way for free churches such as Baptist and Pentecostal groups, who most often are following the "thin" theology of Christ's presence after the "memorial" or symbolic understanding, to establish a more robust theology of Christ's spiritual presence.[199] For Pentecostals, quite surprisingly, the robust "Spirit Christology" at the core of their spirituality seems to strongly support this direction.[200]

In the debates about the presence of Christ, theology has too often missed the point that, however one may understand that matter, something

---

194. For Orthodox theology, see Meyendorff, *Byzantine Theology*, pp. 201–2.

195. Stephenson, "The Lutheran View"; while this essay represents the Missouri Synod–Lutheran viewpoint, it also gives an introduction to other Lutheran orientations.

196. Calvin, *Institutes of the Christian Religion* 4.17.31; see also *Heidelberg Catechism*, Q. 79; Schaff, *Creeds*, 3:334–35; for historical details and sources, see Pannenberg, *ST* 3:312–14.

197. Pannenberg, *ST* 3:312–14. An important rapprochement has already been reached in the Lutheran-Reformed "Arnoldshain Theses" (1957), for whose importance see Welker, *What Happens in Holy Communion*, pp. 36–37. Another major milestone is the *Leuenberg Concord* (1971); see particularly ##18–20 (p. 246). Cf. the highly critical assessment of a leading (late) Lutheran theologian, Mannermaa, *Von Preussen nach Leuenberg*.

198. An accurate, accessible discussion is van Dyk, "The Reformed View," pp. 67–82; citation on p. 70.

199. See R. Olson, "The Baptist View."

200. See Kärkkäinen, "The Pentecostal View."

deeper is taking place at the table, as there "we become the body of Christ by consuming it." Already Augustine saw this clearly — or to be precise: he claimed to have been given this truth in a "message." He surmised that unlike in regular eating, where food is being incorporated into the one who eats, at the Eucharist the one who eats becomes one with the bread and wine: "I am the food of strong men; grow, and thou shalt feed upon me; nor shall thou convert me, like the food of thy flesh, into thee, but thou shall be converted into me."[201]

As emphasized throughout the project, everything that the church is and does is related to mission. So even the most sacred sacrament, the Eucharist, bears a connection to the church's missional existence. That theme will be the focus of the next section.

"The Eucharist and Human Liberation"

Unlike in almost all contemporary celebrations of the Eucharist, the socioeconomic aspect was part of the New Testament church's sacramental life. This is why Paul's exhortation and rebuke come as prelude to what we now know as the words of institution (1 Cor. 11:20–22): "When you meet together, it is not the Lord's supper that you eat. For in eating, each one goes ahead with his own meal, and one is hungry and another is drunk. What! Do you not have houses to eat and drink in? Or do you despise the church of God and humiliate those who have nothing? What shall I say to you? Shall I commend you in this? No, I will not."[202]

Similarly, as much idealized as Luke's description of the early church's life might be, remarkable is the link between economic sharing and spiritual *koinonia*, including the Word, prayers, and Eucharist (Acts 2:42–46; 4:32–37).[203] In the patristic church's life, the socioeconomic sensibility was still there, as is evident in *Didache*. Advising catechumens on how to live the Christian life, the author makes a strong appeal for sharing, including sharing at the table:

> Do not turn your back on the needy, but share everything with your brother and call nothing your own. For if you have what is eternal in common, how much more should you have what is transient! (4.8)
>
> On every Lord's Day — his special day — come together and break bread and give thanks, first confessing your sins so that your sacrifice may

---

201. Augustine, *Confessions* 7.10.[16], cited in Cavanaugh, *Torture and Eucharist*, p. 231.
202. For comments, see Knoch, "Do This in Memory of Me!"
203. See further R. Finger, *Of Widows and Meals*; Yoder, *Body Politics*, chap. 2.

be pure. Anyone at variance with his neighbor must not join you, until they are reconciled, lest your sacrifice be defiled. (14.1–2)[204]

This is what the feminist scholars A. Bieler and L. Schottroff call "*Eucharistic life* — a way of living with regard to food, body politics, economic exchange, and memory practices that flows out of liturgical practice." It is sacramental life deeply "embedded in micro- and macro-structures that shape individual bodies as much as they shape the global economy."[205] To help discover the meaning and significance of this kind of eucharistic life, they introduce the twin concepts of "sacramental permeability" and "eschatological imagination." The former concept refers to the many ways the physical matters (say, bread) and actions (say, eating) radiate and help make transparent the divine, the sacramental. "Sacramental worship embraces a permeability in which the bread we consume at our kitchen tables, the bread we steal from the poor, and the bread that is consecrated and consumed during Holy Communion are related." This may lead to conflict or harmony. The latter concept, eschatological imagination, means the experience of Christ's resurrection and eschatological consummation as a foretaste in the sacramental celebration. "Bodies in pain are and will be transformed into resurrected bodies at the table — bodies that are indeed the temple of the Holy Spirit (1 Cor. 3:16) abundantly filled with divine life." Bread that decays will be transformed into the bread of life, the bread of eternal life.[206]

A momentous shift in the conception of the Eucharist happened in later history, argues the Sri Lankan Catholic theologian and churchman Tissa Balasuriya in a provocative book from which the title for this section has been taken, *The Eucharist and Human Liberation*. Differently from Jesus, to whom what became the Christian Eucharist was "the supreme symbol of his self-offering unto death," the church fairly soon lost this concrete sharing and self-sacrifice aspect of the table and, instead, involved itself with endless speculations about the mode of Christ's presence and related theological issues.[207] Balasuriya wonders how it can be that during colonial times, once a week

204. I am indebted to Balasuriya, *The Eucharist and Human Liberation*, pp. 25–26; for other such early texts, see pp. 26–27.

205. Bieler and Schottroff, *The Eucharist*, p. 4. See also Hellwig, *The Eucharist and the Hunger of the World*; Grassi, *Broken Bread and Broken Bodies*.

206. Bieler and Schottroff, *The Eucharist*, pp. 4–7 (5, 6); for details on the eschatological imagination, see chap. 1.

207. Balasuriya, *The Eucharist and Human Liberation*, p. 33. See also the Latin American Catholic liberationist Juan Luis Segundo's *The Sacraments Today*.

those who colonized and those colonized were brought into the same place to share in the common bread and wine — European wine and bread baked according to the recipe of the old continent — "while the rape of these colonial countries was going on." How come this "domestication of the sacraments within the colonial system" could be tolerated by Christian missionaries?[208] Even more ironic, he continues, in the meantime, the most complex, minor doctrinal issues and liturgical arrangements were widely and heatedly debated in the homelands!

Eucharist and the Unity of Christian Communion

Throughout history — from the *Didache* (10.6), to the Middle Ages with its sophisticated penitential system, to the Pietist movements — the Pauline "unworthiness" ban on partaking of the Lord's Supper (1 Cor. 11:27) has been conceived in terms of moral lapses; even the Lutheran Confessions, despite their strict rejection of what they saw of the excesses of Rome's penitential practices, presupposed confession and absolution as the precondition.[209] Although there is no reason to deny the importance of minding one's moral and spiritual condition when approaching the Lord's Table, contemporary exegesis is unanimous that what Paul had in his mind when urging his hearers to discern "the body" (v. 29) had to do primarily with church unity. The celebrants are warned seriously not to split or divide the one church body. Hence, the advice about self-examination (v. 28) is less about scrutiny of one's own conscience as an individual person and more about paying attention to one's behavior and attitudes with regard to unity.[210]

That interpretation also brings to surface weighty ecumenical issues — keeping unity among all who wish to come to the table. In the words of Pannenberg, "When a celebration of the Supper does not preserve the fellowship with all who belong to Jesus Christ, there is an offense against the duty of fellowship that has its basis in the very nature of the Supper. Hence the urgent question arises whether the divisions in Christianity that manifest themselves in mutual or one-sided exclusion from the Lord's table are not to be regarded as offenses against the commandment of fellowship."[211] Not without reason,

---

208. Balasuriya, *The Eucharist and Human Liberation*, pp. 4–5 (5).
209. CA 25; *BC*, pp. 62–63.
210. See also Pannenberg, *ST* 3:326–28.
211. Pannenberg, *ST* 3:329.

then, a call has been issued to open the Eucharist to all Christians as long as they desire fellowship with the Lord and his people.[212]

Some go even further and, like Moltmann, call for a totally "open table," that is, not only are all Christians welcome but all people, whether of faith or not. His main argument is that it is Christ's meal, not the church's, and therefore, "[b]ecause he died for the reconciliation of 'the world,' the world is invited to reconciliation in the supper." That invitation would reach even non-Christians.[213] What to think of that? While it certainly is true that the Lord's Supper is the *Lord's* rather than the church's, that does not mean it should be opened indiscriminately to everyone. How, then, could it be a *memorial* of Christ? How could it embody the unity of *Christ's* body? How could it anticipate the gathering of Christians at the *Lamb's* festal banquet in the eschaton? There is not the slightest indication in the New Testament data to suggest that kind of openness. From the beginning, it was the meal for those who had publicly aligned their lives with Jesus. Baptism could and should be normally set as a prerequisite, as it has been from the beginning.[214] A certain theological interpretation of the meaning of the Lord's Supper, however, should not be made a condition as long as the guest intends to celebrate the Lord's meal.[215]

Finally, although there is no need to reject in principle the traditional belief in "concomitance," that is, the equal presence of Christ in *both* elements, it should not be interpreted in the way the medieval Latin Church did (of course building on a much older tradition), namely, withholding the cup from laypersons. Regretfully, the rightful demand by Luther to return both elements to the laity was a main item in the papal condemnation of the bull *Exsurge Domine* (1520). It took an amazingly long time for Rome to reinstate the ancient practice of serving wine and bread to all congregants, indeed until Vatican II.[216]

Having now reflected on the church's missional existence gathered around the gospel and sacraments in liturgy and worship, we highlight in the following chapter the missional nature of the church by looking specifically at her ministry.

---

212. Pannenberg, *ST* 3:329.
213. Moltmann, *The Church in the Power of the Spirit*, pp. 244-46 (246).
214. See, e.g., *Didache* 9.5.
215. In agreement with Pannenberg, *ST* 3:329-32.
216. For details and historical sources, see Pannenberg, *ST* 3:293-95.

18. Missional Existence as the Charismatic-Diaconal Ministry

The People of God as the Missional Minister

The Multidimensional Mission as the Church's Ministry

Constantly nurtured, sanctified, sustained, and empowered by prayerful liturgical-sacramental life as well as biblical study and preaching, the missional communion, shaped after the triune communion, graciously drawn to the sending of the Son by the Father in the power of the Spirit, is engaged in the manifold, diverse, and multilayered missional ministry, as established above (chap. 16):

- mission as evangelism and common witness
- mission as healing and restoration
- mission as social justice and equality
- mission as integrity and flourishing of nature
- mission as reconciliation and peace building
- mission as dialogue and interfaith engagement[1]

This is an interrelated and mutually conditioned network of dimensions and aspects of the missional community's ministry, integrally interwoven with

1. For useful listings of the tasks, see Bevans and Schroeder, *Constants in Context*, pp. 349–52. I greatly appreciate the authors' own listing of aspects of what they call "mission as prophetic dialogue," namely, witness and proclamation; liturgy, prayer, and contemplation; justice, peace, and the integrity of creation; interreligious dialogue; inculturation; and reconciliation (pp. 348–95).

sacramental-liturgical life. Ideally — although in practice rarely — each local communion, in communion with other communions, is engaged simultaneously in all these tasks. That said, for the sake of diversity and plurality, some local communions may major in one or a few aspects and others in other dimensions (without, however, dropping any of the tasks as far as the life conditions and context allow for it). For example, it is clear that a Christian communion in a war-stricken area may invest more time and efforts toward reconciliation, peace, justice, and healing, whereas a church placed on the borderline between various faiths is likely to concentrate more on dialogue.

Having discussed in much detail all the dimensions and tasks of the mission listed above (to which will be added in the last chapter the focused look at dialogue and interfaith engagement), we now ask who in the local communion ought to be doing this ministry. In other words, who are the ministers executing mission? The shorthand and foundational answer is this: the whole community serves as the minister. Even when tasks vary and some persons are dedicated to a lifelong and full-time ministry, everything is part of the common calling and vocation of the whole church.

The "Priesthood" of the Whole Community

According to the New Testament testimonies and teaching, the basis for all talk about ministry is "the common calling of all Christians to bear witness to Jesus Christ as salvation for all people. All are called and sent to give prophetic witness to the gospel of Jesus Christ, to engage together in worship of God, and to serve others."[2] Passages such as 1 Peter 2:9 make this clear, as it speaks of all Christians as "a chosen race, a royal priesthood, a holy nation, God's own people, that you may declare the wonderful deeds of him who called you out of darkness into his marvelous light."[3]

As established in the context of the doctrine of election (*Spirit and Salvation*, chap. 9), there is an integral link between divine calling, election, and sending for mission.[4] Thanks to election, in itself a trinitarian event, "Christian life is life in movement toward a goal. God not only justifies and sanctifies human life in the power of the Spirit but also gives it a particular vocation

---

2. Pannenberg, *ST* 3:372-73.

3. For a careful examination of this passage and relevant NT texts, see Muthiah, *Priesthood of All Believers*, pp. 6-16. A defining exegetical study is Schweizer, "Priesthood of All Believers." For a succinct recent theological look at issues, see Lakeland, "The Laity."

4. Suggested but not developed by Pannenberg, *ST* 3:438.

and a great hope. When this aspect of God's work of liberation and reconcil-iation is neglected, a certain narrowness and even narcissism creeps into the life of faith and the work of theology."[5] The connection between election and missionary calling of the people of God is of course evident already in the beginning of biblical history (Gen. 12:2-3).[6] With the vocational orientation we need to couple the empowering and charismatic nature of electing grace as the "empowering presence of the Holy Spirit."[7] To those called to new life and the mission of God to the world, charismatic gifting is also given with a view to making them fit for the vocation, a theme to be developed below.

The "priesthood" of all believers, which is well known but not always ac-curately understood, became a leading theological theme in Luther's theology.[8] He considered all Christians as sharing in Christ's royal and priestly offices.[9] In the programmatic early pamphlet *On Christian Freedom* (1520), Luther called all "who believe in Christ . . . priests and kings in Christ."[10] Differently from Catholic theology — including even Vatican II's *Lumen Gentium* (#10) — Luther's theology of ministry refused to grant any special status to minis-ters; they are merely set apart by the community for the community.[11] Other Reformers, like later Protestant movements, as well as Anabaptists, materially affirmed Luther's theology of the ministry of all.[12]

Despite all the differences between churches on issues of ministry, there is currently an important ecumenical consensus that the whole people of God are the ministers of the church.[13] Notwithstanding making ministry (ordina-tion) sacramental and thus in one sense separating the clergy qualitatively from the rest, even the Roman Catholic Church at Vatican II famously ex-panded and deepened the theology of the ministry to encompass the whole church.[14] In line with this, the Catholic-Lutheran statement *The Apostolicity of*

---

5. Migliore, *Faith Seeking Understanding*, p. 246.

6. For Christian life as "costly service," see Bonhoeffer, *The Cost of Discipleship*, p. 48.

7. Heading in Henderson, "Election as Renewal," p. 153.

8. Luther, *To the Christian Nobility of the German Nation* (1520), WA 6:407-10; LW 44:125-31.

9. Luther, *The Freedom of a Christian* (1520), WA 7:56-57; LW 7:354-55; see also Pan-nenberg, *ST* 3:373-74.

10. Luther, *On Christian Freedom*, LW 31:354; WA 7:56.37-38.

11. Luther, *The Babylonian Captivity* (1520), LW 36:113; WA 6:564.6-14.

12. For Calvin, Anabaptists, and later Protestant movements, see Muthiah, *Priesthood of All Believers*, pp. 19-22. For a contemporary free church (Baptist) view, see George, "Priest-hood of All Believers."

13. For the important missional implications and background debates and issues, see Bosch, *Transforming Mission*, pp. 467-74.

14. A highly formative work was the French Dominican Yves Congar's *Lay People in the*

the Church (2006) affirms "that all the baptized who believe in Christ share in the priesthood of Christ and are thus commissioned to 'proclaim the mighty acts of him who called you out of darkness into his marvelous light' (1 Pet. 2:9). Hence no member lacks a part to play in the mission of the whole body."[15] The ecumenical consensus document *Baptism, Eucharist and Ministry* (1982) makes a similar kind of statement: "The Church lives through the liberating and renewing power of the Holy Spirit. . . . The Spirit calls people to faith, sanctifies them through many gifts, gives them strength to witness to the Gospel, and empowers them to serve in hope and love."[16]

Behind the primacy of the priesthood of all believers is the idea of the nature of the church as the people of God. Notwithstanding different charisms and callings, there are no classes or hierarchies in the sense of compromising the equal status of all men and women regardless of sex, ethnicity, social status, or other human markers (Gal. 3:28). According to the New Testament, the "*whole* people, filled with the Spirit of Christ, becomes a priesthood set apart; all Christians are priests."[17] Differently from pagan cults and Judaism, there is direct access to God for all Christians. All of them are called to offer "spiritual sacrifices" as priestly people, including the preaching of the Word.

What about the administration of sacraments? It is clear without any debate that in the New Testament there are no restrictions: all baptized men and women have the right to baptize and serve the Lord's Supper. This is simply because what the entire church has the authority to do pertains to all members of the priestly people.[18] That most churches have in the course of history reserved the right to the ordained clergy may be justifiable for the reason of order,[19] but even then the New Testament teaching and practice should be kept in mind as the leading principle.[20] Concerning the royal status, Luther importantly opined, "every Christian is by faith so exalted above all things that, by virtue of a spiritual power, he is lord of all things without exception."[21] As

---

Church. It is highly significant that *Lumen Gentium* devoted a whole chapter (4) to the laity. See Rausch, *Towards a Truly Catholic Church*, pp. 27–29.

15. *The Apostolicity of the Church* (2006), #273, p. 10 (in Kasper, *HTF*, #50).

16. *BEM-M*, #3. See also Muthiah, *Priesthood of All Believers*, p. 46.

17. Küng, *The Church*, pp. 473–76 (475), emphasis in original.

18. In agreement with Küng, *The Church*, pp. 476–86.

19. So, e.g., CA 14.

20. For the first time in the *Didache*, the Lord's Supper is presided over by the leaders (and for the first time the meal is called a "sacrifice"; 14.1); see Küng, *The Church*, pp. 488–89.

21. Luther, *On Christian Freedom*, LW 31:354; WA 7:56.4–6.

a result, as "priests we are worthy to appear before God to pray for others and to teach one another divine things."[22]

Diaconal-Charismatic Ministry of the "Polycentric Community"

It is curious that the New Testament does not use any particular term equivalent to our term "ministry."[23] It seems to me we can learn something important about the "theology of ministry" by giving attention to that curious fact. Namely, the two terms used in the New Testament that come closest to "ministry" are highly informative about the distinctive features of what we call "ministry." The first one is "charism." For Paul (Rom. 12; 1 Cor. 12; 14; Eph. 4) and others (1 Pet. 4), a normal part of the church's worship and ministry is the exercise by the body of believers of various types of charisms, spiritual gifts. The second one is *diakonia*, "service." Indeed, Küng claims that the most unique way the New Testament describes ministry is with this term *diakonia*. Unlike other terms drawn from Greek secular or religious usage, which would imply privilege and special status, *diakonia* refers to the work of serving food and waiting at table, including at times also being responsible for managing food. It was a kind of service freed from all notions of glamour, despised by all free Greek citizens. In Jesus' teaching and example, it focuses on living for and serving others, even to the point of self-sacrifice.[24]

With the focus on lowly and unselfish service, following Küng, we may speak of the "diaconal structure" of the church as the template for church ministry and link it tightly with the charismatic structure of the church. Indeed, *diakonia* and *charisma* are mutually related and presuppose each other: "Diakonia is rooted in charisma, since every diakonia in the Church presupposes the call of God. Charisma leads to diakonia since every charisma in the Church only finds fulfillment in service."[25]

Miroslav Volf says the same when he sets forth the participatory principle of ministry: "The church lives through the participation of its members, that is, the laity and the office holders, and is constituted through them by the Holy Spirit."[26] This leads to a "polycentric community" model of the com-

---

22. Luther, *On Christian Freedom*, LW 31:355; WA 7:57.25-26. For comments and details, see Pannenberg, *ST* 3:126.

23. See Moltmann, *The Church in the Power of the Spirit*, p. 295.

24. Küng, *The Church*, pp. 497-502. See further Mette and Gardiner, *Diakonia*.

25. Küng, *The Church*, p. 502.

26. Volf, *After Our Likeness*, p. 222.

munion with the participation, gifting, and responsibility of all instead of the traditional "bipolar" model in which those in office do the church work and the laity observes.[27]

If charismatic endowment and diaconic service are taken as leading principles, then it becomes evident that whatever different types of assignments, ministries, and offices there might be in the church, they "only come into being by virtue of the common commissioning of the community itself." As a result, those people are not separated or isolated from the community but rather render service among the people and on their behalf.[28] It is also clear, following the New Testament testimonies and intuitions, that any commission, charge, or ministry can "be full-time or part time. They can be carried out by men and women, by the married and the unmarried, by the theologically trained and people without any theological training. They can be exercised by individuals and groups. None of these circumstances and aptitudes amount to a law."[29]

Lutheran ecclesiology, rightly in my mind, anchored the need for ordained ministers in the need to take care of the public ministry and order. Importantly, it presupposes a "general call" by the church.[30] In that sense — and only in that sense — as representatives of the church, ministers act *in persona Christi* (though never above it).

Yet another noteworthy contribution of the Protestant Reformation to the theology and practice of ministry is its emphasis on preaching and proclamation, as particularly in the medieval church the cultic function of the priest had taken over. Vatican II moved definitely in the same direction with a remarkable emphasis on proclamation.[31]

In light of the import of charismatic gifting and endowment for the church's mission, repeatedly mentioned so far, let us take a focused look at its meaning and nature before reflecting on missional structures and offices for the sake of ministry.

---

27. Volf, *After Our Likeness*, pp. 223–28 and passim. For the meaning of "laity" in the NT and its surroundings, see Muthiah, *Priesthood of All Believers*, p. 12 (and literature therein).

28. Moltmann, *The Church in the Power of the Spirit*, pp. 302–3 (302).

29. Moltmann, *The Church in the Power of the Spirit*, p. 308.

30. CA 14 (*BC*, p. 36): "It is taught among us that nobody should publicly teach or preach or administer the sacraments in the church without a regular call."

31. See, e.g., the emphasis on proclamation in the introduction of the priestly office in *Presbyterorum Ordinis*, #2; in #4 preaching is mentioned as "the primary duty"; and so forth. See also Pannenberg, *ST* 3:384.

The Charismatic Structure of the Church

The Church Is Charismatic

As distant as it may sound to most contemporary churches, "[f]or Paul the congregation is the place where the Spirit manifests itself (I Cor. 14) in an overflowing wealth of spiritual powers (charismata)";[32] the same charismatic experience continued to be vivid during the early centuries.[33] The term "charism" (from the Greek *charis*, "grace") is used loosely and nontechnically in the New Testament with reference to various types of charismatic endowments, giftings, and capabilities.[34] Many and various examples of charisms are given in the New Testament testimonies, from more extraordinary (miraculous works, words of wisdom, prophetic words) to fairly "mundane" (teaching, exhortation, giving generously), and it is clear that there is no fixed number of them.[35]

Indeed, in New Testament theology, everybody is a "charismatic," not just some![36] Hence, it is appropriate to speak of "the charismatic structure of the church."[37] Importantly, *Baptism, Eucharist and Ministry* materially says the same when speaking of the equipping of all men and women for ministry: the "Holy Spirit bestows on the community diverse and complementary gifts. These are for the common good of the whole people and are manifested in acts of service within the community and to the world."[38]

These charisms are gifts and energies of the Spirit.[39] Ultimately — in

32. Moltmann, *The Church in the Power of the Spirit*, p. 294. See also the important essay by the NT scholar Käsemann, *Essays on New Testament Themes*, pp. 63–94.

33. Speaking in tongues was well in use in the third century, as is evident in Irenaeus, *Against Heresies* 5.6.1. For other accounts of various charismatic experiences and listing of gifts in the church, see Tertullian, *A Treatise on the Soul* 9; Origen, *On First Principles* 2.7.3. The anonymous early writing (related to Tertullian) *The Passion of the Holy Martyrs Perpetua and Felicitas* is a collection of charismatic, ecstatic experiences and visions. For a number of other examples and textual evidence, see my *Spirit and Salvation*, chaps. 1–5.

34. Küng, *The Church*, pp. 247–48; see also Garijo-Guembe, *Communion of the Saints*, pp. 39–41.

35. For a highly useful detailed biblical-theological investigation, see M. Turner, "Spiritual Gifts Then and Now."

36. Moltmann, *The Church in the Power of the Spirit*, p. 296. See also Dussel, "Differentiation of Charisms."

37. Section title in Küng, *The Church*, pp. 236–50 (exactly: "The Continuing Charismatic Structure of the Church"); see also Volf, *After Our Likeness*, pp. 228–33; Haight, *CCH*, 1:116–18, 121–23.

38. *BEM-M*, #5.

39. So also Muthiah, *Priesthood of All Believers*, p. 68.

keeping with the trinitarian ecclesiology constructed in this project — it can be said that "the charisms bestowed by the Spirit on the people of God are a point of concrete trinitarian correspondence in the church. The nature of the Trinity is imprinted on the charisms."[40] Commensurately, the Spirit's charismatic work in the church is widely and deeply related to that of the risen Christ, in keeping with the promise of the Johannine Jesus (John 14 and 16). Indeed, "the exalted Christ himself is acting in the gifts of the Spirit," and Christ himself is present in the church also in the form of the gifts of the Spirit. No wonder Paul ties the charismatic energies and workings of the Spirit in 1 Corinthians 12 tightly with the confession of Christ's lordship (vv. 1–3) for the sake of the work of the united body of Christ (vv. 4–26).[41]

Charisms are not only for the individual believers, although they of course are that; they are first and foremost gifts for the whole church.[42] Importantly, Kilian McDonnell, OSB, reminds us that "the charisms of the Spirit play an indispensable role in the life of the Church because they create the shared faith consciousness of the Christian community."[43] In keeping with the focus on the whole church as the minister and in light of the charismatic gifting and endowment of all, it is clear that "there is no division between office bearers and the people."[44]

The marginal role and at times even omission of the topic of the charismatic in most contemporary systematic theological presentations of the doctrine of the church is inexcusable — and another sad testimony to the reductionism of the allegedly "critical" Western theological scholarship.[45] Just think of what is by any standard one of the most important and certainly most comprehensive Protestant systematic theologies of the church by the Lutheran Pannenberg: in a text of well over three hundred pages encompassing all possible aspects of ecclesiology, the index lists only a couple of passing references to charisms! The only two exceptions to this omission from the latter part of the twentieth century are the Catholic Küng's detailed discussion of charisms and the charismatic structure of the church in *The Church* (section C.II) and the Reformed theologian Moltmann's constant engagement of the topic not only in his ecclesiology, *The Church in the Power of the Spirit* (the long section

---

40. Muthiah, *Priesthood of All Believers*, p. 68.

41. Volf, *After Our Likeness*, pp. 228–29 (228). Käsemann, "Amt und Gemeinde im Neuen Testament."

42. See Laurentin, "Charisms."

43. McDonnell, "Communion Ecclesiology and Baptism in the Spirit," pp. 671–75.

44. Moltmann, *The Church in the Power of the Spirit*, p. 298.

45. See my *Spirit and Salvation*, chap. 12.

VI), but also in pneumatology (chap. 9, "The Charismatic Powers of Life," in *The Spirit of Life*), and to a smaller extent in other "contributions" to theology. The other theologians leave it to Pentecostals and charismatics to speak of spiritual gifts and charismatic manifestations with the mistaken implication that the topic does not belong to every church.

Christian communities that have followed more closely the ministry patterns present in the Pastoral Epistles have tended to prefer order over spontaneity, structures over improvisation, and the body of Christ metaphor over that of the temple of the Spirit. Those communities in the footsteps of the Pauline teaching for the Corinthian and Thessalonian congregations have sought a continuing, fresh experience of the charisms and spiritual manifestations. Without pitting these New Testament traditions against each other, it is vital for the church of the third millennium to rediscover the charismatic structure of the church and its integral link with the diaconic structures of ministry.

Taking the charismatic structure of the church as the starting point means that the Spirit, rather than human persons and committees, is the leader of the church. The Spirit's work is not set against or as an alternative to the church structures. Rather, it reminds us that any church and her structures need the constant invigorating, testing, and renewal of the Spirit: "Structure is essential to the life of the church and can provide effective conduits through which the Spirit might work. But while essential, church structure is in constant need of renewal because it always moves towards calcification and rigidity, which tries to contain the movement of the Spirit." Hence, the church should strive to promote "ecclesial structures that have enough freedom and opportunity in and around them to allow for the Spirit to work in an unrestricted manner."[46]

The Charismatic Workings of the Spirit in the Church

Three important principles can be drawn from the New Testament teachings and testimonies, particularly in Pauline literature.[47] First and foremost, the charisms are distributed and delivered by the sovereign Spirit of God, "who apportions to each one individually as he wills" (1 Cor. 12:11). This means that it is not the church, nor even bishops or other leaders, who dispense charisms

---

46. Muthiah, *Priesthood of All Believers*, p. 69.

47. I am following closely Volf, *After Our Likeness*, pp. 228-33; Küng, *The Church*, pp. 236-50; Muthiah, *Priesthood of All Believers*, pp. 70-73.

but the Spirit — and yet, according to the Pauline exhortation, it is right and appropriate to "earnestly desire the higher gifts" (v. 31).

Second, charisms are not only exceptional and sensational phenomena — although there are also those, including glossolalia, powerful works, exorcisms, and healings (1 Cor. 12 and 14; Acts 10:46; Mark 16:17) — but also everyday ministry energies and giftings, from giving and exhortation to helping and leading, from teaching and discernment of spirits to acts of mercy and administration (Rom. 12:7-8; 1 Cor. 12:8, 10; 1 Pet. 4:10-11). The main goal of both types of charisms is the common good of the church (1 Cor. 12:7).[48]

Charisms are not all of one type, but rather are diverse and plural. There is absolutely no definite or exhaustive list of gifts anywhere in the New Testament, but rather we find various types of descriptions, open-ended in nature (Rom. 12:6-8; 1 Cor. 12:28-31; Eph. 4:11-13; 1 Pet. 4:10-11). Volf speaks of two kinds of plurality: "synchronic," that is, the possibility of having several gifts at the same time, and "diachronic," which means that "[i]n contrast to calling, charismata in the theological sense of a combination of calling and endowment for a specific ministry in church and world not 'irrevocable' (Rom. 11:29)," but gifts may vary over time and replace others, as the Spirit chooses.[49]

Third, there is a universal distribution of charisms, as every Christian is charismatic (Rom. 12:3; 1 Cor. 12:7; Eph. 4:7; 1 Pet. 4:10). No members are without any charisms, although there might be some — perhaps many — who are yet to discern and acknowledge them. Hence, the principle of "common responsibility" for the life of the church. Christians ought to seek to use their gifts as best they can. Other important guidelines stem from this universal distribution, according to Paul: mutual subordination (Eph. 5:21), that is, all members should submit to each other, not only the laypeople to the leaders, in order to be ministered to and guided by the community. The other guideline is interdependence: while all have been gifted, not every one is gifted in all ways. Because the gifts to each person are different (Rom. 12:6), Paul's teaching about the functioning of the body in 1 Corinthians 12 is emphatic that each and every one be appreciated and everyone's contribution to others be acknowledged. This leads to a life of mutuality.

The community that lives in the power of the Spirit will be characterized by a variety of charisms. The Spirit is the giver of diverse gifts that enrich the life of the community. To enhance their effectiveness, the community will publicly recognize certain of these charisms. While some serve permanent

---

48. See the important teaching in *LG*, #12.
49. Volf, *After Our Likeness*, p. 233.

needs in the life of the community, others will be temporary. Men and women in the communities of religious orders fulfill a service that is of particular importance for the life of the church. The ordained ministry, which is itself a charism, must not become a hindrance to the variety of these charisms. On the contrary, it should help the community discover the gifts bestowed on it by the Holy Spirit and equip members of the body to serve in a variety of ways.[50]

Minding the common calling of the whole people of God and the charismatic endowment of every church member determines the kinds of governance and community structures appropriate for missional existence. This is the following topic, before we delve into the question of ordination and full-time ministry.

The Missional Organization of the Community Structures

If missional existence is the nature of ecclesial existence — and vice versa — that means ministry patterns, leadership models, administrative procedures, and other decisions concerning the structures of the community should be in the service of mission.[51] As C. Van Gelder aptly puts it, "the church organizes what it does."[52] As practical and hands-on as the question of structures is, ultimately it is a deeply *theological* and *ecclesiological* question. *The Nature and Mission of the Church* saw this clearly: "Therefore the visible organizational structures of the Church must always be seen and judged, for good or ill, in the light of God's gifts of salvation in Christ, celebrated in the Liturgy (cf. Heb 12:18–24)."[53] Rather than fixed patterns, Scripture clearly underdetermines instructions concerning structures and what we call polity.[54]

The missional orientation comes to the fore immediately in the New Testament. It is highly important to acknowledge the improvised and fluid emergence of church structures in the New Testament and early Christianity.[55]

---

50. *BEM-M*, #32.

51. Consult chap. 11 in Harper and Metzger, *Exploring Ecclesiology*.

52. Van Gelder, *The Essence of the Church*, p. 37; significantly, this principle is endorsed by the leading Catholic ecclesiologist Bevans, "Beyond the New Evangelization," p. 19. This order is wonderfully illustrated in the argument (and title) of Power, *Mission, Ministry, Order: Reading the Tradition in the Present Context*.

53. *NMC*, #45.

54. See Ensign-George, "Denomination as Ecclesiological Category," pp. 11–12.

55. For a detailed study, see Garijo-Guembe, *Communion of the Saints*, pp. 37–57; Hood, "Governance," pp. 536–49.

Just consider the long-term and still-continuing scholarly debates about the diverse list of "offices" and ministers in 1 Corinthians 12:28–29 alone: "And God has appointed in the church first apostles, second prophets, third teachers, then workers of miracles, then healers, helpers, administrators, speakers in various kinds of tongues. Are all apostles? Are all prophets? Are all teachers? Do all work miracles?"[56]

Even in the latter part of the New Testament, routinely named "early Catholicism," the organizational structures are still flexible.[57] Along with the simple need in the church (as evinced in the selection of the first deacons in Acts 6),[58] the unity of and need to care for the fledgling communities seemed to have been the major catalyst behind the appointment of leaders.[59] In that sense, Lutheran ecclesiology's refusal to endorse any particular kind of ministry pattern or church structure[60] is in keeping with the New Testament witness, whereas both the Catholic insistence on divinely sanctioned offices and the Reformed, as well as Baptist, ecclesiology's claim for a specific kind of biblical mandate for offices and structures are unfounded.[61] On this basis, the in-many-ways highly useful discussion of ministry and ordination in *Baptism, Eucharist and Ministry*, with its assumption that in practice the traditional threefold office structure of bishop, pastor/priest, and deacon should be normative,[62] does not do justice to either the biblical diversity or the complexity of historical evolvement; neither does it honor the widening plurality and diversity of the global church. What matters is the theological judgment by the community as to which structures in the given religio-cultural and societal context best facilitate missional ministry.

That said, historically it is undisputed that as early as the second century the office of the bishop — and a fairly straightforward three-tiered ministry, with priests and deacons as assistants — emerged.[63] As is well known, Ignatius of Antioch played an important role in the rise of the episcopacy, which he saw

---

56. For debates and literature, see Dunn, *The Theology of Paul the Apostle*, pp. 566–71.

57. Consult Dunn, *Unity and Diversity in the New Testament*, pp. 106–7.

58. So also Haight, *CCH*, 1:194.

59. MacDonald, *The Pauline Churches*, p. 203, cited in Haight, *CCH*, 1:84.

60. CA 7.3 (*BC*, p. 32).

61. For the Catholic tradition, see, e.g., twenty-third session of Trent (1563; Schaff, *Creeds*, 2:186–94). On the Reformed side, Calvin, *Institutes of the Christian Religion* 4.3.1; for the Baptists, see Smyth, *Principles and Inferences*, p. 252.

62. *BEM*-M, part III.

63. Among other early shapers of the episcopacy and related ministries were Irenaeus, Justin Martyr, Hippolytus, Tertullian, and Cyprian; for details, see Haight, *CCH*, 1:148–76; for an extended study of Cyprian's views, see also pp. 182–85.

first and foremost as the needed instrument for ensuring unity with regard to internal struggles, not least related to the still-developing self-identity and leadership problems, as well as external challenges.[64] The central tasks given to the bishop included presiding over the liturgy, particularly the Eucharist, teaching, and governance, and that assignment has continued throughout history.[65]

Notwithstanding the need to honor flexibility and diversity, in light of this early emergence of the episcopal office, it is theologically appropriate to hold a special place for it within the ministerial structuring. That acknowledgment, however, should not lead to attempts to establish an appeal to any kind of (semi)technical understanding of apostolic succession in terms of historical continuity with the first apostles. In light of contemporary scholarship, that claim cannot be supported at all.[66] Furthermore, we do not yet have a firm knowledge of the extent that our contemporary conception of the bishop corresponds to the early episcopacy, as that undoubtedly had its origin in ministry to the local church, even when bishops' influence and ministry also took them beyond that one community.[67]

A highly important ministerial-structure decision, theologically-ecclesiologically speaking, is the setting apart of some members of the communion for full-time ministry, or other special category of ministry, usually called ordained. That will be the topic of the last section of the chapter; it will focus especially on integrating the theology of ordination widely and deeply within the ministry of the whole communion. This discussion also seeks to make a strong appeal for an inclusive understanding of ordination, that is, that both men and women have access to all ministerial tasks.

Ordained Ministers in the Service of the Community

The Missional Reassessment of the Nature and Role of the Ordained Ministry

As argued, the question of structures and organization is a theological issue. With some justification, M. Volf contends, "an entire ecclesiology is always reflected in a certain understanding of office, that is, of what officeholders are

64. Just consult Ignatius, *To the Philadelphians* (particularly 1–4) and *To the Magnesians* (particularly 3–7).
65. For details, see Haight, *CCH*, 1:153–54.
66. Similarly the Catholic Haight, *CCH*, 1:193.
67. Consult Küng, *The Church*, pp. 510–28; Pannenberg, *ST* 3:377–82.

to do in the church and how they are to become officeholders."[68] With that theological criterion in mind, we have to assess also the historical developments of patterns of ministry.

Although, as is well known, the term "priest" in the New Testament is not applied to any specific persons (except for Christ) but rather to all Christians,[69] as early as the time of Tertullian, priests as ordained persons are mentioned along with bishops, presbyters, and deacons.[70] On how the presbyter developed into the priest, we do not know enough details; suffice it to say that only after Nicea (325) did that office become established firmly.[71] From the second- or third-century manual *The Apostolic Tradition* (routinely attributed to Hippolytus), we can gather that at the time a fairly organized structure was in place with "procedures of initiation, the ordination of ministers and their functions, Eucharistic celebration, the agape meal, and a regime of prayer." It is of course left to later Christians to decide if this is prescriptive and normative or merely descriptive.[72]

With much justification Luther was troubled about the way the theology and practice of the priesthood had developed in his former church. He refused to include ordination as a sacrament not only because in his understanding there was no promise of grace attached to it in the New Testament,[73] but also — polemically — because he found the contemporary view of ordination into a sacrificial priesthood repulsive to evangelical faith.[74] It is clear in light of the New Testament teaching that Luther's rejection of a sacrificial priesthood was correct.[75] At the same time, Luther did not of course reject ordination per se. Furthermore, he was also right about making the laying on of hands the main ordination rite, following the New Testament pedigree (1 Tim. 4:14).[76] Indeed,

68. Volf, *After Our Likeness*, p. 221.

69. Faivre, *Emergence of the Laity*, p. 7; see also the detailed discussion in Küng, *The Church*, pp. 466-73; see also Muthiah, *Priesthood of All Believers*, p. 17.

70. Rankin, *Tertullian and the Church*, p. 163.

71. Bernier, *Ministry in the Church*, pp. 58-81; Haight, *CCH*, 1:195-96.

72. Haight, *CCH*, 1:161.

73. Luther, *The Babylonian Captivity of the Church*, WA 6:560.20-23; *LW* 36:106. But interestingly, Melanchthon was more open to it in the Apology of the Augsburg Confession, 13.7-11 (*BC*, p. 212); see Pannenberg, *ST* 3:396.

74. The Ecumenical Council of Florence: "Receive the power of offering sacrifice in the church for the living and the dead."

75. So also Pannenberg, *ST* 3:393-94.

76. Luther, *Concerning the Ministry*, WA 12:191.23-34; *LW* 40:37. Laying on of hands as a way of setting apart for ministry is common in Acts; a defining passage historically is 1 Tim. 4:14. For the biblical witness of laying on hands, see the detailed discussion in Warkentin,

it is deplorable that the medieval church did not consider laying on of hands, which also has a long Old Testament history, suitable and valid for ordination; astonishingly, it took until the mid-twentieth century for Catholic ecclesiology to acknowledge it as a proper sign.[77]

Although it is common particularly in Catholic ecclesiology to speak of the office as a form of charism, biblically and theologically it is more useful to make a distinction but not a separation between them. For an appointment into a certain office, charisms are given by the Spirit of God for equipping and power. In a particular office, the minister exercises various charisms she or he has received from God.[78] Furthermore, I think it is best not to make any kind of categorical distinctions between charisms meant as an aid for a certain office, say, bishop or deacon, and charisms among laypersons.[79]

Ordination as the Divine-Human Commissioning and Gifting

Placing the ordained ministry within the missional communion rather than over it or separate from it honors the mutuality principle that I take as a leading ordination theological guideline. *Baptism, Eucharist and Ministry* puts it well:

> All members of the believing community, ordained and lay, are interrelated. On the one hand, the community needs ordained ministers. Their presence reminds the community of the divine initiative, and of the dependence of the Church on Jesus Christ, who is the source of its mission and the foundation of its unity. They serve to build up the community in Christ and to strengthen its witness. In them the Church seeks an example of holiness and loving concern. On the other hand, the ordained ministry has no existence apart from the community. Ordained ministers can fulfil their calling only in and for the community.[80]

Ordination, pp. 109–56; for theological and ecclesiological implications, see also Muthiah, *Priesthood of All Believers*, pp. 75–77; Grenz, *Theology for the Community of God*, pp. 564–65.

77. See Pope Pius XII's 1947 encyclical *Mediator Dei*, ##40, 43, etc.; this whole section is indebted to Pannenberg, *ST* 3:393–97.

78. In agreement with Muthiah, *Priesthood of All Believers*, pp. 77–78.

79. Contra Volf, *After Our Likeness*, pp. 246–47, and in agreement with Muthiah, *Priesthood of All Believers*, pp. 79–80.

80. *BEM-M*, #12; see also #44. Materially similar is Muthiah, *Priesthood of All Believers*, p. 82.

This is to say that "ordination denotes an action by God and the community by which the ordained are strengthened by the Spirit for their task and are upheld by the acknowledgment and prayers of the congregation."[81] Hence, ordination at the same time is a "public reception of a charisma given by God and focused on the local church as a whole . . . [and] an act of the entire local church led by the Spirit of God."[82]

In summary, we can list the following interrelated aspects and effects of ordination:

- the reception of the gift of the Spirit (1 Tim. 4:14; 2 Tim. 1:6-7)[83]
- public commissioning (Acts 13:3)
- the acknowledgment of God's gifting and calling in the ordained person's life
- the commissioning of the person by the local church
- the mutual commitment between the community and the ordained
- the public declaration to the world outside the church, as the minister will minister in and to the world[84]

The reason Protestant Reformers were cautious about speaking of the conferring of a "gift" in the rite of ordination, notwithstanding the biblical references that have been traditionally connected with ordination (1 Tim. 4:14; 2 Tim. 1:6), was that Trent used it as a basis for calling ordination a sacrament. As long as the gift was understood as the reception of the gift of the Holy Spirit rather than as something in the nature of an "indelible mark" and thus related to the function rather than the person of the minister, the Reformers could affirm it.[85] That conception of the gift is biblically and theologically sustainable.

Although the New Testament has no definite ministry patterns to endorse, no more than it endorses particular forms of governance, it is clear about what it takes and means to be the holder of a church office: rather than above the people of God in their own category, ministers are but cobelievers, and rather than dignitaries to be served, they are servants willing to minister

---

81. *BEM*-M, #40.

82. Volf, *After Our Likeness*, p. 249; so also *BEM*-M, #42.

83. Thus, the act of ordination should include *epiklesis*, the prayer for the Spirit (as recommended by *BEM*-M, #42).

84. I am indebted to Volf, "Systematic Theology III"; I also wish to acknowledge Pannenberg, *ST* 3:397-99.

85. For details and sources, see Pannenberg, *ST* 3:397-98.

to others.[86] All appeals to superiority over others are totally foreign to the biblical teaching (see Mark 9:33–35; 10:42–45; and par.).[87]

An Inclusive Theology and Practice of Ordination

On the Conditions and Context of an Inclusive Ordination Theology. Although there have existed deeply negative attitudes toward women in Christian history,[88] which are alive and well even in contemporary churches, only a few women theologians have gone as far as urging women to withdraw (at least for the time being) from the male-dominated churches.[89] Instead, a growing number of women are looking for a more inclusive, affirmative way of conceiving the Christian community and her ministry.[90] While the place of women in the church touches wider issues than just ministry and ordination, these two stand at the heart of contemporary discussions.

Orthodox and Catholic churches — joined by a number of the most conservative Protestant churches, such as many Baptist and some Lutheran churches — do not allow female ordination, whereas Anglican and most mainline Protestant churches do.[91] Linked with the blocking of ordination for half of the church members, a cluster of traditional orientations in theology and ecclesiastical practices continues to hinder an inclusive theology of ordination. These include the support for patriarchal top-down structures dominated by males,[92] a strongly biased androcentric writing of church history,[93] and so forth.

As an important theological call for churches to open up to inclusivity, I find highly useful the late American Reformed feminist L. Russell's celebrated *Church in the Round*, which utilizes the symbolism of the table to create new

86. So also Küng, *The Church*, p. 465.

87. See further *BEM*-M, ##15, 16.

88. Schüssler Fiorenza, *Discipleship of Equals*, pp. 19–22.

89. Ruether, *Women-Church*.

90. L. Russell, *Church in the Round*, p. 11; for Asian women's experiences, see Pui-lan, "Women and the Church."

91. Understandably — but regretfully — the in-many-ways innovative and bold *Baptism, Eucharist and Ministry* document leaves open the question of women's ordination. All other appeals for inclusivity and for the church to better minister to women sound shallow (see *BEM*-M, #318).

92. For details, see Schüssler Fiorenza, *Discipleship of Equals*, chaps. 15 and 17.

93. A good case in point is Schüssler Fiorenza, *Discipleship of Equals*, chap. 11, which unpacks the use of "father" in early Christianity.

images of the church by employing the common cultural image of hospitality. So much in the home happens around the kitchen table, and some of the most precious memories go back to table fellowship. Table represents inclusivity.

An inclusive understanding of ministry takes it for granted that both the reception and the recognition of God's gifting for ministry apply to women and men alike. Consequently, at the heart of the issue is not only the insistence on the right of ordination for women but also a revision of the whole concept of ordination.[94]

In patriarchal styles of leadership, authority is exercised by standing above in the place of power. Feminist styles of leadership draw their model from a partnership paradigm that is oriented toward community formation. In feminist styles of leadership, authority is exercised by standing with others and seeking to share power and authority. Power is seen as something to be multiplied and shared rather than accumulated at the top. In this search for a new approach to leadership in the church, feminist ecclesiologists are again drawing from the example of Jesus, who literally turned the tables.[95]

The inclusive and hospitable vision of the communion would help us imagine an inclusive theology of ordination. Notwithstanding the sad history of blocking ministry opportunities for women, recent history has uncovered significant examples of precedents of ministry opportunities for women throughout the church's existence,[96] most probably also including some women's access to the ordained office here and there. In his groundbreaking recent study, *The Hidden History of Women's Ordination: Female Clergy in the Medieval West*, Gary Macy contends that "[t]here is no question that women were considered to have been ordained by a large number of Christians over several centuries."[97] That includes those women presiding over the Eucharist. Of course, the counterargument insists that, although those kinds of memories and records cannot be erased, this is not about "real" ordinations.[98] While I have to leave it to historical scholars to pursue both the historical records and

94. I found highly useful two essays by Watson, "Reconsidering Ecclesiology" and "Faithful Dissenters?"

95. L. Russell, *Church in the Round*, chap. 2: "Leadership in the Round." Still formative is also the short essay by Schüssler Fiorenza, *Discipleship of Equals*, chap. 5.

96. Schüssler Fiorenza, *Discipleship of Equals*, chap. 3.

97. Macy, *Hidden History of Women's Ordination*, p. 4; for a critical assessment of earlier studies, see pp. 8–21. See also the important formative work of Schüssler Fiorenza, *In Memory of Her*.

98. Macy, *Hidden History of Women's Ordination*, p. 5; for engaging that argument, see pp. 15–17.

their setting in the theological-ecclesiological understanding of their time, these indications of an inclusive view should be remembered and appreciated.

Typical Arguments against Women's Ordination — and Why They Fail. Having acknowledged that women have played a decisive role in the life of the church and accomplished tasks of outstanding value, the (in)famous 1976 Catholic document *Inter Insigniores*[99] lists a number of reasons why the Roman Catholic Church does not ordain women: first, "[t]he Catholic Church has never felt that priestly or episcopal ordination can be validly conferred on women"; second, neither Christ nor the apostles "ordained" and commissioned women, but rather men, and these actions are *normative* and not subject to historical relativity; third, only with regard to men is there the "'natural resemblance' which must exist between Christ and his minister," as the minister represents Christ, whose incarnation "took place according to the male sex."[100] Furthermore, the document notes, there is no confusing the calling and access to priesthood; despite a genuine calling to ministry for many women, no "individual can of itself give access to it [ordination]: it is of another order." Having acknowledged the diversity of interpretations concerning contested New Testament passages and the presence of sociocultural influences in theological considerations, the document reaches a final conclusion that only male ordination is legitimate and is the normative divine plan for the church.

This widely debated Catholic rebuttal of female ordination includes many of the most typical biblical and historical-traditional arguments presented among the traditions opposing female ordination. For the sake of clarity, let us divide them into three broad categories: (1) biblical-exegetical (focused on well-known New Testament passages seemingly barring women from ministry: 1 Cor. 11:3–16; 14:34–35; 1 Tim. 2:11–15); (2) traditional-historical (related to the beliefs about the lack of access of women to ministry during history); and (3) anthropological/gender-related assumptions (based on conceptions of women's nature and role in Christian theological understanding).[101]

Since all these and related arguments in favor of exclusive male ordination have been so thoroughly investigated and rebutted in contemporary theological scholarship — which in turn has opened access to ministry for women among most Protestant and Anglican-Episcopalian communities (except for fundamentalist-oriented ones) — I will give the shortest possible response and

99. Sacred Congregation, *Inter Insigniores*.

100. Materially similar argumentation can be found, e.g., in Mascall, "Some Basic Considerations," p. 23; so also Archbishops' Council, *Women Bishops in the Church of England?* p. 139; I am indebted to Cornwall, "Sex Otherwise," pp. 24–25.

101. This structure is present, e.g., in Stroda, "Ordination of Women."

point further to some major resources. Indeed, I simply take female ordination for granted in this constructive ecclesiology. Or, to be more precise, I assume an inclusive view of ordination for Christian ministry; that is, both men and women may be ordained in any ecclesiastical office.

Concerning the alleged biblical prohibitions, exegetes and theologians have presented the following types of counterarguments and rebuttals that — if not absolutely convincing one by one — seriously undermine their credibility as a whole and, indeed, have convinced the supporters of the inclusive view:

- The equality in Christ of both men and women is a central affirmation (Gal. 3:28).
- The gifts of the Spirit have been promised for both men and women (Joel 2:28–29; Acts 2:17–18).
- The hermeneutics of passages used to prohibit female ordination in the New Testament (particularly in 1 Cor. 11 and 14, as well as 1 Tim. 2) have been successfully defeated with reference to lack of authenticity, cultural conditioning of texts, the occasional nature of prohibitions, translation alternatives, and so forth.
- The presence of female leaders in the New Testament such as Lydia (Acts 16:40), the four daughters of Philip (Acts 21:9), Priscilla (Acts 18:18; Rom. 16:3), Euodia and Syntyche (Phil. 4:2–3), among others, is established.[102]
- Furthermore, the appeal to the precedent of twelve apostles lost its scholarly credibility long ago; this is even acknowledged by some Catholic critics of their own church.[103]
- We have to agree with the feminist theologians that the gender of Jesus is not a problem; the way Jesus' maleness is used in tradition to establish hierarchy, exclusivity, and power structures is the problem.[104]

The minimal conclusion by those who continue supporting exclusion of women should be that since arguments in favor of their position are nonconclusive at their best, the matter should at least be left inconclusive, that is, open for continuing discussion.[105] Although that conclusion is too little for the current project, it would at least make it possible to continue constructive proposals.

---

102. Any major critical commentary can be consulted for details of exegesis and hermeneutics, including arguments pro and con; for wider considerations of issues, see the literature mentioned in this chapter.

103. Schüssler Fiorenza, *Discipleship of Equals*, chap. 8.

104. See E. Johnson, *She Who Is*, pp. 151–52.

105. Cardman, "Non-conclusive Arguments," pp. 92–97.

As argued in this project, the question of ordination and ministry should be placed in the wider context of the equality, inclusivity, and hospitality of the Christian communion vision: "Where Christ is present, human barriers are being broken. The Church is called to convey to the world the image of a new humanity. There is in Christ no male or female (Gal. 3:28). Both women and men must discover together their contributions to the service of Christ in the Church."[106] As Pannenberg convincingly argues, although inequalities typical of this world are not erased per se, among all the baptized in the Christian communion, these earthly limitations and blockages "are transcended by the mutuality of human relations grounded in the love of Christ."[107] He continues with an important theological note: "We have here a fundamental matter for Christians that is of more than ordinary significance for the liberation of women to equal dignity with men and also for debate with other religions. By setting aside distinctions that otherwise divide people our eschatological determination for fellowship in the kingdom of God declares itself in the church's life. The exclusion of women from the church's ordained ministry for what are now outdated reasons does not sit well with this principle."[108] This project couldn't agree more with that wise counsel!

Although the unity of the church has been a recurring theme in the discussion so far, it is so essential as to deserve a chapter of its own. Like everything else in ecclesial existence, it is deeply and widely connected with mission as well. Indeed, as will be detailed below, lack of unity may be the more serious challenge to the church's missional existence.

106. *BEM*-M, #18.
107. Pannenberg, *ST* 3:390.
108. Pannenberg, *ST* 3:390-91.

19. Missional Existence as the Pursuit of the Diversified and Plural Unity of the Church

The Task and Landscape in the Search for the Unity of the Church

A Trinitarian Vision of Diversified Unity

Any credible and energetic work on the continuing healing of divisions and working for the unity of the church has to acknowledge honestly that "[f]or the first time . . . the scandal of divided Christendom has reached such a head that it has become intolerable for the faith consciousness of countless modern Christians." Rightly, Pannenberg raises this important question: "How can we recognize and treat one another as Christian brothers and sisters united by faith in the one Lord and its trinitarian exposition in the church, yet at the same time say nothing about full communion with one another?"[1] Promisingly, the same spirit of honesty and desire to engage were evident in the recent evangelical mission gathering in Cape Town, South Africa; often considered to be interested merely in "spiritual unity" at the cost of concrete ecumenical labor, the declaration stated: "We lament the dividedness and divisiveness of our churches and organizations. We deeply and urgently long for Christians to cultivate a spirit of grace and to be obedient to Paul's command to 'make every

---

1. Pannenberg, *ST* 3:411. The highlighting of current urgency is not to naively imagine that divisions are in any way a new phenomenon; indeed, diversity and divisions have been there from the very beginning, indeed already in the NT (Gooder, "In Search of the 'Early Church,'" p. 23). It is rather the size of the Christian religion and the plurality of the world that make the current situation unprecedented historically.

effort to maintain the unity of the Spirit in the bond of peace.'"[2] Indeed, so much is at stake with the issue of divisions and unity that only "[if] Christians succeed in solving the problems of their own pluralism, they may be able to produce a model combining pluralism and the widest moral unity which will also be valid for political life."[3]

Faced with this painful reality and urgent mandate, we should recall that the Christian church — each local communion in communion with other communions — shaped after the triune communion and drawn graciously into the sending of the Son by the Father in the power of the Spirit for the salvation of the world, anticipates the final gathering of all God's people in the new Jerusalem under one God. This eschatological gathering will consist of a ransomed people "from every tribe and tongue and people and nation" (Rev. 5:9). This means that the ultimate vision for the unity of God's people will be unity characterized by diversity and plurality — without divisions, tensions, and strife pertinent to even the best attempts for oneness on this side of the eschaton. Hence, the somewhat counterintuitive expression in the chapter title: "The Diversified and Plural Unity of the Church." That diversified unity is based on the plurality in the triune God as established above (chap. 13 and passim).[4] It opens up the path toward the vision of the ecumenical movement "as a conciliar fellowship of local churches which are themselves truly united. In this conciliar fellowship each local church possesses, in communion with the others, the fullness of catholicity, witnesses to the same apostolic faith and therefore recognizes the others as belonging to the same Church of Christ and guided by the same Spirit."[5]

With this trinitarian/eschatological communion ecclesiology as the guide and framework, we devote this chapter to deepening our understanding of and commitment to seeking the oneness of Christ's church — before, in the last chapter, we dialogue with other religions and their claims for the community. Writing as we are in the beginning of the third millennium, with the results and insights of the first century of the modern ecumenical move-

---

2. Lausanne Movement, *The Cape Town Commitment*, II.F.1.a.

3. Pannenberg, "Christian Morality and Political Issues," p. 38.

4. See also *NMC*, ##60-63; materially similar is the leading American ecumenist Michael Kinnamon, *Vision of the Ecumenical Movement*, p. 5. While enthusiastically endorsing the trinitarian orientation in the provocative proposal of Ingle-Gillis, *The Trinity and Ecumenical Church Thought*, this project also refuses to follow its conclusion according to which, therefore, any attempt for (visible) unity between denominations is futile and counterproductive.

5. WCC, "Concepts of Unity and Models of Union." See also the highly informative and insightful discussion in Saarinen, "Concept of Communion in Ecumenical Dialogues."

ment behind us (heuristically beginning after the 1910 Edinburgh Missionary Conference), the continuing deep visions of the global church facing us, and unprecedented new challenges and opportunities lying ahead of us, we cover three interrelated tasks:

1. to attempt a critical and sympathetic assessment of where we are currently with regard to the work toward the unity of the church
2. to highlight the impending and urgent theological and ecumenical tasks for today
3. to envision new resources and emerging opportunities for the sake of the globalized church as well as the secular and religiously plural(istic) world

Unity in Mission — Mission in Unity

Before we proceed, we should remember the deep and integral connection of unity with mission, as evinced so clearly in the emergence of the modern ecumenical movement.[6] Theologically, that connection has been established in this project over and over again. Just recall these shorthand statements: the church is drawn into the mission of the triune God, whose ultimate purpose is the reconciliation of the world and final gathering of God's people under one God in the new Jerusalem. As a result, the church is missionary by her very nature, and therefore, not only her liturgical and ministerial existence but also her very calling — as the anticipation of the eschatological gathering of one people, diverse as it may be — is rooted in God-given unity and its search on this side of the eschaton. Unity is not something we humans create; it is a gift of God.[7] As established in the context of the "marks" of the church, unity as gift is also a task for us; the Christian communion seeks to become unified because it is made one.

Birthed by the enthusiasm of the 1910 Edinburgh Missionary Conference, the initial vision for the unity of Christ's church was fueled by the "practical" missionary need to collaborate and remove obstacles, including questions of ethics and reconciliation. The Life and Work movement, beginning the

---

6. Bosch, *Transforming Mission*, p. 460. See also WCC, "Mission and Evangelism in Unity Today," pp. 59–89.

7. For a fine recent discussion, see Kinnamon, *Vision of the Ecumenical Movement*, chap. 1; see also O'Gara, *Ecumenical Gift Exchange*.

following decade, also embodied the first phase of the modern ecumenical movement. This first stream can be called "ecumenism of life." As important as it is, in itself it hardly yet results in visible unity. Hence, in the second stage of the emergence of the modern ecumenical movement, it was further guided since 1927 by the Faith and Order movement, which concentrated on doctrinal and ecclesiological issues and can thus be named the "ecumenism of truth" or "ecumenism of dialogue."[8]

Since the beginning, the lofty goal of the ecumenical movement has been to "proclaim the oneness of the Church of Jesus Christ and to call the churches to the goal of visible unity in one faith and one Eucharistic fellowship, expressed in worship and in common life in Christ, in order that the world may believe."[9] In the 1948 founding of the World Council of Churches,[10] this vision was commonly accepted as the shared goal.[11] Standing in the widening river of these (and related) streams, the current ecumenical movement in the beginning of the third millennium lives the third phase, with several emerging paradigms as aids toward a fuller unity, as will be discussed in this chapter. Though constantly debated as to nuances and emphases, the tight link between unity and mission still lies at the movement's heart. Recall the wise words of D. Bosch: "Since mission and unity belong together, we may not view them as consecutive stages; if this is not consistently kept in mind, we would only be converting people to our own 'denomination' while at the same time administering to them the poison of division." Indeed, he adds importantly: "It is through the universality of the gospel it proclaims that the church becomes missionary." The conclusion thus is inevitable: "Therefore, to claim — as some do — that the ecumenical age has now taken the place of the age of mission, is to misunderstand both; and to neglect one of the two is to lose both."[12]

Now, after this crucial reminder of the integral link of unity with mission and mission with unity, let us attempt a brief look at where this search for the unity is in the beginning of this millennium.

8. This nomenclature is from P. Murray, "Introducing Receptive Ecumenism," p. 2.

9. Faith and Order Commission, "Faith and Order By-Laws, 3.1," p. 450; for its importance, note the inclusion of the passage in the beginning of *NMC* (#1).

10. For a number of initiatives and developments prepared for the coming into existence of the contemporary ecumenical movement, see Saarinen, "Ecumenism," pp. 263–69.

11. This was again affirmed in the 1997 statement *Towards a Common Understanding and Vision of the WCC*, #1.

12. Bosch, *Transforming Mission*, p. 460.

On Different Perceptions of the Unity among Church Traditions

The somewhat technical-sounding expression "models of unity" means "statements of the nature and form of the full visible unity of the church, which is the final goal of the ecumenical movement."[13] As mentioned, visible unity is the stated goal of the ecumenical movement. That said, no one (at the moment at least) knows or has the authority to formulate in any authoritative manner what that might imply. That is why there are various — take them either as competing or complementary — notions of what that unity may imply. All ecumenists agree that visible unity means more than a mere generic acknowledgment of "spiritual unity," as important as that in itself is (the idea that all believers throughout the ages belong to the one and same body of Christ).

All ecumenists also agree — against common misconceptions and "rumors" — on what visible unity does not entail: no credible vision of visible unity in the modern ecumenical movement has ever meant canceling out denominational markers (unless, as in some uniting church processes, that has been agreed to out of a common desire to form one new body — another "denomination"); nor does it mean an effort to eradicate distinctive features between different traditions; and, needless to say, visible unity has nothing to do with the caricature of a "world church" taking over other churches. Those and related misconceptions about the goal of the ecumenical movement are not worth discussing further. Highly useful, in contrast, for the sake of assessing how far ecumenical work has advanced and what are the urgent tasks, is to attempt a brief but comprehensive look at the models of unity and their usefulness.[14]

The effort to discern the Eastern Orthodox Church's "model of unity" is highly challenging due to the scarcity of official pronouncements (similar to the hesitancy of this church family to provide doctrinal definitions in general). What is clear is that schism is taken as a grave problem, on the one hand, and, on the other hand, that the church itself is confident it stands in the unbroken line of the apostolic tradition and church.[15] With-

---

13. N. Lossky et al., eds., *Dictionary of the Ecumenical Movement*, p. 1041; for details, consult L. Fuchs, *Koinonia and the Quest*, pp. 53-68.

14. This section draws directly from my recent essay "Growing Together in Mission," which utilizes chap. 7 of my *Introduction to Ecclesiology*. For supporting sources, see Meyer, *That All May Be One*, pp. 15-36. I am also indebted to Saarinen, *Johdatus Ekumeniikkaan*, pp. 81-110, 113-21.

15. See the statement of the Third Pan-Orthodox Pre-Conciliar Conference, 1968.

out recognition of the apostolic succession and, related, the sacramental priesthood, the Orthodox are hardly able or willing to proceed in full mutual recognition.[16]

No other church has defined as carefully and publicly its model of unity than the Roman Catholic Church. Recall that "[t]he restoration of unity among all Christians" was "one of the principal concerns" of Vatican II.[17] Along with the Orthodox, Catholics affirm only one church of Christ on the earth. Importantly, *Lumen Gentium* helped correct and balance three issues for better facilitating the search for unity. First of all, rather than considering the church as the "perfect society" (after Vatican I), it imagines the church as a "pilgrim people" on the way, not yet arrived.[18] Second, rather than equating the church of Christ with the Catholic Church, it teaches that Christ's church "subsists in the Catholic Church,"[19] leaving open the possibility of the same for other Christian communities.[20] Third, although the council affirmed that the church "is necessary for salvation,"[21] it also famously set forth the most comprehensive and inclusive vision of the levels with which other Christians and even followers of other faith traditions may be linked to the Catholic Church. Of other Christians with whom the Catholic Church shares so much in common, from its Scriptures to the triune God to the sacraments, it says, "in many ways she is linked with those who, being baptized, are honored with the name of Christian."[22] What remains a grave challenge to other communities is that even though the Vatican I mentality of the "return of separated brethren" was qualified by Vatican II, it still is part of the Catholic ecumenical view. "The unity, we believe, subsists in the Catholic Church as something she can never lose, and we hope that it will continue to increase until the end of time."[23]

For the Anglican communion, as explicated in the Thirty-Nine Articles of 1563 and 1571, the unity of the church is based on the preaching of the Word of God and the sacraments (##19, 34). However, the later Chicago-Lambeth Quadrilateral from 1870 went further in its specifications regarding unity and outlined four aspects that shift the ecclesiological identity

---

16. See further Patelos, ed., *The Orthodox Church in the Ecumenical Movement.*
17. *UR,* #1.
18. *LG,* chap. 7.
19. *LG,* #8.
20. Cf. *LG,* #13.
21. *LG,* #14.
22. *LG,* #15.
23. *UR,* #4.

definitely toward the Roman Catholic and Orthodox view (and away from the Protestant one): Scripture, the Apostles' Creed, the two sacraments, and the episcopate.[24] In that respect, the churches of the Reformation differ from the Anglicans, as they build on a very minimum for Christian unity, namely, the preaching of the Word of God and the right administration of the sacraments.

The youngest Christian churches, the free churches, have entertained many kinds of suspicions, even doubts, concerning the idea of ecumenism. The guiding principle for them has been the idea of "spiritual union," according to which the God-given unity already exists among "true" churches, or at least among "true" individual believers. The free churches have not located unity in creeds or even the Bible, although for most of them these two have been very important, but rather in the believing hearts of individuals.[25] Four aspects of this unity are highlighted in the free churches: first, the personal faith of every Christian; second, the local church as the focus; third, the priesthood of all believers; and fourth, reservations with regard to the idea of visible unity.[26]

Having taken up the urgency of the ecumenical task, the development of that vision in the twentieth-century ecumenical movement, and the perceptions of unity that have emerged in the process, we will spend the rest of the chapter discussing the constructive task. A major new resource in the search for the unity of the church is the concept of recognition, which is the focus of the following section. Thereafter, a set of other recent — some still emerging and developing — resources will be brought into ecumenical service, namely,

- "receptive ecumenism," closely related to the widely used concept of reception;
- "partial communion," rather than full communion, as the (first) stated goal, related to the acknowledgment of the "provisional" nature of churches and denominations; and
- "interdisciplinary" approach to the search for unity, utilizing behavioral sciences' insights into the behavior of groups and communities, related to the paradigm of "ecclesiology as ethnography."

---

24. *Book of Common Prayer*, Resolution 11. The Lambeth Quadrilateral can be found at "The Chicago-Lambeth Quadrilateral," last updated February 21, 2011, http://anglicansonline .org/basics/Chicago_Lambeth.html.

25. For the Baptists, see Pitts, "The Relation of Baptists to Other Churches." For the Pentecostals, see Kärkkäinen, *Spiritus ubi vult spirat*, chap. 5.

26. Meyer, *That All May Be One*, pp. 24-27.

Toward Mutual Recognition of Churches

"Recognition" in Philosophical and Interdisciplinary Perspectives

Along with the issues related to deep theological convictions about the ecclesiality of the church, sacraments, and ministry, questions related to identity,
unity, otherness, and difference loom large in any ecumenical (and interfaith)
enterprise. Now that the rise of the modern ecumenical movement as well as
the complexity of cultural-religious plurality of the contemporary world have
placed these questions at the center of theological conversations, it is useful
to recall that by no means are they new ones.[27] Issues related to negotiating
between the "one" and "many," "we" and "they," or "unity" and "diversity" have
been on the menu of thinkers from the ancient Greek philosophers all the way
up to leading modern thinkers.[28] In addition to contemporary multiculturalism, the most obvious arena, recognition has been employed in the discourse
on human rights,[29] peacemaking,[30] education,[31] social and political theory,[32]
and philosophy, among others.[33] More recently, its relevance and potential
are being unearthed also in theology,[34] Christian ethics,[35] and ecumenism.[36]

Among the modern philosophers, no thinker scrutinized the problematic of recognition with greater influence than Hegel.[37] His sustained re-

27. An excellent guide is Bush and Zurn, eds., *The Philosophy of Recognition*.

28. For examples, see Lim, "Ecclesial Recognition," pp. 52–53.

29. Yeager, "Recognition, Human Rights."

30. Stassen, *Just Peacemaking*.

31. Sardoc, *Toleration, Respect, and Recognition*.

32. In addition to works by Axel Honneth, see Thompson, *Political Theory of Recognition*; Fraser, "Rethinking Recognition"; Ikäheimo and Laitinen, "Analyzing Recognition."

33. Ricoeur, *The Course of Recognition*; Ikäheimo, *Anerkennung*.

34. Henriksen, *Desire, Gift, and Recognition*; G. Walter, *Being Promised*.

35. Moses, "The Ethics of Recognition." A highly important interdisciplinary theological
work is Hoffman, *Toward Mutual Recognition*.

36. A massive current study is Lim, "Ecclesial Recognition." For specific ecumenical
topics, see Tucker, "Baptism and Ecumenism," pp. 1–12; Saarinen, "Living Sola Fide" (doctrine
of justification).

37. There is a scholarly consensus that the main locus for Hegel's philosophy of recognition is to be found in his *Phenomenology of Spirit* (1807), also known as the *Jena Lectures
on the Philosophy of Spirit* (available in English in various versions; the one used here is translated by J. B. Baillie). The master-slave analogy is in B.IV, "The True Nature of Self-Certainty"
("Self-Consciousness" in other translations). Of course, Descartes and Kant (especially) contributed to what became a full-scale philosophy of recognition in Hegel; see Lim, "Ecclesial
Recognition," pp. 46–53.

flections on the intersubjective concept of recognition, particularly through the lens of the master-slave analogy, have continued to inspire generations of thinkers.[38] At the heart of Hegel's conception is reciprocal recognition and the idea that in a real sense of the word, one receives one's own personhood from the other — and commensurately, helps the other to have the same.[39] The space of the other, so to speak, is not so foreign a territory that one could not inhabit it in some sense, and it is the same from the other's perspective. The main lesson from the complicated reasoning of Hegel's master-slave analogy is simply that self-consciousness develops in three stages: First, there is a complete identification of oneself with the other, the slave's sublation of his or her personhood with that of the master. Second, self-recognition in relation to others emerges slowly, as threatening as that may be to the slave. Third, at the end, there is a mutual recognition without inferiority-superiority condition.[40]

A current programmatic statement that has inspired much useful thinking on recognition in the sociopolitical area is the Canadian philosopher Charles Taylor's 1994 essay "Multiculturalism and the Politics of Recognition." The essay notes that recognition is a felt need in society, whether for feminists or those concerned about racial divisions or the challenges of multiculturalism. So important is recognition for one's identity that "[n]onrecognition or misrecognition can inflict harm, can be a form of oppression, imprisoning someone in a false, distorted, and reduced mode of being."[41] Particularly impending is this need in the midst of intensifying multiculturalism, Taylor argues.

In addition to Taylor, a leading contemporary political philosopher who has made unusually significant contributions to recognition theory is the German Axel Honneth. His theory of recognition consists basically of three parts: love, respect, and esteem. What can be called "emotional recognition" emerges in the early years of one's life at home in an intimate relationship of love and worth. "Rights-based" recognition is related to learning to respect and receive respect in the legal structures of society. Esteem is related to a "community

---

38. Anderson, *Hegel's Theory of Recognition*; from a theological perspective, see De Nys, *Hegel and Theology*, chaps. 1 and 2 particularly.

39. Hegel, *The Phenomenology of Mind*, #126.

40. Hegel (*Phenomenology of Mind*, ##176–77) summarizes the three stages; thereafter, the full explanation of the analogy (##178–96); for a useful introduction of the main figures, see #189.

41. C. Taylor, "The Politics of Recognition," p. 25. The original title of this essay was "Multiculturalism and the Politics of Recognition," from which the citation here has been taken.

of values" in a society that values one's accomplishments. Honneth's conviction is that only through recognition from the most important social groups and communities can our personal being emerge and develop. This puts the obligation to love, respect, and show esteem — or solidarity, as he also calls it — on others in relevant contexts in the society, or else denial of recognition or misrecognition takes place.[42] After this brief detour into secular recognition discourse, let us now inquire into its ecumenical potential.

Ecumenical Recognition

Briefly and nontechnically put, following secular recognition theories, ecumenical recognition "focuses on the possibility of recognizing the other [church] as a true church," and as such it is a key "part of a conscious process of changing the identification of the other [church]."[43] This is exactly what *The Church: Towards a Common Vision* (2013) does: "Visible unity requires that churches be able to recognize in one another the authentic presence of what the Creed of Nicea-Constantinople (381) calls the 'one, holy, catholic, apostolic Church.'"[44] With that lofty goal in mind, let us now briefly mine related ecclesiological and ecumenical resources from the work of representatives of interdisciplinary inquiry in the category of recognition.

Implications of Taylor's relevance to ecumenical work are obvious. His "main concern is how various minorities may coexist and flourish within a majority culture so that neither the majority nor the minorities have their rights to authentic existence diminished. In a similar manner, ecumenical recognition is seriously concerned with the authenticity of the Church both as universal and contextual manifestations." What makes his approach a fitting aid for ecumenical work is that neither his nor the modern ecumenical movement's goal is "the annihilation of particular ecclesial identities in the name of reconciling differences," but rather it seeks to resist that kind of oppressive uniformity.[45]

42. Honneth, *The Struggle for Recognition*; *The I in We*; and also his *Disrespect*. For a detailed and lucid exposition in the wider context of political theory of recognition, see chap. 4 in Lim, "Ecclesial Recognition."

43. Hietamäki, "Recognition and Ecumenical Recognition," p. 458. The term "recognition" had also been employed in ecumenism earlier; for this see Meyer, "Anerkennung." For the current state of discussion, see Saarinen, "Anerkennungstheorien und Ökumenische Theologie." Useful still is also G. Kelly, *Recognition*.

44. *CTCV*, p. 9.

45. Hietamäki, "Recognition and Ecumenical Recognition," p. 461.

Putting Hegel's philosophical reflections on recognition in ecumenical perspective, T. Lim summarizes: "The ecclesial struggle for recognition analogously resembles the multilayered consciousness of the master and the slave's struggle for recognition to be the bearer of its identity, to win the battle/struggle, and to be recognized ideally as equally valid members of society."[46] Clearly this entails a long-term struggle, given the possibility and risks of "misrecognition" and "nonrecognition" when dealing with the otherness of the other and one's own identity.[47] What is especially important for the ecumenical context is that this struggle concerns both parties, not only the "weaker" one (slave) but also the "stronger" one (master), albeit differently. The reason is obvious in light of Hegel's thought: "The lord who was free became dependent on the slave when the lord desired the recognition from the slaveman in order to uphold his status of lordship."[48] In other words, both parties need recognition, mutual recognition, in order to solve the dilemma.[49] Ecumenical recognition can never be a one-way street. T. Lim summarizes succinctly: "[J]ust like the recognition struggle between the master and the slave could terminate prematurely or progress to a mutual and equal reciprocal recognition of the other if parties are not aware of the often unconscious instincts and dynamics in the struggle, the churches' process of seeking unity could be terminated prematurely or could be expanded gradually if churches are not sensitive to the many insurmountable (theological and non-theological) obstacles."[50]

As explained, ecumenical recognition "examines whether churches may accept the legitimacy and authenticity of other churches as the Church in the dialogical process towards fuller communion."[51] As also established, this is a two-way street because, "[i]n order for the Churches to move further towards complete mutual recognition and full communion, they need to reflect on how they understand and claim their own ecclesial identity and how they regard the ecclesial status of other churches and other Christians."[52] Working toward full mutual recognition includes recognition of each other's

---

46. Lim, "Ecclesial Recognition," p. 62.

47. Lim, "Ecclesial Recognition," p. 75; for a careful reading and interpretation of Hegel's theory of recognition (and its implications for ecumenism), see chap. 2.

48. As paraphrased by Lim ("Ecclesial Recognition," p. 86, on the basis of Hegel's *Phenomenology of Mind*, pp. 194–96).

49. For debates about interpreting Hegel, see Lim, "Ecclesial Recognition," pp. 88–96 particularly.

50. Lim, "Ecclesial Recognition," p. 84; see also pp. 62–63.

51. Lim, "Ecclesial Recognition," p. 7.

52. "Limits of Diversity?" point d. in *NMC*, #63.

baptism,[53] source(s) of authority,[54] ministry, liturgy, and so forth. Particularly in this pluralistic and multicultural world of ours, to this goal also belongs the capacity to "recognize the gospel being faithfully proclaimed in another culture."[55] What would a path toward this kind of multilayered mutual recognition mean, and what kinds of attitudes and procedures would it entail? Building on Honneth's theory of recognition, the following questions could be asked to inspire and offer guidelines for application to ecumenism:

- What historical patterns or practices of nonrecognition exist between churches?
- Do churches love and care for each other as Jesus' brethren and friends, respect each other as the Abba Father's creatures of equal worth on the road, and esteem each other as the Spirit's indwelled agents and co-laborers of the kingdom?
- Do denials assault, denigrate, and decenter the value of themselves and the other as part of the body of Christ, people of God, and temple of the Spirit?
- If divisions were multilayered, would churches examine more deeply the sociocultural and political causes that are more than theological?
- Is there a hidden and not immediately recognizable hegemonic rhetoric of suppressing alternative voices in the churches?
- Do church members' natural approach of yielding to the perspectives of the avant-garde (or leadership or official position) of the churches compound the problems of recognition between churches of different traditions?[56]

The need for this kind of honest and careful scrutiny of churches' attitudes would be a significant step to heal the division. Mind that, at the moment, "full mutual recognition thus far only occurs among certain Protestant denominations but not outside of Protestantism."[57] Even full recognition would not entail canceling out differences; it would entail working toward "the diversified and plural unity of the church." Küng takes this diversity-in-unity/unity-in-diversity as a main ecumenical guideline in his useful summary:

53. *NMC*, #74; see also *OBTMR*.
54. *NMC*, #107.
55. *NMC*, #61.
56. Lim, "Ecclesial Recognition," p. 181 (I have changed the style of the list).
57. See Lim, "Ecclesial Recognition," p. 4.

As long as these Churches recognize one another as legitimate, as long as they see one another as part of one and the same Church, as long as they are in fellowship as Churches with one another and hold common services, and especially celebrate the Eucharist together, and as long as they are helping one another, working together and standing together in times of difficulty and persecution, there can be no objection to their diversity. All the differences, however profound, between the individual Churches are then swallowed up by the certainty that all are one in the unity of the Church of Christ.[58]

As outlined above, along with the recognition paradigm, other new and emerging ways of negotiating unity will be utilized in this project for the sake of a constructive ecumenical proposal, including "receptive ecumenism," "partial communion" as the stated goal, and interdisciplinary investigation in behavioral sciences regarding the behavior of groups, institutions, and movements. The rest of the chapter highlights and develops these perspectives.

Further New Resources and Fresh Perspectives on the Way toward Recognition and Unity

The Promise of "Receptive Ecumenism"

"Reception" as an Ecumenical Category. The new paradigm of "receptive ecumenism" is related to the standard ecumenical term "reception," although it also goes beyond it. By "reception" is meant "the process by which the churches make their own the results of all their encounters with one another, and in a particular way the convergences and agreements reached on issues over which they have historically been divided."[59] The proliferation of doctrinal statements and their reception are of course a well-attested phenomenon in the New Testament; just think of Paul's note about receiving core christological doctrines (1 Cor. 15:3) and the words of institution of the Eucharist (11:23). Reception was also a key issue in the early centuries, particularly with regard to the ways the churches embraced and understood the pronouncements of ecumenical

---

58. Küng, *The Church*, pp. 356–57.

59. "The Nature and Purpose of Ecumenical Dialogue," #59 (pp. 82–83) (appendix D); for background, see Kilmartin, "Reception in History"; Rusch, *Reception*.

councils.[60] No wonder the question of reception has received a lot of attention in the modern ecumenical movement.[61] Not only doctrinal reception but also "the broader process which churches can receive elements such as liturgy, spirituality and forms of witness from one another's traditions" relate to this task.[62]

Reception, if it really is true and genuine, does not leave the church the same; it may lead to renewal and change.[63] This is exactly what happened in the historic agreement on justification between the Vatican and Lutherans in 1999 as both parties' self-understanding and way of embracing a formative doctrinal stance were impacted.[64]

As practical and hands-on as the work around ecumenical reception may be, it is also a deeply *theo*logical affair. The recent major ecumenical document on reception reflected this clearly as it reminded us that true reception is rooted in the life of the trinitarian God and "takes place in the Holy Spirit . . . in and through events of communion (*koinonia*)."[65] Similarly to recognition, divine-human synergy is at work, ultimately rooted in and empowered — even in the midst of human frailty and sinfulness — in the same trinitarian origin from which the church herself derives: divine communion.

Receptive Ecumenism as Mutual Learning and Exchange. The leading idea behind the new approach to seeking unity stemming from the collaborative work of the British Catholic theologian Paul D. Murray of Durham University called "receptive ecumenism" is simple and profound, stating that "the primary ecumenical responsibility is to ask not 'What do the other traditions first need to learn from us?' but 'What do we need to learn from them?'"[66] The impetus behind receptive ecumenism is "to take seriously both the reality of the contemporary ecumenical moment — wherein the hope for structural unification in the short to medium term is, in general, now widely recognized as being unrealistic — and the abiding need for the Christian churches precisely in this situation to find an appropriate means of continuing to walk the way of conversion towards more visible structures and sacramental unity."[67]

60. See G. Kelly, "A New Ecumenical Wave."

61. The most recent ecumenical document is WCC, *Reception.*

62. WCC, *Reception,* #2.

63. WCC, *Reception,* #13.

64. See Lutheran World Federation and the Catholic Church, *Joint Declaration on the Doctrine of Justification,* #7 (in the preamble).

65. WCC, *Reception,* ##5, 7 (7).

66. This definition can be found, e.g., in Durham University, "About Receptive Ecumenism."

67. P. Murray, "Introducing Receptive Ecumenism," p. 1; see further P. Murray, ed.,

For that to happen, receptive ecumenism recommends the following kinds of attitudes and postures: willingness to change oneself rather than the other; "[t]o learn *from* and *across* our denominational differences in a mutually enriching way that fosters growth *within* traditions by finding the beauty of another tradition's focus"; and openness to continuing growth and change of tradition.[68] To make the basic idea of receptive ecumenism more concrete, consider the two following "real-life" statements concerning the acknowledgment of the marks of the church in other church families; the first statement comes from a leading Catholic ecumenist, and the second from the ecclesiastically diverse body of drafters of the *Princeton Proposal for Christian Unity.*

> Unity, holiness, catholicity, and apostolicity are dynamic realities that depend on the foundational work of Christ and on his continued presence and activity through the Holy Spirit. Evangelical communities that excel in love for Jesus Christ and in obedience to the Holy Spirit may be more unitive, holy, catholic, and apostolic than highly sacramental and hierarchically organized churches in which faith and charity have become cold.[69]
>
> Evangelical and Pentecostal Christians and their institutions also have a unique role. All churches may benefit from their vitality, their zeal for evangelism, and their commitment to Scripture. They demonstrate a spirit of cooperation with each other and sometimes with others that breaks down old barriers, creates fellowship among formally estranged Christians, and anticipates further unity. The free-church ecclesiologies of some Evangelicals bring a distinct vision of unity to the ecumenical task.[70]

Clearly, in these statements the key principle of receptive ecumenism — desire to learn from the other and even be impacted by that learning — is at work. Recognition is also there, as this kind of approach makes "reception" a fully two-way street, materially similarly to recognition.

A differently formulated goal of the ecumenical work, namely, "partial" rather than full communion, can be linked with the tactics of recognition and mutual reception, particularly when connected with the concept of "provisionality" of ecclesiastical traditions and communities on this side of the eschaton. In the spirit of receptive ecumenism, in that kind of approach one would

---

Receptive Ecumenism and the Call to Catholic Learning; P. Murray, "Receptive Ecumenism and Ecclesial Learning." For an assessment, see Barrett, ed., *Unity in Process.*

68. Durham University, "About Receptive Ecumenism," emphasis in original.
69. Dulles, "The Church as 'One, Holy, Catholic, and Apostolic,'" p. 27.
70. Braaten and Jenson, eds., *In One Body through the Cross*, #67 (pp. 55-56).

be willing to have one's own identity and self-understanding be affected and transformed rather than working from an assumption that only fully arriving according to the ready-made plan would qualify as a result.

"Partial Communion" and "Provisionality": The Turn toward Modest and Humble Goals

What If Full Communion Were Unattainable as a Goal? Without cynicism or an attempt to "lower standards," most all ecumenists agree that full communion[71] seems to be too ambitious a goal of unity — at least for the time being. If so, why not seek a partial communion? That is a more modest and realistic standard to begin with. Partial communion "means mutual recognition despite substantial or significant differences or disagreements."[72] That kind of goal may better help a church enter into a relationship of communion with another church that may seriously differ from it. The principle of partial communion seeks to steer between the Scylla of a "simplistic celebration of the *different* [that] provides no resources for appropriate attachment" and the Charybdis of an "anxious fusion to *the same* ... [that] hinders us from appropriate differentiation."[73] While diversity is a high value both theologically and culturally, we also need to beware of diversity that "is easily conscripted to sinful purposes"; at times, it is not so easy to see the difference between a diversity that is valuable and one that is to be deplored.[74]

This notion of communion admits many degrees. Consider the principle of partial communion in relation to one of the defining aspects of ecclesiality, apostolicity, which is also the foundation for the church's missionary nature. According to the American Jesuit R. Haight, "The apostolic character of common ecclesial existence provides the grounds for partial communion.... [A]s a common apostolic dimension in all the churches, this ecclesial existence contains the possibility to serve as a basis for partial communion among the churches. Indeed, it urges such communion and even demands it."[75]

In keeping with the modest call of partial communion, ecumenism could envision flexible, creative, and diverse processes and structures in the service of seeking unity. That kind of imagination, rather than rigid structures, better fits

71. See O. C. Edwards, "Meanings of Full Communion," p. 11.

72. Haight, *CCH*, 3:277.

73. Shults, "Theological Responses to Postmodernities," p. 3, emphasis in original.

74. Braaten and Jenson, eds., *In One Body through the Cross*, #22 (pp. 27–28); see also *NMC*, #63.

75. Haight, *CCH*, 3:285–86.

the mosaic of the Christian church at both local and global levels. That would allow for new kinds of ecumenical players, such as the Global Christian Forum,[76] to be engaged as a full partner. It would also allow for free churches, emerging communities, Christian coalitions, and similar groups to have a stronger voice. Flexible structures and processes with partial communion as the goal would much better fit the diverse and globalized church than rigid and fixed agendas.

Partial communion as the goal is based on the conviction that diversity in itself is not the problem; exclusivity is. As established above (chap. 14), as long as the Christian communities are willing to honor the principle of "*openness* of every church toward all other churches as an indispensable condition of ecclesiality," remaining differences should not necessarily lead to insurmountable problems of mutual recognition and reception. Again, the act of isolating from all other communions and unwillingness to acknowledge their belonging to the one and the same body of Christ under one Head would frustrate the integrity of the church as a communion of communions. Even if full communion were out of sight, setting partial communion (at least for the time being) as the guide would put the church on "a path on which it is to express and deepen its communion, that is, its differentiated unity, with all other churches through the common confessions of faith and appropriate structures of communion (see Eph. 4:2, 13-16)."[77] Rather than one church to which all others are invited to "return" — the archenemy of mutual recognition and reception — the diversity and plurality of the communions in the communion would be the hallmarks of such unity. Indeed, the diversity and plurality of churches in communion with others are the normal mode of the Christian church. Only at the eschaton will there be one church under one God.[78] Diversity and plurality of the communion of communions are also fostered by the provisionality of each communion in itself.

The Provisionality of Christian Traditions and Denominations

All denominational identities and claims for the ecclesiality of any particular church (family) are by definition provisional. This is for two reasons. First of all, on this side of the eschatological consummation, each communion, as well as the communion of communions, as an anticipation of the final gathering of all people and churches, is just that, an *anticipation*. Second, each

---

76. See the official Web site: http://www.globalchristianforum.org/.
77. Volf, *After Our Likeness*, pp. 156-57.
78. So also Volf, *After Our Likeness*, pp. 157-58.

local communion, while a full church in the sense of being an authentic, fully funded expression of ecclesiality, can only be so when turned toward the other communions, as established above. Under one Head (Christ), there cannot be such independent "bodies" that they are not members of the body of Christ.

This is the proper context for theological understanding of the ecclesial category of "denomination" that, astonishingly, has escaped the notice of ecumenists and systematicians as far as its theological meaning and significance are concerned;[79] curiously, theologians have left the issue to sociologists (of religion) and church historians.[80] So, what is a denomination in ecclesiology? Briefly put, it is "a primary mode of trans-congregational structure and life within the church today,"[81] "a middle term between 'congregation' and [universal] 'church,'" and as such, an intermediary structure.[82] According to the useful analysis of B. Ensign-George, there are five features involved with the concept:

- "intermediary," as explained above
- "contingent" rather than necessary, in that denominations have not always existed (at least in the sense we have them today) and that they arose to meet a particular need
- "interdependent," in that they depend on each other for their existence and only make sense thus
- "partial," in that each and every one can never claim to be the full embodiment of the church
- "permeable," as denominations allow for movement in and out as well as within themselves[83]

All these features are linked with and support the principle of provisionality.[84] On top of theological reasons, provisionality is also to be minded for the sake of the complexity and diversity of the contemporary global church. There

79. For this omission, see the new collection of essays edited by P. Collins and Ensign-George, *Denomination*, and particularly its lead essay by Ensign-George, "Denomination as Ecclesiological Category."

80. Well-known classic and standard works are H. R. Niebuhr, *Social Sources of Denominationalism*; Richey, ed., *Denominationalism*; Mullin and Richey, eds., *Reimagining Denominationalism*.

81. Ensign-George, "Denomination as Ecclesiological Category," p. 1.

82. Ensign-George, "Denomination as Ecclesiological Category," p. 4, with my addition in parentheses.

83. Ensign-George, "Denomination as Ecclesiological Category," pp. 6–7.

84. The meaning and significance of "provisionality" of denominations (and churches) are in keeping with that of the Canadian Catholic Christian Duquoc, *Provisional Churches*.

is no doubt that as inevitable as it may be that denominational markers will be with us "until the end," there are also a widespread and increasing loosening and fluidity of those markers, particularly due to the constant emergence of new ecclesial structures and experiments. Regrettably, the contemporary ecumenical movement at large has basically ignored the significance of reflecting theologically on both the category of the denomination and the radical transformation of its meaning in the consciousness of the faithful. Modern (and contemporary) ecumenism is still focused on negotiating merely between solid identities; it is blind to the emerging hybrid identities of local communions, networks of communions, and even more recent denominations.[85] Even worse, contemporary ecumenism also operates as if "denominations" were composed only of established, mainline communities and provides little room for the significance of many free churches, Pentecostal/charismatic groups, emerging churches, and other newcomers.[86]

In the spirit of receptive ecumenism's goal of learning from others in order to better understand oneself and so to make a contribution to a common search for mutual recognition and reception, the last set of resources will be briefly studied as the last task of this chapter. These resources have to do with the rise of a new desire to combine empirical (or practical or congregational) studies with theological reflection. Therein the theologian may learn from and employ the results and insights of behavioral sciences and related fields.

The Role and Significance of Nontheological Factors in Divisions and Unity: An Interdisciplinary Inquiry

Although the employment of empirical methods and interdisciplinary studies as an aid to theological-ecumenical reflection may be a more recent idea, the acknowledgment of nontheological factors is not. Consider this example: studying the central ecumenical problem in *After Nine Hundred Years: The Background of Schism between the Eastern and the Western Churches*, the late French Dominican Yves Congar focused the investigation on political, cultural, and ecclesiological reasons, in other words, on bases other than typical theological-doctrinal issues.[87] Others have agreed that the role of nontheo-

---

85. See further Volf, *After Our Likeness*, pp. 19–20.

86. So also Volf, *After Our Likeness*, pp. 20–21.

87. Congar, *After Nine Hundred Years*, p. 39; discussed in detail in Lim, "Ecclesial Recognition," chap. 5.

logical factors, whether psychological-personal or group dynamics or socio-cultural or similar, may be much more pronounced than theologians have routinely allowed for.[88] Indeed, there is a growing consensus that, along with theological, biblical, and tradition-driven reasons, "a complex dynamics of inclusionary and exclusionary intersubjectivities lie behind the ecumenical project since churches also fail to recognize each other for many reasons."[89] In other words, "non-theological factors (such as the instinctive struggle for recognition, intragroup and intergroup dynamics, and various political notions impacting churches' witness of the gospel and churches' mutual ecclesiastical diplomacy) impact the churches' recognition process."[90]

To acknowledge and unearth those and related nontheological reasons, interdisciplinarily informed theologians and ecumenists have been willing to consult the findings and insights of behavioral and social sciences. Psychology, social psychology, and sociology have served well and been beneficial to congregational and other empirical studies, including ethnography.[91] Another way of naming this orientation is to speak of doing ecclesiology "From Below" by carefully observing what is happening in local congregations and drawing lessons from that.[92] This is what Timothy Lim has sought to do in his recent massive study titled "Ecclesial Recognition." While not engaging in empirical study, Lim taps into various psychological, sociopsychological, and intergroup studies (along with philosophical, political, and theological investigations) with the goal of helping remove obstacles on the way toward full(er) mutual recognition and attaining unity among the churches.

The benefit of the "social recognition" model, as studied by behavioral and sociological disciplines, is that it "registers the complex, inter-subjective, social-psychological, and relational dynamics involved in the process of recognition. These dynamics operate multi-dimensionally: individual, interpersonal, group, intra-group, and intergroup levels,"[93] thus also corresponding to the multilayered arena of ecumenical actors. Gleaned from a wide array of interdisciplinary literature on social (re)cognition, group and intergroup

88. Zamfir, "Is There a Future for the Catholic-Protestant Dialogue?" pp. 87–92.

89. Lim, "Ecclesial Recognition," p. 39.

90. Lim, "Ecclesial Recognition," p. 42.

91. See Scharen, "'Judicious Narratives,' or Ethnography as Ecclesiology"; P. Ward, ed., *Perspectives on Ecclesiology and Ethnography*; Brittain, "Why Ecclesiology Cannot Live by Doctrine Alone."

92. For the continuing international collaborative project and network Ecclesiology and Ethnography, see http://www.ecclesiologyandethnography.com/.

93. Lim, "Ecclesial Recognition," p. 103.

and relationship dynamics, the following concepts and observations might be useful for ecumenical work:[94]

- *Social categorization*,[95] the process of sorting people and things in the complex environment into neat categories, facilitates adaptation, group cohesion, and productivity; but it also may lead to intergroup discrimination and intensify intergroup conflict. In addition, it may enhance stereotypes, sticking with "the party line," and an us-*versus*-them attitude.[96]
- *Social comparison*, the process of assessing the worth of other groups as well as one's own, is often linked with social (or intergroup) competition to enhance one's own group's value.[97] It may easily lead to overly positive valuing of one's own group and overly negative assessment of other groups.
- *Social identification* "further distinguishes groups cognitively, affectively, and behaviorally. Like social comparison, it emphasizes or reinforces the distinct and positive identity of their groups from other groups, so as to improve the value of their social identity."[98] For an individual balancing between assimilating into the group and distinguishing oneself from it (in order to affirm self-identity), social identification may easily turn into discrimination or favoritism, among other vices.
- *The theory of socially shared cognitions* refers to the ways people process information together in groups. At their best, these cognitions help deal with complex and confusing situations. At their worst, because shared cognitions are more than just the sum of the individuals' conceptions, they also have more power to exclude, stigmatize, and attach labels. Particularly important in the formation of group cognition is the role of strong leaders, whose opinions are often followed without much questioning.
- *Group conformity* is a related (inter)group dynamic that significantly influences one's choices, opinions, likings, and decisions. Conformity is particularly important in the case of (perceived or real) threats.[99]

---

94. Based on chap. 3 of Lim, "Ecclesial Recognition." Because of the rich documentation therein, references are kept to a minimum here.

95. For basics, see Ellemers and Haslam, "Social Identity Theory."

96. See further Dovidio et al., eds., *Sage Handbook of Prejudice*.

97. See Brewer, "Ingroup Identification and Intergroup Conflict."

98. Lim, "Ecclesial Recognition," p. 126.

99. See Stephan, Ybarra, and Morrison, "Intergroup Threat Theory."

It does not take much imagination to find examples of each of these features of group dynamics in the ecumenical world, in which people from different backgrounds, doctrinal convictions, and tastes associate with each other — or refuse to do so. Those behavioral patterns and attitudes have everything to do with reception, recognition, and mutual acknowledgment. One can only hope that as systematic/constructive theological paradigms are widening in approach and scope — as has been attempted throughout this project[100] — the fruits of interdisciplinary collaboration will be adopted where relevant for the theological task.

Recall that in the listing of the tasks of the missional community in the previous chapter — from evangelization and church planting, to healing, to social justice, to caring for the environment, to seeking reconciliation and peace — the last one was named "mission as dialogue and interfaith engagement." Whereas the current chapter has focused on dialogue and mutual engagement within the global Christian church, the last chapter of this volume will venture into the domain of four living faiths and secular ideologies reigning in the Global North. This will build on some insights of this chapter — particularly the theory of recognition — but also understandably move into a different world and set of questions.

100. For the purposes of this chapter, consult particularly the multidisciplinary investigation of forgiveness in chap. 10 of my *Spirit and Salvation*.

20. Missional Existence as Hospitable Dialogue: The Church among Religious Communities and Secularisms

A Methodological Orientation: Christian Theology as Comparative Theology

This lengthy final chapter breaks into the following main sections: First, clarification of the need and ways to do Christian theology as comparative theology and engaging the religious other will be attempted. Second, the meaning and significance of religious pluralism(s) will be discussed. Thereafter, third, a set of guidelines based on a trinitarian theology of hospitality will be presented as aids to the church in her twofold task of witnessing to the gospel amid religious diversity and building relationships and communitarianism. The rest of the chapter, indeed, more than half of it, will be devoted to actual comparative theological discussion between the Christian tradition and four other living faiths.

The Theological Mandate of Engaging Other Faith Traditions

There are certainly many "practical" reasons for the church to engage the religious other, from establishing a pedagogical contact and preparing to witness to Christ in the matrix of religious convictions, to helping Christians live in a civil way with the other and so alleviating conflicts.[1] These reasons alone would suffice; indeed, missiological, pastoral, and other disciplines of

---

1. See Locklin, "A More Comparative Ecclesiology?"

the theological curriculum tackle many of those pressing issues.[2] On top of those, there are also weighty theological and "methodological" reasons, that is, reasons related to the way systematic theology is to be conducted according to this project. They mandate a robust engagement of the religious other and religious diversity.[3] Let us summarize them under three interrelated rubrics, in no particular order:

- the essential task of (systematic) theology to pursue the question of the truth (of God) for the sake of all people
- the common origin and destiny of humanity in one God
- the theology of hospitality

The first task, pursuing the question of the truth of God for the sake of all, may strike one not only as a hybrid sort of task, but also as something easily leading to violence and oppression. How could any theologian (of any faith tradition) claim such a task? Before dismissing the argument, let us be reminded of the obvious yet all-too-often-neglected necessary connection between monotheism — whether Islamic, Jewish, or Christian — and the assumption of the location of truth (and beauty and goodness, among other virtues) in the one and same God. The English philosopher of religion R. Trigg reminds us of this: "Christianity and Islam both believe that they have a universal message. If there is one God, one would expect that He would be regarded as the God of all people, and not just some." Consequently, there is an assumption of "only one world, one version of reality": "Monotheism can have no truck with relativism, or alternative gods. Beliefs may construct gods, but those who believe in one God cannot allow for other parallel deities, even in the sense that other people have their gods while monotheists look to their one deity. Monotheism must not only imply the falsity of all other alleged gods, but, if it is true to itself, it has to proclaim it to all, loud and clear. Otherwise, by definition, it is not monotheism, or even realism."[4]

Out of this uncompromising monotheism arises not only Islam's and Christianity's missional task but also the mandate for theology to pursue God's truth. As explained in some detail in the introduction to volume 1, *Christ and Reconciliation* (and more briefly in the orientation to each subse-

---

2. For background issues and debates concerning the rise of the ecumenical "mission as witness to people of other living faiths," see Bosch, *Transforming Mission*, pp. 474-89.

3. See Berger and Zijderveld, *In Praise of Doubt*, p. 7.

4. Trigg, *Religious Diversity*, p. 115.

quent volume), that pursuit of truth does not have to be "foundationalist" in terms of expecting indubitable Cartesian certainty after modernity. Rather, our approach is postfoundationalist; therefore, questioning and confidence mutually shape and inform each other, and the personal search and the communal search for truth critically cohere. Neither does this pursuit have to expect final arrival, as it were: ultimately, the search for the truth of God is eschatological and anticipatory in nature — also in keeping with the Christian communion's anticipatory nature. Nor should it be coercive or violent; rather, it should be guided by hospitality and gift giving. It is done for the sake of others and their well-being, without subsuming the other under one's own explanation. Dialogue and mutual engagement in a peaceful and honoring posture are the key.

Consequently, we should seriously critique the common tendency to assume that since there are so many religions and ideologies with competing truth claims, none of them can be true and, therefore, relativism is the only way out — the view according to which "[e]ach group must live by their own truth, but there is no overarching 'truth' that all should recognize."[5] Should relativism be adopted, it would mean that religious commitments, similarly to, say, personal tastes, are merely subjective choices but have no role to play in the public arena.[6] That argument fails in light of the fact that "[r]eligions that only express the personal attitudes of the believer cannot claim any truth that can be rationally assessed. Faith then is merely an idiosyncrasy that some have and some do not."[7] The very fact that we continue speaking of *different* religions indicates that they are something bigger than just one person's — or even a group's — personal "tastes." There is a necessary intersubjective side to religion — as there is also to secularism, as far as that is thoughtfully and rationally defended. Indeed, "total subjectivism brings the threat of nihilism."[8] Common sense tells us that the content of faith matters. Just think of everyday nonreligious life: the content matters with regard to the kind of doctor or car mechanic we put our faith in. I agree with R. Trigg's argument

---

5. Trigg, *Religious Diversity*, p. 2.

6. Trigg, *Religious Diversity*, pp. 15-18. A strong appeal to the subjective nature of religions is presented by the Italian philosopher Vattimo, *A Farewell to Truth*; for a critique, see Trigg, *Religious Diversity*, pp. 26-27. For a wider critique of subjectivism, see Trigg, *Religion in Public Life*. For a convincing defeat of relativism due to its incoherence, see Trigg, *Reason and Commitment*.

7. Trigg, *Religious Diversity*, p. 23. This has also been the persistent argument throughout Pannenberg's theological career; see, e.g., chap. 1 in *ST* 1.

8. Trigg, *Religious Diversity*, p. 13.

that "all faith has to be faith in something or somebody. There is no such thing as undirected faith."[9]

Nor does doubt or uncertainty, that is, the difficulty or even seeming impossibility of establishing the basis of one's beliefs, constitute relativism.[10] It just makes the pursuit of truth a lifelong, communal, and painstaking task for all. Only if one is an ontological nonrealist, that is, if one holds that all there is, is a result of human construction, could a link between doubt and relativism be made. Most of us, however, are realists (of some sort), which simply means that "reality is independent of all our knowledge and not a construction out of human knowledge." As a result, the jump from epistemology (how we know) to ontology (how things are) cannot be taken for granted.[11]

In keeping with these presuppositions, this project builds on the conviction that in order for constructive theology to pursue the task of coherent argumentation regarding the truth of Christian doctrine, its claims must be related to not only the internal but also the external spheres. Religions certainly form an essential part of human experience and the experience of the world. In this process, the self-understanding of Christian faith may also be clarified and deepened — and if the engagement is done in an authentic and respectful way, the religious other may also benefit. A hospitable relating to the other not only makes space for a genuine presentation and identification of one's own position but also opens one for a careful listening to the testimonies and convictions of the other.[12] All faith traditions may learn from the Jewish distinction between arguing for victory and arguing for God.[13]

The second theological reason for robust engagement with the religious other lies in the common origin and destiny of humanity, an offshoot from monotheism. This was clearly set forth in the beginning of Vatican II's statement on other religions (*Nostra Aetate*, #1): "One is the community of all peoples, one their origin, for God made the whole human race to live over the face of the earth. One also is their final goal, God. His providence, His manifestations of goodness, His saving design extend to all men, until that time when the elect will be united in the Holy City, the city ablaze with the glory of God, where the nations will walk in His light." Because of this common origin and

9. Trigg, *Religious Diversity*, p. 18. See further Trigg, *Rationality and Religion*; Netland, *Christianity and Religious Diversity*, chap. 7.

10. For thoughtful reflections, see Netland, *Christianity and Religious Diversity*, chap. 6.

11. Trigg, *Religious Diversity*, pp. 23–30 (27); Trigg uses the term "antirealism" for what I call here nonrealism.

12. See further Kärkkäinen, "Dialogue, Witness, and Tolerance."

13. Firestone, "Argue for God's Sake."

destiny, the Holy Spirit is at work among religions in ways unknown to men and women in helping them be connected with the love of God and seek for salvation and truth.[14] As a result, all men and women "should constitute one family and treat one another in a spirit of brotherhood,"[15] including mutual love and care for one another. This reaching out and engaging in the spirit of hospitality is particularly important for the church in light of the growing interdependence of our globalizing world.[16]

Third, on the basis of these two "foundational" convictions, the mandate for hospitable relating to the other establishes itself. It seeks to cultivate inclusivism, welcoming testimonies, insights, and interpretations from different traditions and contexts, and so foster mutual dialogue. A hospitable posture honors the otherness of others as human beings created by the same God and reconciled by the same Lord. Hospitality also makes space for an honest, genuine, authentic sharing of one's convictions. In pursuing the question of truth as revealed by the triune God, constructive theology also seeks to persuade and convince with the power of dialogical, humble, and respectful argumentation. Ultimately, comparative theology itself becomes an act of hospitality, giving and receiving gifts. This kind of hospitable dialogue is a "relationship where both parties are recognized by each other as someone not determined by the conditions of one's own horizon, but rather as an Other, a relationship that is not part of the world and the concrete expectations (or anticipations) of the Other. Hence, in such a relationship one is invited into the world of the Other by means of an open invitation."[17]

Some Methodological Desiderata

The God-centered pursuit of truth, acknowledging the deep belonging together of all men and women, leading to hospitable dialogue and mutual engagement, facilitates the scholarly work of comparative theology. Whereas comparative religion seeks to be "neutral" and look "objectively" at the features of religious traditions, comparative theology is "*comparative* and *theological* beginning to end . . . [and] marks acts of faith seeking understanding which are rooted in a particular faith tradition but which, from that foundation,

14. For the Catholic Church's christocentric inclusivistic interpretation, see *Gaudium et Spes*, #22. For my proposal, see *Spirit and Salvation*, chap. 5.

15. *Gaudium et Spes*, #24.

16. See further *Gaudium et Spes*, #23.

17. Henriksen, *Desire, Gift, and Recognition*, pp. 44–45.

venture into learning from one or more other faith traditions. This learning is sought for the sake of fresh theological insights that are indebted to the newly encountered tradition/s as well as the home tradition."[18]

Comparative theological work does not brush aside or undermine deep dynamic tension concerning religions and their claims for truth; in the spirit of hospitality they are brought to the dialogue table. That said, it acknowledges that "there is a tradition at the very heart of [many living] . . . faiths which is held common. It is not that precisely the same doctrines are believed, but that the same tendencies of thought and devotion exist, and are expressed within rather diverse patterns of thought, characteristic of the faiths in question."[19] Nor does the comparative work reject tradition, as is typical in modernist epistemology with its alleged "neutrality" and "objectivity."[20] Rather, remaining "tied to specific communities of faith without being trapped by these communities,"[21] the investigation honors contextuality and the locality of human knowledge.[22]

Religious Pluralisms in a Theological Assessment

The Plurality of Religious Pluralisms

Similarly to terms such as "modern" and "postmodern," "pluralism" is polyvalent and subject to differing interpretations.[23] Notwithstanding diverse meanings, there is a scholarly consensus that the roots of contemporary pluralistic theologies can be found in the philosophical-religious views of leading (post-) Enlightenment thinkers from Hume, Kant, and Hegel to his famed pupil D. F. Strauss and others who revised the original quest of the historical Jesus.[24] Building on his teacher's idiosyncratic philosophical idealism with "incarnation" as a formative idea,[25] Strauss's massive two-volume *Life of Jesus Critically Examined* widened the manifestation of the divine to encompass in some way

---

18. Clooney, *Comparative Theology*, p. 10, emphasis in original; see also p. 12.

19. K. Ward, *Images of Eternity*, p. 1.

20. See Zimmermann, *Incarnational Humanism*, pp. 35–36.

21. Van Huyssteen, *Alone in the World?* p. 12.

22. See Van Huyssteen, *Alone in the World?* p. 36 and passim.

23. See Larson, "Contra Pluralism."

24. For a highly useful recent account, see Netland, *Christianity and Religious Diversity*, pp. 47–54.

25. For an important investigation, see Hodgson, "Hegel's Christology."

the whole of the human race.[26] In twentieth-century pluralistic interpretations,[27] this program of nonexclusive Christianity was taken to its logical end with alleged openness to embrace the religious other without any demanding Christian identity.[28]

In investigations of christological and *theo*logical pluralisms (*Christ and Reconciliation*, chap. 9, and *Trinity and Revelation*, chap. 14, respectively), the somewhat clumsy expression "first-generation pluralisms" refers to the pluralistic Christian theologies of religions that arose in the second half of the last century, building on the modernist epistemology and ethos. These emerged both in the Global North (by the Protestant John Hick and the Roman Catholic Paul F. Knitter)[29] and in Asia (by the Protestants Stanley Samartha and M. M. Thomas, as well as the Roman Catholic Aloysius Pieris).[30] Even those coming from Asian soil, while shaped by the multireligious context of that continent, draw their main inspiration from the European Enlightenment and its subsequent developments, including classical liberalism. They represent by and large the replacement of Christocentrism with theo-centrism.

Although what I call "second-generation pluralists" share a common vision with their predecessors, namely, negotiating the interfaith impasse of exclusivism, their approach differs significantly in that they are not willing to leave behind Christian identity, nor do they try to subsume the religious other under their own explanation but rather make every effort to honor both identities. The late Hindu-Christian Catholic Raimundo Panikkar, half Indian, half Spanish, and the American Baptist S. Mark Heim represent those orientations in their own distinctive ways. Since these and other views and representatives have been engaged in detail in other volumes, there is no need to repeat the discussions here.

Rather, let us briefly review the main reasons for the failure of pluralisms as a way to prepare for a robustly trinitarian approach to dialogue and interfaith engagement.

---

26. Strauss, *Life of Jesus*, pp. 779–81; this par. (151) comes under a telling heading, "The Last Dilemma."

27. A leading contemporary example is Hick, ed., *Metaphor of God Incarnate*; see also Knitter, *No Other Name?*

28. For a typical statement (by the Catholic pluralist), see Knitter, *No Other Name?* p. 205.

29. In *Christ and Reconciliation*, chap. 9, I have engaged the American Roman Catholic Knitter's eco-liberationist pluralism particularly from the perspective of Christology.

30. In *Christ and Reconciliation*, chap. 9, I have engaged the Sri Lankan Roman Catholic Pieris's liberationist pluralism particularly from the perspective of Christology.

Healing the Broken Promises of Pluralism(s)

The leading Roman Catholic comparative theologian of England, Gavin D'Costa, has offered a sharp criticism of pluralisms, which this project affirms. He considers pluralisms at their core to be representations of modernity's "hidden gods." Ultimately, these pluralisms fail to deliver the promises of the Enlightenment: "Despite their intentions to encourage openness, tolerance, and equality they fail to attain these goals (on their own definition) because of the tradition-specific nature of their positions." Why so? Because, "in granting a type of equality to all religions, [the Enlightenment] ended up denying public truth to any and all of them."[31] Not for nothing, D'Costa laments the fact that even though pluralists present themselves as honest "brokers to disputing parties," they in fact conceal the fact "that they represent yet another party which invites the disputants to leave their parties and join the pluralist one, namely, liberal modernity." In the true sense of the word, this represents a concealed form of exclusivism and even "liberal intolerance."[32]

With D'Costa, I contend that the remedy to pluralisms is not exclusivism but rather an attitude that takes delight in the potential of an encounter with the other without denying either party's distinctive features. "The other is always interesting in their difference and may be the possible face of God, or the face of violence, greed, and death. Furthermore, the other may teach Christians to know and worship their own trinitarian God more truthfully and richly."[33] The aim is to make room for a "critical, reverent, and open engagement with otherness, without any predictable outcome."[34] That kind of engagement does not water down real differences, as happens when modernity's epistemology is followed. Too easily, pluralisms tend to deny the self-definitions of particular religions and to do so from a distance.[35] In contrast, the pluralism-defeating approach aims at openness that becomes "taking history seriously." Differences are honored rather than dismissed or suspended. Tolerance, rather than denying tradition-specific claims for truth — which in itself, ironically, is one more truth claim among others — becomes the "qualified establishment of civic religious freedom for all on the basis of Christian revelation and natural law." Equality becomes the "equal and inviolable dignity of all persons," which

31. D'Costa, *Meeting of Religions*, pp. 1–2.
32. D'Costa, *Meeting of Religions*, pp. 20, 22, 24 (24).
33. D'Costa, *Meeting of Religions*, p. 9.
34. D'Costa, *Meeting of Religions*, p. 9.
35. See further D'Costa, "Christian Theology and Other Religions," pp. 161–78, and Hick's response: "Possibility of Religious Pluralism," pp. 161–66.

naturally leads to taking the other seriously, dialoguing with the other with willingness to learn from the other and teach the other.[36]

Plurality and diversity of religions itself is not the problem. On the contrary, ultimately it is the case that "[f]or a religious person, to *accept* disagreement is to see it as within the providence of God" — even disagreement due to diversity of religious beliefs and convictions. Religions are not here without God's permission and allowance. The continuing challenge, particularly for the staunch monotheist, is how to reconcile the existence of one's own deeply felt (God-given?) beliefs with different, often opposite, kinds of convictions.[37]

A Trinitarian Theology of Interfaith Hospitality of Witness and Dialogue

The Trinitarian Shape of Interfaith Engagement

In keeping with the trinitarian ecclesiology attempted in this project — following the trinitarian unfolding of Christian theology in the whole project — Trinity is a proper framework for interfaith dialogue and hospitality.[38] As discussed above (chaps. 13 and 15), in the triune God there is both unity and plurality, communion and diversity. The Trinity as communion allows room for both genuine diversity (otherwise we could not talk about the Trinity) and unity (otherwise we could not talk about one God). The Trinity "unites transcendence and immanence, creation and redemption," thus facilitating true dialogue.[39]

Borrowing from the biblical scholar Walter Brueggemann, I make the term "other" a verb to remind us of the importance of seeing the religious other not as a counterobject but rather as a partner in "othering," which is "the risky, demanding, dynamic process of relating to one that is not us."[40] What matters is the capacity to listen to the distinctive testimony of the other, to patiently wait upon the other, and to make a safe space for him or her. Similarly, that

36. For a brief statement, see D'Costa, *Meeting of Religions*, p. 13.

37. K. Ward, *Religion and Community*, p. 25, emphasis in original.

38. This section borrows directly from my two earlier essays "Theologies of Religions," in *Witnessing to Christ*, and "Theologies of Religions," *Evangelical Interfaith Dialogue*. For a theologically and missiologically fruitful application of the doctrine of the Trinity to interfaith hospitality, see Doan, "Participating in and Witnessing to Triune Hospitality."

39. Jukko, *Trinitarian Theology in Muslim-Christian Encounters*, p. 221.

40. Brueggemann, *The Covenanted Self*, p. 1.

kind of encounter gives the Christian an opportunity to share the distinctive testimony of the love of God. An important aspect of the process of "othering" is to resist the tendency, so prevalent in secular societies of the Global North and in the various forms of religious pluralisms, to draw the other under one's own world explanation and thus deny the existence and possibility of genuine differences among religions. It is an act of insult rather than a sign of tolerance to tell the believer of another faith that — contrary to his or her own self-understanding — no real differences exist in beliefs, doctrines, and ultimate ends.

In a profound reflection titled "The Holy Spirit's Invitation to Relational Engagement,"[41] D'Costa speaks of the Spirit's call to "relational engagement." Other religions are important for the Christian church in that they help the church penetrate more deeply into the divine mystery and so also enrich their own spirituality and insight. While testifying to the salvation in Christ, the trinitarian openness toward other religions fosters the acknowledgment of the gifts of God in other religions by virtue of the presence of the Spirit — as well as the critical discernment of these gifts by the power of the same Spirit. "[I]f the Spirit is at work in the religions, then the gifts of the Spirit need to be discovered, fostered, and received into the church. If the church fails to be receptive, it may be unwittingly practicing cultural and religious idolatry."[42] This kind of mutual engagement holds great promise. In the words of the postcolonial feminist Mayra Rivera, there is the "possibility of transformation . . . in the encounter with the transcendence in the flesh of the Other."[43] Similarly, another postcolonial feminist, Luce Irigaray, speaks of "touching which respects the other."[44]

At the same time, as argued in other volumes of this project, the Trinity not only determines the Christian view of God, it also shapes our understanding of Christ. Only when Christ is confessed as truly divine and truly human, following the ancient symbols (creeds) of faith confessed by all Christian churches, can the Christian doctrine of the Trinity be maintained. Making Jesus merely an ethical teacher, as in classical liberalism, or only one "Incarnation" among others — as in extreme pluralisms, an embodiment of the Deity, a.k.a. Hindu *avataras* — truncates not only the confession of the Trinity but also the biblical understanding of Christ.[45]

41. Section title in D'Costa, *Meeting of Religions*, p. 109.
42. D'Costa, *Meeting of Religions*, p. 115.
43. Rivera, *Touch of Transcendence*, p. 118.
44. Irigaray, *I Love to You*, p. 124.
45. See also Heim, *Depth of the Riches*, p. 134.

Many problems in theologies of religions derive from a less than satisfactory conception of the Trinity, including the typical pluralistic pitfalls of turning to "theo-centrism" in an effort to replace Jesus as *the* Way, or turning to the "Spirit" in order to get around the centrality of Jesus and the Father, as if the Spirit's ministry were independent from the other trinitarian members. Similarly failing are approaches to other religions and mission that have a tendency to minimize the church and only speak of the kingdom of God and the building of the kingdom as the only goal.[46] That constitutes a failure to recognize the fact that the kingdom, the rule of God, is in itself a trinitarian process: the Son comes in the power of the Spirit to usher in the Father's righteous rule, graciously allowing the church, the body of Christ, to participate in its coming. Of course, the kingdom is far wider than the church; but the church serves as sign, anticipation, and tool of the coming rule of God.

Witness, Dialogue, and Tolerance

Although they are too often juxtaposed with each other, there is ecumenical consensus that mission and dialogue, proclamation and interfaith engagement belong together and are not alternatives: "In mission there is place both for the proclamation of the good news of Jesus Christ and for dialogue with people of other faiths,"[47] including common service, healing, and reconciliation,[48] in keeping with the multilayered ministry of the missional communion. In accord with this ecumenical consensus, the recent Catholic interreligious document "Dialogue and Proclamation" encapsulates in a few pregnant sentences a holistic understanding of interfaith engagement by listing the principal elements of mission in terms of Christian "presence and witness; commitment to social development and human liberation; liturgical life, prayer and contemplation; interreligious dialogue; and finally, proclamation and catechesis." The document stresses that "[p]roclamation and dialogue are thus both viewed, each in its own place, as component elements and authentic forms of the one evangelizing mission of the Church. They are both oriented towards the com-

46. For a critique of the Roman Catholic pluralist Paul F. Knitter in this respect, see my *Christ and Reconciliation*, pp. 231–35.

47. "Mission and Evangelism in Unity Today," #61. So also *CWMRW*, "A Basis for Christian Witness," #4. For important current ecumenical discussions, see further "Theme Two: Christian Mission among Other Faiths."

48. Duchrow and Hinkelammert, *Transcending Greedy Money*; Sinaga, ed., *A Common Word*.

munication of salvific truth."[49] In other words, interfaith dialogue includes and makes space for both proclamation, with a view to persuasion by the power of truth and love, and dialogue, with a view to facilitating mutual understanding, reconciliation, and harmony.

In this respect I find useful and fully affirm the veteran American evangelical philosopher and missiologist H. Netland's wise principles for how to do witnessing in our kind of world:

1. Bearing witness to the gospel of Jesus Christ among religious others is not optional, but rather is obligatory for the Christian church.
2. Christians are to bear witness to the gospel in accordance with God's love.
3. Christian witness must be respectful of others and be conducted with humility and moral integrity.
4. Christian witness should include appropriate forms of interreligious dialogue.
5. Christians are to reject violence and the abuse of power in witness.[50]

A true dialogue does not mean giving up one's truth claims but rather entails patient and painstaking investigation of real differences and similarities. The purpose of the dialogue is not necessarily to soften the differences among religions but rather to clarify similarities and differences as well as issues of potential convergence and of impasse. A successful and fruitful dialogue often ends up in mutual affirmation of differences, divergent viewpoints, and varying interpretations.

The contemporary secular mind-set often mistakenly confuses tolerance with lack of commitment to any belief or opinion. That is to misunderstand the meaning of the term "tolerance." Deriving from the Latin term meaning "to bear a burden," tolerance is needed when real differences are allowed. Tolerance means patient and painstaking sharing, listening, and comparing notes — as well as the willingness to respectfully and lovingly make space for continuing differences.[51] To foster tolerance and heal conflicts between religions, in collaboration with representatives of other faiths of good will, Christians should do their best to help governments and other authorities to secure a safe, noncoercive place for adherents of religions to present their testimonies with-

49. Pontifical Council for Inter-Religious Dialogue, "Dialogue and Proclamation."
50. Netland, *Christianity and Religious Diversity*, pp. 234-42.
51. A highly useful discussion is Netland, *Encountering Religious Pluralism*, chap. 4.

out fear. The late missionary bishop Lesslie Newbigin reminds us that while for Christians the gospel is a "public truth," it has nothing to do with a desire to return to the Christendom model in which the state seeks to enforce beliefs.[52] That should be unacceptable to all religions. In a truly pluralist society, decision for beliefs can never be a matter of power-based enforcement. When Christians, Muslims, Hindus, Buddhists, Sikhs, Confucians, and followers of other faiths can without fear and threat meet each other in a free "marketplace" of beliefs and ideologies, genuine missionary encounters are also possible.[53]

Having now clarified Christian theological guidelines for interfaith engagement and constructed some directives for continuing comparative theological work, we move in the rest of the chapter from methodology toward actual material interfaith engagement with Jewish, Muslim, Hindu, and Buddhist traditions from a Christian perspective with the focus on community and its mission, if any. In so doing, we assume the "neutral" description of each tradition's views of community as set out above in chapter 12 and engage in intentional dialogue and mutual recognition.

The Church and the Synagogue

The Pain and Promise of Christian-Jewish Relations: A Theological Assessment

Having outlined above (chap. 12) the main Jewish ideas of community life and liturgy in the synagogue, including the idea of relationship to the religious other, we engage in this section the sister faith from the perspective of Christian ecclesiology. Three interrelated tasks await: first, a brief up-to-date assessment of Jewish-Christian relations from a theological perspective; second, the theological-ecclesiological implications of Christians and Israel forming one people of God with a lasting covenant; and third, the uniqueness of Christian mission to Israel.

What unites the Jewish and Christian parent-child traditions is not only their common origins and Scripture but also the strict monotheism of one and the same God, as well as messianism. What separates these faiths most deeply is the Christian reading of the First Testament in light of the messianic interpretation of Jesus of Nazareth, which also leads to a trinitarian monothe-

---

52. For details, see my "The Church in the Post-Christian Society."
53. See the WCC document "Religious Plurality and Christian Self-Understanding," #27.

ism.[54] Indeed, at its core, when raising the question of "what separates Jews and Christians from each other, the unavoidable answer is: a Jew."[55] That is because Jews from the beginning rejected the Christian claim for Jesus' messiahship and deity.[56] However, what makes this dilemma ironic is that when "Jesus came to move the covenant people to conversion to its God,"[57] it was only after the rejection by his own people that the crucified and risen Messiah became the "Savior of the nations."[58] This fact alone puts Christian-Jewish engagement in a unique interfaith context.[59]

Along with these and related theological reasons, what has damaged the relations between the two Abrahamic communities is the "supersessionist ideolog[y] of Christian identity," which rejects that Israel continues to be the people of God,[60] and its corollary, Christian anti-Semitism — which, in its most horrific form, led some churches to turn their backs on or even collaborate in the criminal act of the Shoah.[61] The anti-Semitic stream in Christianity has a painfully long and variegated history, stretching all the way from the earliest fathers to the twentieth century.[62]

It is against this sad and regrettable background — including also Jewish omission until modern times of a thoughtful engagement of Christianity and the proliferation of caricatures and prejudices — that "[s]ince the beginning of the twentieth century, the relationship between Judaism and Christianity has changed dramatically and is one of the few pieces of encouraging news

---

54. See my *Christ and Reconciliation*, pp. 238-50.

55. Lapide, *Resurrection of Jesus*, p. 30.

56. Heschel, "Jewish Views of Jesus," p. 149; see also Kogan, *Opening the Covenant*, pp. 90-95.

57. Pannenberg, *ST* 2:311.

58. Pannenberg, *ST* 2:312; so also Moltmann, *Way of Jesus Christ*, p. 34; see also J. G. Kelly, "The Cross," pp. 166-67.

59. Fortunately, we are now served with a most wonderful resource in all-things-Jewish-Christian-engagement, namely, Kessler and Wenborn, eds., *Dictionary of Jewish-Christian Relations*. A highly useful compendium is Kessler, *Introduction to Jewish-Christian Relations*. For a comparative theological engagement, other useful titles are Greenberg, *For the Sake of Heaven and Earth*; Poorthuis, Schwartz, and Turner, eds., *Interaction between Judaism and Christianity*; Wyschogrod, *Abraham's Promise*. For a thoughtful theological analysis of the conditions, foci, and boundaries of the mutual engagement, see Rosner, "Healing the Schism," pp. 39-51.

60. J. G. Kelly, "The Cross," p. 168.

61. For the role of Christian theology behind the events leading to the Holocaust, see Klein, *Anti-Judaism in Christian Theology*. For a historical and theological account, see also Idinopulos, "Christianity and the Holocaust."

62. For a thorough survey, see chaps. 3, 6, and 7 in Kessler, *Introduction to Jewish-Christian Relations*.

that can be reported today about encounter between religions." Factors contributing to this emerging rapprochement and healing of relations include "the Holocaust, the creation of the state of Israel, the development of the ecumenical movement and the work of the Second Vatican Council."[63] This affirming statement by Edward Kessler, a leading Jewish expert, is strongly supported by testimonies from other scholars, including the highly important *Dabru Emet: A Jewish Statement on Christians and Christianity* (2002), as well as from a growing number of Christian theologians.[64] The rediscovery of the Jewishness of Jesus and Paul and other correctives in Christian theology have further fueled mutual engagement.[65] All this means that we are in a promising place to attempt a brief constructive proposal.

Jews and Christians as the People of God

It was established above (chap. 13) that the concept of the "people of God" includes both Jews and Christians.[66] Consequently, the idea of the church as the "new" people replacing Israel as the "old" people[67] is to be rejected. As will be argued below, the inclusive view of the people of God is in keeping with Paul's vision in Romans 9–11. This theological conviction should guide constructive Christian theology in negotiating a proper relation to the Jewish mother faith.

As orientation to this complex discussion, it may be useful to outline briefly (but hopefully not in an oversimplified manner) the main options among Christian theologians with regard to this issue:[68]

- In the *supersessionist* (or traditional) view, the church as the "new people" replaces Israel and takes her place in the divine economy.[69]

---

63. Kessler, *Introduction to Jewish-Christian Relations*, p. 1. For Vatican II, see *Nostra Aetate*, #4, among others.

64. See, e.g., Flanagan, "Jewish-Christian Communion," p. 303.

65. For details, see Kessler, *Introduction to Jewish-Christian Relations*, pp. 10–15, 177–79, and passim.

66. Consistently affirmed by both Christian and Jewish contributors to Braaten and Jenson, eds., *Jews and Christians*.

67. *Epistle of Barnabas* (5.7; 7.5) goes so far as to reject that Israel ever was the people of God; see Pannenberg, *ST* 3:470–71.

68. I am following with minor modifications Bloesch, *Last Things*, pp. 43–46 and chap. 10, to which I acknowledge my indebtedness regarding this section, including some of the bibliographic references.

69. For a strong statement along this line, see Little, *The Crucifixion of the Jews*, p. 30;

- *Dispensationalists* make a categorical distinction between God's dealings with church and Israel, and they expect a literal fulfillment of Old Testament prophecies, including the rebuilding of the temple and its cult in the eschaton before the final consummation.[70] Because this view is novel and therefore marginal in Christian theology (and it was critiqued above), I do not consider it worth further critical engagement.
- For the *revisionists*, there is ultimate redemption for both Israel and church, and while for the latter it is through Christ, for the former it is not; indeed, the nonacceptance of Jesus as the Messiah for Israel is made a matter of obedience to God in this scheme.[71]
- In *reunionism*, God's covenant with Israel will never be annulled but rather fulfilled through Christ, Israel's and all peoples' Messiah; ultimately both peoples of God, that of the Old Testament and of the New Testament, will be reunited and saved.

In support of the reunionist vision — and thus rejecting supersessionism[72] — it seems clear and unambiguous in the biblical testimonies, first, that God's covenant with Israel is irrevocable, which is clearly and unambiguously testified to both in the Old Testament (Amos 9:14-15) and in the New Testament (Rom. 11:1, 29). In keeping with this point is the fact that although for Paul the church embodied the true Israel (Rom. 2:29; 9:6; Phil. 3:3; see also 1 Cor. 10:1-12), this did not mean God put Israel aside (Gal. 3:17) after the supersessionist scheme.[73] The inviolability of the covenant has of course other New Testament testimonies as well (Luke 1:72; Acts 3:25; and so forth). It is also undisputed in the biblical testimonies, second, that in the divine plan of salvation, Israel plays a unique role as the "light" to the nations (Isa. 42:6; 49:6; Acts 13:47; cf. 26:23). That commission is not made void by Israel's disobedience and failure in carrying out the mandate (although the importance of obedience for the covenant people is emphasized throughout biblical testimonies). Third, the New Testament teaches that in Jesus Christ, Israel's Messiah and the Savior of the whole world, the line of enmity between the chosen people and Gentiles has been eradicated forever (Eph. 2:12-22), hence making possible the coming eschatological reunionism.

---

see also Rowley, *Biblical Doctrine of Election*, p. 149. For an analysis of supersessionism, see Soulen, *The God of Israel and Christian Theology*, chap. 1.

70. Clouse, "Fundamentalist Eschatology," pp. 263-77.

71. Eckhardt, *Elder and Younger Brothers*, p. 104.

72. Materially similar is Marshall, "Christ and the Cultures."

73. Similarly Bloesch, *Last Things*, p. 44.

It is against this background of covenant theology that Paul picks up his discussion in the programmatic Romans 9–11. Taking for granted the inviolability of God's covenant, he clearly holds that Israel is the "trunk" of God's tree, and that the church, as the newcomer, can be compared to branches. Paul's concern is not to continue consolidating the trunk's permanent status but rather to show that in God's plan the branches could be united with the trunk (9:25)![74] This is a diametrically opposite angle from later Christian theology. At the same time, Paul is of course deeply troubled with the disobedience of Israel, that is, their unwillingness to embrace Christ as the Messiah. He finds consolation in the Old Testament remnant theology, having already affirmed God's faithfulness earlier in the letter amidst the faithlessness of his people (3:3–4). Paul is confident that Israel's current "hardening" is but temporary and, ironically, is used by God to further God's plans for the salvation of the whole world (11:11): "But through their trespass salvation has come to the Gentiles"; and even more ironically, this in turn has happened "so as to make Israel jealous" for receiving salvation! "In the 'No' of God's rejection is hidden the 'Yes' of his election"[75] (see also 11:28). As a result, God's purposes will be fulfilled: "a hardening has come upon part of Israel, until the full number of the Gentiles come in, and so all Israel will be saved" (11:25–26). There is thus a united eschatological goal for both Israel and the church,[76] and they are set in mutual, yet distinct, roles in relation to each other. On the one hand, the church is "dependent on Israel for the fulfillment of its mission," and on the other hand, "Israel stands in need of the church, for it is through the gospel proclaimed by the church that Israel will come to appreciate anew its glorious heritage and enter into its glorious destiny (Rom. 10:8–17; 1 Cor. 1:21–24)."[77]

All this means that the church should take a careful and self-critical look at herself as the people of God: "In its relations with the Jewish people the church had to decide for the first time whether it would view its own place in God's history of the human race along the lines of a provisional sign of a still awaited consummation, or view itself as the place of the at least initially actualized eschatological consummation itself." Unfortunately, as church history testifies, the church has opted for the latter mistaken alternative, which would frustrate the ultimate eschatological vision of *one* people of God gathered

74. So also Barth, "Jewish Problem and the Christian Answer," p. 200; in Wyschogrod, *Abraham's Promise*, p. 220.

75. Bloesch, *Last Things*, p. 201.

76. So also Barth, *CD* II/2, p. 199.

77. Bloesch, *Last Things*, pp. 203. This and the preceding paragraph are indebted to pp. 198–204 and to Pannenberg, *ST* 3:471–75 particularly.

under *one* God in the new Jerusalem (Rev. 21–22), consisting of both Gentiles and Jews. Furthermore, the exclusion of Israel from the peoplehood has also led during history to horrible consequences, including hatred, intolerance, harassment, and even crimes toward humanity.[78]

While holding to the continuation of God's covenant with Israel, the Christian church and theology also should exercise critical judgment in not identifying that status with the current secular state of Israel. Israel's political sins and wrongdoings, similarly to those of her Arabic neighbors, should be subjected to the same kinds of ethical and theological judgments as are other nations' deeds.[79]

The Unique Nature of the Christian Mission to the Jews

Unlike Judaism, Christianity — like Islam — is an active missionary faith. A central question asks how that essential Christian vocation relates to the Jewish community, which has a special standing. This brings us to the critical rejection of the revisionist view, which, while agreeing with much that has been said above, would oppose any notion of Jewish evangelization.[80] The counterargument to revisionism of this project is twofold. First, it can be easily seen that neither Paul nor the rest of the New Testament was advocating a "special path" for Israel in terms of the Jews not needing Jesus the Messiah. In other words, different salvific avenues have not been opened for Gentiles and Jews, respectively, but rather the contrary: this one people of God will all be saved in and through Christ. The church empowered by the Spirit was sent to begin the task of witnessing in "Jerusalem" on the way to the ends of the world. Similarly, not only did Paul preach to both Gentiles and Jews (Acts 9:15), but he also considered bringing the gospel of Christ to Israel to take priority over other works of mission (Rom. 1:16). In light of this, it can be said — somewhat counterintuitively — that not only is the church "betraying its evangelistic mandate if it withholds the gospel of salvation from the very people who gave us the Messiah and Savior of the world," but also that such "an attitude could be construed as the worst kind of anti-Semitism because it means deliberately bypassing the Jews in giving out the invitation to the banquet of the kingdom

---

78. Pannenberg, *ST* 3:476-77 (476).

79. So also Berkhof, "Israel as a Theological Problem," pp. 344-45; Bloesch, *Last Things*, p. 45.

80. In addition to revisionist advocates mentioned above, see also Osten-Sacken, *Christian-Jewish Dialogue*, pp. 166-75; van Buren, *Discerning the Way*, pp. 180-96.

(cf. Luke 14:15–24). Such an attitude could imply that the Jews are incapable or unworthy of receiving the blessings of the new covenant."[81]

The second response to the revisionist rejection of all proclamation to the Jewish people is equally important, namely, the unique and special nature of Jewish evangelization and mission. The gospel of Christ, even when rejected by Jews, is not calling the people of God into something "new" in the way Gentiles are being called. After all, Jesus Christ is Israel's Messiah before he is the Savior of the world. Mission to the Jews should also include a contrite and repentant spirit and acknowledgment of guilt for the sins in which Christians have participated throughout history. At the same time, Christians should acknowledge their indebtedness to Israel for the message of salvation and the Messiah. The Christian church should also acknowledge the special role and contribution of messianic Jews, the people of Israel who are publicly confessing their faith in Christ and following him in their own communities.[82] D. Bloesch summarizes it well: "The church must learn to incorporate the promises of God to Israel within its own life and mission. It should not see itself as the exclusive fulfillment of the promises of biblical prophecy but recognize that Israel too has a key role in the plan of salvation."[83] This attitude is in keeping with the Faith and Order–sponsored statement "The Church and the Jewish People" (1967):

> We are convinced that the Jewish people still have a significance of their own for the Church. It is not merely that by God's grace they have preserved in their faith truths and insights into his revelation which we have tended to forget. . . . But also it seems to us that by their very existence in spite of all attempt to destroy them, they make it manifest that God has not abandoned them. In this way they are a living and visible sign of God's faithfulness to men, an indication that he also upholds those who do not find it possible to recognize him in his Son. While we see their continuing existence as pointing to God's love and mercy, we explicitly reject any thought of considering their suffering during the ages as a proof of any special guilt. Why, in God's purpose, they have suffered in that way, we as outsiders do not know. What we do know, however, is the guilt of Christians who have all too often stood on the side of the persecutors instead of the persecuted.[84]

---

81. Bloesch, *Last Things*, pp. 209–10.
82. In agreement with Bloesch, *Last Things*, pp. 210–12.
83. Bloesch, *Last Things*, p. 45.
84. "The Church and the Jewish People," section III, n.p.

It seems to me that these two broad theological principles help us better appreciate this continuing dynamic tension facing Christian theology: how "to be faithful to the New Testament command to witness for Christ to all peoples and to convert all nations, while, at the same time, affirming the ongoing validity of the covenant between God and Israel via Abraham and Moses."[85] At the center of this tension, the American Jewish theologian Michael S. Kogan reminds us, lies the obvious but important fact that "historically Christianity has been theologically exclusive and humanistically universal, while Judaism has been theologically universal and humanistically exclusive." Christian theological exclusivism, however, does not entail a view to disqualifying others from salvation but — as the sympathetic Jewish observer further rightly notes — is funded by the conviction that Christ's salvific work is meant for the benefit of all.[86] As long as the Christian community firmly holds both to the christologically driven missionary calling for the sake of the salvation of all and the continuing validity of Yahweh's covenant with Israel, Christians may kindly and humbly put forth this question — again ably formulated by the Jewish theologian himself: Would the Jewish people, God's people, be "ready and willing to affirm that God, the God of Israel and of all humanity, was involved in the life of Jesus, in the founding of the Christian faith, in its growth and spread across much of the world, and in its central place in the hearts of hundreds of millions of their fellow beings"?[87] That many Jews refuse to embrace that Messiah should not in principle stop them from making this acknowledgment for the sake of progress and reconciliation.

Church and *Ummah*

Muslim-Christian Relations in a Theological Perspective: A Brief Assessment

Not only does Judaism stand in a unique position in relation to Christianity in the wider matrix of interfaith relations, so does Islam, albeit differently. As mentioned above (chap. 12), that closeness is also acknowledged by Islam.[88]

---

85. Kogan, *Opening the Covenant*, p. xii.

86. Kogan, *Opening the Covenant*, pp. xii–xiii.

87. Kogan, *Opening the Covenant*, p. xiii; see also p. 13; on p. 32 Kogan makes the striking statement that the existence of "many billions [who] worship Israel's God, only some 15 million of them being Jews" means that "[t]his is either some gigantic accident or the partial fulfillment of God's commission to Abraham."

88. For a concise scrutiny of the Qur'anic perception of Christianity, see Watt,

That said, it is too rarely appreciated how different the Christianity first encountered by the Prophet and the early Muslim *ummah* was from what the contemporary global Christian church is now. In the seventh century, notwithstanding internal differences, there was one undivided church (at least formally). Importantly, the segments of the church that early Islam engaged were either marginal or heretical in the eyes of the mainstream Christianity, namely, churches in Arabia, Egypt, Palestine, Syria, and Iraq, which represented Nestorianism and Monophysitism (of various sorts). Most ironically, many of the objections of Muslims against the orthodox Christian doctrine of the Trinity and Christology either stem from or are strongly flavored by these Christian divergences.[89]

Regretfully, the Christian-Muslim encounters throughout history have been characterized by misperceptions, misrepresentations, and even hostility. That said, "[r]egarding the relations of Muslims and Christians from the seventh century on, it is not sufficiently appreciated — especially by ill-informed or biased publicists — that these relations were characterized by far greater tolerance than western Europe had known during the Middle Ages."[90] The situation, however, worsened dramatically by the time of the Crusades.[91] Illustrative is the fact that whereas for Christian apologists beginning from the seventh century, such as John of Damascus,[92] Islam was represented more like a heresy, from the late medieval period onward it was taken as a false religion, apostasy.[93]

In the contemporary situation, a number of promising signs indicate that concentrated efforts are under way to continue constructive mutual engagement, heal memories, and improve understanding of the two faiths. These include the widely acclaimed "A Common Word" process,[94] the long-standing Building Bridges Muslim-Christian Dialogue,[95] and a growing number of re-

---

Muslim-Christian Encounters, pp. 14-24; Bennett, *Understanding Christian-Muslim Relations*, chap. 2.

89. For details, see Watt, *Muslim-Christian Encounters*, chap. 1. See also my *Trinity and Revelation*, pp. 365-85, and *Christ and Reconciliation*, pp. 250-64.

90. Fakhry, "An Islamic Perspective," p. 394.

91. Fakhry, "An Islamic Perspective," p. 397.

92. See my *Trinity and Revelation*, p. 378, on his engagement of debates concerning Scripture and Trinity, and *Christ and Reconciliation*, pp. 258-59, 388-89, for christological debates.

93. See Watt, *Muslim-Christian Encounters*, pp. 70-72, 83-88.

94. For details concerning the aim, activities, and constant flow of publications, see A Common Word, http://www.acommonword.com/.

95. For details concerning the aim, activities, and constant flow of publications, see

gional, national, and local encounters.[96] We are reminded of the urgency of this important task by the "ACW Letter," signed by over a hundred Muslim and Christian leaders from all over the world, produced by the "A Common Word" dialogue: "Muslims and Christians together make up well over half of the world's population. Without peace and justice between these two religious communities, there can be no meaningful peace in the world. The future of the world depends on peace between Muslims and Christians."[97]

Since excellent historical surveys and assessments of the fifteen-hundred-year encounter between the two traditions exist, there is no need to summarize that in a few paragraphs here.[98] Rather, for the sake of systematic/constructive theological work, let us first briefly map the key areas of doctrinal interest and concern for the sake of future prospects. Thereafter, the important question of mission and its relation to colonialism and political powers, a shared concern for both traditions, will be taken up.

In Search of Common Themes and Shared Convictions

Interfaith engagement should involve both differences and similarities. Never should its goal be a "cheap" compromise in which all parties sell out their distinctive treasures and lose identities. On the other hand, analogously to Christian ecumenism, efforts toward mutual recognition may also build on perceived real differences in the midst of which — and at times, above which, so to speak — are shared convictions and common themes. That is the goal of this section.

I find highly useful a paradigm of the Christian approach to Islam from history in that of Nicholas of Cusa. He testified to the horrendous disaster in the capital of the Eastern Christian church, Constantinople, as the forces of the Ottoman Empire under the leadership of Mehmed II in 1453 brutally conquered the city. Rather than instigating retaliation and hatred — and refusing

---

"The Building Bridges Seminar," Berkley Center for Religion, Peace & World Affairs, http://berkleycenter.georgetown.edu/projects/the-building-bridges-seminar.

96. These are well-documented and analyzed in main surveys listed above, and many of them also have continuously updated Web resources.

97. "The ACW Letter," A Common Word, 2007, http://www.acommonword.com/the-acw-document/; Volf, *Allah*, p. 1.

98. For a brief, useful survey, see Winkler, *Contemporary Muslim and Christian Responses*, chap. 2. Useful broad overviews and assessments include Bennett, *Understanding Christian-Muslim Relations*; Watt, *Muslim-Christian Encounters*.

to give support to another crusade by Pope Nicholas V — this Catholic cardinal penned *De pace fidei* (*On the Harmonious Peace of Religions*). It issued a call to organize a conference "in Jerusalem," under the auspices of the heavenly King of kings, between rival religions, to achieve a "harmony among religions" and "perpetual peace."[99] Against mutual fear and suspicion, Cusa asserted that all people, including the Muslims, worship one and the same God, and that if they fail to do so, it is because of ignorance.[100] That is the core of his celebrated dictum *una religio in varietate rituum*, "one religion in a variety of rites."[101] Importantly, his approach had nothing to do with a pluralism that sells out Christian identity and expects the Muslims to do the same. The Catholic leader was firmly and robustly convinced of Christian truth (and not all aspects of his defense are necessarily a model to us in the third millennium).[102] My point is that — set in the highly conflictual and volatile situation of the times — "[f]rom a Christian perspective . . . his strategy can be seen as an exercise in charitable interpretation";[103] in Cusa's words, he "presupposed not a faith that is other but a faith that is one and the same."[104]

These two Abrahamic communities would do well in their mutual engagement and dialogue to mind the lesson of Cusa's example: honest and open highlighting of differences, yet, because of a shared common belief in one God, a special kind of convergence absent in other faith encounters except for those with Judaism. Recall the wise words from Vatican II's *Nostra Aetate*: "The Church regards with esteem also the Moslems. They adore the one God, living and subsisting in Himself; merciful and all-powerful, the Creator of heaven and earth, who has spoken to men; they take pains to submit wholeheartedly to even His inscrutable decrees, just as Abraham, with whom the faith of Islam takes pleasure in linking itself, submitted to God. Though they do not acknowledge Jesus as God, they revere Him as a prophet. They also honor Mary, His virgin Mother; at times they even call on her with devotion."[105]

The common basis comes to the fore with regard to revelation. What binds together the *ummah* and the church is that both derive their scriptures from the common Israelite source. Whereas the Christians continue holding

---

99. Nicholas of Cusa's *De pace fidei* and *Cribratio Alkorani* 68. For useful comments, see Volf, *Allah*, chap. 2.

100. Nicholas of Cusa, *De pace fidei* 5.

101. Nicholas of Cusa, *De pace fidei* 6.

102. Just think of his critical scrutiny of the Qur'anic teaching in *Cribratio Alkorani*.

103. Volf, *Allah*, p. 50.

104. Nicholas of Cusa, *De pace fidei* 10.

105. *Nostra Aetate*, #3.

to the full scriptural status of the First Testament but see it fulfilled — having reached its goal, so to speak — in the coming of the Messiah as testified to in the Second Testament, Muslim tradition believes that, similarly, the Old Testament forms the basic revelation to be fulfilled in light of the direct final revelation given to the Prophet, yet also that Christianity's understanding is partially wrong and partially incomplete. The relationship, thus, is complex and multilayered, as discussed in detail in *Trinity and Revelation* (chap. 8). For the continuing mutual engagement, a highly recommended venue is one of the theologically most promising initiatives in this respect: "scriptural reasoning." Specifically designed for mutual scriptural study among Abrahamic traditions, it gives opportunities for Jews, Muslims, and Christians to study together on another's and one's own holy book. It proceeds inductively, guided by the text itself. It does not require any organization or logistics of a formal dialogue. Rather, it can take place in homes or worship places, and it is based on personal relationships and trust.[106]

Because of the shared scriptural tradition, specific doctrinal topics can also be studied in common as part of the scriptural-reasoning task. That is highly useful for the purposes of letting each party scrutinize the meaning of later doctrinal/theological developments. This is highly relevant to the church because, as mentioned above (chap. 12), many Muslim objections to Christology and the Trinity may be due to marginal (or even heretical) Christian interpretations that are also rejected by most Christians. Christology, as briefly discussed in part 1 and in much detail in *Christ and Reconciliation* (chaps. 10 and 15), is a unique arena of scriptural and theological engagement. In no other religious tradition — not even Judaism — does Jesus (and his mother, Mary) play any role. Yet for Islam, "christology" — or, to be more precise, "Jesusology," because of the reluctance of the Muslim tradition to go beyond the human Jesus of Nazareth — is so central a theme that one cannot be an orthodox Muslim if one dismisses the numerous references to Jesus in the Qur'an and Hadith. Christology, of course, also brings to surface the deep and seemingly irreconcilable differences in interpretation, highlighting the importance of the principle endorsed above, namely, letting both differences and commonalities guide the mutual engagement.

Closely related to the role of Jesus is the complex but promising question of the doctrine of God, more specifically, first, the relation of Allah, Yahweh,

---

106. For basics, see Ford and Pecknold, eds., *Promise of Scriptural Reasoning*. A highly useful, continuously updated database is the Web site of the *Journal of Scriptural Reasoning*, at http://www.scripturalreasoning.org/; see also my *Trinity and Revelation*, p. 178.

and the Father of Jesus Christ to each other, and second, the conditions for Muslims endorsing in some real sense, or at least working toward easing the seeming impasse for recognizing, the possibility of monotheism also as Christian trinitarianism. The detailed discussion in *Trinity and Revelation* (chap. 15) sought to address these two interrelated questions, also including in the conversation Jewish monotheism. Briefly put, the main result and tentative suggestion was this: if Christians are able to identify Yahweh and the Father of Jesus Christ (a view Christians endorse universally in keeping with the New Testament witness), notwithstanding deep disagreements about the Trinity, it should not be impossible to say mutually that with "Allah" Muslims mean to speak of the same God Christians and Jews know from the Bible. That would leave much room for negotiation and even disagreement, but broad monotheistic embrace along the lines of Cusa would stay intact. The shared yet different basis would serve well the dialogue that, as a form of exchange, "makes us catch sight of a life of fellowship and exchanges in God himself, source of all mission and all dialogue." Recall that in trinitarian ecclesiology and missiology, dialogue corresponds to the being of the triune God, and hence the confession of faith in one God as Father, Son, and Spirit, an eternal loving communion, is an invitation to dialogue and engagement.[107]

Other common areas and concerns that could be addressed by common scriptural study include the doctrine of creation (*Creation and Humanity*, chap. 5); human person, including sin and "Fall" (chap. 14); salvation (*Spirit and Salvation*, chap. 8); as well as eschatology (above, chap. 3). Commonalities and differences also come to the surface in the missional orientation of both traditions, the topic of the next section.

Mission, Colonialism, and Political Power: Shared Concerns

Similarly to Judaism, Islam sees "the appropriate way to human fulfillment in obedience to a divinely revealed law," named in that tradition the Shari'a, which differs from Judaism in that it is "given to be followed by all humanity, and not just by one special community."[108] How does Christian mission relate to that claim? Instead of a divinely given law to govern all of life as in a theocracy, Christian mission aims at providing a holistic way of life based on

---

107. Jukko, *Trinitarian Theology in Muslim-Christian Encounters*, p. 214; see also pp. 221-22.

108. K. Ward, *Religion and Community*, p. 31.

love of God and neighbor, leaving open issues of government (most inclusively understood). From a Christian perspective, it is highly ironic that the Islamic pursuit of global Shari'a has from the beginning been closely allied with a specific ethnicity and language (Arabic) and, in modern and contemporary times, often allied with nationalism,[109] particularly in the regions of the world colonized by European powers.[110] How would a universal reach to all humanity be reconciled with that? K. Ward poses the following challenge to the contemporary Islamic world, strongly and vehemently setting itself against the West: "If Islam is indeed meant to be a global community, then it is self-defeating for Islam to oppose 'the West,' when Westerners should be Muslims, too, and when many are." And he continues: "One of the major tensions within Islam is between the drive for global community, inclusive of every race and nation, and its alliance in fact with many countries of the developing world, finding in Islam a political tool for rejecting the colonial and economic domination of the white Western nations."[111]

As mentioned in chapter 12, both Islam and Christianity carry the legacy of colonialism as part of their mission history. Unbeknownst to many is the fact that "[w]hile from the first there were considerable numbers of Christians under Muslim rule, yet until the appearance of European colonialism there were virtually no Muslims under Christian rule except for limited periods."[112] Everywhere Christians lived under Muslim rule, the Shari'a law totally forbade Christian sharing of the gospel with Muslims. Indeed, according to Shari'a law, the penalty for apostasy — the Islamic perception of converting to Christianity — is death.[113] Undoubtedly it is a sensitive and at times painful process of mutual engagement and life together that is needed for the wounds to heal, the animosities to be transformed into trust, and the mutual condemnations to be changed into recognition; that path, however, is worth every tear because so much is at stake in the relations between the world's two largest monotheist communities.

The same was affirmed by the French Roman Catholic Church in an extended exchange with local Muslims. Rather than pushing the Trinity to the margins, it was stated that "[t]he Church is committed to dialogue above all because of her faith in the trinitarian mystery of the one God . . . [which] makes us catch sight of a life of fellowship and exchanges in God himself, source of all mission and all dialogue." Dialogue corresponds to the being of

109. See the rejection of nationalism by Maududi, *Nationalism and Islam*, p. 10.
110. See B. Lewis, *Islam and the West*.
111. K. Ward, *Religion and Community*, pp. 32–33 (33).
112. Watt, *Muslim-Christian Encounters*, p. 74.
113. See Watt, *Muslim-Christian Encounters*, p. 70.

the triune God and hence the confession of faith in one God as Father, Son, and Spirit; eternal loving communion is an invitation to dialogue and engagement.[114] The Finnish theologian Risto Jukko, expert in Muslim-Christian relations, summarizes the trinitarian foundation of the dialogue as it came to expression in the French situation: "It seems that only the concept of the trinitarian God can be the basis for fruitful interreligious Christian dialogue with non-Christians . . . [especially] Muslims. Even though the concept is an article of Christian theology . . . it unites transcendence and immanence, creation and redemption in such a way that from the Christian standpoint dialogue becomes possible and meaningful. It is the hermeneutical key to interpret the religious experiences of non-Christians (as well as of Christians)."[115]

The Church and Hindus

Differences of Orientation

Because of the difference of orientations between Hindu and Christian traditions, namely, the former's individualistic pursuit of release and the latter's deeply communal faith, dialogue focused on ecclesiology yields fewer results and areas of shared concerns than between the church and the synagogue or the *ummah*. Individual doctrinal topics between the two traditions have been investigated in detail in other volumes and will not be repeated here:

- Scripture and revelation (*Trinity and Revelation*, chap. 8)
- the notion of the divine and God (*Trinity and Revelation*, chap. 15)
- avatars and Christology, including "atonement" (*Christ and Reconciliation*, chaps. 10 and 15)
- creation (*Creation and Humanity*, chap. 5)
- humanity (*Creation and Humanity*, chap. 14)
- Spirit(s) (*Spirit and Salvation*, chap. 5)
- "salvation" (*Spirit and Salvation*, chap. 8)
- "eschatology" and consummation (part 1, chap. 3, of this volume)

In the discussion on Hindu spiritual life and devotion above (chap. 12), it became evident that in many ways it is oriented differently than Judeo-

---

114. Jukko, *Trinitarian Theology in Muslim-Christian Encounters*, p. 214.
115. Jukko, *Trinitarian Theology in Muslim-Christian Encounters*, pp. 221–22.

Christian tradition — for example, prayer for the Hindu, rather than petition and pleading, as in the Judeo-Christian tradition, is more about chanting the sacred mantra, linked with the search for *darśana* in the divine presence. There is also what can be called "ritual enhancement," that is, a devotional practice that "aims at sustaining or improving the circumstances of the worshiper," whether that means practical life situations like sickness or business or family concerns, or the spiritual aims of liberation and release.[116] This is of course also a common feature of Abrahamic traditions. What is a foundational difference has to do with another common theme throughout Hindu devotional life, namely, "negotiation or exchange, in which devotional performances become occasions for giving human resources of food, gifts, and devotion to supernatural entities and powers in exchange for human well-being, which is understood to flow from those persons and powers as a consequence of the rite."[117] Although this kind of exchange mentality is not unknown in Christian spirituality — just think of the ill-advised "prosperity gospel" mentality in which, for example, tithing may be taken as a means of "demanding" or at least expecting from God a plentiful return — theologically it is a foreign concept.

Religious Diversity: Connections and Disconnections

As discussed above (chap. 12), Hinduism exhibits internal diversity unlike any other living faith tradition, and its relation to the religious other is also more open than in Abrahamic faiths. Its tendency to assimilate others under itself, believing itself to be the "original" and perhaps best revelation, makes it in some real sense a counterpart to Roman Catholicism.[118] At the same time, the Hindu attitude toward Christian faith is more complicated than that. Consider the well-known spokespersons of Hinduism in the West, Swami Vivekananda, India's delegate to the World Parliament of Religions meeting in Chicago in 1893, and Sarvepalli Radhakrishnan, the former president of India. Known for tolerance and religious coexistence, they are also critics of Christianity.[119] Needless to say, the rejection of Christianity among Hindutva advocates and other "orthodox" Hindus, such as the members of the Arya Samaj, "an orga-

116. Courtright, "Worship and Devotional Life," p. 9820.
117. Courtright, "Worship and Devotional Life," p. 9820.
118. Noted by many, e.g., Clooney, "Hindu Views of Religious Others," pp. 306-7.
119. For a detailed and balanced investigation, see Streiker, "Hindu Attitude toward Other Religions"; a similar judgment on Vivekananda can be found in Clooney, "Hindu Views of Religious Others," pp. 320-23.

nization which clings to the infallibility of the Vedas, seeks the extirpation of all foreign religions, and which devotes itself to incessant propaganda,"[120] illustrates the other side of Hinduism's efforts to embrace religious diversity.

Indeed, there is no standard, universal Hindu response to the religious other.[121] In a recent programmatic essay, the Catholic expert on Hindu-Christian relations, F. X. Clooney, SJ, outlined no fewer than five different Hindu positions toward Christianity, from exclusivism,[122] to inclusivism, to "pragmatic interreligious collaboration in search of truth and nonviolence (M. Gandhi)," to Vivekananda's "hierarchical inclusivism," to "oppositional inclusivism" represented by "Ram Swamp's new hindu apologetics."[123] By seeking to build and strengthen Indian and Hindu identity, Swamp countered strongly and sharply what he saw as Christian (and Muslim) attempts at hegemony in India, under which he also counted Vatican II's inclusivism.[124] Although the constitution of India rules that the country is secular and that there is room for religious coexistence, conflicts, even occasional violence,[125] between Hindus and Muslims, occasionally with Buddhists, and continuously with Christians, challenge that coexistence all the time.[126]

In light of the complexity of the Hindu perception of the religious other discussed here and above in chapter 12, it is important to recall that the roots of Hindu-Christian engagement and coexistence go far back in history. It is probable that there was a Christian presence in India as early as the first century. Syrian Christianity is believed to have been present beginning in the fourth century. That said, we do not have any records of mutual dialogue before the colonial era.[127] Although Western colonialism helped poison mutual relations between Hindus and Christians in a number of ways, it is significant that, beginning from the end of the nineteenth century, a new wave of interpretations of Christ related to the so-called Indian renaissance or neo-Hindu

120. Streiker, "Hindu Attitude toward Other Religions," p. 90 n. 85.

121. Daniel, *Hindu Response to Religious Pluralism*, pp. 233–36.

122. Exclusivism in its Brahmanic, Vedic religion form also includes a vehement rejection of Buddhism as a Hindu-originated sect; see Clooney, "Hindu Views of Religious Others," pp. 308–12.

123. Clooney, "Hindu Views of Religious Others."

124. Clooney, "Hindu Views of Religious Others," pp. 323–26. See, e.g., Swamp's *Hindu View of Christianity and Islam*.

125. See Rambachan, "Co-Existence of Violence and Non-Violence in Hinduism."

126. For a recent, thoughtful reflection, see Amaladoss, "Religious Diversity and Harmonious Living"; more extensively, Amaladoss, *Making Harmony*.

127. For details, see Rambachan, "Hindu-Christian Dialogue"; more widely, Coward, introduction to *Hindu-Christian Dialogue*.

reform emerged, testing affinities between the two traditions. Furthermore, several Hindu writers were turned on by the social teachings of Christ but did not make a personal commitment to him. There are also Hindus who have become Christians but insist they have remained Hindus.[128]

These and related experiences in the past both speak to the complexity of relations between the two traditions and open up some possibilities for continuing common exploration of common themes and concerns.[129] I find it highly useful that according to Anand Amaladass, writing in 1988, "the dialogue initiative has come to stay in India" rather than, as with some other major interfaith engagements, predominantly in the Global North's academic settings. He continues:

> During the last two decades this initiative has grown among Hindus and Christians, though it is difficult to give the exact percentage of Indians who are affected by the dialogue movement. In the name of dialogue various centres are opened by the Christian communities and well-informed Hindus participating in inter-religious seminars and prayer meetings are in the increase. They find that more of "living together" for a few days rather than formal discussions and seminars brings about a better result, creating fellowship among participants of different religions. This mode of dialogue is gaining ground among many dialogue groups that have been meeting for a number of years.[130]

The Church and Buddhists

The Slow Emergence of Buddhist and Christian Engagement

In contrast to Christianity's interaction with Judaism and Islam, Christian and Buddhist theologies do not have a history of dialogue and mutual engagement; indeed, until the nineteenth century, very little exchange took place. True, there are some occasional early references in Christian literature, the first known going back to Clement of Alexandria's *Stromata* (around 200), but

---

128. See my *Christ and Reconciliation*, pp. 277–84.
129. See further Klostermaier, "The Future of Hindu-Christian Dialogue." Still useful is also Abhishiktananda, *Hindu-Christian Meeting Point*.
130. Amaladass, "Viewpoints," pp. 7–8.

his comment shows little if any familiarity with Buddha's teachings.[131] From the sixth to the eighth century, the Nestorian Christians had some meaningful encounters with Buddhists in India and China.[132] Franciscan missionaries of the thirteenth and fourteenth centuries gave commending reports of the lifestyle of Buddhist monks in China, but again, theologically they did nothing more than create "the scanty image of Buddhism that prevailed in Western Christianity for centuries." At the same time, ironically, throughout the Middle Ages under the pseudonymous legends of Barlaam and Josaphat, Gautama was widely venerated among Christians![133] The best-chronicled friendship-based and intimate knowledge of Buddhism among Christians comes from the sixteenth-century Jesuit Francis Xavier.[134]

The seventeenth-century Chinese Buddhist scholar Ouyi Zhixu presented weighty criticisms against some key aspects of the Jesus tradition, particularly focusing on the absurdity of the "Lord of Heaven" having been born as a human being.[135] Around the same time in Japan, onetime convert to Christianity Fabian Fucan resorted to the kinds of criticisms well known from other religions, including the illicit status of Mary. He also ridiculed the coming of Jesus at such a late moment of history. Furthermore, Fucan concludes that because followers of Jesus "are preaching a doctrine wicked and contrary to the Way of the Sages . . . the wise ruler has decided to stamp [them] out" of Japan.[136]

Similarly to all other faith traditions, Buddhism in the contemporary world faces massive challenges, and many of those have to do with relations to Christianity:[137] Buddhism "has been shaped through encounters with Western colonialism, Christian missions, and modernization."[138] The effects of modernization are aptly named by D. L. McMahan "detraditionalization," "demythologization," and "psychologization." These tactics, well known and widely tested in post-Enlightenment Christianity, seek to highlight the importance of

---

131. Clement of Alexandria, *Stromata (Miscellanies)* 1.15.

132. For the seventh-century Nestorian bishop Alopen's analogy between Christian apophatic theology and the Buddhist notion of sunyata, see *Discourse on Monotheism* 58, in Saeki, *Nestorian Documents and Relics in China.*

133. Schmidt-Leukel, "Intimate Strangers," pp. 4–5 (4) (this essay title inspired the heading for this section); see further Almond, "The Buddha of Christendom."

134. For comments on Xavier, see Küng, "A Christian Response," pp. 307-8.

135. Zhixu, in *JBC*, pp. 229–30.

136. Fucan, "Deus Destroyed," pp. 223–26 (226).

137. For a thoughtful reflection, see Obeyesekere, "Thinking Globally about Buddhism."

138. Netland, *Christianity and Religious Diversity*, p. 83.

reason and critique over traditional authority patterns and sources; to reinterpret beliefs problematic to modern reason, such as hell, spirits, demons, and
so forth; and to identify connections between Buddhist analysis of humanity
and the world in relation to contemporary Western psychology.[139] Part of this
process is the coming of Buddhism into the Global North in new contextualized forms, from Zen Buddhism to Buddhist theosophical societies, among
others.[140] The growing desire to engage the religious other, as mentioned above
(chap. 12), undoubtedly has to do also with these modernity-related changes
and moves to new locations. It is yet to be seen what the specific implications
for Christian-Buddhist relations may be.

Discerning Differences and Potential Common Concerns

Without repeating the detailed comparisons in other volumes on all main
Christian doctrinal topics,[141] for the sake of continuing dialogue let us regis-
ter these foundational differences, which have to be kept in mind during the
mutual engagement:

- Although the *sangha* is an important part of Buddhist pursuit of spiritual
  liberation, as in Hinduism, spiritual liberation is ultimately a matter
  of each individual's effort. Hence, Buddhism is not, ecclesiologically, a
  religion of "communion," to use the Christian parlance.[142]
- Although not atheistic in the Western sense, God(s) is marginal to Buddhists. One's salvation depends on one's own effort. Even the Buddha is
  not a savior after Christian tradition, just the one who set the example to

---

139. McMahan, *The Making of Buddhist Modernism*, chap. 2; see also McMahan, *Buddhism in the Modern World*. A shining example of such a demythologized version of Buddhism
is S. Batchelor, *Buddhism without Beliefs*. I am indebted to Netland, *Christianity and Religious
Diversity*, pp. 83–86.

140. For details and sources, see Netland, *Christianity and Religious Diversity*, pp. 86–102.

141. For Scripture and revelation, see *Trinity and Revelation*, chap. 8, and on the notion
of the divine/ultimate reality and God, chap. 15; for Christology and atonement, see *Christ
and Reconciliation*, chaps. 10 and 15; for creation, see *Creation and Humanity*, chap. 5, and on
the human being, chap. 14; for the Spirit(s), see *Spirit and Salvation*, chap. 5, and chap. 8 for
salvation/release; and for "eschatology," see part 1 above, chap. 3.

142. A clear indication of *sangha*'s noncentral nature is the almost total lack of references to it in what can be taken as the most authoritative summary of original Buddha's
teachings in the English-speaking world by the Venerable Dr. Walpola Sri Rahula, a Buddhist
monk and scholar from Sri Lanka, *What the Buddha Taught*.

follow and a mighty inspirer through his profound insight. Similarly, his teachings do not constitute divine revelation but rather spiritual-ethical guidance to help human effort.

- Although Buddhism does not lack a social ethic or noble examples of working toward peace, reconciliation, and improvement of the society and world, as a religious-ethical system it is not optimistic about the future consummation, and "Buddhists do not seek to bring the world under the laws of God"[143] after Islam or look for eschatological fulfillment after Christianity. Ultimately, with Hinduism, it is a religion of renouncement (even if the members of the *sangha* necessarily need "householders" to support them and the religious, in turn, give the laypeople the opportunity to gain merit through donations and service).[144]

When it comes to their discernment of Christian tradition, a number of foundational obstacles and differences stand in the way. With all their appreciation of Jesus' ethical life, ministry, and teaching, "the single most problematic aspect of Jesus' identity is his portrayal by Christians as God," says the leading Tibetan Buddhist scholar and practitioner José Ignacio Cabezón. He specifies the problem in this way: "The problem lies not in the claim that Jesus is the incarnation or manifestation of a deity. What I find objectionable is (a) the Christian characterization of the deity whose incarnation Jesus is said to be, and (b) the claim that Jesus is unique in being an incarnation."[145] Related is the Christian doctrine of God as Trinity.

Despite these radical differences of orientation, what is common to both traditions is their missionary nature.[146] Indeed, unbeknownst to many, Buddhism is at its core a missional tradition and, as discussed above (chap. 12), has been conducting missionary work since its inception. That said, its missional nature is nothing like the Christian tradition, whose mission is anchored in and derived from the trinitarian divine movement for the salvation of the world. The *sangha's* mission is to spread the knowledge of the liberating insight of the Buddha for the sake of men and women pursuing a similar path and for the well-being and benefit of all.

Concerning the related topic of women's status in religion and the re-

143. K. Ward, *Religion and Community*, pp. 53–54 (53). For examples of active sociopolitical concern, see, e.g., the Web site for the Soka Gakkai International movement: http://www.sgi.org.

144. Similarly K. Ward, *Religion and Community*, pp. 68–71.

145. Cabezón, "Buddhist Views of Jesus," p. 21.

146. See Mikaelsson, "Missional Religion."

ligious community, the Christian church may be in a position to inspire and instruct the Buddhist community. Despite the inclusive vision of Buddha discussed above, particularly in the Theravada heartlands, but also almost as a rule throughout the Buddhist world, females are either completely banned from the highest religious calling — full monastic life — or relegated to lower monastic levels. Religious authority is kept firmly in men's hands.[147] It is yet to be seen what accommodation to modernity and our globalized world may mean in this respect. The same challenge faces Islam and is not irrelevant to most Hindu communities either.

Having engaged the four religious communities and their spiritual life from a Christian perspective, we now intend to do the same with secularisms. The following section assumes the short discussion of what secularism is and of its relationship to global religiosity in the introduction to part 2.

Christian Church and Ecclesiology in the "Secular City"

Forms and Ways of Secularisms

With the founding of the United States of America in 1789, a new kind of officially formulated relation between religion and society emerged as the Constitution endorsed freedom of religion and avoidance of privileging any particular faith.[148] The same was reaffirmed with the founding of India and Israel in 1947.[149] The Russian Federation, formerly the atheistic Soviet Union, states that it "is a secular state. No religion may be established as a state or obligatory one. Religious associations shall be separated from the State and shall be equal before the law."[150] Whereas particularly in the United States the desire not to affiliate the state with religion was motivated mostly by need for tolerance and freedom of choice, in France, Spain, and Italy it was "a secularism of protest against the privilege" of the dominant religion, the Roman Catholic Church,

147. See Lai, "Engendering Buddhism"; Kabilsingh, *Thai Women in Buddhism*; Ito, "New Beginnings."

148. The First Amendment to the Constitution is available at Legal Information Institute, https://www.law.cornell.edu/constitution/first_amendment.

149. For comments, see K. Ward, *Religion and Community*, pp. 103–5.

150. The Constitution of the Russian Federation, First Section: Main Provisions, #14:1–2, http://www.constitution.ru/en/10003000-02.htm. For the need to exercise caution when applying the term "secularization" in general and to the American context in particular, see Haight, *CCH*, 1:33–35.

with much power, wealth, and influence.[151] The cruelty of religious wars also lies behind the modern movement to separate church and state.[152]

These and similar decisions by a number of states in the post-Enlightenment world testify to a growing desire to ensure freedom of religion, including the choice not to follow any faith tradition.[153] The rise of democratic forms of government is undoubtedly linked with this development, although the relationship between freedom, toleration, and democracy is a complex issue.[154] That said, as mentioned in the introduction to part 2, even though secularism enjoys overwhelming influence in the Global North,[155] religions are not being marginalized; rather, the opposite is true.[156] As the British philosopher R. Trigg aptly summarizes: "Growing religious diversity, coupled with further moves to a more active secularism in the West, has been coupled with a marked growth in commitment to various religions, not least Christianity and Islam, in other countries across the globe."[157] Linked with that is the rise of fundamentalist and ethnic projects to endorse the "religion of the land," whether by Islamic, Hindu, and some right-wing American constituencies; at least one country, Sri Lanka, still holds Buddhism as the state religion (albeit with at least formal endorsement of freedom of religion).[158]

Unknown to many, secularization is not limited to the Global North, although its epicenter definitely is in Europe and North America. The meaning and manifestations of secularism, however, are quite different in various contexts of the Global South. As is well known, traditional religions are "part and parcel of the whole fabric of African cultural life."[159] Unlike in the West, reli-

---

151. The classic tracts from John Locke are *A Letter concerning Toleration* (1685) and *Two Treatises on Government* (1690). For the 1689 Act of Toleration in England and its significance to freedom and diversity, see Trigg, *Religious Diversity*, pp. 7–8; for the religious "dissenters" in colonial America, see pp. 8–9. Useful wider treatments are Zagorin, *How the Idea of Religious Toleration Came to the West*; A. Levine, ed., *Early Modern Skepticism and the Origin of Toleration*.

152. K. Ward, *Religion and Community*, pp. 107–8 (107).

153. For a thoughtful philosophical reflection, see Trigg, *Equality, Freedom, and Religion*.

154. For a short discussion, see Trigg, *Religious Diversity*, pp. 11–15.

155. A persistent believer in the advance of secularism (at least in the Global North, although he seems to assume a wider appeal to it as well) is Bruce, *God Is Dead* and *Secularization*.

156. See Toft, Philpott, and Shah, *God's Century*. For a highly thoughtful theological reflection, see Netland, *Christianity and Religious Diversity*, chap. 2.

157. Trigg, *Religious Diversity*, p. 3.

158. See the Constitution of the Democratic Socialist Republic of Sri Lanka, chap. 2, #9, http://www.priu.gov.lk/Cons/1978Constitution/Chapter_02_Amd.html.

159. Metuh, *African Religions in Western Conceptual Schemes*, p. 4.

gion in Africa is not separate from the rest of life; it is part of everything: "To be an African in the traditional setting is to be truly religious."[160] Hence, a separate word for "religion" is not needed.[161] The pervasive nature of traditional religion helps explain the lack of appeal of atheism or even a Western type of secularism in that continent. Even when gods do not intervene in people's lives and defeat the opposing powers, as happened during the colonial oppression of Africa, faith in gods does not disappear among the traditionalists.[162] This is not to say necessarily that secularism is unknown in Africa. It is to say that its appearance and meaning differ vastly from that of European and North American contexts. One may guess that it has to do only partially with the loosening of the power of traditional religiosity and more with its continuing creative adaptation into the modern world, including syncretistic infiltration with African Instituted Churches and other forms of popular Christian (and Muslim) religiosity.[163]

As one may expect, secularism in the vast continent of Asia comes in various forms.[164] What does it mean in India and the Hindu world? In a bold recent study with a telling title, *Secularism's Last Sigh?*, the authors argue that "secularism has never been taken for granted in India," notwithstanding the nation's secular constitution; a telling example, they argue, is the official recognition of the Hindutva party (with its stated desire to make India Hindu) by the Supreme Court.[165] However, another recent major study argues the contrary, namely, that secularism has played and continues to play a central role in Indian politics and religious tolerance. At the same time, the author outlines the existence of several attitudes toward secularism in India, from endorsement to ambiguity to virtual rejection.[166]

This brief global survey of secularization in the Global North and Africa and Asia reaffirms what was already indicated above (chap. 11): secularism comes in many forms and with various meanings.[167] Although — unfortu-

---

160. Mbiti, *Introduction to African Religion*, p. 30; Mbiti, *African Religions and Philosophy*, p. 1.

161. Kibicho, "Nature and Structure of African Religion," p. 39.

162. See Kibicho, *God and Revelation in an African Context*, pp. 91-95.

163. See Mmassi, "Secularism in the Face of African Traditional Religions."

164. J. Hodge, "Church, State and Secularism in Asia."

165. Cossman and Kapur, *Secularism's Last Sigh?* p. 1; for comments, see Selvanayagam, "Indian Secularism."

166. Tejani, *Indian Secularism*. I am indebted to Selvanayagam, "Indian Secularism."

167. For an attempt at terminological precision, see Casanova, "The Secular, Secularizations, Secularism"; I do not find that necessary or useful, and will not follow it.

nately — limited to the Global North and therefore not to be taken as globally representative, highly useful is the nuanced analysis of versions of secularism by the Canadian philosopher Charles Taylor. He traces carefully the history of the European-American cultural shift away from a culture in which it was virtually impossible not to believe in God to an era in which belief in God is but one option — and to many a marginal one.[168] Public spaces "have been allegedly emptied of God, or of any reference to ultimate reality." On the other hand, alleged tolerance is the new norm.[169] Taylor distinguishes three notions of secularism: the retreat of religion from the public space (type 1), the decline in belief and practice (type 2), and the change in the conditions of belief (type 3).[170] Secularism, even in the Global North, does not necessarily entail leaving behind all notions of God/transcendence, although that takes place in many persons' lives. What makes the difference with regard to the context for God-talk in the Global North is that belief in God is made a matter of personal choice.[171] This change of the conditions of belief (type 3), while of course related to and influenced by the changed role of religion in the public sphere (type 1) and the diminishing degree to which people practice religion (type 2), is what the original advocates of the secularization theory missed and what really makes the difference.[172]

Taylor's nuanced analysis grasps some key aspects of secularism's diversity in the Global North. For the sake of ecclesiological reflection, we also need to go further back in history. As is well known, secularism's roots go back much further than the "secular decade" of the 1960s. All analysts agree that its genesis lies in the (European) Enlightenment and subsequent modernity — in itself far from a monolithic phenomenon.[173] Even further back, the Protestant Reformation certainly played a role with the promotion of literacy and personal freedom of faith.[174]

---

168. Materially similar is P. Berger, *Heretical Imperative*; see also C. Smith, ed., *The Secular Revolution*.

169. C. Taylor, *A Secular Age*, pp. 1–3 (2).

170. See also chap. 15 in *Secular Age*.

171. To that "choice" also belongs the freedom to doubt — and so, to be "heretic" (P. Berger, *Heretical Imperative*).

172. This paragraph draws directly from my *Trinity and Revelation*, pp. 182–86.

173. For the complexity and nuances of the "Enlightenment," see Schmidt, "What Enlightenment Project?"; Schmidt, ed., *What Is Enlightenment?*; Dupré, *The Enlightenment*.

174. B. Gregory, *The Unintended Reformation*.

What's Next: Postsecularism?

The latest "turn" in secularism discourse owes to the leading German philosopher Jürgen Habermas and the concept of the postsecular that he has helped launch.[175] Taking notice of the obvious "multifaceted transformation" in the landscape of religions in the Global North and beyond,[176] as a result of which "religious symbols and language games are being transposed into other, not genuinely religious domains," including literature, performing arts, and advertisement, among others, he observes the ways "the semantic and symbolic potentials of religions are becoming a universal social resource which shapes public and cultural life in a whole variety of ways."[177] At the global level, this social significance of religions is getting even more robust, as religious communities play more and more significant roles in societies.[178]

No wonder a change in the secularization discourse is needed:[179] notwithstanding the "enduring trends towards secularization in certain regions of the world . . . today almost nobody speaks of an imminent 'extinction' of religions or of the religious any longer."[180] Rather, we speak of "the return of the gods."[181] In light of the failure of the secularization thesis to explain the role (and alleged demise) of religion in the contemporary pluralistic world in general and the Global North in particular, it is better to speak of the "secular and sacred"[182] as cohabiting forces in the beginning of the third millennium. Somewhat counterintuitively, "orthodox" and even fundamen-

175. A programmatic essay that helped widely publicize the idea was Habermas, "Faith and Knowledge." An important recent contribution is Habermas, *Between Naturalism and Religion.*

176. For a highly insightful global assessment, see Barbato and Kratochwil, "Habermas's Notion of a Post-Secular Society." Another important critical engagement is Gorski et al., eds., *The Post-Secular in Question.*

177. As paraphrased by Reder and Schmidt, "Habermas and Religion," pp. 1–2; see also Harrington, "Habermas and the 'Post-Secular Society.'"

178. For religious institutions' role as "communities of interpretation" at national and global levels, see Habermas, "Notes on Post-Secular Society," p. 20. See also the important work by Casanova, *Public Religions in the Modern World.*

179. See Habermas, "Notes on Post-Secular Society," pp. 17–18.

180. Reder and Schmidt, "Habermas and Religion," p. 2.

181. Graf, *Die Wiederkehr der Götte.* Note that Habermas himself is a staunch "nonmetaphysical" thinker (as outlined in his *Postmetaphysical Thinking*), and therefore, talk about "gods" by him should be understood in that perspective. Cf. Puntel, "Habermas' Postmetaphysical Thinking," pp. 1–43.

182. Norris and Inglehart, *Secular and Sacred.*

talist expressions of Christian,[183] Muslim, and other religions are flourishing and gaining strongholds.[184]

What would the Christian church's response look like? Understandably, a number of strategies have been tried, to which we turn in the last section of this chapter.

Churches Respond to (Post)secularism(s)

Classical liberals sought to encounter the emerging secular age with the strategy of accommodation or "correlation" in which Christian doctrines were reinterpreted in ways that were believed to be appealing to those who rejected religion. Think of young Schleiermacher's lament in his *On Religion: Speeches to Its Cultural Despisers* (1799) about how "unexpected" it must be to his modern audience to hear talk about religion, which was "so entirely neglected by them." Old religion seemed hardly to appeal anymore to the "cultivated people" of the times; for them "the only sacred things to be met with are the sage maxims of our wise men, and the splendid compositions of our poets." Consequently, "no room remains for the eternal and holy Being that lies beyond this world."[185] Continuing the liberal program but also tweaking it, the Harvard theologian Harvey Cox advocated in a nuanced manner "secularization" as "an authentic outcome of the impact of biblical faith on Western history."[186] In contrast to "secularism," which denotes an ideology or closed worldview that functions like a new religion, *secularization* takes the biblical faith's turn to the "word" seriously and seeks to avoid secularism in its normal sense.[187]

A much more radical option was put forth by the short-lived "death of God" movement, whose response to the 1960s' secularism was neither interesting nor sustainable.[188] In some sense the "death of God" ideology is continued in a totally new form by the advocates of "postreligion" Christianity, heralded by titles such as D. B. Bass's *Christianity after Religion: The End of Church and*

183. As reported widely by Jenkins, *The Next Christendom*, among others.

184. Habermas, "Notes on Post-Secular Society," pp. 18–19; Habermas, "An Awareness of What Is Missing," pp. 19–20.

185. Schleiermacher, *On Religion*, p. 1.

186. Cox, *Secular City*, p. 18.

187. Cox, *Secular City*, pp. 16–32 especially.

188. Altizer, *The Gospel of Christian Atheism*.

the Birth of a New Spiritual Awakening (2012)[189] and Phil Zuckerman's *Faith No More: Why People Reject Religion* (2012).[190]

Not all churches, not even a majority of them, are excited by these versions of accommodation (some may say, capitulation of faith). Briefly put: those strategies would not only mean compromising the identity of the church and her missional calling, but they would also mean basically constructing a new "secular religion" not based on any known tradition. On the other extreme of the spectrum (on the American scene) stands the "Constantinian" project of the Religious Right, which seeks to reestablish a "Christian nation" in alignment with political powers.[191] There is no need to elaborate why this project cannot follow it. Another, very different extreme strategy is recommended by the British Radical Orthodoxy movement, which rejects any project of correlation and apologetic. It not only opposes but also denies secularism. For this British theological program, there is no "neutral" secularism. Instead, academic, political, and other spaces are "temples of other gods"[192] of modernity.[193] Rather than correlation, a robustly and distinctively *Christian* theological vision is put in place. Understandably, the current project cannot follow that — in itself admirable — strategy, as it cuts off bridges with non-theological disciplines and can hardly avoid the impression of dogmatism. Rightly, Radical Orthodoxy's approach has been described as "reason within the bounds of religion."[194]

Although I will not follow the American ethicist Stanley Hauerwas's call for building "Christian colonies" in the world, which would lead to an insular and somewhat isolated ecclesial existence, I affirm his critique of secularism: "secular liberalism" has caused the church to capitulate under its claim that only if religion is privatized may true democracy and (religious) freedom occur.[195] In this respect, somewhat similarly, L. Newbigin critiqued tirelessly the Western church for retreating into a harmless position of caring for individuals' "souls" rather than arguing for the truth of the Christian message.[196] I also agree with the Orthodox theologian Alexander Schmemann, in that at its

---

189. See, e.g., Butler Bass, *Christianity after Religion*.

190. Zuckerman, *Faith No More*.

191. For a discussion and critique, see Hauerwas and Willimon, *Resident Aliens*, pp. 17–24.

192. See J. K. A. Smith, *Introducing Radical Orthodoxy*, p. 42.

193. Milbank, *Theology and Social Theory*.

194. Hedley, "Should Divinity Overcome Metaphysics?" p. 274.

195. Hauerwas, *Dispatches from the Front*.

196. For the ingenious and insightful program of Newbigin's, see Kärkkäinen and Karim, "Community and Witness in Transition" (and the original literature cited therein).

heart, secularism is but "a negation of worship" of God:[197] "It is the denial, both ontologically and epistemologically, of the true meaning of human beings' existence being found in the worship of God."[198] In that sense, atheistic secularism is not about denying God but rather about denying the human person as "a worshipping being."[199] The missional calling outlined in this project leads to a robust, hospitable encounter with (post)secularism(s) through the church's missional existence as a worshiping-liturgical and diaconal-charismatic communion, presenting a credible Christian gospel for religionless secularists, the nones, and followers of other religious paths.[200]

197. Schmemann, "Worship in a Secular Age," p. 118, cited in McCall, *The Greenie's Guide to the End of the World*, p. 233. See also Alfeyev, "European Christianity and the Challenge of Militant Secularism," pp. 82–91.

198. As paraphrased by McCall, *The Greenie's Guide to the End of the World*, p. 233.

199. Schmemann, "Worship in a Secular Age," p. 118.

200. For a thoughtful attempt by the Catholic Church to cope with the nones and the influence of secularism, see Cascoigne, *The Church and Secularity*. For Protestant evangelicalism, see White, *The Rise of the Nones*. For the Orthodox, see Hovorun, "Church and Nation." And for the Anglican-Episcopal tradition, see Sempell, "God, Society and Secularism."

Epilogue: In the End — the Beginning

The Trinitarian Unfolding of Divine Economy

The popular version of Moltmann's massive eschatology, *The Coming of God*, is wittily titled *In the End — the Beginning*.[1] Apart from its aptness for materially describing the core of the Christian doctrine of eschatology — and to which hopefully part 1 of the current project also makes a modest contribution — the title also reflects well my feelings and intuitions at the end of the current five-volume constructive project in Christian doctrine. Far from reaching the "end" of the theological construction, this milestone is rather an occasion not only to take stock of where we are but also to envision a wider, deeper, and more ambitious vision for the future. As discussed in the introduction to part 1, "end" has the dual meaning of "reaching the goal" and "coming to an end."

I have been asked by my reviewers, colleagues, and students why the project started with Christology (*Christ and Reconciliation*, vol. 1) rather than with what is more common, either God or revelation. There is no dogmatic reason for it, and it could have been otherwise as well. The main reason had to do with the biblical intuition that our knowledge of God — and even in that sense, the reception of revelation — comes through the portal of Christ. Indeed, only he or she who has seen Jesus the Christ has seen the Father (John 14:6). That said, I could have also started with the Spirit (*Spirit and Salvation*, vol. 4), as after the departure of the Son, the Spirit is the "contact point" between God and the world. Choosing Christology, however, seemed warranted

---

1. With the subtitle *The Life of Hope*.

because — unlike with pneumatology — therein we speak of incarnation and, hence, an "embodied" and concrete form of divine manifestation. This naturally leads to inquiring into the nature of the Father, including the gracious sharing of God's own life with us (*Trinity and Revelation*, vol. 2) and God's work of creation (*Creation and Humanity*, vol. 3). With the Spirit, then, it seemed appropriate to delve deeper into the mystery of salvation as well (part 2 of vol. 4), continuing the inquiry started already in the context of Christology (part 2 of vol. 1). Finally, as with most all systematic presentations, the final consummation (*Hope and Community*, vol. 5, part 1) of the trinitarian unfolding of the divine economy followed. But since salvation and consummation are deeply communal (and even cosmic) in nature, the church has to be tightly linked with that discussion (part 2 of vol. 5). Again, differently from tradition, I chose to speak of consummation first, and only then of the community's place. That was to follow the trinitarian logic of moving from the "beginning" (creation) via present work (salvation) to fulfillment (eschatology) and draw the church, the missional community, into that divine movement to heal and reconcile the world God has created. In sum: as emphasized throughout, the presentation of Christian doctrine is but the theological observation and following of the trinitarian logic in the interrelated and mutual works of Father, Son, and Spirit. The whole economy and each "locus," from revelation to creation to atonement to salvation to ecclesiology, are triune-shaped, as evident in these five volumes.

This sounds all good and coherent. But what about the truth and reliability of the trinitarian Christian vision? How credible is it in the matrix of religious pluralisms and ideological secularisms? What about the sciences? Although this project — as first expounded in much detail in the introduction to volume 1 and subsequently clarified in the beginning of each volume, including the one at hand — builds on humble and modest explanations rather than the dream of modernity's (followed by fundamentalisms of various sorts) indubitable certainty,[2] I am also convinced that mere "intrasystemic" coherence does not suffice. Even if any talk about "correspondence" (with "reality") after the advent of late modernity/postmodernity and pluralisms has to be handled with utmost care, the inner coherence of trinitarian Christian doctrine has to be tested, or at least put in constant questioning, against all other beliefs and, ultimately, against the way things are in the world, as it were. This (widely speaking and inclusively understood) epistemological critical questioning does

---

2. Recall that "postfoundationalism" rather than foundationalism or nonfoundationalism has been adopted as the epistemological framework in this project.

not stop at the end when finishing the writing of this five-volume work; it is a constant task for theology and the church, and thus an integral task looking beyond the "end." Let us delve briefly into this problematic once again for the sake of this epilogue, which is also as much a new prologue!

In Search of a Proper Confidence Rather Than Indubitable Certainty[3]

In the last year of his life, the Austrian philosopher Ludwig Wittgenstein penned the work *On Certainty*, in which he investigates the meaning of statements such as "that I know" and "that I know that I know" something with certainty or confidence.[4] Wittgenstein wonders if "all enquiry on our part is set so as to exempt certain propositions from doubt, if they were ever formulated" (88), and hence, that "'I know' has a primitive meaning similar to and related to 'I see'" (89). Is this the mature philosopher's way of trying to tell us that there is something in "knowing" that is very basic, reliable, and, rightly understood, beyond doubt? Perhaps, as he says, his thoughts "do form a system, a structure" (102) rather than being there merely randomly (see also 105). Is it the case that "in that system some things stand unshakeably fast" (144)? In a tentative conclusion, in the middle of his book, the philosopher comes to this conclusion:

> Here I have arrived at a foundation of all my beliefs. (246)
>   ... I have arrived at the rock bottom of my convictions. And one might almost say that these foundation-walls are carried by the whole house. (348)

The all-important implication, then, is that "[a]t the foundation of well-founded belief lies belief that is not founded. Any 'reasonable' person behaves like this" (253–54).

Are the aging Wittgenstein's reflections on certainty, thus, another exercise in epistemological foundationalism, in the search of an indubitable certainty of the Enlightenment? Far from it. Writing before the advent of postmodernism, the Viennese philosopher acknowledged the situational ("a language-game does change with time," 256) and fallibilistic (using as meta-

---

3. The first part of the heading borrows from the book title of Newbigin, *Proper Confidence*.

4. Wittgenstein, *On Certainty*, #18 (numbers in the text refer to paragraphs). I was inspired to investigate this piece of Wittgenstein by K. Ward (*Religion and Revelation*, pp. 8–10), although my own reading goes in somewhat different directions from his.

phor the shifting of a riverbed, as on p. 144) nature of knowledge, including more than one type of picturing of the world/reality. If so, then it means that the mature Wittgenstein is reminding us that in the final analysis, our basic, most "foundational" beliefs cannot be fully justified by neutral, noncommittal reasoning. Rather, these basic beliefs are partially given; we are drawn to them; they are based on something given; and they form some kind of "system" that supports us as much, or more, than we can support them. Furthermore, these beliefs, far from being merely answers to intellectual curiosity, have everything to do with our way of life, our practice.[5] Indeed, when it comes to religion and faith, I would like to add that the basic beliefs not only support our search for the good life in this age but also the life to come, and that they are answers to questions of life and death. Belief in God emerges out of and is based on these deepest beliefs and convictions — as well as questions and doubts.[6] The best that the theologian has to be willing to live by is a "proper confidence" (to borrow L. Newbigin's book title). There is always the possibility of misplacing one's trust. Recall the nagging acknowledgment by Thomas Hobbes in his 1661 *Leviathan* that "to say God hath spoken to him [a man] in a dream, is not more than to say he dreamed that God spoke to him."[7]

So, what kind of certainty can be expected of religious claims? As mentioned above, in light of the diversity of religions of our age and the advent of modernity's principle of doubt, "it is useless to say that God makes his revelation self-authenticating."[8] If it was self-authenticating, then not only all who trust scientific reasoning but also believers in different faith traditions would be persuaded, perhaps even honest agnostics! On the other hand, this acknowledgment does not mean that there is no place for certainty and confidence in religion, but its specific nature and quality have to be assessed anew in the intellectual and religious milieu of each age. According to K. Ward, "such certainty cannot be a matter of simple self-evidence (available when the denial of a proposition is self-contradictory); or of immediate intuition (possible only for immediately experienced non-inferential truths); or of universally agreed and testable observation."[9] If it is of any consolation to theologians, the Cartesian "indubitable certainty" hardly is available in any other humanistic

5. It seems to me K. Ward (*Religion and Revelation*, p. 9) is materially agreeing with this general conclusion.
6. For an important discussion of belief in God in this kind of framework, see K. Ward, *The Concept of God.*
7. Hobbes, *The Leviathan*, part 3, chap. 32; p. 271.
8. K. Ward, *Religion and Revelation*, p. 7.
9. K. Ward, *Religion and Revelation*, p. 7.

disciplines and intellectual pursuits, including history, philosophy, and arts.[10] This does not have to mean there is therefore no difference between an ideological presentation of a nation's history and a careful, scholarly pursuit. There is certainly a difference, but it is a matter of degree of objectivity. Furthermore, with regard to philosophy, some opinions command more respect and hold greater validity and interest than others.[11]

While intellectually rigorous in its pursuit, the certainty in theology — as in other disciplines in the humanities — readily acknowledges its relatedness to a wide and comprehensive network of basic beliefs that sustains our thinking. It is situated and fallible in nature and aims at "proper confidence." Ultimately, it awaits the eschatological confirmation of the final divine manifestation. It is deeply value-driven and has to do with the deepest and most ultimate questions of death and life. In that sense, it is living by faith, rather than seeing. On the other hand, as an academic discipline, theology's claims, including claims concerning revelation, also have to be subjected to proper critical scrutiny and debate. To theology, as well as philosophy and similar fields, disagreements and different viewpoints belong as an essential part of the inquiry. That is simply because theological "views are extremely wide-ranging beliefs about the nature of things in general; they aim at unrestricted generality and comprehensiveness."[12] These kinds of statements are not easy to formulate and verbalize, and they can be understood in so many ways. Following Polanyi, Keith Ward rightly notes, "Theology can be seen as the articulation of a tacit framework of beliefs."[13] Add to that the existence of religious diversity, which makes it mandatory — and possible — to acknowledge that "[t]here is no intrinsic reason . . . why a 'science of God' should be confined to one religious tradition," and therefore, one should acknowledge that theology is not purely a Christian discipline, as other living faiths are also setting forth claims to ultimate questions of life and death, including the question of the divine.[14]

While faith and reason should not be juxtaposed, ultimately theological convictions and beliefs are just that: *convictions* and beliefs. They are person-related. The American philosopher William James's classic essay "The Will to

10. The late British missionary bishop Lesslie Newbigin (*Gospel in a Pluralist Society*, p. 35) put it well: "We have to abandon the idea that there is available to us or any other human beings the sort of certitude that Descartes wanted to provide and that the scientific part of our culture has sometimes claimed to offer."

11. See further K. Ward, *Religion and Revelation*, p. 8.

12. K. Ward, *Religion and Revelation*, p. 12.

13. K. Ward, *Religion and Revelation*, p. 15.

14. K. Ward, *Religion and Revelation*, p. 15.

Believe" sets forth some characteristics of a commitment to believe when one is faced with a lack of conclusive evidence. The three basic conditions James outlines are that, first, the decision to believe does not leave any choices ("belief is forced") because of its urgency; second, that it makes a vital difference in life; and third, that it presents itself as a plausible or realistic option.[15] It is easy to see the application of James's reasoning to the discussion of certainty with regard to revelation and faith. Although there is no conclusive evidence available — and in this sense, to quote Kierkegaard, the believer lives in "objective uncertainty" — the call of the gospel comes to one's life as a total call for surrender. Even when intellectual and rational homework is done, that alone will persuade no one to surrender, particularly when the Christian gospel also calls for moral obedience, similarly to Jewish and Islamic traditions. In his discussion James refers to French philosopher Blaise Pascal's famous wager metaphor, which introduces the concept of risk as well — but risk worth taking. Advises the French philosopher: "Let us weigh the gain and the loss in wagering that God is. Let us estimate these two chances. If you gain, you gain all; if you lose, you lose nothing. Wager, then, without hesitation that He is."[16] The recommendation to take up this wager is another fitting way of repeating the message of this epilogue: "In the End — the Beginning."

---

15. James, "The Will to Believe," pp. 1–31 (see esp. pp. 1–4 for a brief presentation and discussion of these conditions). I am indebted to K. Ward (*Religion and Revelation*, pp. 26–27) for turning my attention to this essay for the consideration of this topic.

16. Pascal, "Of the Necessity of the Wager," in *Pensées*, section 3, citation in #233.

Bibliography

Abe, Masao. *Buddhism and Interfaith Dialogue*. Edited by Steven Heine. Honolulu: University of Hawai'i Press, 1995.

———. "Kenotic God." In *DEHF*, pp. 25–90.

Abhishiktananda [Henri le Saux, OSB]. *The Hindu-Christian Meeting Point*. Bombay: Institute of Indian Culture, 1969.

"Abū 'l-ʿAlā al-Mawdūdi on the Verse of Light." Translated by Feras Hamza and Sajjad Rizvi. In *Islamic Theological Themes: A Primary Source Reader*, edited by John Renard. Oakland: University of California Press, 2014.

Adams, Daniel J. "Universal Salvation? A Study in Myanmar Christian Theology." *Asia Journal of Theology* 22 (2008): 219–36.

Adams, Marilyn McCord. *Horrendous Evils and the Goodness of God*. Ithaca, N.Y.: Cornell University Press, 1999.

Adeel, Ghulam Husayn. "Divine Justice and the Problem of Evil." *Message of Thaqalayn: A Quarterly Journal of Islamic Studies* 11, no. 2 (Summer 2010): n.p. http://www.al-islam.org/message-of-thaqalayn/vol-11-n-2/divine-justice-problem-evil-ghulam-husayn-adeel/title.htm.

Adelman, Howard. "Jews, Eschatology, and Contemporary Visions of a World Order." *Religious Studies and Theology* 29 (2010): 49–62.

Adiswarananda, Swami. *Vivekananda, World Teacher: His Teachings on the Spiritual Unity of Humankind*. Woodstock, Vt.: Skylight Paths, 2006.

Adogame, Afe. *The African Christian Diaspora: New Currents and Emerging Trends in World Christianity*. London: Bloomsbury, 2013.

Adogame, Afe, Roswith Gerloff, and Klaus Hock, eds. *Christianity in Africa and the African Diaspora: The Appropriation of a Scattered Heritage*. New York: Continuum, 2008.

Afsaruddin, Asma. "Death, Resurrection, and Human Destiny in Islamic Tradition." In *Death, Resurrection, and Human Destiny: Christian and Muslim Perspectives*, edited by David Marshall and Lucinda Mosher, pp. 43–60. Washington, D.C.: Georgetown University Press, 2014.

Ahluwalia, Kewal. "Shudhi Movement: 85th Shardhanand Shudhi Divas — December 23rd." Accessed November 11, 2016. http://www.aryasamaj.com/enews/2012/jan/4 .htm.

Ahmad, Khurshid, and David Kerr, eds. *Christian Mission and Islamic Da'wah: Proceedings of the Chambésy Dialogue Consultation.* Leicester: Islamic Foundation, 1982.

Alam, Mehmood. "Signs of Hour." Darussalem Web site. Accessed July 23, 2014. https:// blog.darussalampublishers.com/signs-of-hour/.

Aland, Kurt. *Did the Early Church Baptize Infants?* Translation and introduction by George Beasley-Murray. Philadelphia: Westminster, 1963.

Albrecht, Daniel E. "Pentecostal Spirituality: Looking through the Lens of Ritual." *Pneuma: The Journal of the Society for Pentecostal Studies* 14, no. 2 (Fall 1996): 107–25.

————. *Rites in the Spirit: A Ritual Approach to Pentecostal/Charismatic Spirituality.* Sheffield: Sheffield Academic Press, 1999.

Aletti, Jean-Noël, SJ. "God Made Christ to Be Sin (2 Corinthians 5:21): Reflections on a Pauline Paradox." In *The Redemption: An Interdisciplinary Symposium on Christ as Redeemer,* edited by Stephen T. Davis, Daniel Kendall, SJ, and Gerald O'Collins, SJ. Oxford: Oxford University Press, 2004.

Alexander, Kimberly Ervin. *Pentecostal Healing: Models in Theology and Practice.* Dorset, UK: Deo Publishing, 2006.

Alfeyev, Hieromonk Hilarion. *Christ the Conqueror of Hell: The Descent into Hades from an Orthodox Perspective.* New York: St. Vladimir's Seminary Press, 2009.

————. "Eschatology." In *The Cambridge Companion to Orthodox Christian Theology,* edited by Mary B. Cunningham and Elizabeth Theokritoff, pp. 107–20. Cambridge: Cambridge University Press, 2008.

————. "European Christianity and the Challenge of Militant Secularism." *Ecumenical Review* 57 (January 2005): 82–91.

"Alī on the Vision of God." Translated by I. K. A. Howard. In *Islamic Theological Themes: A Primary Source Reader,* edited by John Renard, p. 211. Oakland: University of California Press, 2014.

Almond, P. "The Buddha of Christendom: A Review of the Legend of Barlaam and Josaphat." *Religious Studies* 23 (1987): 391–406.

Althaus, Paul. *Die christliche Wahrheit: Lehrbuch der Dogmatik.* 6th ed. Gütersloh: Gerd Mohn, 1959.

Altizer, Thomas. *The Gospel of Christian Atheism.* Philadelphia: Westminster, 1966.

Amaladass, Anand. "Viewpoints: Dialogue in India." *Journal of Hindu-Christian Dialogue* 1, no. 7 (June 1988): 7–8.

Amaladoss, Michael, SJ. *Making Harmony: Living in a Pluralist World.* Chennai, India: IDCR, 2003.

————. "Religious Diversity and Harmonious Living: The Indian Story and Challenge." *Religions/Adyan* (August 2, 2015): 92–103. https://religionsadyan.wordpress

.com/2015/08/02/religious-diversity-and-harmonious-living-the-indian-story
-and-challenge-michael-amaladoss-s-j/.

Amanat, A., and M. Bernhardsson, eds. *Imagining the End: Visions of Apocalypse from the Ancient Middle East to Modern America*. London and New York: I. B. Tauris, 2002.

Amini, Ayatollah Ibrahim. *Al-Imam al-Mahdi: The Just Leader of Humanity*. Toronto: Islamic Education and Information Center, 1996. http://yamahdi.com/new1/pdf /justlead.pdf.

Ammar, Abu. "Principles of Dawah — Its Principles and Practices in History." Islamic Information Center, 2002. http://www.islamicinformationcentre.co.uk/dawah.htm.

Anderson, Sybol Cook. *Hegel's Theory of Recognition: From Oppression to Ethical Liberal Modernity*. London and New York: Continuum, 2009.

Anglican-Lutheran International Continuation Committee. *The Niagara Report, 1987*. London: Anglican Consultative Council; Geneva: Lutheran World Federation, 1988. http://www.anglicancommunion.org/media/102175/the_niagara_report.pdf.

The Apostolicity of the Church (2006). In Kasper, *HTF*, p. 50.

Aran, Gideon. "From Religious Zionism to Zionist Religion: The Roots of Gush Emunim." *Studies in Contemporary Jewry* 2 (1986): 116–43.

Archbishops' Council. *Women Bishops in the Church of England? A Report of the House of Bishops' Working Party on Women in the Episcopate*. London: Church House Publishing, 2004.

Ariel, Yaakov. "Born Again in a Land of Paradox: Christian Fundamentalists in Israel." *Fides et Historia* 28, no. 2 (Summer 1996): 35–49.

—————. "Radical Millennial Movements in Contemporary Judaism in Israel." In *OHM*, pp. 1–15.

Arjomand, Said Amir. "Thinking Globally about Islam." In *OHGR*, pp. 401–10.

Arnold, Bill T. "Old Testament Eschatology and the Rise of Apocalypticism." In *OHE*, pp. 23–39.

Asad, Muhammad. *The Message of the Qur'ān*. Gibraltar: Dar al-Andalus, 1980.

Asamoah-Gyadu, J. Kwabena. "Mission to 'Set the Captives Free': Healing, Deliverance, and Generational Curses in Ghanaian Pentecostalism." *International Review of Mission* 93, nos. 370–71 (2004): 389–406.

Asimov, Isaac. *A Choice of Catastrophes: The Disasters That Threaten Our World*. New York: Simon and Schuster, 1979.

Aulén, Gustav. *The Drama and the Symbols: A Book on Images of God and the Problems They Raise*. Philadelphia: Fortress, 1970.

Aune, David. *Revelation 6–16*. Word Biblical Commentary. Dallas: Word, 1986.

Ausmus, Harry J. "Nietzsche and Eschatology." *Journal of Religion* 58, no. 4 (1978): 347–64.

Austin, J. L. *How to Do Things with Words*. Edited by J. O. Urmson and Marina Sbisà. 2nd ed. Cambridge, Mass.: Harvard University Press, 1975.

Averill, James R., George Catlin, and Kyum Koo Chon. *Rules of Hope*. New York: Springer, 1990.

Avery-Peck, Alan J., and Jacob Neusner, eds. *Death, Afterlife, and the World-to-Come*. Part 4 of *Judaism in Late Antiquity*. Leiden: Brill, 2000.

Ayre, Clive M. "Where on Earth Is the Church? Theological Reflection on the Nature,

Mission, Governance and Ministry of the Church amidst the Global Environmental Crisis." In *Christian Faith and the Earth: Current Paths and Emerging Horizons in Ecotheology*, edited by Ernst M. Conradie, Sigurd Bergmann, Celia Deane-Drummond, and Denis Edwards, chap. 8, pp. 137–56. London: Bloomsbury, 2014.

Badham, Linda. "A Naturalistic Case for Extinction." In *DIRW*, pp. 158–70.

Badham, Paul, and Linda Badham. "Death and Immortality in the Religions of the World: An Editorial Survey." In *DIRW*, pp. 1–8.

Bae, Choon-Sup. *Ancestor Worship: The Challenges It Poses to the Christianity Mission and Ministry*. Saarbrücken, Germany: VDM Verlag, 2008.

Baillie, John. *The Belief in Progress*. New York: Scribner, 1951.

Baker, Lynne Rudder. *Persons and Bodies: A Constitution View*. Cambridge: Cambridge University Press, 2000.

———. "Persons and the Metaphysics of Resurrection." In *PIR*, pp. 161–76.

Balasubramanian, R. "The Advaita View of Death and Immortality." In *DIRW*, pp. 109–27.

Balasuriya, Tissa. *The Eucharist and Human Liberation*. Maryknoll, N.Y.: Orbis, 1977.

Balthasar, Hans Urs von. *Theo-Drama: Theological Dramatic Theory*. Translated by Graham Harrison. 5 vols. San Francisco: Ignatius, 1988–1998.

Banchoff, Thomas, ed. *Religious Pluralism, Globalization, and World Politics*. Oxford: Oxford University Press, 2008.

"Bāqillāni on the Vision of God in the Next Life." Translated by Richard J. McCarthy, SJ. In *Islamic Theological Themes: A Primary Source Reader*, edited by John Renard, pp. 209–10. Oakland: University of California Press, 2014.

Bar, Shmuel. "Sunnis and Shiites: Between Rapprochement and Conflict." In *Current Trends in Islamist Ideology*, edited by Hillel Fradkin et al., 2:87–96. Washington, D.C.: Center on Islam, Democracy, and the Future of the Muslim World, Hudson Institute, 2005.

Barbato, Mariano, and Friedrich Kratochwil. "Habermas's Notion of a Post-Secular Society: A Perspective from International Relations." European University Institute Working Papers. 2008. http://cadmus.eui.eu/bitstream/handle/1814/9011/MWP _2008_25.pdf?sequence=1.

Barnhart, J. E. *Religion and the Challenge of Philosophy*. Totowa, N.J.: Littlefield, Adams, 1975.

Barr, Stephen M. "Modern Cosmology and Christian Theology." In *BCSC*, chap. 16.

Barrett, Clive, ed. *Unity in Process: Reflections on Receptive Ecumenism*. London: Darton, Longman and Todd, 2012.

Barrett, David B., George T. Kurian, and Todd M. Johnson. *World Christian Encyclopedia*. 2 vols. 2nd ed. New York: Oxford University Press, 2001.

Barrow, John D. "Cosmology: A Matter of All and Nothing." *Astronomy and Geophysics* 43, no. 4 (2002): 4.8–15. http://onlinelibrary.wiley.com/doi/10.1046/j.1468-4004 .2002.43408.x/pdf.

———. "The Far, Far Future." In *FFU*, pp. 23–40.

Barrow, John D., and Frank J. Tipler. *The Anthropic Cosmological Principle*. Oxford: Oxford University Press, 1986.

Barth, Karl. *The Epistle to the Romans*. Translated by Edwyn C. Hoskyns. 6th ed. London: Oxford University Press, 1968 [1933].

———. "Jewish Problem and the Christian Answer." In *Against the Stream: Shorter Postwar Writings, 1946–52*. London: SCM, 1954.

Bartholomew I. "Called to Be One Church." Opening address to the plenary of the World Council of Churches, Crete, Greece, October 7, 2009. http://www.oikoumene.org /en/resources/documents/commissions/faith-and-order/x-other-documents-from -conferences-and-meetings/plenary-commission-meeting-crete-2009/opening -address-by-the-ecumenical-patriarch-bartholomew-i.

Bashear, Suliman. "Muslim Apocalypses and the Hour: A Case-Study in Traditional Interpretation." *Israel Oriental Studies* 13 (1993): 75–99.

Basil the Great. *A Treatise on Baptism: With an Exhortation to Receive It, Translated from the Works of St. Basil the Great, to Which Is Added a Treatise on Confirmation*. Translated by Francis Patrick Kenrick. 1843. Accessed November 11, 2016. https:// archive.org/details/treatiseonbaptis00basi.

Batchelor, Martine. "Meditation and Mindfulness." *Contemporary Buddhism* 12, no. 1 (May 2011): 157–64.

Batchelor, Stephen. *Buddhism without Beliefs: A Contemporary Guide to Awakening*. New York: Riverhead Books, 1997.

Bauckham, Richard. *Living with Other Creatures: Green Exegesis and Theology*. Waco: Baylor University Press, 2011.

———. "The Millennium." In *God Will Be All in All: The Eschatology of Jürgen Moltmann*, edited by Richard Bauckham, pp. 123–47. Edinburgh: T. & T. Clark, 1999.

———. "Theodicy from Ivan Karamazov to Moltmann." *Modern Theology* 4 (1987): 83–97.

———. *The Theology of the Book of Revelation*. Cambridge: Cambridge University Press, 1993.

———. "Universalism: An Historical Survey." *Themelios* 4 (1978): 47–54.

Bauckham, Richard, and Trevor A. Hart. *Hope against Hope: Christian Eschatology at the Turn of the Millennium*. Grand Rapids: Eerdmans, 1999.

Bauer, Walter. *A Greek English Lexicon of the New Testament and Other Early Christian Literature*. Revised by F. W. Danker, W. F. Arndt, and F. W. Gingrich. 3rd ed. Chicago: University of Chicago Press, 2000.

Bauman, Zygmunt. *The Individualized Society*. Malden, Mass.: Blackwell, 2001.

———. *Liquid Modernity*. Malden, Mass.: Blackwell, 2000.

Beasley-Murray, G. R. *Baptism in the New Testament*. 1962. Reprint, Grand Rapids: Eerdmans, 1973.

Bechert, Heinz. "Samgha: An Overview." In *ER*, pp. 8071–76.

———. "The Theravada Buddhist Sangha: Some General Observations on Historical and Political Factors in Its Development." *Journal of Asian Studies* 29, no. 4 (1970): 761–78.

Becker, Ernest. *The Denial of Death*. New York: Free Press, 1973.

Beker, J. Christiaan. *Paul's Apocalyptic Gospel*. Philadelphia: Fortress, 1984.

Bell, Rob. *Love Wins: A Book about Heaven, Hell, and the Fate of Every Person Who Ever Lived*. New York: HarperOne, 2012.

Bellah, Robert N., et al. *Habits of the Heart: Individualism and Commitment in American Life*. New York: Harper and Row, 1986.

Bendavid, Naftali. "Europe's Empty Churches Go on Sale." *Wall Street Journal*, January 2, 2015. Up-to-date statistics and analysis are available at http://www.wsj.com/articles /europes-empty-churches-go-on-sale-1420245359.

Benedict XII. *Benedictus Dei* (On the beatific vision of God). 1336. Accessed November 11, 2016. http://www.papalencyclicals.net/Ben12/B12bdeus.html.

Benedikt, Michael. *Cyperspace: First Steps*. Cambridge, Mass.: MIT Press, 1991.

Bennett, Clinton. *Understanding Christian-Muslim Relations: Past and Present*. London: Continuum, 2008.

Berdyaev, Nicolas. *Truth and Revelation*. Translated by R. M. French. New York: Collier, 1962.

Berentsen, J.-M. *Grave and Gospel*. Leiden: Brill, 1985.

Bergant, Dianne, CSA. "Does the Church Have a Mission, or Does the Mission Have a Church?" In *Creating a Welcoming Space: Reflections on Church and Mission; Essays in Honor of Larry Newer, SVD*, edited by Ross Fishburn and Michael Kelly, pp. 49–62. Eugene, Ore.: Wipf and Stock, 2015.

Berger, David. "Reflections on Conversion and Proselytizing in Judaism and Christianity." *Studies in Jewish-Christian Relations* 3 (2008): R1–R8. https://ejournals.bc.edu/ojs /index.php/scjr/article/viewFile/1502/1355.

Berger, Peter L. "The Desecularization of the World: A Global Overview." In *The Desecularization of the World: Resurgent Religion and World Politics*, edited by Peter Berger, pp. 1–18. Washington, D.C.: Ethics and Public Policy Center; Grand Rapids: Eerdmans, 1999.

———. *The Heretical Imperative: Contemporary Possibilities of Religious Affirmation*. Garden City, N.Y.: Anchor Press, 1980.

———. *The Sacred Canopy: Elements of a Sociological Theory of Religion*. New York: Doubleday, 1967.

Berger, Peter, and Anton Zijderveld. *In Praise of Doubt*. New York: HarperOne, 2009.

Berkhof, Hendrikus. "Israel as a Theological Problem in the Christian Church." *Journal of Ecumenical Studies* 6 (1969): 329–47.

———. *Well Founded Hope*. Richmond, Va.: John Knox, 1969.

Berkouwer, G. C. *The Return of Christ*. Translated by James Van Oosterom. Grand Rapids: Eerdmans, 1972.

Berkovits, Eliezer. *Faith after the Holocaust*. Jersey City, N.J.: KTAV, 1973.

Bernier, Paul. *Ministry in the Church*. Mystic, Conn.: Twenty-Third Publications, 1992.

Berry, Thomas. *Befriending the Earth: A Theology of Reconciliation between Humans and the Earth*. Mystic, Conn.: Twenty-Third Publications, 1991.

Berzin, Alexander. "A Buddhist View of Islam." In *Islam and Inter-Faith Relations*, edited by P. Schmidt-Leukel and L. Ridgeon, pp. 225–51. London: SCM, 2007.

Best, T. F., and G. Gassmann, eds. *On the Way to Fuller Koinonia: Official Report of the Fifth World Conference on Faith and Order*. Faith and Order Paper no. 166. Geneva: WCC, 1994.

Bevans, Stephen, SVD. "Beyond the New Evangelization: Toward a Missionary Ecclesiology for the Twenty-First Century." In *A Church with Open Doors: Catholic Ecclesiology for the Third Millennium*, edited by Richard R. Gaillardetz and Edward P. Hahnenberg, pp. 3–22. Collegeville, Minn.: Liturgical Press, 2015.

———. "What Does Rome Have to Do with Pasadena? Connecting Roman Catholic Missiology with SWM/SIS Innovations." Presentation at the Missiological Lectures, School of Intercultural Studies, Fuller Theological Seminary, Pasadena, Calif., October 22–25, 2015.

Bevans, Stephen B., and Roger P. Schroeder. *Constants in Context: A Theology of Mission for Today*. Maryknoll, N.Y.: Orbis, 2004.

Bhardwaj, Surinder M. *Hindu Places of Pilgrimage in India*. Berkeley: University of California Press, 1973.

Bieler, Andrea, and Luise Schottroff. *The Eucharist: Bodies, Bread, and Resurrection*. Minneapolis: Fortress, 2007.

Bijlefeld, W. "Eschatology: Some Muslim and Christian Data." *Islam and Christian-Muslim Relations* 15, no. 1 (2004): 35–54.

Birch, C., W. Eaking, and J. B. McDaniel, eds. *Liberating Life: Contemporary Approaches to Ecological Theology*. Maryknoll, N.Y.: Orbis, 1990.

Blanchard, Laurence Malcolm. "Universalism: Its Historic Development and Its Contemporary Expression in Western Theology." PhD diss., Fuller Theological Seminary, 2007.

Blankinship, Khalid. "The Early Creed." In *CCCIT*, pp. 33–54.

Bleich, David J. "Establishing Criteria of Death." In *Ethical Issues in Death and Dying*, edited by Tom L. Beauchamp and Robert M. Veatch, pp. 28–32. 2nd ed. Upper Saddle River, N.J.: Prentice-Hall, 1996.

Blichfeldt, Jan-Olaf. *Early Mahdism: Politics and Religion in the Formative Period of Islam*. Leiden: Brill, 1985.

Blidstein, Gerald J. "Maimonides and Mei'iri on the Legitimacy of Non-Judaic Religion." In *Scholars and Scholarship: The Interaction between Judaism and Other Cultures*, edited by Leo Landman, pp. 27–35. New York: Yeshiva University, 1990.

Bloesch, Donald G. *The Church: Sacraments, Worship, Ministry, Mission*. Downers Grove: InterVarsity, 2002.

———. *The Last Things: Resurrection, Judgment, Glory*. Downers Grove: InterVarsity, 2004.

Boersma, Hans. "Irenaeus, Derrida and Hospitality: On the Eschatological Overcoming of Violence." *Modern Theology* 19 (April 2003): 163–80.

———. *Violence, Hospitality, and the Cross: Reappropriating the Atonement Tradition*. Grand Rapids: Baker Academic, 2006.

Boff, Leonardo. *Ecclesiogenesis: The Base Communities Reinvent the Church*. Maryknoll, N.Y.: Orbis, 1986.

———. *Ecology and Liberation: A New Paradigm*. Maryknoll, N.Y.: Orbis, 1995.

———. *Liberating Grace*. Translated by John Drury. Maryknoll, N.Y.: Orbis, 1979.

———. *Trinity and Society*. Translated by Paul Burns. Maryknoll, N.Y.: Orbis, 1988.

———. *Was kommt nachher? Das Leben nach dem Tode*. Translated from Portuguese to German by Horst Goldstein. Salzburg: Otto Müller Verlag, 1982.

Boisvert, Kate Grayson. *Religion and the Physical Sciences.* Westport, Conn., and London: Greenwood, 2008.

Bonhoeffer, Dietrich. *The Cost of Discipleship.* London: SCM, 1959.

Bonino, José Míguez. *Doing Theology in a Revolutionary Situation.* Philadelphia: Fortress, 1975.

Boomgaarden, Jürgen. "Können Säuglinge glauben? Luthers Begründung der Fides Infantium als Lehrstück über den Glauben." *Kerygma und Dogma* 59, no. 1 (2013): 45-64.

Borg, Marcus J. *Jesus, A New Vision: Spirit, Culture, and the Life of Discipleship.* San Francisco: Harper and Row, 1987.

—————. *Jesus in Contemporary Scholarship.* Valley Forge, Pa.: Trinity, 1994.

Borowitz, Eugene B. *Reform Judaism Today.* Book 2, *What We Believe.* 3 vols. in 1. Springfield, N.J.: Behrman House, 1983.

—————. *Renewing the Covenant: A Theology for the Postmodern Jew.* Philadelphia: Jewish Publication Society, 1991.

Bosch, David J. *Transforming Mission: Paradigm Shifts in Mission.* Maryknoll, N.Y.: Orbis, 1991.

Bowker, John Westerdale. *Problems of Suffering in Religions of the World.* Cambridge: Cambridge University Press, 1970.

Boyd, Gregory A. *Satan and the Problem of Evil: Constructing a Trinitarian Warfare Theodicy.* Downers Grove: InterVarsity, 2001.

Boyd, Robin. "The End of Eschatology? Questions on the Future of Interfaith Relations — Part 1." *Expository Times* 123, no. 5 (February 2012): 209-17.

—————. "In the End — Which God? Questions on the Future of Interfaith Relations — Part 2." *Expository Times* 123, no. 6 (March 2012): 261-71.

Boyle, Joseph M., Jr. "Toward Understanding the Principle of Double Effect." *Ethics* 90 (1980): 527-38.

Braarvig, Jens. "The Buddhist Hell: An Early Instance of the Idea?" *Numen: International Review for the History of Religions* 56, nos. 2-3 (2009): 254-81.

Braaten, Carl E., and Robert W. Jenson, eds. *In One Body through the Cross: The Princeton Proposal for Christian Unity.* Grand Rapids: Eerdmans, 2003.

—————. *Jews and Christians: People of God.* Grand Rapids: Eerdmans, 2003.

Bracken, Joseph A., SJ, ed. *World without End: Christian Eschatology from a Process Perspective.* Grand Rapids: Eerdmans, 2006.

Bradshaw, David. *Aristotle East and West: Metaphysics and the Division of Christendom.* Cambridge: Cambridge University Press, 2004.

Braiterman, Zachary. *(God) after Auschwitz: Tradition and Change in Post-Holocaust Jewish Thought.* Princeton: Princeton University Press, 1998.

Braswell, George W., Jr. *Islam: Its Prophet, Peoples, Politics, and Power.* Nashville: Broadman and Holman, 1996.

Brewer, Marilynn B. "Ingroup Identification and Intergroup Conflict." In *Social Identity, Intergroup Conflict, and Conflict Reduction,* edited by Richard D. Ashmore, Lee Jussim, and David Wilder, pp. 17-41. New York: Oxford University Press, 2011.

Brierly, Peter. *The Tide Is Running Out.* London: Christian Research, 2000.

Brill, Alan. "Judaism and Other Religions: An Orthodox Perspective." Paper commis-

sioned by the World Jewish Congress for the World Symposium of Catholic Cardinals and Jewish Leaders, January 19–20, 2004, New York City. https://www.bc.edu/content/dam/files/research_sites/cjl/texts/cjrelations/resources/articles/Brill.htm.
———. *Judaism and Other Religions: Models of Understanding*. New York: Palgrave Macmillan, 2010.
Brittain, Christopher Craig. "Why Ecclesiology Cannot Live by Doctrine Alone." *Ecclesial Practices* 1, no. 1 (2014): 5–30.
Brown, Dee. *Bury My Heart at Wounded Knee*. New York: Holt, Rinehart and Winston, 1971.
Brown, R. E. *The Virginal Conception and Bodily Resurrection of Jesus*. New York: Paulist, 1992.
Brown, Warren S., and Brad D. Strawn. *The Physical Nature of Christian Life: Neuroscience, Psychology, and the Church*. Cambridge and New York: Cambridge University Press, 2012.
Bruce, Steve. *God Is Dead: Secularization in the West*. Oxford: Blackwell, 2002.
———. *Secularization*. New York: Oxford University Press, 2011.
Brueggemann, Walter. *The Covenanted Self: Explorations in Law and Covenant*. Minneapolis: Augsburg Fortress, 1999.
———. *Theology of the Old Testament: Testimony, Dispute, Advocacy*. Minneapolis: Augsburg Fortress, 1997.
Brunn, Stanley D., ed. *The Changing World Religion Map: Sacred Places, Identities, Practices, and Politics*. 5 vols. Dordrecht and New York: Springer, 2015.
Brunner, Daniel L., Jennifer L. Butler, and A. J. Swoboda. *Introducing Evangelical Ecotheology: Foundations in Scripture, Theology, History, and Praxis*. Grand Rapids: Baker Academic, 2015.
Brunner, Emil. *The Christian Doctrine of the Church, Faith, and the Consummation*. Vol. 3 of *Dogmatics*. Translated by David Cairns. Philadelphia: Westminster, 1960.
———. *Dogmatics*. Vol. 1, *The Christian Doctrine of God*. Translated by Olive Wyon. Philadelphia: Westminster, 1949.
———. *The Misunderstanding of the Church*. Cambridge: Lutterworth, 2002 [1952].
Brunner, Rainer. "Shi'ite Doctrine. iii. Imamite-Sunnite Relations since the Late 19th Century." *Encyplopaedia Iranica*. November 12, 2010. http://www.iranicaonline.org/articles/shiite-doctrine-iii.
Brüntrup, Godehard, SJ. "3.5–Dimensionalism and Survival: A Process Ontological Approach." In *Personal Identity and Resurrection*, edited by Georg Gasser, pp. 67–85. Surrey, UK: Ashgate, 2010.
Budde, Michael L. *The (Magic) Kingdom of God: Christianity and Global Culture Industries*. Boulder, Colo.: Westview, 1997.
The Buddha-Carita or The Life of Buddha by Ven. Aśvaghoṣa. Edited and translated by E. B. Cowell. Last updated August 2005. http://www.ancient-buddhist-texts.net/Texts-and-Translations/Buddhacarita/index.htm.
Buddhagosa. *Visuddhi Visuddhimagga, the Path of Purification: The Classic Manual of Buddhist Doctrine and Meditation*. Translated by Bikkhu Nanamoli. Kandy, Sri

Lanka: Buddhist Publication Society, 2011. http://www.accesstoinsight.org/lib/authors/nanamoli/PathofPurification2011.pdf.

Buenting, Joel, ed. *The Problem of Hell: A Philosophical Anthology.* Surrey, UK: Ashgate, 2009.

Bujo, Bénézet. *African Theology in Its Social Context.* Translated by John O'Donohue. Nairobi: Paulines Publications Africa, 1992.

Bultmann, Rudolf. *Theology of the New Testament.* Translated by Kendrick Grobel. Vol. 1. Waco: Baylor University Press, 2007 [1951].

Burgess, Stanley M., and Eduard M. van der Maas, eds. *New International Dictionary of Charismatic and Pentecostal Movements.* Revised and expanded ed. Grand Rapids: Zondervan, 2010.

Burns, Charlene. "'Soul-Less' Christianity and the Buddhist Empirical Self: Buddhist-Christian Convergence?" *Buddhist-Christian Studies* 23 (2003): 87–100.

Burton, David. "A Buddhist Perspective." In *OHRD*, pp. 321–36.

Bush, Hans-Christoph Am, and Christopher F. Zurn, eds. *The Philosophy of Recognition: Historical and Contemporary Perspectives.* Lanham, Md.: Lexington Books, 2010.

Butler Bass, Diana. *Christianity after Religion: The End of Church and the Birth of a New Spiritual Awakening.* San Francisco: HarperOne, 2012.

Bynum, Caroline Walker. *The Resurrection of the Body in Western Christianity, 200–1336.* New York: Columbia University Press, 1995.

Cabezón, José Ignacio. "Buddhist Views of Jesus." In *JWF*, pp. 15–24.

Calvin, John. "Psychopannia." In *Tracts and Treatises in Defence of the Reformed Faith*, translated by H. Beveridge, 3:414–90. Grand Rapids: Eerdmans, 1958.

Camporesi, Piero. *The Fear of Hell: Images of Damnation and Salvation in Early Modern Europe.* Translated by Lucinda Byatt. University Park: Pennsylvania State University Press, 1990.

Caplan, Eric. *From Ideology to Liturgy: Reconstructionist Worship and American Liberal Judaism.* Cincinnati: Hebrew Union College Press, 2002.

Cardman, Francine. "Non-conclusive Arguments: Therefore, Non-conclusion?" In *Women Priests: A Catholic Commentary on the Vatican Declaration*, edited by Leonard Swidler and Arlene Swidler, pp. 92–97. New York: Paulist, 1977. Also at http://www.womenpriests.org/classic/cardman.asp.

Carnes, Bruce A., and S. Jay Olshansky. "Evolutionary Perspectives on Human Senescence." *Population and Development Review* 19 (December 1993): 793–806.

Caron, Ann M. "Towards an Inclusive Communion Ecclesiology." In *Comparative Ecclesiology: Critical Investigations*, edited by Gerard Mannion, pp. 106–24. London and New York: T. & T. Clark, 2008.

Carson, D. A. *Becoming Conversant with the Emerging Church: Understanding a Movement and Its Implications.* Grand Rapids: Zondervan, 2005.

Carter, Stephen L. *The Culture of Disbelief in the Nineteenth Century.* New York: Basic Books, 1993.

Casanova, José. *Public Religions in the Modern World.* Chicago: University of Chicago Press, 1994.

———. "The Secular, Secularizations, Secularism." In *Rethinking Secularism*, edited by

Craig Calhoun, Mark Juergensmeyer, and Jonathan VanAntwerpen, pp. 54–74. New York: Oxford University Press, 2011.

Cascoigne, Robert. *The Church and Secularity: Two Stories of Liberal Society*. Washington, D.C.: Georgetown University Press, 2009.

Castles, Stephen, and Mark J. Miller. *The Age of Migration: International Population Movements in the Modern World*. 4th ed. New York: Guilford Press, 2009.

Cavanaugh, William T. *Torture and Eucharist: Theology, Politics, and the Body of Christ*. Oxford and Malden, Mass.: Blackwell, 1998.

Cha, Peter. "Ethnic Identity Formation and Participation in Immigrant Churches: Second-Generation Korean American Experiences." In *Korean Americans and Their Religions: Pilgrims and Missionaries from a Different Shore*, edited by Ho-Youn Kwon, Kwang Chung Kim, and R. Stephen Warner, pp. 141–56. University Park: Pennsylvania State University Press, 2001.

Chadwick, Owen. *The Secularization of the European Mind in the 19th Century*. Cambridge: Cambridge University Press, 1975.

"The Challenge of Proselytism and the Calling to Common Witness." *Ecumenical Review* 48, no. 2 (April 1996): 212–21.

Chanda, Nayan. *Bound Together: How Traders, Preachers, Adventurers, and Warriors Shaped Globalization*. New Haven: Yale University Press, 2007.

Chandngarm, Saeng. *Arriyasatsee* (The four noble truths). Bangkok: Sangsan Books, 2001.

Chaplin, Jonathan. *Multiculturalism: A Christian Retrieval*. London: Theos, 2011.

Chappell, D. W. "Buddhist Interreligious Dialogue: To Build a Global Community." In *The Sound of Liberating Truth: Buddhist-Christian Dialogues in Honor of Frederick J. Streng*, edited by S. B. King and P. O. Ingam, pp. 3–35. Richmond, UK: Curzon, 1999.

Charles, R. H. *A Critical History of the Doctrine of a Future Life in Israel, in Judaism, and in Christianity*. London: Adam and Charles Birch, 1913.

Childs, B. S. *Biblical Theology of the Old and New Testaments: Theological Reflection on the Christian Bible*. London: SCM, 1992.

Chittick, William C. "Muslim Eschatology." In *OHE*, pp. 132–50.

Ch'oe, Ki-bok. "Ancestor Worship: From the Perspective of Confucianism and Catholicism." In *Ancestor Worship and Christianity in Korea*, edited by Jung Young Lee, pp. 35–43. Lewiston, N.Y., and Lampeter, UK: Edwin Mellen Press, 1988.

Chuang, D. J. "9 Things about Asian American Christianity." *The Exchange: A Blog by Ed Stetzer*, November 7, 2013. http://www.christianitytoday.com/edstetzer/2013/november/9-things-about-asian-american-christianity.html.

Chung, Paul S. *Christian Mission and a Diakonia of Reconciliation: A Global Reframing of Justification and Justice*. Minneapolis: Lutheran University Press, 2008.

———. "Engaging God's Mission and Diakonia in Life of Public Spheres: Justification and Economic Justice." *Dialog* 49, no. 2 (2010): 141–54.

———. *Reclaiming Mission as Constructive Theology: Missional Church and World Christianity*. Eugene, Ore.: Cascade Books, 2012.

"The Church and the Jewish People." Faith and Order of WCC, 1967. Accessed November

11, 2016. http://www.bc.edu/content/dam/files/research_sites/cjl/texts/cjrelations/resources/documents/protestant/WCC1967.htm.

"The Church as Community of Common Witness to the Kingdom of God." *Reformed World* 57 (2007): 105–207. Report of the third phase of the International Theological Dialogue between the Catholic Church and the World Alliance of Reformed Churches (1998–2005).

Church of England. *Mission-Shaped Church: Church Planting and Fresh Expressions of Church in a Changing Context*. London: Church House Publishing, 2004.

Clark, S. R. L. "Deep Time." In *FFU*, pp. 177–95.

Clark, Victoria. *Allies for Armageddon: The Rise of Christian Zionism*. New Haven: Yale University Press, 2007.

Clark-Soles, Jaime. "The Afterlife: Considering Heaven and Hell." *Word & World* 31, no. 1 (Winter 2011): 65–74.

———. *Death and Afterlife in the New Testament*. New York: T. & T. Clark, 2006.

Clayton, Philip C. *Adventures in the Spirit: God, World, Divine Action*. Edited by Zachary Simpson. Minneapolis: Fortress, 2008.

———. "Eschatology as Metaphysics under the Guise of Hope." In *World without End: Essays in Honor of Marjorie Suchocki*, edited by Joseph Bracken, pp. 128–49. Grand Rapids: Eerdmans, 2005.

———. *Mind and Emergence: From Quantum to Consciousness*. Oxford: Oxford University Press, 2004.

Clayton, Philip, and Steven Knapp. "Divine Action and the 'Argument from Neglect.'" In *PC*, pp. 179–94.

Cleary, Edward, and Timothy J. Steigenga, eds. *Conversion of a Continent: Contemporary Religious Change in Latin America*. New Brunswick, N.J.: Rutgers University Press, 2007.

Clooney, Francis X., SJ. *Comparative Theology*. West Sussex, UK: Wiley-Blackwell, 2010.

———. *Hindu God, Christian God: How Reason Helps Break Down the Boundaries between Religions*. Oxford and New York: Oxford University Press, 2001.

———. "Hindu Views of Religious Others: Implications for Christian Theology." *Theological Studies* 64, no. 2 (2003): 306–33.

———. "Restoring 'Hindu Theology' as a Category in Indian Intellectual Discourse." In *Blackwell Companion to Hinduism*, edited by Gavin Flood, pp. 447–77. Malden, Mass.: Blackwell, 2003.

A Cloud of Witnesses: Opportunities for Ecumenical Commemoration; Proceedings of the International Ecumenical Symposium, Monastery of Bose, 29 October — 2 November 2008. Edited by Tamara Grdzelidze and Guido Dotti. Faith and Order Paper no. 209. Geneva: WCC Publications, 2009. http://www.academia.edu/7564644/A_Cloud_of_Witnesses.

Clouse, Robert G. "Fundamentalist Eschatology." In *OHE*, pp. 263–77.

———, ed. *The Meaning of Millennium: Four Views*. Downers Grove: InterVarsity, 1977.

Coakley, Sarah. "Kenosis: Theological Meanings and Gender Connotations." In *The Work of Love: Creation as Kenosis*, edited by John Polkinghorne, pp. 192–210. Grand Rapids: Eerdmans, 2001.

―――. "The Resurrection and the 'Spiritual Senses': On Wittgenstein, Epistemology and the Risen Christ." In *Powers and Submission: Spirituality, Philosophy, and Gender*, pp. 130–52. Oxford: Blackwell, 2002.

Cobb, John B., Jr. *Christ in a Pluralistic Age*. Philadelphia: Westminster, 1975.

―――. "The Resurrection of the Soul." *Harvard Theological Review* 80, no. 2 (1987): 213–27.

Cohen, A. O. *Self-Consciousness: An Alternative Anthropology of Identity*. London: Routledge, 1994.

Cohen, Arthur A. "Resurrection of the Dead." In *20th Century Religious Thought: Original Essays on Critical Concepts, Movements, and Beliefs*, edited by Arthur A. Cohen and Paul Mendes-Flohr, pp. 807–13. Philadelphia: Jewish Publication Society, 2009.

Cohen, Charles L., and Ronald L. Numbers, eds. *Gods in America: Religious Pluralism in the United States*. New York: Oxford University Press, 2013.

Cohn-Sherbok, Daniel. "Death and Immortality in the Jewish Tradition." In *DIRW*, pp. 24–36.

―――. "Jewish Faith and the Holocaust." *Religious Studies* 26 (1990): 277–93.

―――. "Jewish Religious Pluralism." *Cross Currents* 46, no. 3 (1996): 326–42.

Cohon, Samuel S. *Essays in Jewish Theology*. Cincinnati: Hebrew Union College Press, 1987.

Collins, John J. "Apocalyptic Eschatology in the Ancient World." In *OHE*, pp. 40–55.

―――. *The Apocalyptic Imagination*. Rev. ed. Grand Rapids: Eerdmans, 1998.

Collins, Paul M., and Barry Ensign-George, eds. *Denomination: Assessing an Ecclesiological Category*. London: T. & T. Clark, 2011.

Collins, Steven. *Selfless Persons: Imagery and Thought in Theravada Buddhism*. Cambridge: Cambridge University Press, 1982.

―――. "What Are Buddhists *Doing* When They Deny the Self?" In *Religion and Practical Reason: New Essays in the Comparative Philosophy of Religions*, edited by Frank E. Reynolds and David Tracy, pp. 59–86. Albany: SUNY Press, 1994.

Colwell, John E. "Proclamation as Event: Barth's Supposed 'Universalism' in the Context of His View of Mission." In *Mission to the World: Essays to Celebrate the 50th Anniversary of the Ordination of George Raymond Beasley-Murray to the Christian Ministry*, edited by Paul Beasley-Murray, pp. 42–46. Didcot, UK: Baptist Historical Society, 1991.

Cone, James H. *A Black Theology of Liberation*. 2nd ed. Twentieth anniversary ed. Maryknoll, N.Y.: Orbis, 1986.

―――. *God of the Oppressed*. Rev. ed. Maryknoll, N.Y.: Orbis, 1997; originally New York: Seabury Press, 1975.

―――. *The Spirituals and the Blues: An Interpretation*. New York: Seabury Press, 1972.

Congar, Yves. *After Nine Hundred Years: The Background of Schism between the Eastern and the Western Churches*. New York: Fordham University Press, 1959.

―――. *I Believe in the Holy Spirit*. Translated by David Smith. New York: Seabury Press, 1983. 3 vols. in 1, New York: Herder, 1997.

―――. *Lay People in the Church: A Study for a Theology of the Laity*. Westminster, Md.: Newman, 1957 [1953].

Conniry, Charles J. "Identifying Apostolic Christianity: A Synthesis of Viewpoints." *Journal of the Evangelical Theological Society* 37 (June 1994): 247–61.

Conradie, Ernst M., ed. *Creation and Salvation: A Companion on Recent Theological Movements.* Berlin: LIT Verlag, 2012.

——. *Hope for the Earth: Vistas for a New Century.* Eugene, Ore.: Wipf and Stock, 2005.

——. "What Is the Place of the Earth in God's Economy? Doing Justice to Creation, Salvation and Consummation." In *Christian Faith and the Earth: Current Paths and Emerging Horizons in Ecotheology,* edited by Ernst M. Conradie, Sigurd Bergmann, Celia Deane-Drummond, and Denis Edwards, pp. 65–96. London: Bloomsbury, 2014.

Cook, David. *Contemporary Muslim Apocalyptic Literature.* Syracuse, N.Y.: Syracuse University Press, 2005.

——. "Early Islamic and Classical Sunni and Shi'ite Apocalyptic Movements." In *OHM,* pp. 267–83.

——. *Studies in Muslim Apocalyptic.* New York: Syracuse University Press, 2005.

Corcoran, Kevin. "Physical Persons and Postmortem Survival without Temporal Gaps." In *Soul, Body, and Survival: Essays on the Metaphysics of Human Persons,* edited by Kevin Corcoran, pp. 201–17. Ithaca, N.Y., and London: Cornell University Press, 2001.

Cornwall, Susannah. "Sex Otherwise: Intersex, Christology, and the Maleness of Jesus." *Journal of Feminist Studies in Religion* 30, no. 2 (2014): 23–39.

Cossman, Brenda, and Ratna Kapur. *Secularism's Last Sigh? Hindutva and the (Mis)Rule of Law.* Oxford University Press India, 2001.

Courtright, Paul B. "Worship and Devotional Life: Hindu Devotional Life." In *ER,* pp. 9820–26.

Coward, Harold. Introduction to *Hindu-Christian Dialogue: Perspectives and Encounters,* edited by Harold Coward, pp. 1–9. Maryknoll, N.Y.: Orbis, 1989.

——. *Pluralism in the World Religions: A Short Introduction.* Oxford: OneWorld, 2000.

Cox, Harvey G. *The Secular City: Secularization and Urbanization in Theological Perspective.* Twenty-fifth anniversary ed. New York: Collier Books, 1990.

——. "Thinking Globally about Christianity." In *OHGR,* pp. 245–54.

Coyne, George V., SJ. "Seeking the Future: A Theological Perspective." In *FFU,* pp. 12–19.

Cragg, Kenneth. *The House of Islam.* 2nd ed. Encino, Calif.: Dickenson, 1975.

Craig, William Lane. *Time and Eternity: Exploring God's Relationship to Time.* Wheaton, Ill.: Crossway, 2001.

Cranston, Sylvia. "Reincarnation: The Lost Chord of Christianity?" In *Immortality and Human Destiny: A Variety of Views,* edited by Geddes MacGregor, pp. 143–60. New York: Paragon House, 1985.

Cray, Graham, and Ian Mobsby. *Fresh Expressions and the Kingdom of God.* Norwich, UK: Canterbury, 2012.

Creel, Richard E. *Divine Impassibility: An Essay in Philosophical Theology.* Cambridge: Cambridge University Press, 1985.

Crevier, Daniel. *AI: The Tumultuous History of the Search for Artificial Intelligence.* New York: Basic Books, 1993.

Crockett, William, ed. *Four Views on Hell*. Grand Rapids: Eerdmans, 1997.

Crone, Patricia. *God's Rule: Government and Islam*. New York: Columbia University Press, 2004.

Crossan, John Dominic. *The Birth of Christianity: Discovering What Happened in the Years Immediately after the Execution of Jesus*. San Francisco: HarperSanFrancisco, 1998.

Crüsemann, Frank. "Scripture and Resurrection." In *RTSA*, pp. 89–102.

Csordas, Thomas J., ed. *Transnational Transcendence: Essays on Religion and Globalization*. Berkeley: University of California Press, 2009.

Cunningham, Lawrence S. "Saints and Martyrs: Some Contemporary Considerations." *Theological Studies* 60 (1999): 529–37.

Dabney, Lyle. "Justified by the Spirit: Soteriological Reflections on the Resurrection." *International Journal of Systematic Theology* 3, no. 1 (2001): 46–68.

Daley, Brian E. "Apocalypticism in Early Christian Theology." In *The Encyclopedia of Apocalypticism II: Apocalypticism in Western History and Culture*, edited by Bernard McGinn, pp. 3–47. New York: Continuum, 2000.

———. "Apokatastasis and 'Honorable Silence' in the Eschatology of St. Maximus the Confessor." In *Maximus Confessor*, edited by F. Heinzer and C. Schönborn, pp. 309–39. Freiburg: Éditions Universitaires, 1982.

———. "Eschatology in the Early Church Fathers." In *OHE*, pp. 91–109.

———. "A Hope for Worms: Early Christian Hope." In *RTSA*, pp. 136–64.

———. *The Hope of the Early Church: A Handbook of Patristic Eschatology*. Rev. ed. Peabody, Mass.: Hendrickson, 2003 [1991].

Daneel, M. L. *African Earthkeepers*. Vol. 2, *Environmental Mission and Liberation in Christian Perspective*. Pretoria: University of South Africa Press, 1999.

Daniel, P. S. *Hindu Response to Religious Pluralism*. Pitam Pura, Delhi: Kant Publications, 2000.

David, John Jefferson. "The Holocaust and the Problem of Theodicy: An Evangelical Perspective." *Evangelical Review of Theology* 29 (2005): 52–76.

Davies, Paul C. "Eternity: Who Needs It?" In *FFU*, pp. 41–52.

———. *God and the New Physics*. New York: Simon and Schuster, 1983.

———. *The Last Three Minutes: Conjectures about the Ultimate Fate of the Universe*. New York: Basic Books, 1994.

Davies, W. D. *Paul and Rabbinic Judaism*. London: SPCK, 1955.

Davis, Cyprian, OSB. "Roman Catholic Ecclesiology." In *The Cambridge Companion to Black Theology*, edited by Dwight N. Hopkins and Edward P. Antonio, pp. 198–210. Cambridge: Cambridge University Press, 2012.

Davis, Elizabeth Gold. *The First Sex*. Baltimore: Penguin, 1971.

Davis, John R. *Poles Apart: Contextualizing the Gospel in Asia*. Bangalore, India: Theological Book Trust, 1998.

Davis, Stephen T. "Resurrection, Personal Identity, and the Will of God." In *PIR*, pp. 19–31.

———. *Risen Indeed: Making Sense of the Resurrection*. London: SPCK, 1993.

D'Costa, Gavin. "Christian Theology and Other Religions: An Evaluation of John Hick and Paul Knitter." *Studia Missionalia* 42 (1993): 161–78.

———. *The Meeting of Religions and the Trinity*. Maryknoll, N.Y.: Orbis, 2000.

Deane-Drummond, C. *Eco-Theology.* London: Darton, Longman and Todd, 2008.

De Lange, Nicholas. *An Introduction to Judaism.* Cambridge: Cambridge University Press, 2000.

Deleuze, Gilles, with Fanny Deleuze. "Nietzsche and Saint Paul, Lawrence and John of Patmos." In Gilles Deleuze, *Essays Critical and Clinical,* translated by D. W. Smith and M. A. Greco, pp. 36–53. Minneapolis: University of Minnesota Press, 1997.

Denison, Jim. "100,000 Atheists Are 'Unbaptized.'" Christian Headlines.com, October 20, 2014. http://www.christianheadlines.com/columnists/denison-forum/100-000 -atheists-are-unbaptized.html.

Denny, Frederick Mathewson. *An Introduction to Islam.* 2nd ed. New York: Macmillan, 1994.

—. "The Meaning of Ummah in the Qur'ān." *History of Religions* 15, no. 1 (1975): 34–70.

De Nys, Martin J. *Hegel and Theology.* New York: T. & T. Clark, 2009.

Derrida, Jacques. "Faith and Knowledge: The Two Sources of 'Religion' at the Limits of Reason Alone." Translated by Samuel Weber. In *Religion,* edited by Jacques Derrida and Gianni Vattimo. Cultural Memory in the Present. Stanford: Stanford University Press, 1998.

—. "Hospitality, Justice, and Responsibility: A Dialogue with Jacques Derrida." In *Questioning Ethics: Contemporary Debates in Continental Philosophy,* edited by Richard Kearney and Mark Dooley, pp. 65–83. London: Routledge, 1999.

De Silva, Lily. "The Buddhist Attitude towards Nature." *Access to Insight (Legacy Edition),* November 30, 2013. http://www.accesstoinsight.org/lib/authors/desilva/attitude .html#fnt-lds.

Devji, Faisal. *Landscapes of the Jihad: Militancy, Morality, Modernity.* Ithaca, N.Y.: Cornell University Press, 2005.

DeVries, Dawn. "Providence and Grace: Schleiermacher on Justification and Election." In *Cambridge Companion to Friedrich Schleiermacher,* edited by Jacqueline Mariña, pp. 189–208. Cambridge: Cambridge University Press, 2005.

Dharmasiri, Gunapala. *A Buddhist Critique of the Christian Concept of God: A Critique of the Concept of God in Contemporary Christian Theology and Philosophy of Religion from the Point of View of Early Buddhism.* Colombo, Sri Lanka: Lake House Investments, 1974.

Dhavamony, Mariasusai. "Death and Immortality in Hinduism." In *DIRW,* pp. 93–108.

Dienstag, Jacob I. *Eschatology in Maimonidean Thought: Messianism, Resurrection, and the World to Come.* New York: Ktav Publishing House, 1983.

DiNoia, Joseph A. "Varieties of Religious Aims: Beyond Exclusivism, Inclusivism, and Pluralism." In *Theology and Dialogue: Essays in Conversation with George Lindbeck,* edited by Bruce D. Marshall, pp. 249–74. Notre Dame: University of Notre Dame Press, 1990.

Doan, Linh. "Participating in and Witnessing to Triune Hospitality: Toward a Theology of Interreligious Engagement." PhD diss., Fuller Theological Seminary, 2014.

The Doctrine Commission of the Church of England. *The Mystery of Salvation: The Story of God's Gift.* London: Church House Publishing, 1995.

Dodd, C. H. *The Coming of Christ — Four Broadcast Addresses for the Season of Advent.* Cambridge: Cambridge University Press, 1951.

Doniger, Wendy. *On Hinduism.* Oxford: Oxford University Press, 2014.

———. *The Origins of Evil in Hindu Mythology.* Berkeley: University of California Press, 1976.

Donner, Fred M. *Muhammad and the Believers: At the Origins of Islam.* London and Cambridge, Mass.: Belknap Press of Harvard University Press, 2010.

Dotti, Brother Guido. "The Bose Monastery's Ecumenical Martyrology." Lecture, Bose, Italy, July 9, 2013. www.strasbourginstitute.org/wp-content/uploads/2013/08/Bose -Monastery.docx.

Dovidio, John F., Miles Hewstone, Peter Glick, and Victoria M. Esses, eds. *The SAGE Handbook of Prejudice, Stereotyping, and Discrimination.* Los Angeles: SAGE Publications, 2010.

Doyle, Dennis M. *Communion Ecclesiology.* Maryknoll, N.Y.: Orbis, 2000.

Doyle, Dennis M., Timothy J. Furry, and Pascal D. Bazzell, eds. *Ecclesiology and Exclusion: Boundaries of Being and Belonging in Postmodern Times.* Maryknoll, N.Y.: Orbis, 2012.

Drees, Willem B. "A Case against Temporal Realism? Consequences of Quantum Cosmology for Theology." In *QCNL*, pp. 331–65.

Dubrovsky, D. I. "Cybernetic Immortality: Fantasy or Scientific Problem?" 2045: Strategic Social Initiative, February 11, 2012. http://2045.com/articles/30810.html.

Duchrow, Ulrich, and Franz J. Hinkelammert. *Transcending Greedy Money: Interreligious Solidarity for Just Relations.* New York: Palgrave Macmillan, 2012.

Duffy, Regis A. "Sacraments in General." In *Systematic Theology: Roman Catholic Perspectives,* vol. 2, edited by Francis Schüssler Fiorenza and John P. Galvin. Minneapolis: Fortress, 1991.

Dufoix, Stéphane. *Diasporas.* Berkeley: University of California Press, 2008.

Dulles, Avery. "The Church as Communion." In *New Perspectives on Historical Theology: Essays in Memory of John Meyendorff,* edited by Bradley Nassif. Grand Rapids: Eerdmans, 1996.

———. "The Church as 'One, Holy, Catholic, and Apostolic.'" *Evangelical Review of Theology* 23, no. 1 (1999): 14–28.

Dunn, James D. G. *The Theology of Paul the Apostle.* Grand Rapids: Eerdmans, 1998.

———. *Unity and Diversity in the New Testament: An Inquiry into the Character of Earliest Christianity.* 2nd ed. London: SCM, 1990.

Dupré, Louis K. *The Enlightenment and the Intellectual Foundations of Modern Culture.* New Haven: Yale University Press, 2004.

Duquoc, Christian. *Provisional Churches: An Essay in Ecumenical Ecclesiology.* London: SCM, 1986.

Durham University. "About Receptive Ecumenism." Accessed November 11, 2016. https:// www.dur.ac.uk/theology.religion/ccs/projects/receptiveecumenism/about/.

Dussell, Enrique. "The Differentiation of Charisms." *Concilium* 109 (1978): 38–55.

Dyrness, William A. *Poetic Theology: God and the Poetics of Everyday Life.* Grand Rapids: Eerdmans, 2010.

Dyson, F. J. "Life in the Universe: Is Life Digital or Analogue?" In *FFU*, pp. 140–57.
———. "Time without End: Physics and Biology in an Open Universe." *Reviews of Modern Physics* 51, no. 3 (1979): 447–60.
Ebeling, Gerhard. *Word of God and Tradition: Historical Studies Interpreting the Divisions in Christianity*. Translated by S. H. Hooke. London: Collins, 1968.
Eckardt, Alice I. "The Holocaust: Christian and Jewish Responses." *Journal of the American Academy of Religion* 42, no. 35 (1974): 453–69.
Eckhardt, A. Roy. *Elder and Younger Brothers*. New York: Charles Scribner's Sons, 1967.
Eckstein, Hans-Joachim. "Bodily Resurrection in Luke." In *RTSA*, pp. 115–24.
Ecumenical Council of Florence. "Session 8 — 22 November 1439 [Bull of union with the Armenians]." Eternal Word Television Network. Accessed November 12, 2016. https://www.ewtn.com/library/COUNCILS/FLORENCE.HTM.
Eddington, Arthur S. *The Nature of the Physical World*. Cambridge: Cambridge University Press, 1928.
Edwards, Denis. "Where on Earth Is God?" In *Christian Faith and the Earth: Current Paths and Emerging Horizons in Ecotheology*, edited by Ernst M. Conradie, Sigurd Bergmann, Celia Deane-Drummond, and Denis Edwards, pp. 11–30. London and New York: Bloomsbury T. & T. Clark, 2014.
———. "Why Is God Doing This? Suffering, the Universe, and Christian Eschatology." In *PC*, pp. 247–66.
Edwards, O. C., Jr. "Meanings of Full Communion: The Essence of Life in the Body." *Speaking of Unity* 1 (2005): 9–35.
Edwards, Paul. "Heidegger and Death as 'Possibility.'" *Mind*, n.s., 84, no. 336 (October 1975): 548–66.
Eickelman, Dale F. "Rites of Passage: Muslim Rites." In *ER*, pp. 7824–28.
Eliade, Mircea. *The Myth of the Eternal Return, or Cosmos and History*. Translated by W. R. Trask. Princeton: Princeton University Press, 1971.
Eliott, Jaklin A., ed. *Interdisciplinary Perspectives on Hope*. Hauppauge, N.Y.: Nova Science Publishers, 2005.
Ellemers, Naomi, and S. Alexander Haslam. "Social Identity Theory." In *The Handbook of Theories of Social Psychology*, edited by Paul A. Van Lange, Arie W. Kruglanski, and E. Tory Higgins, 2:379–98. New York: SAGE, 2012.
Engel, Mary P., and Susan B. Thistlethwaite. "Introduction: Making Connections among Liberation Theologies around the World." In *Lift Every Voice: Constructing Christian Theologies from the Underside*, edited by Susan B. Thistlethwaite and Mary P. Engel. Rev. ed. Maryknoll, N.Y.: Orbis, 1998.
Ensign-George, Barry. "Denomination as Ecclesiological Category: Sketching an Assessment." In *Denomination: Assessing an Ecclesiological Category*, edited by Paul M. Collins and Barry Ensign-George, pp. 1–21. London and New York: Bloomsbury, 2011.
Erb, Peter C. "Responses to 'The Spirit and the Church' by Miroslav Volf and Maurice Lee." *Conrad Grebel Review* 18, no. 3 (Fall 2000): 55–62.
Erikson, Millard J. *A Basic Guide to Eschatology: Making Sense of the Millennium*. Grand Rapids: Baker, 1998.

"Evangelical and Roman Catholic Dialogue on Mission, 1977-1984: A Report." *International Bulletin of Missionary Research* 10, no. 1 (1986): 2-21.

Evans, C. F. *Resurrection and the New Testament*. London: SCM, 1970.

Evans, Gillian R. *Augustine on Evil*. Cambridge: Cambridge University Press, 1982.

————. "The Church in the Early Christian Centuries: Ecclesiological Consolidation." In *RCCC*, pp. 28-47.

Evans, James H., Jr. *We Have Been Believers: An African-American Systematic Theology*. Minneapolis: Fortress, 1992.

Evans, Michael D., with Jerome R. Corsi. *Showdown with Nuclear Iran: Radical Islam's Messianic Mission to Destroy Israel and Cripple the United States*. Nashville: Nelson Current, 2006.

Faith and Order Commission. "Faith and Order By-Laws, 3.1." In *Faith and Order at the Crossroads: Kuala Lumpur 2004; The Plenary Commission Meeting*, edited by Thomas F. Best. Faith and Order Paper no. 196. Geneva: WCC, 2005.

Faivre, Alexandre. *The Emergence of the Laity in the Early Church*. Translated by David Smith. New York: Paulist, 1990.

Fakhry, Majid. "An Islamic Perspective." In *OHRD*, pp. 393-402.

Farley, Margaret A., and Serene Jones, eds. *Liberating Eschatology: Essays in Honor of Letty M. Russell*. Louisville: Westminster John Knox, 1999.

Ferguson, Everett. *Baptism in the Early Church: History, Theology, and Liturgy in the First Five Centuries*. Grand Rapids: Eerdmans, 2009.

————. *The Church of Christ: A Biblical Ecclesiology for Today*. Grand Rapids: Eerdmans, 1996.

Ferguson, Sinclair B. "Infant Baptism View." In *Baptism: Three Views*, edited by David F. Wright, pp. 77-111. Downers Grove: InterVarsity, 2009.

Feuerbach, Ludwig. *The Essence of Christianity*. Translated by George Eliot. New York: Harper and Brothers, 1957.

Finger, Reta Halteman. *Of Widows and Meals: Communal Meals in the Book of Acts*. Grand Rapids: Eerdmans, 2007.

Finger, Thomas N. *Christian Theology: An Eschatological Approach*. Scottdale, Pa.: Herald, 1985.

————. *A Contemporary Anabaptist Theology: Biblical, Historical, Constructive*. Downers Grove: InterVarsity, 2004.

Firestone, Reuven. "Argue for God's Sake — or a Jewish Argument for Argument's Sake." *Journal of Ecumenical Studies* 39, nos. 1-2 (2002): 47-57.

Fischer, John Martin. "Why Immortality Is Not So Bad." *International Journal of Philosophical Studies* 2 (1994): 257-70.

Flanagan, Brian P. "Communion Ecclesiologies as Contextual Theologies." *Horizons* 40, no. 3 (June 2013): 53-70.

————. "Jewish-Christian Communion and Its Ecclesiological Implications." *Ecclesiology* 8, no. 3 (2012): 302-25.

Fleischer, Ezra, and Ruth Langer. "Controversy." *Prooftexts* 20, no. 3 (2000): 380-87.

Flett, John G. *The Witness of God: The Trinity, Missio Dei, Karl Barth, and the Nature of Christian Community*. Grand Rapids: Eerdmans, 2010.

Flew, Anthony. "The Logic of Mortality." In *DIRW*, pp. 171–87.

Flood, Gavin D. *An Introduction to Hinduism.* Cambridge: Cambridge University Press, 1996.

Florovsky, Georges. "The Elements of Liturgy in the Orthodox Catholic Church." *One Church* 13, nos. 1–2 (1959).

———. "The Last Things and the Last Events." In *Collected Works of Church History*, vol. 3, *Creation and Redemption*, pp. 243–65. Belmont, Mass.: Nordland Publishing, 1976.

Ford, David F., and C. C. Pecknold, eds. *The Promise of Scriptural Reasoning.* Oxford: Blackwell, 2006.

Ford, Lewis S. *The Lure of God: A Biblical Background for Process Theism.* Philadelphia: Fortress, 1978.

Fraser, Nancy. "Rethinking Recognition." *New Left Review* 3 (2000): 107–20.

Freston, Paul. "Globalization, Southern Christianity, and Proselytism." *Review of Faith and International Affairs* 7, no. 1 (2009): 3–9.

Freud, Sigmund. *Reflections on War and Death.* Translated by A. A. Brill and Alfred B. Kuttner. New York: Moffat, Yard and Co., 1918. http://www.gutenberg.org/ebooks /35875.

Friedman, William. *About Time: Inventing the Fourth Dimension.* Cambridge, Mass.: MIT Press, 1990.

Friedman, Yohanan. *Tolerance and Coercion in Islam: Interfaith Relations in the Muslim Tradition.* Cambridge: Cambridge University Press, 2006.

Frogacs, David, ed. *The Antonio Gramsci Reader: Selected Writings, 1916–1935.* New York: New York University Press, 2000.

Fromherz, Allen. "Judgment, Final." In *The Oxford Encyclopedia of the Islamic World*, edited by John L. Esposito. Oxford: Oxford University Press, 2009. http://www .oxfordislamicstudies.com/article/opr/t236/e1107.

Froom, L. E. *The Conditionalist Faith of Our Fathers.* Washington, D.C.: Herald and Review, 1966.

Frost, Michael, and Alan Hirsch. *The Shaping of Things to Come: Innovation and Mission for the 21st-Century Church.* Peabody, Mass.: Hendrickson, 2003.

Frykholm, A. J. *Rapture Culture: Left Behind in Evangelical America.* Oxford and New York: Oxford University Press, 2004.

Fucan, Fabias. "Deus Destroyed." In *JBC*, pp. 223–26.

Fuchs, Lorelei F., SA. *Koinonia and the Quest for an Ecumenical Ecclesiology: From Foundations through Dialogue to Symbolic Competence for Communionality.* Grand Rapids: Eerdmans, 2008.

Fuchs, Stephen. *Rebellious Prophets: A Study of Messianic Movements in Indian Religions.* New York: Asia Publishing House, 1965 [1908].

Fudge, Edward W. *The Fire That Consumes: A Biblical and Historical Study of Final Punishment.* Houston: Providential, 1982.

Fudge, Edward W., and Robert A. Peterson. *Two Views of Hell: A Biblical and Theological Dialogue.* Downers Grove: InterVarsity, 2000.

Fukuyama, F. *The End of History and the Last Man.* New York: Free Press, 1992. This is an expanded version of the noted 1989 essay "The End of History," *National Interest* (Summer 1989): 3–18. http://www.wesjones.com/eoh.htm.

Fuller, Daniel. *Easter Faith and History.* London: Tyndale Press, 1968.

Fuller, Graham E. *The Future of Political Islam.* New York: Palgrave Macmillan, 2003.

Gaine, Simon Francis, OP. *Will There Be Free Will in Heaven? Freedom, Impeccability, and Beatitude.* London: T. & T. Clark, 2003.

Gallup, George, Jr., and D. Michael Lindsey. *Surveying the Religious Landscape.* Harrisburg, Pa.: Morehouse, 2000.

Garijo-Guembe, Miguel M. *Communion of the Saints: Foundation, Nature, and Structure of the Church.* Translated by Patrick Madigan, SJ. Collegeville, Minn.: Liturgical Press, 1994.

Gasser, Georg. Introduction to *PIR*, pp. 1–17.

Geach, Peter. *Providence and Evil.* Cambridge: Cambridge University Press, 1977.

Geaves, Ron. "The Community of the Many Names of God: *Sampradaya* Construction in a Global Diaspora or New Religious Movement." *Religions of South Asia* 1, no. 1 (2007): 107–25.

Gebara, Ivone. *Out of the Depths: Women's Experience of Evil and Salvation.* Minneapolis: Fortress, 2002.

George, Timothy. "The Priesthood of All Believers." In *The People of God: Essays on the Believers' Church,* edited by Paul Basden and David S. Dockery, pp. 85–95. Nashville: Broadman, 1991.

Geraci, Robert. *Apocalyptic AI: Visions of Heaven in Robotics, Artificial Intelligence, and Virtual Reality.* Oxford: Oxford University Press, 2010.

Gerloff, Roswith I. H. "The Significance of the African Christian Diaspora in Europe: Selected Bibliography." *International Review of Mission* 89 (2000): 498–510.

Ghaly, Mohammed. *Islam and Disability: Perspectives in Theology and Jurisprudence.* New York: Routledge, 2009.

Ghazali [Ghazzali], Abu Hamid Muhammad al-. *The Alchemy of Happiness.* Translated by Henry A. Homes. Albany, N.Y.: Munsell, 1853.

———. *The Remembrance of Death and the Afterlife.* Cambridge: Islamic Texts Society of Cambridge, 1995.

———. *Tahafut Al-Falasifah: The Incoherence of Philosophers.* Translated by Michael E. Marmura. Provo, Utah: Brigham Young University Press, 2000.

Gibbs, Eddie. *ChurchNext.* Downers Grove: InterVarsity, 2000.

Gibbs, Eddie, and Ryan Bolger. *The Emerging Churches: Creating Christian Community in Postmodern Cultures.* Grand Rapids: Baker Academic, 2005.

Giblet, Jean. "Baptism — the Sacrament of Incorporation into the Church according to St. Paul." In *Baptism in the New Testament: A Symposium,* translated by David Askew, pp. 161–88. Baltimore: Helicon, 1964.

Giddens, Anthony. *Runaway World: How Globalization Is Reshaping Our Lives.* New York: Routledge, 2003.

Gillman, Neil. *The Death of Death: Resurrection and Immortality in Jewish Thought.* Woodstock, Vt.: Jewish Lights Publishing, 1997.

————. "How Will It All End?" In *Faith, Science and the Future*, edited by Charles P. Henderson, pp. 39–51. New York: Association of Religion and Intellectual Life, 2007.

Godzliher, Ignaz. *Introduction to Islamic Theology and Law*. Translated by Andras Hamory and Ruth Hamory. Princeton: Princeton University Press, 1981.

Goetz, Stewart, and Charles Taliaferro. *Naturalism*. Grand Rapids: Eerdmans, 2008.

Goheen, Michael W. *As the Father Has Sent Me, I Am Sending You: J. E. Lesslie Newbigin's Missionary Ecclesiology*. Zoetermeer: Uitgeverij Boekencentrum, 2000.

Goldberg, Robert. "Bound Up in the Bond of Life: Death and Afterlife in the Jewish Tradition." In *DAR*, pp. 97–108.

Goldman, Robert P. "Karma, Guilt, and Buried Memories: Public Fantasy and Private Reality in Traditional India." *Journal of the American Oriental Society* 105, no. 3 (1985): 413–25.

González, Justo L. *Mañana: Christian Theology from a Hispanic Perspective*. Nashville: Abingdon, 1990.

Gooder, Paula. "In Search of the 'Early Church': The New Testament and the Development of Christian Communities." In *RCCC*, pp. 9–27.

Goosen, Gideon. *Spacetime and Theology in Dialogue*. Milwaukee: Marquette University Press, 2008.

Gorenberg, Gershom. *The End of Days: Fundamentalism and the Struggle for the Temple Mount*. New York: Oxford University Press, 2000.

Gorski, Philip, David Kyuman Kim, John Torpey, and Jonathan Vanantwerpen, eds. *The Post-Secular in Question: Religion in Contemporary Society*. New York: New York University Press, 2012.

Goudzwaard, Bob. *Globalization and the Kingdom of God*. Grand Rapids: Baker, 2001.

Gowan, Donald E. *Eschatology in the Old Testament*. Philadelphia: Fortress, 1986.

Graf, Friedrich Wilhelm. *Die Wiederkehr der Götte: Religion in der Modernen Kultur*. Munich: C. H. Beck, 2004.

Graham, Elaine. "Liberation or Enslavement?" *GeneWatch*. Accessed November 12, 2016. http://www.councilforresponsiblegenetics.org/genewatch/GeneWatchPage .aspx?pageId=227.

Grassi, Joseph A. *Broken Bread and Broken Bodies: The Lord's Supper and World Hunger*. Maryknoll, N.Y.: Orbis, 1985.

Green, Ronald M. "Theodicy." In *ER*, pp. 9111–21.

Greenberg, Irving. *For the Sake of Heaven and Earth: The New Encounter between Judaism and Christianity*. Philadelphia: Jewish Publication Society, 2004.

Greggs, Tom. "Exclusivist or Universalist? Origen the 'Wise Steward of the Word' (*Comm-Rom.* V.1.7) and the Issue of Genre." *International Journal of Systematic Theology* 9 (2007): 315–27.

Gregory, Brad S. *The Unintended Reformation: How a Religious Revolution Secularized Society*. Cambridge: Belknap Press of Harvard University Press, 2012.

Gregory, D. *The Colonial Present*. Oxford: Blackwell, 2004.

Gregory of Nyssa. *Song of Songs*. Translated by Casimir McCambley. Brookline, Mass.: Hellenistic College Press, 1987.

Grenz, Stanley J. "Ecclesiology." In *Cambridge Companion to Postmodern Theology*, edited by Kevin J. Vanhoozer, pp. 252–68. Cambridge: Cambridge University Press, 2003.

———. *The Millennial Maze*. Downers Grove: InterVarsity, 1994.

———. *Rediscovering the Triune God: The Trinity in Contemporary Theology*. Minneapolis: Fortress, 2004.

———. *The Social God and Relational Self: A Trinitarian Theology of the Imago Dei*. Louisville: Westminster John Knox, 2001.

———. *Theology for the Community of God*. Grand Rapids: Eerdmans, 1994.

Grey, Aubrey de. "The War on Aging." In *The Scientific Conquest of Death: Essays on Infinite Lifespans*, edited by Immortality Institute, pp. 29–46. Buenos Aires: Libros EnRed, 2004. http://www.imminst.org/SCOD.pdf.

Griffel, Frank. "Al-Ghazali." In *Stanford Encyclopedia of Philosophy* (Winter 2014 edition), edited by Edward N. Zalta. Revised September 22, 2014. http://plato.stanford.edu /archives/win2014/entries/al-ghazali/.

Griffin, David Ray. "Process Eschatology." In *OHE*, pp. 295–307.

Grönvik, Lorenz. *Die Taufe in der Theologie Luthers*. Abo: Abo Academy University, 1968.

Gross, Rita M. "Meditation and Prayer: A Comparative Inquiry." *Buddhist-Christian Studies* 22 (2002): 77–86.

Grossman, Susan, and Rivka Haut, eds. *Daughters of the King: Women and the Synagogue*. Philadelphia and Jerusalem: Jewish Publication Society, 1992.

Guder, Darrell, ed. *Missional Church: A Vision for the Sending of the Church in North America*. Grand Rapids: Eerdmans, 1998.

———. "Missional Hermeneutics: The Missional Authority of Scripture — Interpreting Scripture as Missional Formation." *Mission Focus: Annual Review* 15 (2007): 106–21.

———. "The Nicene Marks in a Post-Christendom Church." In *Called to Witness: Doing Missional Theology*, pp. 78–89. Grand Rapids: Eerdmans, 2015. https://www.pcusa .org/site_media/media/uploads/reformingministry/pdfs/nicene_marks.pdf. Page numbering in the online version (pp. 1–16), which has been used above in the notes, differs from that in the published article.

Gundry, Robert. "The New Jerusalem: People as Place, Not Place for People (Revelation 21:1–22:5)." *Novum Testamentum* 29 (1987): 254–64.

Gündüz, Sinasi. "Problems on the Muslim Understanding of the Mandaeans." *ARAM Periodical* 11 (1999): 269–79.

Gunton, Colin E. *The Actuality of Atonement: A Study of Metaphor, Rationality, and the Christian Tradition*. Edinburgh: T. & T. Clark; Grand Rapids: Eerdmans, 1989.

———. *The Triune Creator: A Historical and Systematic Study*. Edinburgh Studies in Constructive Theology. Grand Rapids: Eerdmans, 1998.

Gurmann, Joseph, and Steven Fine. "Synagogue." In *ER*, pp. 8920–26.

Gutiérrez, Gustavo. *On Job: God-Talk and the Suffering of the Innocent*. Translated by Matthew J. O'Connell. Maryknoll, N.Y.: Orbis, 1995.

———. *A Theology of Liberation: History, Politics, and Salvation*. Translated and edited by Sister Caridad Inda and John Eagleson. Maryknoll, N.Y.: Orbis, 1986 [1973]; rev. ed. with a new introduction, 1988.

Guyatt, N. *Have a Nice Doomsday: Why Millions of Americans Are Looking Forward to the End of the World.* New York: Harper Perennial, 2007.

Habermas, Jürgen. "An Awareness of What Is Missing." In Jürgen Habermas et al., *An Awareness of What Is Missing: Faith and Reason in a Post-Secular Age*, translated by Ciaran Cronin, pp. 15–23. Cambridge, UK, and Malden, Mass.: Polity, 2010 [2007].

———. *Between Naturalism and Religion.* Translated by Ciaran Cronin. Cambridge: Polity, 2008.

———. "Faith and Knowledge." In *The Future of Human Nature*, translated by William Rehg, Max Pensky, and Hella Beister. Cambridge: Polity, 2003.

———. "Notes on Post-Secular Society." *New Perspectives Quarterly* 25, no. 4 (2008): 17–29. Available at http://www.staff.amu.edu.pl/~ewa/Habermas,%20Notes%20on%20Post-Secular%20Society.pdf.

———. *Postmetaphysical Thinking: Philosophical Essays.* Translated by William Mark Hohengarten. Cambridge, Mass., and London: MIT Press, 1992.

Habito, Maria Reis. "The Notion of Buddha-Nature: An Approach to Buddhist-Muslim Dialogue." *Muslim World* 100 (April/July 2010): 233–34.

Habito, Ruben L. F. "Environment or Earth Sangha: Buddhist Perspectives on Our Global Ecological Well-Being." *Contemporary Buddhism* 8, no. 2 (2007): 131–47.

———. "Japanese Buddhist Perspectives and Comparative Theology: Supreme Ways in Intersection." *Theological Studies* 64 (2003): 362–87.

Hackett, Rosalind I. J., ed. *Proselytization Revisited: Rights Talk, Free Markets, and Culture Wars.* New York: Routledge, 2014 [2008].

Haddad, Yvonne Y., and Jane I. Smith. "The Anti-Christ and the End of Time in Christian and Muslim Eschatological Literature." *Muslim World* 100, no. 4 (October 2010): 505–29.

Haider, Najam. *Shīʿī Islam.* Cambridge: Cambridge University Press, 2014.

Haitch, Russell. *From Exorcism to Ecstasy: Eight Views of Baptism.* Louisville and London: Westminster John Knox, 2007.

Halberstam, Judith, and Ira Livingston, eds. *Posthuman Bodies.* Indianapolis: Indiana University Press, 1995.

Haleem, Muhammad [A. S.] Abdel. "Commentary on Selected Qurʾānic Texts." In *Death, Resurrection, and Human Destiny: Christian and Muslim Perspectives*, edited by David Marshall and Lucinda Mosher, pp. 147–52. Washington, D.C.: Georgetown University Press, 2014.

———. "Life and Beyond in the Qurʾan." In *Beyond Death*, edited by D. Cohn-Sherbok and C. Lewis, pp. 66–79. New York: St. Martin's Press, 1995.

———. "Qurʾan and Hadith." In *CCCIT*, pp. 19–32.

Hall, Douglas John. *Thinking the Faith.* Minneapolis: Fortress, 1991.

Hall, Lindsay. *Swinburne's Hell and Hick's Universalism: Are We Free to Reject God?* Aldershot, UK: Ashgate, 2003.

Hall, Stuart G. "The Early Idea of the Church." In *The First Christian Theologians: An Introduction to Theology in the First Centuries*, edited by G. R. Evans, pp. 41–57. Oxford: Blackwell, 2004.

Hallett, Garth L. "The Tedium of Immortality." *Faith and Philosophy* 18 (2001): 279–91.

Hamza, Feras. "Unity and Disunity in the Life of the Muslim Community." In *The Community of Believers*, edited by Lucinda Mosher and David Marshall, pp. 65-80. Washington, D.C.: Georgetown University Press, 2015.

Hanciles, Jehu J. "'Africa Is Our Fatherland': The Black Atlantic, Globalization, and Modern African Christianity." *Theology Today* 71 (2014): 207-20.

———. *Beyond Christendom: Globalization, African Migration, and the Transformation of the West*. Maryknoll, N.Y.: Orbis, 2008.

Handbook of Thanatology: The Essential Body of Knowledge for the Study of Death, Dying, and Bereavement. 2nd ed. New York: Routledge, 2013.

Hanson, John Wesley. *Universalism: The Prevailing Doctrine of the Christian Church during Its First Five Hundred Years, with Authorities and Extracts*. Boston and Chicago: Universalist Publishing House, 1899. https://archive.org/details/universalismprevoohans.

Hardacre, Helen. "Ancestor Worship." In *ER*, pp. 320-25.

Hardt, Michael, and Antonio Negri. *Empire*. Cambridge, Mass.: Harvard University Press, 2000.

———. *Multitude: War and Democracy in the Age of Empire*. New York: Penguin, 2004.

Hargrove, Thomas, and Guido H. Stempel III. "Most Americans Doubt the Resurrection of the Body." *Scripps Howard News Service*. April 5, 2006. NewsPolls.org. http://www.newspolls.org/articles/19603.

Harper, Brad, and Paul Louis Metzger. *Exploring Ecclesiology: An Evangelical and Ecumenical Introduction*. Grand Rapids: Brazos, 2009.

Harrington, Austin. "Habermas and the 'Post-Secular Society.'" *European Journal of Social Theory* 10, no. 4 (2007): 543-60.

Hart, David Bentley. *The Beauty of the Infinite: The Aesthetics of Christian Truth*. Grand Rapids: Eerdmans, 2003.

———. "Death, Final Judgment, and the Meaning of Life." In *OHE*, pp. 476-88.

Hart, Kevin. "'Without World': Eschatology in Michael Henry." In *Phenomenology and Eschatology: Not Yet in the Now*, edited by Neal DeRoo and John Panteleimon Manoussakis, pp. 167-92. Surrey, UK: Ashgate, 2009.

Hartman, David. "Suffering." In *Contemporary Jewish Religious Thought: Original Essays on Critical Concepts, Movements, and Beliefs*, edited by Arthur A. Cohen and Paul Mendes-Flohr, pp. 939-46. New York: Free Press, 1987.

Hartshorne, Charles. *Omnipotence and Other Theological Mistakes*. Albany: State University of New York Press, 1984.

Harvey, David. *The New Imperialism*. Oxford: Oxford University Press, 2003.

Harvie, Timothy. "Living the Future: The Kingdom of God in the Theologies of Jürgen Moltmann and Wolfhart Pannenberg." *International Journal of Systematic Theology* 10 (April 2008): 149-64.

Hasker, William. *The Triumph of God over Evil: Theodicy for a World of Suffering*. Downers Grove: InterVarsity, 2008.

Hassan, Riaz. "Globalization's Challenge to Islam: How to Create One Islamic Community in a Diverse World." *YaleGlobal Online*, April 17, 2003. http://yaleglobal.yale.edu/content/globalizations-challenge-islam.

———. "Globalisation's Challenge to the Islamic 'Ummah.'" *Asian Journal of Social Science* 34, no. 2 (2006): 311–23.

Hassan, Riffat. "Messianism and Islam." *Journal of Ecumenical Studies* 22 (Spring 1985): 261–91.

Hastings, Ross. *Missional God, Missional Church: Hope for Re-evangelizing the West.* Downers Grove: InterVarsity, 2012.

Hauerwas, Stanley. *Dispatches from the Front: Theological Engagements with the Secular.* Durham, N.C.: Duke University Press, 1995.

———. *The Peaceable Kingdom.* Notre Dame: Notre Dame University Press, 1983.

———. *The State of the University: Academic Knowledges and the Knowledge of God.* Malden, Mass.: Blackwell, 2007.

———. *With the Grain of the Universe: The Church's Witness and Natural Theology; Being the Gifford Lectures Delivered at the University of St. Andrews in 2001.* Grand Rapids: Brazos, 2001.

Hauerwas, Stanley, and Samuel Wells. "How the Church Managed before There Was Ethics." In *The Blackwell Companion to Christian Ethics,* edited by Stanley Hauerwas and Samuel Wells, pp. 39–50. Malden, Mass.: Blackwell, 2004.

Hauerwas, Stanley, and William H. Willimon. *Resident Aliens: A Provocative Christian Assessment of Culture and Ministry for People Who Know That Something Is Wrong.* Nashville: Abingdon, 1989.

Haught, John F. *Is Nature Enough? Meaning and Truth in the Age of Science.* Cambridge and New York: Cambridge University Press, 2006.

———. *The Promise of Nature: Ecology and Cosmic Purpose.* Mahwah, N.J.: Paulist, 1993.

Hawk, Matthew C. "Recent Perspectives on the Holocaust." *Religious Studies Review* 22, no. 3 (1996): 197–208.

Hawking, Stephen. *The Universe in a Nutshell.* London: Bantam Books, 2001.

Hayes, R. P. "Gotama Buddhism and Religious Pluralism." *Journal of Religious Pluralism* (1991): 65–96.

Hays, Richard B. "'Why Do You Stand Looking Up toward Heaven?' New Testament Eschatology at the Turn of the Millennium." In *Theology and Eschatology at the Turn of the Millennium,* edited by James Buckley and L. Gregory Jones, pp. 113–33. Oxford: Blackwell, 2001.

Healey, Joseph, and Donald Sybertz. *Towards an African Narrative Theology.* Maryknoll, N.Y.: Orbis, 1996.

Healing and Wholeness: The Churches' Role in Health. The report of a study by the Christian Medical Commission. Geneva: WCC, 1990.

"The Healing Mission of the Church." In *"You Are the Light of the World" (Matthew 5:14): Statements on Mission by the World Council of Churches, 1980-2005,* edited by Jacques Matthey, pp. 127–62. Geneva: WCC, 2005.

Hebblethwaite, B. *The Christian Hope.* Grand Rapids: Eerdmans, 1984.

Hedley, Douglas. "Should Divinity Overcome Metaphysics? Reflections on John Milbank's Theology beyond Secular Reason and Confessions of a Cambridge Platonist." *Journal of Religion* 80 (2000): 271–98.

Heemskerk, Margaretha T. *Suffering in the Mu'tazilite Theology: 'Abd-al-Jabbār's Teaching on Pain and Justice*. Leiden: Brill, 2000.

Hefner, Philip. *The Human Factor: Evolution, Culture, and Religion*. Minneapolis: Augsburg Fortress, 1993.

———. *Technology and Human Becoming*. Minneapolis: Fortress, 2003.

Hegel, G. W. F. *The Phenomenology of Mind*. Translated by J. B. Baillie. San Francisco: Harper Torch Paperbacks, 1967 [1910]. https://www.marxists.org/reference/archive/hegel/phindex.htm.

Heidegger, Martin. *Being and Time*. Translated by J. Macquarrie and E. Robinson. Harper Perennial Modern Classics. 1962. Reprint, New York: HarperCollins, 2008.

Heim, S. Mark. *The Depth of the Riches: A Trinitarian Theology of Religious Ends*. Grand Rapids: Eerdmans, 2001.

Hejzlar, Pavel. *Two Paradigms for Divine Healing: Fred F. Bosworth, Kenneth E. Hagin, Agnes Sanford, and Francis MacNutt in Dialogue*. Leiden and Boston: Brill, 2010.

Heller, Michael. "Time of the Universe." In *FFU*, pp. 53–64.

Hellwig, Monika. *The Eucharist and the Hunger of the World*. New York: Paulist, 1976.

Helm, Paul. *Eternal God: A Study of God without Time*. Oxford: Clarendon, 1988.

Henderson, James M. "Election as Renewal: The Work of the Holy Spirit in Divine Election." PhD diss., Regent University, School of Divinity, 2012.

Henriksen, Jan-Olav. *Desire, Gift, and Recognition: Christology and Postmodern Philosophy*. Grand Rapids: Eerdmans, 2009.

Heppe, Heinrich. *Reformed Dogmatics: Set Out and Illustrated from the Sources*. Revised and edited by Ernst Bizer. Translated by G. T. Thomson. London: Allen and Unwin, 1950.

Herberg, Will. *Judaism and Modern Man*. New York: Farrar, Straus, and Young, 1951.

Herman, Arthur L. *The Problem of Evil and Indian Thought*. Delhi: Motilal Banarsidass, 1993.

Hermansen, Marcia. "Eschatology." In *The Cambridge Companion to Classical Islamic Theology*, edited by Tim Winter, pp. 308–24. New York: Cambridge University Press, 2008.

Herrin, Judith. *The Formation of Christendom*. London: Fontana, 1989.

Hershenov, David B. "Van Inwagen, Zimmerman, and the Materialist Conception of Resurrection." *Religious Studies* 38 (2002): 451–69.

Herzfeld, Noreen. "Cybernetic Immortality versus Christian Resurrection." In *RTSA*, pp. 192–201.

Heschel, Susannah. "Jewish Views of Jesus." In *JWF*, p. 149.

Hesse, D. T., ed. *After Nature's Revolt: Eco-Justice and Theology*. Philadelphia: Fortress, 1992.

Hick, John. *Death and Eternal Life: With a New Preface by the Author*. Louisville: Westminster John Knox, 1994 [1976].

———. *Evil and the God of Love*. 2nd reissued ed. New York: Palgrave Macmillan, 2010.

———, ed. *The Metaphor of God Incarnate: Christology in a Pluralistic Age*. London: SCM, 1993.

———. "The Possibility of Religious Pluralism: A Reply to Gavin D'Costa." *Religious Studies* 33 (1997): 161–66.

Hiebert, Paul G. "Conversion in Hinduism and Buddhism." In *HRC*, pp. 9–21.

Hietamäki, Minna. "Recognition and Ecumenical Recognition — Distinguishing the Idea of Recognition in Modem Ecumenism." *Neue Zeitschrift für systematische Theologie und Religionsphilosophie* 56 (2014): 454–72.

Hill, C. E. *Regnum Caelorum: Patterns of Future Hope in Early Christianity.* Oxford: Clarendon, 2002.

Hill, Graham. *Salt, Light, and a City: Introducing Missional Ecclesiology.* Eugene, Ore.: Wipf and Stock, 2012.

Hiltebeitel, Alf. "The 'Mahābhārata,' and Hindu Eschatology." *History of Religions* 12, no. 2 (1972): 95–135.

Himes, Michael J. *Ongoing Incarnation: Johann Adam Möhler and the Beginnings of Modern Ecclesiology.* New York: Crossroad, 1997.

Hinze, Bradford E. "Releasing the Power of the Spirit in a Trinitarian Ecclesiology." In *Advents of the Spirit: An Introduction to the Current Study of Pneumatology*, edited by Bradford E. Hinze and D. Lyle Dabney, pp. 347–81. Marquette Studies in Theology 30. Milwaukee: Marquette University Press, 2001.

Hippolytus. *The Apostolic Tradition of Hippolytus.* Edited and translated by Burton Scott Easton. Cambridge: Cambridge University Press, 1934.

Hobbes, Thomas. *The Leviathan (Or the Matter, Forme & Power of a Commonwealth, Ecclesiastical and Civil).* Edited by A. R. Waller. Cambridge English Classics. Cambridge: Cambridge University Press, 1904 [1651]. https://archive.org/details /leviathanormatto2hobbgoog.

Hodge, Charles. *Systematic Theology.* Vol. 3. Grand Rapids: Eerdmans, 1973 [1872].

Hodge, Joel. "Church, State and Secularism in Asia: The Public Nature of the Church in Timor-Leste." *International Journal of Practical Theology* 16 (2012): 323–48.

Hodgson, Peter C. "Hegel's Christology: Shifting Nuances in the Berlin Lectures." *Journal of the American Academy of Religion* 53, no. 1 (1985): 23–40.

Hoekema, Anthony A. *The Bible and the Future.* Grand Rapids: Eerdmans, 1979.

Hoffman, Marie T. *Toward Mutual Recognition: Relational Psychoanalysis and the Christian Narrative.* New York: Routledge, 2011.

Hollenweger, W. J. "From Azusa Street to Toronto Phenomenon: Historical Roots of Pentecostalism." *Concilium* 3 (1996): 3–14.

Holliday, Lisa R. "Will Satan Be Saved? Reconsidering Origen's Theory of Volition in *Peri Archon*." *Vigiliae Christianae* 63 (2009): 1–23.

Hollinger, David. *Postethnic America: Beyond Multiculturalism.* Tenth anniversary, revised and updated ed. New York: Basic Books, 2006 [1995].

Honneth, Axel. *Disrespect: The Normative Foundations of Critical Theory.* Malden, Mass.: Polity, 2007.

———. *The I in We: Studies in the Theory of Recognition.* Translated by Joseph Ganahl. Malden, Mass.: Polity, 2012.

———. *The Struggle for Recognition: The Moral Grammar of Social Conflicts.* Translated by Joel Anderson. Cambridge: Polity, 1995.

Hood, Adam. "Governance." In *RCCC*, pp. 536–49.

Hoover, Jon. *Ibn Taymiyya's Theodicy of Perpetual Optimism*. Leiden and Boston: Brill, 2007.

———. "The Justice of God and the Best of All Possible Worlds: The Theodicy of Ibn Taymiyya." *Theological Review* 28, no. 2 (2006): 53–75.

Horton, Michael. *A Better Way: Rediscovering the Drama of God-Centered Worship*. Grand Rapids: Baker, 2002.

Horvath, Tibor, SJ. *Eternity and Eternal Life: Speculative Theology and Science in Discourse*. Waterloo, Ont.: Wilfrid Laurier University Press, 1993.

Hospital, Clifford G. "The Contribution of Keshub Chunder Sen toward a Global and Inductive Christology." *Journal of Ecumenical Studies* 19, no. 1 (1982): 1–17.

Hovorun, Cyril. "Church and Nation: Looking through the Glasses of Post-Secularism." *St. Vladimir's Theological Quarterly* 57, no. 3 (2013): 423–30.

Howell, Brian. "Multiculturalism, Immigration and the North American Church: Rethinking Contextualization." *Missiology: An International Review* 39 (2011): 79–85.

Hudson, Hud. "Multiple Location and Single Location Resurrection." In *PIR*, pp. 87–101.

Hudson, W. Donald. *A Philosophical Approach to Religion*. London: Macmillan, 1974.

Hunt, Stephen, ed. *Christian Millennialism: From the Early Church to Waco*. Bloomington: Indiana University Press, 2001.

Hunter, Harold D. "Ordinances." In *The New International Dictionary of Pentecostal and Charismatic Movements*, edited by Stanley M. Burgess and Eduard M. van der Maas. Revised and expanded ed. Grand Rapids: Zondervan, 2002.

Huntington, Samuel, and Peter Berger, eds. *Many Globalizations: Cultural Diversity in the Contemporary World*. New York: Oxford University Press, 2002.

Huovinen, Eero. *Fides infantium: Martin Luthers Lehre vom Kinderglauben*. Göttingen: Vandenhoeck & Ruprecht, 2013 [1991].

———. "Fides infantium — fides infusa?" *Lutheran Forum* 30, no. 4 (1996): 37–42.

Husserl, Edmund. *On the Phenomenology of the Consciousness of Internal Time (1893–1917)*. Translated by John Barnett Brough. Dordrecht, Boston, and London: Kluwer Academic, 1991.

Huxley, Aldous. *The Perennial Philosophy: An Interpretation of the Great Mystics, East and West*. First Perennial Classics Edition. New York: HarperCollins, 2004 [1945].

Hvidt, Nils Christian. "Historical Developments of the Problem of Evil." In *PC*, pp. 1–35.

Ibn Hanbal, Ahmad. "Hanbalī Traditionalist Creed." Translated by William Montgomery. In *Islamic Theological Themes: A Primary Source Reader*, edited by John Renard, pp. 104–9. Oakland: University of California Press, 2014.

Ibn Khaldun. *Muqaddimah: An Introduction to History*. Translated by Franz Rosenthal. 3 vols. New York: Pantheon, 1958.

Idinopulos, Thomas A. "Christianity and the Holocaust." *Cross Currents* 28, no. 3 (Fall 1978): 257–67.

Igenoza, Andrew Olu. "Universalism and New Testament Christianity." *Evangelical Review of Theology* 12 (1998): 261–75.

Ikäheimo, Heikki. *Anerkennung*. Translated by Nadine Mooren. Berlin: De Gruyter, 2014.

Ikäheimo, Heikki, and Arto Laitinen. "Analyzing Recognition: Identification, Acknowledgement, and Recognitive Attitudes towards Persons." In *Recognition and Power: Axel Honneth and the Tradition of Social Theory*, edited by Bert van den Brink and David Owen, pp. 33–56. New York: Cambridge University Press, 2007.

Immortality Project Organization. http://www.immortality-project.org/.

Ingle-Gillis, William C. *The Trinity and Ecumenical Church Thought: The Church-Event*. Burlington, Vt.: Ashgate, 2007.

International Conference on Environmental Pollution and Remediation. *3rd International Conference on Environmental Pollution and Remediation, July 15–17, Toronto, Ontario, Canada*. http://icepr2013.international-aset.com/index.html.

International Council of Christians and Jews. "Dabru Emet: A Jewish Statement on Christians and Christianity." July 15, 2002. http://www.jcrelations.net/Dabru _Emet_-_A_Jewish_Statement_on_Christians_and_Christianity.2395.0.html.

Inwagen, Peter van. *Material Beings*. Ithaca, N.Y.: Cornell University Press, 1990.

————. "The Possibility of Resurrection." *International Journal for Philosophy of Religion* 9 (1978): 114–21.

Iqbal, Muzaffar. "Islam and Modern Science: Questions at the Interface." In *God, Life, and the Cosmos: Christian and Islamic Perspectives*, edited by Ted Peters, Muzaffar Iqbal, and Syed Nomanul Haq, pp. 3–41. Surrey, UK: Ashgate, 2002.

Irigaray, Luce. *I Love to You: Sketch of a Possible Felicity in History*. Translated by Alison Martin. New York and London: Routledge, 1996.

Islam, Jamal N. *The Ultimate Fate of the Universe*. London: Cambridge University Press, 1983.

Ito, Tomomi. "New Beginnings: The *Bhikkhuni* Movement in Contemporary Thailand." In *Bridging Worlds: Buddhist Women's Voices across Generations*, edited by Karma Lekshe Tsomo, pp. 120–24. Taipei: Yuan Chuan Press, 2004.

Ives, Christopher. "Liberating Truth: A Buddhist Approach to Religious Pluralism." In *Deep Religious Pluralism*, edited by David Ray Griffin, pp. 178–92. Louisville: Westminster John Knox, 2005.

Jabbar, Abd al-. "Five Principles." In "Abd al-Jabbār on God and Humanity in the Hereafter," translated by Richard Martin, in *Islamic Theological Themes: A Primary Source Reader*, edited by John Renard, pp. 212–14. Oakland: University of California Press, 2014.

Jackelén, Antje. *Time and Eternity: The Question of Time in Church, Science, and Theology*. Translated by Barbara Harshaw. West Conshohocken, Pa.: Templeton Foundation Press, 2005.

Jackson, Sherman. *On the Boundaries of Theological Tolerance in Islam*. Oxford: Oxford University Press, 2002.

Jacobs, Louis. *A Jewish Theology*. London: Darton, Longman and Todd, 1973.

Jacobsen, Knut A. "Three Functions of Hell in the Hindu Traditions." *Numen: International Review for the History of Religions* 56, nos. 2–3 (2009): 385–400.

Jacoby, Susan. *Freethinkers: A History of American Secularism*. New York: Metropolitan, 2004.

James, William. "The Will to Believe." In *"The Will to Believe" and Other Essays in Popular*

Philosophy [1897] *and Human Immortality* [1898], pp. 1–31. Mineola, N.Y.: Dover Publications, 1956.

Jaspers, Karl. *The Origins and Goal of History.* Translated by Michael Bullock. New Haven and London: Yale University Press, 1965 [1949].

Jenkins, Philip. *The New Faces of Christianity: Believing the Bible in the Global South.* New York: Oxford University Press, 2006.

————. *The Next Christendom: The Coming of Global Christianity.* Oxford: Oxford University Press, 2001.

Jenks, G. C. *The Origin and Development of the Antichrist Myth.* London and New York: De Gruyter, 1991.

Jenson, Robert W. *Systematic Theology.* 2 vols. New York: Oxford University Press, 1997, 1999.

————. *The Triune Identity: God according to the Gospel.* Philadelphia: Fortress, 1982.

Jeung, Russell. *Faithful Generations: Race and New Asian American Churches.* New Brunswick, N.J.: Rutgers University Press, 2005.

Johann-Albrecht, Meylahn. "Ecclesiology as Doing Theology in and with Local Communities but Not of the Empire." *Studia Historiae Ecclesiasticae* 37 (2011): 287–313.

John Chrysostom. *Baptismal Instructions.* In *Ancient Christian Writers,* translated by Paul W. Harkins. Mahwah, N.J.: Paulist, 1962.

Johnson, Elizabeth. *Friends of God and Prophets: A Feminist Theological Reading of the Communion of Saints.* New York: Continuum, 1998.

————. *She Who Is: The Mystery of God in Feminist Theological Discourse.* New York: Crossroad, 1993.

Johnson, Todd M., and Brian J. Grim. *The World's Religions in Figures.* Oxford: Wiley-Blackwell, 2013.

Joint Lutheran–Roman Catholic Study Commission. *Malta Report "The Gospel and Church,"* 1972. In *Growth in Agreement: Reports and Agreed Statements of Ecumenical Conversations on a World Level,* edited by H. Meyer and L. Vischer. New York and Ramsey, N.J.: Paulist; Geneva: WCC, 1984.

Jones, Serene. *Feminist Theory and Christian Theology: Cartographies of Grace.* Minneapolis: Fortress, 2000.

Jones, Tony. *The Church Is Flat: The Relational Ecclesiology of the Emerging Church Movement.* Minneapolis: JoPa Group, 2011.

Jongeneel, Jan A. B. "The Mission of Migrant Churches in Europe." *Missiology: An International Review* 31 (2003): 29–33.

Juergensmeyer, Mark. "Thinking Globally about Religion." In *OHGR,* pp. 3–12.

Jukko, Risto. *Trinitarian Theology in Christian-Muslim Encounters: Theological Foundations of the Work of the French Roman Catholic Church's Secretariat for Relations with Islam.* Helsinki: Luther-Agricola-Society, 2001.

Jüngel, Eberhard. *Death: The Riddle and the Mystery.* Translated by I. Nichol and U. Nichol. Edinburgh: T. & T. Clark, 1975.

————. "The Last Judgment as an Act of Grace." *Louvain Studies* 15 (1990): 389–40.

Kabilsingh, Chatsurmarn. *Thai Women in Buddhism.* Berkeley, Calif.: Parallax Press, 1991.

Kalin, Ibrahim. "Mulla Sadra on Theodicy and the Best of All Possible Worlds." *Oxford Journal of Islamic Studies* 18 (2007): 183–201.

Kankanamalage, Indunil Janakaratne Kodithuwakku. "Conversion and Proselytism in the Light of 'Christian Witness in a Multi-religious World.'" *International Review of Mission* 103, no. 398 (April 2014): 109–15.

Kant, Immanuel. "The End of All Things." In *Religion and Rational Theology*, translated and edited by Allen W. Wood and George di Giovanni, pp. 217–31. Cambridge: Cambridge University Press, 2001.

———. "On the Miscarriage of All Philosophical Trials in Theodicy" (1791). In *Religion and Rational Theology*, translated and edited by Allen W. Wood and George di Giovanni, pp. 24–37. Cambridge: Cambridge University Press, 2001. http://cas .uchicago.edu/workshops/germanphilosophy/files/2013/02/Kant-On-the-Mis carriage-of-all-Philosophical-Trials-at-Theodicy.pdf. Also titled "On the Failure of All Philosophical Attempts at a Theodicy."

———. *Religion within the Limits of Reason Alone.* Translated by Theodore M. Greene and Hoyt H. Hudson. Harper Torchbook/The Cloister Library edition. New York: Harper and Row, 1960.

———. *Universal Natural History and Theory of the Heavens.* Translated by W. Hastie. New York: Greenwood, 1968.

Karamustafa, Ahmet T. "Community." In *Key Themes in the Study of Islam*, edited by Jamal J. Elias, pp. 93–103. Oxford: Oneworld, 2010.

Kärkkäinen, Veli-Matti. *Ad ultimum terrae: Evangelization, Proselytism, and Common Witness in the Roman Catholic–Pentecostal Dialogue (1990–1997).* Studien der Interkulturellen Geschichte des Christentums 117. Frankfurt: Peter Lang, 1999.

———. "The Apostolicity of Free Churches: A Contradiction in Terms of an Ecumenical Breakthrough?" *Pro Ecclesia* 10, no. 4 (2001): 389–400.

———. *Christ and Reconciliation.* A Constructive Christian Theology for the Pluralistic World, vol. 1. Grand Rapids: Eerdmans, 2013.

———. "The Church in the Post-Christian Society between Modernity and Late Modernity: L. Newbigin's Post-Critical Missional Ecclesiology." In *Theology in Missionary Perspective: Lesslie Newbigin's Legacy*, edited by Mark T. B. Laing and Paul Weston, pp. 125–54. Eugene, Ore.: Pickwick, 2013.

———. *Creation and Humanity.* A Constructive Christian Theology for the Pluralistic World, vol. 3. Grand Rapids: Eerdmans, 2015.

———. "Dialogue, Witness, and Tolerance: The Many Faces of Interfaith Encounters." *Theology, News & Notes* 57, no. 2 (Fall 2010): 29–33. Fuller studio. Accessed November 14, 2016. https://fullermag.fuller.edu/dialogue-witness-tolerance-many -dimensions-interfaith-encounters/.

———. "Growing Together in Mission." In *Called to Unity for the Sake of Mission*, edited by John Gibaut and Knud Jørgensen, pp. 59–70. Oxford: Regnum, 2014.

———. "Hope, Theology of." In *Global Dictionary of Theology*, edited by Veli-Matti Kärkkäinen and William Dyrness, pp. 404–5. Downers Grove: InterVarsity, 2008.

———. *An Introduction to Ecclesiology: Ecumenical, Historical, and Contextual Perspectives.* Downers Grove: InterVarsity, 2002.

————. *An Introduction to the Theology of Religions: Biblical, Historical, and Contemporary Perspectives*. Downers Grove: InterVarsity, 2003.

————. "Pentecostalism and the Claim for Apostolicity." *Evangelical Review of Theology* 25, no. 4 (2001): 323–36.

————. "Pentecostal Mission and Encounter with Religions." In *The Cambridge Companion to Pentecostalism*, edited by Cecil M. Robeck and Amos Yong, pp. 294–312. Cambridge: Cambridge University Press, 2014.

————. "The Pentecostal View." In *The Lord's Supper: Five Views*, edited by Gordon T. Smith, pp. 117–35. Downers Grove: InterVarsity, 2007.

————. *Spirit and Salvation*. A Constructive Christian Theology for the Pluralistic World, vol. 4. Grand Rapids: Eerdmans, 2016.

————. *Spiritus ubi vult spirat: Pneumatology in Roman Catholic–Pentecostal Dialogue (1972–1989)*. Schriften der Luther-Agricola-Gesellschaft 42. Helsinki: Luther-Agricola Society, 1998.

————. "Theologies of Religions." *Evangelical Interfaith Dialogue* 1, no. 2 (Fall 2011): 3–7. http://cms.fuller.edu/EIFD/issues/Spring_2010/Theologies_of_Religions.aspx.

————. "Theologies of Religions." In *Witnessing to Christ in a Pluralistic World: Christian Mission among Other Faiths*, edited by Lalsingkima Pachuau and Knud Jørgensen, pp. 110–18. Edinburgh 2010 Studies. London: Regnum, 2011.

————. *The Trinity: Global Perspectives*. Louisville: Westminster John Knox, 2007.

————. *Trinity and Revelation*. A Constructive Christian Theology for the Pluralistic World, vol. 2. Grand Rapids: Eerdmans, 2014.

————. "Unity, Diversity, and Apostolicity: Any Hopes for Rapprochement between Older and Younger Churches?" In *Believing in Community: Ecumenical Reflections on the Church*, edited by Peter de Mey, pp. 487–506. Bibliotheca Ephemeridum Theologicarum Lovaniensium. Leuven: Leuven University Press, 2013.

Kärkkäinen, Veli-Matti, and Michael Karim. "Community and Witness in Transition: Newbigin's Missional Ecclesiology between Modernity and Postmodernity." In *The Gospel and Pluralism Today: Reassessing Lesslie Newbigin in the 21st Century*, edited by Scott W. Sunquist and Amos Yong, pp. 71–100. Downers Grove: InterVarsity, 2015.

Karras, Valerie A. "Eschatology." In *Cambridge Companion to Feminist Theology*, edited by Susan Frank Parsons, pp. 243–60. Cambridge: Cambridge University Press, 2002.

Käsemann, E. "Amt und Gemeinde im Neuen Testament." In *Exegetische Versuche und Besinnungen*, 1:109–34. Göttingen: Vandenhoeck & Ruprecht, 1970.

————. *Essays on New Testament Themes*. Translated by W. J. Montague. London: SCM, 1964.

Kassis, Hanna. "Islam." In *LDWR*, pp. 48–65.

Kateregga, Badru D., and David W. Shenk. *Islam and Christianity: A Muslim and a Christian in Dialogue*. Ibadan, Nigeria: Daystar Press, 1985.

Katz, Steven T., ed. *The Impact of the Holocaust on Jewish Theology*. New York and London: New York University Press, 2005.

Kaufman, Gordon. *In Face of Mystery: A Constructive Theology*. Cambridge, Mass.: Harvard University Press, 1993.

―――. *Systematic Theology: A Historicist Perspective*. New York: Scribner, 1968.

Keller, Catherine. *Apocalypse Now and Then: A Feminist Guide to the End of the World*. Boston: Beacon Press, 1996.

―――. "Eschatology, Ecology, and a Green Ecumenacy." *Ecotheology: Journal of Religion, Nature & the Environment* 5 (January 1997): 84–99.

―――. *Face of the Deep: A Theology of Becoming*. London and New York: Routledge, 2003.

―――. "No More Sea: The Lost Chaos of the Eschaton." In *Christianity and Ecology: Seeking the Well-Being of Earth and Humans*, edited by Dieter T. Hessel and Rosemary Radford Ruether, pp. 183–98. Cambridge, Mass.: Harvard University Press, 2000.

―――. "Women against Wasting the World: Notes on Eschatology and Ecology." In *Reweaving the World: The Emergence of Eco-Feminism*, edited by I. Diamond and F. Orenstein, pp. 249–63. San Francisco: Sierra Club Books, 1990.

Keller, James A. *Problems of Evil and the Power of God*. Surrey, UK: Ashgate, 2007.

Kelly, Gerard. "A New Ecumenical Wave." Public lecture at the National Council of Churches Forum, Canberra, July 12, 2010. http://www.ncca.org.au/index.php/faith -and-unity/46-a-new-ecumenical-wave/file.

―――. *Recognition: Advancing Ecumenical Thinking*. New York: Peter Lang, 1996.

Kelly, J. N. D. *Early Christian Creeds*. 3rd ed. London and New York: Continuum, 2006 [1972].

―――. *Early Christian Doctrines*. Rev. ed. New York: Harper and Row, 1978 [1960].

Kelly, John G. "The Cross, the Church, and the Jewish People." In *Atonement Today*, edited by John Goldingay, pp. 166–84. London: SPCK, 1995.

Kelsey, David H. *Eccentric Existence: A Theological Anthropology*. 2 vols. Louisville: Westminster John Knox, 2009.

Kenney, Jeffrey T. "Millennialism and Radical Islamist Movements." In *OHM*, pp. 688–716.

Kessler, Edward. *An Introduction to Jewish-Christian Relations*. Cambridge: Cambridge University Press, 2010.

Kessler, Edward, and Neil Wenborn, eds. *A Dictionary of Jewish-Christian Relations*. Cambridge: Cambridge University Press, 2005.

Kibicho, Samuel G. *God and Revelation in an African Context*. Nairobi: Acton Publishers, 2006.

―――. "Nature and Structure of African Religion." In *A Comparative Study of Religions*, edited by J. N. K. Mugambi. Nairobi: Nairobi University Press, 1990.

Kiblinger, Kristin Beise. *Buddhist Inclusivism: Attitudes toward Religious Others*. Burlington, Vt.: Ashgate, 2005.

Kierkegaard, Søren. *Attack upon "Christendom."* Translated by Walter Lowrie. Princeton: Princeton University Press, 1944.

Kilmartin, Edward J. "Reception in History: An Ecclesiological Phenomenon and Its Significance." *Journal of Ecumenical Studies* 21, no. 1 (1984): 34–54.

Kim, Myung Hyuk. "Ancestor Worship: From the Perspective of Korean Church History." In *Ancestor Worship and Christianity in Korea*, edited by Jung Young Lee, pp. 21–34. Lewiston, N.Y., and Lampeter, UK: Edwin Mellen Press, 1988.

King, Anna. "The Glorious Disappearance of Vaishnavas: ISKCON's Vision of Exemplary Death." *Religions of South Asia* 6, no. 1 (2012): 103–28.

King, Winston L. "No-Self, No-Mind, and Emptiness Revisited." In *Buddhist-Christian Dialogue: Mutual Renewal and Transformation*, edited by Paul O. Ingram and Frederick J. Streng, pp. 155–76. Honolulu: University of Hawai'i Press, 1986.

Kinnamon, Michael. *The Vision of the Ecumenical Movement and How It Has Been Impoverished by Its Friends*. Saint Louis: Chalice, 2003.

Kinnamon, Michael, and Brian E. Cope, eds. *The Ecumenical Movement: An Anthology of Key Texts and Voices*. Geneva: WCC Publications; Grand Rapids: Eerdmans, 1997.

Klein, C. *Anti-Judaism in Christian Theology*. Translated by Edward Quinn. Philadelphia: Fortress, 1978.

Klostermaier, Klaus. "The Future of Hindu-Christian Dialogue." In *Hindu-Christian Dialogue: Perspectives and Encounters*, edited by Harold Coward, pp. 262–74. Maryknoll, N.Y.: Orbis, 1989.

———. *A Survey of Hinduism*. 3rd ed. Albany: State University of New York Press, 2010.

Knipe, David M. "Hindu Eschatology." In *OHE*, pp. 170–90.

Knitter, Paul F. *No Other Name? A Critical Survey of Christian Attitudes toward the World Religions*. Maryknoll, N.Y.: Orbis, 1985.

Knoch, Otto. "'Do This in Memory of Me!' (Luke 22:20; 1 Cor. 11:24–25): The Celebration of the Eucharist in the Primitive Christian Communities." In *One Loaf, One Cup: Ecumenical Studies of 1 Cor. 11 and Other Eucharistic Texts; The Cambridge Conference on the Eucharist, August 1988*, edited by Ben F. Meyer, pp. 1–10. Macon, Ga.: Mercer University Press, 1993.

Kogan, Michael S. *Opening the Covenant: A Jewish Theology of Christianity*. Oxford: Oxford University Press, 2008.

Kohler, Kaufman. *Jewish Theology: Systematically and Historically Considered*. New York: Ktav, 1968 [1918].

Komonchak, Joseph. "The Church Universal as the Communion of Local Churches." In *Where Does the Church Stand? Concilium 146*, edited by G. Alberigo and G. Gutiérrez, pp. 30–35. New York: Seabury Press, 1981.

Körtner, Ulrich. *The End of the World: A Theological Interpretation*. Louisville: Westminster John Knox, 1995.

Koyama, Kosuke. *Mount Fuji and Mount Sinai: A Critique of Idols*. Maryknoll, N.Y.: Orbis, 1985.

Krabill, Matthew, and Allison Norton. "New Wine in Old Wineskins: A Critical Appraisal of Diaspora Missiology." *Missiology: An International Review* 43 (2015): 442–55.

Küng, Hans. "A Christian Response [to Heinz Bechert: Buddhist Perspectives]." In *Christianity and the World Religions: Paths to Dialogue with Islam, Hinduism, and Buddhism*, by Hans Küng, with Josef van Ess, Heinrich von Stietencron, and Heinz Bechert, translated by Peter Heinegg, pp. 306–28. New York: Doubleday, 1986.

———. *The Church*. Garden City: Doubleday, 1976 [ET 1967].

———. *Islam: Past, Present, and Future*. Oxford: OneWorld, 2007.

Kurzweil, Ray. *The Age of Spiritual Machines: When Computers Exceed Human Intelligence*. New York: Penguin Group, 1999.

————. *The Singularity Is Near: When Humans Transcend Biology*. New York: Penguin, 2005.

Kvanvig, Jonathan L. "Hell." In *OHE*, pp. 413–26.

————. *The Problem of Hell*. New York: Oxford University Press, 1993.

Kydd, Ronald A. N. *Healing through the Centuries: Models for Understanding*. Peabody, Mass.: Hendrickson, 1998.

Kyrtatas, Dimitris J. "The Origins of Christian Hell." *Numen: International Review for the History of Religions* 56, nos. 2–3 (2009): 282–97.

LaBute, Todd S. "The Ontological Motif of Anticipation in the Theology of Wolfhart Pannenberg." *Journal of the Evangelical Theological Society* 37 (June 1994): 275–82.

Lacoste, Jean-Yeves. "The Phenomenality of Anticipation." In *Phenomenology and Eschatology: Not Yet in the Now*, edited by John Panteleimon Manoussakis and Neal DeRoo, chap. 1. Surrey, UK: Ashgate, 2009.

Ladd, G. E. *The Presence of the Future: Eschatology of Biblical Realism*. Rev. ed. Grand Rapids: Eerdmans, 1996 [1974].

Lai, Suat Yan. "Engendering Buddhism: Female Ordination and Women's 'Voices' in Thailand." PhD diss., Claremont Graduate University, 2011.

Lakeland, Paul. "The Laity." In *RCCC*, pp. 511–23.

————. *Postmodernity: Christian Identity in a Fragmented Age*. Minneapolis: Fortress, 1997.

Lamotte, E. "The Assessment of Textual Interpretation in Buddhism." In *Buddhist Hermeneutics*, ed. D. S. Lopez, pp. 11–28. Honolulu: University of Hawai'i Press, 1992.

Lampe, Peter. "Paul's Concept of Spiritual Body." In *RTSA*, pp. 103–14.

Langer, Ruth. "Revisiting Early Rabbinic Liturgy: The Recent Contributions of Ezra Fleischer." *Prooftexts* 19, no. 2 (1999): 179–94.

————. "Worship and Devotional Life: Jewish Worship." In *ER*, 14:9805–9.

Langmead, Ross. "Transformed Relationships: Reconciliation as the Central Model for Mission." *Mission Studies* 25, no. 1 (2008): 5–20.

The Lankavatara Sutra: A Mahayana Text. Translated by Daisetz Teitaro Suzuki (1932). Last correction June 16, 2008. http://lirs.ru/do/lanka_eng/lanka-nondiacritical .htm.

Lapide, Pinchas. *The Resurrection of Jesus: A Jewish Perspective*. Minneapolis: Augsburg, 1983.

Largen, Kristin Johnston. *What Christians Can Learn from Buddhism: Rethinking Salvation*. Minneapolis: Fortress, 2009.

Larson, G. "Contra Pluralism." *Soundings: An Interdisciplinary Journal* 73, no. 2/3 (1990): 303–26.

Lauber, David. *Barth on the Descent into Hell: God, Atonement, and the Christian Life*. Aldershot, UK: Ashgate, 2004.

Laurentin, R. "Charisms: Terminological Precision." *Concilium* 109 (1978): 3–12.

Lausanne Committee for World Evangelization and the World Evangelical Fellowship. *Evangelism and Social Responsibility: An Evangelical Commitment*. Lausanne Occasional Paper 21. Exeter, UK: Paternoster Press, 1982.

Lausanne Movement. *The Cape Town Commitment.* January 25, 2011. http://www.lausanne
.org/en/documents/ctcommitment.html#p2-6.

Learman, Linda, ed. *Buddhist Missionaries in the Era of Globalization.* Honolulu: University of Hawai'i Press, 2005.

Lee, Daniel. "Karl Barth, Contextuality, and Asian-American Context." PhD diss., School of Theology, Fuller Theological Seminary, Pasadena, Calif., 2014.

Lee, Jung Young. "Ancestor Worship: From a Theological Perspective." In *Ancestor Worship and Christianity in Korea,* edited by Jung Young Lee, pp. 83–91. Lewiston, N.Y., and Lampeter, UK: Edwin Mellen Press, 1988.

Legenhausen, Muhammad. *Islam and Religious Pluralism.* London: Al-Hoda, 1999.

Leibniz, Gottfried Wilhelm von. "Theodicy." In *The Philosophical Works of Leibniz,* edited by G. Duncan, pp. 194–204. New Haven: Tutle, Morehouse and Taylor, 1890. http://openlibrary.org/books/OL7119462M/The_philosophical_works_of_Leibnitz.

Leirvik, Oddbjørn. *Images of Jesus Christ in Islam.* 2nd ed. London and New York: Continuum, 2010.

The Leuenberg Concord. Translated by John Drickamer. 1971. In *The Springfielder* 35 (March 1972). http://www.ctsfw.net/media/pdfs/drickamertheleuenbergconcord
.pdf.

Levine, Alan, ed. *Early Modern Skepticism and the Origin of Toleration.* New York: Lexington Books, 1999.

Levine, Lee I. *The Ancient Synagogue: The First Thousand Years.* New Haven: Yale University Press, 2000.

Levitt, Peggy. *God Needs No Passport: How Immigrants Are Changing the American Religious Landscape.* New York: New Press, 2007.

Lewis, Bernard. *Islam and the West.* Oxford: Oxford University Press, 1993.

Lewis, C. S. *God in the Dock: Essays on Theology and Ethics.* Grand Rapids: Eerdmans, 1972.

Lieberman, Philip. *Uniquely Human: The Evolution of Speech, Thought, and Selfless Behavior.* Cambridge, Mass.: Harvard University Press, 1991.

Lim, Timothy T. M. "Ecclesial Recognition: An Interdisciplinary Proposal." PhD diss., Regent University, School of Divinity, 2014.

Linzey, Andrew. *Animal Theology.* London: SCM, 1994.

―――. "Is Christianity Irredeemably Speciesist?" Introduction to *Animals on the Agenda: Questions about Animals for Theology and Ethics,* edited by Andrew Linzey and Dorothy Yamamoto, pp. xi–xx. Urbana and Chicago: University of Illinois Press, 1998.

Lipner, Julius J. "Ancient Banyan: An Inquiry into the Meaning of 'Hinduness.'" *Religious Studies* 32, no. 1 (1996): 109–26.

Little, Franklin H. "The Concept of the Believers' Church." In *The Concept of the Believers' Church,* edited by James Leo Garrett, pp. 15–33. Scottdale, Pa.: Herald, 1969.

―――. *The Crucifixion of the Jews.* New York: Harper and Row, 1975.

Locke, J. *An Essay concerning Human Understanding.* Translated and edited by P. Nidditch. In *Clarendon Edition of the Works of John Locke.* Oxford: Oxford University Press, 1979 [1689].

Locklin, Reid B. "A More Comparative Ecclesiology? Bringing Comparative Theology to the Ecclesiological Table." In *Comparative Ecclesiology: Critical Investigations*, edited by Gerard Mannion, pp. 125–49. London and New York: T. & T. Clark, 2008.

Lossky, Nicholas, et al., eds. *Dictionary of the Ecumenical Movement*. 2nd ed. Geneva: WCC, 2002.

Lossky, Vladimir. "Concerning the Third Mark of the Church: Catholicity." In *In the Image and Likeness of God*, edited by J. H. Erickson and T. E. Bird, pp. 169–81. Crestwood, N.Y.: St. Vladimir's Seminary Press, 1985.

————. *The Mystical Theology of the Eastern Church*. New York: St. Vladimir's Seminary Press, 1997.

Lovelock, James. *The Revenge of Gaia: Earth's Climate in Crisis and the Fate of Humanity*. New York: Basic Books, 2006.

Löwith, Karl. *Meaning in History: The Theological Implications of the Philosophy of History*. Chicago: University of Chicago Press, 1949.

Luckmann, Thomas. *The Invisible Religion: The Problem of Religion in Modern Society*. New York: Macmillan, 1967.

Ludwig, Frieder, and J. Kwabena Asamoah-Gyadu, eds. *African Christian Presence in the West: New Immigrant Congregations and Transnational Networks in North America and Europe*. Trenton, N.J.: Africa World Press, 2011.

Ludwig, Theodore M. *The Sacred Paths: Understanding the Religions of the World*. 4th ed. Upper Saddle River, N.J.: Pearson, 2006.

Lutheran World Federation and the Catholic Church. *Joint Declaration on the Doctrine of Justification*. October 31, 1999. http://www.vatican.va/roman_curia/pontifical_councils/chrstuni/documents/rc_pc_chrstuni_doc_31101999_cath-luth-joint-declaration_en.html.

MacDonald, Margaret Y. *The Pauline Churches: A Socio-Historical Study of Institutionalization in the Pauline and Deutero-Pauline Writings*. Cambridge: Cambridge University Press, 1988.

MacIntyre, Alasdair. *Whose Justice, Which Rationality?* London: Duckworth, 1988.

Mackie, J. L. "Evil and Omnipotence" [1955]. In *PE*, pp. 25–37.

Macy, Gary. *The Hidden History of Women's Ordination: Female Clergy in the Medieval West*. Oxford: Oxford University Press, 2008.

Madan, T. N. "Thinking Globally about Hinduism." In *OHGR*, pp. 15–24.

Maguire, Daniel. *The Moral Core of Judaism and Christianity: Reclaiming the Revolution*. Philadelphia: Fortress, 1993.

Maharaj, Swami B. H. Bon. *Origin and Eschatology in Hindu Eschatology*. Delhi: Narenda Printing Press, n.d.

Mahmud, Abdel Haleem. *The Creed of Islam*. London: World of Islamic Festival Trust, 1978.

Mahmutcehagic, Rusmir. *The Mosque: The Heart of Submission*. New York: Fordham University Press, 2007.

Maimonides, Moses. "Teshuva — Chapter 3." Translated by Eliyahu Touger. Chabad.org. http://www.chabad.org/library/article_cdo/aid/911896/jewish/Teshuvah-Chapter-Three.htm.

———. "The Thirteen Principles of Jewish Faith." N.d. Chabad.org. http://www.chabad
.org/library/article_cdo/aid/332555/jewish/Maimonides-13-Principles-of-Faith
.htm.

Majjhima Nikaya Sutta. In *The Middle Length Discourses of the Buddha.* A new translation
of *Majjhima Nikāya.* Translated by Bhikkhu Ñānamoli and Bhikku Bodhi. Kandy,
Sri Lanka: Buddhist Publication Society, 1995.

Majumdar, A[soke] K[umar]. *Bhakti Renaissance.* Bombay: Bharatiya Vidya Bhavan, 1965.

Mannermaa, Tuomo. *Von Preussen nach Leuenberg: Hintergrund und Entwicklung der
theologischen Methode der Leuenberger Konkordie.* Hamburg: Lutherisches Ver-
lagshaus, 1981.

Manning, Patrick. *The African Diaspora: A History through Culture.* New York: Columbia
University Press, 2009.

Mannion, Gerard. *Ecclesiology and Postmodernity: Questions for the Church in Our Time.*
Collegeville, Minn.: Liturgical Press, 2007.

———. "Postmodern Ecclesiologies." In *RCCC,* pp. 127–52.

Mannion, Gerard, and Lewis S. Mudge. "Introduction: Ecclesiology — the Nature, Story
and Study of the Church." In *RCCC,* pp. 1–6.

Manoussakis, John Panteleimon. Introduction to *Phenomenology and Eschatology:
Not Yet in the Now,* edited by John Panteleimon Manoussakis and Neal DeRoo,
pp. 1–12. Surrey, UK: Ashgate, 2009.

A Manual of Abhidhamma (Abhidhammattha Sangaha). Translated and edited by Nàrada
Mahà Thera. 5th ed. Kuala Lumpur: Buddhist Missionary Society, 1987. http://www
.buddhanet.net/pdf_file/abhidhamma.pdf.

Maqsood, Ruqaiyyah Waris. *The Problem of Evil: A Study of Evil, Fate, Freewill, and Predestination, Forgiveness, and Love.* New Delhi: Adam Publishers, 2003.

Marcel, Gabriel. *Homo Viator: Introduction to a Metaphysic of Hope.* Translated by Emma
Crawford. New York: Harper Torchbooks, 1962.

Marion, Jean-Luc. *God without Being.* Translated by Thomas A. Carlson. Chicago: University of Chicago Press, 1991.

Marsden, George M. *The Soul of the American University: From Protestant Establishment
to Established Nonbelief.* New York: Oxford University Press, 1994.

Marshall, Bruce D. "Christ and the Cultures: The Jewish People and Christian Theology."
In *The Cambridge Companion to Christian Doctrine,* edited by Colin E. Gunton,
pp. 81–100. Cambridge: Cambridge University Press, 1997.

Martin, David. *A General Theory of Secularization.* Oxford: Blackwell, 1979.

Martin, Ralph, and Peter Williamson, eds. *John Paul II and the New Evangelization.* San
Francisco: Ignatius, 1995.

Martínez, Juan. "Historical Reflections on the 'In-Betweenness' of Latino Protestantism."
Common Ground Journal 12, no. 1 (Spring 2015): 26–30.

———. *Los Protestantes: An Introduction to Latino Protestantism in the United States.*
Santa Barbara, Calif.: ABC-CLIO, 2011.

Martos, Joseph. *Doors to the Sacred: A Historical Introduction to Sacraments in the Catholic Church.* Garden City, N.Y.: Doubleday, 1981.

Marty, Martin E., and R. Scott Appleby, eds. *The Fundamentalism Project.* 5 vols. Chicago: University of Chicago Press, 1991–1995.

Mascall, E. L. "Some Basic Considerations." In *Man, Woman, and Priesthood,* edited by Peter C. Moore, pp. 9–26. London: SPCK, 1978.

Maududi, Abul Ala. *Nationalism and Islam.* Lahore: Islamic Publications, 1947.

Mavrodes, George I. "The Life Everlasting and the Bodily Criterion of Identity." *Nous* 11 (1977): 27–39.

Maybaum, Ignaz. *The Face of God after Auschwitz.* Amsterdam: Polak and Van Gennep, 1965.

Maynard, Dorow. "Worship Is Mission Seeing the Eucharist as the Drama of God's Mission to the World." *Missio Apostolica* 9, no. 2 (2001): 78–83.

Mbiti, John S. *African Religions and Philosophy.* 2nd ed. Oxford: Heinemann, 1990.

———. *Introduction to African Religion.* London: Heinemann Educations, 1975.

———. *New Testament Eschatology in an African Background.* London: Oxford University Press, 1971.

McCall, Theodore David. *The Greenie's Guide to the End of the World.* Adelaide: ATF Theology, 2011.

McClendon, James, Jr. *Doctrine.* Vol. 2 of *Systematic Theology.* Nashville: Abingdon, 1994.

McDaniel, Jay Byrd. *Of God and Pelicans: A Theology of Reverence for Life.* Louisville: Westminster John Knox, 1989.

McDannell, Colleen, and Bernhard Lang. *Heaven: A History.* New York: Vintage, 1990.

McDermott, Gerald R. "Will All Be Saved?" *Themelios* 38, no. 2 (2013): 232–43. http://tgc -documents.s3.amazonaws.com/themelios/Themelios38.2.pdf#page.

McDermott, John M. *The Bible on Human Suffering.* Middlegreen Slough, UK: St. Paul Publications, 1990.

McDonald, Gregory [Robin A. Parry]. *The Evangelical Universalist.* 2nd ed. Portland, Ore.: Cascade Books, 2012.

McDonnell, Kilian, OSB. "Communion Ecclesiology and Baptism in the Spirit: Tertullian and the Early Church." *Theological Studies* 49 (1988): 671–93.

———. "The Determinative Doctrine of the Holy Spirit." *Theology Today* 39, no. 2 (July 1982): 142–62.

McFague, Sallie. *The Body of God: An Ecological Theology.* Minneapolis: Fortress, 1993.

McGinn, Bernard. *Antichrist: Two Thousand Years of the Human Fascination with Evil.* New York: Columbia University Press, 2000.

McGrath, Alister E. *A Brief History of Heaven.* Oxford, UK, and Malden, Mass.: Blackwell, 2003.

———. *A Scientific Theology.* Vol. 1, *Nature.* Vol. 2, *Reality.* Vol. 3, *Theory.* Grand Rapids: Eerdmans, 2001–2003.

McIntyre, Alison. "Doctrine of Double Effect." In *Stanford Encyclopedia of Philosophy* (Winter 2014 edition), edited by Edward N. Zalta. Substantively revised September 23, 2014. http://plato.stanford.edu/archives/win2014/entries/double-effect/.

McKnight, Scot. "Five Streams of the Emerging Church: Key Elements of the Most Controversial and Misunderstood Movement in the Church Today." *Christianity Today*

51 (January 19, 2007). http://www.christianitytoday.com/ct/2007/february/11.35 .html.

McLeod, Hugh, and Werner Ustorf, eds. *The Decline of Christendom in Western Europe, 1750-2000*. Cambridge: Cambridge University Press, 2003.

McMahan, David L. *Buddhism in the Modern World*. London: Routledge, 2012.

——. *The Making of Buddhist Modernism*. New York: Oxford University Press, 2008.

McNamara, Patrick, and Wesley Wildman, eds. *Science and the World's Religions*. Vol. 1, *Origins and Destinies*. Vol. 2, *Persons and Groups*. Vol. 3, *Religions and Controversies*. Santa Barbara, Calif.: Praeger, 2012.

Mead, George Herbert. *Mind, Self, and Society*. Edited by Charles W. Morris. Chicago: University of Chicago Press, 1962 [1934].

Melanchthon, Philip. Apology of the Augsburg Confession 2.47. In *BC*, 119.

Merad, M. A. "Christ according to the Qur'an." *Encounter* (Rome) 69 (1980): 14, 15.

Merleau-Ponty, Maurice. *Phenomenology of Perception*. Translated by Colin Smith. London: Routledge and Kegan Paul; New York: Humanities Press, 1962 [1945].

Merricks, Trenton. "The Resurrection of the Body." In *The Oxford Handbook of Philosophical Theology*, edited by Thomas P. Flint and Michael C. Rea, pp. 476-90. Oxford: Oxford University Press, 2009.

Mette, Norbert, and James Aitken Gardiner. *Diakonia: Church for Others*. Concilium. Edinburgh: T. & T. Clark, 1988.

Metuh, Emefie Ikenga. *African Religions in Western Conceptual Schemes: The Problem of Interpretation; Studies in Igbo Religion*. 2nd ed. Jos, Nigeria: Imico Press, 1991.

Metz, Johann Baptist. "Facing the Jews." In *The Holocaust as Interruption* (Concilium, 175), edited by David Tracy and Elisabeth Schussler Fiorenza. Edinburgh: T. & T. Clark, 1984.

——. *Faith in History and Society: Toward a Practical Fundamental Theology*. Translated by David Smith. New York: Seabury Press, 1980.

——. "Theology as Theodicy?" In *A Passion for God: The Mystical-Political Dimension of Christianity*, translated by J. Matthew Ashley. New York: Paulist, 1998.

Meyendorff, John. *Byzantine Theology: Historical Trends and Doctrinal Trends*. New York: Fordham University Press, 1987.

——. "The Orthodox Church and Mission: Past and Present Perspectives." *St. Vladimir's Theological Quarterly* 16, no. 2 (1972): 59-71.

Meyer, Harding. "Anerkennung — ein 'Ökumenischer Schlüsselbegriff.'" In *Dialog und Anerkennung: Hanfried Krüger zu Ehren*, edited by Peter Manns, pp. 25-41. Frankfurt am Main: Lembeck, 1980.

——. *That All May Be One: Perceptions and Models of Ecumenicity*. Grand Rapids and Cambridge: Eerdmans, 1999.

Miconi, Thomas. "Evolution and Complexity: The Double-Edged Sword." *Artificial Life* 14 (Summer 2008): 325-44.

Middleton, J. Richard. *New Heaven and New Earth: Reclaiming Biblical Eschatology*. Grand Rapids: Baker, 2014.

Migliore, Daniel L. *Faith Seeking Understanding: An Introduction to Christian Theology*. 2nd ed. Grand Rapids: Eerdmans, 2004.

Mikaelsson, Lisbet. "Missional Religion — with Special Emphasis on Buddhism, Christianity and Islam." *Swedish Missiological Themes* 92 (2004): 523–38.

Milbank, John. *Theology and Social Theory: Beyond Secular Reason.* Oxford: Basil Blackwell, 1990.

Miller, Patrick D. "Judgment and Joy." In *EWEG*, chap. 11.

Miller, William D. "Da'wah." In *ER*, pp. 2225–26.

Milner, Murray, Jr. "Hindu Eschatology and the Indian Caste System: An Example of Structural Reversal." *Journal of Asian Studies* 52 (May 1993): 298–319.

Min, Anselm Kyongsuk. *The Solidarity of Others in a Divided World.* New York: T. & T. Clark, 2004.

Minear, Paul S. *The Images of the Church in the New Testament.* London: Lutterworth, 1960.

Mitchell, Donald William. *Buddhism.* Oxford: Oxford University Press, 2002.

Mmassi, Gabriel. "Secularism in the Face of African Traditional Religions." *African Ecclesial Review* 55, nos. 3–4 (2013): 227–42.

Mohler, Albert. "Do Christians Still Believe in the Resurrection of the Body?" Albert Mohler.com. April 7, 2006. http://www.albertmohler.com/2006/04/07/do-christians-still-believe-in-the-resurrection-of-the-body/.

———. "Modern Theology: The Disappearance of Hell." In *Hell under Fire: Modern Scholarship Reinvents Eternal Punishment*, edited by Christopher W. Morgan and Robert A. Peterson, pp. 15–42. Grand Rapids: Zondervan, 2004.

Moltmann, Jürgen. *The Church in the Power of the Spirit: A Contribution to Messianic Ecclesiology.* Translated by Margaret Kohl. London: SCM, 1977.

———. *The Coming of God: Christian Eschatology.* Translated by Margaret Kohl. Minneapolis: Fortress, 1996.

———. "Cosmos and Theosis: Eschatological Perspectives on the Future of the Universe." In *FFU*, pp. 249–65.

———. *The Crucified God: The Cross of Christ as the Foundation and Criticism of Christian Theology.* Translated by Margaret Kohl. Minneapolis: Fortress, 1993.

———. *Experiences in Theology: Ways and Forms of Christian Theology.* Translated by Margaret Kohl. Minneapolis: Fortress, 2000.

———. *God in Creation: A New Theology of Creation and the Spirit of God.* Translated by Margaret Kohl. Minneapolis: Fortress, 1993.

———. *In the End — the Beginning: The Life of Hope.* Translated by Margaret Kohl. Minneapolis: Fortress, 2004.

———. *Is There Life after Death?* Milwaukee: Marquette University Press, 1998.

———. "Is There Life after Death?" In *EWEG*, pp. 238–55.

———. *The Spirit of Life: A Universal Affirmation.* Translated by Margaret Kohl. Minneapolis: Fortress, 2001.

———. *Theology of Hope: On the Ground and the Implications of a Christian Eschatology.* London: SCM, 1967 [1964].

———. *The Trinity and the Kingdom of God: The Doctrine of God.* Translated by Margaret Kohl. San Francisco: Harper and Row; London: SCM, 1981.

————. *The Way of Jesus Christ: Christology in Messianic Dimensions.* Translated by Margaret Kohl. Minneapolis: Fortress, 1993 [1989].

Moore, Susan Hardman. "'Towards Koinonia in Faith, Life and Witness': Theological Insights and Emphases from the Fifth World Conference on Faith and Order, Santiago de Compostela 1993." *Epworth Review* 22 (January 1995): 88–97.

Moravec, Hans. *Mind Children: The Future of Robot and Human Intelligence.* Cambridge, Mass.: Harvard University Press, 1988.

————. *Robot: Mere Machines to Transcendent Mind.* Oxford: Oxford University Press, 1999.

More, Max. "On Becoming Posthuman." 1994. Accessed November 14, 2016. http://eserver .org/courses/spring98/76101R/readings/becoming.html.

Morenz, Siegfrid. *Egyptian Religion.* Translated by Ann E. Keep. Ithaca, N.Y.: Cornell University Press, 1973.

Morgan, Mardon Lee. "Eschatology for the Oppressed: Millenarianism and Liberation in the Eschatology of Jürgen Moltmann." *Perspectives in Religious Studies* 4 (2012): 379–93.

Morgan, Robin. "The Women's Creed." *Canadian Woman Studies* 16, no. 3 (1996): 37.

Morris, Simon Conway. "Does Biology Have an Eschatology, and If So Does It Have Cosmological Implications?" In *FFU*, pp. 158–74.

Moseley, Carys. *Nations and Nationalism in the Theology of Karl Barth.* New York: Oxford University Press, 2013.

Moses, Sarah. "'The Ethics of Recognition': Rowan Williams's Approach to Moral Discernment in the Christian Community." *Journal of the Society of Christian Ethics* 35, no. 1 (2015): 147–65.

Moule, C. F. D. *The Meaning of Hope: A Biblical Exposition with Concordance.* Philadelphia: Fortress, 1953.

Moussalli, Ahmad S. *Radical Islamic Fundamentalism: The Ideological and Political Discourse of Sayyid Qutb.* Beirut: American University of Beirut, 1992.

Mukhtar, Gohar. "A Comparative and Critical Analysis of the Story of Job as Found in the Bible and the Quran." *Gohar Mukhtar's Weblog.* July 22, 2011. http:// goharmukhtar.wordpress.com/2011/07/22/a-comparative-and-critical-analysis -of-the-story-of-job-as-found-in-the-bible-and-the-quran/.

Muktar, Bedru Hussein. "Response: Communities in Mission — the Church and the Ummah." In *Anabaptists Meeting Muslims: A Calling for Presence in the Way of Christ,* edited by James R. Krabill, David W. Shenk, and Linford Stutzman, pp. 59–62. Scottdale, Pa.: Herald, 2005.

Müller, Tobias. *Gott, Welt, Kreativität: Eine Analyse der Philosophie A. N. Whitehead.* Paderborn: Schöningh, 2009.

Mullin, Robert Bruce, and Russell E. Richey, eds. *Reimagining Denominationalism: Interpretive Essays.* New York: Oxford University Press, 1994.

"Multicultural Ministry: Report of the First International Network Forum." Edited by Seongja Yoo-Crowe and Colville Crowe. Sydney: Uniting Church in Australia, 2000.

Munday, John C., Jr. "Animal Pain: Beyond the Threshold?" In *Perspectives on Evolving Creation*, edited by K. B. Miller, pp. 435–68. Grand Rapids: Eerdmans, 2003.

Murphy, Nancey. *Beyond Liberalism and Fundamentalism: How Modern and Postmodern Philosophy Set the Theological Agenda*. Valley Forge, Pa.: Trinity, 1996.

———. "The Resurrection Body and Personal Identity: Possibilities and Limits of Eschatological Knowledge." In *RTSA*, pp. 202–18.

Murray, Michael. *Nature Red in Tooth and Claw: Theism and the Problem of Animal Suffering*. Oxford: Oxford University Press, 2008.

———. "Three Versions of Universalism." *Faith and Philosophy* 16 (1999): 55–68.

Murray, Paul D. "Introducing Receptive Ecumenism." *Ecumenist: A Journal of Theology, Culture, and Society* 51, no. 2 (2014): 1–8.

———. "Receptive Ecumenism and Ecclesial Learning: Receiving Gifts for Our Needs." *Louvain Studies* 33 (2008): 30–45.

———, ed. *Receptive Ecumenism and the Call to Catholic Learning: Exploring a Way for Contemporary Ecumenism*. Oxford: Oxford University Press, 2008.

Murray, Stuart. *Post-Christendom: Church and Mission in a Strange New World*. Carlisle, UK: Paternoster, 2004.

Muthiah, Robert A. *The Priesthood of All Believers in the Twenty-First Century: Living Faithfully as the Whole People of God in a Postmodern Context*. Eugene, Ore.: Pickwick, 2009.

Nagao, Gajin. "The Life of the Buddha: An Interpretation." *Eastern Buddhist*, n.s., 20, no. 2 (1987): 1–31.

Nagel, H. M. T. "Some Considerations concerning the Pre-Islamic and the Islamic Foundations of the Authority of the Caliphate." In *Studies on the First Century of Islamic Society*, edited by G. H. A. Juynboll, pp. 177–97. Carbondale: Southern Illinois University Press, 1982.

Nakamura, Hajime. *Gotama Buddha: A Biography Based upon the Most Reliable Texts*. Vol. 1. Translated by Gaynor Sekimori. Tokyo: Kosei, 2000.

Nalunnakkal, George Mathew. "Come Holy Spirit, Heal and Reconcile: Called in Christ to Be Reconciling and Healing Communities." *International Review of Mission* 94, no. 372 (2005): 7–19.

Ñāṇamoli, Bhikkhu, and Bhikku Bodhi. Introduction to *The Middle Length Discourses of the Buddha*, pp. 19–60. A new translation of *Majjhima Nikāya*. Translated by Bhikkhu Ñāṇamoli and Bhikkhu Bodhi. Kandy, Sri Lanka: Buddhist Publication Society, 1995.

National Conference of Commissioners on Uniform State Laws. "Uniform Determination of Death Act." Approved by the American Medical Association October 19, 1980; approved by the American Bar Association February 10, 1981. Accessed January 6, 2017. http://www.uniformlaws.org/shared/docs/determination%20of%20death /udda80.pdf.

Nattier, Jan. "Buddhist Eschatology." In *OHE*, pp. 151–69.

"The Nature and Purpose of Ecumenical Dialogue." In *The Joint Working Group between the Roman Catholic Church and the World Council of Churches: Eighth Report, 1999–2005*. Geneva: WCC Publications, 2005.

Ndingwan, Sammuel Anye. "Ancestor Veneration among the Mankon of the Cameroon Republic." PhD diss., Fuller Theological Seminary, School of World Mission, 1981.

Neill, Stephen. *Creative Tension*. London: Edinburgh House Press, 1959.

Nelson-Pallmeyer, Jack. *Is Religion Killing Us? Violence in the Bible and the Quran*. Harrisburg, Pa.: Trinity, 2003.

Nesbitt, Eleanor, and Elisabeth Arweck. "Retrospect and Prospect: Sampradayas and Warwick Fieldwork in Religions and Education." *Fieldwork in Religion* 2 (April 2006): 49–64.

Netland, Harold A. *Christianity and Religious Diversity: Clarifying Christian Commitments in a Globalizing Age*. Grand Rapids: Baker Academic, 2015.

―――. *Encountering Religious Pluralism: The Challenge to Christian Faith and Mission*. Downers Grove: InterVarsity, 2001.

Neusner, Jacob. *Judaism in Modern Times: An Introduction and Reader*. Cambridge: Blackwell, 1995.

―――. "Theodicy in Classical Judaism." In *Encyclopaedia of Judaism*, edited by Jacob Neusner, Alan J. Avery-Peck, and William Scott Green. New York: Continuum; Leiden: Brill, 2006.

Newbigin, Lesslie. *The Gospel in a Pluralist Society*. Grand Rapids: Eerdmans; Geneva: WCC, 1989.

―――. *The Household of God: Lectures on the Nature of the Church*. London: SCM, 1953.

―――. *Proper Confidence: Faith, Doubt, and Certainty in Christian Discipleship*. Grand Rapids: Eerdmans, 1995.

―――. "Religious Pluralism and the Uniqueness of Jesus Christ." *International Bulletin of Missionary Research* 13, no. 2 (1989): 50–54.

Newman, Carey C., ed. *Jesus and the Restoration of Israel: A Critical Assessment of N. T. Wright's "Jesus and the Victory of God."* Downers Grove: InterVarsity, 1999.

Nicholas of Cusa. *De Pace Fidei and Cribratio Alkorani: Translation and Analysis*. Edited and translated by Jasper Hopkins. 2nd ed. Minneapolis: Arthur J. Banning Press, 1994. http://jasper-hopkins.info/DePace12-2000.pdf.

Nickelsburg, George W. E. *Resurrection, Immortality, and Eternal Life in Intertestamental Judaism*. Cambridge, Mass.: Harvard University Press, 1972.

Niebuhr, H. Richard. *The Social Sources of Denominationalism*. New York: Meridian, 1957 [1929].

Niebuhr, Reinhold. *Nature and Destiny of Man: A Christian Interpretation*. 2 vols. New York: Charles Scribner's Sons, 1941.

Niederbacher, Bruno, SJ. "The Same Body Again? Thomas Aquinas on the Numerical Identity of the Resurrected Body." In *PIR*, pp. 145–59.

Nietzsche, Friedrich Wilhelm. *Beyond Good and Evil*. In *The Complete Works of Friedrich Nietzsche*, edited by Oscar Levy. New York: Russell and Russell, 1964.

―――. *The Use and Abuse of History*. Translated by Adrian Collins. New York: Bobbs-Merrill, 1957.

Nikojlasen, Jeppe Bach. *The Distinctive Identity of the Church: A Constructive Study of the Post-Christendom Theologies of Lesslie Newbigin and John Howard Yoder*. Eugene, Ore.: Pickwick, 2015.

Nisbet, Robert, and Robert G. Perrin. *The Social Bond*. 2nd ed. New York: Knopf, 1977.

Norris, Frederick W. "Universal Salvation in Origen and Maximus." In *Universalism and the Doctrine of Hell*, edited by Nigel M. de S. Cameron, pp. 35–72. Grand Rapids: Baker, 1992.

Norris, Pippa, and Ronald Inglehart. *Secular and Sacred*. Cambridge: Cambridge University Press, 2004.

Novak, David. *The Election of Israel: The Idea of the Chosen People*. New York: Cambridge University Press, 1995.

————. "Jewish Eschatology." In *OHE*, pp. 113–31.

Nürnberger, K. *Regaining Sanity for the Earth*. Pietermaritzburg: Cluster Publications, 2011.

Nyang, Sulayman S. "The Teaching of the Quran." In *Death and Immortality in the Religions of the World*, pp. 71–85. New York: Paragon House, 1987.

Obeyesekere, Gananath. "Thinking Globally about Buddhism." In *OHGR*, pp. 69–82.

Ocker, Christopher. "Ecclesiology and the Religious Controversy of the Sixteenth Century." In *RCCC*, pp. 63–84.

O'Collins, Gerald, SJ. *Jesus Risen: An Historical, Fundamental, and Systematic Examination of Christ's Resurrection*. New York: Paulist, 1987.

Oden, Patrick. *The Transformative Church: New Ecclesial Models and the Theology of Jürgen Moltmann*. Minneapolis: Fortress, 2015.

Oden, Thomas C. *Life in the Spirit: Systematic Theology*. Vol. 3. San Francisco: Harper-Collins, 1992.

O'Gara, Margaret. "Apostolicity in Ecumenical Dialogue." *Mid-Stream: Ecumenical Movement Today* 37, no. 2 (April 1998): 175–212.

————. *The Ecumenical Gift Exchange*. Collegeville, Minn.: Liturgical Press, 1998.

Ogutu, Gilbert E. M. "An African Perception." In *Immortality and Human Destiny: A Variety of Views*, edited by Geddes MacGregor, pp. 102–11. New York: Paragon House, 1985.

Olson, Eric T. *The Human Animal: Personal Identity without Psychology*. New York: Oxford University Press, 1997.

————. "Immanent Causation and Life after Death." In *PIR*, pp. 51–66.

————. *What Are We? A Study in Personal Ontology*. New York: Oxford University Press, 2007.

Olson, Roger E. "The Baptist View." In *The Lord's Supper: Five Views*, edited by Gordon T. Smith, pp. 91–108. Downers Grove: InterVarsity, 2007.

O'Neill, Michael. "Karl Barth's Doctrine of Election." *Evangelical Quarterly* 76 (2004): 311–26.

Organ, Troy W. *The Hindu Quest for the Perfection of Man*. Athens: Ohio University Press, 1970.

Ormerod, Neil J., and Shane Clifton, eds. *Globalization and the Mission of the Church: Ecclesiological Investigations*. New York: T. & T. Clark, 2009.

Ormsby, Eric L. *Theodicy in Islamic Thought: The Dispute over al-Ghazali's "Best of All Possible Worlds."* Princeton: Princeton University Press, 1984.

Orobator, Agonkhianmeghe E. *Theology Brewed in an African Pot.* Maryknoll, N.Y.: Orbis, 2008.

Ortner, Sherry B. "Is Female to Male as Nature Is to Culture?" In *Women, Culture, and Society*, edited by Michelle Zimbalist Rosaldo and Louise Lamphere, pp. 67-87. Stanford: Stanford University Press, 1974.

Osten-Sacken, Peter von der. *Christian-Jewish Dialogue.* Translated by Margaret Kohl. Philadelphia: Fortress, 1986.

Pagitt, Doug, and Tony Jones, eds. *An Emergent Manifesto of Hope.* Grand Rapids: Baker, 2007.

Pandey, Rajbali. *Hindu Saṁskāras: Socio-Religious Study of the Hindu Sacraments.* 2nd ed. Delhi: Motilal Banardisass Publishers, 1969.

Panikulam, George. *Koinōnia in the New Testament: Expression of Christian Life.* Rome: Biblical Institute Press, 1979.

Pannenberg, Wolfhart. *Anthropology in Theological Perspective.* Translated by Matthew J. O'Connell. Philadelphia: Westminster, 1985.

―――. "Christian Morality and Political Issues." In *Faith and Reality*, translated by J. M. Maxwell. Philadelphia: Westminster, 1977.

―――. "Contributions from Systematic Theology." In *OHRS*, pp. 359-71.

―――. "Eternity, Time and Space." In *The Historicity of Nature: Essays on Science and Theology*, edited by Niels Henrik Gregersen, pp. 163-74. Philadelphia: Templeton Foundation Press, 2008.

―――. *Jesus — God and Man.* Translated by Paul L. Wilkins and Duane A. Priebe. 2nd ed. Philadelphia: Westminster, 1977.

―――. "Laying Theological Claim to Scientific Understandings." In *Beginning with the End: God, Science, and Wolfhart Pannenberg*, edited by Carol Rausch Albright and Joel Haugen, pp. 51-64. Chicago and La Salle, Ill.: Open Court, 1997.

―――. "Theological Questions to Scientists." In *Beginning with the End: God, Science, and Wolfhart Pannenberg*, edited by Carol Rausch Albright and Joel Haugen, pp. 37-50. Chicago and La Salle, Ill.: Open Court, 1997.

―――. *Theology and the Kingdom of God.* Translated by Richard John Neuhaus. Philadelphia: Westminster, 1969.

―――. *Theology and the Philosophy of Science.* Translated by Francis McDonagh. London: Darton, Longman and Todd, 1976.

―――. "What Is Truth?" In *Basic Questions in Theology*, translated by George H. Kehm, 2:1-27. Philadelphia: Fortress, 1970.

Parfit, Derek. *Reasons and Persons.* Oxford: Oxford University Press, 1986.

Park, Chan Ho. "Transcendence and Spatiality of the Triune Creator." PhD diss., Fuller Theological Seminary, School of Theology, 2003.

Park, M. Sydney, Soong-Chan Rah, and Al Tizon, eds. *Honoring the Generations: Learning with Asian North American Congregations.* Valley Forge, Pa.: Judson, 2012.

Parry, Robin. *Worshiping the Trinity: Coming Back to the Heart of Worship.* Eugene, Ore.: Wipf and Stock, 2012.

Parry, Robin A., and Christopher H. Partridge, eds. *Universal Salvation? The Current Debate.* Grand Rapids: Eerdmans, 2003.

Pascal, Blaise. "Of the Necessity of the Wager." In *Pensées*, translated by W. F. Trotter, section 3. 1944 [1690]. ccel.org.

Patelos, C. G., ed. *The Orthodox Church in the Ecumenical Movement*. Geneva: WCC, 1978.

Pattison, George. *Heidegger on Death: A Critical Theological Essay*. Surrey, UK: Ashgate, 2013.

Pauley, Garth E. "Soundly Gathered Out of the Text? Biblical Interpretation in 'Sinners in the Hands of an Angry God.'" *Westminster Theological Journal* 76 (Spring 2014): 95–117.

Pauw, Amy Plantinga. "The Graced Infirmity of the Church." In *Feminist and Womanist Essays in Reformed Dogmatics*, edited by Amy Plantinga Pauw and Serene Jones, pp. 189–203. Louisville: Westminster John Knox, 2006.

Payne, J. D. *Strangers Next Door: Immigration, Migration, and Mission*. Downers Grove: InterVarsity, 2012.

Payne, Richard K. "Worship and Devotional Life: Buddhist Devotional Life in East Asia." In *ER*, pp. 9834–39.

Payutto, P. A. [Venerable Phra Dammapitaka]. *Dependent Origination: The Buddhist Law of Conditionality*. Translated by Bruce Evans. Bangkok: Buddhadhamma Foundation, 1995. http://www.dhammatalks.net/Books3/Payutto_Bhikkhu_Dependent_Origination.htm.

Peacocke, Arthur. *Paths from Science towards God: The End of All Our Exploring*. Oxford: Oneworld, 2001.

———. "Theology and Science Today." In *Cosmos as Creation: Theology and Science in Consonance*, edited by Ted Peters. Nashville: Abingdon, 1989.

———. *Theology for a Scientific Age: Being and Becoming — Natural, Divine, and Human*. Theology and the Sciences. Enlarged ed. Minneapolis: Fortress, 1993.

Perspectives on Koinonia. The report from the third quinquennium of the dialogue between the Pontifical Council for Promoting Christian Unity of the Roman Catholic Church and some classical Pentecostal churches and leaders, 1985–1989. http://www.vatican.va/roman_curia/pontifical_councils/chrstuni/pentecostals/rc_pc_chrstuni_doc_1985-1989_perspectives-koinonia_en.html.

Peters, Ted. *Anticipating Omega: Science, Faith, and Our Ultimate Future*. Göttingen: Vandenhoeck & Ruprecht, 2006.

———. *God — the World's Future: Systematic Theology for a Postmodern Era*. Minneapolis: Fortress, 1992.

———. *God as Trinity: Relationality and Temporality in Divine Life*. Louisville: Westminster John Knox, 1993.

———. "Introduction: What Is to Come." In *RTSA*, pp. viii–xvii.

———. "The Trinity in and beyond Time." In *Quantum Cosmology and the Laws of Nature: Scientific Perspectives on Divine Action*, edited by Robert J. Russell, Nancey Murphy, and C. J. Isham, pp. 263–89. Vatican City and Berkeley, Calif.: Vatican Observatory and Center for Theological and the Natural Sciences, 1993.

Peterson, Daniel C. "Eschatology." In *The Oxford Encyclopedia of the Islamic World*, edited by John L. Esposito. Oxford: Oxford University Press, 2009; Oxford Islamic Studies Online. http://www.oxfordislamicstudies.com/article/opr/t236/e0223.

Peterson, M. "Religious Diversity, Evil, and a Variety of Theodicies." In *The Oxford Handbook of Religious Diversity*, edited by C. Meister, pp. 154–68. New York: Oxford University Press, 2010.

Pew Research Center. "America's Changing Religious Landscape: Chapter 1; The Changing Religious Composition of the U.S." May 12, 2015. http://www.pewforum .org/2015/05/12/chapter-1-the-changing-religious-composition-of-the-u-s/.

———. "Faith on the Move — the Religious Affiliation of International Migrants." March 8, 2012. http://www.pewforum.org/2012/03/08/religious-migration-exec/.

———. *The Global Religious Landscape: A Report on the Size and Distribution of the World's Major Religious Groups as of 2010*. December 2012. http://www.pewforum .org/files/2014/01/global-religion-full.pdf.

———. "'Nones' on the Rise." October 9, 2012. http://www.pewforum.org/2012/10/09 /nones-on-the-rise/.

Phan, Elaine, and Peter C. Padilla, eds. *Contemporary Issues of Migration and Theology*. New York: Palgrave Macmillan, 2013.

Phan, Peter C., ed. *Christianities in Asia*. Blackwell Guides to Global Christianity. Oxford: Wiley-Blackwell, 2011.

———. "Roman Catholic Theology." In *OHE*, pp. 215–29.

Phillips, D. Z. *The Problem of Evil and the Problem of God*. London: SCM, 2004.

Phillips, Derek L. *Looking Backward: A Critical Appraisal of Communitarian Thought*. Princeton: Princeton University Press, 1993.

Pinnock, Clark H. "Annihilationism." In *OHE*, pp. 462–75.

———. "The Conditional View." In *Four Views on Hell*, edited by William Crockett, pp. 135–66. Grand Rapids: Zondervan, 1992.

———. *Flame of Love: A Theology of the Holy Spirit*. Downers Grove: InterVarsity, 1996.

———. *A Wideness in God's Mercy: The Finality of Jesus Christ in a World of Religions*. Grand Rapids: Zondervan, 1992.

Pinnock, Sarah Catherine. *Beyond Theodicy: Jewish and Christian Continental Thinkers Respond to the Holocaust*. Albany: State University of New York Press, 2002.

Pirkei Avot. ("Ethics of the Fathers"). Chabad.org. http://www.chabad.org/library/article _cdo/aid/682518/jewish/English-Text.htm.

Pittenger, Norman. *After Death — Life in God*. New York: Seabury Press, 1980.

Pitts, William L. "The Relation of Baptists to Other Churches." In *The People of God: Essays on the Believers' Church*, edited by Paul Basden and David S. Dockery, pp. 235–50. Nashville: Broadman, 1991.

Plantinga, Alvin. "God, Evil and the Metaphysics of Freedom." In *PE*, 83–109.

———. *God, Freedom, and Evil*. London: Allen and Unwin, 1975.

Polanyi, Michael. *Personal Knowledge*. New York: Harper Torchbooks, 1964.

Polkinghorne, John. "Anthropology in an Evolutionary Context." In *God and Human Dignity*, edited by R. K. Soulen and L. Woodhead, pp. 89–103. Grand Rapids: Eerdmans, 2006.

————. "Eschatological Credibility: Emergent and Teleological Processes." In *RTSA*, pp. 43–55.

————. "Eschatology: Some Questions and Some Insights from Science." In *EWEG*, pp. 29–41.

————. *The Faith of a Physicist*. Princeton: Princeton University Press, 1994.

————. *The God of Hope and the End of the World*. New Haven and London: Yale University Press, 2002.

————. "Introduction to Part 1: Eschatology and the Sciences." In *EWEG*, pp. 17–18.

————. *Quarks, Chaos, and Christianity: Questions to Science and Religion*. Rev. ed. New York: Crossroad, 2005.

————. *Science and Christian Belief / The Faith of a Physicist*. London and Princeton: Princeton University Press, 1994.

————. *Science and Religion in Quest of Truth*. London: SPCK, 2011.

————. *Science and Theology: An Introduction*. London: SPCK; Minneapolis: Fortress, 1998.

————. *The Way the World Is*. Grand Rapids: Eerdmans, 1983.

Polkinghorne, John, and Michael Welker. "Introduction: Science and Theology on the End of the World and the Ends of God." In *EWEG*, pp. 1–13.

Pontifical Council for Inter-Religious Dialogue. "Dialogue and Proclamation." May 19, 1991. http://www.vatican.va/roman_curia/pontifical_councils/interelg/documents/rc_pc_interelg_doc_19051991_dialogue-and-proclamatio_en.html.

Poon, Michael Nai-Chiu, ed. *Christian Movements in Southeast Asia: A Theological Exploration*. Singapore: Genesis Books and Trinity Theological College, 2010.

Poorthuis, Marcel, and Joshua Schwartz, eds. *A Holy People: Jewish and Christian Perspectives on Religious Communal Identity*. Leiden and Boston: Brill, 2006.

Poorthuis, Marcel, Joshua Schwartz, and Joseph Turner, eds. *Interaction between Judaism and Christianity in History, Religion, Art, and Literature*. Leiden and Boston: Brill, 2008.

Porter, Andrew. "Cultural Imperialism and Protestant Missionary Enterprise, 1780–1914." *Journal of Commonwealth and Imperial History* 25, no. 2 (1997): 367–91.

Porterfield, Amanda. *Healing in the History of Christianity*. New York: Oxford University Press, 2005.

Power, David M. *Mission, Ministry, Order: Reading the Tradition in the Present Context*. New York and London: Continuum, 2008.

Prebish, Charles. "Councils: Buddhist Councils." In *ER*, pp. 2034–39.

Price, R. M. *The Paperback Apocalypse: How the Christian Church Was Left Behind*. Amherst, N.Y.: Prometheus, 2007.

Pui-lan, Kwok. "Mending of Creation: Women, Nature, and Eschatological Hope." In *Liberating Eschatology: Essays in Honor of Letty M. Russell*, edited by Margaret A. Farley and Serene Jones, pp. 144–55. Louisville: Westminster John Knox, 1999.

————. "Women and the Church." In *Introducing Asian Feminist Theology*, pp. 98–112. Cleveland: Pilgrim Press, 2000.

Puntel, Lorenz B. "Habermas' Postmetaphysical Thinking: A Critique." 2012. http://www

.philosophie.uni-muenchen.de/lehreinheiten/philosophie_1/personen/puntel
/download/2013_habermas.pdf.

Putnam, Robert D. *Bowling Alone: The Collapse and Revival of American Community.* New York: Simon and Schuster, 2000.

Putnam, Robert D., and Lewis M. Feldstein. *Better Together: Restoring the American Community.* New York: Simon and Schuster, 2003.

Quinn, Philip L. "Personal Identity, Bodily Continuity and Resurrection." *International Journal for Philosophy of Religion* 9 (1978): 101–13.

Quitterer, Josef. "Hylomorphism and the Constitution View." In *PIR*, pp. 177–90.

Radhakrishnan, Sir Sarvepalli. *Indian Philosophy.* Vol. 2. New York: Macmillan; London: George Allen and Unwin, 1958 [1927].

Rahman, Fazlur. "Appendix II — the People of the Book and Diversity of Religion." In Rahman, *Major Themes of the Qur'an*, pp. 112–17. 2nd ed. Chicago: University of Chicago Press, 2009.

———. *Major Themes of the Qur'ān.* Minneapolis: Bibliotheca Islamica, 1980. http://www.geocities.ws/islamic_modernist/Major_Themes_of_the_Quran.pdf.

Rahner, Karl. "Anonymous Christians." In *Theological Investigations*, vol. 6, translated by Karl-H. Kruger and Boniface Kruger, pp. 390–98. Baltimore: Helicon, 1969.

———. *Foundations of Christian Faith: An Introduction to the Idea of Christianity.* Translated by William W. Dych. New York: Crossroad, 1982.

———. "Hell." In *Sacramentum Mundi: An Encyclopedia of Theology*, edited by Karl Rahner et al., translated by W. J. O'Hara et al., 3:8. New York: Herder and Herder, 1969.

———. "The Hermeneutics of Eschatological Assertions." In *Theological Investigations*, vol. 4, translated by Kevin Smyth. Baltimore: Helicon, 1966.

———. *On the Theology of Death.* Translated by Charles H. Henkey. New York: Herder and Herder, 1961.

———. "Resurrection." In *Encyclopedia of Theology: A Concise Sacramentum Mundi*, edited by Karl Rahner, executive editor J. Cumming, pp. 1438–42. Freiburg: Herder and Herder; London: Burns and Oates, 1975.

———. "The Theology of the Symbol." In *Theological Investigations*, vol. 4, translated by Kevin Smyth, pp. 221–52. Baltimore: Helicon Press, 1966.

———. "Word and Eucharist." In *Theological Investigations*, vol. 4, translated by Kevin Smyth, pp. 253–86. Baltimore: Helicon Press, 1966.

Rahula, Walpola. *What the Buddha Taught.* Rev. ed. New York: Grove Press, 1974.

Rambachan, Anantanand. "The Co-Existence of Violence and Non-Violence in Hinduism." *Ecumenical Review* 55, no. 2 (2003): 115–221.

———. "Hindu-Christian Dialogue." In *Wiley-Blackwell Companion to Inter-Religious Dialogue*, edited by Catherine Cornille, pp. 325–45. Oxford: Wiley-Blackwell, 2013.

———. "Hinduism." In *LDWR*, pp. 66–86.

Rankin, David. *Tertullian and the Church.* Cambridge: Cambridge University Press, 1995.

Raphael, Simcha Paull. *Jewish Views of the Afterlife.* Northvale, N.J., and London: Jason Aronson, 1994.

Rashed, Rashdi. "The End Matters." In *ISCHP*, 1:37–50.

Rasmussen, Tarald. "Hell Disarmed? The Function of Hell in Reformation Spirituality." *Numen: International Review for the History of Religions* 56, nos. 2–3 (2009): 366–84.

Ratzinger, [Cardinal] Joseph. *Death and Eternal Life.* Translated by Michael Waldstein. Edited by Aidan Nichols. Washington, D.C.: Catholic University of America Press, 1987.

————. *Eschatology: Death and Eternal Life.* Washington, D.C.: Catholic University of America Press, 2007.

————. *The Ratzinger Report: An Exclusive Interview on the State of the Church; Joseph Ratzinger and Vittoria Messori.* San Francisco: Ignatius, 1985.

Rausch, Thomas P. *Towards a Truly Catholic Church: An Ecclesiology for the Third Millennium.* Collegeville, Minn.: Liturgical Press, 2005.

Reat, Noble Ross. "Karma and Rebirth in the *Upanisads* and Buddhism." *Numen* 24 (December 1977): 163–85.

Reder, Michael, and Josef Schmidt, SJ. "Habermas and Religion." In *An Awareness of What Is Missing: Faith and Reason in a Post-Secular Age,* by Jürgen Habermas et al., translated by Ciaran Cronin, pp. 1–14. Cambridge, UK, and Malden, Mass.: Polity, 2010 [2007].

Rees, Martin J. "The Collapse of the Universe: An Eschatological Study." *Observatory* 89 (1969): 193–98. http://articles.adsabs.harvard.edu/full/1969Obs....89..193R.

————. "Living in a Multiverse." In *FFU,* pp. 65–88.

————. *Our Final Hour.* New York: Basic Books, 2003.

Reese, Robert. "John Gatu and the Moratorium on Missionaries." *Missiology* 42, no. 3 (2014): 245–56.

Renard, John, ed. *Islamic Theological Themes: A Primary Source Reader.* Oakland: University of California Press, 2014.

Reumann, John. "Koinonia in Scripture: A Survey of Biblical Texts." In *On the Way to Fuller Koinonia: Official Report of the Fifth World Conference on Faith and Order,* edited by Thomas F. Best and Günther Gassman, pp. 38–69. Geneva: WCC, 1994.

Richardson, Joel. *The Islamic Antichrist: The Shocking Truth about the Real Nature of the Beast.* Los Angeles: WND Books, 2009.

Richey, Russell E., ed. *Denominationalism.* Eugene, Ore.: Wipf and Stock, 2010 [1977].

Ricoeur, Paul. *The Course of Recognition.* Translated by David Pellauer. Cambridge, Mass.: Harvard University Press, 2005.

Riga, Peter J. "The Ecclesiology of Johann Adam Möhler." *Theological Studies* 22, no. 4 (1961): 563–87.

Ripsman, Dina Eylon. *Reincarnation in Jewish Mysticism and Gnosticism.* Lewiston, N.Y.: Edwin Mellen Press, 2003.

"Rise of Hispanic Evangelical Church: *Time* Magazine Discusses Influence of Latinos in America's Religion." *Huffington Post.* April 10, 2013. http://www.huffingtonpost .com/2013/04/10/hispanic-evangelical-church_n_3055752.html, which discusses the April 15, 2013 issue of *Time,* "The Latino Reformation: Inside the New Hispanic Churches Transforming Religion in America."

Ritzer, George. *The McDonaldization of Society: An Investigation into the Changing Character of Contemporary Social Life*. Rev. ed. Thousand Oaks, Calif.: Pine Forge, 2000.

Rivera, Mayra. *The Touch of Transcendence: A Postcolonial Theology of God*. Louisville: Westminster John Knox, 2007.

Rizvi, Sajjad. "Mulla Sadra." *Stanford Encyclopedia of Philosophy* (Summer 2009 edition), edited by Edward N. Zalta. http://plato.stanford.edu/archives/sum2009/entries /mulla-sadra/.

Ro, Bong Rin, ed. *Christian Alternatives to Ancestor Practices*. Taichung, Taiwan: Asia Theological Association, 1985.

Ro, Young-chan. "Ancestor Worship: From the Perspective of Korean Tradition." In *Ancestor Worship and Christianity in Korea*, edited by Jung Young Lee, pp. 7–20. Lewiston, N.Y., and Lampeter, UK: Edwin Mellen Press, 1988.

Robeck, Cecil M. "Mission and the Issue of Proselytism." *International Bulletin of Missionary Research* 20, no. 1 (1996): 2–8.

———. "A Pentecostal Perspective on Apostolicity." Paper presented to Faith and Order, National Council of Churches, Consultation on American-Born Churches, March 1992.

Roberts, Arthur O. *Exploring Heaven: What Great Christian Thinkers Tell Us about Our Afterlife with God*. San Francisco: Harper, 2003.

Roberts, J. Deotis. "Dignity and Destiny: Black Reflections on Eschatology." In *Cambridge Companion to Black Theology*, edited by Dwight N. Hopkins and Edward P. Antonio, chap. 15. Cambridge: Cambridge University Press, 2012.

Robinson, Neil. "Ash'ariyya and Mu'tazila" (1998). Accessed November 14, 2016. http:// www.muslimphilosophy.com/ip/rep/H052.

Root, Michael. "The Communion Statement in Its Context." In *CC-LCE*, pp. 31–42.

Rose, Michael R. "Biological Immortality." In *The Scientific Conquest of Death: Essays on Infinite Lifespans*, edited by Immortality Institute, pp. 17–28. Buenos Aires: Libros EnRed, 2004. http://www.imminst.org/SCOD.pdf.

Rosin, H. H. *Missio Dei: An Examination of the Origin, Contents, and Function of the Term in Protestant Missiological Discussion*. Leiden: Interuniversity Institute for Missiological and Ecumenical Research, 1972.

Rosner, Jennifer Marie. "Healing the Schism: Barth, Rosenzweig and the Jewish-Christian Encounter." PhD diss., Fuller Theological Seminary, School of Theology, 2012.

Ross, Kenneth R. "Christian Mission and the End of Poverty: Time for Eschatology." *Mission Studies* 24 (2007): 79–97.

Rossing, Barbara. "Models of Koinoina [*sic*] in the New Testament and Early Church." In *CC-LCE*, pp. 65–80.

Roth, John K. "A Theodicy of Protest." In *Encountering Evil: Live Options in Theodicy*, edited by Stephen T. Davis. Atlanta: John Knox, 1981.

Rowe, William L. "The Problem of Evil and Some Varieties of Atheism." In *PE*, chap. 7.

Rowley, H. H. *The Biblical Doctrine of Election*. London: Lutterworth, 1950.

Royce, Josiah. *The World and the Individual*. Gloucester, Mass.: Peter Smith, 1976 [1899–1901].

Rubenstein, Richard. *After Auschwitz: Radical Theology and Contemporary Judaism.* Upper Saddle River, N.J.: Prentice-Hall, 1966.

Ruether, Rosemary Radford. "Ecofeminism — the Challenge to Theology." *DEP: Deportate, esuli, profughe* 20 (2012): 22–33.

———. "Eschatology in Christian Feminist Theologies." In *OHE*, pp. 328–42.

———. *Gaia and God: An Ecofeminist Theology of Earth Healing.* San Francisco: HarperCollins, 1992.

———. *New Woman, New Earth: Sexist Ideologies and Human Liberation.* New York: Seabury Press, 1975.

———. *Sexism and God-Talk: Toward a Feminist Theology.* Boston: Beacon Press, 1983.

———. *Women-Church: Theology and Practice of Feminist Liturgical Communities.* San Francisco: Harper and Row, 1985.

Rusch, William G. *Reception: An Ecumenical Opportunity.* Philadelphia: Fortress, 1988.

Russell, Bertrand. "A Free Man's Worship." In *Mysticism and Logic, and Other Essays.* London: Allen and Unwin, 1963.

———. *Why I Am Not a Christian, and Other Essays on Religion and Related Subjects.* London: Allen and Unwin, 1957.

Russell, Jeffrey Burton. *A History of Heaven.* Princeton: Princeton University Press, 1997.

Russell, Letty M. *Church in the Round: Feminist Interpretation of the Church.* Louisville: Westminster John Knox, 1993.

Russell, Robert J. "Bodily Resurrection, Eschatology and Scientific Cosmology." In *RTSA*, pp. 3–30.

———. *Cosmology: From Alpha to Omega; The Creative Mutual Interaction of Theology and Science.* Minneapolis: Fortress, 2008.

———. "Cosmology and Eschatology." In *OHE*, pp. 563–80.

———. "Cosmology and Eschatology: The Implications of Tipler's 'Omega-Point' Theory for Pannenberg's Theological Program." In *Beginning with the End: God, Science, and Wolfhart Pannenberg*, edited by Carol Rausch Albright and Joel Haugen, pp. 195–216. Chicago and La Salle, Ill.: Open Court, 1997.

———. "Eschatology and Physical Cosmology: A Preliminary Reflection." In *FFU*, pp. 266–315.

———. "Physics, Cosmology, and the Challenge to Consequentialist Natural Theodicy." In *PC*, pp. 109–30.

———. "Quantum Physics in Philosophical and Theological Perspective." In *Physics, Philosophy, and Theology: A Common Quest for Understanding*, edited by Robert J. Russell, William R. Stoeger, and George V. Coyne, pp. 343–74. Vatican City: Vatican Observatory, 1988.

———. *Time in Eternity: Pannenberg, Physics, and Eschatology in Creative Mutual Interaction.* Notre Dame: Notre Dame University Press, 2012.

Rustomji, Nerina. *The Garden and the Fire: Heaven and Hell in Islamic Culture.* New York: Columbia University Press, 2009.

Saarinen, Risto. "Anerkennungstheorien und Ökumenische Theologie." In *Ökumene — Überdacht (Quaestiones Disputate 259)*, edited by Thomas Bremer, pp. 237–61. Freiburg: Herder, 2013.

———. "The Concept of Communion in Ecumenical Dialogues." In *CC-LCE*, pp. 287–316.

———. "Ecumenism." In *GDT*, pp. 263–69.

———. *Johdatus Ekumeniikkaan*. Helsinki: Kirjaneliö, 1994.

———. "Living Sola Fide: Features of Religious Recognition." *Dialog* 52 (Fall 2013): 204–11.

———. "Lutheran Ecclesiology." In *RCCC*, pp. 170–86.

Sachedina, Abdulaziz Abdulhussein. *Islamic Messianism: The Idea of Mahdi in Twelver Shi'ism*. Albany: State University of New York Press, 1981.

———. *The Islamic Roots of Democratic Pluralism*. New York: Oxford University Press, 2001.

———. *The Role of Islam in the Public Square: Guidance or Governance?* Amsterdam: Amsterdam University Press, 2006.

Sacred Congregation for the Doctrine of the Faith. *Instruction on Christian Freedom and Liberation*. Given at Rome, March 22, 1986. http://www.vatican.va/roman_curia/congregations/cfaith/documents/rc_con_cfaith_doc_19860322_freedom-liberation_en.html.

———. *Inter Insigniores: Declaration on the Question of Admission of Women to the Ministerial Priesthood*. 1996. http://www.vatican.va/roman_curia/congregations/cfaith/documents/rc_con_cfaith_doc_19761015_inter-insigniores_en.html.

Saeed, Abdullah. "The Nature and Purpose of the Community (Ummah) in the Qur'ān." In *The Community of Believers: Christian and Muslim Perspectives*, edited by Lucinda Mosher and David Marshall, pp. 15–28. Washington, D.C.: Georgetown University Press, 2015.

Saeki, Y. P. *The Nestorian Documents and Relics in China*. Tokyo: Academy of Oriental Culture, 1937.

Said, Edward. *Culture and Imperialism*. New York: Knopf, 1993.

Sanneh, Lamin. *Translating the Message: The Missionary Impact on Culture*. Maryknoll, N.Y.: Orbis, 1989.

———. *Whose Religion Is Christianity? The Gospel beyond the West*. Grand Rapids: Eerdmans, 2003.

Sanneh, Lamin, and Joel A. Carpenter, eds. *The Changing Face of Christianity: Africa, the West, and the World*. Oxford: Oxford University Press, 2005.

Sardoc, Mitja. *Toleration, Respect, and Recognition in Education*. Oxford: Wiley-Blackwell, 2010.

Saritoprak, Zeri. *Islam's Jesus*. Gainesville: University Press of Florida, 2014.

Sartre, Jean-Paul. *Being and Nothingness: An Essay on Phenomenological Ontology*. New York: Philosophical Library, 1956.

Sathianathan, Clarke. "Hindutva, Religious and Ethnocultural Minorities, and Indian-Christian Theology." *Harvard Theological Review* 95, no. 2 (2002): 197–226.

Sauter, Gerhard. "The Concept and Task of Eschatology: Theological and Philosophical Reflections." *Scottish Journal of Theology* 41 (1988): 499–515.

Saward, John. *Sweet and Blessed Country: The Christian Hope for Heaven*. Oxford: Oxford University Press, 2005.

Schaff, Philip, ed., *Creeds of Christendom*. 3 vols. New York: Harper and Row, 1877. www .ccel.org.

Scharen, Christian Batalden. "'Judicious Narratives,' or Ethnography as Ecclesiology." *Scottish Journal of Theology* 58, no. 2 (2005): 125-42.

Schärtl, Thomas. "Bodily Resurrection: When Metaphysics Needs Phenomenology." In *PIR*, pp. 103-25.

Scherer, James A. *Missionary, Go Home! A Reappraisal of the Christian World Mission*. Englewood Cliffs, N.J.: Prentice-Hall, 1964.

Schillebeeckx, Eduard. *Church: The Human Story of God*. New York: Crossroad, 1990.

———. *The Eucharist*. New York: Burns and Oates, 1968.

Schirrmacher, Christine. "They Are Not All Martyrs: Islam on the Topics of Dying, Death, and Salvation in the Afterlife." *Evangelical Review of Theology* 36 (2012): 250-65.

Schleiermacher, Friedrich. *On Religion: Speeches to Its Cultural Despisers*. Translated and edited by Richard Crouter. Glasgow: Cambridge University Press, 1996.

Schlink, Edmund. *Ökumenische Dogmatik: Grundzüge*. Göttingen: Vandenhoeck & Ruprecht, 1983.

Schloss, Jeffrey P. "From Evolution to Eschatology." In *Resurrection: Theological and Scientific Assessments*, edited by Ted Peters, Robert J. Russell, and Michael Welker, pp. 65-85. Grand Rapids: Eerdmans, 2002.

Schmemann, Alexander. *For the Life of the World*. Crestwood, N.Y.: St. Vladimir's Seminary Press, 1988.

———. "Liturgy and Eschatology." *Sobornost* 7, no. 1 (1985): 9-10.

———. "Worship in a Secular Age." In *For the Life of the World: Sacraments and Orthodoxy*. Crestwood, N.Y.: St. Vladimir's Seminary Press, 1973.

Schmid, Heinrich. *The Doctrinal Theology of the Evangelical Lutheran Church*. Translated by Charles A. Hay and Henry E. Jacobs. 3rd ed. Minneapolis: Augsburg, n.d. www .ccel.org.

Schmidt, James. "What Enlightenment Project?" *Political Theory* 28, no. 6 (2000): 734-57.

———, ed. *What Is Enlightenment? Eighteenth-Century Answers and Twentieth-Century Questions*. Berkeley: University of California Press, 1996.

Schmidt-Leukel, Perry. "Intimate Strangers: An Introduction." In *Buddhism and Christianity in Dialogue*, edited by Perry Schmidt-Leukel, pp. 1-26. London: SCM, 2005.

Schnackenburg, R. "Apostolizität: Stand der Forschung." In *Katholizität und Apostolizität*, ed. Reinhard Groscurth, pp. 51-73. Kerygma und Dogma: Beihefte 2. Göttingen: Vandenhoeck & Ruprecht, 1971.

Schneider, David J. *The Psychology of Stereotyping*. New York: Guilford Press, 2004.

Scholem, Gershom. *Major Trends in Jewish Mysticism*. 3rd rev. ed. New York: Schocken, 1961.

Schrag, Calvin O. "Transversal Rationality." In *The Question of Hermeneutics: Essays in Honor of Joseph J. Kockelmans*, edited by T. J. Stapleton. Dordrecht: Kluwer, 1994.

Schrank, B., G. Stanghellini, and M. Slade. "Hope in Psychiatry: A Review of the Literature." *Acta Psychiatrica Scandinavica* 118, no. 6 (2008): 421-33. doi:10.1111/j.1600-0447.2008.01271.x. Epub 2008 Oct 10.

Schreiter, Robert J. "Reconciliation and Healing as a Paradigm for Mission." *International Review of Mission* 94, no. 372 (January 2005): 74-83.

Schubel, Vernon James. "Worship and Devotional Life: Muslim Worship." In *ER*, pp. 9815-20.

Schuele, Andreas. "Transformed into the Image of Christ: Identity, Personality, and Resurrection." In *RTSA*, pp. 219-35.

Schultz, Kevin M. "Secularization: A Bibliographic Essay." *Hedgehog Review* 8, nos. 1-2 (Spring-Summer 2006): 170-77.

Schüssler Fiorenza, Elisabeth. *Discipleship of Equals*. New York: Crossroad, 1993.

————. *In Memory of Her: A Feminist Theological Reconstruction of Christian Origins*. New York: Crossroad, 1983.

Schwaller, John Frederick. *The History of the Catholic Church in Latin America: From Conquest to Revolution and Beyond*. New York: New York University Press, 2011.

Schwartz, Matthew B. "The Meaning of Suffering: A Talmudic Response to Theodicy." *Judaism* 32 (1983): 444-51.

Schwarz, Hans. *Christology*. Grand Rapids: Eerdmans, 1998.

————. *Eschatology*. Grand Rapids: Eerdmans, 2000.

————. *On the Way to the Future*. Rev. ed. Minneapolis: Augsburg, 1979.

Schweizer, Eduard. "The Priesthood of All Believers: 1 Peter 2:1-10." In *Worship, Theology, and Ministry in the Early Church: Essays in Honor of Ralph P. Martin*, edited by Michael J. Wilkins and Terence Paige, pp. 285-93. Sheffield: JSOT Press, 1992.

Scott, Mark S[tephen] M[urray]. "Guarding the Mysteries of Salvation: The Pastoral Pedagogy of Origen's Universalism." *Journal of Early Christian Studies* 18 (2010): 347-68.

————. "Theodicy at the Margins: New Trajectories for the Problem of Evil." *Theology Today* 68 (2011): 149-52.

Sefer haBahir. "The Book of Illumination." ET: http://www.servantsofthelight.org/QBL/Books/Bahir_1.html.

Segal, Eliezer. "Judaism." In *LDWR*, pp. 11-30.

Segundo, Juan Luis. *An Evolutionary Approach to Jesus of Nazareth*. Maryknoll, N.Y.: Orbis, 1988.

————. *The Sacraments Today*. Translated by John Drury. Maryknoll, N.Y.: Orbis, 1974.

"Selected Passages from al-Ghazālī's *The Remembrance of Death and the Afterlife*." In *Death, Resurrection, and Human Destiny: Christian and Muslim Perspectives*, edited by David Marshall and Lucinda Mosher, pp. 153-59. Washington, D.C.: Georgetown University Press, 2014.

Sells, Michael A. "Armageddon in Christian, Sunni, and Shia Traditions." In *The Oxford Handbook of Religion and Violence*, edited by Michael Jerryson, Mark Juergensmeyer, and Margo Kitts, pp. 467-95. Oxford: Oxford University Press, 2012.

Selvanayagam, Israel. "Indian Secularism: Prospect and Problem." *Implicit Religion* 15, no. 3 (2012): 357-61.

Sempell, Andrew. "God, Society and Secularism." *St. Mark's Review* 221 (September 2012): 56-65.

Sennett, James F. "Is There Freedom in Heaven?" *Faith and Philosophy* 16, no. 1 (1999): 69-82.

Seo, Bo-Myung. *A Critique of Western Theological Anthropology: Understanding Human Beings in a Third World Context.* Lewiston, N.Y.: Edwin Mellen Press, 2005.

"The 72 Signs of Doomsday (Qayamat)." IslamiCity.com. May 12, 2006. http://www.isla micity.com/forum/printer_friendly_posts.asp?TID=4825.

Shaar HaGilgulim. "Gates of Incarnation." Kabbalah Online. Accessed November 15, 2016. http://www.chabad.org/kabbalah/article_cdo/aid/380302/jewish/Gate-of-Reincar nations-Introduction.htm.

Shakespeare, Steven. *Radical Orthodoxy: A Critical Introduction.* London: SPCK; Perseus Books Group: Kindle Edition, 2007.

Sharma, Arvind. "Apostolic Islam and Apostolic Christianity: An Eschatological Comparison." *Dialogue & Alliance* 19, no. 1 (2005): 39–46.

⸻. *Classical Hindu Thought: An Introduction.* Oxford: Oxford University Press, 2000.

⸻. "A Hindu Perspective." In *OHRD*, pp. 309–20.

Shatz, David. "A Jewish Perspective." In *OHRD*, pp. 365–80.

Shenk, Wilbert. *Write the Vision: The Church Renewed.* Christian Mission and Modern Culture. Valley Forge, Pa.: Trinity, 1995.

Sherwin, Byron L. "Theodicy." In *Contemporary Jewish Religious Thought: Original Essays on Critical Concepts, Movements, and Beliefs,* edited by Arthur A. Cohen and Paul Mendes-Flohr, pp. 959–70. New York: Free Press, 1987.

Shiver, Terry D. "Ken Sumrall and Church Foundational Network: A Modern-Day Apostolic Movement." PhD diss., Regent University, School of Divinity, 2014.

Shults, F. LeRon. *The Post Foundationalist Task of Theology: Wolfhart Pannenberg and the New Theological Rationality.* Grand Rapids: Eerdmans, 1999.

⸻. "Theological Responses to Postmodernities or Tending to the Other in Late Modern Missions and Ecumenism." Presentation for Nordic Institute for Missiological and Ecumenical Research Annual Meeting at the University of Abo, Turku, Finland, August 19–22, 2007.

Siddiqui, Mona. "Death, Resurrection, and Human Destiny: Qur'ānic and Islamic Perspectives." In *Death, Resurrection, and Human Destiny: Christian and Muslim Perspectives,* edited by David Marshall and Lucinda Mosher, pp. 25–38. Washington, D.C.: Georgetown University Press, 2014.

Sigālaka Sutta: To Sigālaka; Advice to Laity. In *The Long Discourses of Buddha,* translated by Maurice Walshe, pp. 461–69. London: Wisdom Publications, 1987.

Simons, Menno. *Reply to Gellius Faber (1552).* In *The Complete Writings of Menno Simons (c. 1496-1561),* edited by H. S. Bender. Scottdale, Pa.: Herald, 1956.

Simut, Corneliu C. "Understanding Death beyond Religion in the Thought of John Shelby Spong." *Expository Times* 125, no. 8 (2014): 375–82.

Sinaga, Martin L., ed. *A Common Word: Buddhists and Christians Engage Structural Greed.* Minneapolis: Luther University Press, 2012.

Sivalon, John C. *God's Mission and Postmodern Culture: The Gift of Uncertainty.* Maryknoll, N.Y.: Orbis, 2012.

Sivaraman, K. "The Meaning of *Moksha* in Contemporary Hindu Thought and Life." In

Living Faiths and Ultimate Goals: Salvation and World Religions, edited by S. J. Samartha, pp. 2–11. Maryknoll, N.Y.: Orbis, 1974.

Sizer, Stephen. *Christian Zionism: Road Map to Armageddon?* Leicester, UK: Inter-Varsity, 2004.

Skilling, Peter. "Worship and Devotional Life: Buddhist Devotional Life in Southeast Asia." In *ER,* pp. 9826–34.

Smith, Brian K. *"Samsāra."* In *ER,* pp. 8097–99.

Smith, Christian, ed. *The Secular Revolution: Power, Interests, and Conflicts in the Secularization of American Pubic Life.* Berkeley: University of California Press, 2003.

Smith, Gordon T. *The Lord's Supper: Five Views.* Downers Grove: InterVarsity, 2008.

Smith, James K. A. *Desiring the Kingdom: Worship, Worldview, and Cultural Formation.* Cultural Liturgies, vol. 1. Grand Rapids: Baker Academic, 2009.

———. *Imagining the Kingdom: How Worship Works.* Cultural Liturgies, vol. 2. Grand Rapids: Baker Academic, 2013.

———. *Introducing Radical Orthodoxy: Mapping a Post-Secular Theology.* Grand Rapids: Baker Academic, 2004.

Smith, Jane Idleman, and Yvonne Yazbeck Haddad. *The Islamic Understanding of Death and Resurrection.* Albany: State University of New York Press, 1981; Oxford: Oxford University Press, 2002.

Smyth, John. *Principles and Inferences concerning the Visible Church.* In *The Works of John Smyth, Fellow of Christ's College 1594-8,* vol. 1, edited by W. T. Whitley. Cambridge: Cambridge University Press, 1915. https://archive.org/stream/cu31924092458995 /cu31924092458995_djvu.txt.

———. *The Works of John Smyth, Fellow of Christ's College 1594-8.* Edited by W. T. Whitley. 2 vols. Cambridge: Cambridge University Press, 1915. https://archive.org /stream/cu31924092458995/cu31924092458995_djvu.txt.

Snyder, C. Richard, ed. *Handbook of Hope: Theory, Measures, and Applications.* San Diego: Academic Press, 2000.

———. *Psychology of Hope: You Can Get from Here to There.* New York: Free Press, 1994.

Snyder, Howard A. "The Marks of an Evangelical Ecclesiology." In *Evangelical Ecclesiology: Reality or Illusion?* edited by John G. Stackhouse Jr. Grand Rapids: Baker Academic, 2003.

Sölle, Dorothee. *Suffering.* Translated by Everett R. Kalin. Minneapolis: Fortress, 1975.

Soloveitchik, Joseph B. "On Interfaith Relationships." In *Community, Covenant, and Commitment,* edited by Nathaniel Helfgot, pp. 259–65. New York: Toras HoRav Foundation, 2005.

Soskice, Janet Martin. "The Ends of Man and the Future of God." In *EWEG,* chap. 6.

Soulen, R. Kendall. *The God of Israel and Christian Theology.* Minneapolis: Fortress, 1996.

"The Soul's Journey after Death." Abridgment of *Kitabar-Ruh* by Ibn Qayyim al-Jawziya. Accessed November 15, 2016. https://ia600409.us.archive.org/6/items/KitabAlRuh Summary-IbnAlQayyim/23713846-The-Souls-Journey-After-Death.pdf.

Southgate, Christopher. "God and Evolutionary Evil: Theodicy in the Light of Darwinism." *Zygon: Journal of Religion and Science* 37, no. 4 (2002): 803–21.

Spinks, Bryan D. *Early and Medieval Rituals and Theologies of Baptism: From the New Testament to the Council of Trent.* Burlington, Vt.: Ashgate, 2006.

Spong, John Shelby. *Eternal Life: A New Vision; Beyond Religion, Beyond Theism, Beyond Heaven and Hell.* New York: HarperOne, 2009.

Stander, Hendrick F., and Johannes P. Louw. *Baptism in the Early Church.* Rev. ed. Pretoria: Didaskalia Publishers; Leeds, UK: Reformation Today Trust, 1994 [1988].

Stanley, Brian. *The Bible and the Flag: Protestant Missions and British Imperialism in the Nineteenth and Twentieth Centuries.* Trowbridge, UK: Apollos, 1990.

———. "Conversion to Christianity: The Colonization of the Mind?" *International Review of Mission* 92, no. 366 (July 2003): 315–31.

Staples, Russell Lynn. "Christianity and the Cult of the Ancestors: Belief and Ritual among the Bantu-Speaking Peoples of Southern Africa; An Interdisciplinary Study Utilizing Anthropological and Theological Analyses." PhD diss., Princeton Theological Seminary, 1981.

Stark, Rodney. *The Rise of Christianity.* San Francisco: HarperCollins, 1997.

Stassen, Glen. *Just Peacemaking: The New Paradigm for the Ethics of Peace and War.* Cleveland: Pilgrim Press, 2008.

Steinkellner, Ernst. "Buddhismus: Religion oder Philosophie? und Vom Wesen der Buddha." In *Der Buddhismus als Anfrage an christliche Theologie und Philosophie,* edited by Andreas Bsteh, pp. 251–62. Studien zu Religionstheorie 5. Mödling, Austria: Verlag St. Gabriel, 2000.

Stenmark, Mikael. "How to Relate Christian Faith and Science." In *BCSC,* chap. 6.

Stephan, Walter G., Oscar Ybarra, and Kimberly Rios Morrison. "Intergroup Threat Theory." In *Handbook of Prejudice, Stereotyping, and Discrimination,* edited by Todd D. Nelson, pp. 43–59. New York: Psychology Press, 2009.

Stephenson, John R. "The Lutheran View." In *The Lord's Supper: Five Views,* edited by Gordon T. Smith, pp. 41–58. Downers Grove: InterVarsity, 2007.

Stern, David. "Afterlife: Jewish Concept." In *ER,* pp. 152–56.

Stevenson, Tyler Wigg. "Revelation's Warning to Evangelicals: *Left Behind* May Be Hazardous to Our Health." *Reflections* 92 (Spring 2005): 35–39.

Stieglecker, Hermann. *Die Glaubenslehren des Islam.* Paderborn: Ferdinand Schöningh, 1962.

Stoebe, Michael. "Transformative Suffering, Destructive Suffering and the Question of Abandoning Theodicy." *Studies in Religion/Sciences Religeuses* 32 (2003): 429–47.

Stoeger, William R., SJ. "Scientific Accounts of Ultimate Catastrophes in Our Life-Bearing Universe." In *EWEG,* pp. 19–28.

Strauss, David F. *The Life of Jesus Critically Examined.* Translated from the fourth German ed. by George Eliot. 2nd ed. in 1 vol. London: Schwann Sonnenschein; New York: Macmillan, 1892.

Strawson, P. F. *Individuals: An Essay in Descriptive Metaphysics.* London: Methuen, 1959.

Streiker, Lowell D. "The Hindu Attitude toward Other Religions." *Journal of Religious Thought* 23, no. 1 (1966/1967): 75–90.

Stroda, Una. "The Ordination of Women: The Experience of the Evangelical Lutheran Church of Latvia." Master's thesis, Catholic Theological Union, Chicago, 2008.

Stromberg, Jean S. "Responding to the Challenge of Migration: Churches within the Fellowship of the World Council of Churches (WCC)." *Missiology: An International Review* 31, no. 1 (January 2003): 45–50.

Stump, Eleonore, and Norman Kretzmann. "Eternity." *Journal of Philosophy* 78, no. 8 (1981): 429–58.

Suchocki, Marjorie Hewitt. *The End of Evil: Process Eschatology in Historical Context.* Albany: State University of New York Press, 1988.

———. *God, Christ, Church: A Practical Guide to Process Theology.* Rev. ed. New York: Crossroad, 1989.

Sullivan, Francis A., SJ. *The Church We Believe In: One, Holy, Catholic, and Apostolic.* New York and Mahwah, N.J.: Paulist, 1988.

Sullivan, Lawrence E. Preface to *Hinduism and Ecology: The Intersection of Earth, Sky, and Water,* edited by Christopher Key Chapple and Mary Evelyn Tucker. Religions of the World and Ecology. Cambridge, Mass.: Harvard University Press, 2000.

Sumegi, Angela. *Understanding Death: An Introduction to Ideas of Self and the Afterlife in World Religions.* Malden, Mass.: Wiley-Blackwell, 2014.

Summers, Steve. *Friendship.* New York: T. & T. Clark, 2009.

"Summons to Witness to Christ in Today's World: A Report of the Baptist–Roman Catholic International Conversations, 1984–1988." Vatican Web site. Accessed January 18, 2017. http://www.vatican.va/roman_curia/pontifical_councils/chrstuni/Baps tist%20alliance/rc_pc_chrstuni_doc_19880723_baptist-convers_en.html.

Sundkler, Bengt, and Christopher Steed. *A History of the Church in Africa.* Cambridge: Cambridge University Press, 2000.

Swamp, Ram. *Hindu View of Christianity and Islam.* New Delhi: Voice of India, 1992.

Swinburne, Richard. *Faith and Reason.* Oxford: Clarendon, 1981.

———. "A Theodicy of Heaven and Hell." In *The Existence and Nature of God,* edited by Alfred J. Freddoso. Notre Dame: University of Notre Dame Press, 1983.

Swinton, John. *Raging with Compassion: Pastoral Responses to the Problem of Evil.* Grand Rapids: Eerdmans, 2007.

Szabolcs, Nagypál. "Proselytism and Religious Freedom: The Case of Russia, Ukraine and Poland." In *Communicating Vocation: Spirituality Down to Earth,* edited by Rebecca Blocksome and Nagypál Szabolcs, pp. 186–202. Vienna and Budapest: BGÖI & WSCF-CESR, 2009.

Tabor, James D. "Ancient Jewish and Early Christian Millennialism." In *OHM,* pp. 252–53.

Talbott, Thomas. "Christus Victorious." In *Universal Salvation? The Current Debate,* edited by Robin A. Parry and Christopher H. Partridge. Grand Rapids: Eerdmans, 2003.

———. "Freedom, Damnation, and the Power to Sin with Impunity." *Religious Studies* 37 (2001): 417–34.

———. *The Inescapable Love of God.* Portland, Ore.: Cascade Books, 2014 [1999].

———. "Punishment, Forgiveness, and Divine Justice." *Religious Studies* 29 (1993): 151–68.

———. "Universalism." In *OHE,* pp. 446–61.

Tanner, Kathryn. "Eschatology without a Future." In *EWEG,* pp. 222–37.

Tapp, Christian. "Joseph Ratzinger on Resurrection Identity." In *PIR,* pp. 207–24.

Taylor, Charles. *A Secular Age.* Cambridge, Mass., and London: Belknap Press of Harvard University Press, 2007.

———. "The Politics of Recognition." In *Multiculturalism: Examining the Politics of Recognition,* edited by Amy Gutman, pp. 25–73. Princeton: Princeton University Press, 1994. http://elplandehiram.org/documentos/JoustingNYC/Politics_of _Recognition.pdf.

Taylor, John B. "Some Aspects of Islamic Eschatology." *Religious Studies* 4 (October 1968): 57–76.

Tejani, Shabnum. *Indian Secularism: A Social and Intellectual History, 1870–1950.* Bloomington: Indiana University Press, 2008.

Tennent, Timothy C. *Theology in the Context of World Christianity.* Grand Rapids: Zondervan, 2007.

Thatamanil, John J. *The Immanent Divine: God, Creation, and the Human Predicament; An East-West Conversation.* Minneapolis: Fortress, 2006.

"Theme Two: Christian Mission among Other Faiths." In *Edinburgh 2010,* vol. 2, *Witnessing to Christ Today,* edited by Daryl Balia and Kirsteen Kim, pp. 34–60. Oxford: Regnum, 2010.

Thielicke, Helmut. *Death and Life.* Translated by Edward H. Schroeder. Philadelphia: Fortress, 1970.

Thiessen, Elmer John. *The Ethics of Evangelism: A Philosophical Defense of Proselytizing and Persuasion.* Downers Grove: InterVarsity, 2011.

The Third Panorthodox Pre-Conciliar Conference in Chambesy, Switzerland, 1986, statement of. In *Episkepsis,* no. 369 (December 1968).

Thiselton, Anthony C. *Life after Death: A New Approach to the Last Things.* Grand Rapids: Eerdmans, 2012.

Thomas, Günther. "Resurrection to New Life: Pneumatological Implications of the Eschatological Transition." In *RTSA,* pp. 255–76.

Thomassen, Einar. "Islamic Hell." *Numen: International Review for the History of Religions* 56, nos. 2–3 (2009): 401–16.

Thompson, Simon. *The Political Theory of Recognition: A Critical Introduction.* Cambridge: Polity, 2006.

Tillard, J. M. R. *Church of Churches: The Ecclesiology of Communion.* Collegeville, Minn.: Liturgical Press, 1992.

Tilley, Terrence W. *The Evils of Theodicy.* Washington, D.C.: Georgetown University Press, 1991.

———. "The Problems of Theodicy: A Background Essay." In *PC,* pp. 35–51.

Tillich, Paul. *Systematic Theology.* Vols. 1–2. Chicago: University of Chicago Press, 1951, 1957.

Tipler, F. J. *The Physics of Immortality.* London: Weidenfeld and Nicolson, 1994.

Toft, Monica Duffy, Daniel Philpott, and Timothy Samuel Shah. *God's Century: Resurgent Religion and Global Politics.* New York: Norton, 2011.

Tolonen, Miika. *Witness Is Presence: Reading Stanley Hauerwas in a Nordic Setting.* Eugene, Ore.: Wipf and Stock, 2013.

Torrance, James B. *Worship, Community, and the Triune God of Grace*. Downers Grove: InterVarsity, 1997.

Torrance, Thomas F. *Space, Time, and Incarnation*. Edinburgh: T. & T. Clark, 1968.

———. *Space, Time, and Resurrection*. Grand Rapids: Eerdmans, 1998.

Toynbee, Arnold J. *Civilization on Trial*. London: Oxford University Press, 1949.

Tractate Sanhedrin. Translated by Herbert Danby. 1919. Accessed November 15, 2016. http://www.sacred-texts.com/jud/tsa/tsa37.htm#fr_388.

Travis, Stephen H. *I Believe in the Second Coming of Jesus*. Grand Rapids: Eerdmans, 1982.

Trigg, Roger. *Equality, Freedom, and Religion*. Oxford: Oxford University Press, 2012.

———. *Rationality and Religion: Does Faith Need Reason?* Oxford: Blackwell, 1998.

———. *Reason and Commitment*. Cambridge: Cambridge University Press, 1973.

———. *Religion in Public Life: Must Religion Be Privatized?* Oxford: Oxford University Press, 2007.

———. *Religious Diversity: Philosophical and Political Dimensions*. Cambridge: Cambridge University Press, 2014.

Trumbower, Jeffrey A. *Rescue for the Dead: The Posthumous Salvation of Non-Christians in Early Christianity*. Oxford: Oxford University Press, 2001.

Tsirpanlis, Constantine N. "The Concept of Universal Salvation in Saint Gregory of Nyssa." *Studia Patristica* 17, no. 3 (1982): 1131–44.

Tucker, Karen Westerfield. "Baptism and Ecumenism: Agreements and Problems on the Journey towards Mutual Recognition." *Studia liturgica* 42, nos. 1–2 (2012): 1–12.

Tug, Salih. "Death and Immortality in Islamic Thought." In *DIRW*, pp. 86–92.

Turner, Max. "Spiritual Gifts Then and Now." *Vox Evangelica* 15 (1985): 7–63.

Turner, V. *The Ritual Process: Structure and Anti-Structure*. Ithaca, N.Y.: Cornell University Press, 1979 [1969]. http://monoskop.org/images/9/90/Turner_Victor_The _Ritual_Process_Structure_and_Anti-Structure.pdf.

Tuveson, Ernest L. *Redeemer Nation: The Idea of America's Millennial Role*. Chicago: University of Chicago Press, 1968.

Twelftree, Graham H. *People of the Spirit: Exploring Luke's View of the Church*. Grand Rapids: Baker Academic, 2009.

Umansky, Ellen M. "Election." In *ER*, pp. 2744–49.

Unamuno, Miguel de. *Tragic Sense of Life*. Translated by J. E. Crawford Flitch. New York: Dover Publications, 1954 [1913]. http://archive.org/stream/tragicsenseofli fi4636gut/14636.txt.

"Uniatism, Method of Union of the Past, and the Present Search for Full Communion." Joint International Commission for the Theological Dialogue between the Roman Catholic Church and the Orthodox Church: Seventh Plenary Session, Balamand School of Theology, Lebanon, June 17–24, 1993. *Information Service* 83 (1993): 95–99.

The Uppsala Report 1968: Official Report of the Fourth Assembly of the World Council of Churches, Uppsala July 4–20, 1968. Edited by Norman Goodall. Geneva: WCC, 1968.

Urban, Hugh B. "Millenarian Elements in the Hindu Religious Traditions." In *OHM*, pp. 369–81.

Uzukwu, Elochukwu E. *A Listening Church: Autonomy and Communion in African Churches.* Eugene, Ore.: Wipf and Stock, 2006.

——. *Worship as Body Language: Introduction to Christian Worship, an African Orientation.* Collegeville, Minn.: Liturgical Press, 1997.

Vail, Eric Michael. "Using 'Chaos' in Articulating the Relationship of God and Creation in God's Creative Activity." PhD diss., Marquette University, 2009. http://epublications .marquette.edu/cgi/viewcontent.cgi?article=1004&context=dissertations_mu.

Vainio, Olli-Pekka. *Beyond Fideism: Negotiable Religious Identities.* Surrey, UK: Ashgate, 2010.

Van Buren, Paul M. *Discerning the Way.* New York: Seabury Press, 1980.

Van Dyk, Leanne. "The Gifts of God for the People of God: Christian Feminism and Sacramental Theology." In *Feminist and Womanist Essays in Reformed Dogmatics*, edited by Amy Plantinga Pauw and Serene Jones, pp. 204–20. Louisville: Westminster John Knox, 2006.

——. "The Reformed View." In *The Lord's Supper: Five Views*, edited by Gordon T. Smith, pp. 67–82. Downers Grove: InterVarsity, 2007.

Van Engen, Charles. "Church." In *Evangelical Dictionary of World Christian Missions*, edited by A. Scott Moreau et al., p. 193. Grand Rapids: Baker Academic, 2000.

——. *God's Missionary People.* Grand Rapids: Baker Academic, 1991.

Van Gelder, Craig. *The Essence of the Church.* Grand Rapids: Baker, 2000.

Van Gelder, Craig, and Dwight J. Zscheile. *The Missional Church in Perspective: Mapping Trends and Shaping the Conversation.* Grand Rapids: Baker Academic, 2011.

Vanhoozer, Kevin J. *The Drama of Doctrine: A Canonical-Linguistic Approach to Christian Theology.* Louisville: Westminster John Knox, 2005.

——. *Faith Speaking Understanding: Performing the Drama of Doctrine.* Louisville: Westminster John Knox, 2014.

Van Huyssteen, Wentzel J. *Alone in the World? Human Uniqueness in Science and Theology.* Grand Rapids: Eerdmans, 2006.

Vattimo, Gianni. *After Christianity.* Translated by Luca D'Isanto. New York: Columbia University Press, 2002.

——. *A Farewell to Truth.* New York: Columbia University Press, 2011.

Vélez de Cea, Abraham. "A Cross-Cultural and Buddhist-Friendly Interpretation of the Typology Exclusivism-Inclusivism-Pluralism." *Sophia* 50, no. 3 (2011): 453–80.

Vivekananda, Swami. "The Real Nature of Man." In *Complete Works of Swami Vivekananda*, vol. 2, chap. 2. N.d. http://www.ramakrishnavivekananda.info /vivekananda/complete_works.htm.

Viviano, Benedict T. "Eschatology and the Quest for the Historical Jesus." In *OHE*, pp. 73–90.

Volf, Miroslav. "After Moltmann: Reflections on Eschatology." In *God Will Be All in All: The Eschatology of Jürgen Moltmann*, edited by Richard Bauckham, pp. 233–58. Edinburgh: T. & T. Clark, 1999.

——. *After Our Likeness: The Church as an Image of the Trinity.* Grand Rapids: Eerdmans, 1998.

——. *Allah: A Christian Response.* New York: HarperCollins, 2011.

———. "Enter into Joy!" In *EWEG*, pp. 256–78.

———. *Exclusion and Embrace: A Theological Exploration of Identity, Otherness, and Reconciliation*. Nashville: Abingdon, 1996.

———. "The Final Reconciliation." *Modern Theology* 16, no. 1 (2000): 91–113.

———. "Forgiveness, Reconciliation, and Justice: A Theological Contribution to a More Peaceful Social Environment." *Millennium — Journal of International Studies* 29 (2000): 861–77.

———. "Systematic Theology III: Ecclesiology and Eschatology." Unpublished lecture notes, Fuller Theological Seminary, Pasadena, Calif., Summer 1988.

———. "'The Trinity Is Our Social Program': The Doctrine of the Trinity and the Shape of Social Engagement." *Modern Theology* 14, no. 3 (1998): 403–23.

———. *Work in the Spirit: Toward a Theology of Work*. Eugene, Ore.: Wipf and Stock, 2001.

Volf, Miroslav, and Maurice Lee. "The Spirit and the Church." In *Advents of the Spirit: An Introduction to the Current Study of Pneumatology*, edited by Bradford E. Hinze and D. Lyle Dabney, pp. 382–409. Milwaukee: Marquette University Press, 2001.

Wagner, C. Peter. *Churchquake! How the New Apostolic Reformation Is Shaking up the Church as We Know It*. Ventura, Calif.: Regal, 1999.

———. *The New Apostolic Churches*. Ventura, Calif.: Regal, 1998.

Wainwright, Geoffrey. *Doxology: The Praise of God in Worship, Doctrine, and Life*. New York: Oxford University Press, 1980.

———. *Eucharist and Eschatology*. New York: Oxford University Press, 1981.

Walker, D. P. *The Decline of Hell*. Chicago: University of Chicago Press, 1964.

Walls, Andrew F. *The Missionary Movement in Christian History: Studies in the Transmission of Faith*. Maryknoll, N.Y.: Orbis, 1996.

Walls, Jerry L. "Heaven." In *OHE*, pp. 399–412.

———. *Heaven: The Logic of Eternal Joy*. Oxford: Oxford University Press, 2002.

———. *Hell: The Logic of Damnation*. Notre Dame: University of Notre Dame Press, 1992.

———. Introduction to *OHE*, pp. 3–18.

Walter, Gregory. *Being Promised: Theology, Gift, and Practice*. Grand Rapids: Eerdmans, 2013.

Walter, Jonathan S. "Missions: Buddhist Missions." In *ER*, pp. 6077–82.

Wan, Enoch, ed. *Diaspora Missiology: Theory, Methodology, and Practice*. Portland, Ore.: Institute of Diaspora Studies, Western Seminary, 2011.

"Wang Daiyu on Translating *Tawhīd* in Chinese Traditional Terms." Translated by Sachiko Murata. In *Islamic Theological Themes: A Primary Source Reader*, edited by John Renard, pp. 214–26. Oakland: University of California Press, 2014.

Ward, Keith. *The Concept of God*. Oxford: Basil Blackwell, 1974.

———. "Divine Action in an Emergent Cosmos." In *SPDA*, pp. 285–98.

———. "God as a Principle of Cosmological Explanation." In *QCNL*, pp. 247–62.

———. *Images of Eternity: Concepts of God in Five Religious Traditions*. London: Darton, Longman and Todd, 1987. Reissued as *Concepts of God: Images of the Divine in Five Religious Traditions*. Oxford: Oneworld, 1998.

———. *Religion and Community*. Oxford: Oxford University Press, 1999.

————. *Religion and Human Nature*. Oxford: Clarendon, 1998.

————. *Religion and Revelation: A Theology of Revelation in the World's Religions*. Oxford: Clarendon, 1994.

Ward, Pete. *The Liquid Church*. Peabody, Mass.: Hendrickson, 2002.

————, ed. *Perspectives on Ecclesiology and Ethnography*. Grand Rapids and Cambridge: Eerdmans, 2012.

Ward, Peter D., and Donald Brownlee. *The Life and Death of Planet Earth: How the New Science of Astrobiology Charts the Ultimate Fate of Our World*. New York: Owl Books, 2004.

Ward, Wayne. "Baptism in a Theological Perspective." *Review and Expositor* 65, no. 1 (1968): 43–52.

Ware, [Timothy] Bishop Kallistos. "Dare We Hope for the Salvation of All? Origen, St. Gregory of Nyssa and St. Isaac the Syrian." In *The Inner Kingdom*, pp. 193–215. New York: St. Vladimir's Seminary Press, 2000.

————. *The Orthodox Church*. New York: Penguin Books, 1993.

Warkentin, Marjorie. *Ordination: A Biblical-Historical View*. Grand Rapids: Eerdmans, 1982.

Warren, Rick. *The Purpose-Driven Church: Growth without Compromising Your Message and Mission*. Grand Rapids: Zondervan, 1995.

Waters, Brent. "Whose Salvation? Which Eschatology? Transhumanism and Christianity as Contending Salvific Religions." In *Transhumanism and Transcendence: Christian Hope in an Age of Technological Enhancement*, edited by Ronald Cole-Turner, pp. 163–75. Washington, D.C.: Georgetown University Press, 2011.

Watson, Natalie K. "Faithful Dissenters? Feminist Ecclesiologies and Dissent." *Scottish Journal of Theology* 51, no. 4 (1998): 464–84.

————. "Reconsidering Ecclesiology: Feminist Perspectives." *Theology and Sexuality* 14 (March 2001): 59–77.

Watt, William Montgomery. *Islamic Philosophy and Theology: An Extended Survey*. Edinburgh: Edinburgh University Press, 1962.

————. *Muhammad in Medina*. Oxford: Oxford University Press, 1956.

————. *Muslim-Christian Encounters: Perceptions and Misperceptions*. London and New York: Routledge, 1991.

Watts, Fraser. "Subjective and Objective Hope: Propositional and Attitudinal Aspects of Eschatology." In *EWEG*, pp. 47–60.

Weatherhead, Leslie. *The Christian Agnostic*. London: Hodder and Stoughton, 1965.

Weber, Max. *Economy and Society*. Edited by Guenther Roth and Claus Wittich. Berkeley: University of California Press, 1978.

Weber, Otto. *Versammelte Gemeinde: Beiträge zum Gespräch über die Kirche und Gottesdienst*. Neukirchen: Buchhandlung des Erziehungsvereins, 1949.

Weber, Timothy P. "Millennialism." In *OHE*, pp. 365–83.

————. *On the Road to Armageddon: How Evangelicals Became Israel's Best Friend*. Grand Rapids: Baker Academic, 2004.

Weder, Hans. "Hope and Creation." In *EWEG*, chap. 13, pp. 184–202.

Weinberg, S. *The First Three Minutes: A Modern View of the Origin of the Universe*. New York: Basic Books, 1988.

Welker, Michael. "Creation: Big Bang or the Work of Seven Days?" *Theology Today* 52 (1995): 173-87.

———. "Resurrection and Eternal Life: The Canonic Memory of the Resurrected Christ, His Reality, and His Glory." In *EWEG*, pp. 279-90.

———. "Springing Cultural Traps: The Science-and-Theology Discourse on Eschatology and the Common Good." *Theology Today* 58 (2001): 165-76.

———. "Theological Realism, and Eschatological Symbol Systems." In *Resurrection: Theological and Scientific Assessments*, edited by Ted Peters, Robert J. Russell, and Michael Welker, pp. 31-42. Grand Rapids: Eerdmans, 2002.

———. *What Happens in Holy Communion?* Translated by John F. Hoffmeyer. Grand Rapids: Eerdmans; London: SPCK, 2000.

Wenz, Gunther. *Introduction to Pannenberg's Systematic Theology*. Bristol, Conn.: Vandenhoeck & Ruprecht, 2013.

Werblowsky, R. J. Zwi. "Eschatology: An Overview." In *ER*, pp. 2833-40.

Westhelle, Vítor. "Liberation Theology: A Latitudinal Perspective." In *OHE*, pp. 311-27.

Wetzel, James. "Predestination, Pelagianism, and Foreknowledge." In *Cambridge Companion to Augustine*, edited by Eleonore Stump and Norman Kretzman, pp. 49-58. Cambridge: Cambridge University Press, 2001.

Wheeler, Brannon. "Ummah." In *ER*, pp. 9446-48.

Wheeler, Michael. "Martin Heidegger." *Stanford Encyclopedia of Philosophy* (Fall 2014 edition), edited by Edward N. Zalta. October 12, 2011.

White, James Emery. *The Rise of the Nones: Understanding and Reaching the Religiously Unaffiliated*. Grand Rapids: Baker Books, 2014.

Whitehead, Alfred North. "Immortality." *Harvard Divinity School Bulletin* 7 (1941-1942): 5-21.

———. *Process and Reality: An Essay in Cosmology*. Edited by David R. Griffin and Donald W. Sherburn. Corrected ed. New York: Free Press, 1978 [1929].

Wiesel, Elie. "A Plea for the Dead." In *A Holocaust Reader: Responses to the Nazi Extermination*, edited by Michael L. Morgan, pp. 67-77. New York: Oxford University Press, 2001.

Wiggins, David. *Identity and Spatio-Temporal Continuity*. Oxford: Clarendon, 1967.

Wildman, Wesley J. "Incongruous Goodness, Perilous Beauty, Disconcerting Truth: Ultimate Reality and Suffering in Nature." In *PC*, pp. 267-94.

Wilkinson, David. *Christian Eschatology and the Physical Universe*. London: T. & T. Clark, 2010.

Williams, Bernard. "The Makropulos Case: Reflections on the Tedium of Immortality." In *Metaphysics of Death*, edited by John Martin Fischer, pp. 73-92. Stanford: Stanford University Press, 1993.

Williams, George H. "The Believers' Church and the Given Church." In *The People of God: Essays on the Believers' Church*, edited by Paul Basden and David S. Dockery, pp. 325-32. Nashville: Broadman, 1991.

Willis, Robert E. "Christian Theology after Auschwitz." *Journal of Ecumenical Studies* 12, no. 4 (1975): 493–519.

Wilson, Monica. "Nyakyusa Ritual and Symbolism." *American Anthropologist* 56 (1954).

Winkler, Lewis E. *Contemporary Muslim and Christian Responses to Religious Plurality: Wolfhart Pannenberg in Dialogue with Abdulaziz Sachedina.* Eugene, Ore.: Pickwick, 2011.

Winter, Tim. "Al-Ghazālī' on Death." In *Death, Resurrection, and Human Destiny: Christian and Muslim Perspectives,* edited by David Marshall and Lucinda Mosher, pp. 161–65. Washington, D.C.: Georgetown University Press, 2014.

Witherington, Ben, III. *Jesus, Paul, and the End of the World.* Downers Grove: InterVarsity, 1992.

Wittgenstein, Ludwig. *On Certainty.* Edited by G. E. M. Anscombe and G. W. Wright. Translated by Denis Paul and G. E. M. Anscombe. Oxford: Basil Blackwell, 1969–1975. http://thatmarcusfamily.org/philosophy/Course_Websites/Readings/Wittgenstein%20On%20Certainty.pdf.

Wood, Susan. "Baptism and the Foundations of Communion." In *Baptism and the Unity of the Church,* edited by Michael Root and Risto Saarinen, pp. 37–60. Grand Rapids: Eerdmans; Geneva: WCC, 1998.

———. "Ecclesial *Koinonia* in Ecumenical Dialogues." *One in Christ* 30, no. 2 (1994): 124–45.

———. "The Liturgy: Participatory Knowledge of God in Liturgy." In *Knowing the Triune God: The Work of the Spirit in the Practices of the Church,* edited by James J. Buckley and David S. Yeago, pp. 93–116. Grand Rapids: Eerdmans, 2001.

Woodberry, J. Dudley. "Conversion in Islam." In *HRC,* pp. 22–41.

———. "The Kingdom of God in Islam and the Gospel." In *Anabaptists Meeting Muslims: A Calling for Presence in the Way of Christ,* edited by James R. Krabill, David W. Shenk, and Linford Stutzman, pp. 48–58. Scottdale, Pa.: Herald, 2005.

Woollaston, Victoria. "We'll Be Uploading Our Entire MINDS to Computers by 2045 and Our Bodies Will Be Replaced by Machines within 90 Years, Google Expert Claims." DailyMail.com. June 19, 2013. http://www.dailymail.co.uk/sciencetech/article-2344398/Google-futurist-claims-uploading-entire-MINDS-computers-2045-bodies-replaced-machines-90-years.html#ixzz3RZJ4OIjP.

World Council of Churches. *Church and World: The Unity of the Church and the Renewal of Human Community.* Faith and Order Paper no. 151. Geneva: WCC, 1970. https://www.oikoumene.org/en/resources/documents/commissions/faith-and-order/vi-church-and-world/church-and-world.

———. "A Cloud of Witnesses: Message to the Churches from a Symposium in Bose." November 2, 2008. https://www.oikoumene.org/en/resources/documents/wcc-programmes/unity-mission-evangelism-and-spirituality/visible-unity/a-cloud-of-witnesses-message-to-the-churches-from-a-symposium-in-bose.

———. *Common Understanding and Vision of the WCC.* February 14, 2006. http://www.oikoumene.org/en/resources/documents/assembly/2006-porto-alegre/3-preparatory-and-background-documents/common-understanding-and-vision-of-the-wcc-cuv.

————. *Common Witness and Proselytism* (1970). In *The Ecumenical Movement: An Anthology of Key Texts and Voices*, edited by Michael Kinnamon and Brian E. Cope, pp. 351–53. Geneva: WCC Publications; Grand Rapids: Eerdmans, 1997.

————. "Concepts of Unity and Models of Union." Faith and Order Conference in Santiago de Chile, 1993. In *Documentary History of Faith and Order, 1963–1993*, edited by Günther Gassman, pp. 37–38. Geneva: WCC, 1993.

————. "Mission and Evangelism in Unity Today." In *"You Are the Light of the World" (Matthew 5:14): Statements on Mission by the World Council of Churches, 1980–2005*, edited by Jacques Matthey, pp. 59–89. Geneva: WCC, 2005.

————. *Mission and Evangelism: An Ecumenical Affirmation*. Geneva: WCC, 1982.

————. "Mission as Ministry of Reconciliation." In *"You Are the Light of the World" (Matthew 5:14): Statements on Mission by the World Council of Churches, 1980–2005*, edited by Jacques Matthey, pp. 90–126. Geneva: WCC, 2005.

————. *The "Other" Is My Neighbor: Developing an Ecumenical Response to Migration*. Geneva: WCC, 2013.

————. *Reception: A Key to Ecumenical Progress*. Joint Working Group between the Roman Catholic Church and the World Council of Churches. Geneva: WCC, 2014.

————. "Religious Plurality and Christian Self-Understanding." February 14, 2006. https://www.oikoumene.org/en/resources/documents/assembly/2006-porto-alegre/3-preparatory-and-background-documents/religious-plurality-and-christian-self-understanding.

————. *Towards Koinonia in Faith, Life, and Witness: A Discussion Paper*. Faith and Order Paper no. 161. Geneva: WCC, 1993.

————. "A Treasure in Earthen Vessels: An Instrument for an Ecumenical Reflection on Hermeneutics." January 1, 1998. http://www.oikoumene.org/en/resources/documents/commissions/faith-and-order/iv-interpretation-the-meaning-of-our-words-and-symbols/a-treasure-in-earthen-vessels.

Worthing, Mark William. *God, Creation, and Contemporary Physics*. Theology and the Sciences. Minneapolis: Fortress, 1996.

Wright, David F. *Infant Baptism in Historical Perspective: Collected Studies*. Carlisle, UK: Paternoster, 2007.

————. *What Has Infant Baptism Done to Baptism? An Enquiry at the End of Christendom*. Carlisle, UK: Paternoster, 2005.

Wright, J. Edward. *The Early History of Heaven*. New York: Oxford University Press, 2000.

Wright, Jeremiah, Jr. "Protestant Ecclesiology." In *The Cambridge Companion to Black Theology*, edited by Dwight N. Hopkins and Edward P. Antonio, pp. 184–97. Cambridge: Cambridge University Press, 2012.

Wright, N. T. *Evil and the Justice of God*. Downers Grove: InterVarsity, 2006.

————. *For All the Saints: Remembering the Christian Departed*. Harrisburg, Pa.: Morehouse, 2003.

————. *Jesus and the Victory of God*. Vol. 2 of *Christian Origins and the Question of God*. Minneapolis: Fortress, 1996.

————. *The New Testament and the People of God*. Vol. 1 of *Christian Origins and the Question of God*. London: SPCK; Minneapolis: Fortress, 1992.

―――. *The Resurrection of the Son of God*. Minneapolis: Fortress, 2003.

―――. *Surprised by Hope: Rethinking Heaven, the Resurrection, and the Mission of the Church*. New York: HarperOne, 2008.

Wyschogrod, Michael. *Abraham's Promise: Judaism and Jewish-Christian Relations*. Grand Rapids: Eerdmans, 2004.

Yazicioglu, Isra Umeyye. "Affliction, Patience and Prayer: Reading Job (P) in the Qur'an." *Journal of Scriptural Reasoning* 4, no. 1 (2004).

Yeager, D. M. "Recognition, Human Rights, and the Pursuit of Peace." *Perspectives in Religious Studies* 40, no. 2 (2013): 167–79.

Yoder, John Howard. *Body Politics: Five Practices of the Christian Community before the Watching World*. Harrisonburg, Va.: Herald, 1992.

―――. "The Meaning of the Constantinian Shift." In *Christian Attitudes to War, Peace, and Revolution*, edited by Theodore J. Koontz and Andy Alexis-Baker, pp. 57–74. Grand Rapids: Brazos, 2009.

Yong, Amos. *The Spirit Poured Out on All Flesh: Pentecostalism and the Possibility of Global Theology*. Grand Rapids: Baker Academic, 2005.

Young, D. N. De L. "The Sangha in Buddhist History." *Religious Studies* 6, no. 3 (1970): 243–52.

Zaehner, R. C. *Mysticism, Sacred and Profane*. Oxford: Clarendon, 1957.

Zagorin, Perez. *How the Idea of Religious Toleration Came to the West*. Princeton: Princeton University Press, 2003.

Zaleski, Carol. "In Defense of Immortality." *First Things* 105 (August/September 2000): 36–42. http://www.firstthings.com/article/2000/08/in-defense-of-immortality.

Zamfir, Korinna. "Is There a Future for the Catholic-Protestant Dialogue? Non-Reception as Challenge to Ecumenical Dialogue." In *Receiving "The Nature and Mission of the Church": Ecclesial Reality and Ecumenical Horizons for the Twenty-First Century*, edited by Paul M. Collins and Gerard Mannion, pp. 85–102. New York: T. & T. Clark, 2008.

Zhixu, Ouyi. In *JBC*, pp. 229–30.

Zimmerman, Dean. "Bodily Resurrection: The Falling Elevator Model Revisited." In *PIR*, pp. 33–50.

―――. "The Compatibility of Materialism and Survival: The 'Falling Elevator' Model." *Faith and Philosophy* 16 (1999): 194–212.

―――. "Immanent Causation." *Nôus* 31, supplement: *Philosophical Perspectives 11: Mind, Causation, and World* (1997): 433–71.

Zimmermann, Jens. *Incarnational Humanism: A Philosophy of Culture for the Church in the World*. Downers Grove: InterVarsity, 2012.

Zizioulas, John D. *Being as Communion: Studies in Personhood and the Church*. Crestwood, N.Y.: St. Vladimir's Seminary Press, 1985.

―――. "Communion and Otherness" (1993). *In Communion*. July 23, 2012. https://incommunion.org/2012/07/23/communion-and-otherness-2/.

―――. "The Doctrine of the Holy Trinity: The Significance of the Cappadocian Contribution." In *The Trinity Today*, edited by Christoph Schwöbel. Edinburgh: T. & T. Clark, 1996.

———. "Human Capacity and Human Incapacity: A Theological Exploration of Person-hood." *Scottish Journal of Theology* 28, no. 5 (1975): 401–47.

Zuckerman, Phil. *Faith No More: Why People Reject Religion.* New York: Oxford University Press, 2012.

Index of Authors

Index of Subjects